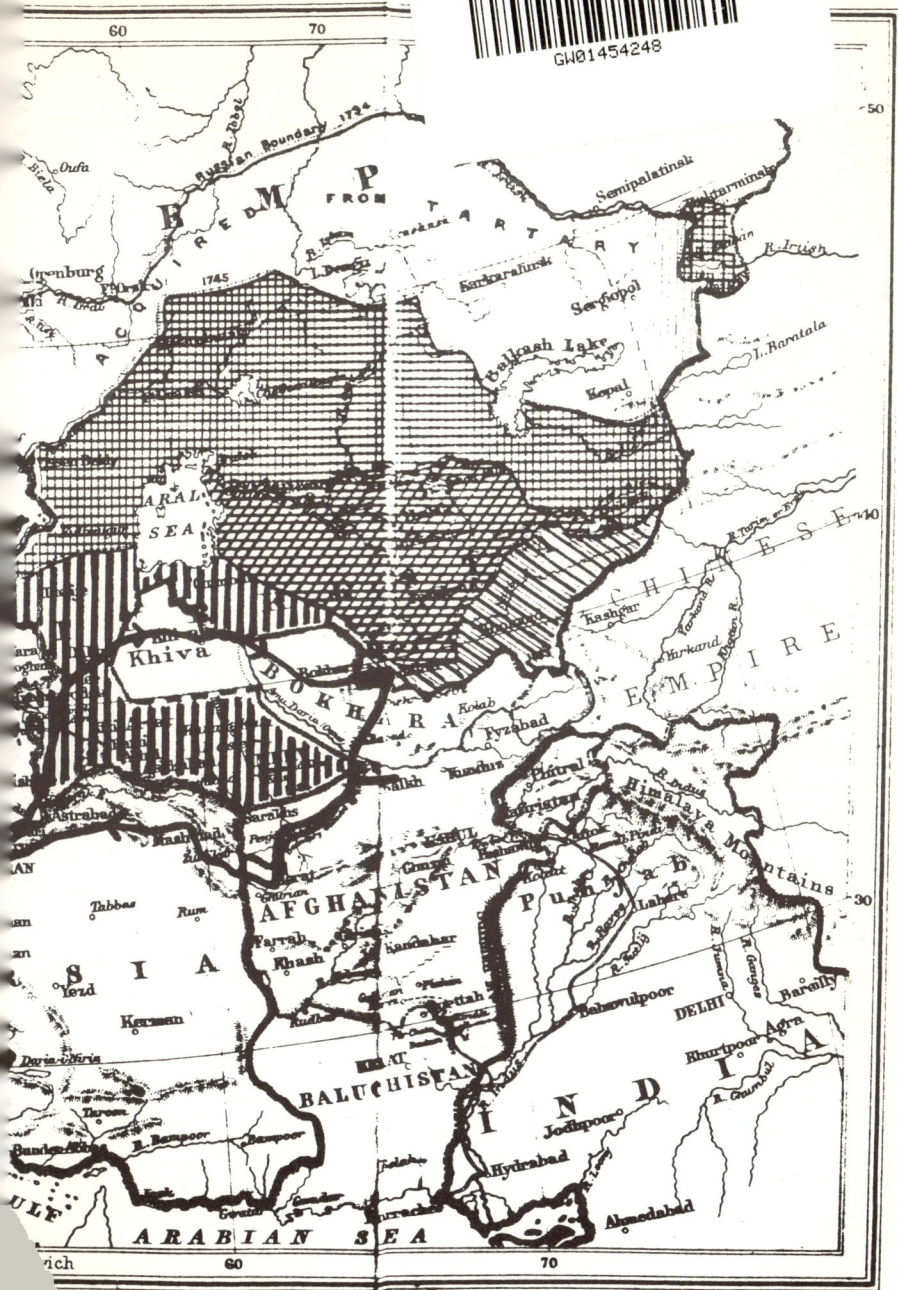

ANCE TOWARDS INDIA.

60   70   50

Orufa

E M P
Russian Boundary 1724

FROM

A C Q U I R E D

Orenburg   Forbu   1745   L. Deng

T A R T A R Y

Semipalatinski   Toldgarminsk

R. Irtish

Sarkaralinsk

Serghopol

Balkash Lake

L. Baratala

Kopal

ARAL SEA

C H I N E S E

Khiva   B O K H A R A

Kashgar   E M P I R E

Yarkand

Kolab

Pyzabad

Chitral   Himalaya Mountains

Astrabad

Kabul   Indus

A F G H A N I S T A N   P u n j a b

P E R S I A

Tebbes   Rum

Yezd

Kerman

Ghazni   Herat   Lahore

Kandahar

DELHI   Bareilly

Khash   Khelat

Bahawulpoor   Khurtpoor   Agra

Farrah

I N D I A

B A L U C H I S T A N   Jodhpoor

Bunder Abbas   R. Bompoor

Hydrabad

Ahmedabad

A R A B I A N   S E A

60   70

Edwd Weller Lith.

1878   1883   1884

THE DERVISH OF WINDSOR CASTLE

THE DERVISH OF WINDSOR CASTLE

The Life of Arminius Vambery

Lory Alder and Richard Dalby

Bachman
& Turner

Bachman & Turner Ltd.
London

Bachman and Turner Ltd
The Old Hop Exchange
1/3 Central Buildings
24 Southwark Street
London S.E.1

ISBN 0 85974 045 5

First published 1979

Typeset by Inforum Ltd, Portsmouth
Printed in Great Britain by litho at The Anchor Press Ltd
and bound by Wm Brendon & Son Ltd
both of Tiptree, Essex

CONTENTS

'A man of many parts' — *from an English magazine circa 1885. When Arminius Vambery was at the height of his fame.*

ACKNOWLEDGEMENTS

Our sincerest thanks are due to Her Majesty The Queen for her gracious permission to quote from documents in the Royal Archives, Windsor; and we should also like to express our gratitude for the assistance given by Her Majesty's Librarian, Sir Robin Mackworth-Young, KCVO.

Transcripts from letters and documents in the Public Record Office (F.O. 800, volumes 32 & 33) appear by permission of the Controller of H.M. Stationery Office.

Our grateful thanks also go to Mr. Robert Vambery for his invaluable assistance, and for sending copies of unpublished family letters and photographs;

to Professor Gyula Germanus, the last surviving pupil of Vambery, for giving us several hours of his time and for sharing with us his fascinating personal reminiscences of his teacher in the first decade of this century;

to Professor Laszlo Bogsch for his great patience in translating unpublished letters in the archives of the Hungarian Academy of Sciences, and other relevant matter;

to Miss Margit Lanc for her indefatigable energy and initiative in helping us with our research;

to Mr. Anthony Hern literary editor of the *Evening Standard* for his kindness in reading and correcting the draft version and making helpful suggestions; and to the following individuals, all of whom have gone out of their way to help us:

to Mr. John Murray CBE, for allowing us to quote from unpublished Vambery letters in the archives of John Murray Ltd., Publishers;

in Budapest, Dr. Eva Apor (of the Hungarian Academy of Sciences); Dr. Annie Barat; Mrs. Agnes Fedor; Dr. Tibor Frank (head of the English Department of the Eotvos Lorand University); Mrs. Lajos Hatvany; Dr. Zoltan Jokay; Dr. Zsuzsa Kakuk (of the Turkish Department of the Eotvos Lorand University); Professor Sandor Scheiber (Head of the Rabbinical College); Dr. Gyorgy Vambery; Dr. Aurel Varannai; and Dr. Miklos Wesselenyi; and in England, Mr. T.H. Aston (Keeper of the Archives, University of Oxford); Mr. Robert H.E. Brown; Mr. R.A. Downie; Mr. Charles Elwell; Mr. Philip Hainsworth (Bahai Centre); Mrs. Rose Katona; Lord Kaldor, MA, FBA (Cambridge); Professor Nicholas Kurti, CBE, FRS (of Brasenose College, Oxford); Mr. Harry Ludlam; Mr. R.R. Mellor (Public Record Office, Kew); Mr. John Prest; Mrs. Ruth Robbins; Mr. Harvey Satty; Mr. G. Schofield (of the School of Oriental and African Studies); Mrs. Elisabeth Simms; Mr. Stephen Simpson; Mr. K.J. Sommerfeld ("Deus ex Machina"); Mrs. Margaret Tauszig; and the late Sir Stanley Unwin; as well as to Professor David Vital, of the University of Tel Aviv, and to Mr. H. Clark of London.

Our thanks are also due to the staffs of the British Museum and Library; of the Bodleian Library; of the India Office Library and Records; of the Kensington Public Library; of the Royal Geographical Society; of the Royal Society for Asian Affairs; of the School of Oriental and African Studies; of the Westminster Public Library; and of the Wiener Library; for patiently dealing with our endless enquiries.

For loaning us previously unpublished photographs, our additional thanks go to Professor Kurti for the Vambery 'graffiti' photograph (taken at Persepolis in 1964); to Professor Germanus; to Mr. Laszlo Tokes, of the Hungarian Academy of Sciences; to Mr. Emil Horn, of the Magyar Munkasmozgalmi Muzeum; to Mr. Jozsef Kis, for photographs of Central Asia from his film 'Vambery' (1970); and to the Mansell Collection (E.O. Hoppe collection).

We should also like to thank Mrs. Magda Vamos for allowing us to use material from the final chapter of her book *Resid Efendi*; to MALEV Hungarian Airlines, for a most enjoyable two-hour flight to Budapest; and, last but not least, to Mr. Donald Copeman and Mr. Cecil Turner without whom this book would never have seen the light of day; and to *Dracula* who brought us all together.

We should also like to thank the Press sections of the Hungarian and Turkish embassies for their help.

Publisher's Note: With a few exceptions, accents in French and Hungarian words, as well as German umlauts, have been omitted.

INTRODUCTION

When we were asked to write a biography of Arminius Vambery, we had no idea of how startling a story we would uncover. All we knew was that he was a celebrated Hungarian traveller of the nineteenth century, a great scholar and Orientalist. But at that stage we could not know how actively involved in British politics he was, if only in an advisory capacity.

This D'Artagnan of the Puszta shot to fame through his adventurous journey across Central Asia, disguised as a dervish, a unique feat made even more astounding by the fact that he was lame. A tribute to his profound knowledge of the Koran and his histrionic abilities was the fact that towards the end of his life Moslem pilgrims passing through Budapest would still believe that he was one of them, a genuine dervish in disguise who had chosen to settle in Europe. Chameleon-like he had taken on protective colouring and merged with the surroundings on his journey.

In an age of explorers that alone would have been sufficient to secure him a hero's welcome in London. But he had more to offer. Phenomenal linguist, fully conversant with Turkish, Persian, Arabic and various Central Asian languages, he brought back information of the greatest interest to British politicians. Turkestan was virtually uncharted in those days. Not much news reached Europe. But Vambery had been there and seen for himself; he had met the fierce local khans, whose cruelty was legendary, face to face; he had kept his eyes and ears wide open, listening to political gossip in bazaars and tea-shops. He could report on Russian steamers on the Oxus; on Russian military moves, threats to the still independent khanates of Khiva and Bokhara and on pro — or anti — British feeling in the market-place. Commerce in Central Asia was of great interest to Britain and Russia a rival.

From 1864, when Vambery first arrived in London, to 1878

when the last Central Asian Khanate fell to Czarist troops — as he had so accurately prophecied — he was undisputed master; but as the Russians progressively 'pacified' the region, with unparalleled ferocity, it finally became safer for travellers to venture there. And in the eighties a bevy of gallant British officers set forth on horseback (one even from Charing Cross) to reconnoiter the frontiers of distant Persia and Afganistan.

The role of Afghanistan was vital to the fate of British India and the second Afghan war resulted in the installation of a pro-British Emir: Vambery had met him . . . but beyond the Afghan frontiers in Turkestan, lurked the ever-present menace of Czarist designs on British India.

By the late eighties his name was made; he wrote, lectured and in the best manner of a retired British colonel (the comparison would please him) wrote innumerable letters to *The Times*. British Government circles took increasingly notice of his views and opinions on the political issues of the day. He never ceased to sound a warning note, for his interest in politics had led him to defend passionately the country of his adoption — England and to set himself up as a self-proclaimed defender of the British Empire. He was not alone in seeing a threat to British India in the relentless southward drive of the Tsarist troops deep into Turkestan.

His unique personal relations with Eastern rulers, such as Abdul Hamid and the Shahs of Persia, his knowledge of languages which enabled him to read newspapers in Russian, Persian, Turkish and Arabic, his wide-flung network of correspondents in the East made him a useful source of information in Whitehall. In 1889 the British fleet steamed to the Bosporus as a precautionary measure: Vambery's advice behind the scenes was almost certainly a contributory factor.

His worth was fully recognised in Whitehall although his quixotic tendency to tilt at 'Russian spies' instead of windmills must have caused some amusement in the corridors of powers, but he remained a useful source of information to the end of his life.

By this time he had reached the peak of his fame; he had become a friend of Edward VII, had been invited to Sandringham, figured in Court circulars, was a guest at Windsor and on his 70th birthday he was made a C.V.O.

Yet, he was never quite able to believe he had arrived, nor could he ever forget his origin: the theme of "struggles" and "suffering" occurs again and again.

Vambery was born in a small Hungarian village, of Jewish orthodox parents, a fact he himself considered a "problematic blessing". But the typically Jewish love of learning he had inherited from his father and his mother's unceasing exhortations and loving encouragements were jointly responsible for shaping his character. No doubt he also owed much of his later success to his fierce determination to overcome the handicap of his birth until in later life he felt defeated by the anti-semitism of his day and espoused the cause of the Jews. On the way, however, he passed in turn as a member of the Moslem, Christian and other faiths — a formal convert to none, while passionately proclaiming himself a free-thinker.

He was vain and he was boastful, at times a snob, a social climber and an inveterate name-dropper (who would turn a Colonel into a General and a Sir into a Lord if it suited his book); he showed a marked lack of humour on most occasions and developed an elephantine memory for grudges. Age did not mellow him, but made him increasingly irascible and touchy.

But before judging him too harshly one must try to see him against the background of his times. If he was pushful it was because he knew full well that, if he was to succeed — and he was avid for recognition he could rely on no one but himself. This was the lesson his early hardships had taught him, apart from serving as a useful training for his dervish journey. Vambery, characteristically, put his deprived childhood to good use.

Nature had not favoured him. He was of less than average height and walked with a limp. But he made up in mental equipment for what he lacked in physical stature. A complete autodidact with a phenomenal memory and gift for languages (he claimed to speak sixteen, write twelve and know a score more) coupled with an inborn "talent for talking") saved his life on many occasions in the East.

He was of robust good health (although he worried about it a good deal) and did not suffer a day's illness. He was resourceful, persevering, determined and hard-working and, unable to forget his deprived childhood, basically insecure, he made money his god.

Vambery wrote many books of travel and scholarly works. He also wrote two autobiographies which became bestsellers. Though richly varied in detail, they tell only half the story. They bear the imprint of his famed egotism and it must have cost him much to suppress the most interesting part of his later career. The times were not opportune for him to discuss, among other things, his links with Zionism. And though rumours were rampant for many years — and still are today in his native land — concerning his secret agent activities, he kept an unaccustomed silence — yet he could not resist dropping hints, unable to resist boasting.

As a scholar he won great acclaim in his lifetime. For many years writers and scholars in western Europe and the U.S.A. believed he was the leading authority in the field, and even in this century Sir Ronald Storrs called him *the* greatest Orientalist in the world.

Today he is remembered paradoxically not by the country he loved so well — England, but by the country of his origin where recognition only came after a long struggle and his acceptance abroad. In his old age he became a respected figure in Hungary, only to be laid in cold storage for a number of years after his death. Today his contribution to Oriental philology is universally acknowledged and stands as a lasting memorial.

The full story of his extraordinary career is told in this volume for the first time. It is the first critical biography of Arminius — alias Hadji Reshid, alias Reshid Effendi, alias 'Hermann' Wamberger — to appear in English and draws to a large extent on completely unpublished material.

PART 1

Dervish
In
The
Making

1

TUTOR AT ELEVEN

"Noblesse oblige!" the short, bearded man muttered, nervously tugging at his tie as he craned to see his reflection in the mirror of the first-class railway compartment.

He had to stand on tiptoe, for he was not only short of stature but also lame in one leg. He grimaced at his reflection in the mirror. He felt most uncomfortable in his high, stiff collar, and feared he looked ridiculous in his frock-coat.

Wind and rain rattled the windows. The weather that 6th of May 1889 was as unsettled as he was. For although he was indubitably a great man and justifiably famous, he almost could not believe that he was on his way from London to Windsor Castle — invited there personally by Queen Victoria.

Yet in his portmanteau was the irrefutable evidence, bearing the Royal crest die-stamped in gold: the invitation that was a command. Professor Arminius Vambery was invited by Victoria, Queen of the United Kingdom of Great Britain and Ireland and Empress of India, to dine at Windsor Castle, and to spend the night there.

Vambery was one of the most colourful and unusual characters of a colourful and unusual century. Celebrated as 'ex-Dervish', traveller, scholar, author and political journalist, he was nevertheless unable to convince himself that, socially, he had 'arrived'. At every step — so it still seemed to him — he was confronted by the invisible yet insurmountable barriers thrown up by his obscure Jewish birth.

He was to be reminded of it within the hour. After being met at the railway station by a royal carriage, ushered into one of Windsor Castle's splendid drawing rooms by a liveried footman and welcomed by Sir Henry Ponsonby, the Queen's Private Secretary, he was immediately plunged into a situation profoundly embarrassing to him.

As it was the custom at the Castle to ask distinguished visitors to sign the Queen's Birthday Book, Sir Henry offered it to him. But what was he to enter? He could not even be sure of the year of his birth. Was it 1831, or 1832?

Encouraged by the Queen's Secretary, he paused for a moment's reflection, and then entered 19 March 1832 as his birth-date, in a spidery hand. But whether it was right or wrong he had no means of knowing.

His earliest memories were of a poverty-stricken childhood in a Hungary scourged by cholera. The great epidemic of the early 1830s, which had its origins in India, had swept across the Russian steppes into Europe, and had even reached Britain — where anxious readers could chart its progress in *The Times* and heave a sigh of relief when the news moved from the front to an inside page. In Britain, the epidemic was dealt with in a modern and enlightened way, but in Hungary things were different.

Then still part of the Austrian Empire, the country was despotically ruled by the Emperor Francis I. His paternal 'care and protection', so the papers said, 'would prevent the propagation of the cholera'. But the peasants, had they been able to read, could have told his Imperial Majesty that it was to no avail. They knew better. They knew who the real culprits were. It was the Jews who had poisoned the wells . . .

The cholera, however, chose its victims with commendable impartiality. It carried off Jew and Christian alike. One of its victims was Vambery's own father.

In such a social climate it is not surprising that few official records of Jewish births were kept. After all, who cared? The Jews were not compelled by law to register them and, in any case, wanted as little truck with authority as possible. Dealings with officialdom only led to trouble.

So when a date was officially recorded for a Jewish birth it was not always correct. A father might enter a false date, or even register a son's birth under a girl's name, in the hope that by the time his boy grew up he would have escaped conscription and the consequences of a future war.

Thus Vambery was never able to obtain a certificate of his birth. All he learned from his mother was that he had been born on St. Joseph's day which, with the aid of a Catholic calendar, he discovered was March 19th. He knew that he had been born shortly before his father's death, when the cholera epidemic was at its height, but the plague struck annually during the early 1830s, so he could not be sure of the actual year. It was either 1831 or 1832.

Arminius Vambery was born Hermann — or Chaim — Wamberger, 'Haschele' in the family circle, the second child and only son of a pious young Talmud scholar. The name Wamberger was a corruption of Bamberger, which indicated that his ancestors had originally come from the town of Bamberg in Germany. But Vambery's grandfather had been born in Hungary and, on his mother's side, the Malavan family came from Moravia.

Vambery himself was born in a small town then called St. Georghen.* Most works of reference, however, give his birthplace as Duna Szerdahely,† to which the family moved when he was three. Indeed Vambery himself preferred to do so, dating from Duna Szerdahely his 'intellectual awakening'.

Vambery's mother described his father as a shy and studious young man, so odd and unworldly in appearance that he excited the derision of her family. Nevertheless, she fell in love with this 'bashful young scholar, who had bright eyes and pleasant features to recommend him', and was ready to accept him when he asked for her hand in marriage. She was then eighteen.

The young couple moved to Wamberger's native St. Georghen, but he was too shy and retiring to bring himself to compete for the coveted post of assistant rabbi. He therefore had to try and make his living in some other way.

In those days, Jewish activities in Hungary were severely circumscribed. Certain agricultural pursuits were open, as was the brewing and sale of alcoholic beverages. Jews were also permitted to keep inns, and even to exercise the profession of doctor. But considering the primitive state of medicine in Hungary at that time, this last was not surprising. Doctors were generally held in low esteem.

Vambery's mother encouraged her husband to start a fruit and corn business, but it failed. They tried keeping an inn, but this failed too. Finally, his father had to stoop to hawking. "... Des-

---

* St. Georghen (now Jur pri Bratislave, in Czechoslovakia).
† Duna Szerdahely (now Dunjaska Streda, in Czechoslovakia).

cending to the vulgar occupation of bargaining and bartering for a sack of beans, or peas, a sheep, or a goatskin!" Vambery's mother told him this with tears in her eyes, for she shared her husband's enthusiasm for study.

But he was not humiliated for long. The cholera struck, Vambery's father died; the young widow — then only twenty-two — proved herself an extremely competent businesswoman almost at once. She was again keeping an inn and "In the second year of her widowhood," Vambery writes," she had the satisfaction of seeing her cellar stacked with good wine, her store-room full of corn, and her inn one of the most frequented in the little town of St. Georghen."

Nonetheless, she felt she needed a companion at her side. Unfortunately, her choice fell upon a Mr Fleischmann, whom Vambery describes as kind-hearted and easy-going, but who otherwise seems to have been clumsier in practical matters than even Vambery's father — and with no great religious knowledge to redeem him.

Fleischmann blamed his inability to make a living on the fact that he was among strangers. He would do better, he declared, in his native Duna Szerdahely. But he didn't. He did no better there than in St. Georghen and soon, moreover, the family had increased from four to seven.

He tried trading in leeches. First the leeches had to be bought from peasants, then sorted out according to size and washed twice in twenty-four hours. Finally, they were sold to neighbouring pharmacies. Later, Vambery recalled how the slimy creatures would often escape from badly tied bags and crawl around the floor — on which some of the children would be sleeping. Then there would be a frantic search for them with a torch, some of the children shrieking in fright, and others howling with laughter.

But always Fleischmann was unlucky. Suddenly 'bleeding' fell into disrepute, and the demand for leeches decreased. The poverty of the family grew in proportion.

Vambery remembered this as a desperate time when they were always hungry. Nevertheless, he grew up strong and bright-eyed, tough in mind and body. In the market-place, the peasants' wives were apt to make a great fuss of him, patting his rosy cheeks and stroking his dark, curly hair, murmuring: "A pity the little Jew is crooked . . ."

For one morning he had woken up with pain in his left foot.

"Coxalgia had taken hold of me," he writes, "and I began to go lame in my left leg, an affliction for which no cure could be found." From that day he walked with a pronounced limp, frequently having to resort to a crutch. Was it rickets?

His mother, who loved her son dearly, was at her wit's end. To make her son whole again, she would try anything — even magic. The first 'cure' she could think of was to 'sell' her son for a small sum to another woman — "in the hope that this would please God and that he would show mercy to this possibly sinless new mother". But the 'cure' did not work.

So she tried a host of other bizarre remedies: potions, herbs, and magic charms. Miracle-mongers and quacks with which the Hungarian countryside abounded were all appealed to in turn. On one occasion the boy was spreadeagled at a crossroads at midnight whilst a gypsy woman chanted incantations. On another, a so-called doctor tried a 'cure' so barbariously cruel and drastic that no man with any feeling would have subjected even an animal to it.

This was the treatment: for five days the boy's lame leg was held over hot steam "to soften the sinews and fibres", then, on the sixth day, he was made to lie on the floor. While two strong gypsies held him by the shoulders and the feet, the doctor threw all his weight onto the rigid right-angle of the crippled knee.

"A terrible crash —" Vambery wrote later "— and I knew no more." Mercifully, he had lost consciousness. He awoke to find his weeping mother kneeling beside him, offering him something to drink. The injured leg was put between rough wooden splints and tightly bandaged. But when, eventually, the splints were removed Vambery was as lame as ever and, much to his chagrin, had to continue to use his crutch.

Characteristically, he considered his bodily defect a challenge, even trying to run races with the village children. Inevitably he lost and, when he limped home in tears, his mother would comfort him — "My child you will do better than any of them, but you must have patience and perseverance."

Her words were prophetic.

At the age of eight, Vambery could read and translate Hebrew, knew much of the Pentateuch (the five books of Moses) by heart, and could recite the commentary. He was acquainted with the Prophets, and biblical stories, and spoke Hungarian and German and could read and write in both languages. The bounds of his knowledge seemed only limited by the rigid tenets of the Jewish 'third-rate' school where he was enrolled, for here the prime emphasis was on religion, and all secular knowledge was held to stem from the devil. Nor were his horizons widened to any considerable degree when his natural ability won him a place in the best Jewish school in the district at a greatly reduced fee.

His mother said proudly: "His father was a great scholar, he is bound to have plenty of brains". And at night — an early advocate of sleep learning, of her own brand — she put his school books under his pillow "so that knowledge will get into your head, right through the bloster!"

But she didn't stop there.

Illiterate and, as Vambery describes her, a strange mixture of ancient superstitions and shrewd commonsense, this woman was in many ways far ahead of her time. Spurred on by ambitious plans for her son — for was he not to become a doctor? — she took an unprecedented step. Determined that he was to have every opportunity possible, she took him out of the Jewish school and placed him in a Christian one.

For "devout and God-fearing as she was", Vambery says, "she seemed to have come to the conclusion that the study of Torah and Talmud may be all very well to open the gates of paradise, but they are of little use to help one in the world.

"The boldness of the plan," he adds, "can only be fully appreciated by those who have known . . . the ways of thinking and the horrible fanaticism of the Jews of those days."

At the elementary school run by the Protestant community, a whole new world opened up before him. And now Vambery's mother took an even more astonishing step. She was determined that her son was going to get on in the world. So at all costs he had to stay at this school for as long as it had anything to teach him. Yet how was this to be achieved when they were so desperately poor that there was never enough food to go round?

His elder sister had already left home and gone into service at the age of twelve. This is the only fact he disclosed about her. We do not even know her name. With a heavy heart, Vambery's mother decided to place him as an apprentice with a Jewish tailoress, whose son he was to instruct in Hebrew in exchange for board and lodging. Vambery, then just eleven, was flattered to be placed in the position of tutor to a boy of his own age, even if it was only for three hours a day, but he intensely disliked having to learn to sew.

He described himself as clumsy with a needle and thread, and the others made fun of him. After a month, he ran home to his mother in tears. But she urged him to hold out — if only just for the winter. At least he would have a warm room and tolerable food while, if he stayed at home, he would have to go all the way to school scantily clad and with only a warm potato or two in his pocket for breakfast. Nevertheless, Vambery stayed.

She further admonished him: "You cannot and must not be an ordinary man. The spirit of your learned father is in you. You must study and become a doctor." She told him that when he had learned all he could at the Protestant school he must enter the college at St. Georghen. But to do this he first had to earn some cash, for all his mother could give him to speed him on his way when the time came was a change of linen and a suit of clothes.

His first job was in the house of a Jewish inn-keeper at Nyek, a village about two hours' distance from Duna Szerdahely. He arrived there, accompanied by his mother, a small bundle on his back and leaning heavily on his crutch: a picture of misery. His prospective employer, the inn-keeper, looked him up and down and clearly wasn't impressed. "Too young . . . too small . . ." he muttered. Vambery caught the words. But a man from Szerdahely happened to be present and retorted sharply: "Never mind the outside, it's the inside you want. The lad is crammed full of learning. He knows the Prayer book and the Pentateuch by heart . . ." And he was grudgingly accepted.

He very soon discovered, however, that the job was no sinecure — even by the harsh standards of those hardened times. He was expected not only to teach the son of the house the three 'Rs' and the Pentateuch for four hours a day, but also to be house-servant and waiter and serve the peasant customers brandy early in the morning and late into the night. In addition, on Friday afternoons, before the beginning of the Sabbath, he had to clean the boots of the entire family and brush all their clothes.

Vambery recalled that he performed his duties to the best of his ability, but he wasn't happy. At the outset he had longed desperately for his mother; later, he simply thought he was being given no chance to succeed as a teacher. And so, after six months, he left and returned to Szerdahely, eight florins the richer.

At home, he was received with open arms. His mother was overjoyed to see him again, but immediately started making new

21

plans. She would have wished him to commence his studies at once at the Latin school at St. Georghen — the new term started in autumn. But it was finally decided that he should have his *Bar Mitzvah* in Szerdahely first: the religious ceremony marking a boy's transition to the status and duties of a man, held when he is thirteen.

The ceremony made little impression on Vambery, although he did his best to acquit himself of his religious duties as well as possible, if only for his mother's sake. But by now the hold that Orthodoxy had had upon him was definitely waning.

"Pork and Christian food no longer seemed to poison me, and with the gradual breaking away of the barriers . . . my faith was more exposed to the outward attacks made upon it."

A few days later he again left home, his crutch under his arm, his knapsack bulging with books, and again accompanied by his mother. They hoped to get a lift as far as Pressburg, and then continue on to St. Georghen and, in fact, they succeeded in making their entry in style — on a cart drawn by four oxen. Vambery thought otherise. "(It) . . . was a fitting beginning for the poverty-stricken existence I was destined to lead there."

For if the Jewish community in St. Georghen would have been quite prepared to open its arms to an impecunious but bright lad studying to become a rabbi, it was not quite as willing to do the same for someone planning to engage in heretical — that is to say Christian and secular — studies. In fact, the family friend on whom they called only grudgingly gave the boy free lodging.

And the word 'lodging' was something of a euphemism too. In reality it consisted only of a straw mattress which he was allowed to spread out anywhere in the house. Other charitable people had to supply a pillow and blanket.

However, his mother was satisfied that he had a roof over his head and took him to see the Director of the Piarist's College — a Catholic school — where his name was entered in the Latin class. The entrance fee alone came to nearly half the money he had earned at Nyek and with the remaining amount he had to buy school books. He was penniless again.

In those days it was the custom of the Jewish community to take it in turns to invite students of the Talmud for the midday meal. On Saturdays, Vambery could look forward to being a guest of the community and on Fridays he had a ticket for a meal with one of the richer pillars of Jewish society. But often his presence — as one who was studying secular, even heretical, matters came as a very unpleasant surprise to his hosts. "I ate," he wrote, "with the bitter feeling that I was an unwelcome guest".

But it worked for a time. Even though he might find himself served the same dish on different days of the week, this arrangement did at least mean that he had sufficient to eat and a bit of bread for his supper. He was better off than he would have been at home.

So this second separation was not quite as bad as the first. Vambery's mind was set on school and he enjoyed his first year. He found his studies easy — despite the fact that Latin grammar was taught in Latin as was all the rest of the curriculum. There were heavy penalties for anyone caught using his mother tongue and an espionage system existed. Certain boys carried the *Liber asini* — the donkey's book — hidden in their clothing. Acting as junior *agents provocateurs*, they inveigled smaller children into speaking in their own tongue and, as soon as they fell into the trap, whipped out their books with the words "*Inscribas, amice!*" — "Write your name, friend!" — and the culprit was punished.

In part, this was a throwback to the Middle Ages and the severe monastric regime imposed in religious establishments in Hungary. But principally it was due to the fact that throughout much of the nineteenth century Latin was still the language of the educated Hungarian — and indeed the official language for most State affairs.

As Vambery's college, Catholic religious instruction was compulsory. Neither Lutherans, Calvinists or Jews were allowed to leave the classroom and were forced to repeat Hail Marys and The Lord's Prayer together with the others. No meat was served on Fridays and "a sort of silent pressure exercised on the scholars in the hope of their embracing the Catholic religion.

"A pressure exercised without result, it is true," Vambery commented, "but it had a strange effect upon me, who had been an Orthodox Jew ..."

Nevertheless, Vambery did well. One teacher was a young Piarist friar of twenty who liked him right from the start and would sometimes give him an apple or sometimes, in winter, warm clothing — which he sorely needed.

His teachers praised him and if he was only the second best pupil at school and not the *primus* it was due to one thing alone: he took one subject less than the others — the Catechism.

23

Very soon his resourcefulness was put to a severe test. On account of his Christian studies he was finally thrown out of the house of the family friend and forced to look for other lodgings. Meals were reduced from five a week to four. "Jewish charity," he writes bitterly," was not compatible with Christian education and only among the more enlightened Orthodox Jews . . . did real humanity and pity for the starving boy gain the upper hand."

He finally found lodgings with a childless couple, a cap-maker and his wife, and came to a barter arrangement with his schoolmates: he would accept pieces of bread in return for helping them with their lessons. But he began to look pale, and one or another of his fellow pupils took pity on him and invited him home for a meal. By the end of term, he had become a sort of protege of the school, and very popular with his schoolmates.

During the holidays he hitch-hiked home. Although his mother couldn't read a word, she was overcome with pride when Vambery showed her his end-of-term certificate. She was intoxicated by the sight of his name inscribed on it in letters of gold, and kept repeating: "Of course it's quite natural, for my son has his father's brains, and I'm sure he will be a success."

After two months' holiday, Vambery returned to school to start the new term, and his worries about board and lodging recommenced. To make matters worse, the new professor of the *secunda*, the second form, eyed him with profound distaste and, addressing him with a derogatory nickname for Jews, said: "Well, Moshele, why do you study? Would it not be better for you to become a kosher butcher?"

Unabashed, Vambery produced his certificate and asked the hostile and anti-semitic professor to be kind to him and to protect him. But his stratagem proved useless. The year wore wearily on. But, according to Vambery, the treatment he was receiving was the exception rather than the rule. "The real Magyars," he wrote," were kind and tolerant to Jews. But not so the Slavs."

Despite his good reputation as a scholar, stones were hurled at him in the street and, in short, that second year at college was anything but agreeable. "Full of privations of every kind". He could eat his fill only once or twice a week, and nights in the cap-maker's kitchen were bitterly cold.

Nevertheless, now fourteen, he was busy building castles in the air. While other boys went in for games and sports, he was reading, devouring books. He even found that they drove away hunger. And towards the end of his second year he began to think seriously of leaving St. Georghen and continuing his studies at Pressburg: one thing alone made him hestitate, his father's grave was in the cemetery at St. Georghen, and he visited it frequently, especially when he felt depressed. Now he was to pay it a last visit. He had decided to do without his crutch "which not only gave rise to sarcastic remarks among my school-fellows, but also wore out my coat sleeve". Although alone and unobserved he broke it over his father's grave in a melodramatic gesture, so characteristic of him, and "with a heavy heart, and slow, laborious steps . . . returned to town, hopping most of the way on one foot. And with the help of a stick, "aided by my vanity, I was soon able to overcome all difficulties".

His mother advised him to spend his next holidays with relatives at Lundenburg* rather than at home. He set out, unsure how to get there. He did not have two pennies to rub together when, limping, he arrived in Pressburg. As luck would have it, he bumped into an old acquaintance from Szerdahely and got a free meal. Later he hitched a lift on a cart laden with hay as far as Vienna. A relative there provided the cash and he left after a two-day stay, buying himself plenty of food — fruit, various delicacies and especially butter-cake, his favourite — for his first railway journey. When he arrived at the station, he found to his dismay that he had not enough money left for his railway ticket. An amused booking clerk advised him to approach two well-dressed men in the hall and ask them in Latin for the missing sum.

The train was nearly due to leave when Vambery, in a panic, approached the two strangers and said: "*Domini spectabilis, rogo humillime, dignemini mihi dare aliquanto cruciferos qui iter ferrarium solvendi mihi carent*". ("Kind Sirs, please give me the few pence I lack for my fare"). He had not miscalculated the effect. "This Latin speech from a small, lame boy . . . had its effect, and they soon collected about two shillings for me". He bought his ticket and "hopping gaily through the waiting room, got into the compartment of the train for Lundenburg".

Vambery was now nearly fifteen; his relatives fitted him out with a new suit of clothes, gave him a few florins and sent him back to school at Pressburg.

*   now Breclav in Czechoslovakia.

He spent all the following summer holidays exploring the old Austro-Hungarian monarchy on foot, with the aid of his "travelling stick"; if he could not cadge lifts from cart-drivers, he would limp cheerfully on, putting up at night at the houses of the local clergy, where his Latin conversation earned him "some regard and a few kreutzers as well as some provisions" (Latin had survived in Hungary as a living language and a sign of education well into the 19th century and one is driven to speculate whether Vambery's "latinisation" of his first name was not in some way connected with it.)

In retrospect he was to consider these route marches excellent preparation for his wanderings as a dervish.

He disliked towns. When he returned to Pressburg he felt depressed for his old problem of finding a roof over his head had begun. Finally, after much searching, he found lodgings with a Mr. Lovy, it consisted in half a share of a folding bed.

Lovy ran a cookshop and soon after midday his room was filled with hungry students and tailors' apprentices. Their 1p meal consisted of small portions of soup, meat and vegetables and the heartless Lovy, well aware that Vambery could not pay the 1p, had banished him to a corner of the room where he sat "in vain trying to keep my eyes fixed on my book, and feeling all the gnawing pains of hunger . . ." ("The pangs of hunger . . . (are) . . . the same in Pressburg as in Central Asia"). Customers more charitable than Lovy, would gesture to him to finish the vegetables or other left-overs on the plate, or would press a hunk of bread into his hand . . .

The "eyes of the starving lad" had done the trick.

He now tried to enrol in the third form of a college run by Benedictine monks and his welcome was much the same as at his former school. "Well, Harshel", grumbled the head priest Father Aloysius Pendl, sarcastically "So you want to be a doctor, do you? . . ." and proceeded to make life difficult for Vambery. He was never to forget the three years spent at this college, nor the "endless instances of priestly animosity and disgraceful intolerance".

Under the influence of this teacher Vambery found his desire for study rapidly diminishing and was only happy when he could read and study on his own.

By this time he was quite fluent in Latin and knew Hungarian, German, Slovak and Hebrew; now he started on French since he had heard that it was essential if one wanted to get on in society and one's education was considered incomplete without it. He would make up conversations in his head or read aloud, declaiming the most trivial passages with pathos; in a short time he had acquired the reputation in school of knowing far more French than was actually the case and "conversed in French without restraint, and my volubility surprised not only myself but all who heard me". It developed into such an obsession with him that he would address everyone in sight in French — peasants, tradespeople, Slovaks, Germans and Hungarians, "it was all the same to me and great was my delight if they stared at me and admired me for my learning".

Vambery thought that hunger was the only problem he had to contend with, but one day he caught a skin disease from his bedmate (with whom he slept sardine fashion, head to toe). He was promptly evicted. As he still owed a few pence, Lovy kept all his belongings and Vambery left the house with nothing but his school books under his arm. Wandering around the streets, feeling utterly wretched and "like a pariah dog", not daring to look for lodgings elsewhere, lest he be turned out again, he lay down on a park bench and, exhausted by hunger and tiredness, burst into tears. Footsteps approached. Vambery assumed it was the night watchman, hastily removed his boots which had served him as a pillow, and crept underneath the bench. And there he remained for the rest of the night, peering out anxiously now and again, cowering there until day-break ...

At school the next day he said he was ill and was sent to a hospital run by the Friars of Mercy where he fully recovered.

He finished the third and fourth form at the Benedictine college but was far more interested in the progress of his private studies. He was later to be critical of his lack on method and of a solid college education "but on the other hand it spurred me on to greater industry and perseverance, as, being free from all control, I was master and pupil in one person".

As his circle of acquaintances grew, he found it easier to make a living by teaching. His fame "had spread in the lower classes of Jewish society, and it was chiefly to cooks and housemaids I gave lessons in reading and writing". In some cases he was employed to write *billets-doux*, "and in return for this service I received a good meal, sometimes even dainties". He was greatly in demand "and if I was able to commit to paper a sigh, a longing look, a greeting sweet as sugar, or even a kiss, I was sure of a rich reward, and could reckon on a good dinner or supper for days to come."

From cooks and housemaids his reputation spread to young ladies or even to the lady of the house. One evening, at the request of a cook who was head over heels in love with a shoe-maker, he sang a well-known German song which emphasised the sorrow of parting and accompanied himself on a guitar. He was called into the parlour where the lady and her two daughters made him sing further songs "and when the lady smoothed my curls and praised my voice and hair, I became aware ... that I was in for a good time".

But he was wrong. Etiquette did not allow the cook's teacher to be employed in the house. The lady of the house however recommended him as private tutor of Hungarian, French and Latin to the Jewish society of Pressburg.

In view of his age, the salary he received was less than two florins a month (about one penny an hour). If successful his salary was increased and he managed to live quite comfortably in Pressburg by teaching three hours a day and was filled with pride "when I bought with my own hard-earned money a tolerably threadbare coat and a pair of trousers".

But with eight hours at school and three or four spent daily in teaching he found little time for his own studies, even though he would allow himself a visit to the theatre or a piece of cake as a treat only occasionally.

Vambery had turned sixteen in 1848 and the Hungarian revolt against Austrian despotism had begun; all schools were closed in Hungary and commerce was at a standstill and, once again, the persecution of the Jews had begun.

The situation of the Jews in Pressburg, crammed into their ghetto, was peculiar. The houses on the one side of the main street, the Judengasse, once belonged to the Hungarian nobleman, Count Palffy: he had granted "his" Jews a Charter of Privileges as early as 1714, permitting them to engage in crafts and in all branches of commerce and allowing them freedom of worship. In 1770 the municipality of Pressburg has given the Jews permission to settle on land opposite to these houses and this constituted the Judengasse through which the mob now stormed and rampaged.

Vambery felt himself more a Hungarian than a Jew and was

most distressed by the execution of Hungarian patriots he witnessed. Some of the scenes remained indelibly imprinted on his memory.

It had become impossible for him to stay in Pressburg any longer and he began to look around for other posts as a tutor in the country. Finally he found a job in a quiet village in the Carpathian mountains and had time once more for his studies.

After a few months he had saved enough to continue his schooling but decided against entering the sixth form at the Benedictine College in favour of the Protestant school where the professors were known to be "unprejudiced, humane and intelligent"; he was sick to death "of the everlasting drudgery for the fanatical monks".

At the new school he was taught mainly in German and the lectures were better in every way. He felt he would have got on very well there, had he not had to worry about earning his living as well.

He was now eighteen and heartily sick of the struggles he had endured for eight hard years to make ends meet. "My spirit was so broken", he wrote, "that I decided to pause in my studies for a year and take an engagement with a country family", telling himself that he would take up his studies again when he had saved enough money.

Even though he consoled himself with one of his favourite mottoes "*Docendo dicimus* (by teaching we learn)" he bitterly regretted leaving school and going out into the world, as he felt, "without discipline, without a system, without even the supervision my age demanded".

On a visit to an uncle in the village of Szambokret in northern Hungary he met a Mr. von Petrikovitch, a small landowner and postmaster. He was sufficiently unprejudiced to engage Vambery as a tutor to his two sons, for the salary of 150 florins. Vambery called it "a modest honorarium" (one of his favourite phrases). He was not very happy since he considered his knowledge sadly defective", with the exception of Hungarian and Latin. The lady of the house took a liking to him and set about giving him lessons in etiquette. Now this "unpolished individual" (himself) learnt "how to handle my serviette, fork and knife at table, how to salute, walk, stand and sit".

As a result Vambery would spend whole hours over his toilet, practising "bows, and the elegant movement sof head and hands", without neglecting his duties as a tutor, but his own studies suffered considerably. The money he should have saved to recommence his studies again disappeared and at the end of the year he could not even find the sixteen florins he owed the Lutheran school in Pressburg and without which he could not obtain his school leaving certificate. (He was to berate himself for this bitterly in years to come).

Meanwhile his engagement ended; von Petrikovitch took his two sons to Pest* in the autumn of 1851 to finish their schooling there.

Vambery followed them feeling wretched and miserable.

He found Pest a gloomy, depressing place. Looking for cheap lodgings in miserable backstreets he met with no success: no one would take him in without references or at least part payment in advance. And so, reluctantly, he went in search of a relative who took him in for a few days and then "slipping two florins into my hand gave me the paternal advice to try and find something to do, as his wife objected to my presence there".

There was only thing left: to look for a coffee-house . . . If this sounds strange, it must be remembered that in those days a coffee-house functioned as the Labour Exchange of the ghetto. It was a meeting-place of tradespeople who were likely to know if anyone required a teacher of languages.

The Cafe Orczy was such a place. Prospective employers came there to inspect their wares. The place was dirty and noisy and reeked of tobacco smoke: it was crowded with town and country Jews, all bargaining and shouting and yelling at the top of their voices. "In the afternoon, between two and four, the crush and clatter were at their worst in this paedagogic exchange", wrote Vambery. "At that time everybody of importance was there . . ."

The men who acted as agents, procuring servants, kosher butchers, brandy distillers or tutors for wealthy Jewish families, were themselves merchants or farmers; they came to Pest twice a year, at the time of the big agricultural fairs and when their work was done doubled as agents.

The eligible teachers were seated on a bench, anxiously scanning the agent's face, while the future employer would stand in front of them, looking them up and down and finally deciding on one or the other of the candidates. Vambery felt this to be an

---

* Buda and Pest did not become united until 1873.

extremely humiliating experience and was later to compare it with the slave markets in the bazaars of Central Asia. He shuddered even in his old age whenever he passed the Cafe Orczy.

The first man to employ him here was touched by his "timid and dejected appearance". To Vambery's dismay, however, he found that the family lived a good distance from the Piarist College he wished to attend and that his lodgings consisted of a bed in the servants' room; he shared it with the cook, the chambermaid and one of the children. The food was so extremely poor and scanty that "the memory of the various meals of the day was rather in my thoughts than in my stomach". At night, when he tried to get on with his studies, the cook or the chambermaid began to sing or to quarrel, or to play tricks on him . . . and it finally became so unbearable that he gave notice.

He had only been admitted to the seventh form of the Piarist school as a temporary student and, since he was never able to supply the missing school leaving certificate from his previous school, was compelled to leave this college for good.

This was decisive and he made up his mind to turn his back on towns and schools and to try and find a place in the country as a private tutor. The decision "to leave forever the road which was to lead me to a definite profession in life . . . aimlessly studying foreign languages instead . . ." was, in his own words, extremely painful. He had no inkling how this was to shape his future career.

By now he claimed he could read German, French and Italian, without the help of a dictionary, spoke Hungarian and Slovak and a little Czech, and knew Hebrew and Latin. On the strength of these accomplishments, he writes, "I had the audacity to advertise myself as professor of seven languages, and in my arrogance I even pretended to teach them all".

He was obliged to return to the "bench of shame" at the Cafe Orczy, sitting there for hours "with a heavy heart and deeply ashamed". Finally the agent managed to "sell" him; Vambery had, of course, to pay for his own equipment and travelling expenses.

His prospective employer, a Mr. Rosenberg, was scarcely much older than Vambery himself; he was on the look-out for a teacher for his younger brothers and sisters and Vambery addressed him in fluent French, so he tells us, and was engaged on the spot.

When Vambery arrived at Rosenberg's house, in the village of Kutyevo, his reception was a carbon copy of what had happened in Nyek. Vambery was "too young", his cheeks were "too red"; moreover Mama greatly feared for the moral safety of her sixteen year old daughter, Miss Emily.

However, Vambery was accepted, given a good room, had excellent food and taught for six hours a day and had enough time to devote to his own studies. "It was here that I first began to give my studies a definite direction", he wrote, "for after acquiring a so-called knowledge of several European languages I passed on to Turkish, and turned my attention to oriental studies".

He took a special delight in memorising and set himself a given number of words each day to learn by heart, increasing their number from ten to sixty, and even a hundred. He was still worried about his lack of formal schooling and took himself severely to task for having neglected to save the sixteen florins for his certificate twice over.

Guilt-laden he determined not to waste a single moment in his studies and would scribble admonitions to himself in the margin in his books — using Arabic characters so that no one else could read them — and even on the walls of his room. "Persevere!" "Be ashamed of yourself!" "Work!"

He now could read the various classics in the original and covered the margin of his books with enthusiastic comments. He liked particularly Voltaire's *Henriade*, Petrarch's *Sonnets* or James Thomson's *Seasons*, losing himself in day-dreams. His favourite spot was on a hill, just outside the village underneath a spreading cherry tree, near a stream. There he would sit for hours, declaiming aloud the passages he loved the most oblivious to thunderstorms and rain, often drenched to the skin, holding forth to the birds or flowers or blades of grass . . .

His ardour was heightened for this romantic youth had fallen in love for the first time — with 'Miss Emily', just as Mama had foreseen. Miss Emily, however, "took good care not to give the poor, lame tutor the slightest encouragement". Vambery took a bold step: he took hold of her "plump little hand" to guide it in forming the letters of the alphabet, and the contact "soon sent a fire of passion tingling into my finger-tips . . ." The young lady jumped up, gave Vambery an angry look and left the room. Vambery was dismissed on the spot.

He was exceedingly sorry to leave not only his haven of rest but also to lose the generous salary of 600 florins per annum, most of which he had already spent on books and clothes; he had saved

Cafe Orczy, Budapest (coffee house founded in 1795). This photograph was taken in 1935 (Cafe, lower right part of photo). Cafe destroyed (? in 1945) presumably.

only enough to travel to Pest and to Szerdahely to see his mother. Sadly he took leave of the old cherry tree, under whose shade he had spent "so many blissful hours with the intellectual heroes of Italy, England, France and Spain", and cried for hours; "and with good reason", he adds, "for never again in all my life have I had moments of such pure enjoyment".

He was afraid of facing his mother. What would she say? He had not saved a penny: all he could show for his labour were a few new clothes and a silver watch.

It cut no ice with her that he had taught himself Serbian as well. His mother gave him a good talking to and wanted to know where the knowledge of so many languages would lead him. Could he not get a regular job of some kind? She felt her son would have done better to go on with his schooling, take a degree and become a doctor. In vain did Vambery explain to her (with great foresight) that the knowledge of so many — especially Oriental — languages, might one day make him famous . . .

Meanwhile it was his ambition to become an interpreter. ". . . The acquisition of so many languages, and the stimulus of praise . . . had puffed me up with egotism, I fancied myself worthy of something better than the humble position of tutor in a Jewish family." And so he travelled to Vienna, bent on obtaining from the Ministry of Foreign Affairs an appointment as interpreter. A forlorn hope! That he would fail was a foregone conclusion; how could he, a stranger in Vienna, without introductions or letters of recommendation, ignorant of the pedantic and tortuous passages of Austrian bureaucracy and with the wrong background, obtain State employment? He therefore tried to get private lessons, this time advertising in Viennese newspapers, without any result . . .

His lodgings consisted of a bed in the flat of a tailor, on the fourth floor of a dilapidated house. This man advised Vambery to return to Hungary as long as he had a few books and some clothes left to sell to cover his travelling expenses.

But Vambery did not give up.

He met the celebrated Austrian Orientalist, Baron Joseph von Hammer-Purgstall, who in turn introduced him to Baron Schlechta (a future Austrian Minister). Both men were important influences on Vambery's ambitions. They encouraged him to continue his studies of Turkology, convinced that native Hungarians possessed great linguistic advantages in the study of Oriental languages. Hammer-Purgstall, author of innumerable volumes on

34

the East, had spent many years at the turn of the century in Constantinople, and Vambery must have been enthralled by all the old man's stories.

He returned to Pest and found lodgings at 7 Three Drums Street — though this is again an euphemism. The tenants let out single beds. Vambery's new landlady was a Mrs. Schonfeld, a nurse, who had an invalid husband to look after. She had no less than four beds in one room, accommodating eight persons. The tenants were mostly underpaid artisans, out of work the whole day. As a bedfellow Vambery, "a special favourite of the childless Madame Schonfeld, had the privilege of receiving a thin tailor lad, who, because of his lanky proportions did not take up quite so much room in the bed". They again slept sardine-fashion and sometimes it would happen that the stranger would kick his mate out of bed in his sleep.

Vambery revisited his former "agent", a certain Mr. Mayer, and waited for a well-paid post to turn up. Meanwhile he supported himself as best he could by giving private lessons for two or three florins per month, but his down-at-heel appearance precluded him from gaining entry to the "better circles" of the capital. The more he progressed in his studies the more irksome he found teaching. Hunger plagued him again and he felt depressed; he sought solace in his books.

He was now devoting from ten to twelve hours a day to his studies and had added Russian to the other Slav languages so that he could soon read Pushkin and other Russian classics in the original, taking great pleasure in wandering from "north to south and from east to west" in literature. "My joy and my delight were boundless . . . I tingled with the excitement of the lyric or epic content of these various works".

The people he associated with most were "bartering Jews of the most prosaic type, artisans, day-labourers, and shop-assistants, their only thought how to earn a few coppers, and to spend them straight away . . . menders and cleaners of old clothes, poor women and pedlars . . ."; they looked upon him as half-demented, sometimes pitied him and at other times made fun of him.

In winter he was cold as well as hungry, especially when the public reading room of the University closed and he had to sit in his landlady's unheated parlour. At night he went to the near-by Cafe Szegedin and, huddled up in a corner, tried to read his books by the flickering light of a gas lamp, despite the noise going on around him. In his room he continued his studies by candlelight, "while the sleeping inmates accompanied my recital — for I always read aloud — with a snoring duet or terzet . . ." He got little sleep himself, for in the early morning he gave a lesson to the son of a coffee-house proprietor next door, in return for a mug of hot coffee and two rolls.

Finally his "agent" got him a job with a wealthy family in Kecskemet. He was well paid, well cared for, but also hard worked, teaching for eight or nine hours daily. He spent two to three hours over his appearance and meals, and devoted about six hours daily to his own studies.

Now he had more money at his disposal than ever before and could afford the expensive books he required for the study of Oriental languages; he concentrated mainly on Turkish and Arabic and was lucky in striking up an acquaintance with a professor living in the vicinity, who could lend him Arabic books. He found that his knowledge of Hebrew helped him to progress rapidly in the second semitic language and with the help of Arabic also to perfect to himself in Turkish.

Vambery remained with the family one year, and then returned to Pest, occupying once more the "seat of disgrace" in the Cafe Orczy. His next employer lived in a lonely house on the edge of the Puszta* and there he spent the following spring and summer. "Here I had the first foretaste of the Steppe regions of Central Asia, afterwards to be the scene of my adventurous travels".

He would lie for hours in the shade of a hayrick reading the *Odyssey* (for he claimed to have meanwhile taught himself Greek as well), as a respite from his Oriental studies; stretched out on the grass, he never noticed the shepherd grazing his flock who now stood before him "both hands on his staff, and listening in breathless attention to the strange sounds, half admiring, half pitying me . . ."

They all thought him mad, a man who had learned too much and was now possessed of the devil . . .

His reputation as an eccentric spread and to this he owed his invitation to a wealthy neighbour whose passion was meteorology, and who had set up strange instruments everywhere. He was thought an eccentric as well. A friendship sprang up between

* The Great Plain of Hungary.

Vambery and this man who engaged him as tutor in French and English for his son.

Here Vambery spent the next winter. He had a quiet, large room, overlooking a garden, had good food, his teaching duties occupied only a few hours a day and he had much time and leisure to devote to his studies of Turkish, Arabic and Persian and was enchanted by their poets.

But the idyll soon came to an end. The lady of the house could not bear the idea of a Jewish tutor in her house and took to "sneering at my origin and my want of gentlemanly manners". Unpleasant scenes and family quarrels were the order of the day, with Vambery's employer taking his side, but Vambery decided that he would have to leave and — with a heavy heart — returned to Pest.

After about six months he found a job with a family in the county of Veszprem. This was to be his last post as a tutor and one of the pleasantest. There was one dramatic incident, however, which would stand out in his memory for many years "like some dreadful dream": an encounter with robbers from the Bakonyi forest . . .

One rainy night there was a banging at the door. Vambery opened it and the thugs burst in and held the family to ransom. He was knocked to the floor in the scuffle, yet "with one of the ruffians kneeling on my chest and the barrel of a pistol . . . pressed to my forehead", managed to gain the upper hand. He jumped up, so he tells us, and "placing the weapon on my own breast" cried melodramatically: "If you must kill, kill me: I have neither wife nor children . . ." With the result that the leader of the gang desisted and the robbers left with a booty of 20,000 Florins belonging to Vambery's employer, the family's valuables and Vambery's Hungarian classics . . .

Since it was he who had opened the door and had had only a few books stolen he came in for some suspicion from the Austrian police; he was saved from imprisonment by his employer. Vambery himself believed the robbers to have been political fugitives hiding from the Austrians.

By now his idea to travel to the East had become an obsession. His imagination fired from early youth, he was eager to discover the mysterious origin of the Hungarians and above all their language. He now decided to do something about it. Although sad to leave this "peaceful haven of rest and comfort" he gave notice. A decisive factor had been the death of his beloved mother. "The last link with the land of my birth was broken . . . My name was the last word that passed her lips, and her death left me absolutely alone, with no one to care for me in all the world".

By now Vambery had magyarised his name ("as has been the custom with us for centuries") because he felt his ancestors had been Hungarians for several generations and his education had been "strictly Magyar".

He considered the six years he had spent as a private tutor the most productive of his life, forming the nucleus for his future actions, but with hindsight he realised that his inborn talent for languages had led him astray and that sometimes he had acquired only a superficial knowledge of the languages; his lack of system and method was to invite great criticism on the part of his more staid University colleagues, who had followed a more orthodox academic career, and who turned up their collective nose at an autodidact.

He claimed that he could now speak fluently, read and write moderately well in several of the languages he had taught himself yet he was not satisfied. He was excessively strict with himself and devised a curious system of reprimanding and punishing himself. Many a New Year's Eve he would spend in solitude, and writing out and sealing his resolutions for the coming year. These he would open on the next New Year's Eve and when he saw that he had not kept to one or the other point, would write "bitter reproaches" to himself in the margin of books "and was out of sorts for days". He also kept a daily calendar on which he marked the different subjects to be studied before retiring to bed. If, for one reason or another, he had not been able to stick to this routine, he made up for it the following day, and if he did not do so the next day he would punish himself by leaving the table under the pretext of a headache or indigestion. "With my healthy appetite this was the severest punishment I could think of . . ."

Vambery had begun to plan his journey to the East in Kecskemet. But how was he to accomplish it? His obsession had grown apace with his knowledge of Oriental languages but not so his finances. His delight in Oriental poetry and literature acted as a spur, but he had only 120 florins in his pocket — all his savings. He was weary of teaching and longed for adventure: the time for action had come.

Although he had only half the money for his passage, he determined to set out for Constantinople, treating the fact that once he arrived there (if he arrived at all) he would be penniless, with cavalier disregard. It did not worry him in the least. "I shall manage somehow" he told himself. What worried him far more was how to get a passport from the Austrian authorities who were chary of Hungarians bound for Constantinople, afraid of revolutionary plots being hatched there by the Hungarian refugees.

Vambery realised he would get nowhere without influence.

Fortuiutously Baron Joseph Eotvos, an exceptionally able and far-seeing man, writer and scientist and later Minister of Religion and Education, had heard of Vambery and wished to meet him personally. When the appointment was fixed, Vambery was greatly embarrassed for his clothes were terribly shabby; his shoes had practically fallen apart, and since he had no money to buy a new pair he had tied rags to his feet. Afraid that coming into the Baron's house from the street he would leave marks all over the carpet he tied makeshift cardboard soles to his feet; but his precautions were in vain. Baron Eotvos noticed the footmarks but dismissed the incident with a smile. He put Vambery completely at his ease and asked him what had made him take up the study of philology. Vambery's answers seem to have satisfied the Baron, for the latter promised to take him under his wing, giving him an introduction to the library of the Academy of Sciences, so that he could now borrow books . . .

The matter of the passport was not so easily arranged but Baron Eotvos succeeded. He even tried to start a collection for Vambery: in this he failed. Finally the Baron, who was to become Vambery's protector and guardian-angel, gave him some money and clothing and sent him on his way, with his blessing, merely asking for some news of him from time to time.

The local Hungarian newspaper *Pesti Naplo* (February 1857) devoted a whole article to the young man's adventurous ambitions, complete with a picture headed 'VAMBERGER ARMIN'. The article described the career of the "talented young man" on his way to Constantinople to study the Turkish language and literature.

Now Vambery was in possession of the most important things: a valid travel document and some cash. He soon packed up his dictionaries, a few favourite books and some underwear, and was ready for his first journey to the East. At the recommendation of Baron Eotvos he was given a ticket to Galatz* at half price; he booked second class, boarding the Danube steamer at Pest one fine Spring morning. Delighted with the great variety of passengers of different nationalities he saw, he remained on deck, talking to all and sundry and trying to address everyone in their mother-tongue. This called forth much admiration "which sometimes expressed itself in the offer of a drink, sometimes in the invitation to a modest repast which I always gladly accepted". After a good meal, Vambery felt euphoric and began to recite long passages from his favourite classics — mostly it was Petrarch's *Sonnets* — with an eye on the ship's cook who was Italian. Soon he was invited to sit by the kitchen door and while Vambery declaimed with fervour the cook, stirring his pots and pans inside, would break into an admiring "Bravo!", *"Ben Fatto!"* ("Well done!") and hand out from time to time "a plateful of the best food his kitchen could produce".

Vambery felt his first journey to the east had got off to an auspicious start.

He soon saw that his pronunciation was often faulty and made ample use of his fellow passengers to improve it and so made rapid progress.

At Widdin* he saw his first Turks come on board. The deck was swarming with Serbians and Bulgarians and at sunset one of the Turks stepped forth, spread his prayer mat in front of him and began to recite his evening devotions. Vambery was deeply impressed by the sight. As soon as the old man had finished his prayers and rolled up his mat Vambery approached and spoke to him. He was not slow in finding out that the old man was on his way to Constantinople to visit his son (later Minister of Justice) and was now on a pilgrimage to Mecca. A useful contact, thought young Vambery and showed him a religious book he had studied, reciting parts of it aloud. The result was an invitation to supper by the old man, who became a good friend.

At Galatz he had to transfer to a Lloyd steamer bound for Constantinople; he could only afford a lower deck ticket. But he was excited: soon he would see with his own eyes "the briny ocean" (the Black Sea) so familiar to him from the descriptions of Byron and other poets. When he actually did so he was "almost giddy

---

* Now Galati (in Rumania).
* Now Vidin in Bulgaria.

41

with delight and admiration". He stationed himself near the bow-sprit and imagined he was riding a dolphin, exhilarated by the salty waves washing all over him. He sang, shouted until far into the night until finally, nearly soaked to the skin, he left his perch and joined a group of sleeping Turks, huddled together in a corner of the deck. About midnight he was suddenly awakened by the pitching and rolling of the ship. "The howling of the wind, the creaking of the planks, the jolting and bumping of the vessel, the sighs and groans of the passengers . . . soon made me realise that I was to have the good fortune of witnessing a real storm . . . Regardless of the consternation round me, the fright, the lamentations, the cries, and the general confusion, I steered my way along the pitch-dark deck, and was beside myself with joy when an occasional flash of lightning gave me the sight of the awful spectacle around, and the black waves towering high above me . . ."

Was it quite by accident that he stood leaning against the railing which separated his deck from the first-class passengers? What prompted him, in his "rapturous excitement" to declaim a few stanzas from Voltaire's *Henriade* just then? Whatever the motive, it had useful results. For his sharp eye had detected a first-class passenger on the other side of the barrier muffled up to his ears, yet occasionally stopping to listen. "Who are you?" shouted the traveller above the storm. "What makes you think of the *Henriade* just now?"

What indeed? The hope of a good meal?

Vambery moved closer to the barrier and soon found out that this distinguished traveller was the Secretary of the Belgian legation at Constantinople. The choice of French had been an inspired one.

The next morning, while admiring the Bosporus, Vambery spent a long time in conversation with this man and was asked to call on him in Pera, the European quarter of Constantinople.

Vambery felt his first journey to the east had got off to an auspicious start.

2

EFFENDI OF CONSTANTINOPLE

With high hopes and not a penny in his pocket, Vambery stepped ashore at Pera. The Danube steamer had cast anchor at the Golden Horn and his last coins had been spent paying for his passage across to the European sector; now not a piastre remained.

This was hardly likely to dismay Vambery who, at twenty-five, was seeing his wildest dreams come true. Besides, lack of money had never disturbed him; he was accustomed to it from early youth and relied on his resourcefulness, which had never failed him yet. On board the steamer he had in any case, he felt, made a valuable contact: he had met the Secretary of the Belgian Legation at Pera; hence his choice of the European sector of Stambul. He was excited and supremely confident as he looked around and took stock of the city, fascinated by the mixture of types, the variety of national costumes he saw around him and all the languages buzzing around his ears. These included Turkish, Greek, Armenian . . . and Hungarian, for in the year 1857 Constantinople was filled with Hungarian refugees who had fled the abortive uprising against Austria in 1848. Vambery felt he would not have long to search before he found a compatriot; and, indeed, he was soon hailed by an individual attracted by the ribbons on his hat, though, he says, the man addressed him in Italian. He wanted to know who Vambery was and where he was bound for. The stranger turned out to be a Mr. Puspoki, a former quartermaster in the Crimean War. He led him to his rat-infested lodgings and, with true Hungarian hospitality, offered Vambery a share in this princely apartment — half a divan. But the most pressing problem was where to eat. Puspoki led him to the grandly named *Cafe Flamm de Vienne*, a basement eating place situated in the Grande Rue de Pera where they sold Austrian innovations such as cafe-au-lait and Viennese rolls. His new friend bought Vambery a cup of coffee and a roll or two, but the urgent problem nevertheless presented itself: how to pay for food in future?

Vambery was never at a loss for long. He decided, for a start, that the Cafe Flamm was not likely to yield good results: a place frequented by emigres and armchair strategists, planning, as everywhere, a triumphant return home, and trying to make a cup of coffee last for half a day, was not a happy hunting ground. He looked elsewhere.

He discovered the old Turkish quarter and talked to everyone, glad to practise his Turkish. Watching the Turks lounging in their coffee-houses, leisurely smoking their *nargilehs* (water pipes) and listening to the story-teller on his high stool gave Vambery the inspiration he required. He entered and began reciting; a crowd soon collected and applauded. Heartened by this success he began frequenting the coffee-houses, emulating the story-tellers, and reading aloud passages from well-known poems "with the right accent and modulation" and reaping a rich harvest, he tells us, of bread, cheese and coffee, with sometimes even a *Kebab* (chunks of beef on a spit) or *Pastirma* (dry, smoked meat) thrown in. His listeners were impressed by his knowledge of Turkish and Persian and were amazed that, only two days after his arrival, he already spoke Turkish "like a gentleman" and could read and write it as well. He claims that many soon took him for a native "and the jokes and jests caused by this muddle of languages gave me many a delicious moment". He went on talking, perfecting his accent and grammar. But his friend Puspoki got another job, and Vambery had to leave his lodgings and his rats. He went to the "Magyar Club" where he was offered a large old divan (to himself) in a draughty hall and — when he complained of the cold — a tattered Hungarian flag to keep him warm.

Vambery looked around for better things.

He had made the acquaintance of a Hungarian Major who lived in a lonely house and who was frequently away on business. His watchdog had recently died and he offered Vambery board and lodging if he would look after the house. "So I was to occupy the vacant position of watchdog! It was not particularly inviting . . . but instead of a dog kennel I had a comfortable room and plenty of coffee and bread for breakfast". Vambery moved in.

He spent the mornings reading Turkish books, did some chores about the house in the afternoons, and in the evenings visited Turkish coffee-houses where he continued earning a piastre or two reciting love-poems. "No sooner was I seated on a high stool, surrounded by Turks and Armenians and had begun to recite in a nasal sing-song tone, when the conversation gradually dropped and the rattling of the water-pipes began to subside . . ."

Vambery had a genuine gift for making friends — a gift which was to prove useful to him on all his future travels. He had already acquired quite a large circle of acquaintances and these included some of the booksellers in Pera. The idea struck him to advertise his services in their shops, offering himself as a teacher "of a whole string of Western and Eastern languages".

Response was immediate. His first student was a Mr. von Hubsch, the Danish Counsul-General, who despite his German-sounding name was of Turkish extraction. His knowledge of Danish was rudimentary and he engaged Vambery to teach him to read Danish court circulars and newspapers. "Not in all my wildest dreams", writes Vambery, "had it entered my head that I would be called upon to teach a representative of Denmark the language of that country!" However, at the end of eighteen months, von Hubsch was able not only to read the newspapers but a novel as well, and no doubt Vambery had also made progress in Danish.

Vambery's next student was a young Bey who had made a good inheritance and was now trying to improve his manners and appearance. "This", says Vambery, "included a fashionable tailored suit, tight patent leather shoes, a small jaunty fez, rakishly worn on one side of the head, gloves, correct deportment — and a knowledge of French." (For in the Turkey of Vambery's day French was in great demand: France had been one of Turkey's allies in the Crimean war.) Vambery did not approve of his pupil. "He was lazy and frivolous," he comments testily, ". . . his object was merely to have a French *maitre* come to his house . . .", adding, characteristically, ". . . but I need hardly say that the instruction I imparted was highly profitable to myself". He also liked the "well-cooked and abundant breakfast" at the end of each lesson and the daily ride on horseback and — since everything European was fashionable in Turkey at the time — lost no time in riding his hobby-horse as well: the superior virtues of western culture. One of his greatest defects was, in fact, this tendency to judge everything he came across by this yardstick. This prejudice was often to hamper any deeper understanding of Oriental mentality and customs.

45

High officials of the Porte* and effendis used to frequent the young Bey's house at Chamlidjia, on a hill above Scutari (on the Asian shore of the Bosporus). This gave Vambery good practice in Turkish conversation and enabled him to learn "the manners and customs in Turkish society and the elegancies of Osmanli speech". After only three months, he claimed, he could act the effendi not only in outward appearance, manners and gesticulation but could hold a conversation in Turkish as well.

Through the intervention of Ismail Pasha (who was in reality General Kmethy, a Hungarian freedom fighter Vambery had known at home) he got a job in the household of Hussein Daim Pasha, as tutor to his son, Hassan Bey, moving from his scruffy lodgings in Pera to the patrician villa of the Pasha at Fyndykli, in a strictly Mohammedan part of the town. From the window of his room he could see the magnificent palace of Bekitash which housed the Sultan's harem — enough to fire the romantic imagination of any young man.

"Henceforth", he writes, "I became a regular Turk. Only the name was now wanting . . ."

This was soon to follow.

After some instruction in Turkish etiquette, ". . . how to sit decorously, i.e. cross-legged . . . how to hold my head, hands . . . how to yawn, sneeze and so forth" by the kindly old Majordomo, the Pasha must have thought Vambery's transformation complete, for he ordered his household to call him "Reshid" (the brave, the discreet) from now on.

Vambery was not always able to live up to his new name.

At the time there was a plot to dethrone Sultan Abdul Medjid and the conspiracy was hatched in this house. Hussein Daim Pasha was at its head and one of the fiercest among his followers was Ahmed Effendi, a Mollah (lay teacher) of whom Vambery was terrified. But the zealot, "always barefoot and half naked, his eyes scattering flames," armed with sword and lance, unbent a little when he heard Vambery being called by his new name. He became a little friendlier and finally even allowed him to visit him in his cell at the mosque, believing Vambery to be on the point of conversion. "A very false inference!" writes Vambery, "but I did not destroy his hopes, thus gaining his good will and getting him to give me instruction in Persian".

---

* Porte: the Turkish Imperial Government; the *Sublime Porte* (Gate) was the chief office of the Ottoman government at Constantinople.

This man was a thorough Persian and Arabic scholar, and Vambery was indebted more to him than to anyone else for his external transformation into an Asiatic. Spellbound, he used to sit at his feet, listening — "it seemed as if I had got hold of a fairy key unlocking to my dazzled eyes the whole of Mohammedan Asia" — for the dream of his youth to explore Central Asia had never left him. Soon he was joining in religious ceremonies and discussing abstruse religious questions with Mohammedans — the question of whether he ever intended to become one was never put to him by any of the educated who were in any case sceptical, he says, as far as the genuine conversion of any European was concerned (but the uneducated gave him endless trouble at first). A formal conversion is not required in Islam. There is a minimum of ritual. The first precept is circumcision: as an orthodox Jew by birth he fulfilled it. The second one is to profess belief in Allah and in his prophet, Mohammed. He gave lip service to it, rehearsing the role, as it were, which he was later to play to perfection on his travels.

Was he a hypocrite? A ruthless opportunist? Even though he was a freethinker at heart, one must remember that the hardships of his early youth had taught him one great lesson: there was no one he could rely on but himself. All means were fair to him if they would help to achieve his objective, and if religion was going to help in furthering his plans then he was certainly going to use it.

He therefore seized the unusual opportunity to study at a Medresseh (Islamic college) and later claimed with pride to have been the first European to have done so.

This was a result of his second job: tutor to Kiamil, the son of Afif Bey, Chief Chancellor of the Imperial Divan. Afif's house was the Rendezvous of Turkish society, and here Vambery met diplomats, high civil servants and celebrated writers. Among the prominent men he met was Midhat Effendi (later to become Midhat Pasha, founder of the Turkish constitution in 1877) who was then secretary to his Pasha. Vambery helped him with his French studies and in return received help in deciphering difficult Turkish historical texts and corrected his essays. Midhat Effendi also enabled him to attend the Medresseh, impressed perhaps by Vambery's intellectual gifts and interest in Eastern things. Here Vambery attended lectures by famous Islamic exegists, grammarians and lawyers, unsuspected by the other students of divinity and

This unique photograph shows Arminius Vambery during his life at Constantinople (1861) together with Daniel Szilanyi, former officer in the Army of the Hungarian Liberty (1849). Vambery with the tarbush on his head is on the left.

acquired a practical knowledge of Islam — "the talisman which had been my guide in all subsequent journeys and wanderings".

With his orthodox background the method of study must have hardly seemed strange to him, even though the subject matter was different. At an orthodox Jewish *Yeshiveh* — as at an Islamic college — endless discussions on the finer points of the law took place; they argued with one another, the discussed the minutest detail or ritual, they spoke for and against . . . and he who could hold out longest with his arguments in these "disputations" was reckoned to be the best scholar. Vambery, obviously, was top of the class. Soon he was called "Mukhtedi" (one brought to the truth, or properly converted) and his teachers and fellow students "were particularly obliging to me, and all my remarks were applauded".

By 1859 (he was then 27) he could take part in "single disputations" and he tells us that his name began to be frequently mentioned in society. As Reshid Effendi he had been able to move about freely in Turkish society without in any way binding himself. In the space of two years he really began to look the part. This was possible because, in the Turkey of Vambery's day, the language of the elite was a mixture of Arabic and Persain — Turkish was the every day language.

More and more doors were open to him. He was impressed by the absence of aristocratic pride and class distinction and flattered to be received by "vizier, marshal, minister or the son-in-law of the Sultan". No questions were asked regarding his antecedents (which he himself seemed unable to forget) and he, "an obscure Jewish teacher at home", had become in the space of two years, "the confidential friend of the most distinguished and wealthiest dignitaries". Here was a country, he felt, where a man was judged on his merits alone.

It certainly helped that he now had a job in the house of Rifat Pasha, a former Minister of Foreign Affairs, as teacher of history, geography and French of his son, Reouf Bey. This house, "the richest in Stambul" was also the focus of the literary elite of the time, a centre where the celebrated *Kiatibs* (writers and calligraphers) embellished the all-important document called *Tugra*: this was the Sultan's seal, the 'passport' destined to extricate Vambery from many a dangerous situation on his travels.

Vambery's quarters were on the top floor of his rich and powerful protector's house, only a few paces away from the curtain separating the harem from the other apartments; and since he had access to not only one but several noble families and was known as a man "who knew how to respect holy customs", his (sharp and observant' eye was able to roam "far more freely than it would otherwise have been able to in view of the difference in sex and origin". He made many mental notes and filed them for future use.

Since he was known to be so familiar with Turkish custom and could be trusted "not to infringe upon the strict rules of the harem" he was chosen to teach a royal pupil, "Princess F ..." (Fatma, daughter of Sultan Abdul Medjid and sister of Abdul Hamid). His acquaintance with the young Abdul Hamid dates from this day.

Vambery was still tutor in the house of Rifat Pasha and would go three times a week to the palace on the bay of Bebek, Dr. Ahn's *First French Course* in hand. This was a revolutionary language teaching method for the times, a kind of forerunner of Berlitz, for it gave priority to conversation over grammar. ("Learn a foreign language as you learn your mother tongue".) Vambery gives us an amusing account of the lessons: "Madame la Princesse F ... daughter of a sultan and daughter-in-law of a Vizier always sat behind the heavy curtain of her chamber in her palace of white marble while I taught into the curtain, Ahn's French grammar in hand, watched by fierce-looking eunuchs: *Pere-baba; mere-ana; mon pere est bon* ... whereupon the delicate voice of a lady would respond with *Benim baba eji dir.*" Teacher and student never set eyes on each other.

He made frequent visits to Pera, the European quarter, and renewed his influential contacts there; one of them was the Austrian ambassador, Baron von Schlechta whose acquaintance he had made in Vienna. By now Vambery's fame as the only European masquerading as the perfect effendi was such that people began to take notice of him, regarding him as a useful source of information, both on the European and on the Turkish side. He was given introductions to the Prussian, Italian and British embassies. He taught Turkish to the naturalist Count Keyserling (grandfather of the famous philosopher). At the British embassy he met Count Pisani, first head interpreter to the British ambassador, Lord Stratford de Redcliffe (formerly Stratford Canning, the celebrated 'Great Elchi'): the "man of the iron mien" was amazed when he heard the supposed effendi "talk English fluently". How fluent?

And with what accent? one is tempted to ask, for many years later Vambery was forced to admit that he "murdered the language of Byron and Shakespeare".

By then he was teacher of a son-in-law of Mahmud Nedim Pasha, nicknamed 'Nedimoff' on account of his pro-Russian sympathies.

In the Turkey of Vambery's day great importance was attached to the knowledge of French "and not much to the knowledge of geography, history, mathematics and other sciences . . . I positively blushed", he writes, "when I had to translate the Pasha's ignorant remarks about the Suez canal . . ."

Turkey was also being urged by the West to carry out an intensive program of reform" in the school, in the harem, in religion and in government" and Vambery was very much in favour of this but believed it could only be carried out gradually, arguing that the differences between Asiatic and European civilisation were too great to be overcome by a hasty outward assimilation. He was to ridicule these attempts at a later date.

He met the reform leaders at the house of his employer: Reshid Pasha, a "well-bred, fair and patriotic" man; and Ali Pasha (of whom Napoleon III said that he wrote better French than many a French diplomat) was "very able", but a "paragon of Oriental intriguers and dissimulators". Whenever Vambery was in earshot Ali Pasha would lower his voice and it was not until Vambery had borrowed some Chagataic (or Eastern Turkish) books from his well-stocked library that he spoke uninhibitedly in his presence "in the full conviction that I, the philologist, took no interest whatever in politics."

Vambery, too, could dissimulate when it suited his (Chagataic) books!

The third reform leader was Fuad Pasha, a "tall, stately man, with refined, thoroughly *European* manners." He gives him full marks. "With his sparkling wit and humorous *apercus* he was more like a Frenchman than a Turk".

He met many others in the reform movement and argued his case with conviction at these "nightly assemblies". Among them was Damad Kiamil Pasha, a Turkish gentleman of the old school, immensely rich who wavered in his sympathies between East and West. Nevertheless he wanted to learn French "in advanced age" and "was fond of me", writes Vambery, "because in his attempts to translate Fenelon's *Telemaque* I had served him instead of a dictionary". Vambery must have known whole passages of this book by heart. It was standard equipment for those who taught according to Dr. Ahn's method.

The old Pasha seems to have been pleased with the results and "took great delight" in Vambery's recitations of Turkish poems. Modesty was not one of his strong points.

He suffered greatly at the hands of the servants. Uncorking his bottled-up resentment years later in a book entitled *Moral Pictures from the Orient*, designed to appeal to an untravelled mass-readership in Central Europe (it was never translated into English) and written in a florid style, he believed that he had genuinely "contributed to a knowledge of the Orient". But how could someone blinkered by prejudice, who judged everything he saw from the lofty pinnacle of the "superior" European do so? Often he derides the funny customs of the "backward" Orientals, in a painful effort, one feels, to be entertaining. However, the passages dealing with Stambul gives a fascinating picture of life there in the middle of the 19th century.

Servants were all-powerful.

Presiding over all, at the top of the hierarchy, whether at home or in the office, was the *Tchibuktchi* — the pipe servant, forever at his master's beck and call, with long-stemmed pipe, fire and bowl, and virtually his shadow for tobacco and pipe denoted rank and status. (Abdul Medjid is reputed never to have taken more than three puffs from any one pipe, Ali Pasha never to have smoked a pipe to the end.)

The almighty pipe-servant was also entrusted with bringing home highly important documents. "Their first place in the house", writes Vambery sardonically," was in the chest storing tobacco; there it got lost and was eventually found, if at all, hidden underneath some dirty linen. I myself was witness to this more than once. You then either greased the palm of the servant or had to submit your petition afresh".

Equally powerful was the *Karakulak* (a kind of secret agent of the Vizier, his sinister functions paralleled at home by the *Kaftan-Agasi*, or holder of overcoats, employed to spy and to snoop). Next in the pecking order came the *Kapidshi*, the keeper of shoes, who could tell at a glance what rank, status and occupation the owner of the shoes (left at the door) might occupy.

"The stuffer of pipes, the keeper of shoes, the holders of Kaftan or overcoat have more influence on the Pasha or Effendi's mind and heart and purse than his wives ..." wrote Vambery with annoyance. "I was always astonished at how much influence these servants usually had ... people who had not the slightest notion of European affairs or of diplomacy or administration ... people who were often illiterate could often influence their master and give counsel. Only after a lengthy stay did I understand the reason ..."

The reason was, he felt — expressing it with delicate Victorian circumlocution — "an unqualifiable vice which the ancient Greeks were addicted to as well ...", for the constant quarrels and intrigues of the women drove the master to seek refuge in the men's quarter. Boredom and solitude, coupled with the fact that in the east a servant was a friend and not a machine, did the rest ... (though it seems questionable whether these reasons alone would turn a man into a homosexual.)

He was well ahead of his times, as far as women's rights and his belief in their equality was concerned, and roundly condemned the "ominous institution of the harem" which turned women into "inferior creatures, devoid of will, obeying the whims of their master".

At first Vambery suffered at their hands, as at those of the servants who "malevolent and fanatic" made him the butt of their ill-chosen jests. One of them threw a boot at his head, because he had not polished it enough to his liking.

He considered the women more fanatical than the men. Most of them could not at first understand how their master could tolerate an unbeliever in such close proximity to them and — even worse — entrust to an infidel the education of his children.

"However much I tried to inculcate the elementary notions of physics, history and geography into my highborn pupils", he writes, "all my efforts failed with pupils who had been instructed for three or four years by a fanatical *Khodja* (teacher) and whose imagination was being constantly stirred by romantic legends from the harem". For the purpose of explaining natural phenomena he used a small French booklet called *Les pourquois et les parceques* and no sooner had the boys listened to the explanation of lightning, thunder and rainbow "than they jumped up from their chairs in order to rush to the harem to tell their mother ... the strange ideas of the Frankish teacher ... and the end of the story was always that the *Ferenghi-Khodja* (foreign teacher) was always declared an ass born in the blackest unbelief and that God may forgive the sin of the *pater familias* to have employed such a teacher".

In the early days Vambery had also trouble following Turkish harem etiquette which required that a man cast his eyes down when facing a lady and whenever he absentmindedly looked up at his (often beautiful) interlocutor he would be met by the master's thunderous roar: "*Edebli Ol!*" (Be decent!) .

He was sharply critical of this "forced and unnatural modesty, this appraisal and treatment which differs so totally from European ideas . . ." He gave it a black mark. Often pompous in his writing, he added sententiously: "The European misses everywhere the harmony, friendship and love which is the main goal of family life . . . in the Orient it always reminded me of the gloomy halls of an Occidental monastery".

These thoughts Vambery kept to himself. He had trouble enough familiarising himself with Oriental ways. Between the *Selamlik* (the men's quarters) and the harem was the *Dolab*, "a round, revolving sort of cupboard". Everything intended for the *Selamlik* was placed there and when the ladies wished to converse with the outside world they did so through the *Dolab*. When Vambery heard the shout of a female voice and shouted "*Buyurun!*" (At your service!) he either received no answer at all or a rude reply: and only much later, when he had learnt how to phrase a polite reply or pay a flowery compliment did they deign to answer. "My youthful fire could not fail to take effect", he writes, "and the ladies, most of them very beautiful Circassian slaves, who were much neglected by the old, invalid master, gradually began to praise my willingness to oblige them and my linguistic proficiency, and proofs of their favours were also forthcoming".

What sort of favours? Vambery is discreetly silent.

But Vambery was by no means unreceptive to feminine charms; prudently — and from a distance — he admired the "naked foot in the tiny slipper . . .", the "exposed breasts", and listened to the "rustle and crackling of silks . . . a libidinous tune in Turkish ears . . .", and admired the "dainty headdress from which locks and ringlets escape", which the women tied so becomingly "without the aid of a mirror . . . their charms so justly sung by the poets . . ."

One day an inmate "long past the spring of her youth" had tooth-ache and Vambery was entrusted with taking her to a dentist. He did so — in Pera — and on the way stopped at the house of a Hungarian friend. This welcome diversion from the routine of harem life so enchanted the lady that soon after many more ladies of the harem were suddenly seized with toothache.

In the homes of the rich a room called *mabejn* separated the *selamlik* from the harem. Normally no outsider was allowed to cross the *mabejn* and if a doctor or a visiting friend was permitted to do so he was always preceded by an eunuch who called out "*Kimze olmazin!*" (Let there be nobody in the way!))

Occasionally however Vambery was called upon to accompany a doctor as interpreter (for upper class Turks preferred to employ a *Hekimi-Frengi*, a European doctor). "... such visits were rather more comical than serious", he writes, "... and often when the doctor's visit was over, we would find the entire troop of black and white slaves lined up at the harem exit. There they stood, showing their tongues and hands, to have them examined or to have their pulse taken — an extremely comic picture". (One can imagine the conspiratorial sniggers that went on behind their backs).

As fiercely opposed as he was to the institution of slavery, believing it to be inhuman and degrading, he still thought that once inside the harem the young slaves were less to be pitied than was the custom in the West. "They receive some rudiments of education and are instructed in singing, dancing and embroidery, and if their character is kind and adaptable they are treated as members of the family". He was indignant at the idea of the purchase of a human being. When slaves were bought the *mabejn* was a scene of feverish activity. The harem women considered it a means of making money and would sell the young and undeveloped slaves they had bought later at twenty to forty times the price (even the imperial harem was not exempt from this practice). Buyer and seller never set eyes on each other, separated as they were, by the harem curtain.

Life in a noble household was a series of elaborate rituals. Several thumps on the *Dolab* (that revolving cupboard separating the harem from the *Selamlik*) summoned a servant who was informed by a female slave that the master had risen from his bed, taken his bath and would now honour the *Selamlik* with his presence, in order to smoke the first pipe of the day. Here he held court, bills were presented and domestic matters were dealt with and the "real work" began — "from 11 am up to breakfast-time or lunch or whatever you may like to call it the *Selamlik* is filled with a crowd of visitors and their servants . . ." A second pipe is smoked . . . a third . . . coffee is served . . . and another thump on the *Dolab* might indicate that the young Bey (four or five years old) has left the harem and wishes to be led into his father's presence (where he must await several invitations to sit down before he is permitted to do so)."

Vambery thought highly of the natural intelligence of Turkish children but not much of their education. The fact that the children showed more respect than love for their parents seemed a sad thing to him. He put it down to harem intrigues.

Not only the men, but the ladies as well, as Vambery could observe, started smoking at a tender age. (They had their own — female — pipe servants). There were strict rules governing the use of pipes in the harem (sometimes circumvented). "According to the poet", Vambery remarks acidly, "the mouth of the fair one should exhale only musk and amber in her youth — but around her fortieth year she spreads so acrid and foul a smell around her that you can smell her from afar like a weatherbeaten sailor".

Sometimes there was an outing for the harem ladies. He describes it graphically. "All slicked up, the eunuchs are waiting in the courtyard, swinging their inevitable canes, ready to mount their horses . . . the younger wives have appeared one by one . . . finally the chief wife arrives on the scene, accompanied by a considerable troop of women and girls . . . They get into the richly decorated carriages . . . the procession . . . moves slowly and sedately through the streets, under the watchful eye of the eunuch, obviously at pains to repel the Christian admirer, though he turns a blind eye to the nods and winks of the true believers . . . these winks and jests are seldom directed at the wives, more frequently they are meant for the merry troop of slaves who have hardly hands enough to indulge in the so-called language of colours: brightly coloured scarves and ribbons are held ready in the carriage . . .

"When they arrive at the chosen picnic spot the slaves spread carpets on the grass and everyone sits down . . . The ladies engage in a dialogue with their admirers strolling in the distance by means of the coloured kerchiefs or by the clever use of their fingers." (The way a veil was held at the corner of the eye, whether with two, three or four fingers, had a deep meaning in the sign language, which the apparently unheedful Effendi or Bey, strolling along, knew well how to interpret. Even the way the edges of a silk wrap were held together had a secret meaning.)

Another diversion for the ladies was the *Hammam*, the Turkish bath. "Some women", Vambery wrote disapprovingly, "spend six hours there ... gossiping ... using four pieces of soap for their hair and although their flesh could be compared to that of an overcooked fowl after a visit nevertheless they indulge in this pleasure three or four times a week ... in winter the *Hammam* is their chief meeting place and replaces the opera and concerts of Europe ..."

Vambery liked the baths in Constantinople. He found them elegant and richly appointed, a kind of home from home. "People", he wrote, with astonishing frankness, "returning from a long and tiring journey, wanting to relax or to recuperate after the over-indulgence of sexual pleasure, proceed to the baths. Young and old, rich and poor alike, are devoted to this passion." He gives a sardonic account of the bath ritual. "Many an effendi steps out proudly, as if on parade, his chest decorated with medals. The naked master is followed by the naked servant carrying the pipe and the cup ..." Massages were carried out by young boys, mostly Georgians (those with moustaches were excluded); after this the master would drink coffee, smoke a pipe, play chess or Tric-Trac (a card game) or sing and the cleverly built *Hammams* supplied an echo "which gives the singer the illusion of having a beautiful voice".

Naked or fully clothed, Vambery ridicules the Europeanised effendi. "Take Reouf Bey, for example ... in top hat and tails a complete European — you will be unable to tell him apart from a southern Frenchman or a Spaniard on the Boulevard Montmartre. But let us take a closer look at this pseudo-Oriental ... he sits cross-legged on a divan, wears a fez and has learnt only enough Arabic grammar and Persian at school to enable him to enter the civil service — he is usually totally ignorant of Turkish literature or history and has only a most superficial knowledge of French."

He continued: "Instead of carrying a rosary the modern (effeminate) young Turk now carries a dainty riding whip in his hand ... while the older generation waddles sedately behind ... the younger Turk strolls along waving his walking stick in the air, the older one is accompanied by two servants, one of whom holds the long pipe, wrapped in cloth (or silk, according to rank) and a tobacco pouch, the other carries the documents ..."

Physically handicapped as he was by his lameness, Vambery admired such "manly virtues" as courage, dash and bravado. He therefore deplored the pipe-servant "swinging the long pipe stem in its silken cover with a martial air", replacing the bearer of arms "of what was once a warrior nation".

He loathed drinking parties and found them "objectionable and abominable". Turkish society had found a way to circumvent the Koran's strict prohibition of wine by serving *Raki* or *Mastika* (brandy) instead. As glasses were filled and re-filled, inhibitions were slowly cast aside. Fezes and turbans were rakishly pushed to one side, distinctions of rank forgotten and talk became "coarse and vile in the extreme, and things were discussed before young people which would have brought a flush of shame to the cheek in the most degraded European society".

For this Vambery blamed the absence of women. "To be nailed to one's chair for hours together, without daring to move — for to show restlessness is a breach of good manners — to be obliged to listen to all sorts of disgusting stories, generally bearing upon sexual intercourse and to trivial and absurd conversation is of all things the most terrible penance which can be inflicted upon a young enthusiastic European striving after higher ideals ..."

The call "*Jemek Tchiktchi*! (the meal is ready)" summoned every-one to table and brought relief to Vambery, who could put up with all this "as long as the language offered fresh charms." But he was frustrated: ... "Just as you are about to enjoy a dish you hear the *Kaldir*! (take it away) being called out and the delicacy is whisked away from under your nose", for the normally slow and leisurely Turks ate "ten to fifteen dishes in a quarter of an hour."

"If our dear Orientals had a lady at their side", he sighs, "who would engage them in conversation ... if they had to be of service to a witty and charming woman they would make longer pauses between their numerous dishes and realise that stimulating con-versation increases delights of the table."

After four years as a private tutor he entered Government ser-vice, working in the Correspondence Office of the Foreign Min-istry as a translator. As always he kept his eyes and ears open, putting his experiences down later with near-total recall.

The higher civil servants arrived at 10 a.m., some "in a light phaeton" or sauntering past on horseback, accompanied by a troop of servants. The higher the rank the deeper the *temenna*, a respectful form of greeting carried out with a flourish to head and heart whose deeper meaning Vambery failed to grasp, considering it extremely humiliating instead. "They bow down to the earth in their devotion and probably regret that they cannot sink a few feet deeper into the earth . . . Some are on foot: they are considered eccentric by the Turks. The groom walks by the side of his master on horseback — long years of training have taught him how to keep step with the horse".

In the Correspondence Office, the writing materials were all neatly displayed: ". . . eight to ten little porcelain saucers, containing black and red ink, water, small sponges, golden or blue sand, usually arranged according to size and surrounded by pens, pen sharpeners, pocket knives and paper scissors . . . between 9 and 10 in the morning you would not find many in the office, the room begins to fill up towards 11 o'clock. And then a hullaballoo begins, shouting all over the place, a chorus of greetings, in short an indescribable confusion. One stands by the divan, another sits; there is a group having a lively conversation, there is another thinking up childish pranks. One eats his elevenses, the other drinks his coffee, the third sharpens his pen, the fourth quarrels with his servant. When the head of department appears . . . everything is suddenly quiet."

He found the seriousness which characterised European official meetings was absent from the Turkish ones, except in those of the highest Council (where discussions of so secret a nature took place that the pipe servants were chosen from the ranks of the deaf and dumb).

In Government offices things were at their liveliest around 2 pm. The corridors, painted in the most garish colours, were full of bizarre figures running hastily to and fro: clients, idlers, country folk, beggar women and orphans . . . "You might find one selling cheese, the other sherbet or sweetmeats, and yet another writing material, books, clothing, ornaments . . ."

On days when salaries were paid — for wages were paid most irregularly, every three months or so — all these rooms were more like a bazaar than like an office; there were buffoons, satirists, poets of sorts who had come to entertain the effendis, while at the same time arranging marriages and forwarding love-letters — even beggars and lay-abouts managed to get themselves paid in some way — "a sorely misplaced charity," as Vambery remarks drily.

In his day, one might find "a mass of high-born young Beys lolling around on sofas or standing around — you would think you had strayed into an Infant's school rather than into a Government department".

After the young effendis had frequented "the official creche run by the State" their suitability as civil servants was supposed to manifest itself. Those who were able to read Fenelon's *Telemaque* fluently and could even make out news items in the *Journal de Constantinople*, began to dream of becoming an attache at an embassy or a very high-ranking civil servant, he wrote sarcastically. They might be sent to Paris to learn French — "unfortunately in most cases they frequent the *Jardin Mabil* and the *Cafe chantant* far more frequently than their college and bring home with them — instead of Western civilisation — vices which do not honour us Europeans".

Vambery himself was dreaming of becoming attached to an (European) embassy, preferably as an interpreter. He had watched those powerful individuals, who arrogantly swishing their canes, could be found later in a huddle in some corner, conferring with the *Tchibuktchis*, "and in no time the telegraph wires would buzz . . . and would transmit to this Court or to that what the pipe servant had said, days in advance of the official report."

How marvellous "to ride on a high horse and be attended by servitors . . . to be honoured and feared at the *Porte!*" But the dream was short-lived. He came to the realistic conclusions that his background and lack of private means ruled out any career of this sort. No European embassy would have employed him.

He cast about in his mind what else he could do. There remained a career in the Turkish State service to consider. This would have been open to him. "I cannot tell why", he writes, "but an official career in Turkey, an appointment in a State which was merely tolerated in Europe had no attractions whatever for me".

Perhaps we can tell him why. The clue lies in just those four words "merely tolerated in Europe". As ambitious a man as Vambery did not wish to be associated with a power Europeans did not consider first-rate. He wanted prestige and recognition, even by proxy.

In any case, he told himself consolingly, his "unbounded sense of freedom" would not have tolerated any interference by superiors (on whose every whim his promotion would depend), that he felt attracted "by the extraordinary alone" and that he was "an incorrigible enthusiast and visionary". "State service held no charm for me".

"State service held no charm for me . . .": especially a state that paid its servants once every three months — if at all!

Meanwhile he continued to visit Pera daily and was in great demand as the bearer of news and information, a link between Turkish and European circles. Nearly accidentally he became a journalist, supplying at first small news items to the Prussian correspondent of the *Augsburger Allgemeine Zeitung* and later writing letters for the *Pesti Naplo* in Budapest, under the name of "Reshid". Instead of a fee he received "only patriotic acknowledgements". He felt slighted. But Vienna's attention had been drawn, so he says, "to the originality of my Hungarian correspondence" — and soon he began to write for the Austrian *Wanderer* as well.

He now published his first book, a Germano-Turkish Dictionary: containing about 14,000 words, it was the first German book to be published in Stambul. It was soon followed by a Chagataic-Turkish Dictionary.

At heart he was a scholar and his main interest had remained the study of languages. He had found that Hungarian contained a rich eastern Turkisc vocabulary and that the similarity between the Hungarian and Turkisc languages increased "as we advance farther into the interior of Asia I could not help being convinced . . . that the *terra incognita* of Central Asia held quite unexpected surprises for me".

Vambery had deciphered ancient Oriental manuscripts and studied Turkish history, practically from the day he had entered noble Turkish households; now he threw himself with characteristic thoroughness and the respect for learning inherent in his race, into the study of Chagataic — ("the language of Central Asia", as Vambery described it) — "greedily devouring every scrap of Chagataic writing" he could lay hands on; ". . . and when I was admitted to the private library of Ali Pasha, which was rich in this subject, my joy knew no bounds".

He began to frequent the *Tekkes* (cloisters), where pilgrims from Central Asia congregated. They belonged to the *Sunni** sect

---

*   The schism in Islam goes back to the death of the Prophet and fights over his rightful descendants. The Caliphate should have devolved upon *Ali*, his son-in-law, claim the *Shi'ite*, while the *Sunnis* claim that Abubekr, the Prophet's father-in-law is the next in line.

of Islam, as did the Turks, and they recognised the sovereignty of the Sultan. In the streets of Stambul Vambery could see these "grotesque Orientals of the interior of Asia" but he was thrilled to deduce from their "proud, dignified bearing" that they might be the "warlike ancestors of the present Hungarians" and happy to claim kinship.

He redoubled his visits to the many libraries he had access to and found so many references to Hungarian history in the Turkish manuscripts that he intended to begin his literary career by translating Turkish literary and historic texts into Hungarian.

At one of the *Tekkes* he met Mollah Khalmurad, a native of Bokhara, who became his teacher. He used to hang on his lips and was "in a fever of excitement" at the mere mention of Bokhara and Samarkand, the Oxus and the Yaxartes.*

Vambery hoped and expected to find among the languages in Central Asia elements which would show a relationship with Hungarian and had secretly been turning over the idea of a journey to Central Asia in his mind for many years; now he redoubled his efforts to contact the Mecca pilgrims who came to Stambul from Central Asia and when some of his Turkish friends would see him in the company of these "half-naked ragged dervishes" they would turn their head away. But Vambery did not mind. "My adopted Turkdom, my pseudo-Oriental character, were after all confined to external things, in my inmost being I was filled through and through with the spirit of the West".

Although he had been doing well for himself in Constantinople any more grandiose scheme (such as a journey to Central Asia) was held up by the usual lack of funds.

Then, in 1860, quite unexpectedly, he was nominated corresponding member of the Academy of Sciences in Budapest, as a reward for his translations of Turkish texts. He travelled to Budapest the following year to deliver his address before the Academy, mulling over his problems.

In Count Emil Dessewffy, then the President of the Academy, "an energetic and unprejudiced man" he found a ready ear. Although the Academy was rather hard up they had set aside a certain sum "for scientific travels" and Vambery was granted 1000 Florins by the Count on condition that he travelled to Central Asia to investigate the relationship of Hungarian with the lan-

---

* Now the Amu-Dar'ya and the Syr-Dar'ya.

guages spoken there. Some members objected: Vambery was frail and walked with a limp. How would he be able to do it? "These gentlemen were not aware", Vambery comments, "that travelling in Asia requires neither legs nor money but a clever tongue".

To help him along the learned men of science gave him a letter of introduction "to all the Sultans, Khans and Begs of Tartary — drawn up for the surer enlightenment of the Tartars in the Latin tongue". Vambery was scathing: "A ready gallows or executioner's sword, forsooth, this document meant if I had produced it anywhere in the desert or along the Oxus!"

Three months later Vambery left Budapest for Constantinople where he intended to spend the winter preparing for his journey "through Asia Minor and Persia".

An unfavourable exchange rate shrank Vambery's reserve from 1000 Florins to 700 and his several months' stay in Stambul depleted it still further.

He found it hard to part from his Turkish friends who thought him mad to leave a life of ease for the unknown. Nevertheless they did all they could to help and advised him to limit his travels to Persia for a start. They gave him letters of introduction to Haidar Effendi, the Turkish Minister at the Court of Teheran and an intimate friend of Reouf Bey, his former pupil. He was also armed with letters from Ali Pasha, as well as with a collective letter from several high officials at the *Porte*. None of them mentioned that he was a European or breathed a word about the aim of his journey: to all intents and purposes he was "Reshid Effendi", gentleman traveller.

When he finally left he was so excited that he hardly knew what he was doing.

Only in retrospect did he marvel at the fact that he should have voluntarily returned to the "school of misery and wretchedness" of his youth, when he had "a comfortable home, plenty to eat and even a horse" at his disposal. He was driven on, as he admitted, by feverish restlessness, a desire to excel and outstrip his fellow men, and a thirst for adventure and the unknown.

And when he embarked on the Lloyd steamer, aptly named "Progresso" in March 1862, his girdle, worn next to his skin, contained, true to type, only enough cash to take him as far as Teheran.

3

ON THE ROAD TO PERSIA

When the 'Progresso' docked at Trebizond cannons boomed, flags waved and a cheering populace thronged the quayside. This rousing welcome was for Emir Muhlis Pasha, the new governor, who had been a fellow passenger of Vambery whose acquaintance he had made in Constantinople. When the governor stepped ashore and mounted the waiting, gaily caparisoned, horse the music struck up a rousing march and a long procession formed behind the governor to ride in state to his palace while, upon the Pasha's orders, largesse was distributed in the form of a rain and silver coins.

Vambery observed all this with an amused eye. He had joined the new governor's retinue since he was to be his guest during his three-day stay in Trebizond, and took it all to be an extremely good omen. He determined to buy his travel equipment without further delay. It consisted of a horse (hired), a carpet bag, containing two shirts, a few books, some unspecified trifles, two carpets — one to be used as a mattress, the other as a cover — a tea service, kettle and one cup, all of which he considered essential for his travels through Turkey and Persia. No real plan of how he was to reach Central Asia had yet matured in his mind. He resolved to keep up his role of Effendi as far as Teheran — a thing he was not able to do.

Declining the escort of two policemen pressed upon him by the Pasha, more for the sake of prestige than for safety, Vambery engaged the services of an Armenian muleteer named Hadjator.

On 21 May 1862 he set off for Teheran — "the paved road and the sea were the last memories of Europe". And as he caught sight of the 'Progresso', "the flag on the masthead beckoning a farewell to me", he was overcome by a feeling of melancholy . . .

After leaving the Governor of Trebizond's hospitable roof, Vambery was in for a shock. For the first time he experienced "that internal struggle between the craving for adventure and a sickening dread of the perilousness and uncertainty for my undertaking." Besides, at night, forced to put up at a "dirty, loathsome caravansery", he had to spread his carpet on the bare floor and, tired as he was, prepare his evening meal. "My rice was burnt, the fat rancid, and the bread one of the worst kinds I had ever tasted in Turkey . . ." Vambery realised that there was a vast difference between dreams and reality.

The other muleteers, chattering and scrubbing their horses, kept him awake and he ached in every limb. He tried sitting up picturing to himself even worse trials to come. "'A fine traveller this!' I hear the reader say", he writes with self-mockery. 'He intends to wander across the steppes of Turkestan to the distant shores of the Oxus! Truly, he does not look the type! And to be quite honest I would never have believed myself in Trebizond that I would be able to overcome all the hardships and dangers that my journey from Constantinople to Samarkand entailed."

Hadjator called him after a short rest and gave him the well-meant advice to negotiate the steep paths of the Pontine mountains on foot, rather than face another four hours in the saddle. What this can have meant for Vambery with his lame leg can be imagined.

He found the steep ascent extremely painful, even without a load to carry and wondered how the overloaded mules descending on the same path, egged on by screaming Persian drivers, managed to keep their foothold and avoided falling into the abyss flanking the mountain path. This was the commercial road that linked Armenia with Persia and (in an extended sense) Central Asia with Europe: Vambery thought there could hardly be a worse road in all Asia.

At the next station his title of effendi procured him better sleeping quarters and on Hadjator's advice he "bathed in salt water those parts of my body which were sore with my riding exertions", noting meticulously "the sensation was at first a stinging one"; but the cure proved effective — the next day riding was not so uncomfortable as before.

On 23 May they reached the third station and were joined by two Armenian merchants, of whom one had been trading with London and spoke English of a sort (as well as French). Vambery was pleased with this opportunity to air his languages, but he was even more pleased with the fact that his new friends seemed to know their way about and were familiar with the road along which they were travelling.

These Armenians were addicted to hunting and would gallop off as soon as a deer was in sight. Vambery disliked this intensely: his sympathies lay with the hunted and he found stories of hunting exploits supremely boring, preferring instead "to listen to the nightingales or to ride quietly through the green meadow. This valley is a veritable paradise . . ."

Suddenly there came into view a caravan from Shiraz. Vambery recognised them as Persians by their tall hats and as they came near, he could hear snatches of songs by Hafiz, the great 14th century Persian poet Vambery had so admired in his youth. He was, in his own words, childishly delighted and immediately tried to strike up a conversation with them but, to his great disappointment, got no reply. Singing they went on their way, trudging along the rough road, and Hadjator explained that the mules travelled more cheerfully to the sound of song.

The next two days Vambery spent at the house of a Turkish peasant who refused all payment for his hospitality. Vambery was nostalgically reminded of the days when he had "read aloud by the light of a torch from a grubby old book . . . and young and old, woman and child, master and servant were gathered around me . . . (listening) . . . with bated breath . . ."

On 28 May he rode into Erzerum. The commanding officer was Hussein Daim Pasha, whose son he had instructed in French "and the European sciences" in Constantinople. He was to be the Pasha's guest for the next three days and went straight to his house, trying to shake the dust of the journey off his feet and looking forward to a rest. He was relieved that his efforts at ingratiating himself with his fellow travellers, "mainly . . . raw, dirty, fanatical mule drivers . . ." were now over and that he could look forward to a clean bed without "the vermin with which every night's lodging swarmed". But here he was faced with a problem of a different sort.

Hussein Daim Pasha, his former boss, was an extremely kind man who had the best of intentions towards Vambery. But he was a mystic and a member of the Naquishbendi order whose headquarters were (and are to this day) in Bokhara. He had kept this a secret in Turkey and was now firmly convinced that the real object of Vambery's journey was a pilgrimage to the grave of the founder of the sect, Bahaeddin Naqsheband.* Both he and his adjutant, Hidayet Effendi, tried for hours to initiate Vambery "into the mysteries of the various orders" but Vambery remained firm: he was not interested. The Pasha had been made Governor of Erzerum after a two year exile in Rhodes and tried to read into Vambery's journey undercover political, motives such as a secret European mission, and was extremely annoyed at not being able to discover anything.

Nevertheless the Pasha offered him letters of introduction to important Sheikhs of Bokhara, but Vambery prudently refused. He had a healthy distaste for fanatics of any kind.

The farewell was extremely cold.

Vambery was not sorry to leave Erzerum. Although he noted that he had now really entered Asia — the houses built of mud were irregular, surrounded by high walls and had windows facing interior courtyards — he was disgusted by the dirt and squalor and the pervading smell of food cooked on a fire fuelled by tezek (cattle dung).

He was revolted by the abject poverty of the town's inhabitants "and when I heard that this place, compared with Persian towns, could be called beautiful, I was frightened to death".

Before leaving, he visited the local bazaar, and was interested in the fine workmanship of the medieval weaponry on show and fascinated by the dashing appearance of the swarthy Kurds on horseback, the first he had seen.

On 29 May he left Erzerum feeling unprepared to face a ride across the Armenian heights to the frontier of Persia which he considered one of the most troublesome etapes of Asiatic travels. He was shocked by the hovels he saw from the roadside, "underground holes, looking from the outside more like molehills than anything else . . . (consisting) . . . of one apartment in which the inmates live, crowded together with from ten to twenty buffaloes . . ." But worse was to come. At the first night stop they were all quartered in the village chief's windowless barn", together with from forty to fifty buffaloes . . . and the first night I spent in company with these evil-smelling animals, tormented by smoke and heat and vermin, will ever remain vivid in my mind". When they rose at dawn the next morning "everyone was lined up . . . the

* One of the great Sufis (the mystics of Islam) of the 15th century.

67

chief, his wife, who had not removed her nose-rings during the night . . . the whole troop . . . and when we totted up the cost we found that the milk and bread in the Kurdish mountains had been as expensive as in the French capital".

But the fresh air of the high Armenian plateau acted like a tonic and if, the night before, Vambery had ridden fearlessly ahead, over ditches and over bushes, he was now to face intrepidly his baptism of fire: an encounter with the robbers of Kurdistan.

In one highly-coloured version the travellers had crossed the river Araxes and reached the frontier of Kurdistan, where letters of introduction and polite requests would no longer have any effect; they began loading their guns. At a village called Eshek Elias they hired two men to accompany them and started out at dawn, sent the loaded animals ahead and followed on after they had their tea. ("In the damp and chilly hours of the early dawn tea is a most refreshing beverage . . .") Remounting their horses they rode on when Vambery's eagle eye detected a certain uneasiness in the behaviour of one of the Kurdish escorts, when lo and behold! armed robbers pounced, "rushing in on us from the right and left and making straight for the animals laden with precious and valuable goods". Vambery was still wearing his fez, denoting his "dignity as an effendi". No sooner had the robbers caught sight of him than they stopped dead in their tracks. "'What do you want?' I asked them in a voice of thunder.'" And old, one-eyed man stepped forward and explained that their oxen had strayed. "'Shame on thee!'" Vambery thundered on. "Has thy beard turned grey to be soiled by thieving and robbery . . .?" and very soon the band of marauders consisting of eight men, "understood with whom they had to deal".

Elsewhere, he freely admitted that "this first meeting made me turn all shades of the rainbow. It made me feel like a soldier undergoing his baptism of fire . . . A deathly cold shiver came over me when at the request of my Armenian fellow-travellers I took up my pistol to act the protector . . . Bravery, quick decision, and contempt of death are noble virtues, but one is not always born with them . . ." However, these were later, self-critcal considerations.

Meanwhile the Armenians had overwhelmed him with expressions of gratitude and some Persian merchants who had joined them the day before pressed large quantities of sweetmeats upon him. At the next village (Mollah Suleiman) the story of Vambery's bravery made the rounds and he was congratulated on his lucky escape, for their 'escorts' — as Vambery soon realised — had been in league with the robbers of the Dagar mountains. A "sumptuous supper" was prepared for the travellers to which all the village elders came to pay their respect . . .

As is the habit with dreams, their realisation is often shattering, Vambery was no exception. After fording the Euphrates, the Persian frontier at Diadin was reached the following day and he actually found himself in Iran — "the land which hitherto I had only viewed in the light of poetic fancy — the bare and barren wilderness which met my eye . . . rudely tore away the last vestige of the glamour which my imagination had woven around this blissful spot". His dignity of effendi had now become a distinct disadvantage for as a *Sunni* he was open to abuse by the fanatical *Shi-ite* Persians. Effendi-baiting was a welcome sport for those he encountered. "*Segi Sunni!*" they shouted ("Sunni dog!"), made scornful remarks, laughed derisively and insulted him whenever they could.

The form this persecution took was by no means new to him. "The villainy and knavery of the Persian merchants and Mollahs", he writes, "were not less offensive than the stones thrown by the Christian street-boys and the invectives of the Catholic college instructors".

At Diadin a surprise awaited him.

The Kurdish village chief explained respectfully that he could offer him no accommodation unless he was prepared to share it with a "soldier-pasha". After a ride of ten hours, Vambery replied, he would be prepared to share it with "a very Satan". He was taken to what looked like a lumber room. Imagine his surprise (and delight) when he discovered the 'soldier-pasha' was none other than Fedjzi Pasha — his old friend and compatriot, General Kolmann, one of the first Hungarian emigres with whom Vambery had made friends in Constantinople. There was an emotional reunion. The general knew of Vambery's plans and was happy to have a chance of bidding him farewell at an outpost of the Ottoman Empire (where he was surperintending the building of barracks). They talked half the night and next morning Vambery left with a heavy heart, depressed at leaving his friend and the country he felt he belonged to "if only for the time being".

After leaving Diadin, the travellers reached the base of Mount Ararat (where Noah's Ark could still be seen marooned on top, according to the inhabitants of the village). "During my travels in Asia I came across four other places of which sacred tradition tells that Noah's Ark had rested there", writes Vambery drily, "and at least four other places again, where people have discovered the unmistakable traces of scriptural paradise".

At the next village he encountered further proof of the hostility towards *Sunnite* effendis. Outside the frontier guard's house stood four stuffed bears and the guard, as Vambery writes abrasively, quickly ranged himself along their side as the fifth, as soon as he saw his fez, subjecting him to jeers and mockery. Vambery wisely decided to stop wearing his fez for the time being.

Khoy, the first important town on Persian soil, was reached on 5 June. Vambery was enchanted by the landscape, the flowering trees, the meadows covered by flowers and found the town completely oriental, ". . . as it was a thousand years ago . . . exactly as described in 1001 Nights . . . just as I had imagined life in an Eastern town to be . . ."

Here, he felt, you could see bazaar life in its ancient splendour. He was fascinated. The noise, the din, the seething life everywhere were things he had never seen before. In the bazaar, topped by a cupola, about thirty coppersmiths were striking away with a will, each at a kettle or pan, and he was amazed to see that despite this infernal din there were two schools in progress. In one corner, the children sat grouped in a half-circle around the skinny teacher, who was armed with a long stick. Vambery went quite close and listened with the utmost attention but could not catch a single word, although both teacher and pupils were screaming at the top of their voices, "with their inflated red faces and starting veins they looked like so many infuriated turkeys".

But he was frightened by the "looks of anger and disdain" with which the Persians looked at him in the bazaar or in the streets. The language of Khoy was Turkish in those days, but as soon as Vambery opened his mouth his accent betrayed him as coming from Stambul — a hated *Sunni*. By most he was considered as unclean as a Christian and only after prolonged and violent arguments would they sell him anything at all. The women were even worse than the men, spitting at him as he passed.

He was agreeably surprised however by the standard of cleanliness of the caravansery at which they put up. During the day a bustling crowd thronged the arcades and the courtyard was filled with bales of merchandise when a camel train arrived . . . pedlars, beggars, Mollahs, children all ran around in confusion while a Persian, sitting calmly at his cell window, smoking his pipe watched the gesticulating crowd bargaining outside . . .

The little caravan left on the eve of 8 June for fear of encountering difficulties on their journey the following day, for this was the start of *Kurban Bairam* (a month of merrymaking after the fast of *Ramadan*). At the next village the peasants were too poor to sell them meat or other victuals and only with difficulty could they obtain some bread.

Finally they reached Tebriz. It was hot and oppressive and Vambery was beginning to feel extremely depressed; he was weary and found it a several trial "to ride for 1½ hours in unbearable heat between solid mud walls surrounding . . . gardens . . . into the city".

Where was the Persia of his dreams? "Whoever has travelled through Persia in the middle of July will sympathise with me", he writes, ". . . it is fearfully fatiguing . . . (to) . . . toil from station to station under a scorching sun, mounted upon a laden mule, and . . . (seeing) . . . nothing but such drought and barrenness as characterise almost the whole of Persia. How bitter is the disappointment to him who has studied Persia only in Saadi, Khakani, and Hafiz . . ."

Tebriz, the ancient town said to have been built by the wife of Harun el Rashid, he found to be nothing but a collection of flat-roofed houses built of dried mud. But the huge bazaar enthralled him. There were traders in linen, leathergoods, locksmiths and tailors, merchants of all descriptions, ironmongers, grocers, cap and shoe makers, sword fashioners, jewellers, stone-masons and so on, all working among the most indescribable confusion. ". . . In the corner of a blacksmith's shop where the bellows are in full swing a public letter writer has installed himself; the infernal din has made him a little hard of hearing — (probably due to the eternal hammering) — and it remains a mystery how he can manage to understand the whispered dictation of a veiled lady — perhaps a *billet-doux* — and turn it into a letter. Facing him is a barber's shop. The face and head of one of the customers is covered in soap and is being worked on by Master Figaro himself with a miserably bad razor; nonchalantly he wipes the remaining soap off his fingers and flings it into the street without the slightest consideration for the passing vendor of steaming pancakes. Another customer is yelling mightily while the operation of pulling a tooth is being performed, while in an adjoining booth a merchant selling weapons pounds on the blade he is offering for sale in order to convince the customer of the silvery quality of the blade from Khorasan ..."

Bazaars sometimes had gruesome sights to offer: Persian punishments were severe and could involve the severing of a hand or a limb; the condemned man would carry his severed limb on a salver through the bazaar in an effort to solicit alms and sympathy.

Elsewhere quarrelling women would take their stand, each shouting her side of the story, in an effort to gain sympathisers.

The bazaar acted like a magnet for any kind of rumour and gossip; all the most secret details of royal private life were discussed here openly with great relish. And the future dervish kept his eyes and ears wide open. "In the broadest sense", he writes, "the bazaar is not only the market place but public life in general." He compared it to the Roman Forum and the European coffee-house. "What has become known in the bazaar is public knowledge." And although he was to find the bazaars of Central Asia far less colourful than those of Persia the information he picked up there was invaluable for his future career.

Vambery was sorry to part with his Armenian companions. They had ordered a modest cell for him at a caravansery, promising to return the following day and show him their native city. A curious crowd had started to collect around him: some took him for a merchant or a money-changer, others (judging him by his clothes) for a member of the Turkish legation at Teheran. Vambery found this "catechising from all sides" extremely wearisome, preferring the role of attentive spectator.

He was reluctant to start cooking for himself so he bought a dish of *Pilaff* (rice) with some *Lule Kebab* (chopped meat, baked in fat and speared on thin rods) but found it far too heavy for his digestion and on the second day started using the cooking utensils he had brought with him and tried to prepare a meal for himself. He found his own cooking tastier and better for his health. His knowledge of Persian customs and language soon gained him friends. He felt lonely in the evenings but decided to stay two weeks in Tebriz "in order to study the peculairities of the dialect of Azerbaidjan".

Vambery was naturally fascinated by the tales he heard about Bokhara from the mouths of European travellers passing through Tebriz. He had met the British Consul, Keith Abbott whose brother (Captain James Abbott) rode from Herat to Khiva in

1840. The Consul told him everyone in Tebriz doubted that he (Vambery) would be able to carry out his plan. He also heard many stories, which amused him greatly, about "that eccentric, Dr. Wolff, the 'Pope of Bayreuth' (who was the son of a Bavarian rabbi and became an Anglican clergyman, setting out on his own in 1843 from Richmond Green to find out the fate of Conolly and Stoddart, victims of the Emir of Bokhara). This remarkable man had been twice to Bokhara, so he claimed, each time with the intention of converting the Khan and the Uzbegs to Christianity, in addition to his self-imposed mission. What helped him most among the fanatical Mohammedans was his extreme sloppiness in dress and his remarkable predilection for dirt — "in short, he was a faithful prototype of a true dervish" Vambery wrote acidly. And indeed he was nicknamed the 'Dervishi frengi' — the foreign dervish — and since in the East, people are used to being told many things by dervishes which another person would not be permitted to say, they listened patiently to everything Dr. Wolff had to say and even called him *Mollah Jussuf* (Joseph). Once he was sold for an old pair of trousers, another time he was exchanged for a lame donkey, but he was always able to show his master the error of his ways, to obtain his freedom and to reach Bokhara.

These tales smack of the exploits of *Baron von Munchhausen* and no doubt Vambery, while amused, considered some of them as such. But it is a fact that Dr. Wolff rode into the city of Bokhara in full clerical regalia (those of an Anglican clergyman), sitting on a donkey and holding a bible. And not long afterwards Vambery was to follow suit, except that on his head he wore an outsize turban "that could have served as a parasol by day and a pillow by night" and around his neck hung a well-thumbed copy of the Koran.

On the whole Vambery seems to have enjoyed his stay in Tebriz, but he disliked intensely the fanaticism he encountered and the bigoted attitude displayed towards Europeans. He was horrified to see that a basin of water, placed in the middle of the caravansery for ritual ablutions, was used for a variety of other purposes as well: washing dirty clothes, soaking half-tanned skins, washing a baby ... "while one even drank of this dark green fluid". Vambery was disgusted.

He was equally revolted by the Persian bathing establishments which, in his eyes, bore no comparison to those in Turkey. Heaps of horse manure was piled outside, used for heating, and when he went inside he felt even more nauseated. Although battle scenes from the epic of *Firdusi* were painted on the walls, "everywhere dirt stared you in the face, camouflaged as luxury". In the early morning the blowing of a trumpet announced that the bathing pool had been filled with warm water, "thus in the same way as the animals are driven out to pasture in Europe", he writes sarcastically "the faithful are called to bathe in Persia".

The pungent smell of henna pervaded everything — the Persians dyed their hair, beard, soles of their feet and even the palms of their hands bright red as Vambery commented caustically: "The coat of paint hides the dirt; and a gentleman, or lady, having made use of it can manage to do without washing for several days". He found the smell even more unbearable in the wash room where the water was changed only once a day in a small basin. "When I saw eight to ten Persians sitting next to each other in a small pool, how they touched each other and scraped each other's skin, I began to understand the revulsion the Turks felt towards their Eastern neighbours.'

He was impatient with the women. "If men take two hours for their toilet in the bath, no wonder that the women take from four to six hours ... but the Western reader must not imagine that they emerge presenting an improve appearance. They tattoo a kind of beauty mark on to their cheeks or necks and courtesans even paint daring scenes on their breasts ... in Isfahan an emancipated daughter of Iran had an entire hunting scene engraved on her bosom."

Vambery witnessed in Tebriz the solemn investiture of the heir apparent, Muzaffar-ed-Din Mirza, then a frail nine-year old. He was delighted to witness at first hand all the oriental pomp and circumstance and gives a detailed description of the splendour of the pageant. But what interested him most was linguistics and he listed carefully to the melodramatic way the various poems of glorification were delivered, regardless of their bombastic contents.

An Italian mission which included diplomats, military men, scientists and merchants had taken great pains to appear before the Persians in full regalia, their chests resplendent with medals. Vambery who had mingled with the crowd, curious to hear their opinion, heard nothing but rude remarks about their tight-fitting uniforms (which they thought plain and even indecent since they outlined the contours of the body) and their plumed hats, ridiculous in Persian eyes . . . Vambery, for once, could see their point, "for the European with his protruding chest looks like a caricature besides one who sits with easy grace on his steed".

During his stay in Tebriz two incidents stood out. At the Emir caravansery, where he mingled with dervishes, traders, artisans, beggars and jugglers — having changed from European into semi-Persian dress — his eye fell on a European who was supervising the unloading of his goods and fumbling around with a phrase-book, at loss for a Turkish word. Vambery watched him thumb impatiently through the slim little volume and not a little amused to recognise his own Germano-Turkish dictionary printed in Constantinople a few years earlier; not having found what he was looking for the stranger flung the booklet aside with some not very flattering comments. Suddenly Vambery spoke up (in German) and informed him that "the writer of this little dictionary was not exactly a fool" but that he had been looking in the wrong place. The stranger, a Swiss by the name of Wurth (who, together with a Herr Hanhardt had business interests in Tebriz) was staggered, according to Vambery, to be addressed in German" by a ragged, semi-Persian, semi-Turkish individual and the affair ended with profuse apologies on the part of the Swiss and an invitation to his house, offering lavish hospitality for the next few days.

Vambery claims that "amusing adventures of a similar nature" befell him on other occasions as well and that it was "always and everywhere" his linguistic skill and the ease with which he could produce "foreign accents, intonations and constructions", as well as being able to quote maxims from the Koran, together with the appropriate gesticulations, which enabled him to pass for a native, despite his foreign features.

In Tebriz, however, all went well and through the "two Swiss gentlemen of culture" he met other Europeans in the town and was "delighted to converse with them in a Western tongue" — and then suddenly put on his Fez again to "become an Effendi in a Persian society . . . my fancy was tickled by this almost theatrical transformation from the East to the West and back again".

At the Emir caravanserai another incident took place. He was sitting outside his cell door, one particularly hot day, trying to "deliver (his) linen of certain animals" when "two Englishmen, whom I recognised by their Indian hats, and who were strolling in the caravanserai stopped suddenly before me and after admiring for a while my patient and untasteful occupation, the younger said to the older: 'Look at the hunting zeal of this fellow!' I raised my eyes and said in English: 'Will you join me, Sir?' Amazed, nay, bewildered, one of them immediately asked me: 'How did you learn English and what countryman are you?'" But he shut up like a clam . . .

This little adventure had a sequel. Years later, on the crest of fame in London, at a dinner party in the house of an English nobleman, he met a distinguished man in tails. Vambery thought he recognised in him his interlocutor at Tebriz but was not sure and kept his mouth shut. Invited to speak about his journey he later asked to be introduced to this man. "Oh, that is Lord R . . .", said his hostess. She acceded to his request and "Lord R . . ." was polite but non-committal: Vambery's face meant nothing to him. But as soon as Vambery said: "My lord, you have been to Tebriz and do not remember the dervish who addressed you in English?" he claimed to recognize him at once and "related the whole adventure to the highly amused company".

Lord R . . .'s identity remains a mystery. Was it Lord Ripon (future viceroy of India)?

Vambery soon felt restless again, anxious to press on and see Teheran, the capital and the residence of the Court, "the place where the great, the rich and the learned of this strange country meet," adding with a good deal of insight, "I was quite aware of my delusion . . . (but) . . . there was sufficient charm left to make up for the unbearable heat . . . the monotony of the scenery and the beggarly way in which I was forced to travel . . ."

He was sure that his personal safety lay precisely in the fact that he had hardly any money: "Nothing is safer against all danger than a small saddle-bag and a ragged dress".

His European contacts had revived the old nostalgia for the West, but there was no turning back.

There were many travellers on the road. Sometimes Vambery would join a group for a few hours, sometimes for several days; "Persians, Turks, Arabs or people of any nationality were on the most intimate terms with me in the shortest time". At the nightly stopping places he always looked for the most modest quarters and after a few days' practice, even got used to travelling on his own, not missing the company he had thought he could not do without.

Two days after leaving Tebriz he reached the village of Turkmantchay and continued on to a place called Miane. Here a *Seid** accused Vambery of having poisoned him with too strong tobacco, but he soon talked himself out of this situation, only to become the victim of some practical jokers. The villagers explained gleefully to a complaining Vambery that the local bedbugs (called *Meleh*) only attacked strangers . . . and Vambery was kept awake by "the ghost of this insect" a whole night long.

"Apart from these insects", Vambery wrote matter-of-factly, "Miane is famed for its numerous whores. They flock to this place from all over the country in order to offer their charms to the passing traveller. Two of my companions with whom I lodged could not resist this temptation and I was most astonished when towards evening two witch-like harpies appeared, painted and dressed grotesquely; soon after a priest made his appearance: he read the *Siga* (temporary marriage contract), for, oh wonder, this shameful traffic is considered legal here. Priests and prostitutes share the spoils. Surrounded by revellers and musicians the most disgraceful orgies took place not far from my camp and my feelings may readily be imagined. Tortured by *melehs* and drunken orgies, I awaited the dawn impatiently and continued on my journey the next morning . . ."

At the city gate next morning he ran into a religious procession of *Shi-ites* whose frenzy and fanaticism, blood-curdling yells and wild antics so frightened him that he withdrew into a corner of the bazaar, waiting prudently until the screaming mob had passed.

Persia was not turning out according to his expectations.

At the next caravanserai along the road, Vambery witnessed his first *Tazie*, a kind of Persian miracle play. It was performed by *Sunnite* Moslems in *Shi-ite* disguise — the female roles acted by men — and may have given Vambery an idea or two. "Religion was their business", he wrote; and the performers later pocketed the "shining gold pieces". It confirmed him in his belief that in one thing the East and West, Christians and Mohammedans were alike: they were the dupes of the clergy.

By the time he reached Kazvin, the ancient capital of Iran, he was virtually penniless — and very hungry. So, pocketing his Magyar pride, he decided to beg. ("I preferred begging to starv-

---

* *Seids* claimed they were rightful descendants of the Prophet.

ing.") He was very displeased with the niggardly alms he got from those "close-fisted Persians".

The oppressive July heat now compelled the caravan to travel at night. In the flat country between Kazvin and Teheran, the quiet was shattered by voices in the distance and the steadily approaching clatter of horses' hooves. According to his highly-coloured account, he held his pistols ready for firing and called out to the three horsemen who, brandishing their arms, had come swooping down upon them: "Get out of the way or I will shoot you down!" And lo! and behold! the horsemen meekly turned tail and galloped off, "frightened either by the strange sound of the foreign dialect, or our costume . . ."

His companions laughed but the episode left Vambery feeling uneasy. His overheated imagination had turned harmless travellers into brigands, as happened to his Persian companions who mistook two old women out gathering thistles for "imposing horsemen . . . armed with spears and double barrelled guns . . ." He ridiculed the Persian "Don Quixote and Sancho Panza" and laughed at himself — "the third hero . . . on his donkey".

He was nervous and extremely worried, "inwardly shaky", impatient to reach Teheran yet full of mixed feelings. What would his reception by the Turkish envoy, Haidar Effendi, be like? He felt that the entire success of his journey depended solely on the Sultan's representative. The truth of the matter was that he was committed; he had undertaken to travel into Central Asia and accepted cash from the Hungarian Academy of Sciences. This money was now all but gone . . .

The whole outcome of his journey depended on the impression he would make on the Turkish envoy. Everything was at stake.

Vambery's pockets were stuffed with letters of introduction to the envoy, for Haidar had been a friend of one of his former employers in Constantinople. They described him as an eccentric who, tired of the idyllic life in Stambul, "was looking for excitement in the wilds of Persia". Some of the letters stressed that he was travelling east impelled by the strange idea of studying Eastern Turkic languages (and these letters were nearer the truth). In brief they tried to satisfy Haidar Effendi that Vambery was in no way engaged on a political mission.

While these thoughts passed through Vambery's mind, the dawn mists suddenly dispersed and Teheran came into view, in his own words "a few bricks varnished with green and some golden cupolas . . . the residence of the king of kings . . . lying before me in its naked poverty."

His disappointment was immense.

And so, on 13 July, 1862 he rode into Teheran "in the condition of a half-boiled fish", entering it through a narrow gate in the mud wall and pushing his way through a throng of pedestrians, horsemen and heavily laden mules. Already his first impression was disastrous. Houses were built of dried mud and were only one storey high, windows were barred and only the pavements, consisting of sharp stones, reminded him of Europe.

After many enquiries he found his way to the Turkish embassy only to be told by the soldiers mounting guard outside that the entire staff had gone to the mountain resort of Djizer to escape the heat.

He followed suit; hiring a donkey with the remnants of his cash, he arrived there two hours later. The members of the Turkish embassy were in the garden, taking their evening meal "beneath a tent of silk". The cordiality with which he was received exceeded his most sanguine expectations. Everyone, from the envoy downwards, was avid for news from Constantinople.

When Vambery told them of his plans, they only stared at him, incredulous, unable to understand "how a sensible man should wish to go to Central Asia . . . a region spoken of . . . as . . . dreadful desert and the dwelling place of all that is most savage and barbarous". His plan was called eccentric and in order to try and drive this mad scheme out of his mind they surrounded him with every possible luxury, giving him a tent to himself and providing him with a horse and a servant. Now Vambery had ample time to look at Teheran. He was disgusted.

"The streets of the capital are filthy", he wrote, "and the interior of the houses dirty, despite the costly carpets decorating the walls . . ."

He thought Persian table manners revolting and was shocked by the drinking parties in Teheran. If he had found the "smoking room conversations" barely tolerable in Constantinople, here the sexually orientated talk revolted him. No longer could he put it down to the "artificial separation of the sexes" ("how beneficial is the influence of women on society") for here women were actually *present*. "Decency and constraint is usually dropped and the activities of uneducated women present an unpleasant, even a repulsive spectacle". In the *Enderun* (the harem) "women have no scruples concerning their choice of topics and nothing is more embarassing than to hear old matrons and young girls discuss themes which would bring a blush to the cheeks of even the most degraded of their sex in Europe".

If the guests wearied of talking, dances were performed. Vambery considered them "plastic embodiments of sensual feelings . . . even more despicable in their base meanings than lewd talk in unwashed mouths . . ."

It was a fact, though, that dancing was despised as an art all over the Orient in Turkey it was open only to Jewish lads and gypsies; in Teheran, too, dancers were considered the lowest of the low.

Vambery tells an amusing story concerning a Persian diplomat, accredited to the *Porte* in Constantinople. A ball was given in his honour. The band struck up a lively waltz, the master of the house, with a bow and a flourish, invited a pretty girl to the next dance. The Persian diplomat who had watched all this, was horrified; he jumped up and rushed towards him. "Sir! No!", he cried, "I will not have it! I refuse to permit you to exhibit yourself in a dance for my sake . . ."

In Teheran, however, the Persians applauded every dance with gusto. The only one which seems to have found favour with Vambery and one he termed "graceful" was the coy "Herati dance". The dancer appeared, wrapped from head to toe in a sheet and was bundled on to a dais: in tune with the music she would lift a corner of the veil, peering coquettishly from behind it and wrap and unwrap herself in her sheet. Vambery thought it charming. "Her graceful movements in time with the music", he wrote, "would have done honour even to the *Corps de Ballet* or to dancers in one of our own theatres . . ."

High praise indeed.

Vambery thought the "fine ladies of the Persian capital far, very far behind those of Constantinople as far as gracefulness and cleanliness is concerned".

"These charming ladies cover themselves to such an extent with a dark sheet called *Tchadir* that you would take them for ambulating mummies rather than attractive women". He preferred a coy Turkish lady "her face half hidden by a veil, her rustling silk trousers, her billowing coat and her little yellow slippers . . ."

The Persian lady went out dressed "in a blue sack, wearing two stockings reaching to her breast (sic), her face covered by a veil or a linen cloth . . . a thick paste on her hair . . . imagine how a Persian beauty smells during the hot season!"

At home it was even worse. Here she ambled around in bare feet, wearing a short skirt "which hangs in loose, wide folds from her hips, her breast covered by a shirt which leaves her belly bare . . . This indecent costume is worn by young and old and those not used to it will find it hard to hide their disgust".

He found the Persians much given to outer pomp and display but dirty. "People will spend fifty or a hundred ducats on an outer garment and will not possess more than two or three changes of shirt", he wrote, "lice are rampant here in the highest circles . . .

"Soap is considered a luxury, the poorer classes use clay. I have often seen a highly educated Khan use the handkerchief of a servant as a towel in which he packs he meat ration for the following day.

"People spend thousands of ducats on ornaments and dress and usually own only one change of underwear; wealthy businessmen, even noble Khans and Ministers possess less underwear than our poorest citizens".

The colour of the underwear was uniformly blue, he wrote, "it shows the dirt less . . ."

"Nothing is more revolting than to see a mighty lord, followed by his retinue covered in the most expensive diamonds and rubies and from the folds of his silken garment the tail of a dirty shirt peeps forth . . ."

In Vambery's day "even His Majesty did not possess more than ten European shirts which — to the horror of all *Shi'ites* — were washed, starched and ironed by the hands of an infidel".

He ridiculed the etiquette attaching to pipe smoking, the servants appearing with a military step and approaching each guest in turn, after which the master of the house would begin to smoke "with a groaning sound . . . spluttering and gargling as he drew on his pipe". The law of hospitality required the pipe to be passed from mouth to mouth and Vambery was revolted.

Persian ladies too would smoke like chimneys, matrons and young girls alike, "and the unpleasant smell of the breath is noticeable in princess and peasant women alike . . ."

The pipe played a part even in tender tete-a-tetes, wrote Vambery, for smoking was considered a sign of special intimacy.

Vambery was impressed by their horsemanship and their skill

of drinking tea in the saddle. He watched whole troops of ladies on horseback charging along on their way to romantic picnic spots near the tomb of a poet or saint.

"Were it not the little slippers in the stirrups and the fire in the eyes which penetrates the narrow grille of the veil" he wrote, "you would take those seated on their gaily caparisoned horses for plump navy blue sacks of linen ... Suddenly a horseman comes galloping along: like a flash of lightning he flies past the fair one (sometimes only recognising her by a brooch on her veil) ... a few words are exchanged. ... a little later there appears again a cloud of dust in the distance, again the horseman nears ... more words are exchanged ... now he trots by her side, now by the side of another navy blue sack, a little broader in the beam this time ... her aunt or her maid ... and begins a conversation" ... but the loose daughters of Iran certainly had no inkling at the time that the dervish trotting behind them on a humble little donkey was pricking up his ears intending to describe their behaviour later to the world of the Franks.

"I was an eye-witness to such scenes and they always had my fullest attention".

Vambery felt that he had his fill of Teheran. He had become bored by the lavish hospitality offered by the Turkish legation, and was restless. But way to Central Asia was barred. Back in Constantinople already he had read reports of a war between Dost Mohammed, tte ruler of Afghanistan, and his son-in-law, Sultan Ahmed Khan, the ruler of Herat. He reasoned that his European features, suspect in times of peace would be the end of him in times of war and that he stood a chance of being massacred on the spot as soon as he crossed the Afghan border. He therefore decided to postpone his journey into Central Asia until the following spring, hoping that the situation would have changed meanwhile.

He decided on a tour of southern Persia. This was not as simple as it sounds, for although he was fairly safe under Turkish protection in Teheran, he was at risk further south where Turks were few and far between and where they were particularly loathed as *Sunni* Moslems.

He considered this "self-imposed hardening system" — the "dry saddle, dry bread and dry soil" which now attracted him more than all the luxury, the riches and the wealth of the Turkish embassy* indispensable, for without this preparation he felt that the journey into Central Asia risked total failure — and failure meant a certain (and unpleasant) death.

In Teheran Vambery had been introduced to the Persian authorities in the semi-official character of an attache at the Turkish legation, had been invited home by Persian aristocrats and had been presented to the king. Now the Persian Government gave him a Letter of Safe Conduct, signed by Mirza Khan, the Minister of Foreign Affairs, which explained that the "high-born and noble Reshid Effendi" was on his way to the province of Fars and that he should be afforded all possible protection.

Vambery did not attach very much importance to this letter, for "even the very highest official commands" were treated offhandly in the provinces; only occasionally did this letter in fact protect him from suspicion, and then in Isfahan and Shiraz alone.

The decision he had made was therefore a courageous one. He knew that he would face trouble of every kind, but he told himself sternly that "a future Dervish must not be afraid of anything" Furthermore, "in the character of a Stamboul effendi and under State protection" he would obtain a more intimate knowledge of the land and people of Persia than was usually possible for a European".

Yet when he eventually left, it was not in the dress of a "Stamboul Effendi".

* Vambery insisted on calling the legation an embassy.

4

DRESS REHEARSAL IN PERSIA

When Vambery left on 2 September 1862 and set out for Isfahan and Shiraz he was in yet another disguise — that of a *Sunnite dervish from Baghdad*. The preparation had taken him seven weeks.

He joined a small caravan consisting of about thirty mules, a couple of horsemen, mollahs, pilgrims returning from Meshed and included a young *Seid* from Baghdad towhom he immediately attached himself.

This man was making as a *rawzekhan*, a singer of holy songs. The *Seids* were among the most fanatical of men. Vambery knew that coming from Baghdad he was a subject of the Turkish Sultan and thus would most likely be honoured by the presence of a Turkish Effendi. Vambery seldom took uncalculated risks.

At first the road was bad, uneven and rocky; they crossed ditches and ravines during the night and at dawn halted for their ritual ablutions and morning prayers in which they young *Seid* took a prominent part. Their next stop, in scorching heat, was on the edge of the salt desert of *Deshti Kuvir* about which the caravan had to cross in its entire length and about which tales of devils and evil spirits abounded. Vambery was less horrified by these than by his evening meal, a *pilaff* (rice and meat) drowned in mutton fat (which was to nauseate him not a little on his travels). Otherwise he thought the dercish fared better than anyone else for his nose told him when a meal was ready and he enjoyed making the rounds of the various groups holding out his *keshkul* (a vessel made out of the coconut shell) shouting *YA HU! YA HAKK!* and piling what he was given into his begging bowl. An hour later, in the cool of evening, the caravan started off again.

Vambery was not frightened by the eerie stillness of the night, nor by the columns of sand, piled up by the wind, which blown from place to place turned them into so many spectres. But his companion drew his cloak about him, not daring to look to the left or the right . . .

And indeed, towards midnight, the sound of bells was heard . . . and as a larger caravan neared theirs "an intolerable stench, as if of dead bodies, filled the air".

It was the caravan of the dead, taking corpses to Kerbela, a place of pilgrimage, for burial.

"Even the animals", wrote Vambery, "with their sad burden of coffins, hung their head, trying to bury their nostrils in their breasts . . ."

Vambery's new friend, the *Seid*, always intervened on Vambery's side in any religious dispute which Vambery wisely sought to avoid as much as possible. "Since I could look forward to continued and repeated religious disputes I went off to look at the magnificent buildings of the caravanserai".

In the first three days Vambery already had made many friends.

On the fourth day they reached Kum, "the sacred city for the female world, for here, in the company of 444 saints repose . . . the remains of Fatima, a sister of Imam Riza" (a *Shi'ite* saint) and many pious Persian women wished to be buried there. "Nowhere else," Vambery remarked dryly, "were there quite as many prostitutes as in the holy city of Kum".

"Ladies' men lie buried there as well", he continued with an attempt at humour, "one of them reputed to have had 800 legal wives — no wonder that he wished to rest in female company even after death".

Devout pilgrims left scraps of material on a bush and Vambery's eagle eye noted at once that some of them bore the stamp of manufacture in India, England or America . . . He stored this scrap of information up for further use.

He claimed to have been the first European to have visited the interior of Fatima's tomb. But in Kum it was the bazaar again which held his attention.

He found it remarkable for its abundance of water melon, a local produce, and also for earthenware.

Despite his costume he was unmasked. Watching a Persian artisan dyeing material blue, the man suddenly turned on him and shouted: "We shall get rid of your expensive fabrics . . . and when the Persians will be able to do without *Frengistan** manufacture . . . you will come begging to us". Vambery's reply is not recorded.

After a two-day rest the caravan left for Kashan where they arrived after a tiring march of a further two days. Vambery's first visit, despite his recent experiences, was to the bazaar of the braziers, where the famous kettles of Kashan were made. He was also interested in the brass wares and highly polished bricks whose solid workmanship and elegance he admired and for which Kashan was famous: these bricks were used as chief ornaments on all the architectural monuments in Central Asia.

Finally, after encountering strolling players, dancing bears, and surviving a shoot-out in the desert, he arrived at Isfahan on September 13. He was not surprised to find . . . in Isfahan the same crooked lanes, the identical dirt as in Teheran and in all Persian towns I have seen so far".

The people of Isfahan had the reputation for shrewdness and craftiness and a great talent for getting up to all sorts of tricks. On closer acquaintance Vambery found this to be quite justified. But he seems to have liked them and to have made friends quite easily.

His first visit was again to the bazaar but here he was bitterly disappointed: nothing had remained of its former magnificence but a few stray water-melon sellers . . .

He lodged with the singer of elegies who "by day had found another outlet for his talents: the bazaar and the courtyard of mosques. He shouted, lamented and wept with all his might and I often wondered from where he took his flood of tears". But in the evenings his songs took a frivolous turn.

He found the middle-class remarkably cultivated and was impressed that "shoemakers, tailors and shopkeepers . . . knew hundreds of verses of their best poets . . ."

He had many invitations and among many others was invited to the house of *Imam Djuma*, the "Pope of Isfahan", an influential priest, on the strength of the letters of recommendation he had brought with him from Teheran.

He particularly enjoyed his stay in this house since he was "a regular problem" to the high priest who did his best to unmask him but failed. This "cunning and most skilful man" also took a great amount of trouble to convert him to the *Shiite* sect and, with this in view, organised evenings of "disputations" during which

* Saadi, born in Shiraz (1184–1291), author of "Gulistan or The Garden of Roses".
* European.

86

all the religious leaders present tried to overpower Vambery by their subtle arguments. But Vambery once again, proved more than a match for them. On another occasion wrote Vambery, "the pious songs were replaced not only by songs of the most trivial kind but became thoroughly obscene". And he continues: "Despite his enormous green turban and his wild outbursts in public on behalf of the family of the Prophet's descendants he took in quite a lot of intoxicants at night". On this particular evening, in the house of a civil servant, whose guests included other officials and mollahs, the drinks began to show their effect as soon as the first hour had pased, spent in the usual polite phrases of courtesy and a show of good manners. Vambery was horrified to see "a veritable orgy" take place: off came the caps, turbans and outer garments and in came four dancing girls (offered by courtesy of one of the guests). The prettiest of the girls came from Shiraz. He thought their dances "less devoted to Terpsichore, the goddess of the dance, than a series of lewd gyrations and gymnastics ... Our pen revolts", he writes primly" against describing the obscene tricks these revellers got up to". And to his amazement, just as he, feigning drunkenness, was trying to "suppress his inner revulsion", two half-inebriated guests sitting next to him, stood up, and without more ado, proceeded to say their evening prayers then and there, "not only in the very room where so many heinous sins were taking place, but right next to the sinners!"

"What disgraceful hypocrisy!" he thunders. "And this they call religion!"

Vambery had to spend another three days at a caravanserai outside the town, waiting for a new caravan to be formed: it consisted of about 60 travellers and 150 animals. Vambery spent the time sight-seeing.

Finally the caravan moved off. Stories of brigandage abounded. Vambery discounted them but was scathing about Persian cowardice. The singers of holy songs continued to sing, wringing floods of tears from the women and making the men beat their breasts in anguish.

On the way to Shiraz Vambery experienced his first *Fata Morgana* (he was to consider them inferior to those of the Turkestan deserts). Vambery saw tall buildings floating before his eyes and found himself transported back to Hungary, to the *Alfold* (Lowland), where on the edge of the vast *Puszta* (Great Plain) he had dreamt of the sea ... But a sudden wind whirled up clouds of sand "which descended on the beautiful performance like a curtain".

The caravan had now entered the southern province of Fars, where the inhabitants were livelier and more excitable than in the north. Very little Turkish was understood here.

Vambery struck up a friendship with a distinguished Khan who joined the caravan: he had been sent by the Shah to collect a debt of 50,000 ducats from the governor of the province who had numerous servants attending to his pipes; Vambery was impressed by the skilful way in which such "pipe servants" were able to assemble the various parts of the pipe on horseback and would offer the pipe to their master with outstretched arm during the fastest gallop . . .

These caravans, bound either for Kerbela in the west or Meshed in the east — both places of pilgrimage — could include women of over eighty and children of ten, some in charge of a group and Vambery admired their independence.

Vambery describes vividly the meeting of two such caravans in the stillness of the desert night and the exchange of pious greetings of *"Iltimasi dua"* ("Pray for me!") to be *"Ziaret Kabul!"* ("May your pilgrimage be accepted!").

Vambery remained the detached and sceptical observer: ". . . if in the stillness of the night you hear them singing their *"Illahie"* (songs of God) it arouses the same feelings as the statue of the miracle-working Virgin Mary, carried around in procession, does in the breasts of the devout in Europe whom they move deeply . . ."

But soon his thoughts turned to more prosaic things. He was hungry and somewhere along the way he bought some quail and had them prepared for him at the next halt. "A meal worthy of Lucullus", he commented. Later he was joined by others, all squatting round him on their haunches, and "engaged . . . in a conversation for which I gladly sacrificed some hours of sleep".

The continuous nightly marches had begun to tire him and he found it difficult to keep in the saddle. Although he was to achieve the remarkable feat of leaping into the saddle (despite his lame leg) he still thought it impossible to compete with the Persians who could sleep in the saddle, and when the caravan arrived at the caravansery of Chane Kergun he was so exhausted that he dropped off immediately, even forgetting to feed his donkey or take the saddle off him . . . He awoke hours later — it had barely seemed minutes to him — and heard with great excitement that the next station would be Maderi Suleiman in the plain of Pasargada. Vambery claimed that this was the village "where the tomb of the great Persian king Cyrus is believed to be".

So great was his excitement that, impatient with the slow progress of the caravan, he left his fellow travellers with the first rays of the rising sun, and set off on his own. And when the caravan finally caught up with him he had found the tomb and was seated on one of the steps of the mausoleum, lost to the world . . .

His lame leg caused him some trouble and he had great difficulty climbing up the huge steps in order to enter the mausoleum built on top. He was awe-struck and describes it meticulously: the low entrance was always open, for the Mohammedans used it as a place of prayer, as evinced by the number of Korans lying around. He lost no time trying to decipher the Arabic and Persian inscriptions when a nomad approached offering his services as a guide in the hope of earning a small baksheesh. "Hadji", said the man "there are no such huge blocks to be seen in Baghdad, are they?" Vambery had successfully passed his test.

As night fell Vambery was preparing his frugal meal when "spurred on by a particular attack of vanity", he tried to drag his cooking pot and provisions of bread up into the inner chamber of the mausoleum. The idea of eating his supper inside the thousands of years old mausoleum filled him with joy and he would have exchanged his place with the most luxurious hotel of any European capital. He sat for a long while on the steps of this strange building, sunk in the splendor of the starry heavens, trying to recall thedays of his early youth when the word "Persia" had already exercised a magical fascination over him and when he had not dared to imagine in his wildest dreams a happiness such as this. Sleep had already overcome him and he would certainly have lain down to sleep, he writes . . . had he not remembered that the cold stones might be bad for his health. He had only a thin carpet with him. Prudently he therefore clambered down the big stones again. Finding a patch of grass some twenty steps further along he lay down. In no time he found his body was covered with an incredible number of flea-bites and unable to stand it any longer he was forced to get up at once. He tried putting his carpet down at another spot but it was the same story. So he ran like mad, now to this ruin, now to that, trying to spread his carpet in different places, but he fared no better. And only then did it dawn on him why the caravan had avoided this spot.

When he asked nomads living in tents nearby how to cope with this affliction, he got the same reply he had got in Miane: these fleas attacked strangers only . . . they left the natives in peace. A standing Persian joke?

There were still two hours to go until the caravan left for Sivend and all this time Vambery tried, like a horse, to sleep standing up. "I would not wish it upon the most boring archaeologist to be similarly tortured by these mindless little insects clad in red . . ."

From Sivend the caravan left for Kenare on October 2. Vambery knew that the ruins of Persepolis were in the vicinity and again, impatient with the slow progress of the caravan, went off on his own. "Why continue with these people", he told himself, "the road is safe enough". He could hardly wait to see the ruins and trotted along on his donkey, at the foot of great mountains, feeling fairly safe from robbers, for his entire fortune consisted of four ducats at the most and his travel equipment, with his donkey thrown in, were hardly worth the trouble. When dawn came he saw in the grey light of early morning a mass of enormously tall figures which looked like phantoms and fear overcame him. All alone, with the clip-clop of the donkey's hooves reverberating, his imagination began to play him all kinds of tricks. But by now he had reached the famous steps he had seen in engravings — with an indescribable feeling of awe and boundless respect, he sat down quietly on a block or stone and remained sitting there for over quarter of an hour surveying the ruins about him in mute admiration, "as if the sight of those dark figures had turned me too into stone".

Vambery spent three days among the ruins and met some tribes in the vicinity who were overjoyed to find someone who could speak Turkish. They provided him with bread and milk during his stay, regaling him with stories of djinns (spirits) and local legends.

Among the names and inscriptions engraved on the ancient columns he found some Hebrew ones, dating allegedly from the time of the first captivity of the Jews. He discovered English names and German ones and was upset not to have found a single Hungarian one, when on the following day he found — to his great delight — the name 'Marothi Istvan, 1839' scrawled in a recess of a window; he could not resist adding: '*Eljen a Magyar!*'

(Long live Hungarians!), and signed his own name with a knife.

Vambery did not have long to wait for a caravan, camping outside the village and consisting mostly of pilgrims returning from Kerbela was due to leave for Zerkum, a place very near Shiraz, at midnight. Vambery joined them and when they reached their home village they were given such a rousing welcome that "even the pilgrims' donkey was carried back in triumph". He heard of an ancient colony of Jews in Zerkum, but was unable to verify it.

He left Zerkum in the company of a *tcharvadar* (muleteer) and his men — all from Shiraz — and was given such glowing descriptions of the city that Vambery's expectations were roused to fever pitch and passages from Hafiz* came to mind, poetic descriptions of Shiraz and its surroundings, but once again reality was disappointing. When he first caught sight of the city, from the famed mountain pass surrounded by bare rocks and called *Tenghi Allah Ekber* he was delighted. There lay Shiraz, with its many mosques, set in a grove of cypress trees and surrounded by luxuriant gardens and high mountains. The air was pure, the sky extraordinarily blue and roses and other flowers bloomed the year round.

He liked it on sight.

The people he found to be unchanged since the days of Hafiz: pleasure-loving, excitable, lively and — despite the strictures of the Koran — extremely fond of wine. Vambery was to take part in some of the more decorous drinking parties himself, thrilled to be in the birthplace of Hafiz, whose poems were in praise of wine. "Everyone drinks wine ... the poor labourer, the artisan, the civil servant, even the pious priests ... they all reach for the goblet and as soon as the sun sets and dusk sets in; drinking continues until the early hours, until midnight and it is really difficult to resist a drinking party held under the starry canopy of the sky in the mild climate of Shiraz ..."

Other drinking parties took place as Musellah, a place of pilgrimage or in the garden of Saadi (another great poet of Persia*) where the pipe gave him so much pleasure "as at no other spot in Persia or anywhere else in the world.

He vividly describes a drinking party around the tomb of Hafiz, where everyone "imbibed the noble liquid of the Chullari" (a wine produced by Armenians) which Vambery compared with the Hungarian Tokay not entirely to its disfavour. "We had

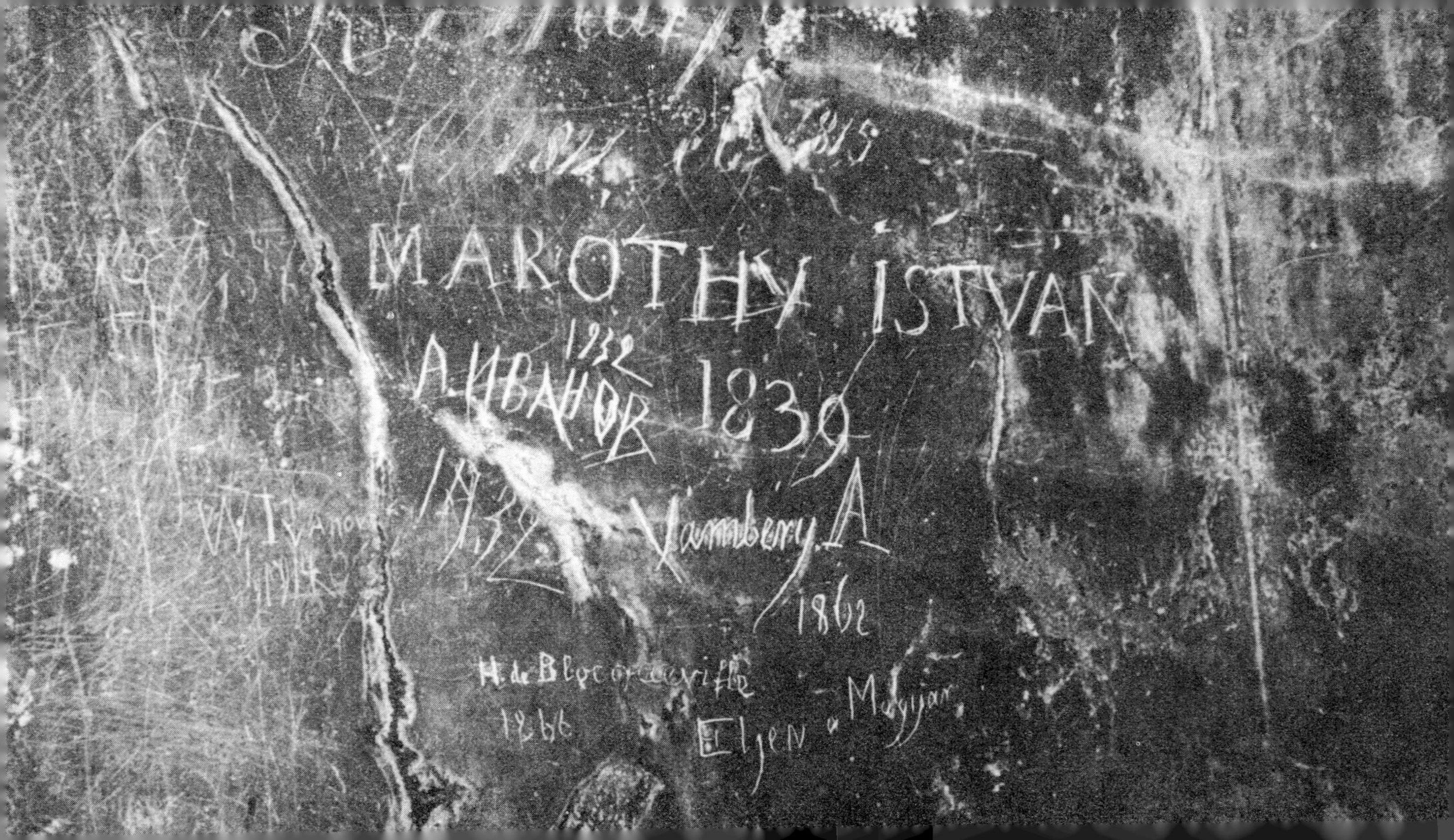

MAROTHY ISTVAN
1839
Vambery A.
1862
1866
Eljen a Magyar

lit a fire nearby and our cup went the rounds till dawn;" the round of drinking could only begin after the last evening prayer had been said, and (only) he who knows the wonderful star-filled sky of southern Persia will understand that the party burst out into exclamations of delight whenever a new group of stars appeared in the night sky. 'One cup for the *Kervanbashi* (caravan leader) . . . one for the *Binat-ul-haash* (the small and the big boar)' one called to the other and in the stillness of the night, surrounded by the stillness of the tomb the melancholy songs of Hafiz inspire ecstasy . . ."

Despite his liking for the Shirazis, he could never forget his European 'superiority'; he witnessed a lesson of geography being taught in a private house "in the and wrote mockingly: ". . . The nomenclature amused me greatly. First the teacher spoke of 'Oster-Lashia' and called it a continent, then of countries the names of which were 'Gujene, Nishaland, Niwiperetin' etc." he mocked. "When I investigated these strange names I found that they were phonetic transcriptions of an English textbook into Persian: 'Oster-Lashia' meant Australasia', 'Gujene' 'Guinea', 'Nisaland' 'New Holland' and 'Niwiperetin' 'New Britain'."

In the ruins of the formerly splendid Islamic college of *Maderi Shah* Vambery got involved in an argument concerning (of course) the superiority of the European school system. How did he dare? The Persian scholar must have seen through his disguise? and kept his mouth shut. Vambery was lucky again.

At any rate the Mollah said: "It is true you have invented the fire waggons (locomotives) in which one flies quicker than the wind from one part of the globe to another; through extending wires . . . you are competing with the speed of lightning (the telegraph). No doubt you will invent machines with which one will be able to fly up to the seventh heaven . . . but tell me, who in the west can make the leaves adhere to the branch of a tree or the rose to its stalk . . .?"

As usual the bazaar drew Vambery like a magnet and he gives his usual graphic description: ". . . the pedlars praise their wares in a loud voice . . . the greengrocer often mixes his business baritone with that of the ambulating cooks, bakers, cheese merchants, vendors of fruit and cakes. This one smacks his lips to advertise his wares, while that one shouts constantly 'Oh how tasty! Oh how good!' . . . each adopts his traditional tone and gesticulation sometimes outdone by the wild shouts of 'YA HU! YA HAKK!' of a

Vambery 'graffiti', Persepolis 1862. 'Eljeu a Magyar' is clearly visible beneath his signature.

dervish hurrying by . . . The concert reaches its highest pitch when a caravan leaves and a long queue of loaded camels beat a path through the crowd thronging the narrow lanes . . . threading their way through the confusion of passers-by, merchants, frightened women and children, sleeping dogs and leaping dervishes, jumping around like mad . . . carefully the camel, like a human being picks his way . . .''

Vambery had arrived at the southernmost point of his journey. He wanted a rest and found lodgings in a large court of a mosque. Wandering through the streets of Shiraz in the costume of a *Sunni* dervish he was again jeered and insulted by the inhabitants, who spat at him and threw stones (reminding him of his experiences in Pressburg.) Yet he remained calm, and bore "the vituperation of my saints very meekly". This made him many friends in a few weeks.

One day he heard of a Swedish doctor living in Shiraz. At once he decided to call on him. But in what guise? As a European or as a dervish? He finally decided on the latter, entering the doctor's room with the customary dervish cry of "Ya Hu! Ya Hakk!" and the doctor automatically put his hand in his pocket for *baksheesh*. Vambery refused to budge. "I seek not money!" he cried out, "but thy confidence! My chief has sent me to convert thee from they false religion and lead thee to the path of true faith".

The doctor was quite frankly amazed. He found Vambery's authoritarian approach a little unusual and, to test him, demanded proof of the miracles worked by his chief . . .

Vambery was not slow to reply. "My master has conferred on me", he told the disbelieving doctor, "the knowledge of all the sciences and languages of the world . . . thou has but to test me . . .''

For a while the doctor stared at him in silence and then spoke a few words in Swedish. Vambery rose to the occasion, delighted to mystify the doctor a little more, and with aplomb recited the opening stanzas of Tegner's *Frithjof's Saga*. (He knew no more.)

The doctor stared at him nonplussed, and tried German. This was an easy one for Vambery; then the doctor tried French and then English and Vambery replied . . . ending with a few verses from the Koran . . . in Persian. The doctor was no fool however and began to guess the truth. When Vambery saw this he abruptly terminated the interview telling the doctor that he would give him until eight o'clock in the morning to make up his mind . . .

And at eight o'clock sharp Dr. Fagergreen called on Vambery in his room. According to Vambery, it was he who decided to drop the mask after having continued the game for a while. The doctor was delighted, they both embraced and he immediately invited Vambery to be his guest and stay as long as he liked. Now the doctor told him that he had suspected as much all along but that Vambery's excellent Persian had made him doubt his European origin.

Vambery was able to give Dr. Fagergreen news of friends and acquaintances in Teheran spent six enjoyable weeks in his house.

But there remained a problem: how to explain his move to his Persian friends? He told them that he was receiving instructions from the doctor . . . in alchemy (thus confirming their belief that all foreigners were in league with the devil).

In Dr. Fagergreen's company Vambery revisited the tombs of Hafiz and Saadi and had many an enjoyable picnic, so much so that he was tempted to spend the winter in Shiraz rather than in Teheran and continue in spring to the neighbouring province of Khorassan, via Yezd and Tebbes. But the arrival of two prominent Europeans upset his plans.

Count Rochechouart, a member of the French embassy in Teheran was on a kind of one-man trade mission touring Persia; the other, the Marquis of Doria (a member of one of the oldest aristocratic families in Rome) was in Persia on a zoological and botanical mission. They were lavishly entertained by the Persian authorities and by Dr. Fagergreen, overjoyed at inviting Europeans to his home. "How could it be otherwise", wrote Vambery, "if one has been banished for fifteen years from Western civilisation and one's spirit has been nourished only by meagre flickerings which Bombay newspapers report of Western intellectual progress . . ."

Vambery met both the Marquis and the Count at the doctor's house. The Count intended to return to Teheran very shortly while the Marquis was planning to spend the winter in Shiraz. If we are to believe Vambery, it was the Count who suggested they both travel back to Teheran together. He accepted with alacrity.

"I was bound to accede to the French nobleman's proposal, although it involved an immediate separation from my friend, as I was nearly destitute of everything, and expected to derive some advantage from making the journey in his company," he wrote, adding quite candidly: "I have come here in the guise of a begging dervish, and here was a chance to go back as a European traveller, sharing in all the comforts at the disposal of a gentleman travelling in an affair of state representing His Majesty the Emperor of France . . ."

Vambery had fallen on his feet again.

The day of their departure was dramatic. Vambery was just saying good-bye to his friend, he had "grasped his friend's hand and they embraced for the last time . . .", when he felt a shock "as if the whole house were falling . . ." And Vambery "heard an underground noise approaching with a hollow roar, as if the bowels of the earth were about to open at our feet". The second shock was even more violent . . . and for a moment all stood stock still, paralysed with fright. An earthquake! Dr. Fagergreen was the first to regain his composure and managed to get his wife and children to a place of safety, in the open . . . but the open spaces were crowded with terrified people shouting "Ya Allah Ya Allah!", followed by shouts of the *mollahs* that it was the *Frengis* who had brought this disaster upon them.

Vambery was afraid and retraced his steps as fast as he could. He had barely reached the yard when he saw birds flying about, flapping their wings wildly and felt there would soon be another shock. And indeed, "very soon we heard the deep roar which usually precedes a violent thunderstorm". The earth shook and the waves became increasingly violent, throwing Vambery and Dr. Fagergreen to the ground. There was a frightful crash and a flood of water was rolling over him — Vambery thought his last moment had come. What with the burst water-tank, the water crushing a dividing wall, and increasing hoarse cries against the foreigners ("The *Frengis* are unclean") the moment had come for action. "To arms'" cried the doctor and Vambery, given no choice, rushed after him into the tottering house, to emerge with rifles and pistols . . . Now they had to defend themselves "both against the rage of the elements and the wickedness of man . . ."

More buildings collapsed amid an ear-splitting noise, a pall of dust descended on the city and the mob scattered.

Half an hour later, no further tremors being felt, Vambery picked up sufficient courage to leave the house.

Count Rochechouart was anxiously waiting and the last taking leave from his friend was "short but affectionate".

As they rode out of the city Vambery saw destruction and misery everywhere; huge boulders had crashed down and houses were flattened. Those who had fled to the open country for safety besieged them with questions anxious for news of their friends and relatives.

Vambery was glad to leave. "Words cannot tell", he wrote, "with what profound satisfaction I descried at last *Tenghi Allah Ekber*, the spot from which I had on my arrival admired the romantic situation of Shiraz ..."

He travelled back the same route he had come, the journey enlivened "by the fascinating conversation of the noble Count" (who claimed he was descended from Cardinal Richelieu and regaled Vambery with stories of the *Quartier St. Germain* in Paris).

He noted with pleasure that Persepolis had escaped destruction.

In Isfahan he was this time quartered in a monastery (run by Catholic Armenians) which stood under the protection of France. There is no record of his doings there but he resisted only with difficulty, he wrote, another visit to Iman Djuma, the "Pope of Isfahan" on whom he had called only a few months earlier in his disguise as a *Sunni* dervish. "It would have amused me to see his face ... *Takije* (or the art of dissimulation) is permitted according to *Shi-ite* law, he would not have condemned it at all, but I felt little inclination for further adventures and was extremely glad when we left here and reached Teheran safely a few days later".

The date was 15 January, 1863. He had covered a thousand miles.

When Vambery returned to Teheran he found that the war in Herat was at an end; another obstacle to carrying out his plan had been eliminated. But the far larger problem remained: how was he to proceed?

His tour of southern Persia had lasted for several months and had been good training. He felt that he now could brave wind and rain, heat and cold "without the slightest risk". His preoccupation with health had diminished and he had further accomplishments to show: not only could he now sleep in the saddle (as did the Persians) but — supreme challenge — he had learnt to swing himself into the saddle in full gallop — no mean achievement for someone with a lame leg. He could also mount heavily-laden mules and camels, "as if he spent his life with tight-rope dancers and with the "roughest specimen of humanity ... vagabonds and robbers ..." and could deal with religious taunts and "impertinent questions". He felt he had learnt to play the part of a wandering dervish to perfection — but was to find that there a big difference between playing the part of a dervish, clad in rags, singing hymns at night in Persian *Tekkes* or Central Asia where endless suspicions were to torment him.

He was now ready to go but felt uncertain how to go about it. Later, in old age, when his head had "cooled down almost to freezing-point" he realised that the execution of his plans had not been "matters of calculation and premeditation, but a leap in the dark", without taking his physical strength or his lame leg into account.

By now Vambery was thoroughly disenchanted. He was impatient to leave and turned over in his mind his earlier plan to go to Bokhara via Herat and across the Turkoman steppes; all words of warning on the part of his European and Turkish friends were of no avail. The fate of the unfortunate Conolly and Stoddart and other Europeans were held up to him, but the warnings fell on deaf ears. ("The sad fate of others had no terror for me").

Among those who discouraged him least was Charles Alison, the British Minister who asked him to find out, if he could, the whereabouts of a Lieutenant or Captain Wyburd, reputed to have fallen into Turkoman hands and was missing presumed lost.

The European colony saw that he was in earnest. Count Gobineau, that arch-racist and envoy of Napoleon III, received him warmly "under his small tent like a caldron" (sic) and tried to discourage him (this Vambery put down to envy and jealousy); at the Turkish legation, however, they were genuinely concerned for him. They recalled the fate of the Shah's French photographer, de Bloqueville, who had returned only recently from Turkoman captivity, ransomed for 10,000 Ducats, and who had horrifying tales to tell . . .

Nevertheless Vambery was all set to go.

Two years earlier he had received from the hands of the Secretary of the Hungarian Academy a travelling stipend of 1000 florins, on condition that he explore the countries beyond the Oxus and discover the relationship between Hungarian and the languages spoken in Turkestan, an ambition that had possessed him since his earliest youth.

Now two years had passed and he was not a step nearer to his goal.

Had he received further payments, as a letter, now in the archives of the Academy testifies: the latest payment made was in January 1863 and it was 43 pieces of gold ... This source had now dried up. He could no longer count on financial aid from the Academy or from Dr. Josef Budenz, the Academy's librarian and a fellow Orientalist (to whom Vambery was to respectfully dedicate his books about Persia). ("I have not told in it a tenth of my sufferings.")

Had he meanwhile had awkward letters from Budapest? What was he *still* doing cooling his heels in Teheran? Holidaying at the Academy's expense?

He was in a tight spot.

When he had so brashly presented himself to the Academy, full of youthful bravado — he had not had the faintest notion of how to put them into practice. In his farewell speech in Budapest (1861) he had said: "You wish me to travel through Central Asia and the Islamic world as Reshid Effendi — the name bestowed on me by the Sultan" (as he untruthfully had boasted) — "to visit the Libraries of Samarkand, Balkh and Bokhara, as well as private houses, to study the spoken language of everyday life".

But the more he had advanced eastward on his journey the more he had realised what a rash promise he had made. And yet he knew the time had come for him to act.

He had toyed with different ideas, trying to evade the issue. (A book about Persia? A Comparative Study of the Oriental Nations?' But there was no way out or around it. His brief was for Central Asia. He was indeed "compelled to go forward" and "compelled" was indeed the operative word.

It was a clear case of Hobson's choice.

The story however was not quite as he had presented it to the Academy.

In a letter dated 20 March 1863* he informed the Hungarian Academy that he was sticking to his earlier plans (to travel to Bokhara via Herat. But he then tore open the letter which had already been sealed and was ready for posting — or so he told the Academy at least — to add with a flourish a characteristically melodramatic P.S. It was in pencil and was subsequently read out by the Secretary of the Academy, Ladislaus Szalay: It read: "I am reopening this letter. A company of Mahommedan pilgrims from Kashgar returning to Mecca, who I met at the Embassy, *have*

---

* Proceedings of the Hungarian Academy, 1863, Vol. I, no. 1, p. 97.

incognito of a dervish. If I succeed in this journey which in its entirety has never been made by a European before, if I am not betrayed, then . . ." (but, tantalisingly, the passage trails off into nothingness).

No doubt this was calculated to have the impact of a bombshell back home and put an end to any embarassing questions demanding to know the reasons for his procrastination.

It was the custom of the Turkish Embassy to assist *Hadjis* on their pilgrimage to Mecca (which lay within the boundaries of the Ottoman empire; besides, as *Sunni* Moslems, the pilgrims — even if from as far away as Central Asia — were subjects of the Sultan). Among them were often dervishes from Bokhara, Khiva and Samarkand who were often given financial help. Vambery even writes that he took "particular pleasure in having these wild and ragged Tartars" come to his room (at the Embassy); he would often intercede on behalf of these travellers from far-off Turkestan and the rumour had spread like wildfire that the effendi was most likely a secret dervish himself. This notion was confirmed by the tales of hardships Vambery regaled them with and his openly professed dislike of the "French dress he wore" (in fact, when eventually he got back to Europe, he was to find it very difficult to accustom himself to European clothing — to "forked garments" — trousers — and the like).

Fortuitously, on March 20, 1863, the same day Vambery wrote the letter to the Hungarian Academy of Sciences, *but before he had added the dramatic P.S.* — four hadjis from Central Asia had come to see Vambery; they had a complaint against the Persians, who, as fierce and fanatical *Shi'ite* Muslims had imposed a tax on hadjis travelling through Persian territory. They explained that they had not come to ask any financial aid for themselves but protest against this unfair tax and to prevent it being collected from their countrymen. These "unselfish words from the lips of an oriental" puzzled Vambery. Was he here confronted with noble savages? And, indeed, a closer look at them revealed, underneath their ragged exterior, a "certain natural nobility". The leader was Bilal, a hadji from Chinese (or Eastern) Tartary, who wore a green *djubbe* over his tattered garments and gigantic white turban. His eyes sparkled with intelligence and vitality. He and the other three were the leaders of a caravan, 24 men strong, who were returning to Turkestan.

Vambery felt they would be useful as guides. He also considered it "something to be known to them as Reshid Effendi . . . and to have been seen as such at the Turkish Embassy". (This piece of snobbery worked in his favour). But he considered it quite out of the question to tell them about the real purpose of his journey — they would have suspected some ulterior motive. He therefore brazenly told them that it had long been his most ardent wish to visit the graves of the saints at Khiva, Bokhara and Samarkand. This confirmed their belief that he really was a dervish in disguise.

When his mind was made up Vambery informed the Turkish ambassador who introduced Vambery to the leader of the "beggar band" as the *Sultan's civil officer* (the italics are Vambery's) and solemnly placed him in their charge. The hadjis promised to look after him; in return the ambassador had 15 gold pieces distributed among them — one for each member of the dervis caravan.

One frequent visitor was Hadji Bilal, the leader who now introduced Vambery's new travelling companions in turn. "His exterior was not apt to inspire confidence", wrote Vambery and resolved to take no chances lest they mark him out as a rich victim to be robbed. He showed Bilal all the money he had, a small sum, asking him at the same time to advise him how to dress and to behave so as to remain as inconspicuous as possible. This pleased Bilal. He recommended the following: first of all Vambery was to shave his head and exchange his Turkish (i.e. "French") dress for that of Bokhara; secondly he was to leave behind him all bedding, linen and "similar articles of luxury".

Vambery carried out these instructions to the letter and was ready to leave three days ahead of time. He made use of this spare time to call on his future travelling companions in their caravensery. "I never saw in my life so much raggedness and dirt crowded into such a small space" he writes.

When Vambery entered their cell they were cleaning themselves "the loathsome description of which I leave to the reader's imagination."

He was very cordially received by them, and immediately offered a cup of green Bokhara tea. Vambery thought it tasted horrible and politely declined a second cup. After suffering their embraces as a "brother" he broke bread with them and sat down to work out the details of their itinerary. There were two roads to choose from — both equally dangerous since they crossed Turkoman territory. One led to Bokhara via Meshed and Merv and was less tiring, but meant crossing territory inhabited by the Tekke Turkomans who were reputed to be capable of selling the "Prophet himself into slavery if he ever fell into their hands"; the other road led through territory inhabited by Yomut Turkomans, who Vambery later considered to be honest and hospitable; but this road meant crossing a desert where for twenty stations not a drop of drinking water could be obtained. Nevertheless, after discussing it all, the latter road was chosen and the decision was ratified by an oath from Bilal: everyone held up his hand to heaven and when the hadji had finished speaking took hold of their beards and said a loud "Amen".

They warned him of the dangers ahead, the risk of being killed or captured as a slave, of hunger, thirst, sandstorms and hurricanes. But Vambery had made up his mind and discounted them. When he had finished speaking the "good Tartars" looked at him and each other in amazement, finding their theory confirmed: he was indeed a secret dervish . . .

Haidar Pasha had given Vambery an authorised passport in the name of *Hadji* Mehemmet Reshid Effendi, with the official signature and seal. He thus became as it were, the first self-made Hadji and says so himself: "Seeing that I had never been in Mecca, and had therefore no legal right to the title of *Hadji* (pilgrim), this official lie may be viewed in various lights . . .

The Sultan's "passport" was of the utmost importance. It bore the *Tugra* — the Sultan's seal — and to this, he owed the success of his enterprise. It was even to save his life on some critical occasions for the official document was the object of pious veneration for the Turkomans. Some came from far and near to behold the holy *Tugra*, and after performing the prescribed ablutions to press the sacred sign against their brow.

The dervishes would therefore not have dared to approach so exalted a person as the *Sultan's civil officer*, Hadji Mehemmed Reshid Effendi, equipped with an official document bearing the Sultan's *Tugra* of their own accord.

But perhaps one should not judge him too harshly if he prevaricated and misrepresented the facts: he knew from experience how little understanding and sympathy he could expect from the Hungarian Academy of Sciences whose members had shown so unrealistic an appraisal of the situation as to equip him with a letter of Safe Conduct — in Latin — addressed to the rulers of Tartary. (And a very unsafe conduct it would have guaranteed him, had he produced it as Vambery had pointed out.

When the first flush of excitement was over, Vambery viewed the coming adventure with some trepidation. He was not unaware of the risks involved. Would the outcome justify them? How would he stand up to the hardships, the insufficient clothing? How would he fare without a safe roof over his head or a change of underwear? No night shirt? These things were real worries to him. "I do not wish to dwell on the struggle which my adventurous decision cost me during the first few days" he writes. How would he fare with his lame leg? He knew he tired easily and that forced route marches might be demanded of him. Would they prove too much?

For months the Academy was to have no news of him. Finally Baron Eotvos wrote to the Turkish legation in Teheran and received a reply from Dr. Bimsenstein Muhlis, the Austrian physician attached to the Turkish legation, dated 5 August 1863 and forwarded through the good offices of the Austrian Consul in Trebizond.

"Contrary to what he said in his last report addressed to the Hungarian Academy, M. Vambery left Teheran on 24 March — directly for Khiva from where he will proceed to Bokhara and to Samarkand. He is making this journey disguised as a Dervish and in the company of a group of pilgrims from Mecca who are returning to their homeland . . .

I must refrain here from indicating the motives and the circumstances which caused M. Vambery to change his itinerary, to go to Bokhara and not to Meshed, as he had announced. I limit myself merely to telling you, M. le Baron, that the Turkish Legation which was anxious to take under its protection your knowledgeable traveller, believes it necessary, for security reasons, to keep his journey a secret and it wishes that it should not yet be made known, not even in Europe, for fear of Russian agents who see political emissaries everywhere compromising its success".

Trusting in the knowledge and the personal qualities which distinguish M. Vambery, we hope that he will succeed completely in the enterprise so full of dangers . . . It is up to him to furnish more details concerning his departure from Teheran which is not without out interest . . ."

This was the physician who supplied him with three strychnine pills in case of capture and torture. Vambery kept them hidden in the wadding of his dress. "I could always reach them with my mouth in case my hands were tied," he explained later. "I knew they could not torture me, then I did not care."

When the time came to leave Vambery's heart was heavy. His friends at the Turkish legation tried again to dissuade him, reminding him of the tragic fate of Stoddart and Conolly and of earlier travellers to Turkestan. But Vambery stood firm. ". . . the fate of others has no terrors and I remained firm in my determination to go".

When all else had failed, Haidar Effendi gave Vambery a banquet he was to remember nostalgically in Central Asia, as he choked on greasy *Pilaff* cooked in rancid mutton fat . . .

Meanwhile he lay back comfortably in an armchair, sipped his wine and smoked his cigar, and tried to put all future hardships out of his mind.

The next morning he was off. Only two persons, Haidar Pasha and Dr. Bimsenstein-Muhlis, knew of his real destination. The rest of the European colony thought he was going to Meshed.

The date of his departure was 28 March.

Whether this discrepancy of dates was due to the Persian calendar or not, one fact is clear: Vambery did not dash off from Teheran a few hours after he had met the dervishes . . .

PART 2

*Dervish
in
Disguise*

5

A NEAR THING IN KHIVA ...

Early in the morning of 28 March 1863, Vambery proceeded to his rendezvous at the caravanserai. Although he was shabbily dressed in the guise of a beggar, he found most of the others in the party had substituted their 'best holiday costume' for their 'travelling dress', consisting of a multitude of rags fastened round their hips by a cord. Vambery had not yet fully acclimatised himself to his travelling companions, having not fully shared their state of poverty and filth.

The caravan numbered twenty-four — everyone entitled to the prefix *Hadji*, as one who had completed the pilgrimage to Mecca: Hadjis Bilal, Sheikh Sultan Mahmoud, Salih Khalifa, and Reshid (Vambery himself) were treated as the four chiefs of the party. There were twelve Chinese Tartars from Khokand, Yarkand, and Aksu (led by Bilal, Court Imam of the Chinese Governor of Aksu); eight in Salih Khalifa's party from Khokand; and Sheikh Sultan Mahmoud was accompanied by two companions from Kashgar (in Chinese Turkestan).

After Bilal had invoked a blessing, the company moved off through the gates in a rush — the pilgrims on foot struggling to keep ahead of those on horseback. The caravan travelled in a north-easterly direction and late in the morning reached a mountain pass. Teheran, its minarets wreathed in misty sunlight, slowly disappeared behind them. Vambery looked back several times at the last outpost of civilization. Doubts again entered his mind. Beyond this pass lay "the extremes of savageness and barbarism", where no 'frengi' with a European complexion was safe.

The day's ride had not disappointed him, but the first night was spent at a station called Kemerd, little more than a rotting, half-ruined mud hut in the middle of a scrubby wilderness. With rain pouring in through the roof, the pilgrims clambered into the few

Vambery disguised as a dervish.

available dry corners. Bilal prepared a small *pilaff* with some candle grease added for fat. Vambery's stomach turned at this sight, so he declined the supper, and sat in a corner of the hut, cold wet mud running down his back. He closed his eyes and thought longingly of the beautiful banquet and sweet wines he had enjoyed only the night before. His friends had been scrutinising his features for betrayal of "inward excitement", but they were very much mistaken. At that moment Vambery had felt that he could carry off the deception successfully, but being a dervish in real life was quite a different affair. Rolled up like a ball, he tried to get to sleep, but this was out of the question since they were packed together like sardines. "First I felt the hand, then the head of one of my neighbours, falling upon me", he wrote, adding with wry humour, "then my opposite companion stretched out his foot, to scratch me behind the ears". To cap it all, a Persian mule driver, afflicted with gout, limped into the hut, sat down beside Vambery, and kept up a steady flow of moans and screams for several hours. This, together with the others' stentorian snoring, kept Vambery awake throughout the night.

In the early morning, Vambery — frozen and wet through — mounted his mule with extreme difficulty. It was usually warm during the day, but in the early hours the cold was unbearable, and Vambery found himself stiffening in his saddle. So he dismounted and warmed himself up by walking with the poorer members of the party. One of these mendicants gratefully borrowed the mule, and he lent Vambery his stick. Stimulated by the fascinating tales and exploits of his fellow Hadjis, Vambery warmed with enthusiasm, and joined in the spontaneous *telkins* (hymns), yelling at the top of his voice "*Allahiya Allah!*" In admiration the Hadjis never ceased repeating: "Hadji Reshid is indeed a genuine Dervish!"

The following night was spent at Ghilar, a drier more comfortable place. Bilal again prepared a foul-smelling supper in a large communal dish. Several pairs of dirty hands dived in vigorously. Vambery's ravenous appetite overcame his squeamishness; he ate his portion, and sank into a refreshing sleep. He rose the next morning much stronger, and less depressed. A bad road took them through beautiful countryside to a place called Surkh Abad where the "mountain tops bathed in the silvery light of the moon", and on to an elevated plateau. Here stood the town of Firuzkuh, an important trading centre. Before reaching this town, Vambery had to brave a very fierce wind, locally known as *Badi Firuzkuh*, of which he had been warned: it had been known to throw travellers off their mules and cast them into the nearby ravines. Brave on so many other occasions, Vambery was genuinely frightened; the storm was so fierce that all the pilgrims had to dismount and the loads had to be taken off the mules.

Beyond Firuzkuh the road stretched through abundant forests, with the distant roar of mountain cataracts. The party ate by the ruins of Div-Sefid, reputedly the favourite resort of the legendary White Giant who Rustem (the hero of Oriental legends) conquered. (Nine years later Vambery named his only son after Rsutem.)

At Zirab, the northern point of the mountainous pass of Mazendran, the pilgrims were warned by local natives that the forest was infested by many kinds of wild animals. When searching for water to make tea, the Hadjis nearly walked into 'two splendid tigers'. Fortunately the tigers appeared to be as startled as the men; they bounded into the thickets, while Vambery — frightened at this new sight — seized a rusty sword to defend himself. Camping at night near a small village, Heften, they lit a large fire and took turns in keeping watch. The thickets resounded with deep roars, while jackals — too numerous to drive away — waited to pounce on unguarded food and clothing. They came so close to Vambery the whole night long that he was obliged "in self-defence, to use both hands and feet to prevent their making off with break-sack or shoes".

In this region there was food in abundance, and next day Vambery bought ten large pheasants for two and a half pence. Most of the other Hadjis bought the same, and for three or four days they had excellent savoury roast dinners. Passing through an unattractive marshy district, the party arrived at Sari, a large market town and trading centre. Here they were met by the local inhabitants, Persian Shiites, who laughed rudely at their dirty appearance. In the caravanserai, where they rested for two days, Vambery and his fellows received — from some friendly Turkomans — gifts of clothing, food and tobacco, for which they bestowed *fatihas* (blessings) "while they were still fresh from the Holy Land". Bilal was delighted to see the Turkomans, saying to Vambery: "Yes, Effendi, we shall be free before long; we are coming to the land of the Turkomans, our brethren in faith, and as much distinction is awaiting us there as we have to suffer shame, insolence and contempt at the hands of the Persians."

Horses had to be hired to take the Hadjis on the nine-hour journey from Sari to Karatepe on the coast — through many marshes and morasses, in normal times impassable by foot. The Hadjis were now accompanied by some notable Afghan merchants, led by a man of some distinction, Nur-Ullah, who seemed to take a particular interest in Vambery. Apparently, he had heard of Vambery's connections with the Turkish Embassy in Teheran.

Consternation grew within Vambery as he arrived in the small port of Karatepe with his fellow travellers. Karatepe was right on the edge of the Persian Empire, situated on the Western flank of Astrabad Bay, the 'Dead Sea', separated from the south-eastern tip of the Caspian Sea by a long neck of land. These waters of the southern Caspian were notorious for rapacious slave-trading Turkoman pirates.

Nur-Ullah insisted that 'Hadji Reshid' — Vambery — come to his house and take tea with him. Vambery accepted, on condition that Bilal came too. No sooner had they sat down when in streamed a horde of Turkoman visitors. They squatted down in a long row right round the room, staring wide-eyed at Vambery, whispering eagerly to each other, and then proclaiming their assorted views and opinions in loud voices: "A dervish he is not. His opinion is anything but that of a dervish; for the wretchedness of his dress contrasts too plainly with his features and his complexion. As the Hadjis told us, he must be a relative of the ambassador, who represents the Sultan at Teheran". Here they all stood up. "Allah only knows what a man who issues from so high an origin has to do amongst the Turkomans of Khiva and Bokhara".

Vambery felt that to contradict his visitors would be unsafe. Instead he sat seemingly buried in thought, with an inscrutable, oblivious expression on his face. This disappointed — and impressed — the inquisitive company. They had failed to tear the mask from Vambery's face. Instead they turned to Bilal, who told them that the strange-looking Reshid was really an Effendi, and a servant of the Sultan; but that he had withdrawn himself from the deceptions of the world, and was now engaged with 'Ziaret' (a pilgrimage to the tombs of the Saints). This did the trick. After two hours of voluble chattering had elapsed, the visitors withdrew, and tea was at last prepared.

On hearing all these disturbing enquiries, Vambery easily pictured to himself, ironically, "the splendid future in store for me further on in the very nest of this people". Before settling down to rest, Vambery was approached by an oily disreputable character, who said he was an Afghan who knew the country of Khiva and Bokhara very well, and proposed that they should travel together on the route to Khiva. The next morning Nur-Ullah warned Vambery that this man, named Emir Mohammed, was an opium-eater with a very bad reputation, and not to be trusted at any cost. This villain would cause Vambery much trouble in the weeks to follow.

The next step for the Hadjis was to find a ship to take them across the Bay to the port of Gomushtepe on the eastern bank of the Caspian. There was an Afghan, named Anakhan, employed by the Russians (at Ashurada, a nearby Russian station), who was willing to ferry them across for a small fee. However he refused to give Vambery a passage, regarding him as a secret emissary of the Sultan, and therefore a danger to his livelihood with the Russians. Vambery was relieved to hear his companions declare that if Anakhan would not take him, they would not go either. Further enquiries brought to light a pious Turkoman who was about to sail to Gomushtepe, and would take all the Hadjis with him for no extra charge, save a blessing. This man, named Yakub, was young and had "an uncommonly bold look". He had a romantic air, and confided to Vambery that he was a victim of unhappy unrequited love, for a girl of his own race. He had been told by a local 'magician', a Jew, that a talisman could be prepared from thirty drops of attar of roses fresh from Mecca. Luckily the Hadjis were able to supply this vital part of the formula — though we do not know if the desired effect was attained.

Provisions were bought, including bread to last as far as Khiva, and a sack of flour each; and two days later, early in the morning of April 10, the pilgrims gathered on the sea-shore. A tiny skiff, hollowed out of the trunk of a tree, took them one mile out to Yakub's boat, a *keseboy*, furnished with a mast and one sail. They were sandwiched into the boat in two rows, port and starboard, so tightly that movement of any kind was practically impossible.

At midday they set sail, the favourable wind driving the tiny vessel like an arrow. As they pulled away from the Persian shore, Vambery's regrets evaporated in the friendly company and good faith of his fellow pilgrims. Towards evening, they anchored near the shore, and each took turns in preparing his tea. Yakub boasted at length of his exploits at sea, the number of heretics he had killed or taken prisoner, and various stories of piracy, rape and murder.

Next morning they sailed into Ashurada, the southernmost point of Russia's possessions in Asia at that time. To guard against piracy, Russian men-of-war were permanently on guard in the harbour, as not only Persian but also Russian sailors were often captured and dragged in chains into slavery to Gomushtepe. Yakub's boat was now called over to one of these large men-of-war to submit to the usual routine examination. As they approached, Vambery placed himself in an inconspicuous position with his back to the Russian vessel. While Yakub's papers were being cleared, Vambery heard to his dismay one of the officers say "See how white this Hadji is": his face was still noticeably less tanned and weatherbeaten than his companions. Luckily no more was said, as the bells ringing on shore denoted this was 'the holiday of the Unbelievers' (the Russian style Easter Sunday), which cut short the Customs examination.

In a few moments the Russian vessel had moved away; and, weighing anchor, Yakub's boat was soon ploughing the waters smoothly towards the north-east. Near them in the water, in a straight line, were several long painted poles. Yakub told Vambery they were sea-marks, placed there by the 'Inghiliz' to mark the limits of the Russian waters. The other side belonged to the Turkomans, whom the 'Inghiliz' would "always protect against the attack of the Russians". This gave food for thought to Vambery on the readiness of the English in this area to stand up against the Russians.

It was not long before the Turkoman coast appeared before them. The boat moored a mile and a half from the mouth of the river Gorghen, either side of which lay the encampment of Gomushtepe, a cluster of tents resembling a hundred beehives lying close together. Yakub disembarked first sending out three small skiffs to relay the Hadjis to shore. Vambery — with Bilal — was the last to land, and was pleased to see that Yakub had already announced their arrival to Khandjan, the chief of Gomushtepe, and that the latter was hastening down at that very moment to receive them.

Khandjan knelt, said his noon-prayers, then came forward and embraced Vambery, Bilal and Salih in turn. The whole population of Gomushtepe swarmed out, like bees from their hives, to greet the travellers. Men, women and children, with dogs barking furiously at their heels, came rushing over to embrace the pilgrims.

Young and old, wrote Vambery, "without distinction of sex or family, all wished to touch the Hadjis on whom the holy dust of Mecca and Medina still rested. Judge, too, of my amazement when women of the greatest beauty, some girls even, hurried up to embrace me."

Khandjan eventually took charge of the situation. He decided where each of the pilgrims should stay, insisting that Vambery and Bilal (together with four other pilgrims) should be his own personal guests. Vambery took an immediate liking to the hospitable, friendly chief. Khandjan was aged about forty, plainly dressed, tall, handsome, and with a long beard. He now took the pilgrims on the long walk to his *Ova*: the Turkoman name for a large tent, the house and family of the local chieftain.

The sun was just setting as an exhausted Vambery reached Khandjan's home, with the others. The pilgrims now had to answer what seemed like a thousand questions from the locals who swarmed inside the *Ova*. Late in the evening, Khandjan's young son brought in a supper of boiled fish and sour milk, which the pilgrims attacked with ravenous appetites.

During his first night in the Turkoman tent, Vambery had a long refreshing sleep on a comfortable couch. Next morning (13 April) Bilal took him for a walk, and confided that Khandjan and the other local inhabitants had been asking some rather tricky questions. They noticed Vambery did not act in quite the same way as the other Hadjis, and were generally of the opinion that he had been sent by the Sultan to Khiva on some anti-Russian mission. However this did not threaten Vambery's safety at this time as the Turkomans here were more friendly to the Sultan than to the Russians.

Bilal said it was most important that Vambery "should lay aside entirely his effendi character, and become body and soul a dervish". He went on: "It will occasion great surprise if, representing yourself to be a dervish, you do not carry out the character to its full extent. You know the form of benediction: assume, therefore, a serious face, and distribute your *Fatiha* (blessings); you can also give the *Nefes* (holy breath) when you are summoned to the sick, only never forget to extend your hand at the same time, for it is well known that we dervishes subsist by such acts of piety, and they are always ready with some little present or other".

The Hadjis were to stay in Gomushtepe for one month, and this gave Vambery useful time to extend his acquaintance with the Turkomans, and also to acquire greater fluency in their language. Within a week, he had made friends everywhere in the district, and very soon he began to cultivate those whom he considered would be of use to him. Among these was Mollah Durdis, who held the rank of judge. It was not long before Vambery became known as "the best informed and most experienced dervish", and he was even consulted about the precise position of the *Mihrab* (altar) when a new mosque was to be constructed! A local scholar and highly respected priest, Satlig Akhond, gave thanks to Allah for allowing him to behold a "Muslim from Roum"; and when a cynic remarked on Vambery's white complexion, this priest said that *that* was the pure light of Islam shining from his countenance!

During the month's stay in Gomushtepe, Vambery also became well acquainted with another locally respected scholar, Kizil Akhond — a Turkoman "savant" — Vambery felt the need to put it in inverted commas. This man had bought (in Bokhara) an important Mohammedan treatise. As it was written in Turkish, he could read it only with extreme difficulty, so when Vambery translated it clearly and gave him the key to the book, he was delighted. Kizil took Vambery on a four-day sight-seeing tour of the local area, and showed him the great wall built by Alexander the Great as a bulwark against the wild nomads of the wilderness over two thousand years before. Vambery was amused to find that Kizil had a different wife and family in each village they visited.

As Bilal had formerly explained, the Turkomans never permitted a dervish to leave empty-handed from their tents, so Vambery soon found himself amassing alms on a large scale — both food and assorted gifts of felt mats and similarly-made local products. Presents of dried fish were most plentiful, as the River Gorghen (which flows through Gomushtepe) was fabulously rich in fish, rendering the fresh water almost undrinkable. Vambery found he had acquired a strong fishy smell after washing briefly on the bank of the river!

Vambery always seems to have been an ardent fighter for personal freedom, so he was appalled at the cruel treatment of Persian slaves which he was forced to witness. Khandjan had two slaves, both Persian youths, compelled to wear heavy chains. Vambery and Bilal, as guests in Khadjan's home, were encouraged to abuse, curse and beat the unfortunate pair — this distressed Vambery more than anything else.

Fortunately for the pilgrims, there was a caravan in the district about to make a return journey to Khiva. The *Kervanbashi* (or caravan-leader) was one Ilias Beg, a cattle-dealer. He made the journey once every year, coming in the late autumn, and returning to Khiva in the spring. He had been instructed by the Khan of Khiva to purchase some buffaloes from Khandjan. (The Khan had been advised by his physicians that drinking buffalo milk would cure his impotence.) Ilias Beg was returning with extra camels — a god-send for the pilgrims, who could hire them for a small additional fee. Each camel carried a *kedjeve* (pair of wooden baskets, hanging down the two sides) — with two pilgrims sharing one camel, each occupying a basket. Vambery was lucky enough to have Bilal as his companion, or 'equipoise'.

The caravan for Khiva was to assemble at Etrek, a district twelve miles north-east of Gomushtepe. The responsibility for the pilgrims had to be transferred from Khandjan to Kulkhan, the head man in Etrek and chief of the Karaktchi, one of the most bloodthirsty tribes in the area. When Kulkhan came to greet the party, he looked at Vambery very suspiciously. This belligerent man, known as *Karaktchilar piri viz* (greybeard of the robbers), had "a morose and repulsive look about him". Apparently, in his youth he had travelled much in Russia and had picked up a lot of informatin concerning Turkish and Eastern European life. He declared hotly that there was nothing Turkish in Vambery's features. Bilal then remarked that he was badly informed, as he himself had been living for a long time in Roum (Turkey), and had never observed the resemblance he spoke about. Kulkhan's doubts seemed to be assuaged for the time being.

The pilgrims were forced to wait an extra day and a half in Gomushtepe, while Kulkhan awaited his son Kolman to return from a horse-stealing raid, across the Persian frontier. Eventally Kolman, with seven of his companions, were seen advancing at the furious gallop towards the opposite shore, bringing with them about ten spare horses. Within a few moments they had crossed swimming the river Gorghen, dismounted, and greeted their friends and relations. Even Vambery could not help being impressed: "However much I despised their occupation I could not help feasting my eyes on the manly forms of these young fellows, who in their short riding costumes, their long fair hair falling in curls on their shoulders, and with defiant looks, were the objects of general admiration". The gloomy Kulkhan cheered up visibly, as he proudly introduced his son to the Hadjis. His suspicions of Vambery seemed to have been forgotten.

Next morning, bidding farewell to Khandjan and his family, the Hadjis left Gomushtepe for Etrek, accompanied by Kulkhan, his son Kolman and the stolen horses, and also a few other miscellaneous travellers including Emir Mohammed (the shifty opium-eater from Karatepe). They proceeded through lush meadows leading past some very old Turkoman burial mounds to a large area of reed-covered marshland which swarmed with wild boar. Vambery was permitted to ride one of the stolen horses — which he much preferred to the discomfort of the camels — but was dismayed to find Emir Mohammed walking at his side. When a particularly wet area of land had to be crossed, Vambery felt obliged to share his horse with this reprobate. On one occasion, according to Vambery, the horse shied, and the two men were hurled together onto the ground, landing right on top of two young wild boars. Vambery and Emir Mohammed were saved by their friends in the nick of time from the onrush of the boars' enraged and savage mother, coming to protect her young.

It was dusk, eight hours later, when the party arrived at a small habitation — and the Hadjis were quartered in the small tent of an aged Turkoman, Allah Nazr. The only thing of value this old man possessed was a goat; but he was so delighted at having the chance to entertain these "heaven-sent guests", that he had no hestitation in killing it for the meal, and to turn the skin into a water-vessel. This he gave to Vambery.* The party were detained in this place for a whole day, while Kulkhan tortured a newly captured Persian slave to ascertain the status and wealth of his family and how high a ransom could be raised to free him.

Next day they resumed the march, and Vambery (for the first time) sat in the basket of the camel he had rented. However, the soil became very soft in the succession of marshes and salt-flats, and Vambery preferred to dismount and trudge through the mud for the remaining one and a half hours walk to Etrek.

On arriving, Kulkhan ushered Vambery into his *Ova* and told him not to leave it. Vambery became greatly alarmed when he

---

* In later years, Vambery was sometimes photographed at his writing-desk in Budapest. Among the objects on the desk was a leather water-vessel — possibly the one given by Allah Nazr.

heard Kulkhan "cursing his women, accusing them of always mislaying his chains, and ordering them to bring them to him immediately". However, the crisis passed when the chains were placed on the new Persian slave, and Vambery was shown to a new tent, which had just been prepared for him and ten of his travelling companions.

Vambery wrote later: "I must confess that this was neither the first nor the last time that the grim look and suspicious doings of the Turkomans, who afterwards turned out to be my best friends, filled my mind with all kinds of horror. I never felt quite safe as to my future, and the only consolation was in my lameness, which made me quite valueless in the eyes of the slave-dealers." He continued boastfully: "Of course, as the time went on, I began to be accustomed to this perpetual anxiety, and in spite of the constant danger in which I found myself, I regained my good humour, and my wit and jokes not only exhilarated my hadji fellows, but even the surliest son of the desert, and the usual remark of the Turkomans was 'That lame Hadji of Roum (Turkey) is a jolly fellow; he would make a capital merry-maker'."

During his stay in Etrek, Vambery was entertained by some of the local notables. One of these, a chieftain named Kotchak Khan, told Vambery: "Now I will give thee a treat. We know the relation in which the Osmanlis stand with the Russians: thou shalt behold one of they arch enemies in chains". A sickly and very sorrowful Russian slave was led in, and was forced down on to the ground before Vambery. "Kiss the Effendi's feet" ordered Kotchak Khan, and the Russian crawled forward to obey. Despite his fierce anti-Russian bias Vambery felt distressed at this treatment of a 'fellow European'. He waved the Russian back, and explained to the surprised Turkoman onlookers that he had only just begun his *Gusl* (great purification), and did not want to soil himself by contact with an unbeliever. It would be more agreeable, he said, if the slave was removed from his presence immediately, as the Russian nation was the one he hated more than any other.

The Persian slave in Kulkhan's tent was being starved and maltreated in a very barbaric manner, especially by Kulkhan's second wife. Years before, she herself had been a Persian slave, and now she was trying to prove to her husband how zealous a convert she had become. The unfortunate slave, who had been subsisting for several days only on dried salt fish instead of bread, desperately implored Vambery for a drop of water when they were alone together for a few minutes in the tent. "The sight of the bearded man bathed in tears made me forget all risks", Vambery remembered. "I handed him my water-skin, and he satisfied his thirst while I kept watch at the door". It would have gone badly with Vambery if this act had been discovered.

The rest of the caravan had now reassembled at Etrek. Vambery and Bilal kissed and hugged their fellow Hadjis from whom they had been separated for a few days. "Although I regarded Bilal as my dearest friend, I was compelled to avow to myself warm attachment to them all, without distinction", noted Vambery. Also new friends were greeted.

Ilias issued orders for all the party to finish their preparations as quickly as possible, as the rendezvous had been arranged with the caravan-leader on the far bank of the River Etrek in two days time, in readiness for their trek across the desert. Everyone spent the final evening in Etrek busily baking bread and salting down camel flesh.

As this was the last outpost before reaching the great desert, Vambery decided it was time to make use of the two sheets of blank paper hidden in his Koran (suspended from his neck in a little bag). He wrote two letters, one to Haidar Effendi — at the Turkish Legation in Teheran — and the second to Khandjan, asking him to forward the other. When Vambery eventually arrived back at Teheran some months later, he was very pleased to find that his letter, and others he had previously written in Gomushtepe, had all reached the Legation safely — thanks mainly to Khandjan.

Leaving Etrek early in the morning, an arduous zigzag journey over marshland took most of the day and covered only four miles. Vambery and Bilal shared the same camel, balancing in panniers one on each side. A four hours' march the next day brought the party to the banks of the river, which they crossed with difficulty, the ground being loamy and soft. Safely on the other side, they were very pleased to see the caravan-leader's party approaching, together with the three very important buffaloes — "to whose health-promising advent the sick Lord of Khiva could hardly look forward with greater impatience than we had done" thought Vambery.

The caravan-leader was a corpulent Turkoman named Amandurdi. He greeted the Hadjis with great cordiality — all except

Vambery who received only a cold stare. Hearing Amandurdi mutter "I know this Hadji already", Vambery was frightened but tried not to show it. He noticed Ilias and some of the other looking angrily at Emir Mohammed, the "crazy opium eater" — who was thus designated as the cause of suspicion. Every day, this malicious Afgtan had seen Vambery make notes with the stump of a pencil on the small pieces of paper concealed in the wool of his Bokhariot dress; and now he reminded Amandurdi of the 'Frenghi envoy' to Khiva who, some years previously, had been discovered making similar notes. Most of this Frenghi's acquaintances had been put to death by the ruthless Khan. During the evening Vambery overheard Emir Mohammed say to the caravan-leader: "I bet you he is a Frenghi or a Russian spy, and with his pencil he makes a note of all the mountains and valleys, all the streams and springs, so that the Russians can later on come into the land without a guide to rob you of your flocks and children. In Khiva, thanks to the precautions of the Khan, the rack will do its part, and the red-hot iron will soon show what sort of metal he is made of".

Fortunately Bilal and some of the other Hadjis argued with Amandurdi successfully on Vambery's behalf. "This wretched sot has already slandered our Hadji Reshid many times. We have assured him that we received him from the hands of the ambassador of our great Sultan, and that he had with him a pass sealed with the Caliph's seal itself". And Bilal whispered to Amandurdi: "This Afghan still refuses to believe and persists in his defamation, but he shall repent it on our arrival in Khiva, where there are Kadis and Ulemas. We shall teach him there what the consequence is of representing a pious Musselman as an unbeliever". Vambery learnt that his enemy had fled from his native city of Kandahar after the occupation by the British, and from the very first meeting had recognised the features of 'Hadji Reshid' as European. Vambery's resolute stand against him naturally made him furious, but at the same time his impiety and opium-eating habits turned all the Hadjis against him, and made them admire Vambery all the more.

Having officially taken command of all the parties, Amandurdi now counted the members, finding the total to be forty travellers and eighty camels. Before starting off, the pilgrims bade a formal farewell to Kulkhan. A prayer was said and both parties stroked their beards. Then Kulkhan and his followers returned to their homes, while the caravan set out on their journey to the north. The course was directed in the day by the sun, and at night by the pole star.

The area they were now traversing was known as *Kizil Takir* (Red Earth), the western edge of the vast wilderness known as *Kara Kum*, or Black Sands.* The pilgrims were often forced to dismount, in order to spare the weary camels, and to trudge beside them for hour after hour, in the soft red sand. This was a particularly severe ordeal for Vambery, with his lame foot.

The party marched without interruption throughout the night, stopping only at the first signs of dawn. "The regulated tread of the distant camels echoed as if someone was beating time in the night", wrote Vambery: he had an ear for rhythm which was nearly to prove his undoing.

In the background, the malicious Afghan Emir Mohammed was still proving indefatigable in his efforts to penetrate Vambery's disguise. He was certain he was European — probably English — and his hatred of all Europeans spurred him on, as before, to turn Amandurdi against the 'strange Hadji Reshid'.

At the next camp, Vambery — while pretending to be buried in thought over his Koran — noticed with some foreboding that Amandurdi was talking in heated tones with Ilias Beg and Hadji Salih, all the time glancing in his direction. A few moments later, Vambery walked over to the group and, drawn to one side by Salih, was told that Amandurdi was having second thoughts and objecting to Vambery remaining with the caravan. The memory of the Khan's wrath at the other 'Frenghi envoy' who made notes was still very fresh in Amandurdi's mind.

Vambery listened in silence to all this. His fate was in the balance — would he be abandoned in the middle of the desert? He decided that attack was the best form of defence. When Salih had finished talking, Vambery answered excitedly in the loudest tones he could muster, so Amandurdi could not fail to hear: "Hadji, you saw me in Teheran and know who I am. Tell Amandurdi that it ill becomes a good honest man like him to listen to the words of that Afghan — that drunken sot who does not even say his prayers! It is not permitted to trifle with religion, and if he calls me a Frenghi infidel once more I will show him in Khiva

---

* The *Kara Kum* desert is now part of Soviet Russia, extensively irrigated by a large reservoir built in the 1950s, and by the navigable Turkmen canal. Farmers can now grow cotton, dates, sugar cane and other crops.

what manner of man I am."

These words, audible now to the whole caravan, roused Vambery's dervish companions to such a pitch, that they were scarcely restrained from assaulting the troublesome Afghan on the spot. Amandurdi was both impressed and baffled. Asked by others who came over to ask what was going on, he could only murmur "Khudaim Bilir" ("God knows!"). In Vambery's opinion, Amandurdi was really an extremely honest, good-humoured man, without malice — but like many Turkomans — he had a fondness for mysteries; and while, at the back of his mind, he may have thought Vambery was a stranger in disguise, he later consulted him on religious matters several times during the journey.

As the mystery of his origins — and his forceful rubuttals — had now become such a matter of discussion with everyone in the caravan, Vambery had now to be much more careful than before. He had to promise to make no secret notes or drawings. From now on, taking even the shortest notes of the journey could be done only with extreme difficulty and danger. Indeed, he was forced to show complete indifference about his surroundings. Vambery wrote (the following year) about his feelings: "I was very much annoyed at not daring to put any questions as to the names of the different stations; for however immense the desert, the nomads inhabiting the various cases have affixed a specific designation to every place, every hill, and every valley, so that if exactly informed I might have marked each place on the map of Central Asia". Some members of the Royal Geographical Society in London, with remarkable incomprehension, were to reproach him for this deficiency.

Whenever humanly possible, he continued to make a few important notes on some pieces of paper (hidden in his Koran?) with the stump of a pencil — "the size of his thumb-nail" — kept hidden in the wadding of his dress. For the rest he had to rely on his prodigious memory.

With Amandurdi becoming increasingly friendly, the Afghan Emir Mohammed became less of a thorn in Vambery's side. However, many years later, Vambery did confess that the idea of murder had been very tempting: "One evening, the Afghan was quietly smoking his opium pipe in the night camp. By the glimmer of the coals on his water-pipe I met his dull, intoxicated gaze, and a diabolical idea took possession of me. 'This man is planning my destruction, and he can effect it; shall I throw one of my strychnine pills into his dish of tea, which he is even now holding in his shaky hand? I could thus save myself, and accomplish my purpose'. I took the pill from the wadding of my cloak, and held it for some time between my fingers close to the edge of the dish . . ." But overcome by the beauty of the night, Vambery stayed his hand, "ashamed of meditating a deed unworthy of a civilised man, and quickly hid the fateful pill again in the lining of my dervish cloak".

The caravan continued on its laborious journey towards Khiva. There were several stops — including one to look for the grave of a brother of one of the pilgrims who had been killed by brigands, and, on finding the place, to exhume the corpse and say prayers over it.

Amandurdi, now anxious at the time he had lost, gave orders that they must march at a faster rate throughout the night, although the track was very difficult to follow in the dark. In the early hours of the morning, Vambery was awakened from deep slumber in his uncomfortable pannier by cries of "Hadji Reshid, look at your compass — we seem to have lost our way!" By the light of a piece of burning wood, Vambery studied his compass, and realised that they were going east instead of north. Amandurdi, very alarmed, ordered that they should not stir from that spot until daylight. They had left the track in the gloom — and were now on the edge of dangerous marshland.

(Apparently, Vambery was the only member of the caravan who possessed a compass. He was convinced that without him the others might never have reached their destination at all!)

Later in the morning (15 May) the caravan regained the track and reached the next station, where Vambery was astonished to see his companions collecting a great number of large, six-inch carrots. They were particularly well flavoured and sweet. Vambery wrote: "I seized the opportunity of giving myself a feast, boiling a good portion of carrots for my breakfast, and storing away a quantity in my girdle".

The track now passed through a very wild terrain intersected, in every direction, by ravines. Vambery had great sympathy for the camels, tethered by ropes from tail to nose: "To spare the poor animals we all dismounted where the route was bad; and although my sufferings were great in the deep sand, I was forced to walk on foot four hours, although slowly, still without a halt."

On one of these marches, Amandurdi's nephew Khali Mollah

asked him several questions concerning Islam. He had no doubts that Vambery was a true dervish. When Khali Mollah requested him to search in his Koran for a *Fal* or prognostic regarding his family, Vambery as usual rose to the occasion. In his own words "I made the usual hocus pocus, shut my eyes, and fortunately opened the book at a place where women are spoken of, in which my explanation of the Arabian text — for here is the whole art — enchanted the young Turkoman. He thanked me, and I was delighted to find that I had won his friendship".

There were three different 'roads' by which travellers could cross the desert, but the caravan-leader Amandurdi had kept his plans secret, against the risk of marauding gangs of bandits. As their water was running short, the party took the middle road on which was situated a good well.

In the morning of 16 May, the caravan saw — to the north-east — the Korentaghi mountain range. Reaching it in the afternoon, they arrived at a village occupied by some friendly Yomut-Turkomans: here the pilgrims stayed the night and the following day. In the vicinity lay the ruins of the Meshedi Misriyan — Vambery's superstitious companions believed this spot to be "an abode of Djinns".

On 18 May, it was estimated that the journey to the twin mountain ranges the Great and Little Balkan* would take two days, and a further twelve days to Khiva. The travellers did not expect to meet a single human being on route, and the only wells would consist of bitter salt water. Their water-skins now contained a very small supply of miry water, which was becoming even more limited through being shaken up on the camels' backs, transformed — as Vambery described — into "a liquid mass of mud, loathsome both to the smell and taste".

Their routine was now regular, each day making three halts: the first (before sunrise) to bake one day's ration of bread; the second (at noon) to seek respite from the heat; and the third (before sunset) to eat a supper consisting of a little bread and a few drops of water carefully doled out. Vambery described the wilderness all around him: "The blazing sun marked the whole surface with a thousand burning cracks. It is frightfully wearisome for the traveller to see before him everlastingly the boundless plain from which every vestige of life is banished, so much so that even the reaching of a new station is quite a relief, as it affords some rest from the rocking motion of the camel".

On 19 May the Little Balkan range came into view on the northern horizon. The slopes were bathed in white mist and the peaks resembled a dark blue cloud suspended between earth and sky. That night, a near-disaster struck the caravan. The usually wakeful and alert Amandurdi nodded off to sleep early in the evening, leaving the camel-leader in charge of the party. In no time at all, this inexperienced substitute brought them into a salt morass. The camels came to a standstill, refusing to move an inch. Their riders leapt down to find the ground shifting under them, as if they were standing on the deck of a boat in a rocky sea. Amandurdi awoke just in time to prevent a general panic. He ordered all to stay exactly where they stood — until sunrise when they would be able to extricate themselves. They remained motionless for three miserable hours, the pungent soda smell from the morass making them feel very dizzy.

Back on the route once more, the caravan travelled on for two days along the western flank of the Little Balkan range. The shady valleys provided a welcome — though temporary — change to the deserts and plains. On their left loomed the southernmost spur of the Great Balkan. On 21 May they passed their spur and, leaving the ranges behind them, entered the true desert.

As they set out, Amandurdi distributed some swords, a lance and two guns among the Hadjis, saying they should not make any loud noises or light fires at night, but should pray to God to watch over them. In previous years Karaktchi bandits had attacked other caravans travelling in this region. Vambery received one of the guns, together with a good supply of powder and shots.

Later Vambery was to sum up his feelings at this point: "The more the Balkan disappeared in the blue clouds in our rear, the greater and more awful became the majesty of the boundless desert. I often tried to brighten the dark hues of the wilderness by picturing, in its immediate vicinity, cities and stirring life, but in vain; the interminable hills of sand, the dreadful stillness of death, the yellowish-red hue of the sun at rising and setting, yes, everything tells us that we are here in a great desert — one of the greatest on the surface of our globe!"

At mid-day on 22 May they encamped near Yeti Siri, which many years before had seven good wells. By this time, four had completely dried up — the other three contained some very fou-smelling salty water. Vambery could not bring himself to exchange the muddy water in his skin (which was still just drinkable) for this bitter nauseous liquid. He was astonished to see some of his companions drink some of this water avidly as if they thought their lives depended on it. Not long afterwards, they were afflicted with the most violent diarrhoea.

A search was made by the Hadjis during the rest of the day for fresh water, but not a drop could be found anywhere. This meant they could scarcely swallow their appallingly dry bread, with no liquid to wash it down. Rancid mutton-fat was more than their stomachs could bear. In the late afternoon, Vambery's sensations "were those of extreme debility; the heat of the day was indescribable. My strength was gone, and I was lying there extended, when I perceived that all were pressing round the caravan-leader". Amandurdi had apparently for years been in the habit of storing away in secret places large quantities of water — to distribute it in times of great need. He now dealt out two glasses of the precious liquid to each member of the caravan — evidently taking great heart in the old Turkoman proverb: "One drop of water given to the thirsting in the desert will wash away the sins of a hundred years".

Much refreshed, the party were able to proceed on the following day across the scorching sands to another dry well at Koymat Ata, and on to Kahriman Ata, a famous place of pilgrimage. Here Vambery was compelled to dismount from his camel and join the procession of pilgrims to a tomb situated on an elevation about a mile distant, and there to shout *telkin* and passages from the Koran like one possessed. "Oh, cruel saint!" thought Vambery, as he sank down to rest by the tomb, breathless and exhausted, "could you not have got yourself interred elsewhere, and spare me the terrible martyrdom of this pilgrimage?" This tomb was surrounded by many smaller graves — those of travellers who had met their end here, either from the heat, or at the hands of bandits.

The sand became so hot in this region, that even the most hardened Asiatic — who had never worn a shoe in his life — was compelled to fasten around his feet pieces of leather, sandal fashion. (Ten years later, a Russian army crossing this same part of the desert recorded a temperature of 152 degrees Fahrenheit.)

A heavy rain storm during the night marked the end of their sufferings for the time being. The next day took them to the edge of the desert, where the keen eyes of Amandurdi spied in the distance a small lake of rain-water. "Su! Su!" they all shouted for

126

joy, "Water! Water!" and were soon slaking their thirst to their hearts' content. From this oasis, Deli Ata, all the way to Khiva (approximately five days' march away), their water skins were constantly full, and that night they pitched their camp in a green meadow amid many little lakes. "The sons of the desert", wrote Vambery, "ascribed the unexpected abundance of water solely to our pious Hadji character".

Invigorated after a rest of several hours, they crossed a broad trench (which the Turkomans declared to be the old channel of the Oxus) and ascended to the Kaflankir (or Tiger Field) plateau, which marked the boundary of the Khanate of Khiva. Here in this very fertile region, so near the barren waste of the desert, were hundreds of gazelles and wild asses, grazing in large herds.

From this place, a day's march brought them, on the morning of 28 May to Shor Gol, a rectangular salt lake. Here the Hadjis halted to wash and perform their ceremonial purification. All of them washed and put on clean shirts except Vambery: he had become firmly convinced that the greater his apparent poverty the less risk he would run. He later claimed his face at this time was covered by a layer of thick dust nearly one inch thick! All the members of the party were disfigured by the *teyemmum* (or washing with the sand), the substitute for the ablutions with water, ordered by the Prophet to travellers in the desert.

A further two days across the plateau brought the caravan to a village, the largest they had seen since leaving the shores of the Caspian Sea. Ilias had some friends here, and they provided the hadjis — in return for their blessings — with ample stores of warm bread, kimis (a sharp acid drink made with mare's milk), and meat (camel, horse, and sheep). After crossing a further fifteen-mile expanse of sand, which marked the termination of the desert between Gomushtepe and Khiva, the caravan passed through much more luxuriant vegetation as they stopped at Akyap (1 June), where the numerous relatives of Ilias came out and wined and dined them most cordially.

After a brief rest much disturbed by a plague of gnats, they resumed their march through green fields and fruitful gardens and orchards until at last through the trees they caught sight of the minarets and watchtowers of the capital. On approaching the city walls, Vambery could not shake off a certain fear of being found out or at least suspected by the Khan of Khiva, whose cruelty was condemned by all other states and tribes, even the Tartars.

It was many years since so large a troop of Hadjis had arrived in Khiva. At the city gates, they were met by several excited citizens who presented them with gifts of bread and dried fruits, and shouted friendly greetings: "*Aman eszen geldin ghiz!*" (Welcome!) and "*Ha Shah bazim! Ha Arszlanim!*" (Ah, my falcon! Ah, my lion!) The narrow, dirty and crooked streets of the city itself contrasted strongly with the beauty of the crystal brooks and well-kept gardens outside. The pilgrims rode into the bazaar, where Bilal intoned a *telkin* (hymn). Vambery joined in as usual, his voice the loudest of all, and the pious Khivans fervently kissed his hands and feet.

However, in spite of their devout and religious standing, the party of Hadjis still had to present themselves for a severe examination at the Customs House, situated in the caravanserai. Here they were met by the Royal Chamberlain — a confidant of the Khan — whose job it was to vet travellers. He had only addressed a few simple questions to the caravan-leader Amandurdi, when a drunken figure pressed forward to put his oar in. It was the troublesome Afghan again! He cried out: "We have brought to Khiva three interesting quadrupeds" — pointing to the buffaloes (animals not seen before in the city) — "*and* a no less interesting biped!" All eyes turned to Vambery — a sure sign that even though he had take superhuman efforts to shed all European traits, he still appeared strangely different from all the others.

Among the suspicious whisperings, he heard the words "Frenghi" (European), "Urus" (Russian), and "Djansiz" (Spy). Trying to prevent the blood rising in his cheeks, Vambery turned away, when the Chamberlain angrily ordered him to stand still. An unpleasant situation was avoided by the entrance of Hadji Salih who — not knowing of the preceding scene — immediately presented Vambery, extolling his virtues, to the Chamberlain. The latter seemed agreeably surprised and satisfied by Salih's words; he changed his attitude and invited Vambery to sit down beside him. However Vambery preferred to decline, and, assuming an air of injured dignity, left the room.

Vambery soon decided to call on Shukrullah Bey, an elderly and revered Khivan, who had recently served as the Ambassador of Khiva in Constantinople for ten years. Vambery had only a hazy recollection of the Ambassador, but if he could persuade him that they had been acquainted, he felt he would be safer in this city of evil reputation.

Khiva type.

Shukrullah Bey was now in retirement and lived in a cell at the Medresseh of Mehemmed Emin, the finest building in the whole of Khiva. When one of his attendants announced the arrival of "a Turkish Effendi from Stamboul, come to pay his respects to you", he came out to greet Vambery, amazed to see this strange, tattered, disfigured mendicant dressed in filthy rags. Exchanging words in the Stamboul dialect, Vambery was plied with questions by the delighted and increasingly amiable Shukrullah Bey, concerning his numerous friends in the Turkish capital. The old man could not contain himself for joy on hearing all the news (some true, some fabricated!) of mutual acquaintences and recent events in Constantinople. Later, he inevitably asked his visitor: "For the love of God, what had induced you, Effendi, to come from Stamboul, that earthly paradise, to these fearful countries?" With a heavy sigh, Vambery explained that, belonging to some dervish order, he had been sent by his *Pir* (chief of the order) upon a journey, which is a duty that every disciple must fulfil at the hazard of his life. He added — on further enquiries — that the name of the order was *Nakishbend*, and that Bokhara was the object of his pilgrimage. Shukrullah Bey seemed very pleased with all that the 'Effendi' had said, and Vambery withdrew — well satisfied with the outcome of the meeting.

Vambery rejoined his companions at the *Toshebaz*, a lodging-house for travelling dervishes. He was gratified to hear that after his departure from the Customs House earlier, all present had angrily turned on his unpleasant Afghan detractor and driven him out with blows and curses. Now by the evening, Vambery had completely restored his position after a shaky uncertain start. "Very good", he thought shrewdly, "the popular suspicion removed, it will be easy enough to deal with the Khan, for he will be immediately informed of my arrival by Shukrullah Bey; and as the rulers of Khiva have always shown the greatest respect for the Sultan, the present sovereign will certainly venture a step towards an Effendi. It is not impossible that the first stranger from Constantinople who had come to Khiva may even be treated with particular distinction".

His expectations proved correct. Next morning he was visited by an official from the Court who brought a small gift from the Khan and instructions to present himself later in the day at the Palace, "as His Majesty attached great importance to receiving the blessing from a dervish born in the Holy Land".

In the afternoon Vambery called on Shukrullah Bey, who wished to be present at the audience, and was conducted by him, through the narrow winding streets of the city to the Palace. On the way they discussed the portocol of the court, and how Vambery should comport himself. There was one tricky point — Shukrullah Bey was not on good terms with the *Mehter* (Minister of the Interior), one of the Khan's right-hand men; and he hoped this would not jeopardise Vambery's standing at the audience.

The great hall of state in the Palace was flanked on either side by a tower ornamented with blue and green tiles. The floor was raised six feet, and the roof was supported by two curved, slender wooden pillars. The other rooms were dark and badly ventilated. To the rear of the great hall was the Khan's treasury, a low vaulted chamber, the walls and ceilings of which were decorated with frescoes of vines and flowers, coloured on the most fantastic principles.

As the two visitors approached, the crowd made way respectfully, whispering to one another: "This is the dervish from Constantinople, who will bestow benediction on our Khan. May the Lord hearken to his words!" Vambery was ushered into the presence of the *Mehter*, a rough-featured man with an off-putting manner. On catching sight of him, the *Mehter* turned with a laugh to those around him. Undeterred by this, Vambery went straight up to him, saluted with due solemnity, and at once assumed the place of honour due to him as a dervish. After intoning the customary prayers, at which all present stroked their beards and added 'Amen', Vambery produced his passport, bearing the Sultan's seal. The *Mehter* took it reverently, kissed it and rubbed it against his forehead.

A few moments later, Vambery was ushered into the throne-room. A curtain was drawn aside to reveal the notorious Khan of Khiva, Seid Mehemmed, seated on a raised platform and holding a short golden sceptre. His cruel eyes, deep-set in his degenerate face, bored hard into Vambery's consciousness — and would give him nightmares for many years to come. "No European can realise", he wrote later, "what it is to stand — a disguised *Frenghi* (this word of terror to the Oriental) — face to face with such a tyrant as the Khan of Khiva and to have to bestow upon him the customary benediction". He trembled to think that this man "with the sallow face and sinister look, as he sat there surrounded by his satellites, might discover the trick".

Vambery first raised his hands, being imitated by the Khan and the others present, then recited a short *sura* from the Koran, followed by two *Allahamu Sellahs* (God be praised) and a prayer. Then the *mussafeha* (the salutation prescribed by the Koran — the two persons in giving a greeting extend an outstretched hand to each other) ended the customary ceremonial.

The Khan then began to question his visitor closely on the object of his journey, and the impression the Turkomans, the desert, the Khiva, had made upon him. Vambery replied that he suffered much, but had been richly rewarded for all he had undergone by being allowed to look upon *Hazrets Djemal* (the beauty of His Majesty)! He added "I thank Allah that I have been allowed to partake of this high happiness, and discern in this special favour of Kismet (fate) a good omen for the safe progress of my journey". Vambery tried to speak in Uzbek (the Turkish of Stamboul was unknown to the Khan) but unavoidably had to have some of his speech translated.

Next the Khan asked him how long he wished to stay in Khiva and whether he was provided with money for his journey. To this Vambery replied that he wanted especially to visit the tombs of the Saints who were buried in the soil of the Khanate, and after this he would prepare for the journey further on. As to his finances, he said: "We dervishes do not trouble ourselves with such trifles. The holy *Nefes* (breath) which was given to me by my *Pir* (chief of the dervish order) will sustain life in me for four or five days without taking any food". His only wish, he added flatteringly, was that God would allow His Majesty to live one hundred and twenty years!

These words seemed to delight the Khan, as he gave orders that he should be given twenty gold ducats and a strong ass. Vambery declined the ducats on the grounds that it was a sin for a dervish to keep money. He gladly accepted the second offer, mentioning the holy commandment which prescribed the use of a *white* donkey on pilgrimages. After the Khan had insisted that he must be his guest during his stay in the capital, Vambery again thanked him profusely, bestowed his blessings on him and took his leave.

As Vambery hurried back to his lodging house, the crowds in the forecourt and bazaar greeted him respectfully with cries of *Sal-aam-aleikum* (peace be with you!) He had carried the interview off so well, in spite of the language handicap, "that all looked at me with astonishment, for submissiveness is befitting to the pious and saints". Back in the comparative safety of his room, Vambery was honoured by the picture of the Khan with his deep-set eyes, with his chin thinly covered with hair, his white lips, and trembling effeminate voice. "How fortunate", he thought, "that the Khan, who in appearance was so fearfully dissolute, and who presents in every feature of his countenance the real picture of an enervated, imbecile, and savage tyrant, had behaved to me in a manner so unobjectionable".

Perhaps the milk from the buffaloes, which had arrived with the Hadjis the previous day, had something to do with the Khan's good mood?

From now on, "the dervish from Turkey" (as they called him) was much in demand. As he had the Khan's favour, everybody wanted to have him as their guest. Every day he was forced to accept at least seven or eight invitations and to eat something in every house. Again and again, before sunrise, he would be woken up and taken to a house nearby, where he would invariably find himself seated in front of a colossal dish of rice, swimming in a gravy of fat from the tails of fat-tailed sheep. On such occasions he began to long for the dry, unleavened bread of the desert! However, his Hadji companions showed no such qualms. As Vambery wrote: "On one occasion I reckoned that each of them had devoured one pound of fat from the tail of the sheep, two pounds of rice, without taking any account of the bread, carrots, turnips, and radishes; and all this washed down, without any exaggeration, by from fifteen to twenty large soup plates full of green tea. In such heroic feats I was naturally a coward; and it was the astonishment of everyone that I, so well versed in books, should have acquired only a half acquaintance with the requisites of polite breeding!"

No less demanding was the constant cross-examination to which Vambery was subjected on all kinds of religious questions. For the Ulemas (theologians) of Khiva, Stamboul set the standard in all such matters and the Sultan of Turkey, as Mohammed's successor, was the ultimate authority on the finer points of Islamic theology. Their questions came thick and fast: how should a devout man walk, sit, lie and sleep? In what way should he wash his hands, his feet, his face and his head? Was it true that a specially consecrated dinner arrived from Mecca for the Sultan miraculously every day? Was it true that the Sultan wore a turban at least fifty ells in length, and that his beard reached half way to his waist? Vambery answered all these questions as well as he could with tact and a sense of self-preservation. He would have placed his life in jeopardy if he had told them some of the facts he knew: that the Sultan had his clothes made for him in Paris by Dusetoye, and that the table of Mohammed's successor was lavishly provided with Chateau Lafite, Margaux, and other fine vintages.

The *Toshebaz,* where the Hadjis were staying, comprised a mosque as well as a lodging-house, and was therefore looked upon as a public place. None of the Hadjis had a moment's rest — from morning to night their monastic cells were besieged by men and women clamouring for blessings and for the Holy Breath, each one giving full descriptions of their maladies and pains. Vambery and the others had to comply with all these requests, breathing or blowing on the sore place three times. On each occasion the patient heaved a deep sigh, and many of them insisted that they immediately felt relieved of pain. All the Hadjis had reason to be pleased with the brilliant success of their dealing in the Holy Breath, and Vambery alone earned fifteen gold ducats for the art.

Among the acquaintances that Vambery made here, the most unusual turned out to be a certain Hadji Ismael. He claimed to have spent no less than twenty-five years in Stamboul, where at one time or another he had plied the trades of tutor, bath-keeper, leather cutter, calligrapher, chemist and conjuror. On the strength of this, he had — since his return — acquired a considerable reputation in Khiva and had been appointed Court Physician to the Khan. He went on to say that he remembered meeting Vambery in Stamboul — and his father as well, a "Mollah in Topkhane" (a suburb of Constantinople) if he recalled correctly. At this, Vambery rose nobly to the occasion and, instead of refuting his statements, embraced him warmly and assured him that he was remembered with much affection in Stamboul and that his return there was anxiously awaited.

But the danger of discovery was always present. It was not long before Vambery learned that the Mehter, the Khan's minister, was plotting against him for no other reason except his hatred for Shukrullah Bey, his patron. He now sought to plant in the Khan's mind the idea that 'Hadji Reshid' was only a dervish in disguise, in reality sent upon some secret mission by the Sultan to Bokhara. Forewarned of these intrigues, Vambery was not surprised to be summoned once again to the Palace and questioned by the Khan on various political subjects. All the time the Mehter stood by, staring hard into Vambery's face and waiting hopefully for him to put a foot wrong. Such an interview was bound to be a great ordeal to anyone who knew how many of the Khan's audiences ended with the fatal words, "*Alib barin*" (Take him away), followed by his visitor's immediate execution. But once again Vambery behaved with caution and assurance, and passed the examination with flying colours.

The Khan told Vambery to apply to the Keeper of the Treasury for a regular daily allowance for his food and lodging. This time Vambery accepted, despite his protestations to the contrary only a few days earlier.

It was while he was on his way to the Treasury that he saw a sight which filled him with horror and greatly increased his own feelings of insecurity. In one of the Palace courtyards were assembled about three hundred prisoners of war who had been captured during some recent fighting. They were raggedly dressed, and already looked half dead from hunger and fear. Those under forty years of age had been separated from those over forty. The former group were being chained together by the neck in batches of ten or fifteen and led away to be sold as slaves. Those over forty — the *Aksakals* or Grey-Beards — awaited their inevitable harsh punishment. As Vambery watched, some were beheaded and a few others were hanged. Then, at a sign from the executioner, eight of the oldest men were forced to lie down on the ground. They were then securely bound hand and foot. The executioner then gouged out the eyes of each in turn, kneeling on his victim's chest as he did so. When he had finished, he wiped his bloodstained knife on the grey beard of the eighth victim. Vambery wrote later "It was a dreadful sight to see these miserable people, after the fetters had been removed from their hands and feet, in their groping attempts to rise from the ground. Some knocked their heads against one another, others sank to the ground again from sheer exhaustion, moaning and beating the ground with their feet in their agony. I shall think with horror of this scene as long as I live".

At the Treasury, Vambery was paid the arranged sum of money due to him. He found the Treasurer sorting out a number of *khalats*, or robes of honour, which were to be awarded to some of Khiva's distinguished warriors. These robes were variously described as four-head, twelve-head, twenty-head and even forty-head. On asking why, Vambery was told that the reason was very simple: a man who had cut off the heads of four enemies received a four-head robe, and so on — the more heads, the finer the robe. The forty-head robe was made of the finest silk and heavily embroidered with gold. The Treasurer told Vambery that the robes would be distributed next day. It might interest him, as a foreigner, to witness the ceremony.

Next morning he reached the main square in time to see the arrival of about a hundred horsemen. Each of them had a prisoner or two with him (women and little children, as well as men) tied to his horse's tail or to the pommel of the saddle, and each carried a sack. First they handed over their prisoners as presents to the Khan. Then, opening their sacks, they shook out the contents on to the ground, as if dealing with potatoes. They were human heads — the heads of slaughtered enemies — some bearded, some beardless. These an accountant kicked on to a pile, at the same time issuing a receipt for the number of heads delivered. These receipts would shortly be exchanged for the *khalats* or robes of appropriate quality.

These scenes of horror and violence, on two successive days, combined with the uncomfortable overcrowding in hot, sultry Khiva, decided Vambery to make a tour in the countryside to the north of the capital. His companion on this trip was a young Mollah, who had joined the caravan in order to reach Samarkand. This tour, which covered about three hundred miles there and back, occupied most of the second half of June.

A journey of eighteen miles took the two travellers through some of the most beautiful country in the whole of the Khanate till they arrived at the bank of the most important river in this part of Asia, the Amu Dar'ya (Oxus). They were able to board a half-laden boat for a moderate fare. A large net served as a canopy to protect them in the daytime from the fierce sun, and at night from the dangerous mosquitoes. There were two other passengers, one of whom was friendly and extremely loquacious — he gave Vambery much information about the area. When unobserved, Vambery was able to make a few more of his surreptitious notes. This could be done when all the crew and passengers (except the steersman) fell fast asleep in the heat of the day.

Kungrat (now Kungrad), the most northerly town in the Khanate of Khiva, and about fifty miles south of the Aral Sea, was reached on the evening of the fifth day. This was the young Mollah's native town; his parents had died the year before, and he now greeted his only remaining relative, together with a few other friends. Vambery was interested to meet two Russians, who had defected from their country, travelled south and taken up residence here. They had both been converted to Islam. Some of the notes Vambery was able to make here on the geography of the area and the Oxus would be incorporated into some of his anti-Russian books and articles in later years.

Vambery and the Mollah decided to return by land to Khiva, as this took nine days — as opposed to the eighteen days which the *up*ward navigation of the Oxus took. They joined a small party of travellers bound for Khiva, and took a road called 'the summer route' on the western side of the river. The scenery was varied, alternating between sandy tracts and fertile regions. One whole day was spent travelling through a very thick forest, supposedly infested with many wild animals including lions, panthers and wild boards. Vambery only saw a few boars, and later on "a fabulous number of guinea-fowl and pheasants, of which we made rich spoil for our evening halt". The Uzbeks proved to be much better cooks than the Persians, and for the whole week Vambery and the others enjoyed some really delicious meals.

When Vambery returned to the city of Khiva, it was the end of June; the heat was becoming even greater and his companions were very anvious to start for Bokhara. From this project his friend Shukrullah Bey did everything he could to dissuade him, recounting stories of the horrible fate which had overtaken so many other travellers to Bokhara. "When I bade him farewell on my last day in Khiva, I saw a tear in his eye", wrote Vambery. Indeed he showed such solicitude for his welfare that Vambery could not help wondering if the old man had not perhaps penetrated his dervish disguise and realised the true nature of the dangers that beset him.

A neighbour of Shukrullah Bey, Mollah Ishak — both occupied cells in the Medresseh of Mehemmed Emin — much absorbed in prayer and the doctrines of Islam, attached himself to Vambery at this point. He was young with a strong desire to travel. He was now in search of a companion on his journey to Mecca. Having listened most attentively to Vambery in the *Toshebaz*, he recognised quickly that here was the most suitable fellow-traveller. In this way Vambery took on a very faithful disciple, and one that was to stay at his side much longer than he ever could have guessed here in Khiva!

Before setting out, Vambery bestowed a final blessing on the Khan, who urged him to come back to Khiva on his return journey. To this he replied only with the single, well-chosen word *Kismet*, enigmatic to the end, as befitted a true dervish.

6

BOKHARA AND SAMARKAND

On 30 June 1863 the pilgrims left the city of Khiva in good spirits.
In spite of the constant danger of discovery, Vambery had
enjoyed his stay there. The Khivans had treated him and his
friends with much kindness and generosity. His 'healing' activities had brought in no less than fifteen gold ducats. Their bags
were full to bursting, and even the poorest Hadji now had a donkey to ride. Spotlessly white turbans took the place of their moth-
eaten fur caps, and new shirts replaced their former tatters.

For some time they were accompanied by a crowd of over-zeal-
ous citizens, seeking to embrace them and crying: "Who knows
when Khiva will again have the great good fortune to harbour in
her walls so many pious men!" After some time, Vambery's white
donkey got fed up with this, and set off at full gallop, leaving the
others a long way behind. When the donkey eventually slowed
down, Vambery was able to pick beautiful ripe mulberries from
the trees as he rode along, as this stretch east of the city was still
fertile and well-cultivated.

At Khanka (the first market-town on the route), Vambery fell
into conversation with two half-naked dervishes who gave him
some tea while they indulged themselves with opium. Within half
an hour, they were both off on their 'trips', and Vambery noted
"while the face of one wore an expression of joy and delight, the
agonies of terrible fear were depicted in the countenance of the
other".

That evening the pilgrims reached the banks of the great river
Oxus, its muddy yellow waters being here so wide that the far
bank was hardly discernible. Next morning they found a ferry
and persuaded a somewhat reluctant ferryman to take them all
across for nothing. The Hadjis shared a joint passport, but Vambery had been given a separate one (in Khiva) which read: "Be it
known to the guards on the frontier and the collectors of customs

and tolls that Hadji Mollah Abdur Reshid Effendi has been granted a license. Let nobody molest or interfere with him".

The crossing took all day — much longer than expected — under a scorching sun. In the labyrinth of side-channels on the far side, the ferry ran aground on one sandbank after another. Each time this happened, all the pilgrims and donkeys had to be unloaded so that the boat could be pushed off and refloated in deeper water again. To make things worse, some of the donkeys — despite much shouting and prodding — refused to budge and had to be carried bodily through the water on the backs of the pilgrims.

By dusk they were all exhausted. After waiting for the camels to be transported across the river, the pilgrims now set out in the south-easterly direction along the right bank of the Oxus with the desert on their left. The caravan-leader thought it best to follow the river southwards as far as possible and then strike due east across the terrible Khalata desert to Bokhara at the narrowest point. If they did this, it was hoped they would only need to spend the last two days of the journey in waterless desert; otherwise there should be adequate supplies of water along the way.

A temporary stop to replenish the provisions was made at Shurakhan, a market town with three hundred shops. Owing to the intense heat of the day, the caravan was now scheduled to travel at night only. Vambery became lyrical: "As we marched on by the light of the moon," he wrote, "the spectacle was indeed entrancing — the moving caravan and its fantastic shadows, upon which the pale moon shed its mysterious silvery light, flanked on the right by the Oxus rolling its darkling waters with a hoarse murmur, on the left the awful desert of Tartary stretching its endless vista".

Next day (4 July) the pilgrims had gone nearly a hundred miles down the willow-covered shores of the Oxus, when, some way past the ruined fort of Tunuklu, they were hailed from a distance by two men. On approaching, they proved to be 'entirely nude' and in a pitiful state as with cries of "Bread! Bread!" they sank exhausted to the ground at the pilgrims' feet. After devouring some bread, water and mutton fat, they recovered enough to tell their story. Both of them were boatmen from further down the river; they had been set upon by a band of Tekke-Turkoman marauders — 150 strong — stripped of their clothes, boat, food and everything else they possessed and left to starve. "For the love of

God", they cried, "run and hide. If you go on, you are sure to come across them in a couple of hours, and although you are pious pilgrims, they will strip you of everything and leave you naked in the wilderness, for the unbelievers — the Tekke — are capable of anything".

Immediately the caravan-leader, who knew the Tekke Turkomans from previous experience, in fear and trembling gave the order to turn about. With their heavily laden donkeys and camels, they could not hope to outdistance the robbers on their swift horses, but — if they could get back to their last halting-place at Tunuklu and there replenish their supplies of water — it was just possible they might have time to 'throw themselves' into the desert before the pursuit caught up with them. Once in the desert, their prospects of escape would improve steadily.

A panic-stricken rush followed over the ground they had just covered, the pilgrims goading their tired overloaded beasts to breaking point. On reaching Tunuklu, three anxious hours were necessary to make preparations for the desert and fill their all-important water-skins. Nearly half the Hadjis were so petrified at the prospect before them, that — on seeing a skiff approaching — they made a confused rush forward in an effort to board it and return to Khiva! These were anxious moments for Vambery who was determined to press on at all costs. Eventually, after much wavering, most of the pilgrims followed the lead of the caravan-leader and by sunset they had already advanced some way into the desert.

All through the night the caravan proceeded in total silence lest any sound should carry and betray them to the Turkoman bandits. The sand became much softer as they struggled along, with the camels sinking in up to their knees. Vambery described the bleak landscape at sunrise ". . . a sea of sand, extending as far as the eye can reach, on one side formed into high hills, like waves lashed into that position by the furious storm; on the other side again, like the smooth waters of a still lake, merely rippled by the west wind. Not a bird visible in the air, not a worm or beetle upon the earth; traces of nothing but departed life, in the bleaching bones of man or beast that has perished, collected by every passer-by in a heap, to serve to guide the march of future travellers!" He was told by his companions that the name of this area was *Adamkirilgan* — 'the place where men perish'!

From this point the caravan-leader calculated it should take them about five days to reach Bokhara, but they would have to march during part of the day as well as the night. Their supplies of water, so plentiful only the day before, were evaporating quickly under the blazing sun, and could last them for only a fraction of the journeyh The camels were now in a distressed condition, and two died on the second day in the desert. The pilgrims' only crumb of comfort came from the thought that they were now safe from the clutches of the Turkoman bandits (who never ventured into this infernal wilderness).

A salt well was situated at the next halt, but it was hopelessly choked with sand and quite unusable. Two of the poorer pilgrims had by now finished all their water and were so weak from thirst that they could neither stand, nor sit on their feeble donkeys. They were strapped down by their companions on to the backs of two camels, and there they remained, feebly begging "Water! Water!" as long as they could articulate. One of them died two days later.

During the brief rest-periods, each pilgrim slept with his own water-vessel tightly clasped to his chest. Vambery wrote: "It is a horrible sight to see the father hide his store of water from the son, and brother from brother; each drop is life, and when men feel the torture of thirst, there is not, as in the other dangers of life, any spirit of self-sacrifice, or any feeling of generosity".

The caravan-leader had hoped to reach the firm plain at the end of the third day, but the beasts were totally exhausted and another whole day was spent in the unbearable heat of the desert. Vambery still had the equivalent of six glasses of water left in his vessel. "These I drank drop by drop, suffering, of course, terribly from thirst. Greatly alarmed to find that my tongue began to turn a little black in the centre, I immediately drank off at a draught half of my remaining store, thinking so to save my life; but, oh! the burning sensation, followed by headache, became more violent towards the morning of the fifth day, and when we could just distinguish, about mid-day, the Khalata mountains from the clouds that surrounded them, I felt my strength gradually abandon me". With these mountains in view, they knew that Bokhara lay only forty miles away to the south-east.

As they approached the mountains, the caravan-leader noticed the approach of 'the tebbad', a swiftly moving cloud of dust. The camels fell on their knees and tried to bury their heads in the sand. There was just time for the pilgrims to dismount and lie down

142

behind their beasts before the blinding, burning sandstorm swept over them.

After they had scrambled up and resumed their course, it was not long before they came to a few wells. The water in all of them was unfit for human consumption, but the animals drank their fill and were refortified enough to continue the trek at a faster pace.

Vambery could no longer mount or dismount without help. Towards midnight on the fifth day, he felt his life ebbing away from him. "I felt a dreadful internal fire and my head stupified by the violence of the headache. My pen has no power to describe the tortures of thirst unallayed which I underwent at that time", he described later. "I was completely broken down; I felt my power of resistance had deserted me and had no hopes of ever surviving the night". Losing consciousness, he awoke several hours later to find himself in a mud hut surrounded by some men with long beards. "*Shuma ki Hadji nistid*" they said in Persian, "You are certainly no Hadji". Seeing he was too weak to answer, they poured down his throat some invigorating tepid milk, followed by a draught of *airan* (sour milk mixed with salt and water).

With miraculous good luck the pilgrims — practically at their last gasp — had met a small party of Persian slaves, sent by their masters in Bohkara to tend sheep in this spot on the edge of the desert. Even though they were naturally very poor and ill-provided, these slaves gave the caravan shelter and freely shared their own frugal supplies of food and drink.

Pressing on much refreshed, the pilgrims were delighted to find at daybreak a lake full of sweet water. This marked the frontier of Bokhara; left behind was the fear of death from thirst, wind, or robbers. The morning's ride took them through a splendid profusion of green fields, gardens and orchards.

News was sent ahead of their approach, and it was not long before three Customs officers of the Emir confronted them on the road. The caravan was escorted to the Customs House — here the pilgrims were taken upstairs and ordered to show the officers all their belongings. Everything was duly listed in great detail. Vambery was the last one to be examined. The resilient impostor had certainly regained his good spirits by this time, as he later described: "When the official looked at my face he laughed, told me to show my trunk, 'for that *we*' (meaning, probably, Europeans, as he took me for one) 'had always fine things with us'. I happened to be in excellent humour, and had on my Dervish or fool's cap. I interrupted the cunning Bokhariot, saying 'that I had, in effect, some beautiful things, which he would see himself when he came to examine my property, movable and immovable'. As he insisted upon seeing everything, I ran into the court, fetched my ass, and led it to him up the stairs and over the carpets into the room; and after having introduced it, amid the loud laughter of my companions, I lost no time in opening my knapsack, and then showed him the few rags and old books which I had collected in Khiva. The disappointed Bokhariot looked round him in astonishment, demanding if I really had nothing more. Whereupon Hadji Salih gave him explanations as to my rank, my character, as well as the object I had in view, in my journey; all of which he noted down carefully, accompanying the act with with a look at me and a shake of the head full of meaning".

The minarets of Bokhara-es-Sherif — Bokhara the Noble, as it was designated by Central Asiatics — came into view later in the afternoon (July 12). All the towers were crowned by nests of storks, sitting "like single-legged sentinels". Skirting round the city walls, the caravan entered the city by the gate called Dervaze Mezar.

Against all odds, Vambery had arrived at the place described by former travellers, including Marco Polo, as one of the greatest jewels among all the world's cities — an Asiatic Rome. In times past, it had been the holiest city in all Central Asia, with 105 medressehs (religious colleges) and 365 mosques, which enabled the faithful to perform their devotions in a different mosque each day in the year. A well-known proverb ran: "In all other parts of the world, light descends upon the earth from above; but in Bokhara it comes from below; it rises".

Hadji Salih took Vambery along to the Tekkie of Khalifa Husein, a monastery built round a spacious courtyard shaded by fine trees. The pilgrims were welcomed by the religious head of the Tekkie, an amiable man who was Court Imam to the Emir and also the grandson of the saint after whom the Tekkie was named. Salih had once been his pupil and he now introduced 'Hadji Reshid' in glowing terms. The Imam conversed with Vambery for half an hour, and seemed delighted with the piety and learning he displayed. He assigned two adjacent cells in the best part of the monastery to Salih and Vambery, who realised he had fallen "into the chief nest of Islamite fanaticism in Bokhara".

Here Vambery had to be on his guard as never before. He

learnt that the Emir's vizier, Rahmet Bi, who was in command in Bokhara during his master's temporary absence, had set spies in the Tekkie, and they were already questioning the Hadjis closely about the origins of the strange dervish from Turkey. Vambery's comrades usually replied: "Hadji Reshid is not only a good Muslim, but also a learned Mollah; to have any suspicion of him is a mortal sin."

Vambery certainly owed his life to the Hadjis' counsels and invaluable suggestions during his stay in Bokhara. He wrote: "I found it a most-perilous place, not only for all Europeans, but for every stranger, because the Government has carried the system of espionage to just as high a pitch of perfection as the population has attained pre-eminence in every kind of profligacy and wickedness".

He did not know at the time that the Emir of Bokhara owned a large gold mine, the location of which was a very jealously-guarded secret. Men who retired from working in this mine had their tongues and eyes put out so that they should be unable to reveal its whereabouts. Anyone suspected of learning its location was immediately put to death — including many local inhabitants and indeed most visitors from other countries. The location was so secret that it was not until nearly a century after Vambery's visit that the mine was rediscovered by the Soviet authorities. (Only in 1965 was the mine put back into production and it is now one of the richest in the Soviet Union.)

The existence of this secret mine may have been an important factor contributing towards the deaths in Bokhara in the early 1840s of Wyburd, Stoddart and Conolly, whose violent deaths had outraged the British public to a very great extent. The official Foreign Office statement declared that Stoddart and Conolly were put to death because they refused to embrace Islam. This did not explain why several Russian missions sent to Bokhara around the same time did not suffer the same fate. For some years before Bokhara became a vassal state of the Czar in 1868, the Emir had received subventions from St. Petersburg; therefore the political influence which the Russians exercised at the Emir's court, could have been a very potent argument for bringing about the deaths of the Englishmen.* Combined with this, had the Emir been given

* However, Colonel Butenyov (or Butenieff), the Russian envoy at Bokhara 1841-2, was appalled by the Emir's excesses and pleaded, unsuccessfully, for the lives of the Englishmen.

reason to suppose that the English envoys had discovered — through bribery or any other means — the location of the secret gold mine, he would certainly never have let them leave alive. In 1842, the British aim to persuade the Emir to place his dominions under British rather than under Russian protection certainly had little hope of success.

Lieutenant-Colonel Charles Stoddart had gone in 1838 to Bokhara, where his brash temper and obstinacy — a bad mixture for a diplomat — landed him in prison very soon after his first audience with Emir Nasrullah, the despot who ruled with a rod of iron from 1826 to 1860. Stoddart, after a long period of sustained torture, had been forced to repeat the *Kulna* or Mohammedan profession of faith, and had subsequently worshipped in public with the Emir — but, as it turned out, this did not save his life. Captain Arthur Conolly arrived in Bokhara three years later (November 1841) and it was not long before he too was imprisoned. After a long spell in prison, the two men were transferred to a well or 'Pit', twenty-one feet deep, in which the Emir kept a selection of specially bred reptiles, enormous sheep-ticks, and other vermin. Eventually, in June 1842, "after masses of flesh had been gnawed off their bones", they were taken out and beheaded in front of the citadel. The corpses of the two martyrs were placed in one grave, which had been dug before their eyes. (To this day, the two Englishmen are remembered in Bokhara. Under the Soviet Government, the Pit is displayed as a monument to the depravity of oriental potentates. At the bottom of the Pit, wax models of Stoddart and Conolly can be seen, their clothes in rags and with snakes and scorpions writhing about the floor to torment them.)

The first full version was given by the Rev. Joseph Wolff, the 'Eccentric Missionary', in his book *'The Narrative of a Mission to Bokhara in the years 1843-1845, to ascertain the fate of Colonel Stoddart and Captain Conolly'* (1846), which was such a runaway success when published that it immediately went into four editions. Wolff also tried to ascertain how another traveller had met his fate in Bokhara: Lieutenant Wyburd, of the Royal Indian Navy, "a fair young Englishman", conversant in both Arabic and Turkish, who was kidnapped on his way to Khiva. He had disappeared without trace shortly before Stoddart arrived on the scene. Wolff gleaned most of his knowledge from one of the chief judges of Bokhara, Kazi Kelaun, who apparently was risking his life talking to the Missionary. This judge related that Wyburd (like Conolly) refused to turn Mohammedan with the words: "Understand that I am an Englishman, and therefore I shall neither change my religion nor enter the service of a tyrant". When led forth to execution, he said: "Now you shall see how an Englishman and Christian can die!" He was then decapitated and the body thrown into a well.

This was the story related by Wolff to Lord Aberdeen (then Foreign Secretary) in a letter dated 18 November 1845. Naturally there was no way to know for certain whether the story was true or a complete fabrication, and the British Government still trying to discover fresh information when Vambery was in Teheran in 1862. He was asked to see what he could find out when he was in the area, but having arrived in Bokhara he found the task very difficult. As he wrote: "(the British) will readily understand that without betraying my real identity it was impossible for me to put the necessary questions to elicit any fresh information". However, ten years later, Vambery did write:* "Wyburd flung himself into the Turkoman steppes without any knowledge of the languages or customs of Central Asia. In vain was he warned at Teheran of the certain death he was encountering. He followed his passionate wish, and met his end in the desert". Apparently Wyburd had gone disguised as a Mohammedan, but — unlike Vambery — met with failure, discovery and death.

During the three weeks which the Hadjis spent in Bokhara Vambery assumed the dress of an *ishan*, or sheikh, wearing an immense turban and with a large copy of the Koran suspended from his neck. Thereby his reputation for sanctity increased, and people pressed round him — wherever he went — to ask his blessing, to praise him for his holiness, and to listen to his preaching. "What extreme piety to come all the way from Stamboul to Bokhara!" they would say as Vambery passed by with his friends. "Their whole life is prayer, piety and pilgrimage!" However, the natives of Bokhara were as close-fisted with their money as the Khivans had been generous.

Not only did the meanness of the inhabitants and the atmosphere of religious bigotry get on Vambery's nerves, but also he detested the heat, dust and dirt in the crowded streets. There was also the ever present threat of tapeworms and other disagreeable

* Vambery, *History of Bokhara* (1873) p. 389.

parasites, which affected approximately one person in every ten. (Wolff caught one of these parasites in Central Asia, and it was not removed till he was back in England.) The bazaars were, in Vambery's opinion, wretched places compared to those in Isfahan and Tebriz, though he was very interested to discover that some of the goods for sale had been made in England. "How my heart beat when I read the words 'Manchester' and 'Birmingham', and how apprenhesive I was of betraying myself by an imprudent exclamation!"

The book bazaar, containing twenty-six shops, was one of Vambery's favourite haunts. Here he saw many treasures and manuscripts which would have been of incalculable value to Oriental historians and philologists in the West. Vambery could not study them too closely as he realised, with Rahmet Bi's spies in the background, that any appearance of worldly knowledge might have prejudiced his disguise. He wrote later: "The few manuscripts that I brought back with me from Bokhara and Samarkand cost me much trouble to acquire, and my heart bled when I found that I was obliged to leave behind me works that might have filled many an important history in our Oriental studies".

Vambery was horrified by the unedifying spectacles he witnessed in the slave-market. At the time of his visit, the price paid for an able-bodied strong man averaged forty-five *tillas* (£30 sterling). Occasionally, when there was a surfeit of slaves, a man could be bought for as low as three or four tillas.

All the time, the vizier Rahmet Bi continued to send out spies to watch Vambery, and *agents provocateurs* whose job it was to engage him in conversation — in the hope of seeing him betray himself through some inadvertent remark. Some of these spies were old Hadjis who had lived some time in Constantinople, and they now tested his knowledge of that place. Vambery usually found it best to display righteous indignation. "Why", he said; "I have left Constantinople for this very reason, to get rid of the sight of these Frenghis who have robbed the devil of his reason. I am now, thank God, in noble Bokhara, and have no wish to waste my time here on speaking about them".

These spies having failed to uncover anything, Rahmet Bi gave Vambery a supreme test when he invited him one day to a dinner at his home. When Vambery arrived, he found all the ulemas (religious heads) of Bokhara assembled as if in judgment, ready with many intricate questions to trap him. Quick as a flash, he turned the tables by assuming the initiative and subjecting them to a vigorous cross-examination on their own religious tenets and priniples. "My zeal met with applause at the hands of the pious assembly", reported Vambery with much satisfaction and self-congratulation. "My trial ended with my triumph. The learned mollahs gave Rahmet Bi to understand that he had been outrageously mistaken, and that there could not be the slightest doubt about my identity!"

Shortly afterwards, it seemed that Rahmet Bi wanted Vambery to become the 'Emir's spy', catching other suspicious characters in the city. "One day, a servant of the vizier brought to me a little shrivelled individual, that I might examine him to see whether he was, as he pretended, really an Arab from Damascus.

"When he first entered, his features struck me much — they appeared to me European: when he opened his mouth, my astonishment and perplexity increased, for I found his pronunciation anything rather than that of an Arab. He told me that he had undertaken a pilgrimage to the tomb of Djafen Ben Sadik at Khoten in China, and wanted to proceed on his journey that very day. His features during our conversation betrayed a visible embarassment, and it was a subject of great regret to me that I had not an occasion to see him a second time, for I am strongly disposed to think that he was playing a part similar to my own!"

Some years later, Herr von Lankenau (a Russian diplomat who went to Bokhara in 1869) interviewed Rahmet Bi, and when the subject arose of "the very pious Hadji" who was lame, Rahmet answered: "Although many pilgrims go to Bokhara and Samarkand every year, I can guess which one you mean. He was a very learned Hadji, much more so than all the other wise men in Bokhara". Concerning Vambery's masquerade, he said "I was quite aware of the fact, but I knew too that he was not dangerous, and I did not want to ruin such a learned man. It was the Mollahs' own fault that they did not guess whom they had with them. Who told them to keep their eyes and ears shut?" Surprisingly, in later years, Vambery wrote of the 'promptings of Rahmet Bi's kindly heart', and not holding the vizier's earlier machinations against him.

When the time came to leave Bokhara, Vambery had the nerve to pay a farewell visit to Rahmet Bi, and to ask him for a letter of recommendation. It read as follows:

"Be it known, that the holder of this letter, the high-born

Hadji Abdurreshid, from Turkey, has come hither with the intention of making a pilgrimage of the graves of the saints in noble Bokhara and in paradisiacal Samarkand. After accomplishing his pilgrimage to the graves of the saints, and having paid homage to his Highness the Emir, he returns to his home. He is in possession of a passport from his Highness the Sovereign of all true believers and the Imam of all Moslems (the Sultan); it is therefore seemly that the said Hadji should not be inconvenienced by any one, neither on the journey nor at any station, but that everyone as he is able should honour and respect him.

Written in the month of Safar, in the year 1280 (1863)."

Several of the Hadjis who had travelled with Vambery from Teheran now left the party, and dispersed to their homes. But Hadjis Bilal and Salih and their companions from Chinese Turkestan still remained, and Vambery was to accompany them on the next stage of their journey to Samarkand. He was still undecided about which route he should take after that — if he travelled east to Kashgar, Aksu and Khoten, he would be reaching areas which no European before had penetrated. As he was more inclined to take the southern route via Afghanistan, Bilal and Salih introduced him to an old friend of theirs, Mollah Zeman, a caravan-leader from Herat. Vambery made a tentative date to meet Zeman three weeks later at Kerki, on the further bank of the Oxus.

Vambery thought Bokhara was "the most shameless sink of iniquity that I know in the East", but his stay there had not been entirely unpleasant. Two new shirts had been made for him, and the daily fare of good bread, tea, fruit, and boiled meats had been quite enjoyable. But owing to the meanness of the Bokharans, the pilgrims' finances were by now at a very low ebb, and many of them — including Vambery himself — had been forced to sell their donkeys. They had to hire two carts in order to continue the journey, and in these they now set out for Samarkand.

The violent jolting of the primitive vehicles made Vambery quite sea-sick, much more so than when on the camels. "Our heads were continually cannoning each other like balls on a billiard table", was Vambery's graphic description. The first stop, a short distance from Bokhara, was at the tomb of Baha-ed-din, the national saint of Turkestan, venerated here as a second Mohammed. Pilgrimages were made to this place even from the most remote parts of China. Vambery wrote that the tomb was approached "through a court filled with blind or crippled mendicants, the perseverance of whose applications would put to shame those of the same profession in Rome or Naples. In the front of the tomb is the famous 'stone of desire' which has been ground away and made smooth by the numerous foreheads of pious pilgrims that have been rubbed upon it."

The road from Bokhara to Samarkand follows the valley of the Zer-Affshan River, and runs through much well-irrigated countryside. "We passed every hour a small market-place, where there were several inns and houses for the sale of provisions, and where gigantic Russian teakettles, even on the boil, are held to be the *ne plus ultra* of refinement and of comfort", wrote Vambery. "My friends seemed to endear themselves to me more and more the nearer the moment of our separation approached; it seemed impossible that I was to journey alone that long way back from Samarkand to Europe!" With his immediate future and chances of survival still most uncertain, Vambery tried to carry on with an ebullient air, as they approached near to Samarkand on the sixth morning.

"All my curiosity and interest revived to see this Mecca of my longings of old". No European had described this vista for centuries: "At last, on toiling up a hill, I beheld the city of Timour in the middle of a fine country. I must confess that the first impression produced by the domes and minarets, with their various colours, all bathed in the beams of the morning sun — the peculiarity, in short, of the whole scene — was very pleasing". On closer examination however, Vambery was less enthusiastic: "But, alas! why need I add that the impression produced by its exterior was weakened as we approached, and entirely dissipated by our entry into the place itself?" His disappointment at the rundown, shoddy appearance of the fabled city was acute. While the party had to cross a large cemetery to gain access to the inhabited parts, Vambery thought of the Persian verse:

"Samarkand is the focus of the whole globe" and burst into a loud fit of sardonic laughter.

On the first evening Vambery was pleased to learn that he and his friends were to be the guests of a high court official. This was a welcome change to the common caravanserai. The Emir was expected to arrive in Samarkand shortly from Khokand, where he had just won a great victory, and the Hadjis decided to await

View of Samarkand.

his return.

During the next eight days, Vambery passed his time looking round the many historic buildings. There were, in all, well over a hundred holy places to be visited. Here, in the early fifteenth century, one of the most beautiful mausoleums in the world was built in honour of Timour (Tamerlane). Embalmed in musk and rosewater and wrapped in linen, the body was laid in an ivory coffin. In the burial-vault beneath the cupola, the place was marked by a solid piece of jade — the largest piece of jade known — six feet long. On one of the walls appeared the following words (in Arabic): "Were I still alive, mankind would tremble".

In the middle of the Old City is the magnificent cobbled expanse of the *Righistan*, which Lord Curzon (who visited Samarkand 23 years after Vambery) called "the noblest public square in the world". On three sides of this square lie three ancient *medressehs*,* richly decorated in gold. Vambery stored much of the information he was told — architectural and historical — in his prodigious memory, for it was a very dangerous and unwise move to produce pencil and paper in public. Inevitably some errors were bound to occur when months later Vambery wrote in great detail of the buildings of Samarkand. (And he was to be taken to task unmercifully by some European critics determined to catch him out, especially since he had described the colour of the *Koktash*, the stone on which the throne was based, as green: a fact which was to cause him much trouble in later years.)

Hadji Bilal was still trying to persuade Vambery to accompany him as far as Aksu, with the 'promise' of a safe route to Yarkand, Tibet and Kashmir. But Hadji Salih was much opposed to this plan, emphasizing the great distance and the scantiness of his means. "As far as Aksu, and even Komul", said Salih, "you would experience no difficulty, for Mussulmans and brothers are living along the road, and they would have regard for you as a dervish from Stamboul; but beyond you will meet unbelievers only, who — it is true — will not harm you, but will not give you anything either. Therefore be advised, and return to Teheran by way of Herat, with the men we have selected for your travelling companions".

Vambery had many long hours of indecision. He tells us of his thoughts at that time: "A journey, I thought, by land to Peking,

---

* They were somewhat decayed in Vambery's time. Recently however, they have been carefully and skilfully restored. (F. Maclean, *To the Back of Beyond*. Cape, 1974).

across the ancient homes of the Tartars, Kirghis, Kalmuks, Mongols, and Chinese — a way by which Marco Polo himself would not have ventured — would be really grand! But moderation whispered in my ear, 'Enough for the moment!' I made a retrospect of what I had done, of what countries I had traversed, what distances I had travelled over, and by ways too, by which no one had preceded me; would it not, I thought, be a pity if I sacrificed the experience which I had acquired, however trifling, in a hazardous and uncertain enterprise? I am but thirty-one years old; what has not happened may still occur; better, perhaps, now, that I should return". So it was that Salih's prudent advice prevailed, with Vambery now definitely deciding to travel back to Persia via Karshi and Herat.

Vambery was in the middle of the preparations for his departure, when the Emir entered Samarkand in triumph at the head of his troops. Mozaffar-ed-din, the son and successor of the bloodthirsty Emir Nasrullah, was then aged forty-two. Vambery noted that he was "of middle size, rather stout, but very pleasant in appearance, with fine black eyes and a thin beard"; and, in his opinion, all the higher functionaries — resplendent in wide silk garments of all the colours of the rainbow — looked more like a chorus of women from an opera than a troop of Tartar warriors. The Emir was known to be an extremely pious Moslem, and his private life — totally unlike that of his father — was reputed to be blameless to the point of austerity. The ladies of his harem were chaste and well trained and were kept fully occupied making their own clothes and those of the Emir.

On the following day it was announced that the Emir would hold a public audience. When Vambery and his friends presented themselves at the Palace, they were disconcerted to be met by a Chamberlain who informed them that His Majesty wished to see Hadji Reshid alone — without his companions. Had the vizier Rahmet Bi alerted the Emir of his suspicions? With a sinking heart, Vambery followed the Chamberlain to an ante-chamber where he was told to wait. Time passed slowly while he nervously wondered what fate held in store for him. A mischievous court official did not help matters by stroking the back of Vambery's neck and remarking in a loud whisper: "Unfortunately I have left my knife at home today." Vambery believed — and hoped — that this was just a casual joke, but it certainly had an ominous ring about it. After an hour had passed, the summons came and he was ushered into the presence of the Emir.

Mozaffar-ed-din was reclining on a divan covered with red cloth, surrounded by books and papers. With his usual presence of mind — so vital in circumstances like these — Vambery immediately recited a short *sura* or prayer (for the welfare of the Sovereign) and then boldly sat down uninvited next to the Emir, which was in fact in perfect keeping with the character of a dervish. The following dialogue then ensued between the two men, a dialogue quoted in much detail later by Vambery:

"Hadji! I hear you have come from Roum (Stamboul) to visit the graves of Baha-ed-din and the other holy saints of Turkestan."

"Yes, Takhsir (Sire); but also I have come to rejoice in the contemplation of Your Majesty's sacred beauty."

"Strange! And you had no other motive in coming here from such distant lands?"

"No, Takhsir. It has always been the warmest wish of my heart to behold noble Bokhara and enchanting Samarkand. Besides I have long been a *djihangeshte* (world-pilgrim). I have no other business in life."

"What, you — with your lame foot — a *djihangeshte*! That is really astonishing!"

"Forgive me, Takhsir, your glorious ancestor Tamerlane — may he rest in peace — was afflicted in the same way, and yet he became a *djihanghir* (world-conqueror)."

Pleased at this last reply, the Emir next asked his visitor some questions about his journey and what impression Bokhara and Samarkand had made upon him. Vambery interlaced his answers with copious citations of Persian poetry. This seemed to make a favourable impression on the Emir, who was a mollah himself and spoke Arabic well. Therefore the conversation flowed much easier than the earlier discourse with the Khan of Khiva. After the audience had lasted some fifteen minutes the Emir summoned a servant to whom he whispered a command. Once again Vambery felt himself on a knife-edge, as he wrote later ". . . my perplexed imagination conjuring up pictures of horror and seeing myself already travelling on the road to the rack and that dreadful death which was ever present in my mind" — and once again his fears were allayed. The servant did not bring the instruments of the executioner, but instead a neatly folded parcel containing a highly ornamental suit of clothing, and an amount of money for

156

the onward journey. The Emir's final word to Vambery was a wish that he should visit him again the next time he was in Bokhara. Thought Vambery: "My triumph was entirely owing to the flexibility of my tongue (which is really quite impudent enough)."

The other Hadjis were overjoyed with Vambery's success at the royal audience, but nevertheless they advised him to leave Samarkand at once, and travel with all haste to the far side of the River Oxus and await there for the caravan bound for Herat. The Hadjis had heard that the Emir had received a message from Rahmet Bi concerning Vambery. Whether the message was for or against Vambery was not known.

It was with genuine grief that Vambery at last took leave of his two closest friends Hadji Bilal and Hadji Salih. The hazards and extreme hardships which they had shared during six months had forged between them the strongest bonds of friendship. They had come to look upon themselves as one family. "My heart nearly broke", wrote Vambery, "at the thought of the double-dealing I had to practise upon these friends of mine — the best I had in the world, who had preserved my life — even in these last moments leaving them in the dark as to my identity." Many tears were shed on both sides when they said farewell outside the city gate in the certain knowledge that they would never see each other again. When Vambery took his seat in the cart with some new companions, and as the vehicle set out at dusk, he waved goodbye to his friends for the last time. "Long did I see them standing there in the same place, with their hands raised to heaven, imploring Allah's blessing upon my far journey. I turned round many times to look back. At last they disappeared from view, and I found I was only gazing upon the domes of Samarkand, illuminated by the faint light of the rising moon!"

7

SUSPECT IN AFGHANISTAN

Apart from a few travellers who stayed with the caravan a short while, Vambery's only constant companion from now on was Ishak, the young Mollah from Kungrat, who Vambery had first met in Khiva. "He was a kind-hearted youth", wrote Vambery, "as poor as myself, and looking upon me as his master, he was always ready to serve and oblige me". This suited Vambery very well.

The road south-west of Samarkand ran through eighteen miles of desert, more like a prairie than some of the terrible wildernesses Vambery had seen recently. There were many deep wells, and herdsmen were numerous. Because of the strict police regulations enforced everywhere by the Emir of Bokhara, there was relatively little danger from robber-bands.

The third day brought them to Karshi, a rambling town noted for the beauty of its gardens and for the cheerfulness of its inhabitants. This place occupied an important position on the trade route between Bokhara and Afghanistan and India. Vambery was interested in the high quality of the knife industry here: "These are not only exported to all parts of Central Asia, but are conveyed by the Hadjis to Persia, Arabia, and Turkey, where they realise three times, and often four times, the cost price. One kind, with Damascus blades, and handles with gold and silver inlaid, is really worked with great taste, and might, both for durability and temper, put to shame the most famous produce of Sheffield and Birmingham."

Among the letters of introduction given to Vambery by Bilal and Salih was one addressed to Ishan Hassan, a man of some importance in Karshi. Vambery sought him out and received a very cordial welcome. He was advised by Hassan to buy an ass (here most asses and cattle were very cheap), and with the remaining money various trinkets and gifts like glass beads, cornelians, needles and thread, and Bokhara-made pocket-handkerchiefs. These, said Hassan, would be very useful when meeting the nomadic tribes along the road to the south, especially as there were so many tolls and levies to be paid. In exchange for two or three glass beads one could get enough bread and melons to last a whole day. Hadjis usually supplemented their diminishing earnings in this way. Vambery and his Mollah Ishak made all the purchases they could afford. "One half of my khurdjin (knapsack) was full of my manuscripts, mostly of literary and historical contents, which I bought in the bazaar of Bokhara; the other half was used by me as a storehouse for my wares", wrote Vambery, "and thus I became at once an antiquarian, a dealer in fashionable articles, a Hadji and a Mollah, deriving an additional source of income from the sale of benedictions, nefesses, amulets, and similar wonderful articles."

After spending three days in Karshi, Vambery set out again with Ishak, their only other companions being two Hadjis. They proceeded at a leisurely pace, sometimes riding, sometimes walking, filling up their vessels with adequate supplies of water along the way. At one of the wells, Vambery noted sardonically that the herdsmen's "cattle, and their children in a complete state of nudity, were splashing about in the water, and spoiling its flavour a little".

It took them nearly three days to cover the sixty miles to the River Oxus. On the opposite bank was situated the small frontier town of Kerki. Vambery noted that the Oxus was here nearly twice the width of the Danube near Budapest.

Owing to the strong current and the numerous sandbanks, it took the ferry a laborious three hours to cross the river. Vambery was gratified not to be asked for any fare on this occasion, but his delight did not last long. He had hardly placed his feet on the riverbank when a *Deryabeghi* (river officer) came up and accused all four of the travellers of being runaway slaves intending to return to Persia. Vambery's three companions were not alarmed — their speech and features proved at once that they originated from the north, not from Persia, and they were allowed to go free. It was not so easy for Vambery, with his unusual appearance. "My surprise and terror may be easily imagined", he wrote. "When I saw that they were about forcibly to take away my ass, I fell into a passion, and, employing alternately the dialects of Tartary and the Turkish dialect peculiar to Constantinople, I handed in my passport, demanding in a violent manner that they should show it to the Bi (governor), or that they should usher me to his presence."

Once again Vambery's presence of mind and command of languages saved the day. "On making this disturbance, I saw that the *Toptchubashi* (commandant of artillery) in the fortress, a Persian by birth, who had elevated himself from the condition of a slave to his present rank, whispered something in the ear of the *Deryabeghi*; he then took me aside, and told me that he had been several times in Stamboul from Tebriz, his native city; that he could distinguish people from Roum very well; I might be easy, nothing would happen here either to me or my property; that all strangers were obliged to submit to the examination, because every emancipated slave on his way home was obliged to pay here, on the frontier, a tax or two ducats, and that often, to smuggle themselves through, they assumed different disguises. Soon afterwards, the servant returned who had shown my pass to the Governor; he gave it me back, with five Tenghe presented to me by the Bi, without any request on my part."

Vambery was expecting to meet here Mollah Zeman, the chief of the Herat-bound caravan, whom he had met in Samarkand. He was disappointed to hear that he would have to wait at least ten days for the arrival of Zeman, so he spent the next week with Ishak exploring the area to the south-east of Kerki, rather than in the town itself. The following day Vambery and Ishak were guests of a hospitable local Ishan, Khalfa Niyaz, a man of self-declared sanctity and rank, who ran a small monastery where a few students were educated in religion. Vambery noted that this Ishan had obtained permission from Mecca to recite the sacred poems (Kaside Sherif): "In reading, he always had a cup filled with water placed by his side, and would spit into the water whenever he had finished reading a poem. The saliva thus permeated by the sanctity of the words he would then sell as a miraculous panacea to the highest bidder."

Waking at dawn, he realised the pain had decreased, and gradually the burning sensation grew less and less violent. His companions assured him that their morning prayers had the effect of "exorcising the devil" which had crept into his body by means of the scorpion bite.

Thanks to his customary resilience, Vambery had recovered sufficiently by the time Mollah Zeman made his long-awaited arrival in Kerki. But the departure was again postponed owing to a heated dispute between Zeman and the Kerki authorities. The governor and the *deryabeghi* were determined to exert the highest tolls possible on all the recently emancipated slaves, of which there were about forty in Zeman's caravan. All the other travellers in the caravan not known to the governor were presumed to be slaves also, and their luggage was unpacked and investigated at length. More exorbitant tolls were ordered, and there seemed no end to the deafening tumult, quarrelling, and shouting.

Eventually the haggling ended in mutual agreement, and the caravan was at last able to proceed on its southward journey. Along the route, and at the various stops for water, Vambery talked with some of the freed slaves, and heard many tales of anguish and suffering. Most of them were from Herat or Persia, and had been kidnapped by Turkoman bandits and sold into slavery at Bokhara.

The caravan now consisted of 400 camels, a few horses, and 190 asses, forming a long chain. Had it not been for the large unassailable size of the caravan, the predatory Kara Turkomans — seen watching like vultures at a distance — would have undoubtedly attacked. When some of the Turkomans approached gingerly, Zeman and a few others in the caravan, fired a few warning shots at the would-be slave-traders.

It was with a feeling of great relief that Vambery crossed the Bokharan frontier* south of Kerki and entered the small Khanate of Andkhuy. "Whilst my heavily-laden ass was trotting on in the still night", he reminisced, "the joyful thought for the first time occurred to me that I had turned my back upon the Khanate of Bokhara, and that I was actually on my way to that West which I loved so well. My travelling experience, thought I, may not be great, but I carry back with me what is worth more than anything — my life." The whole country in these parts was a dry, barren plain, destitute of vegetation with the exception of a species of thistle, the favourite food of the camels.

Owing to the long delay of the caravan-leader Zeman, there was time for Vambery and Ishak to visit, under the guidance of Khalfa Niyaz, the Mezar-i-sharif (the noble grave), a venerated place of pilgrimage. Tradition claimed that this was the tomb of Ali companion and successor of the Prophet. Nearby lay Balkh, the ancient Bactria of the Greeks, reduced to little more than a vil-

---

* This spot now marks the border between the U.S.S.R and Afghanistan (1979).

Afghan type.

lage. Centuries before it had been a famed centre of Islam civilization.

In the evenings, several Turkomans brought with them some of their favourite poems or tales. Vambery was only too pleased to read these out aloud in his best oratorical tones. "It was delightful to have them sitting around me in the stilly night within view of the Oxus rolling onward: they listening to me with rapt attention while I read about the brave feats of one of their heroes." Vambery later recollected one grisly happening which followed one of his recitals.

"One evening the reading had lasted as late as midnight. I was quite fagged out, and, forgetting to heed the advice I had been frequently given not to lie down near a building in ruins, I stretched my weary limbs close to a wall and very soon fell asleep. I might have slept for an hour when I was suddenly roused by a painful sensation. I jumped up screaming; I thought a hundred poisoned needles had run into my leg. The spot from which the pain proceeded was a small point near the big toe of my right foot . . ." He had been bitten by a deadly scorpion, but his life was saved in the nick of time by the swift action of two Turkomans, who applied a tourniquet and took turns in sucking the wound. In his delirium Vambery recollected "that the scorpions of Balkh were known in ancient times for their venomous nature . . ."

"My distress was rendered more intolerable by my fears, and that I had given up every hope during the many hours of suffering was proved by the circumstance that, totally unmindful of my incognito, I had broken out into such moans and plaintive exclamations as seemed to be quite outlandish to the Tartars who, as I subsequently learned, were in the habit of bursting out into shouts of joy on an occasion of this kind. In a few seconds the pain had darted from the tips of my toes to the top of my head, rushing up and down like a stream of fire, but being confined nevertheless to my right side only. The tortures I was suffering beggar all description, and losing all further interest in life I dashed my head against the ground reckless of all consequences, and seeking relief in death. This action of suicidal violence was speedily remarked by the others, and they, taking no heed of my remonstrance, tied me securely to a tree. Thus I continued to be in a prostrate, half-fainting condition for several hours, staring fixedly at the starry vault above me, whilst the cold sweat of agony was gathering in heavy drops on my forehead. The Pleiades were slowly moving towards the west, the beloved West, which I despaired of ever seeing again . . ." But eventually he fell alseep.

It was not long before the caravan arrived at the gates of Andkhuy, a decaying city, famed for its bad climate and terrible drinking water. A Persian verse ran:

"Andkhuy has bitter salt water, scorching sand,
venomous flies, and even scorpions. Vaunt it not,
for it is the picture of a real hell."

This Khanate was a buffer state between the larger powers of Bokhara to the North and Afghanistan to the South, and had suffered much in consequence.

Vambery and the other Hadjis went to the bazaar and set up a stall in an attempt to trade their small stock of cutlery and gifts for an adequate amount of food and money. In the meantime, the caravanleader Mollah Zeman was having another dispute over taxes and tolls, as heated as the one in Kerki, this time with the Vizier of Andkhuy, an unscrupulous man who was seeking to enrich himself in the temporary absence of the ruler, Gazanfer Khan. When Vambery and his companions returned to the caravan from the bazaar, they found that Zeman and the Vizier had come to blows, and it looked as if a pitched battle between the members of the caravan and the Vizier's troops was imminent. A very ugly scene was saved by the sudden unexpected arrival of Gazanfer Khan who proved to be a kindly well-disposed man, who quickly settled the argument and diminished the exorbitant tax imposed by his money-grubbing Vizier.

There were many new recruits in Andkhuy for the caravan, which now swelled to almost double its former size. Now reasonably safe from bandit attacks, the caravan faced other dangers on the three day march to Maymene, the small Khanate lying to the south-west. The land was alternately mountainous and swampy. Mollah Zeman wisely took the caravan on a detour to avoid the town of Khairabad, in order to avoid further sky-high levy and tolls and hard-fought argument. After everyone had crossed safely by the spongy Batkak marshes, Zeman made a present to the Hadjis of two sheep, "as a grateful acknowledgement to God for having happily escaped from the peril to which the caravan had been exposed", Vambery reported. "As the senior, I was charged with the division of the donation". (Vambery did not explain how *he* was the senior Hadji, other than through the power of his personality — the other Hadjis had been to Mecca.)

"We ate that whole day, instead of bread, roast meat, and sang together in the evening some *Telkins* (hymns) to the accompaniment, under my direction, of a Zikr — that is, we shouted out to the full extent of our voices two thousand times, Ya hoo! ya hakk!"

Reaching Maymene, the caravan camped outside the town while Vambery went to the *tekkie* of one Ishan Eyub, to whom he had been given a letter of introduction by his friend Hadji Salih. Vambery knew he had to be on his guard in this city, where most of the inhabitants had never seen a European.* He was especially fearful of meeting here a Mollah he had met three years previously in Constantinople. This Mollah, a native of Maymene named Khalmurad, a mischievous and cunning fellow, knew well that Vambery was a European, and a meeting here could have dire consequences for the dervish impostor. Khalmurad had left Constantinople while Vambery was still there, and was to return to his home in Maymene via Mecca. However, after making a few careful inquiries, Vambery was relieved to hear from his host Ishan Eyub that the Mollah had had "the happiness of dying in Mecca".*

Vambery now moved about Maymene more at his ease. He found the city "extremely filthy and ill built", consisting of 1500 mud huts, and "a bazaar built of brick, that seems about to fall". There was a considerable trade carried on with Persia in raisins, aniseed, and pistachio nuts. Vambery was surprised to see fine horses sold here at very low prices, around 150 tenghis each, less than half the price in Persia. (A tenghi then being about nine-pence.)

The caravan stayed here for ten days, and Vambery made use of the time to set up his small 'shop' at the corner of a street. His stock was becoming very reduced by this time. One of his companions warned him "Hadji Reshid, thou hast already eaten up half of thy knives, needles, and glass beads; thou wilt before long have devoured the other half, and thy ass to boot. What wilt thou then

---

* Col. George Malleson, in his book *Herat* (1880), was only able to trace one previous case of a European visiting Maymene (in peril of his life), a Captain Stirling.

* Presumably an erroneous report. Later when Vambery returned to Teheran he heard that the Mollah from Maymene had passed through the Persian capital only a month previously. The two may have passed on the road without knowing each other. Another lucky escape for Vambery.

do?" Vambery replied that he hoped the proverbial Uzbeg hospitality of never allowing a Hadji to pass by empty-handed would see him through. He always preferred the Uzbegs to the Afghans, whom he described as 'filthy' and 'grasping'. Herat was still 125 miles distant — a very long way in those regions to keep a small budget in the black.

There was only a small toll to pay in the city itself, but at the border of the Khanate a few miles down the road, there was an additional levy to pay under the title of 'whip-money.' The luckless caravanleader Mollah Zeman was again fleeced for more dues after the usual shouting, quarrelling, and negotiations, which lasted a few hours.

From this point, the caravan proceeded under the protection of a troop of Djemshidi horsemen, sent to meet them by their Khan from Bela Murghab, the next place of importance on the road. The countryside was very fertile, with lush meadows covered with flowers, but totally uncultivated. It was impossible for any peaceful villages to exist here, owing to the intolerable number of bandits in the area. On the right side of the road dwelt the Sarik Turkomans, while in the hills on the left roamed the mountaineer robbers, the Firuzkuhi. The travellers journeyed on in great anxiety, cautiously surveying every little hill they passed. It was only due to the great size of the caravan, they surmised, that they were not attacked at all.

At the end of the day the Djemshidi demanded their whip-money, with the unfortunate ex-slaves having to pay a double share. The fertile valley led to a rough mountainous pass, at places so narrow that single loaded camels could wind their way through only with extreme difficulty. The night was spent on the banks of the Murghab, the largest and most important river of the region. It took some time for the party to find a ford through the clear swift-running waters of the river next morning. Vambery described the scene graphically:

". . . I forced my ass into the river. When he made his first step upon the stony bottom of the rapid stream, I felt certain that something awful was going to happen: I strove to get down, but that was unnecessary, for a few steps further on my charger fell, amidst the loud laughter of our comrades standing upon the bank, and then afterwards, in great consternation, he made for the opposite bank, as I wished him to do". Fortunately the knapsack, containing his precious manuscripts, survived the crossing: it was secure on the back of a camel. "This cold morning bath in the clear waters of the transparent crystal Murghab was only so far disagreeable to me that I had no change of clothes, so I was obliged to hide myself a few hours amongst some carpets and sacks until my clothes, which were entirely wet through, should dry in the sun."

Four days were spent along the bank of the Murghab. Vambery, in order to supplement his slender resources, offered his glass beads to the natives in the vicinity, as well as his *fatiha* (blessings) and *nefes* (holy breath). He found it a waste of time. They wanted bread, not items of luxury — and religion here was practically non-existent.

After travelling for some time on the left bank of the river, the caravan veered south again through a narrow pass, and over the lofty Talkhguzar hills. The next morning brought the caravan to a dirty collection of tents, once a prosperous town, called Kale No (now Qala-i-Nau). Here more tolls were paid for the camels and asses, and several of the merchants in the party bought a large quantity of Berek, a renowned light cloth much favoured in Persia.

Herat, their destination, was now less than fifty miles away:* an estimated four-days journey for strong horses, but at least double that time for camels and asses owing to the arduous route over unsafe roads and craggy paths on the lower slopes of the snow covered mountain Serabend. On the third day, there were some particularly dangerous places, with the narrow path passing perilously close to the edge of the precipice. Eventually the steep descent took them, without accident, into the Djolghei-Herat, the fertile plain which surrounds Herat, with its sparkling network of water-courses, its scattered groups of small villages, and its meadows, gardens and vineyards.

The whole caravan was forced to wait a whole day at Kerrukh, one of the border villages, until — as Vambery pointed out impatiently — "the officer of the Customs had, in the overbearing and supercilious manner peculiar to the Afghans, finished making up, with a great deal of ado, an extensive list of every traveller, ani-

---

* The historian Dr. Arnold J. Toynbee travelled along the same 125-mile road from Herat to Maymene, during his Afghan tour in 1960, nearly one hundred years after Vambery. He found it was just possible to cover the distance in two days by land-rover. The road had not improved much over the years — in parts it had liquefied into a skiddy slime. Dr. Toynbee found the road from Maymene to Andkhuy was unusable. (Toynbee, *Between Oxus and Jumna*. Oxford University Press, 1961, pp. 76-89.)

Village in Afghanistan.

mals, and each piece of goods we had with us. I had imagined Afghanistan to be a country with somewhat of a regular administration; nay, I had fondly hoped that my sufferings would terminate here, and that I might dispense henceforth with the assumption of the character of a dervish. Alas! I was sadly mistaken. Nowhere had we been treated in such a brutal manner as we were treated here by the Afghan Customs collectors. We had to pay duty on the very clothes we wore, with the exception of the shirt. On my ass I had to pay a duty of six krans, and he who was not able to pay had simply all this things confiscated".

All the time, Vambery observed those around him, always noting their habits and acquiring new words and idioms. For all his expertise, it took him some time to work out the meaning of the strange names used by the Afghans for their senior military officers: *Mejir, Kornel,* and *Djornel.* He eventually realised that, like the uniforms and the words of command, they were of British origin.

After all the extra tolls had been paid, the Governor of Kerrukh, a man with the rank of *Mejir* (i.e. Major), came over to examine everyone in the caravan. He was wearing a smart British-style uniform, the sight of which cheered Vambery up, albeit momentarily. "At me he took a good long look, evidently being stuck by my foreign features," wrote Vambery, "and immediately summoned the caravanleader to make some whispered inquiries about me. He then called me to come near him, made me sit down, and treated me with marked politeness. Whilst talking with me he studiously turned the conversation on Bokhara, smiling always in a mysterious way as he did so. But I remained faithful to the part I had assumed". Obviously the Governor (whose name was Bator Khan) had made a shrewd guess as to the origins of the unusual figure before him. Vambery acted with his usual panache. The Governor had wanted to shake hands with him in the English fashion, but he anticipated the motion of his hand "by raising . . . mine as if in the act of bestowing a *fatiha* upon him, whereupon he left me with a laugh. We were finally allowed to leave Kerrukh, and entered Herat on the following morning after a toilsome journey of six weeks".

Only a few weeks before, Herat had been finally brought under Afghan domination. There had been a ten months' siege and much fierce fighting, and now the city lay in ruins. Vambery noted that most of the buildings were "little more than heaps of rubbish". He also observed naked Afghans and Hindus squatting in the deserted openings of the houses — "worthy keepers of a city in ruins". The Ark (Citadel) had been half demolished by the Afghan artillery. Only the bazaar still retained signs of its former glory. Afghan soldiers swaggered about the streets arrogantly, some of them dressed in uniforms modelled on those of the British army — scarlet tunics and smart black shakos.

Dost Mohammed Khan (the powerful figure who had ruled Afghanistan on and off for nearly forty years) had died just after the capture of Herat and was buried on the outskirts of the city. The new King, or Amir, Sher Ali, had only just buried his father when he heard that his warmongering brothers were already plotting to overthrow* him. Hastening back to the capital Kabul, Sher Ali entrusted the newly conquered province of Herat to his sixteen-year-old son, Serdar Mohammed Yakub Khan.

Vambery soon realised on his arrival that he would have to visit this young ruler to obtain some kind of assistance in order to continue his journey. He was now completely destitute, and on his first day in Herat, he was forced to sell his ass to pay for food and to settle some small debts. A caravan bound for Teheran, under the charge of a Persian envoy, left that same day with some of the more thrifty Hadjis and other travellers who had accompanied Vambery and Ishak from the banks of the Oxus. As neither Vambery nor his faithful mollah could now pay their way, they were unable to leave with the caravan.

"All abandoned me", wrote Vambery later, "All but Mollah Ishak, my faithful companion from Kungrat, who had believed, when I said that in Teheran better fortunes awaited me, and who stood by me. The honest young man obtained our daily food and fuel by begging, and got ready besides our evening supper, which he refused respectfully to share with me out of the same plate".

When Vambery, accompanied by Ishak, made his way into the courtyard of the palace, he found the daily manoeuvres and military drill taking place there. The words of command, delivered by the Afghan officers, were in impeccable English: "Right shoulder forward! Left shoulder forward!" as the troops marched and counter-marched. At the end of the courtyard, under the Prince's apartments, the band was playing some stirring European tunes. After watching the drill for a few minutes, Vambery and Ishak entered the palace and made their way upstairs to the

large reception-hall.

The young prince Yakub, dressed in uniform, was seated in an armchair by the open window watching the troops' exercises. He was surrounded by a large retinue. On the Prince's right hand sat his Vizier, a corpulent man whose coarse features seemed to Vambery, "the sign-post of stupidity". The internal affairs of Herat were left in his hands, and Vambery had been told that in only two months this corrupt official had so enriched himself he had been able to buy two fine houses with vineyards in his native Kabul. On being consulted about anything, he invariably gave the same answer: "*Her tchi pish bud*" — "Everything as before".

Thanks to Vambery's huge turban and 'anchorite' appearance, everyone made way for him. As became his position as a dervish, he entered with the customary saluation, went straight up the Prince in his usual swashbuckling style, and pushing the corpulent Vizier to one side, sat down between them. There was widespread laughter at this sight, but Vambery kept a serious face while raising his hand to recite his prayer in sonorous tones. During the prayer, he noticed that the young Prince was staring at him fixedly: something was obviously puzzling him. At the concluding Amen, the Prince half rose from his chair, and pointed straight at Vambery suddenly called out "*Vallahi, Billahi Schuma Inghiliz hestid!*" — "By God, I swear you are an Englishman!" A loud burst of laughter followed this remark, after which the Prince jumped up, and looking close into Vambery's face, clapped his hands delightedly, and added: "Hadji ... tell me, you are an Englishman in *Tebdil* (disguise), are you not?"

Vambery kept his head in this distinctly difficult situation. "Have done, Sire!" he replied solemnly, as though the joke had now gone far enough: "You know the saying 'He who takes, even in sport, the believer for an unbeliever, is himself an unbeliever'. Give me rather something for my *fatiha* (blessing), so that I may continue my journey". At this the young Prince sat down again in confusion, excusing himself by saying that he had never seen a Hadji from Bokhara with such features. Vambery then explained that he was from Constantinople and displayed his Turkish passport, which was examined admiringly by all present. The Prince gave him a small amount of money and invited him to come again during his stay in Herat. The audience then came to an end, and Vambery withdrew, having extricated himself once again from an awkward predicament.*

For several days after the meeting with the Prince, Vambery found himself plagued by various Afghans and Persians who asked him many leading questions for the express purpose of finding out whether or not he was an Englishman. "The most boring fellow", wrote Vambery, "was a certain Hadji Sheikh Mehemmed, an old man rejoicing in the reputation of being a great astrologer and astronomer, and really, as far as opportunity enabled me to judge, one well read in Arabic and Persian. He informed me that he had travelled with M. de Khanikoff" (a Russian traveller of note and one of Vambery's rivals) "and had been of much service to him in Herat, and that the latter had given him a letter to the Russian ambassador in Teheran, of which he wished me to take charge. In vain did I try to persuade the good old man, that I had nothing to do with the Russians; he left me with his convictions unshaken".

Time dragged by slowly and the money again evaporated while Vambery waited for the next caravan. "There was a sad and depressing air about the city", he wrote; "terror of the savage conqueror could be read in every face, and the recent siege and devastation continued to form the ever-recurring topics of conversation".*

---

* Many years later the Prince Yakub explained to a British officer that he had guessed Vambery was a European, because he had observed him in the courtyard beating time to the music with his foot — something no Asiatic would ever do. (Sir Robert Warburton: *Eighteen Years in the Khyber.* John Murray, 1900.)

Prince Yakub Khan succeeded to the Afghan throne in 1879, and after a short disastrous reign he spent over forty years exile in India.

* During the Afghan civil war of 1863-1870, it was impossible for Europeans to reach the area. Between Vambery's visit (1863) and the publication of Col. George Malleson's book *Herat* (1880), only one English traveller was able to visit Herat, Captain H.C. Marsh, in 1872.

8

"VAMBERY SAHIB"

At last, on 15 November 1863, Vambery and Ishak left Herat for Meshed with a great caravan numbering two thousand pilgrims and merchants. Their paltry savings from begging were just enough to secure them a place with a group of Afghan merchants from Kandahar, who were conveying their stock of furs and indigo to Persia. "I was utterly destitute of money, of everything", wrote Vambery, "and to satisfy my daily wants I was thrown upon the charity of the Afghans and Tadjiks". One of the merchants' mules was lightly loaded, and Vambery was allowed to ride the beast — on the proviso that he would pay for the 'honour' as soon as the caravan reached Meshed. Through his guarded hints that he would no longer be in a state of destitution in Meshed, he remained a subject of much gossip and curiosity to his fellow-travellers as Herat disappeared from view. But it was still extremely unsafe for him to lay aside his mask completely.

"The dubious light in which I stood afforded a fund of interesting surmises to those by whom I was surrounded", wrote Vambery, "for whilst some of them took me for a genuine Turk, others were disposed to think me an Englishman; the different parties even quarrelled on the subject, and it was very droll to observe how the latter began to triumph over the former, when it was observed that, in proportion as we drew nearer to Meshed, the bent posture of humility of the Dervish began more and more to give way to the upright and independent deportment of the European. Some Afghans, agents of wholesale indigo-houses in Moultan and Shikarpur, seemed quite to accomodate themselves to my metamorphosis . . ."

The caravan took twelve days to travel the rough 230 mile journey from Herat due west to Meshed.* The road ran parallel to the

---

* Now there is a good tarmac road, and the journey by land-rover takes approximately seven hours (including customs check at the Iran/Afghanistan border).

north bank of the river Heri, which formed the southernmost limits of the Turkoman raiders. Every village where the caravan stopped for a while provided Vambery and Ishak with an opportunity to rummage about for food. "My Tartar and I divided the village between us", he wrote; "I would go in one direction and beg for wood and fuel, whilst he would go in another begging for bread and flour". After an hour, they would meet and combine whatever they had been given, and prepare a small meal. "The inhabitants of this region, though very poor themselves, did not turn a deaf ear to our appeals for charity".

At Kuhsun, the last Afghan town, the caravan had to stop two whole days while all the travellers paid the necessary tolls. Then followed a hazardous passage through a 'no man's land', owned neither by Afghanistan nor by Persia. For many miles, there was no sign of life. The country was fertile but there were neither fields nor people. The Turkomans had seen to that. Arriving safely on to Persian soil, near Kafir-Kale, they met a caravan coming from Meshed. Vambery learned from one of the members of this caravan that Colonel Dolmage, an English officer in the Persian service, was still residing in Meshed. This news cheered Vambery up a great deal, as he had been acquainted with the Colonel back in Teheran.

The sharp cold winds from the north-eastern plains caused much acute discomfort to Vambery and all but the wealthy, over-dressed merchants suffered terribly for a few days. "All the way from Shebesh until we were two stations from Meshed, I had to pass the night in the open air, lying on the hard frozen ground, in the ragged dervish dress which I had on me, and which served the purposes of both pillow and coverlet", commented Vambery bitterly. "Many a time I would not dare to close my eyes for fear of freezing to death. I besought the hard-hearted Afghans to let me have one of their spare horse blankets; with chattering teeth and in a most piteous voice I vainly appealed for hours together to the cruel barbarians bundled up in their warm fur skin cloaks. They only jeered at me, saying, 'Dance, Hadji, and thou wilt get warm'. The high plateaus of Eastern Persia will for ever rank in my memory with the sand of the deserts of Central Asia".

After passing by an austere mountain-top called Kelle Munar (Hill of Skulls), the caravan descended to a somewhat warmer region. Here they reached the first village inhabited by Persians, and Vambery was able to thaw out his frozen limbs in a warm stable.

Meshed was now only a short distance away. It was a fine invigorating autumnal morning when Vambery first caught sight of the city as "it lay there like a rich and glittering gem embedded in a rare setting of leafy verdure". As the gilded dome of the mosque and tomb of the Imam Riza came into view, Vambery's spirits rose ecstatically. He later compared his feelings at this point to those of a shipwrecked sailor anticipating rescue. "Meshed was the place where I was at last to shed the mask of my troublesome incognito", he wrote jubilantly, "and to rid myself of the grinding poverty and the many torments of my dangerous adventures . . . and here I was to meet an enlightened Prince, Governor of the province and the uncle of the apparently Europeanized Shah of Persia. I also hoped to embrace an old friend, the only European here in this part of the Far East . . ."

Meshed was the capital of Khorasan, one of the eleven provinces that made up the Persian empire. It is to this day the holiest city in Iran, and the meeting place for the Shi'ite Moslem followers of Western Asia. Whereas in Bokhara every Shi'ite hoped to be taken for a Sunnite, the reverse was true in Meshed. The shrine of the Imam Riza is by far the most important place in the area. Within the high surrounding walls are several mosques, as well as colleges, libraries, and large halls. Imam Riza, one of the descendants of Mohammed's nephew Ali, became a martyred saint and beloved leader of the Shi'ite sect after he was poisoned in Meshed by the Caliph Mamun the Great in the early ninth century. (The name 'Meshed' means 'place of martyrdom'.)

A dense mass of humanity rolling in an endless stream: pedestrians, men on horseback, loaded camels, mules chained to each other, *kedjeves* (travelling baskets) hanging from their sides from which peered coquettishly half-veiling Persian laides, departing pilgrims with cries of "*Aiaret Kabul!*" (May thy pilgrimage be acceptable!) and "*Iltimasidua!*" (Pray for us!) — all these Vambery saw as he entered the busy streets of the city. "In all this noise", he wrote, "in this cacophony of voices, in this deafening confusion the beggars can only obtain alsm from the pious by almight shouting . . ." Vambery was wary of the green-turbaned *Seids* (descendants of the Prophet) "whose fiery eye can detect any newcomer: they crowd around him and offer him their services . . . People sing, shout, howl; the hot-blooded muleteer from Shiraz curses and hits out wildly at his beast; women and children cry out in fear". Vambery commented wryly: "To our European eyes this deafening chaos and confusion gets worse and worse, we believe ourselves in the utmost danger — yet it all sorts itself out in the end!"

Vambery entered the caravanserai, where he had a perfunctory wash before seeking out Colonel Dolmage, his former acquaintance. On the subject of washing and toilet, Vambery gave very few details (bearing in mind his Victorian readers), but one can deduce that he was covered with many layers of ingrained sand and dirt, and a variety of insects and vermin. His accidental dip in the river Murghab, two months earlier, must have been his only bath in nearly a whole year. *Teyemmum* (washing with sand) was now second nature to him.

After tidying himself a little, he made some discreet inquiries as to where Dolmage could be located and a short while later was standing at his old friend's door. He was to describe in great detail the emotions he felt on this day in his book *Meine Wanderungen und Erlebnisse in Persien* (1867):*

"It is impossible to describe my feelings as I seized the front door knocker in my hand in order to hammer on his door . . ." A servant had no sooner opened the door, when he glanced quickly at the tattered creature facing him and, with a volley of oaths, slammed it in his face. Vambery again knocked hard at the door, and when it was opened a second time he barged his way unceremoniously into the hall.

"Who are you, Hadji? What do you want?" demanded the servant, when he had recovered from his surprise. Vambery demanded to see the Colonel.

"What business have you with my master? Don't you know he is an unbeliever?"

"Believer or unbeliever", Vambery retorted angrily, "go quickly, call your master, and tell him a guest has arrived from Bokhara".

When the servant had gone, Vambery wandered into an adjacent room, where he was immediately struck by the friendly sight of European furniture. "I stopped in front of the tables and chairs", he wrote, "staring at them for a long time with moist eyes . . ." Then he picked up the newspaper lying on the table, the *Levant Herald*, which he read avidly from front page to back. As he put the newspaper down, he saw that Colonel Dolmage had

* "My Wanderings and Experiences in Persia".

177

entered and was now looking silently at the ragged Hadji before him, with searching eyes. Vambery waited in vain for a look of recognition. At length he broke the painful silence by suddenly exclaiming in English, "What, Colonel, do you not recognise me?" On hearing the dervish's voice all uncertainty was dispelled, and Dolmage came over and embraced Vambery, weeping at the sight of his miserable appearance.

Vambery was later to write that this first contact covered Dolmage with a mass of those little animals with which his tattered garments were covered. But the Colonel paid little attention to this as he cried: "For God's sake, what have you been doing? What has happened to you? Vambery found him to be a sympathetic listener as he poured out the story of his recent experiences, remaining till late in the evening.

Colonel Dolmage proved to be a staunch friend to Vambery during the four weeks the latter stayed in Meshed. "Although I dare say I occasioned him no little trouble, I found him unflagging in his zeal for my welfare", wrote Vambery later in a report. "Not only did his kind offices largely contribute to making my stay in Meshed an exceedingly pleasant one but to his generosity and active friendship I was chiefly indebted for the means which enabled me to proceed on my journey with renewed vigour and a cheerful mind". In the 1860s Dolmage was a shadowy figure on the periphery of Persian-British politics. He filled many important offices in Meshed for the Prince-Governor, Sultan Murad Mirza. When Vambery later sent his report to the Academy in Budapest, he elevated Colonel Dolmage to the rank of General. (During the rest of his life, Vambery often elevated the rank of officers and politicians he met, to enhance his own importance.) Vambery's report to Baron Eotvos is significant:

"Your Excellency,   Meshed, December 12? 1863.
You will be able to appreciate my feelings when you will have heard the details of the dangers I was exposed during my journey. ... Today I arrived in good health on Persian soil and am staying in the house of the British *General* Dolmage where for the first time I can hear European sounds again and use European writing. I travelled with twenty-eight *hadjis* to Turkmenia where I stayed three months and from there I travelled across the terrible Hyrcanian desert (twenty-two days, three stinking wells);. We arrived in Khiva, the ruler of which received me well ... I was able to

study the Karakalpak, Ychaudor and Khirgiz dialects. Despite all advice to the contrary I covered ground, travelling from Khiva to Bokhara (on which neither Conolly nor Muravieff had ever set foot before). In Bokhara the Emir in residence and the Emir's chief officer were suspicious of me, but could do me no harm since the Sultan's letter and my linguistic ability enabled to thwart his plans. From here I went on to Samarkand . . .

"I stayed ten days in Samarkand and met the Emir personally and although he was outwardly amiable to me he was inwardly convinced of my being a European and therefore wished to kill me, but the God of the Hungarians did not wish it. When I heard of the danger I was in I escaped on foot, with twenty pounds of luggage, and on the way found a cart which took me to Kerki and then I crossed the Oxus. Here I stayed for twenty-four days as a welcome guest of the Ersari Turkomans until a caravan arrived which went to Herat. We reached the ruins of Herat with great difficulty via Andhkoy, Maimene and Balla Murgab. From here I could have proceeded immediately to the Persian frontier but I did not have two pennies to rub together and since I did not want to seel the valuable Oriental manuscripts I had obtained I had to resort to begging, together with a friend from Khiva, to collect the necessary funds.

"After twelve days we arrived in Meshed. The above-mentioned British officer and the ruling prince welcomed me even more warmly because they had heard that two Europeans had been executed in summer in Bokhara and had thought that one of them had been myself. They supplied me with the necessary travelling expenses and I continued my journey to Teheran.

"So much about my journey; as far as the results are concerned only the future can tell. But I can tell you Excellency now already that *my efforts were crowned with unexpected success.* (Underlinings Vambery's.)

"I was able to decide the Finno-Turkish problem without the shadow of a doubt on the strength of my own experience and on the evidence of my manuscripts.

"My unexpected good fortune enables me to throw a spark of light into the darkness in which the origin of my nation is shrouded; this spark does not yet shine but the future will set it aflame and posterity will not forget the *obscure limping Jew*". (Underlinings again Vambery's.)

"I succeeded because I was able to explore central Asia in

depth . . . If my work can be published in Europe I hope that my efforts will not have been in vain.

"Your Excellency, my noble benefactor, the star from the West beckons already . . . but I would be grateful if the Academy would send me another fifty pieces of gold".

There follows a post script: "I beseech your Excellency to show my report to Balloghi and Toldy" (two Hungarian Orientalists and fellow-members of the Academy).

During the first week of December, Vambery felt he had to recuperate and not to exert himself in any way. After a few days rest he felt much invigorated, and he decided to visit a few of the monuments and curiosities in the city. He first went to the Sahni Sherif (the Holy Vestibule). Here there were many *Seids* who crowded round like out-of-work couriers anxious to receive a few coins for their descriptive orations. Without hesitation they hurried Vambery through into the holy sanctuary, a spot no European was ever allowed to see. Conolly, Burnes, Khanikoff, and other visitors to Meshed had been permitted to view this place only from a safe distance.

After admiring the gold-encrusted monument by the Sahni Sherif and the beautiful Mosque of Gowher Shah, Vambery went next to the refectory of Imam Riza (known locally as Ashbaz Khanei Hazret — the Kitchen of His Holiness). Here all beggars and pilgrims were treated to free board and lodging, on lines not unlike those of the Salvation Army, but for a limit of seven days only. Vambery graphically described the huge machinery of the place: the many baths, caravanserais, bazaars, lodgings, soap manufacture, in short, everything for the cofort of all visitors. He could not resist playing the role of the Hadji again here — even though, as he pointed out, the cuisine of Colonel Dolmage left nothing to be desired. Since Vambery still wore his Bokharan tatters it did not seem strange to anyone to see him crouch down with the rest of the Shi'ite and Sunnite dervishes, plunging his fist into a gigantic dish of the ubiquitous steaming rice, swimming in rancid fat.

Vambery noted that only the true believers were allowed to approach all the holy places: Hindus, Armenians and Jews could not even go near them. Local belief had it that "their eyes, even from a distance of five hundred feet, have a desecrating effect

---

*   Edward Eastwick described some of his exploits in his book *Journal of a Diplomate's Three Years' Residence in Persia* (2 vols., 1864).

. . ." On one occasion in Meshed, Vambery was careless enough to shout after one of his fellow-travellers (from Herat), who he knew to be a Jew, "Yehudi! Yehudi!" This man must have had a nasty shock; he begged Vambery to keep quiet: "For God's sake, Hadji, do not call me Jew here. Beyond these walls I belong to my nation, but here I must play the Moslem".

Around the same time, Vambery's belief in his European superiority showed itself again when he despatched a letter, entrusted to some Afghans on the next Herat-bound caravan, to the young prince Yakub Khan, who had seen through his disguise. "I congratulated him on his perspicacity", wrote Vambery, "and told him that, although not an Englishman, I was next door to one, for that I was a European; that he was an amiable young man, but that I would advise him another time, when any person was obliged by local circumstances to travel incognito through his country, not to seek publicly and rudely to tear off his mask". For this ill-advised show of arrogance Vambery was destined to be taken to task in Europe by his critics who pointed out that by admitting his identity direct to the Afghan Crown Prince, he was endangering the lives of any future incognito travellers in the country.

The other pilgrims in Meshed took Vambery for a genuine native of Bokhara for the costume and language he used and the habit of using 'the dialect of Central Asia' had nearly become second nature to him. In vain did he insist that he was a son of the beautiful Stamboul, he wrote later; the pilgrims always answered shrewdly, "Yes, we know you Bokhariots — here with us you want to change your true colours because you fear revenge in return for your cruelties. But you cannot fool us, we can see through your little game".

"So I was a Bokhariot in Meshed", Vambery commented proudly "and in Bokhara a man from Meshed, and on the journey a Russian, European, or some other mysterious character — what will they make of me next?" He feared that, for once, his skill in languages might land him in serious trouble, but reasoned that "here, where there is at least the shadow of a government", the danger was to be discounted. He looked forward greatly to dropping his disguise. "How my heart beat at the thought that I would soon leave this world of deception and pretence, and travel to the West which — with all its vices and malpractices — is still infinitely superior to the Ancient East . . . towards the West where my fatherland lies, the goal of my wishes, for which I so ardently long . . ."

While Vambery was in Meshed, Colonel Dolmage introduced him to the Prince-Governor, Sultan Murad Mirza, uncle of the Shah. This prince bore the proud sobriquet "Sword of the Empire" owing to his successful campaigns in driving the Turkomans out of this corner of the Persian empire. For many years he had tried to keep the public highways safe from Bokhariot raiders, and to advance and encourage commerce and safe travelling. He listened with interest to the account of Vambery's adventures, and his delight knew no bounds when he learned that his detested and bigoted neighbour, the Emir of Bokhara, had actually let himself be blessed by an unbeliever.

After spending Christmas with Colonel Dolmage, Vambery was ready to leave for the Persian capital. Sultan Murad Mirza loaded him with food and presents, so never again would Vambery be compelled to beg for food. He would be able to act the part of a patrician, with Mollah Ishak now well and truly bewildered by Vambery's activities in Meshed and fraternisation with the 'Frenghi' Colonel. As the two of them said goodbye to Meshed, Ishak was still kept in the dark concerning Vambery's true identity, while he shared a strong horse with all the luggage. Vambery had decided to continue wearing his turban and Oriental clothing.

The route from Meshed due west to Teheran runs via the towns of Nishapur and Shahrud. The journey, 565 miles in length, took in those days an average of twenty-four days.* They passed many small caravans coming the other way, and only a few miles out of Meshed Vambery met an old Persian friend — a native of Shiraz who had shown him around Persepolis fifteen months before. The caravan was obliged to stop while the two men enjoyed a long chat over a *kalian* (Persian pipe).

At the first station, Vambery was jubilant that no longer did he have to gather firewood and pronounce prayers and blessings as payment for his night quarters. "Now, on the contrary, I was a great man," he bragged. "I rode proudly into the *tchaparkhane* (post-house or inn), and with a loud voice called for lodgings; for although I was still completely Oriental, so far as outward appearances went, the postmaster could easily observe that he had to do with one who had at his command a sufficiency of the sinews of

* This road is now the Asian Highway A83, and a vehicle can travel the distance in approximately fourteen hours. The railway from Teheran to Meshed was completed twenty years ago.

war. And what will not a Persian do for money?" He always took pains to point out the greed and avarice of the Persians, as he did with the filth and despicability of the Afghans. "My tartar prepared me an excellent supper; rice, sugar, fat, meat — in a word, everything in abundance".

Well armed and riding a good horse, Vambery now felt for the first time the charms of true travelling. On the third day the plain of Nishapur was reached. The beauty and wealth of the place had declined considerably through the years. Nishapur has two claims to fame: it was the home town of Omar Khayyam, who composed the *Rubaiyat* here 850 years ago. And nearby are the large turquoise mines, which for centuries furnished the world with its chief supply of those beautiful stones.

The route from Nishapur to Shahrud, the principal road to Khorasan, was still subject to periodic attacks from bandits. But Vambery was supremely confident; he threw discretion to the winds. "I rode from station to station with my tartar for my only escort — a journey which no European had ever made before me", he boasted. By this he meant the method of travelling — not the route, which had been used by Europeans on several occasions before him in Persia, but always with a strong escort. "Of course I was warned not to do so. But in my Turkoman dress what cared I for Turkoman robbers? As for my tartar, he looked wistfully around in hope that he might espy a countryman of his". It would have been ironic if Vambery had been wrong in his opinion, and had been seized and carried back to Khiva, which he had been so thankful to leave just six months earlier. The provisions and two fine horses they owned would have been tempting to any passing robbers, even those with a religious frame of mind. The monotonous journey through Khorasan was very exhausting. They were in the saddle from dawn till dusk, and Vambery complained at length about "the terrible distance between each station, especially the last between Mejane and Shahrud . . . when I had to sit sixteen hours in the saddle", i.e. between 2 a.m. and 6 p.m. This discomfort troubled him more than fear of the Turkomans.

Shahrud was an important commercial town lying on the border between Khorasan to the east, and Irak Ajemi (the ancient Media) to the west. Vambery and Ishak were tired out when they finnaly dismounted at one of the principal caravanserais. On looking round Vambery saw, to his great astonishment, "a son of Britain, yes, actually an unmistakable living Englishman, with a genuine John Bull physiognomy, sitting — *alone* — at the door of one of the cells. . . . What was the astonishment of the Briton when he heard a man in the dress of a dervish, with an immense turban on his head, greet him in this distant land with a 'How do you do?' In his amazement his countenance assumed all hues; thrice he exclaimed, 'Well, I . . .', without being able to say more. But alittle explanation rid him of his embarrassment . . ." Vambery became his guest, and spent a day with him and another European, a well-informed Russian, who was acting there as agent for the mercantile house of Kawkaz (Caucasus).

From this man Vambery learned that a large Russian factory was located in one of the caravanserais in Shahrud. "In recent times", Vambery wrote later, "it has almost entirely driven English commerce out of Khorasan . . . From the Gulf of Kamtchatka down to Constantinople, throughout all Asia, the influence which the Russians wield is enormous, and there is none other so threatening as that to the rival interests of Great Britain. Inch by inch they gain upon the ground occupied by the British lion, nor is the time far distant when there must ensue a close and bitter contest".

The Englishman at the caravanserai turned out to be a merchant named Longfield, an agent for a large Lancashire firm, for which he purchased wool and cotton. He had to carry a great deal of money with him, and Vambery was later told that (a few months after this meeting) he was robbed and murdered on the road.

By now Vambery had become "more Iranian than the Iranians". The natives could rarely compete with his high-flown rhetoric. "Flowery compliments", he bragged, "I answered with even greater ones. I did indeed accept presents but invited the donor in flowery language to partake of them and he could not resist my bombastic phrases and frequent quotations from Saadi and other favourite posts . . . truly it is a small work of art to deceive a Persian . . . trained as he is in shrewdness and extreme finesse."

From Shahrud, the capital Teheran was only nine or ten days journey distant. A desolate hilly region had to be traversed, and here the temperature was well below freezing. It was now nearly into the middle of January, and snow lay several feet deep in many places near the road. At one particularly remote lodging-house, a station named Ahuan, a memorable night occured, as Vambery described:

184

"After I had taken my tea and felt a pleasant warmth creeping through my whole body I began to undress. I had thrown myself on my couch, my *pilaff* and roast fowl were almost ready, when, about midnight, through the howling of the wind I heard the tramp of a troop of horsemen. I had scarcely time to jump up from my bed when the whole cavalcade dashed into the court with clashing arms, oaths and shouts. In an instant they were at my door, which was of course bolted". Imperious commands rang out and there were repeated blows on the door. Vambery heard that the "lady of Sipeh Salar, the wife of a general and a princess of royal blood" had just arrived, returning home from a pilgrimage to Meshed with a large retinue of servants and troops. Everyone was ordered to leave their rooms and make way for the royal party. Vambery and Ishak stood fast — they did not want to spend the rest of the night in the freezing sub-zero temperatures outside. On learning from the landlord that the occupier of this room was a Hadji, and a Sunnite — a heretic — too, the troops became incensed and began to use the butt-ends of their guns on the door, crying out "Hadji! take thyself off, or wilt thou have us grind thy bones to meal!"

Vambery began to parley with them through the door, in his best Persian accent. According to his description of the scene, not only was the faithful Ishak dumbfounded but also the soldiers fell back in amazement, for the elegance of the Persian he used completely removed their suspicions that he came from Bokhara. Once again his linguistic prowess was to get him out of a tight spot. "Who art thou, then?" cried the soldiers. "Speak man, it seems thou art no Hadji". With the panache he had faced the Khan of Khiva and the Emir of Bokhara and the melodramatic gestures he reserved for great occasions, Vambery roared out: "Who talks about Hadjis? Away with that abusive word! I am neither Bokhariot or Persian. I have the honour to be a European, and my name is Vambery Sahib!"

The name of European — "that word of terror for Orientals" — produced a magic effect. Terms of abuse were followed by expressions of politeness, menaces by entreaties, as Vambery opened the door to the "trembling Persians". Mollah Ishak, however, who so far had looked upon Vambery as a true believer was pale as a ghost: for the first time he had heard from his Hadji-companion's own lips that he was a European. Glaring wildly, his equanimity was restored by "a sharp side-glance" from Vambery so he tells us. A short while later, with some of the Persian soldiers occupying a corner of the room and snoring like horses, Vambery applied himself to the task of explaining matters to his companion. He found to his agreeable surprise that Ishak, who he nearly always referred to as "my tartar", was quite willing to appreciate his explanations.

Next morning they left the stark snow-clad hills, and came to more cheerful scenery in the plain of Damgan. The small town of Damgan had a bedraggled air with two seedy caravanserais and an empty bazaar. Vambery commented: "Damgan is supposed to be the ancient Hecatompylae (city with the hundred gates). If we reduce the hundred gates to twenty, it will still remain a matter of considerable difficulty to discover a city of over twenty gates in the obscure spot now called Damgan". He added: "Of course, one must make large deductions from all assertions made by either Greeks or Persians, who rival each other in the noble art of bragging and exaggerating", a characteristic that Vambery had also developed. He spent a few hours here, observing scornfully that "the strange thing is that the ladies have been made martyrs or holy women in Damgan, where the lack of chastity have earned them quite a reputation."

Damgan was the spot where, over two thousand years before, Alexander the Great had found the dying King Darius in a pool of blood, after laying waste his great Persian empire. Vambery was now travelling — in reverse — on exactly the same route that Alexander had used in 331 B.C. during his great conquests.

On the road to Teheran — via Lazgird, Dahnemek, and over the Chavar pass (believed to be the famous Caspine Pylae of antiquity) — Vambery's tartar grew frightened, for, he said, there were still robbers about, as there always had been since ancient times. The reverberating echoes made the path more eerie. "I saw the impression (made by this scenery) reflected in the features of my tartar", Vambery bragged later, "as we crossed the region quite alone, my weapons in my hand, and meeting (along the road) many a suspicious character ..." There were no ambushes, however, and soon they entered the fertile plain of Veramin (where stood in ancient times the legendary city of Raghes, known also as Rhagae or Rei).

Vambery wanted to speed up the last lap of his journey although he considered a ride of over thirteen hours at one go extremely tiring. Looking forward to being soon at a place where he could rest for two months, and building castles in the air, he rode on lustily from morning to late at night. At last, with dusk approaching, the two of them sighted Teheran, with its glittering cupola of Shah Abdul Azim in the distance. But just as the sun was setting, they took a wrong turning, and the next few hours saw them scrambling furiously among noxious swamps and ditches. Like some terrible dream, Vambery found himself continuously deposited by his horse in freezing murky water up to his hips. "Then again we became entangled in a maze of gardens and enclosures", he despaired, "until at last, late in the night, we contrived to find our way back to the right road".

But all personal discomfort paled in comparison to a new unexpected misfortune, as he recounted bitterly: "Is it not remarkable that no serious accident had marred the success of my journey up to this very moment? Unharmed I had roamed in distant and pathless deserts; I had been able to save my property and above all my manuscripts — the precious prize and reward of all my toils — in spite of most imminent dangers; and yet here, on the very threshold of my abode of rest, at the gates of that spot which my imagination had pictured to me as the land of promise, a most serious mishap befell me. I lost through the immersion one of the manuscripts so highly valued by me. The Oriental is right, after all, in saying that Fate has her caprices, and it is childish to attempt to battle against them! . . ."

When Vambery and Ishak finally arrived at the gates of Teheran after midnight, they found everything barred and shut. They were forced to sink down exhausted and spend the rest of the night at a small caravanserai outside the gates. Vambery gives a swashbuckling picture of himself the next morning on entering the Persian capital:

". . . In riding through the crowded bazaar, midst oaths and clamour, I heard many a Persian remark with surprise and indignation, 'Is not that an impudent Bokhariot!' I fell in, also, during my progress through the streets, with several Europeans who, owing to my strange costume, did not recognize me at first, but later on received me most cordially. I finally came up to the gate of the Turkish Embassy, and my joy was indescribably at finding myself again near the place of my departure and to the same old friends of whom I had taken leave ten months ago, full of uncertain and fantastic plans which had since assumed shape and reality. Those good friends then thought I was boldly engaging in a venture which was sure to prove fatal to me, and at this very moment they supposed that, in my person, another name had been added to the long list of victims to the ferocity and perfidy of Central Asia".

The date was 20 January 1864, and Vambery had travelled well over three thousand miles successfully disguised as a dervish — yet failing completely to grasp this role.

In his eyes a dervish was a cross between a beggar and a madman — at best a humbug.

He had no time for mystics of any description and the dervishes were *Sufis*, the mystics of Islam.

Accustomed, however, to wear from early youth "alternately the mask of Jew, Christian and Moslem" he "prayed, shouted, groaned and raved in pious contrition with the best of them", but — as he wrote candidly — "I lacked the inner faith and it only had a tiring effect on me".

He remained an eternal outsider and a none too sympathetic observer. Privileged to take part in some of the secret rituals and watch feats achieved in a state of trance, he described them as mumbo-jumbo, comparable to medieval belief in witchcraft. What would he make of the scientific twentieth-century explanation which described the remarkable faculty of the human brain to inhibit pain under certain conditions "allowing the martyrs to die happily . . . their minds . . . fixed firmly on the glory of God"?

And although at times he envied the dervishes' state of inner peace and quiet, to him the roads of inner harmony were blocked.

In the beginning his dominant emotion had been fear. He had thought it good policy to make himself agreeable to everyone in the caravan. Often he would dismount giving up his seat to a poorer hadji on foot, and, mix with the others so that, caught up in their conversation, he forgot the dangers of his undertaking; soon he claimed to be able to make puns in their language which made them all laugh heartily.

His tactics soon paid off and he gained the goodwill of his companions, yet at night fear would return. He was so afraid of giving himself away by gesticulating in his sleep (a thing frowned on in Central Asia) that, under some pretext, he would strap his arms down tightly.

He was also afraid of a big meal late at night, for fear of talking in his sleep "in some foreign European language", although he later laughed at himself: who would have understood it? But he could not afford to take chances. At first his companions had watched his every word and gesture, one of them even remarking that his *snoring* sounded different. This unwise *hadji* had been silenced with the words: "Yes. And that is how they snore in Constantinople . . ."

He was afraid even alone in his tent, or even at a considerable distance from the caravan. "I did not dare to eat unleavened bread, mixed with ashes or sand", he wrote, "or to have a draught of the stinking water without accompanying it with the customary Mahometan formulas of blessing . . . The distant hills appeared to me like so many spies . . . which were watching whether I had broken the bread in the proper ritualistic manner and whether I was saying the *Bismillah* . . ."

And not only the distant hills were watching; the way he performed his ritual ablutions, five times a day, was closely scrutinised. "The hairs on the arms of the *Sunni* Moslems tended to grow towards the palms of their hands" (as a consequence of these frequent ablutions), wrote Vambery, tongue-in-cheek; with the *Shi'ites* it was the exact opposite. When they saw Vambery's arms however, they marvelled. "They discovered that my hairs neither inclined upwards nor downwards but grew all around my arm". 'A remarkable Mussulman that!', exclaimed the Bokhariots, 'An unknown race!' and he claimed to have been regarded by many as an "Islamic abortion".

Vambery learnt to consult "the oracle of sticks and stones" and was considered a great divine; he claimed to have learnt to control "blushing and paling" though it seems far more likely that a thick layer of dirt, sand and a deep tan hid any change of colour than that he had learnt to control his autonomous nervous system, for the dirt "collected in the seams of my face formed quite a crust" his beard had grown rugged and coarse, his eyes rolled wildly and his gait had become "as unwieldly, waddling and uncomfortable as if I had lived from early youth with Mongol and Turkish tribes . . .", as lumbering as that of a camel.

His companions thought this noble effendi and pious *Hadji* a great success on foraging expeditions; he scored his greatest triumph with the fierce Tekke Turkomans, approaching them with gifts of *Zemzen* (miracle-working) water, toothpicks and the like", and returning not only with "wheat, rice, cheese and pieces of felt" but getting one of the fearsome nomads "to lead his own donkey with this harvest and take it to our astonished caravan".

He loved the stillness of the desert nights, the tinkling camel bells and plaintive songs which would rise to the heavens, intoned first by the master and then taken up by his servants. Vambery would fall behind, or ride on ahead, "measuring the time this source of pleasure would last by the course of the Pleiades in the heavens".

He grows quite lyrical in his description of night or sunrise in the desert (with the *Muezzin's* call to prayer), and of the haunting greetings exchanged by two carvans meeting in the middle of nowhere. ("May thy pilgrimage be accepted").

Pilgrimages he found full of interest but was sceptical of pilgrims. He compared the pilgrimage to Mount Ararat to a cure at Karlsbad,* "merry and gay. Devout servants of God, keepers of fountains, providers of lodgings, publicans, owners of coffee-houses, entertainers and prostitutes add up the season's takings . . ."

He greatly enjoyed the ovations accorded for the home-coming pilgrims and the respect accorded the *hadjis* but complained bitterly of their nauseating food "swimming in mutton fat . . . And for the delectation of his Victorian readers he gave a recipe from "Chinese Tartary", of a dish called "Mantuy", "a sort of pudding filled with hashed meat mixed with fat and spices", prepared over steam in what sounds like the ancestor of the pressure cooker.

He detested travelling in the *Khedjves* (the baskets hanging from either side of the camel) "stinking of sweat and sores" in the intolerable heat; while commiserating with the plight of the often overloaded camels, he complained their "anti-social habit" of "suddenly leaping into the air and shedding the wooden cage together with the traveller . . ."

He complained of the "jerky trot" of a heavily-laden mule and hated even more travelling by wooden cart with unevenly hewn wheels in central Asia. ("This mode of transport . . . made me extremely seasick in the first few hours . . . one must be equipped with the sinews of a Tartar to get off without cuts or bruises . . ."

Vambery thought a horse better than a donkey. ("Those that bellow loudest come from Bokhara and the most modest donkeys I know are indisputably from foggy England . . .")

* Karlovy Vary.

On the whole — and surprisingly for someone so convinced of European cultural superiority — he liked the leisurely way of travel in the East. "Whoever has experienced the charm of an Oriental journey will agree with me that no camel, horse or mule is so tiring and bad for one's nerves as our railway journeys ... whether by express train between London and Liverpool or on the most miserable train of the Austrian railway ..."

Vambery could always turn a situation to his own advantage. At Kerki, for example, where the governor employed a dervish to call out 'Ya Hu! Ya Hakk!' "from sunset till the break of day, and that with the voice of a stentor", he was able "when the enthusiastic bawler's voice weakened towards dawn" to calculate the distance to daybreak without stepping out of the cell in which he lay ...

But his best effort was doubtless many years later when he gave a widely advertised talk to a group of Hungarian clerics at Sopron. He entitled it: "A dervish is only half a man — a Hungarian clergyman is a whole man" (for he fulfills a social function).

The talk was greatly applauded.

It was left to a latter-day Vambery to describe what life in a harem was like. He visited the summer palace at Shirbudun. The Emir had about twenty bedrooms "now to one, now to another of which he constantly migrated in great secrecy as precaution against assassination, just as ... the Sultans of Constantinople were wont to do".

The specially decorated bedroom in which he used to receive his favourite wife ... (had) ... walls covered with heavy silk carpets ... the ceiling was of juniper and rosewood ... the floor is inlaid with beautifully preserved mosaic patterns in blue and gold.

"A touch of the hidden spring ... and it discloses a secret stair ... A number of small peepholes enabled an observer to spy upon the scene below. While the women of his household were amusing themselves with games, the Emir would watch unseen and make his choice ...

"Next to the private mosque was the ladies' bath ... a neighbouring room is provided with peepholes through which again the Emir could secretly observe his women while they bathed ...

"In the labyrinth the Emir used to play at chasing the beauties whom he had selected from the bath ... If report speaks true it was the dream of every inmate of the harem to hear the eunuchs summons to the labyrinth — because every opportunity of intimacy with the Emir spelt jewels and privileges, and might provide the first step towards the coveted position of favourite".

PART 3

Dervish
of
Distinction

9

HOMECOMING

Flushed with triumph, his bags stuffed with books and with a Tartar who had never seen the West in tow Vambery arrived in Budapest.

He had had a triumphal acclaim in Teheran, welcomed with outstretched arms by the European colony who were happy to see him back safe and sound. It had been a long time since any news had been received from him and the colony had been buzzing with rumours. In fact the last missives received from him had been from Gomushtepe, on the fringe of the Turkoman desert and that had been at the outset of his journey. Little else had been received from him but he now had the satisfaction of finding his sparse letters tidily kept at the Turkish Embassy. Hidden in the wool of his Bokhariot dress as well were other scraps of paper on which he had made his notes, relying for the rest on his remarkable powers of recall.

The wildest rumours had been circulating in Teheran about his fate: he had been made a prisoner by the Turkomans; he had been sold into slavery; executed by the Khan of Khiva; tortured by the Emir of Bokhara. One thing had been certain in people's minds: he had come to a sticky end. This was confirmed by the fact that some pilgrims, returning from Central Asia, who swore he had been taken prisoner and suffered a horrible death in Bokhara. As it turned out they had mistaken him for a member of Signor Meazza's trade mission, Italian silk merchants, who had been trying to do business with the bloodthirsty Emir and who had been reputed to have been executed (as it happened, they were later discovered alive and well). And in fact Vambery writes that some had seen him hanging by his feet; others had been eye-witnesses when the executioner had quartered him and thrown his limbs to the dogs ... The European colony had swallowed the horror stories, hook, line and sinker, and could hardly believe their eyes "when they saw the gay and lively young Hungarian of former days so changed and fallen off" — alive to tell the tale.

The Europeans were delighted to see him and "young and old alike, diplomats and craftsmen" rushed to fling their arms around him, for "with the indisputable marks of excessive suffering upon me, everyone's sympathy went out to me". In short, he was lionised. Among the avalanche of invitations to "festive dinners" and the like which descended upon Vambery from all sides, was an invitation to dine at the "English Legation". His host was Charles Alison, British Minister in Teheran; no doubt much to Vambery's pleasure, he was asked to give an account of his travels and found an attentive and appreciative audience. But something far more important happened and, in Vambery's own words, "largely influenced my further career": Alison gave him official recommendations to Lord Palmerston, Lord Strangford, Sir Justin Sheil, Sir Henry Rawlinson and to many other politicians and scientists of note in London. Though initially impelled by linguistic curiosity alone, the foundations for his meteoric rise to fame had been laid.

But it was not only the British Legation that was anxious to invite so distinguished a traveller. Russia, the nineteenth century rival of England, was not idle and so Vambery was summoned by von Giers, the Russian ambassador in Teheran; during the audience the ambassador conjured up the picture of a brilliant career in Russia — Vambery's Turkoman experiences would be of use in St. Petersburg. But Vambery felt that "all the treasures and all the glory of the Czar's dominions" would never help him to overcome his dislike of Russia, ". . . the oppressor of my fatherland . . . and the personification of despotism and unbridled absolutism". He thus told the Russian ambassador point-blank, he claims, that he could not live under so autocratic a regime as the Russian and that a career in Russia, however glamorous, would be incompatible with his nationality and clash with his own freedom-living political views. He accepted the introductions given him by the British with all the more readiness, "for this nation, with its glorious literature and liberal ideas, had long since become dear to me"; moreover he found them "the only worthy representatives of the West" in Asia — a belief he was to harbour his whole life and for which he was to struggle with pen and persuasion, in lectures and innumerable letters to *The Times* against the, often very real, threat of Russia.

On 3 February 1864 Charles Alison reported home to the British Foreign Secretary, Earl Russell (who was destined to succeed Palmerston as Prime Minister the following year):

"During the year 1862 I made the acquaintance of an Orientalist of some distinction, Mr. Vambery, who was then making preparations for a journey to Bokhara, Khiva, Khokand and Samarkand in the disguise of a mendicant. Among other things Mr. Vambery took an interest in the fates of those Europeans who have preceded him in this perilous enterprise and which formed the subject of our conversation before his departure; that of Lieut. Wyburd was not unknown to him and Your Lordship will observe from the inclosed copy of a letter addressed to me by Mr. Vambery since his return that he has no information to impart on that painful subject".

Vambery's letter is dated 1 February, and his English is still a little less than perfect. It reads:

"Excellency!

The mentioned details on the two unhappy Europeans arrested by order of the Emir of Bokhara I have the honour to present to Your Excellency as follows.

It was about the midst of July when I arrived in Bokhara. Two days after my arrival I heard that two Italians, who came from Orenbourg with the purpose to buy a great quantity of silk, had been taken prisoner by the first Vezir of the Emir, himself being at the same time in the campaign of Khokand. Several false rumours spread out by the treacherous Government reported that the Feringhee had brought fifteen cases of tea, moistened with diamond water, to poison the inhabitants of the very sainted town. Another told that they made night day and day night — yet a third related that they were English spies and that the Russian Government gave the counsel of their arresting".

These Italians were members of a trade mission who had gone to Bokhara to obtain the eggs of the silkworm and, according to a report put out by the Russian Embassy and believed by the Royal Geographical Society, they had been killed. (The Emir had said that they must be Englishmen, for there were no other Europeans except Englishmen and Russians, and so they had executed.)

Vambery's letter continued: "Rahmet Bey, the mentioned Vezir, wrote to the Emir for further orders and he received the resposal to confiscate the 8,000 Tillas they brought with (them) and to arrest at the same time the 4 Nogai Mussulmen (Russian subjects) who accompanied them ... According to the ... Firman of the Emir their money and effects were brought from the Kervanserai Redjeb, their former lodging, to the Ark (Palace of the Emir); they received better treatment and it was settled they shall stay in a Balakhaneh and receive every day once a pillau & twice tea with bread. This all I heard from Rahmet Bey himself and confirmed by the servant, a man of Persian origin ...

"Judging after this behavior of the Emir I would believe they shall not be killed if Russian intrigues dont change the situation of the Tartarian Prince. I hope not the least success from the Mission of the two Sheikhs of Constantinople. Turkey makes this step only to please Europe. The Sublime Porte knows very well that the Princes of Turkestan, like that of Morocco, have only a verbal respect for the religious supremacy of the Sultan".

It already becomes clear how useful Vambery's knowledge of languages was for the British Foreign Office in a climate of intrigue, where rumours and denials were spreading like wildfire. It would eventually make Vambery a rich man in the years to come. However at this juncture he was obliged to admit failure, galling to a man of his temperament.

"I seize at the same time the occasion to announce to Your Excellency", he continued, "that I could not discover any trace nor hear a single word of the unhappy Captain Wyburd whose unknown fate Your Excellency deigned to call to my attention before my starting to Central Asia. It is true the very strong incognito I kept during my journey forbade me strictly to question on the lot of any Feringhee or Christian, but my ears were always open to news concerning my coreligionists and it was by secret inquiry that I saw several Russian captives and took notice of an unfortunate German, a watchmaker, who lived some years at Bokhara and was killed by order of Emir Nasroolah. I was also reported (to) on the fate of a young Englishman (name?) about 24 years old, who came from Baghdad via Herat to Bokhara, passed from here through Samarkand to Khokand where he was murdered by order of Mahomed Ali Khan involved at that time in war with China (25 years before). A Khokhandian who saw him before his imprisonment related to me that the young Feringhee was of a beautiful exterior and a very clever man. He wished to go from Khokhand to

198

Kashgar, which intention gave suspicion that he will make guns for the Governor of Chinese Tartary, and that was the reason of his death".

Was this the unfortunate Lieut. Wyburd?

"As for the lamentable death of Conolly and Stoddart I am sorry I cannot add any important details to those which the late Revd. Dr. Joseph Wolff had delivered to the English public. The papers & effects of these two martyrs came into possession of Abdool Samed Khan, a Persian by origin, and Sirdar Kool ... Chief Commandant of the late Emir, and after the execution of this officer these relics are kept in the Defter Khaneh (archives) of Samarkand. This I am told but did not witness.

"Your Excellency's high reputation on oriental matters and policy, even in the remotest part of Asia, dispenses me from further explanation. I finish these lines having the honor to be yrs. A. Vambery

Member of the Hungarian Academy".

He stayed three months in Teheran and rested. During this time, while the impressions of his journey were still fresh in his mind, he worked on the notes he had secretly taken — the odd scraps of paper hidden in the wool of his Bokhariot dress, written furtively with the stump of a pencil in Turkish (and not in Hungarian, as he claimed). He completed and supplemented them with information he had stored in his prodigious memory and began to map out a systematic account of his travels, hoping to find a publisher in England. At this stage this hope was just one more of his "delightful castles in the air", with no real idea of what his future career would be. He was sure that he had explored regions in Asia "which no European before me had ever set eyes on" — perhaps his fertile imagination magnified their number — he did have the satisfaction of hearing later in London, however, that at least on part of his journey he had indeed broken new ground.

He was dubious about his literary accomplishments. He thus had not made up his mind in which language to write of his travels, but he dreamt of "European fame and honour ... (which would) ... secure for me a position in life, but of what nature this position was to be I knew not, and cared not". But he wanted to be off: "first go home to Hungary and report myself to the Academy at Pest, and then place the account of my wanderings before the European public". He had to wait until spring

Meanwhile Vambery sent off a report to Baron Eotvos; written in Teheran on 5 February 1864 it arrived on 6 April.

Only now did he acknowledge the 43 pieces of gold he had received from the Academy the preceding year.

A negligible sum! "How I suffered can only be understood if one reads the memoirs of Conolly Sandor (Alexander) although he had hundreds of thousands of pounds from the Government".

And he emphasises his sufferings: "Although I came from humble origins I would never have believed I would be obliged to dress in such rags and sleep on the earth . . . Crossing the Oxus the camel looked back and so did I the Oxus reminded me of our Danube . . ."

He told the Baron that his European features had been recognised in Bokhara but that the dervishes had sworn he was a true dervish "whom they took over directly from the hands of the Ambassador of the Great Turkish Sultan"; they were ready to die for their guest.

He informed him that he had stayed five weeks in Bokhara and had studied the libraries there, and then left for Samarkand. "In the south it was not so dangerous for me as I had survived Bokhara . . ." He remained 10 days in Samarkand, inspecting the antiquities "which are overvalued in Europe".

On his return journey he had found it extremely difficult to convince people that he was a dervish.

The main reason for his journey was, he repeats, research into the origin of the Hungarian language and the history of the Magyars.

Hungarian belonged to the Turco-Tartar group of languages, he wrote, for the affinity with Hungarian grew the further east one travelled, and he gave the Baron a detailed explanation of his linguistic theories.

He stressed the dangers he had faced, referring obliquely to "lands where it needs courage to ask a question and where to write things down is a mortal sin" and ending with a patriotic flourish: he was a Hungarian and only his will power had enabled him to carry out his journey.

To a traveller from Bokhara (which in 1864 was 60 days away from Teheran) the Persian capital seemed like Paris. He thought he was back in civilisation and marvelled at the European goods he saw. "My first ride through the Bazaar, after my arrival, made me feel like a child again. Almost with the eagerness of my Tartar companion, my delighted eyes were wandering over articles of luxury from Europen, toys, stuffs and cloths which I saw exhibited there". His travels, he felt, had turned him into half a Tartar himself; the role he had played with such skill now seemed to have become second nature with him. (This was to plague him for some time to come). But not only his outward appearance, his face tanned deeply by scorcing sun and desert wind, his loss of weight had changed him: his salutations, gesticulations, gait, and above all "my mode of viewing things in general" became an object of mirth for his European friends: they teased him unmercifully. Vambery was amused by this good-natured ribbing but there were other things he now found difficult to adjust to. Above all, there was the European "close-fitting dress", which seemed to hamper his movements, accustomed as he had become for so long to wearing the loose-fitting ample, dervish dress. And then there was the problem of hair: he had worn his head shaved (as a precaution against lice) and now found that "the shaved scalp was ill at ease under the burden of hair . . ." Nevertheless it afforded him "a secret pleasure to . . . admire the proud and manly bearing of fellow Europeans". It presented such a gratifying contrast to the slovenly and slouching gait of the Central Asiatics . . ."

When his adventures became more widely known in Teheran his Moslem friends and acquaintances could not contain their surprise, for though *Ketman* — the art of dissimulation allowed by Islam — it had never before happened "that a European should have acquired such a degree of excellence in this peculiarly Eastern art . . . (it) . . . seemed to them incomprehensible". But all the more admirable, for had not their arch-enemies, the Sunni Turkomans had taken in?

They soon plied him with a thousand questions. For although the steppes of Turkestan lay just beyond the Persian border, the tribes that inhabited it were wild and rapacious, forever engaged in man-stealing *alamans* (raids). No man, woman or child was safe and many a Persian had ended up in the slave market, to be ransomed for as high a price as possible. Little wonder therefore that bloodcurdling tales circulated among the Persians, so few had returned to tell the tale. What really happened inside Turkestan? Had Vambery seen any captives? Had they been in chains? Had they been inhumanly treated, kept without food and drink? Had whole families been separated, mothers and daughters, fathers and sons sold separately into slavery? Could you trust a Turkoman to free a slave after ransom was paid? Vambery did his best to reply.

He was invited by several ministers and even had the distinction conferred upon him, he writes ironically, of being presented to his Majesty, Nasr-ed-din, in the garden of the Palace, and was invited to tell the story of his adventures. One imagines Vambery nonchalantly seated in a rose garden, fragrant with the scent of flowers, alive with the song of nightingales and the occasional strident cry of a peacock, with fountains playing and attentive lackeys serving cooling sherbet — was this not the very stuff his dreams had been made of back in Kecskemet? He seems to have slipped back into his European skin, for, in his own words, he "acquitted himself of this task" with no little vivacity and presumably his usual panache. The ministers who graced the interview were in fact quite dumbfounded with the coolness he exhibited (as he was afterwarde told) and could scarcely recover from their astonishment that he had been able to endure without trembling the looks of a sovereign "whose least glance strikes terror into the heart of the boldest mortal".

Nasr-ed-din Shah (whom Vambery was to meet much later again in Europe) seems to have been pleased with Vambery's travelogue for he later sent him the "Order of the Lion and the Sun" and what was more to the purpose, a valuable Persian shawl. The insignia of this order consisted of a plain piece of silver, "but the rapacity of the minister, so characteristic of the court of Teheran", Vambery adds furiously, "confiscated the shawl, worth at least fifty ducats, for his own benefit". In fact, according to Vambery, corruption and bribery were rife at the court of Teheran: "Everyone in the country, lies, cheats and swindles".

Vambery awaited the advent of spring with equanimity. He found his stay pleasant. Had not the European colony made themselves as agreeable to him as possible? What is more, he could count on his fame travelling on ahead of him, for the "embassies did not fail to acquaint their respective governments with my remarkable adventures", as he so modestly declared: ". . . I was quite astonished at the ado made about my performance; nor could I well comprehend the extraordinary importance attached to my dervish trick", which, he claims, 'was more like a comedy brought to a prosperous end".

Understandably he was "not a little proud" to leave Teheran

"provided with letters of recommendation to the principal statesmen of England and France". For, when all is said and done, the
success of his venture was entirely due to his own efforts: from
early youth on he had learnt in a hard school that he could rely on
no one else but himself alone.

With his great talent for making friends with the most dispar-
ate characters he now struck up a friendship with an eccentric
compatriot, a fellow Hungarian whom circumstances had
washed up in Teheran. This man, a tailor by his calling, lured by
adventure had travelled all over Central Asia and India on foot
and was just about to set out for distant China when news of the
Hungarian uprising of 1848 reached him and, like the good patriot
he was, he immediately decided to leave for home and enlist. He
had barely reached Constantinople when he heard of the Hungarian defeat at Villagos. The revolution was over. There was now
no point in continuing his journey, so he retraced his steps and
came to rest in Teheran. This Mr. Szantos took a great liking to
Vambery: they swapped travellers' tales, the former speaking in
"a perfect farrago . . . of Hungarian, German, French . . . (and)
. . . a still more confusing mass of Turkish, Arabic, Persian and
Hindustani words" roundly condemned the Austrians, who, without the aid of the Czar, might not have won.

When Szantos heard of Vambery's impending departure "he
insisted upon my accepting a pair of pantaloons of his own handi-
work, although his circumstances were rather straitened. As I
could not be induced to accept his gift, he persuaded my Tartar to
take it". Mollah Ishak, the faithful Tartar, laughed at first at what
seemed to him a ridiculous garment, a "forked skirt", but then
curiosity prevailed and he put them on: the tailor "was beside himself with delight and pride as having been the first tailor who had
put a Tartar into a pair of European trousers".

He also met another European with whom he could swap stories: this was M. de Bloqueville the Shah's Court photographer
who had been commanded to follow the Persian army on a puni-
tive expedition against the Turkomans. "The 25,000 Rustems
were attacked by 5000 Turkomans", writes Vambery sarcastically, "and shamefully defeated". Bloqueville had had the misfortune to be taken captive and to be sold into slavery: he had been
ransomed for the exorbitant price of 10,000 ducats — "ordinary"
Persians could be ransomed for five to six ducats — after negotiations lasting for one and a half years, prodded by French bayonets.

This man could fully sympathise with the physical hardships Vambery had suffered.

Even though Vambery may have considered the dervish chapter closed, his fame as a wonder-working *Mollah* (priest) was still fresh in the minds of the Turkomans. Some of them happened to be at Astrabad on business and heard that he was in Teheran. They travelled to the capital without delay, called on him in a body, beseeching him for his *fatiha* (blessing) and assuring him that these blessings had worked wonders in the past and that the people in Gomushtepe often wished to have him back. Vambery received them in European dress: they do not appear to have been in the slightest way disturbed, quite on the contrary, they reverently bowed down before him, he tells us, "while I gave each of them a blessing, citing at the same time a few verses from the Koran". These were the last people, he adds, to whom he gave a blessing and this was the last occasion as well on which he performed spiritual functions of the kind.

But *Sheitan* (the Moslem devil) was ready with another temptation for him. "My imagination caught fire at the idea of religious fame" (as it had caught fire at the idea of heading an army of 5000 Turkomans). He dreamt of the things he might achieve among the untutored Children of the Desert, if I had only the will and courage to dare. Such is usually the way in which Oriental heroes commence their career . . ." He was off again on a flight of fancy, momentarily back again under the cherry-tree of Nyek . . .

As soon as the weather was good Vambery left Teheran for Trebizond and the Black Sea, via Tebriz and Erzerum, the same route he had come. Only now he travelled with a difference, no longer full of "anxiety, apprehension and uncertainty", but filled with "joy and delightful anticipation". As he had done on his journey from Meshed to Teheran, he travelled in style, now having been provided with an even better horse, had more funds at his disposal and was treated accordingly. Gone were the greenhorn days: his body was now inured to fatigue and he ound the journey child's play. His triumphant arrival in Tebriz was Teheran all over again. His European friends were all over him, genuinely delighted to see him back. "Warm welcomes, banquets, laudations and undisguised appreciation of my adventure were my greeting. Swiss, French, Germans, English, and Italians — all were proud that a lame European had actually been among the kidnapping Turkomans and the wildly fanatical Central Asiatics and glad that through his discoveries this hitherto obscure portion of the Old World was brought within the reach of Western lands".

From Teheran Vambery had sent an account of his journey to the President of the Hungarian Academy; the various European diplomats had not only informed their Governments about Vambery's activities but had informed various newspapers as well. His fame had indeed preceded him, as he was to find out.

He reached the Persian frontier in high spirits, cracking jokes with his Tartar companion along the road. Before he entered the town of Trebizond he paused awhile at a spot in the Pontic mountains from where the Black Sea was visible, gazing with unalloyed pleasure upon the coast line "upon which I had turned my back with so many strange misgivings two years ago this very month". From this vantage point he could see the flag of the Lloyd steamer fluttering in the breeze: the sight filled him with euphoria. "To reach a harbour where a ship road at anchor ready to start, was the same thing as to reach Europe". The amenities of a "splendid and commodious cabin on board the Lloyd steamer" awaited him and despite the several days' voyage still separating him from Europe, he felt he was home again.

His stay in Trebizond was short. In two days he had disposed "of the larger part of my equipment for Eastern travel", for which he now had no further use, ". . . retaining only a few articles as relics and keepsakes of my roaming".

His first stop was at Constantinople. He was enchanted by the city: "After the howling wilderness of Central Asia" it seemed to him full of sophistication and delight and its inhabitants far superior to their co-religionaries in remote Turkestan. Even their features seemed more European than Asiatic to him.

His fame had preceded him and the European colony welcomed him with open arms, commiserating with him over the "great fatigues I had undergone during my travels".

His first call was on the Austrian Ambassador Count Prokesch-Osten, whom he had met before and who now received him with great cordiality. As Vambery tells the story, the Count gazed at him silently for a few moments without recognising him, so weather-beaten and emaciated had he become; but Vambery, never at a loss, addressed him in German, whereupon the ambas-

sador nearly burst into tears, saying: "For heaven's sake, Vambery, what have you done? What has become of you?" Vambery proceeded to give him an abbreviated account of his travels and adventures" and the good old man, moved to the inmost of his noble heart, tried to persuade me ... to stay a few days in his house, in order to recover my strength ..." before going on to Pest. But Vambery politely declined: he was impatient to return home. He listened attentively to all the advice the ambassador had to give him concerning his next steps in Europe. Vambery mentioned London — this was the advice he had been given in Teheran. "You do quite right to go straight forward to London", said the Count; "England is the only country full of interest for the geography and ethnography of Inner Asia". He assured him that he would find a good reception there, adding a few words of paternal advice: "... You must not forget to style accordingly the account of your travels. Keep yourself strictly to the narrative of your adventures; be short and concise in the description; and particularly abstain from writing a book with far-fetched argumentation or with philological and historical notes".

How right the old Count was and how little Vambery was able to stick to his advice!

Vambery also called on the Grand-Vizier, Ali Pasha who, only a few years back, had lent him rare and valuable manuscripts from his library. It was the story of his meeting with the Old Austrian Count all over again. Ali Pasha was only able to recognise in him the former Reshid Effendi, Vambery tells us, because he had been announced — in fact, on his way to the interview, walking from the European sector in Pera to the old part of Constantinople he had passed many of his former acquaintances ... without being recognised by them. The same had happened as he walked through the corridors of the Sublime Porte.

He was also warmly received by Ali Pasha who wanted to know all about "the hitherto closed districts of inner Asia": he felt that his work had been appreciated and was also proud to be able to report to him first-hand on the political conditions of Persia and Central Asia, as observed by him. Ali Pasha too tried to induce Vambery to stay in longer in Constantinople, but again, he politely declined, in a hurry to be off and board the Danube steamer.

When he arrived at the harbour (at Fyndykly) he steeled himself to dismiss Mollah Ishak, the faithful Tartar, who had become

Vambery on his return in Hungarian national dress, wearing a medal.

a real friend and who was there waiting for him. This man who had never been outside his native Turkestan had decided, out of devotion to Vambery, to follow him as far as Constantinople: from thence he was to continue on his *hadj* to Mecca. From Khiva to the Bosporus he had never left Vambery's side and when Vambery prepared to "say a final good-bye to the sincere and honest young man, who had shared with me all the fatigues and privations of my dangerous journey homewards from the banks of the Oxus and who had really become like a brother to me", he felt genuinely upset. Handing him over nearly all his ready cash and keeping only enough to pay for his food until his arrival in Budapest, he further gave him all his clothes, his equipment, made him a long farewell speech and advised him on how he was to conduct himself on his way to Mecca and on his return journey to Khiva, opening his arms wide to embrace him a last time — then the Tartar "burst out in a torrent of tears and said: 'Effendi! Forgive me, but I cannot separate from you'". And, to Vambery's amazement, Mollah Ishak began to explain that while seeing the holy places was certainly a worthy objective and the sight of the Prophet's tomb worth a whole life he just could not bear to leave him, to travel on alone: he was ready to renounce all the delights of this world and even of paradise and quite prepared never to see his home again — but he could not leave Vambery.

What was Vambery to do? He was thunderstuck. (Or at least, so he pretended.) All he could find to say was: "My dear friend, do you know that I am going to country of unbelievers, to *Frengistan*, where the climate, the water, the language, the manners and customs of the different people will be utterly strange to you . . . and where . . . (you) . . . will have to remain eventually without any hope of revisiting again in your life your paternal seat in Khiva". He bade him consider well what he was doing, "for repentance will be too late, and I should not like to be the cause of your misfortune". The Tartar stood there, pale and dejected, "the great struggle in his soul being noticeable only by the fiery rolling of his eyes", but finally he burst out into the following words: "Believer or unbeliever, I care not which, wherever you go I go with you. Good men cannot go to bad places". In the midst of all this the ship's bell suddenly started to ring furiously and "the time for further consideration and argumentation was gone". Vambery picked up his bags and motioned the Tartar to follow him ("I took my luggage and the Tartar on board the steamer") and no sooner were they on board than the anchors were weighed and away they steamed.

The journey up the Danube in May 1864 was full of delight and interest for with every step nearer to Hungary he met new friends and admirers, who crowded round him, "for the news of my successful travels in Central Asia had already spread throughout Europe".

On arrival he was met by Baron Eotvos, then Vice-President of the Academy of Sciences and his former patron, who was overjoyed to see him again. Vambery himself was overcome by patriotic feelings as he stepped off the ship at the Suspension bridge, his faithful and wondering Tarter in tow.

Now however, filled with happy anticipation, he sped towards the Hotel de l'Europe, as yet unaware that his homecoming was to be "just as lonely and unobserved" as his departure had been. The rousing welcome accorded to returning explorers in London, the articles devoted to them in the press beforehand, the special train bringing the traveller from the coast "feasted as if he were a national hero" was to arouse considerable bitterness in him. Vambery, hurt, retired to his hotel room brooding on his own "gloomy, lonely homecoming" and the "lamentable indifference of his compatriots".

Although "marks of recognition in the papers, invitations to dinner-parties, etc., were not wanting . . ." this was not what he wanted. What he craved was recognition on a national scale.

Lack of interest in his travels he ascribed in part to the political situation of the moment and Hungary's over-riding concern to free herself from the Austrian yoke, and he told himself that "although Asia, from the historical point of view of the old Magyars might be of some interest, geographical and ethnographical researchers . . . could have no special attraction for Hungary just then". The Academy, he reasoned further, "the only national institution" to have escaped the Austrian purges, had at that time rather more a political than a purely scientific character: it felt "more drawn towards the more enlightened, more advanced nations of Western lands than towards the obscure districts of the Oxus and their inhabitants".

Even though his bags might contain specimens of East Turkic languages and the manuscripts he had collected were unknown to the scientific world of Europe and would give him, he hoped, "the character of an explorer and specialist in Turkology" his

GRÓF DESSEWFFY EMIL

return seemed to arouse no interest whatsoever at the Academy; in fact, when he appeared, to take part in a regular Monday meeting and he was warmly embraced only by his patron, Baron Eotvos and the secretary of the Academy, Ladislaus Szalay whom he had kept posted of his progress on his journey and to whom he had addressed his melodramatic P.S. from Teheran — that letter in which he had slightly twisted the facts to present them as he felt they needed to be presented rather than they had actually been; both these gentlemen "did all they could to make up for the neg‹ lect of the others".

His prestige as a serious scholar was not enhanced by the fact that he chose to appear at the Academy with his Fez on — "being used to the heavy turban, my head had to get gradually used to the lighter covering of Europe" — and this particular, characteristic piece of Vambery-showmanship (which was to be appreciated in London) did not go down at all well among the "jealous, narrow-minded people . . . from the Acadamy circles . . . (some of whom) . . . had published scornful remarks about me on the day after my arrival. Some even thought his adventures "fantastic and exaggerated".

After the rousing welcomes accorded to him in Persia and Turkey this was a comedown indeed. And, like a wounded animal, he retired to his lair to lick his wounds. He felt that he had been the first European to explore certain regions in Central Asia, and to bring back valuable scientific information, he was also "not a little proud of the manner in which I had travelled . . .", was this the gratitude of a nation for whom he had risked his life? His joyous homecoming had turned "into one of the most painful experiences of my life". What is more, the gnawing doubt returned that his failure to arouse interest was in some way connected with his obscure Jewish origin; the desire to overcome just this handicap was one of the most powerful driving forces in his nature.

He had arrived penniless in Budapest and he now worried what to do next. He felt he was no nearer to a solution than when he had set out. What were the chances for a career at home? He tried to be realistic in assessing them and he judged them slender indeed. Since Hungary was at that time ruled from Vienna and since, as he writes, he had made intimate friends of some of the Hungarian refugees living in Constantinople, he felt he could not hope for much hope or recommendation on the Austrian side.

Some friends and acquaintances advised him in fact to return to

Constantinople and to resume the official career he had abandoned there; others suggested "that I should apply for a professorship in Oriental languages at Pest University", especially as the position of lector had just become vacant; although he did nothing about it at the time, this was an idea that was to germinate and take root. He kept it firmly fixed in his mind. The idea of returning to Constantinople did not much appeal to him, he felt weary and longed for a rest, anxious above all to find an opportunity "to work out the linguistic and ethnographical results of my travels".

But how? Even though London seemed the best bet, since his pockets were filled with letters of introduction to the high and mighty, where were the funds to come from? The problem was a familiar one. He was only too aware that "travel in the East requires but a knowledge of the languages and the customs, while money is more often dangerous than helpful . . . in the West it is just the reverse", he now approached his "supposed friends", he writes bitterly, for a small loan. In vain. He promised four-fold payment, pointed out the advantages to Hungary if he were to make a personal appearance in the "cultured West"; it fell on deaf ears. No one was willing to advance even a farthing "and there I stood in my native land more forlorn and helpless than in the wildest regions of Central Asia". Even if he had already felt "rudely awakened out of the happy dreams which had been my companions on the homward journey", he now felt his homecoming to have turned "into one of the most painful experiences of my life". But worse was in store.

With the help of Baron Eotvos, the President of the Academy finally advanced him a few hundred florins from the Library Fund — but under one, to him extremely humiliating, condition: he was to deposit his Oriental manuscripts with him as security. Technically the manuscripts were, of course, the property of the Academy (since they considered that they had financed the journey) but Vambery had understandably acquired a certain proprietary interest in them: had he not saved them when, on his homeward trip, a frightened mule had threatened to precipitate him and his luggage into a river? After the "coldness and indifference shown to my travels", here was tangible mistrust and the old spectre, never entirely laid, the old near-paranoid suspicion was back again; and, although he battled in his own mind not to see in it "an intentional non-appreciation of my services", as he so delicately puts it, he could not help asking himself whether "all this humiliation and mistrust . . . this wilful ignoring of all my trouble and labour . . . (was not) . . . due to my obscure origin and the ill-fated star of my Jewish descent?" In time he came to see that he might have been mistaken "but the painful suspicion was there, and could not easily be banished".

So he took his bag of manuscripts to Count Dessewffy's house, inwardly fuming. Never one to easily forget a slight or an imagined insult, he could not let this ultimate humiliation pass without declaiming with false pathos, but true indignation: "So you do not believe me . . . you take me for a vagabond without any feeling of honour; you think that I take the money of the Academy and do not mean to pay it back — I who have been slaving and suffering for the good of the Academy as few have done before me . . . I, the fanatical enthusiast, have to give a guarantee for a paltry few florins!" The Count's reply is not recorded but he was lent some money, most of the manuscripts however remaining in the Count's safe-keeping.

Vambery was ready to move on. He had remained four weeks in Budapest. He knew that in Germany his travels had attracted some attention, but less than in England and in Russia where both political and commercial interests were involved "and where a more intimate knowledge of these hitherto inaccessible regions seemed urgently needed": the foreign papers had in fact been "enthusiastic in their praise and appreciation of my endeavours".

Much to his regret he had to leave his faithful Tartar behind "who would have made a capital figure at Burlington House, before the Royal Geographical Society . . . but I had to accommodate myself to imperious necessity . . .", in other words, there were insufficient funds for two. And so Mollah Ishak stayed behind in Budapest.

When Vambery left, he "was not in the most amiable frame of mind"; packed in his portmanteau were his notes and a few Oriental manuscripts he had been able to salvage from the mistrustful Count or had they perhaps been prudently sewn into the lining of his coat? For Vambery was not to throw off so easily the marks of his dervish days.

10

LION OF THE SEASON

He was still inwardly fuming as he boarded the train but was pleased to see that the "marks of recognition" grew in direct proportion to his westward progress; in Vienna there were articles in the papers about him; in Cologne he was interviewed by a reporter from the *Kolnische Zeitung* and the bitterly disappointing days of his home-coming, he writes, were a thing of the past.

Today it takes little more than two hours by air from Budapest to London. In 1864 it took nearly a week, by train with overnight stops. Vambery never described his emotions on setting foot in England for the first time, but characteristically wrote that his travelling companions in the carriage from Dover to London were most interested in his tales.

Here a mystery man steps in. Among the travellers in his compartment was a certain Mr. Smith. He gave Vambery his visiting card and engaged him in conversation. On arrival in London Vambery had a first-rate opportunity to appreciate both British generosity and splendid eccentricity at its best. "This man seemed so pleased to make my acquaintance", Vambery wrote, "that on our arrival . . . he took me to the Hotel Victoria, engaged a splendid room for me, and that evening and the next day entertained me with regal hospitality". Mr. Smith then found a private house for him and paid the first month's rent. What more could he ask? Vambery never found out who he was, nor did he ever set eyes on him again.

It was a fitting prelude to his meteoric rise to fame which can have surprised no one one as much as himself, for he had come to London with one ambition only: to find a market for his travel experiences — in other words, a publisher. His pockets were crammed with letters of of introduction: from Charles Alison, the British Minister at Teheran, from Thompson and Watson, his aides, ". . . I have to think their recommendation alone", he writes "that on my arrival to publish the narrative of my travels I met with so much unhoped for success".

For once he is too modest.

If in Pest not many had been willing to listen to him, some even disbelieving his adventures, quite the opposite was the case in England. It was the day of the explorer — of Burton and Speke, of Livingstone, Palgrave and Grant — and Vambery arrived on the crest of the wave. In London he was to find not only willing ears to listen to the description of his travels, but interest in government circles as well, for he brought with him news and information of areas that were shrouded in darkness.

The British diplomatic representation in Persia kept a wary weather eye on Afghanistan. But in 1864 Central Asia, divided into several small khanates and emirates, was largely *terra incognita*. Very little news filtered through to the West. Maps of these areas showed huge blank spaces. It was known that there were deserts and inhospitable steppes, but hardly any Europeans had set foot there since 1404 when the Spanish ambassador, Ruiz Goncales de Clavijo, travelling with an exhausted retinue to attend the wedding feast of Timur's elder son, had crossed the treacherous sands and braved the mongol nomads.

For beyond Turkestan, to the north of these small, uncouth and tyrannical princedoms, lay the mighty empire of Russia; and Russia, as history had shown, was on the march . . . How would Turkestan, of which so little was known, react? This was the great question, worrying not only armchair strategists but politicians in England as well. And now here came Vambery, freshly arrived from these countries. He could give first-hand information on matters of political, military and commercial importance (for trade was naturally of paramount importance, even to these distant lands). England needed to find export markets for her goods.

Vambery's importance to England lay above all in the fact that he knew the languages of Central Asia and could eavesdrop not only on gossip in bazaars and tea-rooms but in high places as well.

He was an invaluable asset to Britain in helping her statesmen to assess the friendly or hostile feelings of the strategically placed khanates. And he held a unique position having met, face to face, those dreaded Central Asian despots, known only from hearsay; and though in his dervish role he had had to curb his natural loquacity and curiosity he had still been able to keep his eyes and ears open.

Studio portrait of Vambery in his thirties, note top hat on left.

Vambery had the greatest difficulty in adjusting to European ways. He had already disliked the "rigorous etiquette and stiffness" at the receptions in Pera, the European part of Constantinople; now he felt a deep aversion to European dress, "particularly to the neck-tie and the stiff linen, which were quite an ordeal to me, accustomed as . . . I had been to the wide and comfortable Asiatic garb . . . which gave not the slightest restraint . . either sitting or walking". He disliked the food, and the European manner of eating — he, who had scoffed at the Orientals for using their fingers, now found difficulty in using knife and fork and hated "to observe European table etiquette with all its rigours". (How he must have disliked the lessons in good manners wellmeaning London ladies were to give him!)

He regretted having given up his wandering life, and "the firm and stable house and its furniture seemed to me like fetters, and filled me with disgust after a few days' stay".

He spent the first few days in London trying to get used to all this and trying to get his bearings. His next stop was to make use of the numerous letters of introduction. He laid his plans carefully, first calling on those scholars and politicians who were connected with Central Asia, and who thus could be expected to take an interest in his travels. His first visit was to Sir Henry Rawlinson, who was regarded as one of the greatest living authorities on all scientific and political questions relating to Central Asia. Vambery was very well received at Sir Henry's house in Berkeley Street; the conversation was in Persian (although Vambery writes he was able to speak English sufficiently to hold a conversation) but Sir Henry had been British ambassador in Persia and the choice of the language was a natural one. The topics were Bokhara, Khiva, Herat and Turkestan and the details Vambery could supply regarding the capture of Herat by Dost Mohammed Khan and the campaign waged by the Emir of Bokhara against Khokand — and especially the rumours Vambery had heard about the approach of a Russian detachment led by General Tchernayeff — aroused the greatest interest. Vambery considered it a kind of cross-examination but thought he had not done too badly.

Next he called on Sir Roderick Murchison, the President of the Royal Geographical Society, who lived at 16, Belgrave Square and whose house gave Vambery "for the first time an idea of the comfort and luxury surrounding an English literary man of distinction".

Vambery was received "like a fellow-traveller", but was not happy to see that Sir Roderick "did not care much about the languages, the manners and the habits of Asiatic people, but rather about orographical and hydrographical facts", and — not surprisingly from the latter's point of view — ". . . showed some disappointment on hearing form me that I neither brought cartographical sketches nor specimens of the geological formations". Sir Roderick seems to have shown a certain lack of understanding for in reply to the question whether he had brought any drawings with him, he answered, "not quite to his satisfaction that . . . (he) . . . carried only a small pencil not larger than the half of . . . (his) . . . thumb with . . . (him) . . . concealed under the wadding of . . . (his) . . . dervish dress, and that if people had noticed . . . (his) . . . making use of this contrivance, . . . (he) . . . would certainly not have had the pleasure of . . . (his) . . . present interview with him. But apparently "the good old man" was still unable to understand the dangers Vambery had faced and kept on comparing Vambery's journey with his own to the Ural, which he had made under the protection of the Czar of Russia and provided with ample funds.

Vambery tried to avoid the conversation taking a political turn, for whenever he had alluded to a Russian approach to the frontiers of India, and of the nearing Russian conquest of Central Asia, Sir Roderick had smiled and said: "Oh, you must not believe that; the Russians are nice people; their Emperor is an enlightened prince, and the Russian plans in Asia cannot mean mischief against the interests of Great Britain". Shortly after he noticed two beautiful malachite vases which were a present from the Czar . . .

But apart from this single difference of opinion, Vambery writes his first meeting with the President of the Royal Geographical Society had succeeded beyond his wildest expectations. He was invited to lecture at the society's 14th meeting, and to join a small dinner party at Willis Rooms before that.

The third person on whom Vambery called was Viscount Strangford, who greatly impressed him. ". . . I rarely met a man in my life", Vambery writes, "whose almost supernatural ability to speak and write many European and Asiatic languages caused me much astonishment". Their conversation began in the elegant Turkish of Constantinople, "Where . . . six or eight words out of every ten are certainly either Arab or Persian . . ." To be able to use this language in an elegant way, Vambery thought, required a complete adaptation to Oriental thought and a thorough knowledge of Mohammedan literature, as well to have moved a great deal in the "so-called Effendi society". Lord Strangford fulfilled all these requirements; he was delighted to meet someone who had so recently returned from the East and with whom he could swap reminiscences of Constantinople and give him information about the language and literature of Central Asia. There was one great surprise in store for Vambery, however. "Having flattered myself with the hope that I should become the only authority in Europe on Eastern Turkish", he writes, "the reader may fancy my astonishment when I heard from the mouth of an English nobleman the recital of poems . . . which had hitherto escaped my attention, and when he gave me the explanations of words which I had vainly looked for in the Eastern dictionaries".

Vambery was amazed. For apart from Lord Strangford's knowledge of Eastern languages, he spoke nearly all European ones, he knew Slavic languages, Hungarian — ". . . nay, even the language of the gypsies . . ." And he had a vast store of knowledge concerning their literature and history. He had met more than his match.

Fortunately the attraction that Vambery felt for the "learned Viscount" was reciprocated and Lord Strangford later became one of his most ardent supporters in England. Vambery considers that the recognition he gained in London society was entirely due to him.

Vambery also called on Sir Henry Layard, at that time Under-Secretary for Foreign Affairs, who was another authority on Asia, famous for his excavations at Nineveh. He received Vambery "in his open, straightforward, British manner' and treated him like a colleague and a "former brother in arms".

Another visit was to Sir Justin and Lady Sheil. Sir Justin had been minister in Teheran and was interested to see Vambery. Lady Sheila took him in hand and "was kind enough to give me the necessary hints as to the complicated laws and social tone of the West End . . .", in other words, she instructed him in etiquette and manners.

Vambery was not beset by any scruples of false modesty "Necessity and assistance", he writes," had soon transformed the lame Mohammedan beggar into an admired lion of the British metropolis; and the man, who but a few months ago had to wander about in tatters and to beg his daily bread by chanting hymns and bestowing blessings upon true believers in Asia, became the wonder of the richest and the most civilised society of the Western world!"

But it had not all gone off without a hitch.

A few days after his arrival Vambery had noted with some surprise a certain reserve — not to say downright suspicion — among his new friends and acquaintances. He was used to suspicion and well able to deal with it, but this was something different . . . His curiosity aroused he turned to the only man who he hoped would provide him with an answer, and this was his friend and countryman, General Kmethy — and who now, luckily for Vambery, was living in London and a popular member of London society. Vambery complained to him about the incomprehensible attitude of his new acquaintances. What was the reason? Had he done anything wrong? No, said the general, and laughed; and half jokingly he provided the explanation: Vambery, tanned by the fierce Central Asian sun a deep brown, his skin coarsened by the desert winds had aroused suspicion; his "unmistakable genuine Persian and Turkish conversation" had done the rest. Seeing this swarthy, limping man, his gait still awkward in European dress, no one had believed him to be Hungarian, but had taken him for a Persian vagabond in disguise who had learnt English in India (Vambery's English at the time was heavily accented) who, somehow, had managed to get hold of letters of introduction . . . It was only after General Kmethy had assured people that Vambery really was a countryman of his and a member of the Hungarian Academy of Science that doubts were allayed.

Vambery took the episode with good grace, seeing in it a proof "how an inborn talent for languages, or rather for talking", could deceive even the experts. "In Asia they took me for a Turk, a Persian a Central Asiatic", he reflected, "and very seldom for a European. Here in Europe they thought I was a disguised Persian or Osmanli . . ."

In the wake of Vambery's fame, a certain "Professor William Davies" assumed his identity in America and delivered lectures in his name. (He was eventually unmasked in 1868 by a friend of Vambery's.) There were also several letters printed over his name in the Italian and French press, with opinions contrary to his own; although he repudiated them, they did him great harm.

Except for the first few years, Vambery professed to have

taken no particular pleasure in his popularity.

Finally the great day arrived when Vambery was to appear before the Royal Geographical Society. He confessed to being as afraid as if appearing before the Emir of Bokhara . . .

The dinner at Willis' Rooms went off well. Vambery's health was proposed by Sir Roderick Murchison "and drunk with much cheering"; Vambery consummate showman that he was, ended his little speech "by conferring a Mohammedan blessing upon the dinner party — reciting the first Surah of the Koran with all the eccentricity of the Arabic guttural accent, and with all the queerness of genuine Moslem gesticulation". And in contrast to the wearing of his Fez, greeted by such stony disapproval by the Academicians in Budapest, this was a great success and caused "a good deal of merriment". And after the dinner had ended the little party went straight to Burlington House.

And so on 27 June 1864 Vambery made his "first *debut* before a select English audience". He found it hard to conceal his impatience and anxiety, and was all the more worried, since on the very same evening the question was to be discussed in Parliament whether England should side with Denmark in her struggle against Germany (who wished to annex Schleswig-Holstein)* and he feared that the audience at the Royal Geographical Society would be only small. He was pleasantly surprised: the audience was much larger than he had expected.

The paper Vambery had prepared, a short account of his travels in English, had been revised by Laurence Oliphant, a member of the Royal Geographical Society (on whom Vambery bestowed the title "foreign secretary of the society") and read out by Clements Markham, its secretary.

And so, for the first time, an interested audience could hear an eye-witness account of conditions in Central Asia and a description of the personalities of its rulers, most of whom were dim, shadowy figures at the best and whose military strength and intentions were unknown, since there were no British political agents in Central Asia. Russia already appeared a threatening neighbour and the reactions of these 'natives' were a source of worry.

Vambery painted no reassuring picture of the Khan of Khiva, "a sick tyrant with very frightful features", who did nothing else but slaughter hundreds of his subjects for mere trifles.

221

On the other hand he described Mozaffar-ed-Din, son of the blood-thirsty emir of Bokhara who had murdered Conolly and Stoddart, as "a man of good disposition who was forced for political reasons to commit many tyrannical and barbarous acts". From his lofty pinnacle — as a European — he later mockingly described this emir and all his higher functionaries in their snow-white turbans and their wide silk garments of all the colours of the rainbow "more like the chorus of women in the opera 'Nebuchadnezsar' than a troop of Tartar warriors". More to the point, however, he estimated the strength of the emir's army during the campaign of Khokand as of 30,000 horsemen as against the rumours flying around in Bokhara which had put them at 40,000 or even 60,000 men.

Clements Markham, after a short resume of Vambery's journey, had also alluded to its motive which was "to study the affinity between his native tongue and the languages of Tartary". He emphasised certain points of his journey, highlighting its dangers: how the colour of Vambery's skin had excited the incredulity of the dervish pilgrims; how the Turcomans on the shore of the Caspian Sea had taken him either for an English or for a Russian spy; how his features "had excited the greatest suspicion in the streets of Khiva"; how he had had to pretend that he was a great *mollah* and how the khan had sent for him. How his appearance had again aroused great suspicion in Bokhara and how he had been threatened with death if he did not confess that he was a dervish in disguise and how he had dealt with this "by a display of assurance and tact".

This incident occurs nowhere in the accounts of his travels and one can only surmise that, once again adapting himself to the surroundings he found himself in, he gave a rather more highly coloured description of events for the benefit of the Royal Geographical Society.

The report ended with Vambery's arrival in Herat in October (1863): the country to the north was in turmoil, it said, owing to the revolt of the Afghans after the death of Dost Mohammed.

Vambery was able to supplement this information in his writings and his readers could learn with a shudder than the Emir of Bokhara in Khokand after the successful end of his campaign, had greeted the welcome news of Dost Mohammed's death by ordering the messenger who had brought it to be given a present of 1000 Tenghe and the same day a festival was improvised: that day,

Vambery added, the Emir took to his bed his youngest and fourth wife ...

After Markham had sat down Sir Roderick invited Vambery to speak. Overcoming his nerves and stage fright he rose to speak, comforting himself with the thought that "in case of failure ... the indulgent English public would have expressed its displeasure by benignant laughter" (and not the executioner's axe). But after the first ten or fifteen minutes his stage fright disappeared and he launched into an account of what he calls the salient incidents of his adventures, speaking for more than half an hour with animation. "Oh, glorious language of Shakespeare and Milton! ... nobody has murdered the Queen's English in such a way as the ex-dervish in Burlington House!" he wrote, and probably he was right.

In any case, whether he had mastered the Queen's English or not, the audience clapped and cheered and when, invited by the President to give a blessing Mohammedan style, Vambery complied with the genuine Arabic text, "the whole society burst into a fit of laughter which made the walls nearly tremble". And, swamped by handshakes and congratulations, he heard Lord Strangford's voice ring out: "Well done, dervish!" "(It) will never cease to sound in my ears like the sweetest music I ever heard in my life", he wrote.

When it was Sir Henry Rawlinson's turn to speak he praised Vambery highly not only his competence as an Arabic scholar, but for the fact that he had explored territory of great political interest, since it lay between the two great Asian empires — the Russian empire in the north and the Anglo-Indian empire in the south. Pointing out that now, at certain places, the frontiers were only 600 miles apart, he was careful in saying that he wished by no means to imply that Russia had any hostile intentions towards England. And he quoted what Sir Robert Peel had called "a sort of law of nature": when civilisation impinges upon barbarism, the latter must give way. (A slogan to be taken up by the Liberals many years later).

Dotting his "i"'s and crossing his "t"'s, he left his audience in no doubt as to the importance of Vambery's journey: he was, he said, "deserving of our commendation for having made us acquainted with regions pregnant with so much political importance". No European, he believed, had ever travelled from the Caspian at Astrabad to Khiva. (Conolly had attempted to but had had to turn back after leaving Astrabad).

Vambery had also visited Samarkand, and could fairly claim the honour of having been the first European who had lived in Samarkand and described it since the days of Clavijo.

Vambery had achieved something "exceedingly remarkable" Rawlinson added. He doubted if there was one European in a thousand who could successfully spend three years of probation among bigoted Mohammedans.

Although Vambery had not been able to take astronomical observations (why seemed pretty obvious) he had still brought back a considerable amount of information concerning the geography, statistics, antiquities, commerce and the social conditions of these countries which "that prince of publishers, Mr. Murray, is at present occupied in putting together for publication".

The discussion that followed was lively. Vambery must have squirmed in his seat when one worthy member rose to speak, alleging that Dr. Wolff and he had covered practically the same ground and that his adventures "were precisely similar to those which this Hungarian gentleman has had".

But Lord Strangford quickly contradicted him, remarking that Dr. Wolff had never been to Khiva in his life and that Vambery had taken an entirely different route (by way of Astrabad). "M. Vambery", he declared categorically, "went to Khiva over perfectly new ground; and from Bokhara to Samarkand, a city that had not been visited by a European for several centuries . . ."

The next topic for discussion was the cotton industry. Bokharan and Khivan cotton had been used in English mills . . . and the Russians were trying to teach the natives how to produce better cotton with the help of proper machinery added another member, complacently denying there was any danger to India from Russia.

Vambery must have been ready to leap out of his seat.

Sir Henry rose to speak again, and he spoke of cotton. There could be no doubt, he said, that Russia drew the greater part of her supply from Central Asia. "M. Vambery has not touched upon the commercial part of the question "(but he was to do so in the future); the real rivalry between England and Russia in Central Asia was in commerce, and not in politics". Basing his statements on recent gloomy trade reports he told his audience "that we are entirely driven out of the market. M. Vambery would confirm that in Khiva, Bokhara and Samarkand he saw nothing but Russian goods".

The President agreed sanguinely with Sir Henry, convinced "that the advance of the Russians could be in no way detrimental to our great Indian empire" — a similar line of thought had been pursued by another optimistic member who believed it would be easier "to send an army from the banks of the Thames to the banks of the Indus than for the Russians to send an army from their frontier to Peshawar" — and ended by reminding his friends that "long before we had an empire in the east, the Russians had intercourse with Bokhara". Was England jealous? In any case, the Russians and the English "by advancing their frontier and approximating to each other, only tended to bring savage nations under a regular system of government".*

The next morning *The Times* published a lengthy report of the meeting, with details of his journey "through districts that had not been visited by a European since the days of Marco Polo". His strong foreign accent was remarked upon. Vambery was of great value, it said in substance, because he "would make us acquainted with countries of so much political interest in England". It announced, quite surprisingly, that Vambery was making preparations for another journey, "in which he intended to penetrate into China, taking Samarkand as his starting point".

He does not mention this anywhere else. Perhaps he thought he had to justify the *sobriquet* of "explorer" he had instantly acquired.

Vambery himself dates the beginning of his career in England from this meeting. He basked in the "unanimous approval and admiration", but he now had to get his travel book ready quickly and not keep the public waiting. He claimed to have written it — and to have corrected the proofs — in three months, but said it cost him "more trouble and exertion than many of the most trying parts of my travels". The meagre notes had become nearly illegible through having been for so long hidden in the wadding of his dervish dress, and he had largely to draw on his prodigious memory. He hated being shut up in a room, from which he could see only a small bit of sky and being forced to "sit down to write consecutively for hours every day for weeks and months!" He deplored the fact that he could not add any historical or philosphi-

---

* Proceedings of the Royal Geographical Society, 1863/64.

cal notes since his Oriental MSS had been retained by Count Dessewffy in Budapest as security on the money loan.

He was inundated by publishers' offers, but it was Lord
Strangford who introduced him to John Murray, the publisher of
Byron and Sir Walter Scott, considered "the literary forum of
the elite" — at the time Queen Victoria was negotiating for the
publication of the late Prince Consort's Memoirs and Lord Derby
was publishing his translations of Homer with him. It gave Vambery an introduction to London society for any connection with
this publisher "raised an author to the position of a gentleman,
even if they did not provide him with the means to live as such".

Despite the fact that *Travels in Central Asia* had been written in
so remarkably short a time, the book contained a wealth of information. It was not only a travel book but a political Baedeker and
a runaway success.

"Day after day the post brought piles of invitations to lunch, or
dinner, races, hunting parties, visits to beautiful country houses
and all imaginable pleasures and recreations . . ." Vambery said,
but after the publication of his book he could add: "The post
brought me double as many invitations as before; I was literally
besieged by autograph hunters, and photographers . . ."; and
recalling the hardships of his youth, he added: ". . . for months
together I had invitations for every meal of the day . . ."

Sir William Hardman wrote in his diary:

"Tonight we go over to Tooting to dine with Robert Cook
(Murray's partner) to meet Vambery, the great traveller whose
book was offered to me — to revise the translation and to edit —
who visited Central Asia disguised as a dervish". "I am very curious to see him, for reports say he (has) got so inured to dirty habits
during his Dervish life, that he has abandoned the use of soap and
water for years."†

It was the last chapter of Vambery's book which aroused interest in British Government circles. He had called it: "The Rivalry
of the Russians and English in Central Asia". Always ready to
play to the gallery, he swallowed his religious prejudices and
wrote, most hypocritically: "Christian civilisation, incontestably
the noblest and most glorious attribute that ever graced human
society would be a benefit to Central Asia". But he could not
remain indifferent to the fact that England regarded with indifference Russian's advance towards India . . . for "the continued progress of Russian designs in Central Asia is . . . beyond all doubt".

"The interests of civilisation", he added, with a further hypocritical deference to current public opinion, suppressing his own strongly anti-Russian bias, ". . . make us wish the most entire success to Russian arms . . .", but he doubted that Russia would content herself with Bokhara; sounding a note of warning (which was to become his *Leitmotif*) — he forecast that Russia, once in the possession of Tashkent and Turkestan would not be able to withstand the temptation of advancing . . . into Afghanistan or Northern India".

History was to prove him wrong, but it was strong stuff for Victorians. *Travels in Central Asia* gained him instant recognition, both in Europe and America. Even before the book was published Vambery had taken an interest in the French and German editions. Writing from his London home, 162, Great Portland Street, he told John Murray (11 June 1864):

"I must speak (to the translator) and know his capacities in the two languages as for his character or his discretion I hope you will choice (sic) the man you can trust . . ."

He then dealt with the engravings and map to illustrate the book and added: ". . . I must speak a little more *in extenso* on the German and French edition being much interested in (that) the three editions may appear at once".

In an undated letter the same year he pleads an increasing weakness of his eyes "which obliges me to change my abode for some time" and asks for an advance of twenty guineas. Still writing in execrable English he adds: ". . . I don't know if the Royal Geographical Society will allow me to lecture anything, we do well to let announce my arrival in London with the short relation of my Journey and the manner of the execution, afterwards I'll beg you to let publish my portrait in bokharian dress after a photograph my friends let make at Teheran . . ." And finally expresses "full confidence in the humanity of the gentleman recommended by Sir Henry Rawlinson and Sir Justin Sheel (sic)" — presumably the translator.

A few months later he wrote another letter to his publisher containing minute calculations about the length of the book and suggesting condensing it here and there. "Well, our translator will not be charmed by the procedure", the letter said, "because the diminishing of anticipated ice-crust of English etiquette, a hearty and sincere appreciation of my labours".

Vambery growled that it cost him half his royalties to turn himself into an acceptable "distinguished foreigner".

The trend of political events were to his advantage, and he followed them closely: ". . . Russian aggression in Central Asia is favourable for the sale of our book . . ." he wrote to John Murray on 31 December 1864, with an eye on the jingling cash register, ". . . and as for England I hope she will awaken from her dangerous slumber . . ."

At the request of the British ambassador in Teheran Vambery had written a memorandum about conditions in Central Asia which had been forwarded to Lord Palmerston, Prime Minister at the time. His first remark upon meeting Vambery had been: "You must have gone through nice adventures on your way to Bokhara and Samarkand!" And he had listened with the greatest attention to all that Vambery had to say. Vambery had tried to discuss the question of the Russian advance towards Tashkent and had taken the map out of his book which lay on the table but Lord Palmerston had tried tactfully to change the subject, asking: "And did you not betray your European character?" or "How could you stand that long trial and those privations?" Finally, pressed by Vambery, Lord Palmerston alluded to the barbarity in Central Asia but thought Vambery's idea of Russia's strength in that part of the world exaggerated. Events were to prove Palerston wrong. Tashkent fell to the Russians in the same year.

It was clear to Vambery why other statesmen wished to see him. "The chief point of interest", he writes, "lay in the information which I brought from Khiva, Bokhara and Herat, and more especially with the secret movements of Russia towards southern Asia, so far unknown in England because of the total isolation of Central Asia".

Interest to meet Vambery and to hear from him first-hand the real situation, was the greater since wild rumours were flying around that Russia was on the southward march. How much of it was true?

There was little room left for doubt for even while Vambery was laboriously writing the last chapter of his book by hand news came through that Tashkent had fallen. Vambery himself thought the information doubtful at the time, ". . . but that the Russians are in movement in that quarter is certain". He was right.

He had got on better in his interview with Lord Clarendon, which took place after the fall of Tashkent. Clarendon agreed with the main line of thought expressed in the final chapter of

Vambery's book but added "what has since", said Vambery, "become the standing principle of optimists in England" who compared Russia's policy in Central Asia to British policy in India: she was compelled to move gradually from north to south as England had been obliged to move from south to north in India . . . "she is doing services to civilisation, and we do not much care even if she takes Bokhara", they said, foreshadowing Liberal policy in years to come.

Vambery had been formally introduced to Lord Palmerston at the house of Sir Roderick Murchison, at 16, Belgrave Square and had subsequently been a frequent guest at his private house or had dined with him at a friend's house at Carlton Terrace. He was often the guest of the eccentric Lord Houghton, who delighted in inviting to his luncheon or dinner parties people he knew to hold opposing views (as, for example Lord Stanley of Alderley, according to Vambery, a fanatical admirer of Mohammediaism "and the equally fanatical Protestant Bishop of Oxford, Wilberforce, known as 'Soapy Sam'.) At Ferrybridge (Houghton's country estate in Yorkshire) Vambery met made the acquaintance of Lord Lytton (later to become Viceroy of India), and of the poet Algernon Swinburne, who read to the assembled guests passages from his "Atlanta in Calydon", "over which the slender youth went into ecstasies". In this house, too, Vambery met Richard Burton who had just returned from North-West Africa and who was to spend his honeymoon there. That evening the company included French Orientalist, Jules Mohl (who was working on a translation of the Persian epic — *"The Shah Nameh"*). Both he and his English wife, Mary — who was a witty diarist and whose Parisian Salon was a magnet for all the great names of the day — had been invited in Burton's honour. Burton was the last guest to arrive and Lord Houghton had planned a little surprise. Vambery was to hide behind one of the doors and at a given signal "recite the first *Sura* of the Koran with correct Moslem modulation" before Burton and his wife entered the drawing-room. He did as arranged. Burton, who had meanwhile sat down in a comfortable armchair, looked surprised and jumped up exclaiming: "That is Vambery!" (although he had never set eyes on him or heard his voice before). At least this is Vambery's version of the story.

Vambery was greatly impressed with the comfort and luxury of English country houses (far greater, he wrote, than the largely imaginary splendours of the East). But he found it difficult to get used to the elaborate meals "and the table pomp of the English aristocracy". His mind wandered back to his dervish days "when my meals consisted sometimes of begged morsels and sometimes of *Pilaff* I cooked myself". Now he had to sit through (and consume) an endless series of courses, and drink "the queerest of mixtures". One night stood out particularly in his memory; together with Lord Clarendon and other notabilities he was guest at the magnificent country-house of the Duke of Argyll. After the usual, heavy Victorian 7-course meal, including stuffed pheasant and claret, the men adjourned to the luxuriously furnished smoke room to enjoy their glass of port and cigars "and from their shortly before midnight every guest was conducted to his respective bedroom by a lacky preceding with two huge silver chaneliers. When the powdered footman dressed in red silk velvet had ushered me into the splendidly furnished bedroom, provided with every comfort and luxury, and began to take steps to assist me in undressing, I looked at the man quite dumbfounded and said with a friendly smile, 'Thank you, I can manage alone'. The footman departed. I feasted my eyes upon all the grandeur around me . . . When I turned back the brocaded coverlet and lay down on the undulating bed, my fancy carried me back twenty years, and I thought of my night quarters in the Three Drum Street at Pest with the widow Schonfeld . . ."

But even more than by the wealth and prosperity Vambery was impressed by the spirit of freedom in England. When for the first time he entered the reading room of the Athenaeum Club, and stood reading *The Times* opposite to Lord Palmerston, he was so astonished to see "Mister Pam" so close to him, that he stared more at him than at the columns of *The Times*.

Of all the leading statesmen of the day, he felt most attracted to him. He was impressed by Palmerston's fantastic memory and encyclopedic knowledge, not only of Europe, but of Turkey, Persia and India as well. He liked Palmerston's habit of joking and his *bon mots*. At the dinner parties at 16, Belgrave Square or at Carlton House Terrace. Vambery would often have an opportunity to listen to him after dinner. "When he began to arrange the little knowt of his wide white cravat, and hemmed a little, one could always be sure that some witty remark was on its way", he writes, "and during the absence of the ladies subjects were touched upon which otherwise were but seldom discussed in the prudish English society of the day".

At Lord Palmerston's initiative Vambery was invited to other distinguished houses "for the merry old gentleman was much entertained by my lively conversation and my anecdotes from Asia, which I used to relate after dinner when the ladies had retired. My stories about the white ass of the English embassy, of diplomatic repute and similar amusing details of court life in Persia and the khanates of Central Asia tickled the fancy of the most serious, sober-minded lords and went the rounds in the fashionable West End circles".

Meanwhile Vambery had become an accepted members of London society. He had been taken in hand by Lady Sheil and Mrs. Murray who instructed him "in the ways of fashionable life", and who taught him "how to dress and how to comport myself at table, in the drawing-room and in the street' fully aware that "blunders against the orthodoxy of English customs were resented by many . . ."; occasionally, however, he could not help a little backsliding as on the day a lady saw him on the top deck of an omnibus (from where he thought he had the best view of London). "Sir", she said most severely, "take care not to be seen there again, otherwise you can no longer appear as a gentleman in society". And, indeed, he did his utmost to become one, taking great pains over the cut and colour of his clothes, the shop from where he bought his hat, umbrella and walking-stick and joined a Club. "When I was able to give as my address, 'Athenaeum Club, Pall Mall', the barometer of my importance rose considerably."

Vambery was also well received by Lord Granville (later Minister of Foreign Affairs)" and it always pleased him when I was at table with him to hear me converse with the different foreign ambassadors in their native tongue".

The highlight of his stay however was his meeting with the Prince of Wales, then 23 years old; it took place at the Cosmopolitan Club in London, a Victorian nightclub which did not open its doors until well past midnight. Vambery could not get over the informality. "When I saw the future ruler of Albion sitting there at his ease, without the other members taking the slightest notice of him", he writes, "I fairly gasped at the apparent indifference shown to the Queen's son. I could but approach the young Prince with the utmost reverence and awe". And it was entirely due to the Prince of Wales' "affability and kindness of heart" that Vambery finally plucked up the courage to speak to him for half an hour. Yet this chance meeting was to lead to a life-long friendship between both men.

He found "this specially English characteristic of individual freedom and independence a great contrast with the cringing spirit of Asia and the servility of Eastern Europe".

The attitude of the English towards explorers was a further revelation to him. He was impressed by the fervour with which Livingstone was received on his second return from Africa, marvelled at the role Burton, Speke, Palgrave, Du Chaillu and others played in society and thought that the traveller enjoyed greater fame in England than the scholar or the artist on the Continent.

He became a friend of Richard Burton whom he considered the greatest traveller of the nineteenth century; he also thought he had the most profound knowledge of Moslem Asia, considered him a clever Arabic scholar and was impressed by his — and John Speke's discovery of Lake Tanganyika, source of the Nile.

He became a friend of the explorer-missionary Gifford Palgrave; and met David Livingstone, who told him: "What a pity you did not make Africa the scene of your activity!"

Vambery met Charles Dickens at the Athenaeum Club, and found him "not particularly talkative", but a good listener: he was greatly interested in Vambery's adventures. Perhaps he was gathering material for the article on Vambery in his magazine *All the Year Round* (Volume 13, no. 303: "The Hungarian Dervish").

Travels in Central Asia was mentioned at another meeting of the Royal Geographical Society the following year (22 May 1865) and headed the list of four new publications; the first that had aroused the deepest interest was "that of the ardent and observant Hungarian traveller, M. Vambery, who at the last meeting of the past summer", said Sir Roderick Murchison, "gave us the first sketch of his travels through Central Asia . . . No person, who was then present can forget the effect he produced upon us when he related his racy and lively story . . ." He hoped that Vambery's book would have a much larger sale than it had had so far. He recalled the dangers and hardships Vambery had gone through, "from a pure love of the science of languages and in the hope of tracing his native Magyar tongue", adding: "Since he has come among us, he has so endeared himself to us, by his agreeable conversation, and has so charmed many a society with his sparkling anecdotes . . . that we are no longer surprised that he could pass unscathed through the deserts of the Oxus, or obtain the notice of great Khan . . ."

What followed next was perhaps a surprise for Vambery, as well as a disappointment, for Sir Roderick continued: "Justly, therefore, has the Council acted in awarding a recompense to a bold traveller who ... might have obtained a Gold Medal at my hands, if, as a holy Dervish he had not been interdicted from practising what would be considered as the 'black art' among Mahommedans — the taking of any of those observations which Geographers require".

And after the presentation of the Royal Medal to others (as Vambery, no doubt, bitterly observed) the President handed over a "Testimonial" to Dr. Arminius Vambery — it took the shape of a "honorific donation" of £40 "as a token of our regard and of the high estimation in which we hold your adventurous journey into Central Asia". And although the Society admired "the self-reliance, courage and perseverance", Vambery had displayed, "... our wonder at your successful journey, when first related to us, was modified when we found that you possessed such a marked power of fascinating all those with whom you are brought into contact; and we now understand how the Dervish had his passport in his own hands ..." and he ended his speech, hoping that Vambery's book would be bought by many ...

When Vambery rose to speak, he was his usual fulsome self: "Mr. President and Gentlemen", he replied, "When last year I had the honour of addressing this Society, I could not do it as I wished, because I was then but a half-civilised man. Coming back from Tartary and having been myself half a Tartar and Dervish for many years, on arriving in this wonderful metropolis of the still more wonderful nation, I found I had but little knowledge of the language, and was unable to express myself. But now, after having spent one year in England ... I am a little more civilised, not totally, but sufficiently civilised to express my deepest thanks to this Society for the honour and kindness it has bestowed on me". He ended with renewed thanks for the reception and hospitality he had met with at the Society and which "could never be forgotten by any foreigner in England".

11

FROM NAPOLEON III TO FRANZ-JOSEF

Vambery had begun to grow weary of the "endless series of dinner-parties in London" and of his role of Lion of the Season. Feeling the need to extricate himself from the splendid, but to him already tiresome English hospitality, he crossed the Channel on his first visit to Paris.

His pockets were stuffed with letters of introduction and recommendation: one from Count Rechberg, the Austrian Minister of Foreign Affairs, accredited to the Court of Napoleon III, another from Count Rochechouart, the French envoy at Teheran addressed to Count Drouyn de L'huys, the French Foreign Minister. His English friends had moreover given him introductions to literary figures and prominent men of the day.

He wrote to John Murray, his London publisher, informing him that he had been received by the Emperor only two days after his arrival in the French capital, on 12 January 1865. Vambery appears to have been less than enchanted by the interview. It had all been a most formal affair. Prince Metternich (Austrian ambassador in Paris) had informed him that the Emperor, having read the English edition of *Travels in Central Asia*, wished to see him and to ask a few questions. So, accompanied by Metternich, he left for the Tuileries, entering the palace by the Pavillon d'Horloge gate. Vambery caught sight of Napoleon III on a staircase taking leave from a visitor: the Queen of Spain. The Emperor seized Prince Metternich's arm and beckoned to Vambery to follow. He led them to an apartment, comfortably furnished and crowded with nineteenth-century bric-a-brac, where the Empress Eugenie and her court ladies were waiting.

Metternich remained here while the Emperor took Vambery into his study and motioned him to sit down by his desk — on which Vambery noted the "large quantity of books, papers, maps, etc. not in any particular order", but, prominently dis-

Paris 12/1 865

Dear Sir!

It is only some days I arrived in the french capital — The Emperor has received me the second day of my arrival and the interview dured about 20 minutes. Judging from the questions he put on me, his chief interest is the state of russian — english policy in those remote countries, and although very far from what they call "Le courant Des affaires," he is very clever to conceal his ignorance in certain matters. Next the policy he showed some interest in the ethnographical and social state of those regions

Vambery's letter to John Murray

and as for geographical knowledge Hachette himself tells me, they try to introduce in France the taste for travels, and they are only beginners.

I beg to pay my compliments to Mr R. A. Cooke I hope he will kindly remember the promise he gave me concerning the electro-types and maps for Brockhaus, and will do all his possible to send them soon very soon, to Trübner Paternoster row:

This evening I am at dinner at Prince Metternich, tomorrow at Prince Napoleon but in case of a failure in my business I'll stand yet this week for Hungary and You will get my next letter from Pest.

I am

Dear Sir

Your very devoted

Vámbéry

18th January 1865

played, the English edition of his own *Travels*.

Vambery was not impressed by the Emperor. He describes how this "thick-set man", with his flabby features and whitish-grey eyes, addressed him in a very slow voice and congratulated him on the courage he had shown; he added that seeing him in person he was even more astonished to find that Vambery's slight (and apparently weak frame) could have withstood the great hardships he had endured. "Strange indeed", Vambery wrote to John Murray sarcastically, "like everybody, he paid the most compliments to my lame leg. Why not to my donkey?" And he told the Emperor that he had never been ill in his life, adding — a remark that was to become celebrated — that in Central Asia he did not walk upon his legs but upon his tongue, "for it was only my linguistic study which rescued me out of the clutches of the Central Asia tyrants".

The Emperor concurred but added that Vambery must possess a great deal of dramatic skill to have played the part of mendicant dervish to such perfection.

But the Emperor's chief interest, according to Vambery, was "the state of Russian and English policy in those countries". At first, Vambery claims, Napoleon III tried to conceal this. The Emperor then turned to the ethnology of Central Asia: he wanted to know whether the Parthians were really the ancestors of the present Turkomans. The schoolmaster in Vambery noted that Napoleon III, who had just finished the *Life of Caesar* was "tolerably well versed" in ancient history in general, but that his knowledge of the modern geography of modern Asia was sadly deficient. Vambery further confided to his publisher, "he is very clever to conceal his ignorance in certain matters. Next the policy he showed some interest in the ethnographical and social state of those regions, he opened the map, measured several spots, and noticed several points . . ."

"He had only very dim notions about the principal names of towns and rivers", claimed Vambery "and he had palpably to take care not to betray his ignroance". Vambery took the opportunity, speaking of the river Yaxartes, of skilfully leading the conversation to a subject that was to exercise British minds for the best part of the century and which was to become Vambery's hobby-horse: the threat that Russian advances in Asia presented to India. Napoleon III listened with great interest but did not believe in a collision between England and Russia in the near future.

He then spoke of Persia and Herat and asked various questions and was greatly amused when Vambery assured him that the Persians knew a lot about *Napliun* — (Napoleon I) who was his great-uncle — and considered him a national hero, a direct descendent of the Persian legendary hero Rustem, refusing to believe he was French.

The interview had "dured" (lasted) about twenty minutes. "After a very graceful demission", Vambery writes to John Murray still in broken English, "he let present me to the Empress and the young prince, again same courtesy, and the history was finished".

When Vambery called on Count Drouyn de l'Huys, a few days later, he found him far more interested in Central Asian questions than Napoleon III had been. Vambery, an unknown only a few months earlier, must have been gratified to be asked questions on politics and to be thought to play such an important role in them. Was it true that he had given Lord Palmerston a memorandum on Central Asia affairs? Did he really believe a collision between the two great European powers in the East to be imminent? In reply, he denied that he had passed on any written communication to the British Government, adding that, as far as he had noticed from his conversations with Palmerston they had, on the other side of the Channel, quite different views from the ones held by himself.

When Vambery called on Count Drouyn de L'Huys, he also had an official interview with Prince Napoleon,* who received him in the Palais Royal, seated under a life-size portrait of his great-uncle — apparently watching, writes Vambery ironically, to discover "whether I noticed the likeness to exist between him and his uncle".

But he claimed that the official visits were not at all to his taste and complained bitterly of the manners of the press and of "the intruding reporters" who interviewed him and the next day published totally false reports of his conversations with them which he afterwards had to contradict; one report riled him particularly: it alleged that he had been entrusted by Lord Palmerston with a secret mission to the Tartars "and other similar nonsense".

The inventiveness of the French press, however, was capped by that of a writer — a Polish prince — who wrote a novel about Vambery's travels in which a Tartar princess falls in love with the hero (Vambery) who secures for himself a throne in Asia. He is sent on a political mission to Europe, in order to secure the friend-

ship of England and France against Russia. Vambery laughed heartily at all this, but tired in the end "of this dubious sort of
reputation".

Altogether Vambery was disenchanted with Paris and the
French attitude to travellers, who, he found, were not considered
great men, "as in England", where explorers were on a par with
scientists and artists. In short, he found that the English had more
regard for the self-made man, "the man who had made himself a
name in the field of practical observations", while the French and
Germans had more regard for theoretical knowledge; "in one
word, in England the spirit of Raleigh, Drake and Cook is still
alive, whilst in France and Germany travellers and explorers have
only very recently come into fashion".

Parisian society, he noted, was more impressed with the
novelty of his *manner* of travelling — i.e. his disguise as a dervish
— than by his travels themselves. (In England it was the reverse.)
One thing that impressed them, however, was Vambery's gift for
languages and he boasts that, meeting "representatives of ten different nationalities" at a gathering in Monsieur Guizot's *salon*,
"he was able to converse with them fluently in their mother languages", and was regarded by many as a "real miracle".

He had left London for Paris with a copy of the *Athenaeum* in his
hand and was more than disenchanted with the review of his
book. "'I am a courageous adventurer . . .', he tells John Murray
(11 November 1864) quoting the review — by now his publisher
has become a kind of father confessor. ". . . but the results of my
Journey given in the present volume are nothing. I know languages but am not a good Christian . . . the most pleasing of all is
the counsel to go to Central Asia without disguise . . . why not by
railway with a return ticket?" he mocks. "I see my troubles won't
be appreciated until a second traveller *v*ill succeed in the way I
have done".

He used his stay in the French capital to negotiate with the
publisher Hachette. In several letters addressed to John Murray
he gives details of the financial arrangements proposed, complaining bitterly that he was forced to authorise publication of his book
in the French paper *Le Tour du Monde* as well (at presumably no
extra fee). "Very shabby indeed", he writes, "but what to do, better something than nothing".

In an earlier letter he had already addressed John Murray as
"the prince of publishers"; now he adds: "You must not be aston-

ished that the dervish flatters you, he has seen other publishers and he knows now thousand times better what is John Murray".

"... the leader of *Le Tour du Monde*, the first geographical paper of France", he continues mockingly, "asks me: '*Est-ce-que nous n'avons pas d'Ambassadeur en Asie Centrale?*' France is not England. Paul de Kock" (a very daring writer of the day) "La Mode, and the lectures of Laprade of the *Jardin des Fleurs* are favourite topics — as for geographical knowledge Hachette himself tells me to try and introduce in France the taste for travels, and they are only beginners ..."

Weary of Paris, Vambery left for home, travelling back to Hungary via Germany and visiting a German publisher on the way, to negotiate for the translation of his book. In a letter of 31 October 1864 he told John Murray that the state of publishing in Germany was "lilliputian" compared with England; he also informed him that he has been invited — strangely by "professors of the English language" with whom he had previously been acquainted — to lecture at the "Geografischer Verein" in 'Leipsic' (Leipzig) and talk about his travels. "I did so", he writes, "and succeeded pretty well, although the President and the public have as much notion about Central Asia as the Khan of Khiva has about Germany", signing the letter "your house dervish".

At the same time Vambery was trying desperately to decide what to do: whether he would not settle down quietly (as he yearned to do) or would be driven to "plunge again into new adventures and revisit the interior of Asia".

It was not that Vambery did not know what he wanted: he wanted, passionately, a chair for Oriental Languages at the University of Pest. He might as well have wanted the moon.

Vambery was gratified to see that, in Hungary, he was received "with marked attention" on his return from England. However the country, as part of the Habsburg Empire, was administered from Vienna, that "seat of ancient prejudice." Emboldened by his recent success, he now made a daring move. He travelled to Vienna ...

He had a trump card up his sleeve. He knew that a lectorship for Oriental languages at Pest Universtiy had just become vacant and that the position of professor (his most cherished ambition) would be easier to obtain in this way. This seemed far more attractive to him than continuing his official career in Constantinople, as had been suggested. But he pessimistically sized up his chances as nil; and he knew there was little chance of entering on a political career or obtaining a good diplomatic post — all these doors were closed to him on account of his Jewish and obscure origins. He was fully aware that he was an auto-didact, without any formal academic training, an "upstart" in the university world; and he saw that only one thing would help — that was to go and see the highest authority in the land: the Austrian Emperor. By so doing he made a lot of enemies for himself.

To "solicit the favour of an audience with the Emperor" was not as difficult a thing as it might appear, nor such a great honour as Vambery implied. Although he claimed that it was a special favour granted to him, this was not really so. (Reading his autobiography one has the impression Franz Josef sent for Vambery himself.)

In the old Austro-Hungarian monarchy it had been the custom to receive in audience only nobles of a certain rank, but the Emperor Franz Josef (who ascended the throne in 1848) was an enlightened monarch and extended this right to ordinary citizens too. "He . . . recognized that misfortune had its privileges as well as rank and decided that, under certain conditions, he would grant an audience to those among his subjects . . . who claimed his protection, and whose cases could not, for any reason, be adequately dealt with by means of an ordinary written petition. During more than fifty years, on a fixed day once a week, the Emperor receives one or more such personal applicants. The reception is altogether private, and no official record of it is ever made. Very frequently indeed, even the name of the applicant is known only to the Emperor himself . . . In these audiences there is nothing of the customary ceremonial of the Austro-Hungarian Court. The Emperor receives his subject alone in his private study, and tells him that whatever statements he may make, even though they should entail the confession of a crime, will never be used to his disadvantage, but will be kept as sacredly secret as confession to a priest . . ."* Apparently even the Emperor's bitterest

---

* Palmer (F.H.E.): *Austro-Hungarian Life in Town and Country*, Newnes, 1904.

* Ten years later Vambrey would feel particularly bitter when the two Austrian explorers, Julius Payer and Carl Weyprecht, were feted and lionized on their return to Vienna, while he had been ignored. (During their Arctic exploration 1871-4 Payer and Weyprecht discovered and named Franz Josef Land.) In years to come it would be these two explorers who would call on Vambery at his home in Budapest.

enemies never accused him of betraying in any way the confidence they had placed in 'his honour as a gentleman'.

Vambery's dramatic decision to see the Emperor personally was, from one point of view, a brilliant move — for it enabled him to achieve his objective with one stroke and with a minimum of delay — but was it a wise one? Was it so clever to march straight over the heads of bureaucrats and scholars, thus instantly creating a phalanx of enemies for himself? If these considerations ever entered his mind, they must have been quickly brushed aside, for what mattered most was to *get on*, to achieve his aim and to prove to the world (and, above all, to himself) what the "obscure and limping Jew" could do.

Before he could see the Emperor, he had to overcome the hurdles of Austrian bureaucracy — one of the first of which was epitomised in the word 'antichambrieren'.* (from the French 'anti chambre') Minor officials — and higher ones were not exempt — had made this practice of letting the hapless applicant "cool his heels in the corridors of power" into a fine art: sitting impassably behind their desks, their power increased (in their own eyes) in direct proportion to the time the applicant was kept waiting. It irked Vambery considerably. ". . . I had much to bear from the Austrian bureaucracy and from the fustiness of the medieval spirit which ruled the highest circles of Austrian society . . . perhaps more correctly from their innate ignorance and stupidity." (This was to become a recurrent theme.) It was incarnate, Vambery claimed, in the person of Prince Auersperg (Vambery called him 'Prince A.'), the Lord High Steward he had to see before the audience". Regardless of the recommendations I brought from the Austrian ambassador in London, (he) received me with a coldness and pride as if I had come to apply for a position as lackey", he snorts, adding touchily: "While royal personages of the West and . . . also Napoleon had shaken hands with me and asked me to sit down, this Austrian aristocrat kept me standing for ten minutes . . . spoke roughly to me and dismissed me with the impression that a man of letters is treated with more consideration in Khiva and among the Turkomans than in the Austrian capital!"*

Finally he was ushered in to Franz Josef's study. When the "kind-hearted monarch" asked him whether he intended to remain in the country and what he could do to help, Vambery came straight to the point and asked for an appointment at the

University of Pest, as professor of Oriental languages. This was an unheard of request. Even in Vienna, the Emperor replied, there would be hardly any students — let alone Pest. Where would Vambery find them? If nobody else would learn, Vambery remarked, he would do so himself. This reply seemed to go down well. For after a few questions about his Asian travels the Emperor acceded to Vambery's request, adding: "You have suffered greatly and deserve this post". The Emperor smiled and graciously dismissed him.

Vambery had good reason to feel pleased with the interview.

The Emperor was to keep his word. He left, limping backwards, in conformity with protocol.

But conditions in Hungary were no better than in Austria. "Here also the wall of partition, class distinction and religious differences rose like a black impenetrable screen", wrote Vambery, ". . . and the monster of blind prejudice blocked my way". He considered anti-semitism "one of the darkest stains on the escutcheon in the modern world of culture".

He overlooked the fact that his tactics can hardly have gained him many friends among academicians who had followed a more orthodox career. He himself admitted to a lack of formal theoretical knowledge, offset, he claimed, by his practical experience. But even that began to be questioned.

And indeed the first doubts about the authenticity of his journey began to appear. "Wise and learned men", he wrote bitterly, "professed to have come to the conclusion that my travels in the Far East, and the dangers and fatigues I had professed to have gone through, were a physical impossibility on account of my lame leg".

"The Jew lies", they said roundly; "he is a swindler, a boaster, like all his fellow-believers". Such comments also appeared in the press, but there was worse in store.

12

UNIVERSITY PROFESSOR

Through his audacity and his disregard for the number of enemies he was creating for himself in the academic world, Vambery had succeeded in his most cherished dream: he had obtained an appointment at the University of Pest "by Imperial Cabinet order". For the time being he had to content himself temporarily with the title of 'lector' at the philosophical faculty of the University, teaching Turkish, Arabic and Persian; and with "the modest honorarium of 1000 florins a year — a remuneration equal to that of any respectable nurse in England", he commented bitterly.

At first it looked as if Franz Josef had been right. There were no students. It seemed as if he would have to teach himself, as he had told the Emperor.

He felt disconsolate. On 30 September 1865 he wrote to his publisher John Murray:

"I am already almost in order here, next week I assume my official business, that is to teach the four walls, chairs and tables in Turkish and Arabic; pupils, be well understood, will take care not to present themselves. You might fancy how soon I shall get tired of it and how I long after a career more suitable to my character and to my past time". Shortly after this, his first two students did appear: one turned out to be Ignaz Goldziher, in later years a celebrated Orientalist (and — behind his back — one of Vambery's most vituperative critics).

The following year Vambery sounded even more bitter and disappointed (in a letter to John Murray dated Pest, 6 November 1866): ". . . what do they care here for the East? Last year I had two pupils in the University. This year I have none. My disgust is always increasing . . ." In this letter he also thanked John Murray for settling a five-guinea debt with a London tailor and enclosed a photograph of himself for the Murray family album. He wrote:

"I have the honour to be in the album in my ragged dervish

attire and now I will show myself in a quite different garb", adding humourlessly: "My life presents a very curious comedy but the worse of it is that in my interior I am always playing an unhappy tragedist. My present seclusion in my half-civilised and politically most unfortunate country is all but agreeable, all but not fit neither for my future. With about 60 Gulden a year I must drag on life far from the world — to lose by vant (sic) of society and exchange of ideas, all what I acquired during a most troublesome youth. I am afraid I shall get tired of it finally and throw myself again into the world. Next plans (are) to go to England, France and Italy in spring — should I not succeed I rather return to the East than remain in my present inactivity". (His English was far from perfect at this time, but by all accounts it would steadily improve.)

The ignominy Vambery suffered in his own country was a complete antithesis to the acclaim he received in England. For many years writers and scholars in western Europe and the U.S.A. believed he was the leading authority in his field. Some, including (at a much later date) Sir Ronald Storrs, said Vambery was *the* greatest Orientalist in the world, with the Englishman Edward G. Browne taking second place. Other British writers did not doubt for one minute that Vambery was "the discoverer of the Asiatic birthplace of the Hungarian people and language,"[*] a claim which would have incensed his critics in Budapest.

In view of this, one cannot help asking why he did not settle in England, if he was as unhappy in Budapest as he alleges. There are a number of reasons with a character as devious and complex as Vambery's, it is no easy task to uncover the real ones.

On the surface he disliked two things in England above all: the country's "rigid society manners" and the stuffy "etiquette". He claimed they were utterly foreign to him, and he detested them. Secondly he could not stand the tumultuous uproar of the London traffic — even as long ago as 1864 — with its "incessant hurrying, rushing, bustling crowds ... Standing at the corner of Lombard Street or Cheapside, or mixing with the crowds hurrying along Ludgate Hill, I felt like a man suddenly transported to pandemonium. To see how these masses push and press past one another, how the omnibus drivers swing around the corners, regardless of danger to human life, for the mere chance of gaining a few coppers more ... was enough to make me think with longing of the

---

[*] E.C. Johnson: *On the Track of the Crescent*, Hurst & Blackett, 1885.

indolent life in Eastern lands . . ."

Many of his new acquaintances in London urged him to settle there, including the sister of Lord Granville (Minister of Foreign Affairs): a Mrs. James, who was very influential in London society. But Vambery, sizing up his chances in England with characteristic shrewdness, came to the conclusion that even his contacts in society and his personal acquaintance "with the most powerful and influential persons in England" would not help him to obtain what he most desired: an influential position, combined with financial independence. Nearer the truth was the unpalatable fact that "the English do not give me an independent position and I am not ready to accept a subordinate job in India . . . I would not be prepared to sacrifice my scientific career for such a subordinate position".

He thus decided if no one could make him a firm offer of a good job in London, then he would return home, hoping to make a career in Hungary and that the recognition he had obtained in England would be of use to him there.

While deeply impressed by the spirit of individual freedom and independence in England — "so much more congenial to my own conceptions of life" — he was, like many Hungarians, deeply attached to his native land, even though he found himself at odds with many of the views of his countryman. He felt himself first and foremost to be a Hungarian "and had presented myself to the world as the explorer of the early history and language of my people. As such an expatriation might reasonably have shed a doubtful light upon my character as a man and writer".

This then seems to be the real reason — although Vambery blamed various external causes which compelled him "to remain at home, to persevere . . . in uncongenial surroundings . . . and only occasionally to come to London where the incessant buzzing of machinery . . . this everlasting mad rushing . . . had an exhausting effect on me . . ." The real motive is deeply rooted in his character and in his need for recognition.

During his sojourns in London, Vambery longed for peace and quiet, and his dreams turned to peaceful places nearer home. "I long for the quiet of a Carpathian spa", he wrote in a letter from the Pall Mall Club to the Hungarian Academy of Sciences. He soon found a Carpathian spa to his liking, Koritnitza, where he spent several short holidays. In a letter to John Murray (11 July

* Now in Yugoslavia.

247

1865) he stressed how "*very* modest and retired" this watering-place was, in contrast to the gigantic English metropolis. In later years, Vambery would spend all his summer holidays in the small Tyrolean resort of Muhlbach, situated between the Brenner Pass and the Dolomites.*

Vambery was a cosmopolitan far in advance of the spirit of his age, opposing its narrow nationalism. He held the barriers separating the various nationalities in Europe to be as ridiculous as those separating the various religions. But he believed the existence of a politically independent Hungary as a buffer state in Central Europe to be an absolute necessity.

Time and again he protested his Hungarian patriotism: "Even when a man's horizon has widened one may still cling lovingly to one's native soil . . ." but he felt he was never believed by his numerous critics in Budapest. They used to jeer at him: "People of Jewish origin cannot be Hungarians . . . they can only be Jews and nothing else". When Vambery reminded them of the dangers he had faced to investigate the early history and language of the Magyars, he was greeted by "an ominous sneer, an insidious shrug of the shoulders, an icy indifference, or a silence which had a more deadly effect than any amount of talk".

Is it surprising that he made annual visits to England where he had found acclaim? Here he felt liberalism was not an empty phrase in a land where "the Jew feels thoroughly English and is looked upon as such by the true Briton". But he had made the decision to settle down in Budapest.

If he was at odds with society over the ideas on religion and nationality prevalent in his time, he was even more at loggerheads over the hereditary privileges granted to aristocracy, and his openly expressed views were not likely to make him any more popular. Vambery could not see why the "uneducated born aristocrat" should claim an exceptional position when "study, zeal and persevering intellectual labour . . ." (qualities he felt, with some justification, himself to possess) ". . . (were) not exactly favourite pastimes of the born aristocrat . . ."; and he never missed an opportunity to have a go at them.

"Holding such views," he wrote frankly, "it is only natural that I could never quite fit into the frame of Hungarian society, where aristocratic predilections predominate". For although the

---

* Now in Italy.

Hungarian Parliament had officially abolished the rights of heredity in 1848, this had remained a dead-letter, and in practice everything went on as before.

He also castigated quite severely "the chase after orders and decorations", of which, by the end of his life, he could boast quite a sizeable collection himself, and for which he claimed to have had no use — though he made an exception in the case of British distinctions. "If sovereigns were pleased to confer such distinctions upon me", he wrote, "I have respectfully locked them up in my box, because a public refusal of them seemed to me to be making a useless parade of democracy, and because no one is entitled to respond to a courtesy with rudeness". Holding such maverick views he could not expect to be popular; persistently ignored by many of his colleagues, he reacted by shutting himself off from them and retreating into his shell.

Vambery looked upon a "professorship at Pest and the doctor's chair of Oriental languages" as his salvation — especially since no one in England had made any definite offers to him. However, the title of 'lector' at the philosophical faculty of the University certainly rankled, as did the "modest honorarium". His ego was badly dented, but this did not stop him from signing his early articles (including one "On the Origins of the Hungarians" for the *Ethnological Journal* in 1865) "A. Vambery, *Professor* of Oriental languages in the University of Pest", in no uncertain terms.

He was not made a professor officially until 1867, so as "not to give offence by appointing a *so-called Protestant*, a heretic . . ." For Vambery was the first non-Catholic professor to be appointed to the University of Pest. The Jewish community calls him the first Jewish professor to have been appointed. But Vambery labelled himself a "*so-called* Protestant", the emphasis being on "so-called" — a significant little word one is likely to gloss over in his autobiography. It is revealing.

Vambery was telling the truth. For, as later events were to show, he was never able to produce a Certificate of Baptism. And from what one of his earliest pupils (Ignaz Goldziher) wrote, it is fairly safe to assume that all Vambery did was to *join casually* a circle of Calvinists in Budapest, who were much more tolerant than the Catholics and among whom he readily found acceptance. Once again, all he had done was to 'join' a religion by inference — and, as he had passed himself off as a Moslem in Constantinople and on his Asian journeys, he now passed himself off as a Christian when it suited his purposes. So successful, however, were appearances that he incurred the undying wrath of the Orthodox community who sincerely believed him to be a renegade and a convert, especially as he had severed all connections with them.

There is an amusing anecdote concerning Vambery's religious affiliations still circulating in Budapest today. One day, so the story goes, his benefactor Baron Eotvos (the Minister of Culture) asked Vambery: "What is your religion?"

"I protest!" thundered Vambery.

"All right", the Baron is said to have replied. "Then I shall enter you as a Protestant . . ."

But later, according to Vambery himself, he was not so reluctant to answer an identical question from Benjamin Disraeli (then British Prime Minister) at his London home in Carlton House Terrace.

Disraeli, who had heard many conflicting and fantastic stories about Vambery, asked him to be seated in the centre of a vast forbidding room, as long as a gallery. He himself walked up and down, stopping occasionally to stare at his perplexed guest. Finally he stopped in front of him and asked:

"Pray, Mr. Vambery, what is your nationality?"

"Hungarian", was the reply.

Disraeli began his pacing again, his brows knitted; then he stopped and asked another question:

"And what is your religion, Mr. Vambery?"

"Protestant".

"Indeed!" After more pacing, a final question:

"And was your nationality always Hungarian and your religion always Protestant?"

"No, Mr. Disraeli; I was born a Jew".

"Ah," said Disraeli, beaming, "I knew it. No one but a man of our race could have had the dauntless perseverance to go through all you have gone through and successfully overcome so many difficulties".*

Vambery called the Catholic Church a 'hotbed of intolerance" as he described it. He found it embodied in the person of the Rector of the University, later a bishop of the diocese. When Vam-

---

* This was one of Vambery's favourite anecdotes. He told it to several of his English friends, including Esme Howard who related the story in his memoirs: *Theatre of Life* (1936).

bery introduced himself officially, he was greeted with the following words: "Do you suppose we are not fully informed as to the treacherousness of your character? We are well aware that your knowledge of Oriental languages is but very faulty and that your fitness to fill the chair is very doubtful. But we do not wish to act against His Majesty's commands, and to this coercion only do you owe your appointment".

The situation could not have been brought home clearer to Vambery. He commented bitterly: "Such was the gracious reception I had, and such were the encouraging words addressed to me after the learned Orientalists of Paris and London had loaded me with praise and honour, and after I had accomplished, in the service of my people, a journey which, as regards its perilousness, privations, and sufferings, can certainly not be called a pleasure trip".

In the service of his people? What an extraordinary facility the mind has of twisting facts! No doubt by now Vambery believed this version himself, but had he himself not written, in his report from Meshed dated November 1863 and addressed to Baron Eotvos, in his customary fulsome style: "My unexpected good fortune enables me to throw a spark of light into the darkness in which the origins of my nation are shrouded; this spark does not yet shine but the future will set is aflame and posterity will not forget the *obscure limping Jew*". (Underlinings Vambery's)

The last few words are the key to his character. And indeed his prophecy was to prove right. Posterity has not forgotten "the obscure limping Jew", but meanwhile he was derided or cold-shouldered, and it hurt ...

And for years to come Vambery was to be looked upon with suspicion in his native land.

He was a non-conformist and must have appeared a dangerous radical to the society of his time. Even though there can be no doubt that anti-semitism was a powerful factor in the Hungary of his day, even the most devout Christian holding such progressive ideas on the social structure as Vambery's could hardly have escaped strong criticism.

Religion, he found, "offers but little security against moral degradation", and as an example he quoted Turkoman robbers who were always the first to ask him for a blessing before setting out on a marauding expedition; "... (and) in the towns of Central Asia, Persia and Turkey, I have found in the thickly-turbaned men of God some of the most consummate villains and criminals".

"Ceremonies, usages and superstitions" he found duplicated in many religions and he inveighed heavily against fanaticism and persecution in any form (as he himself experienced in his school-days).

Christianity too came in for a hammering . . . "Our modern culture has developed, not *through*, but *in spite of* Christianity", he wrote.

He proclaimed himself a free-thinker, preferring to occupy his time with "matters of common interest, rather than with the problem of creation, the Deity, etc. which our human understanding can never grasp or fathom". Nevertheless, he added significantly: "when occasion demanded I have always, either of out of respect for the laws of the land, or out of courtesy for the society in which I happened to be, formally conformed to the prevailing religion . . . just as I did in the matter of dress, although it might be irksome at times."

One does well to bear this in mind.

"In certain circles of Hungary", he wrote, ". . . (the fact) that my books of travel . . . in the meantime had been translated for several Eastern and Western nations in their mother-tongue, was simply discredited . . ." Some even expressed doubt that he knew Turkish, but he had the last laugh "when the first Turkish Counsul for Hungary appeared in Budapest; he was asked on all sides whether it was really true that I knew Turkish, and when he replied that I spoke and wrote Turkish like a born Osmanli, everybody was greatly surprised . . . So deplorably low was the standard of Hungarian learning in those days!"

Vambery had originally joined the Hungarian Academy of Sciences as a corresponding member back in 1860. But it took sixteen years — and twelve after his return from Central Asia — before he was elected a full regular member of the Academy and then only, he wrote bitterly, "after several insignificant men had preceded me . . . and I simply could not be passed over any longer".

He need not have worried in the long run. Still during his lifetime, on the 50th anniversary of his first joining the Academy, a commemorative booklet was brought out in his honour.

The idea for the founding of the Hungarian Academy of

Vambery, aged 37.

Sciences goes back to the early nineteenth century. Count Istvan Szechenyi (whose statue can be seen outside in Roosevelt Square donated one year's income. From Constantinople, together with a long list of signatures, collected from Hungarian emigres, Vambery sent three gold pieces. (See letter of 21 March, 1860, in the archives of the Academy.)

The library itself was added in 1864-65, the years of Vambery's great triumph in London and Paris. Today it houses more than half a million volumes: its Oriental section contains over 600 manuscripts and books bequeathed by Vambery and presented by his son, together with over fifty priceless Arabic, Turkish and Persian manuscripts.

At first Vambery taught Turkish, Arabic and Persian at the Philosophical faculty of the University. Later, when the entirely new Turkish department was established, under his charge, the curriculum included the study of Ottoman Turkish and the East Turkic languages — Turkmene, Kazar and Uzbek. But there were never classes filled with eager students. Vambery preferred to teach at his flat, usually accepting only one or two students at a time. From several accounts it seems that he was an impatient, even a reluctant, teacher who did not really want any students at all. His unorthodox teaching methods were certainly curious. He was often known to say, pointing to some Turkish or Persian text: "Read this! Learn that! — and come back later when you know it!" One of his new students, anxious to learn Turkish, was told: "Go home, buy yourself a Turkish grammar, and come back in six months' time when you have learnt it!"

More charitable sources describe him as charming and friendly, filled with benevolence towards his students, helping them where he could, enabling them to obtain grants and go on study tours. The truth, as always, probably lies somewhere halfway between: Vambery, unpredictable, unorthodox in his methods, naturally helped those he liked more than others. At any rate, some of his students were to achieve considerable fame as Orientalists themselves, including Ignaz Goldziher, Bernat Munkacsi, and Ignac Kunos (who became Professor of Turkish in 1891: the only Jew in Hungary to head a state institution of learning).

Vambery himself, unable to see his own shortcomings, complained: "... Had I been able to follow the orthodox path of an Orientalist, things might have been different. I would have grown my Oriental cabbages in peace, in the quiet rut of my professional predecessors . . . ferreting out the grammatical niceties, and (inquiring) into the speculations of theoretical explorers". But he saw himself as a practical man, a self-made man (a fact he never ceased to emphasize, and which he felt to be so appreciated in England), "who as a Dervish, without a farthing in his pocket, had cut his way through the whole of the Islam world . . ."

The dearth of students provided him with ample time for both writing and travelling. (And indeed, seeing the vast amount of letters, books, and reports that emanated from his pen at 'The University', one wonders when he found time to teach at all!) Visitors were often told "Alas, he is away — as always". In retrospect, he seems to have been that kind of man who provoked strong passions: his contemporaries either adored or detested him, as later testimonies were to prove.

Baron Eotvos had advised him to concentrate on foreign markets for his writings, for Central Asia was too little known in Hungary. This was no handicap to Vambery, who by then could claim to both read and write most of "the different European and Asiatic languages without the help of a dictionary". He had assembled a small specialised library and corresponded with his "fellow literati and Orientalists", though he felt the lack of personal contact keenly.

Vambery took to political journalism like a duck to water, considering it a light diversion from his more serious studies in ethnography and ethnology. And he was quick to see that it proved a lucrative undertaking, especially if the articles were printed in British journals. Some of these paid up to twenty or thirty guineas per page, so he quickly came to the conclusion that "one hour of English article-writing was a better proposition than six hours of German literary work . . ."

He wrote innumerable articles, chiefly on political and economic affairs in Central Asia, Persia and Turkey. They were published in English, German, French, Hungarian, Turkish and American newspapers and periodicals. Among the English ones were: *Good Words, The Leisure Hour, The Nineteenth Century, The Fortnightly Review, The National Review, The Army and Navy Gazette, The Journal of the Society of Arts*, and *The Asiatic Quarterly Review*, and several newspapers from *The Daily Telegraph* to *The Reading Advertiser*; in Germany they appeared in the *Munchner Allgemaine Zeitung, Unsere Zeit, Die Deutsche Rundschau, Die Deutsche Revue, Welthandel,* etc.; in France in the *Revue des Deux Mondes*; in America in *Forum* and the *North American Review*; and in Austria-Hungary in the *Neue Freie Presse*, the *Monatsschrift fur den Orient*, and especially to the *Pester Lloyd* (to which he was almost a weekly contributor).

"If (all my articles were) collected", he once boasted, "they would make several volumes". He claimed that a collection of reviews of his work fell into his hands quite accidentally: they contained nearly two hundred articles and reviews in German, French, English, Italian, Hungarian, Turkish, Russian, and Greek. All of them praised his work.*

He came in for his share of criticism as well: "witness the many letters I have received from all parts of the world", he wrote, "and which on the whole have rather burdened than edified me"; adding "... Inspite of gross mistakes, my literary labour has secured me a position far beyond my boldest expectations ...", making no bones about the attraction of a good, solid financial reward.

In this he was quite honest, "I loathed nothing so much as the conventional modesty of scholars", he continued; "... the hypocritical hiding of the material advantage which scholars as much as, if not more, than other mortals have in view ..."

Money became an obsession, his God. But Vambery himself would phrase it more elegantly, writing that he had "preferred to choose that region of literature where not merely laurels but also tangible fruits were to be found ...", and adding quite frankly: "... I have never been able to see why the desire to become independent through the acquisition of earthly goods should be so objectionable in a scholar ..."

Vambery had always expected to make a large fortune out of his book *Travels in Central Asia*, and declared both publicly and privately his disappointment in its "failure" to earn him enough to "ensure his independence". In fact, the book sold well at a guinea a time, and Murray was extremely generous with the royalties. The book was published on the system of two-thirds profits to the author and one-third to the publisher. Vambery's share of the profits was £261 6s. and Murray's was £130 13s. Yet Murray paid him £532 17s.* *in toto*, thus incurring a loss of £140 18s. on the transaction. Nevertheless, Vambery wrote several times to Murray on

---

* Now housed in the New York Public Library.
* The equivalent of over £10,000 today.

financial matters: would more money be forthcoming?

"You offer me £500 as an anticipation from the future gains of my book", he wrote to John Murray on 15 June 1865, "but you say . . . that you expose this money at a risico . . ."; and he went on to ask his publisher if he thought that "the *Season's book* which had been translated into almost all european languages, which contains an adventure not hitherto done . . . would be so unsuccessful in England, and yet presently, when Central Asiatic matters are so much discussioned?"

He continued in a vein not calculated to win support from John Murray: "I would say many statements in the Accounts are contradicted by your best friends". He tried to soften the blow by adding: "No, I trust to you more than to anybody . . ."

Vambery did not give up, but his financial calculations were as devious as his character. Four days later he wrote: "Well, £525 is not quite contemptible sum for Dervishes . . . but you reduce from this £101.10.10 already advanced and make the round bounty a broken, defective thing". He continued: "Bounty is only with perfection a real bounty, says an Arab proverb. You style the offered sum a risque. Could you not give to that £75 more and make me the round sum from which I could easily pay the money you already advanced me . . .?"

Nearly all the reviews of *Travels* were favourable. Vambery felt pleased that the prophecies he had made to Sir Roderick Murchison had been verified by events — and that "Russian aggression is favourable for the sale of our book" (he told John Murray). Vambery hoped England would awake from her dangerous slumber — "I stand prepared for every eventuality".

Travels in Central Asia had a wide sale in America, France, Germany, Sweden, Italy, and other countries, as well as England and Austria-Hungary, but the royalties were small. In Germany the fees paid were especially poor, and 500 Thaler (£75) was the highest sum he ever received for what he termed his popular writings. For purely scientific works, such as his Chagataic and Uiguric studies and his *Sheibaniade* — which would take him ten years' work *during his vacation* at the Imperial Library in Vienna and nearly ruined his eyesight into the bargain — he had to pay all the expenses himself.

Vambery was forever asking his various publishers to settle his debts: Murray was instructed to settle up with Vambery's London tailor; send £20 to somebody else; pay four guineas to a Mrs. Meta

Taylor for debts incurred, etc. If Vambery did not ask for another advance, he would promise to pay the money back out of the fees earned from his other writings. On another occasion he requested his Hungarian publisher to settle a debt of 200 Gulden with a Hungarian aristocrat and to send his son a finely bound copy of his travel book; the new debt thus incurred would be settled when Vambery received payment from his French publisher, Hachette.

Writing to John Murray from Pest on 9 December 1868 Vambery demonstrated a character trait which got him far — persistence — but which cannot have exactly endeared him in the eyes of his publisher: "You can do what you will, you can't get rid of me. I write now the third, perhaps you will get the thousandth letter from me until I get an answer . . ." Vambery had become like the old man of the sea by this time. In fact John Murray *had* got rid of Vambery, at least for the time being. *Sketches of Central Asia*, the sequel volume to *Travles*, was published in London by W.H. Allen instead. (Later T. Fisher Unwin became Vambery's regular London publisher, and John Murray did not publish any of Vambery's works until 1906: *Western Culture in Eastern Lands*.)

The reception of *Sketches* was not uniformly enthusiastic. One of the main objections of the reviewer writing in the *Athenaeum* (4 January 1868) was to refer to the dervishes' repeated cry of "YA HU! YA HAKK!" as "Germanisms". Vambery must have been infuriated. For had the reviewer been less ignorant and more willing to do research than to find fault with Vambery, he would have discovered that "Hu" was a sacred sound in Islam (another word for God) and that "Hakk" meant "the truth" — although the correct Arabic spelling was "Haqq".

While more and more of his political essays appeared in foreign journals and periodicals, Vambery found himself blamed for not sticking to Hungarian topics. He hit back at his critics maintaining that his preparatory and later studies had been international in themselves. "And so it came about", he wrote plaintively, "that mentally I remained a stranger in my native land . . . and lived for years confined to my own society, without any intellectual intercourse, withou interchange of ideas, *without recognition!*"

And recognition was what he craved above all.

He was often asked why he did not take part in Hungarian politics — 1867 was a fateful year for Hungary: Franz Josef was crowned King of Hungary on 8 June that year and the Dual Monarchy was established. Vambery claimed that he had never studied law or economics and that he would therefore have made a poor member of Parliament; but he knew full well that the real obstacles were his birth and origins. "I was bound to reckon with this circumstance", he wrote, "and as my ambition could tolerate no half measures and limitations, I preferred to keep altogether aloof from the political arena of Hungary". He had cause to feel slighted when he was not invited to join in any of the Coronation festivities "when Hungarian literati and artists were picked out". Again he was entirely ignored, and it rankled.

Vambery soon shrugged off the petty "adverse criticism" of his "rivals and ill-wishers", and concentrated on setting up his little home in Pest. His modest flat consisted of two small rooms in the Leopoldgasse.* He wrote later of this time: "Sitting down on the velvet-covered sofa, (as) I surveyed the little domain, which now for the first time I could call my own, I experienced a childish delight, and the possession of my own furniture, my own library, made me exceedingly happy", and his "old indestructible cheerfulness' returned. On his walks in the surrounding countryside he "fancied himself the happiest man on earth".

In spite of this optimism, he retained (in his own words) "a childish sensitivity" to real or imagined slights. He mixed very little with Hungarian society, and was regarded almost as a recluse in Pest. His contracts were limited to a few scholars of comparative philology, visitors from western Europe, pilgrims from the East, and the small trickle of students from the University. In Pest he remained on good terms with the Calvinist community, among whom was Professor Aranyi, head of the pathology department at the University, and his young daughter Cornelia.

Vambery married Cornelia Aranyi in 1868, but one feels practically inclined to put this fact in parenthesis, so little did he ever mention her in his writings. When the engagement was announced, Vambery's critics jeered: "What an unhappy idea; and what a pity for that poor girl!" Many people were sure that the footloose Vambery would desert his wife and his home, to run again after adventures in the depths of darkest Asia. Their fears were unfounded.

He had made a good match — socially she was a cut above him. Professor Lajos Aranyi was well connected and could be a useful father-in-law, but he was known to be fiercely antisemetic.

"You can't exterminate the Jews", Aranyi used to say; "better

to dilute their blood, till it finally disappears, by intermarriage".*
He had put theory into practice, by marrying Johanna Joachim
(sister of the famous Jewish violinist Joseph Joachim, a collaborator of Brahms.)

Vambery soon found he had married into a family of eccentrics
— with a real taste of the macabre into the bargain. It is said that
when he and Cornelia visited Professor Aranyi's flat, a small
silent figure always sat at a desk in a corner of the drawing-room,
dressed in a Pierrot costume. It was a boy who never spoke . . . he
was dead — Cornelia's five-year old brother Zoltan (who had
died of hydrocephalia), emblamed by his doting father. Later Zoltan's body was donated to the Natural History Museum of Budapest, where it was displayed in a glass case for many years,
surrounded by his toys.

Discounting the fact that, like all Hungarian wives of the
period, Cornelia knew her place and kept very much in the background, restricting her activities to running a home and looking
after her husband's welfare, little is known about her — except
through the occasional reminiscence of a family friend. Vambery
himself would only mention her in letters in response to friends'
enquiries about her delicate health: "My Cornelia is still ailing
. . ." he would write.

Their only son, Rustem (named after a Persian legendary
hero), was born on 29 February 1872. A description of his mother
has come down to us. "Mama understood little of father's work",
he said; "she had no interest in it, and only saw to it that there was
no dust on the polished furniture and that there was a tasty meal
on the table".

A favourite meeting-place for the ladies of her class was (and
still is today for those elderly ladies hankering after a bourgeois
past) a famous Budapest *patisserie* named *Gerbeaud* on Vorosmarty
ter (Square), comparable to *Rumpelmayer's* in Paris, or *Demel* and
Gerstner's in Vienna . . . Here the ladies of the leisured class used to
meet over cups of coffee piled high with whipped cream and eat
Dobostorte and *Punschkrapfen*; or she might cross the Danube and
visit the equally enticing *Russwurm*, a *patisserie* in Buda.

Rustem remembered his mother as always ailing (in spite of her
basically strong constitution), ringing interminably for servants.
For a long time she was confined to her bed and had to give her
orders from there. "Pettymindedness was mixed with broad-min-
dedness in mother in an extraordinary way", said Rustem.

By the early 1870s Vambery's income had grown enough to enable him to move into a splendid new flat on the Danube embankment, 33 Ferencz Jozsef Rakpart (Franz Josef Quay). With this change of address, Vambery had really 'arrived'! This superb street (one mile in length), to which carriages were not admitted, was the favourite promenade in Pest, and contained the most fashionable cafes. Throughout the season, and the fine summer evenings, it was thronged with the most colourful society.

The writer Max Nordau visited the new flat in November 1875 and left a vivid record of the Vambery household. "Vambery's flat was on the first floor of a new and stately house on the embankment of the Danube, beyond the Customs buildings, just opposite the Blocksberg", wrote Nordau. "The windows overlooked the river that, wide and proud, flowed past, and the apparently boundless mirror of which was, as with as many coloured jewels, studded with the lights of the boats and of the reflected rows of flames of the street lamps".

Vambery could watch the Danube steamers plying upstream to Vienna and downstream to Constantinople. In unkind moments he would chide his wife: "From my study I can look out on to three continents, but you know only this flat . . ." Another reminder of the East across the river at the foot of the Blocksberg was the *Bruckbad*, the baths surmounted by a remarkable rotunda built by the Turks in the sixteenth century.

Max Nordau described Vambery as a man of middle height, slightly built, wiry and supple; his limp was noticeable. His forehead was high and white, and his face had a healthy colour. At the age of forty-three his beard was still chestnut-coloured and trimmed to a fashionable length, as was his moustache which contained a few red hairs. The thinning hair was brushed down flat on the side and his deep-set grey eyes, overshadowed by thick brows, had a hypnotic brilliance. They could occasionally look at a person with a piercing glance, claimed Nordau, but as a rule they were kind and rather waggish; they were lively and could observe acutely, and knew how to take command of an interlocutor, they spoke of audacity and self-confidence, he added: "Those eyes were never lowered before anything or before anybody. They were lordly eyes . . .", in short, "the eyes of a man who is sure of himself, but is not presumptuous . . ."

His voice was clear and harmonious, strong, but sometimes purposely mellowed, his conversation lively. Here all accounts

Vámbéry Cornélia

agree: Vambery was a born raconteur, capable of holding an audience spell-bound. "He was the Eastern fairy-tale teller who carried his blissful, world-forgetting listeners up to the seventh heaven", commented Nordau. "He was the Scheherazade translated into the masculine and endowed with a precious touch of humour . . ." He claimed that Vambery spoke pure German, without any Hungarian or Austrian accent.

Nordau visited the flat several times and found Mrs. Vambery a very amiable hostess. He was flattering in his description of her: "In her youth she had been strikingly beautiful, a fact that was convincingly suggested by her appearance even in her mature years". She was cultured and well-read, he wrote, but kept well in the shadow, never attempting to outshine her brilliant husband. (She was excluded from his study and workroom.)

Nordau described her as kind and extremely cordial towards her guests, and she would often be inclined to display a lavish generosity — in distinct contrast to her husband's miserliness. He remembered with affection that she never forgot his weakness for a certain kind of Hungarian sweet made with poppy seed, known as *Mohnbeugel*; and whenever he came to dinner Mrs. Vambery would make sure that at the end of the meal a plate full of *Beugels* appeared, "outside brown and crisp, inside dripping with butter, rich with poppy seeds, currants and sugar". She usually prepared this herself, though by then the family coast boast of a cook, maid, and nursemaid (frequently a young peasant girl from the environs) which suggests that, although Vambery so often cried poverty, he was living in some style.

According to his son Rustem's accounts, Vambery was a real workhorse. "When I was a child", he told a friend, "he worked ten hours a day; he hardly ever went to the theatre, and never to a concert". (This clearly adhered to the motto of his juvenile days "*Nulla dies sine linea*" — no day without writing a line. He was to stick to it throughout his life.)

Sometimes one secretary came, his son remembered, or two or three would appear simultaneously; these three secretaries sat at separate tables, and Vambery could then dictate in three different languages — here a German, there a French or a Turkish sentence. He did not muddle his thoughts . . . "I remember that he was over fifty", Rustem continued, "when he told me: 'I had a

Studio portait of Cornelia, Vambery's wife. The signature is in Vambery's own handwriting.

hot flush today — I really must relax and take it easy. Probably I should work with one secretary only from now on.'" And "relaxing" meant working only eight instead of ten hours a day.

Vambery had difficulty in dealing with his entire correspondence in later years — it was so vast, his son said, as if he alone were a whole Foreign Office. He believed that there was hardly any other European who had kept up such a varied correspondence with Orientalists all over the globe.

"In Osmanli (Turkish), Persian, and East Turkish",* he claimed, "I was everywhere taken for a native"; and it was in these three languages that he corresponded with Orientalists throughout the world.

He claimed he had no mother tongue, but stories that he knew twenty Turkish dialects — and as many French ones (on one occasion, for example, astounding his audience by opening a Congress in Geneva in the local patois) — may be apocryphal.

His own assessment of his linguistic talents was by no means modest: he could speak fluently, he alleged, Hungarian, German, Slovak, Serbian, Turkish, Tatar, Persian, French, Italian and English, adding: ". . . and although I could write in several languages, I cannot say that I could write in any one language ready for the Press . . . i.e. without mistakes". But he was by no means blind to the "blunders and defects under which so many of my literary productions laboured because of my mode of working".

In his early days he used to write predominantly in Hungarian, but later mostly in German and English, and all that he published since 1864 was written in either one or the other of these two languages (though the English texts had certainly to be heavily edited, despite his claim that he wrote English quite easily — especially after having spent a few weeks in England. Yet he did admit that in England he was never taken for a native, as had been the case with Turkish, French, German and Persian — and even Central Asian languages).

What had become of the devoted Mollah Ishak, who had been Vambery's companion all the way from Khiva to Constantinople, and right to Pest where they disembarked at the Chain Bridge?

Vambery had observed Ishak's gradual change, and a plan slowly began to form in his mind; he realised how useful Ishak

---

* Joseph Macleod: *The Sisters d'Aranyi*, G. Allen & Unwin, 1969.

would be to him in his linguistic studies. The show he put on at the landing-stage at Constantinople was sheer melodrama for the benefit of the unsuspecting Tartar. And Ishak (by no means to his own detriment) fell into the trap.

So, within three days, Ishak had found himself in Budapest. On board the steamer he had often been absorbed in thought; he had been afraid to taste European food, but gradually he had accustomed himself to the novelty of the scene.

In Budapest, Ishak was a sensation.

He walked the streets of the capital still in his costume of Bokhara. "During the first few days he could scarcely find words, so full was he of amazement. He admired everything, from the square-hewn paving stones in the streets, to the lefty buildings and towers . . ."; he was "much struck with the quick walking of the people in the streets and the rapid movement of the vehicles", but, above all, the women arrested his attention, and he could not understand how the *Frengis*, clever and sensible people as they are, could allow their womenfolk to appear in public in such clumsy and uncouth attire and without protection.

In the daytime Vambery would often see him standing by the telegraph wires, listening to the sounds that passed along them. At night he would stare at the gas lamps, full of curiosity to discover whether it was the iron that was burning.

He was, wrote Vambery, astonished by the luxury and the magnificence of the hotels, and thought every person he met a potentate, judging them by their dress; he thought there were no poor in Hungary.

By now he had lost all shyness and fear of the *Frengis* and had an endearing habit of engaging everyone he met in conversation, forgetting that no one could understand him, "and he would go on talking to his heart's content, without being in the least disturbed by the surprise exhibited by those he was thus addressing".

Naturally Vambery was bombarded with questions.

He would have liked to have taken him to London, but "deemed it better to leave him behind in Hungary — in other words, he had had enough trouble in raising enough money for his own fare, let alone for that of the Tartar! He thus left him in the care of a friend in the country, and when he returned, after a year's absence, he was surprised to find that the Tartar's gradual transformation into a Hungarian was complete: he found him dressed in the Hungarian double-braided national costume "and instead of the turban with his hair nicely curled and trimmed, with a rather droll air and demanour, and a certain still gravity in his manner".

He had learnt Hungarian perfectly in a very short time and was liked everywhere; "When for the first time I saw him smartly dressed, and with gloves on his hands, talking most courteously and earnestly to a lady in her drawing-room, I could scarcely refrain from laughing", wrote Vambery.

Ishak learnt to read and write, as well as speak Hungarian, and proved a most useful aid to Vambery in his philological studies. "Mollah Ishak became an oracle for him in his preparations" wrote one of his pupils. (Ignaz Goldziher).

According to Vambery, Ishak became assistant-librarian at the Academy of Sciences, but there is no evidence for this. There are letters in the Academy's archives* which attest to the Vambery's habit of sending him on errands to his fellow academicians . . .

Rustem recalled this story in later years:

In the flat underneath Vambery's, the neighbours once had a very noisy party with gipsy music that lasted till the small hours. When a furious Vambery sent Ishak down to complain, he was told: "Well, this is a 'Magyar bal'." In the morning after, the guests having left and the hosts presumably retired, Vambery ordered Ishak to stamp loudly on the floor and make a terrific racket. When the neighbours complained, he shouted: "Well, this is a 'Tatar bal'!"

Ishak never lost his wanderlust. On one occasion he wandered off in the direction of Vienna, but returned; another time, eastwards, in the direction of Constantinople, and eventually he disappeared from view . . .

In the beautiful, wooded cemetery of Velence (situated between Budapest and Lake Balaton) lies a Mohammedan grave; as the grave of an unbeliever it lies right at the edge of the Calvinist cemetery. Its tombstone, surmounted by a crescent and a star, bears the following inscription:

---

* Ignaz Goldziher.
† "My Tartar Mollah . . . is living with me at Pesth": letter of 26 April 1886. In March 1869 he wrote to Janos Aranyi, Secretary of the Academy and one of Hungary's greatest poets: "Please send the Uigur manuscript that I left at the Academy through my Tartar"; Arany's letter of reply said: "I have handed the manuscript to the Tartar Mollah".

"Itt Nyugszik	("Here rests
Molla Szadik	Mollah Sadik
Azsia Torok	Turkish Asian
Szerzetes	Monk
Sz. 1836	Born 1836
Megh. 22 majus 1892	Died 22 May 1892
Aldas es beke	Blessings and peace
Hamvaira"	To his ashes")

This Mollah Sadik is known to have married a local girl and become a seller of Oriental sweetmeats, but the peasants who could hardly be expected to know the difference between 'Ottoman Turkish' and 'East Turkish' became suspicious. A rumour soon attached itself to his name; he knew the whereabouts of a buried Turkish treasure, and he may possibly have met a violent death.

Mollah Ishak too was reported to have married a local girl. Are Ishak and Sadik one and the same? 'Ishak' ('Isaac' in Arabic) might have been his Islamic name, and Sadik a family name. Or were there two Mollahs roaming this part of the Hungarian countryside at the same time?

19th century view of the Hungarian Academy of Sciences, Budapest.

13

DEFENDER OF THE EMPIRE

The political issues that aroused such passions in the nineteenth century are now dead and forgotten. Forgotten too is the role Arminius Vambery played in them, giving (at first unsolicited) advice to British statesmen and politicians; he sought to influence British public opinion and to alert it to the one overwhelming danger which in those days seemed to threaten the British Empire: the steady southward march of Czarist Russia into Central Asia.

Of course we can now afford to sit back and smile indulgently: not all he predicted came true. The Russians never set foot in "Mohametan India" — now the independent state of Pakistan; Persia and Afghanistan still exist as independent states in their own right and were not overrun by Russia after all. But the British Empire Vambery so desperately sought to defend exists no more.

To the Victorians, right up to the end of the last century, the fears which Vambery so vociferously expressed in lecture tours and dozens of letters to *The Times* were very real indeed. Russia, the "Northern colossus", was steadily advancing southwards and pushing her frontiers more and more into Central Asia. Where would she stop?

Did Russia really have designs on British India? Would the Cossacks have come pouring down the Khyber and the Bolan passes if Britain had been less vigilant on the North-West frontier? What would their reception have been like? Greeted as liberators or hated as conquerors? Or would India itself have become a battlefield?

In Vambery's mind there was no doubt at all: Russia must be stopped at all costs. And he was to view Russia's relentless southward drive and her desire to extend her borders and subdue the unruly nomads with the greatest of misgivings, for between British India and the Czarist Empire — once Turkestan was conquered — lay only Persia and Afghanistan. His importance to Britain lay in the fact that he had first-hand knowledge of the places in the news and could speak from personal experience as the spotlight shifted from Bokhara and Samarkand to Khiva and Merv and then to Herat, when the danger to the British Raj seemed to loom large indeed. Forever on the alert, watchful as a hawk, he tirelessly followed the political news — with special emphasis on Central Asia.

For nearly ten years, right up to 1873, he was *the* undisputed authority on Central Asia. He forecast accurately the fall of Bokhara and Samarkand (1868) and the campaign of Khiva (1873). But as the Russians (most menacingly, it seemed) built more and more forts in the areas they had captured, bent on "pacifying" (the word has a modern ring) the unruly nomads, the result was that those regions, which Vambery alone could claim to have visited, now became increasingly safe and other travellers, on official or secret missions, ventured there as well. Though he still had the edge over others, through his incredible command of languages. Not only could he read the Russian press (and you could count the people who could do so in London, statesmen included, on the fingers of one hand) but he could read Arabic and Persian papers, as well as those of Turkestan, and he kept up his relations with the East through a net of far-flung correspondents. Thus, whatever else you could call Vambery, you could not call him misinformed. And he made it his job to inform the others: principally the British public.

In 1864, the year Vambery was being feted in London, the Russians had taken Tashkent, the capital of a small khanate called Khokand, and had thus set foot for the first time in Turkestan. The newly won territory was incorporated into the Russian Empire and administered by a Russian military governor.

In the same year Prince Gortchakoff, the Russian Foreign Minister, sent a celebrated but ambiguously worded note to Britain. Vambery distrusted it deeply. The note said that Russia's chief motive was simply to secure an effective boundary, one that could be defended against border raids by the Turkomans. The Russians had therefore to advance until they reached the boundaries of a settled state ...

Vambery never believed that Russia's main reason was to make the borders secure against the slave-stealing raids by the Turkomans. He suspected far more sinister motives. Russian designs on India.

He must have been delighted when in 1864 Lord Palmerston asked him, through the intermediary of Sir Roderick Murchison, President of the Royal Geographical Society, to prepare a memorandum concerning the position of Russia on the Yaxartes* and give his views on politics in Central Asia, as well as in Persia and Turkey. He complied with alacrity, he was flattered but perplexed. It seemed to the young Vambery, serious, ambitious, and unfamiliar with British ways, that he was not being taken seriously enough. He was received by the elder statesman, told not to worry, his fears of Russia were shrugged off (but he was encouraged to persevere in writing letters to *The Times*). However, after the fall of Tashkent — an event he had foreseen — more notice was taken of him in political circles, and more questions were put to him, such as: the defensive strength of the Emir of Bokhara (who was trying to fight Russia's might).

He knew full well that the chief interest in his travels lay "in the information which I brought from Khiva, Bokhara and Herat and more especially of the secret movements of Russia towards Central Asia, so far unknown in England because of the total isolation of Central Asia. In political circles curiosity had reached a high pitch for wild and undefined rumours were afloat about the Northern colossus advancing towards the Yaxartes . . ."

Despite his prodigious output his articles were at first only in demand when the Central Asiatic question became acute — as in 1868 and 1873, and again much later in 1885 when Russian activities caused a tremendous stir in Britain and her annexation of Pendjdeh in Afghanistan led to a war scare. Vambery was by then at the apogee of his power. "For the rest", he admits, "I had to force myself on the public, and not only on the continent, but in England also. I often had difficulty in getting a hearing . . ."

At first he wrote infrequently to *The Times*.

His first letter still signed "A Traveller from Central Asia"* dealt with the Russian designs on Tashkent,† as reported in the Russian press. He indignantly refuted the "Reuter's Express" story reported in *The Times* which gave the news of a great defeat of the Russians in Khokand (of which Tashkent had been the capital) as "bearing all the characteristics of a Hadji tale picked up by a

* 17 June 1865.
† Tashkent is today the capital of the Uzbek Soviet Socialist Republic.

greedy European listener . . ." The Emir of Bokhara would fight, he warned, and "the approach by the Russians to Bokhara and Afghanistan will be much sooner than English politicians believe. Russian outposts have gone so far that they cannot stop . . ."

Yet *The Times* was complacent and Central Asia was far away. A bare four months later it spoke of Herat as "always being besieged by somebody or other . . .", and added unworriedly: ". . . if Russia is advancing in the East, she is not advancing half as rapidly as the British in the Punjab; all this Russian danger is a 'phantom of our own creation' . . ."

Vambery must have danced with rage, but for the next two years during which he was busy establishing himself as a professor in Budapest, he kept silent.

But what he read in the Russian press in the spring of 1867 was obviously more than he could bear and he sat down and wrote to *The Times*" immediately. It was a small news item he had culled from the *Journal de St. Petersburg* and it reported a fight between the Emir of Bokhara and a small town in the south of the khanate: this was Sheri Sebz, the birthplace of Timur.

A year later the Chinese suddenly leapt into the news. They had been reported as about to conclude a treaty with the Turkomans. Vambery grabbed his pen and wrote to *The Times*.* He loftily dismissed the story as so much "Tashkent bazaar gossip". "There are no Turkomans in the neighbourhood of China or Chinese Tartary", he wrote and went on to say that the ruler of Khokand, Yakub Kushbegi, had solicited aid from India in exchange of which he promised free trade over the Karakarum pass. "It remains to be seen", he continued, "whether he has made the same request to the Russians, who", he added sarcastically, "are not acquainted with the noble art of 'masterly inactivity'".

There were old-established trade relations between Russia and Central Asia, which imported pig iron tea kettles and water cans from South Siberia and from the Urals, as well as pig iron, brass, cotton goods, cambric, muslin and cutlery. But Vambery maintained with unflagging zeal that the Central Asiatics preferred the superior quality of English goods. He had seen it with his own eyes.

Calico, plain and dyed, linen and muslin were always in great demand when they reached the bazaars of Khiva, Bokhara and

---

* 31 January 1868.

Samarkand — in fact Uzbek ladies had greatly admired the texture of English chintzes which they found far superior to the Russian. Quite apart from this a pious (and wealthy) Muslim wore at least seven yards of English muslin around his head as a turban.

The road from Peshawar to Cabul across the Khyber was dangerous and the Afghan taxes extortionately high and sometimes communications with India were interrupted for months while Russian goods could come in freely and be sold at a lower price. Yet, despite the obvious advantage with Russian trade, the Asiatics were always in search of English manufacture. He devoted pages and pages in his first travel book to making this point and was meticulous in giving examples.

He urged England to conclude formal commerical agreements with the khanates of Bokhara and Khokand while they were still in possession of their formal independence, so that English agents should enjoy the same privileges Russians had. Above all, however, the security on the roads of Afghanistan must be restored, and this depended entirely on the Anglo-Indian army, and then "instead of arms Anglo-Indian goods may take up the fight for the rivalry in Central Asia".

In a letter to *The Times*** in which he stressed the "urgent necessity for diplomatic relations with Afghanistan", he dealt again with trade between India and Central Asia. He quoted a recent publication by T. Douglas Forsyth. "Whenever I entered on the highly important question of anglo-Russian rivalry in Central Asia", he wrote, "it was judged as emanating from anti-Russian feelings, natural to a Hungarian, but this paper had been written by an Englishman . . ." He drew attention to the concluding chapter of his *Sketches in Central Asia* (which dealt with the same subject) and urged the establishment of diplomatic relations not only with Afghanistan, but with "chinese Tartary" (East Turkestan) as well; in neighbouring Khokand the "demand for English friendship and English goods", he wrote, "increase from day to day. Would it not be a mortal sin to continue in obnoxious inactivity . . .?" And he added a news item that might not have reached the general public. It was already current bazaar gossip, he said, that the Maharajah of Kashmir was not on the best footing with the Government of Calcutta, and "was anxious to grasp the Russian arm . . ." He then addressed himself to Lord Lawrence, the

*   18 April 1868.

272

Viceroy on India, and warned him to "have a watchful eye on the present political constellation in Central Asia".

In 1869 Lord Lawrence put on a Durbar for the Emir of Afghanistan. Vambery seized his pen and sent off a letter to *The Times**
in which he gave much advice to the Indian Government. As a point of interest he was able to add a small, yet not insignificant, detail: the Emir would be surrounded by his Risale troops — "the best beyond the Khyber". He pointed to his own experience of the "Asiatic mentality" and warned the public of the dangers if the new Viceroy, the Earl of Mayo, should be "as lenient and flexible as Lord Canning . . .".

One of his recurrent themes was that leniency would be interpreted as weakness in Central Asia; he felt pleased that "after a long hestitation the anglo-Indian Government had at last decided to take an active part in Asian politics, which did not mea, he added, "to oppose Russia with arms but simply to gain the friendship of Afghanistan as a buffer state".

"To gain the friendship of an Asiatic power", he continued, "means (after his dictionary) to help him . . . England is quite right in spelling the word alliance in an Afghan way . . . and to accord the present ruler money and arms".

"Indulgence in the eyes of an Asiatic is equal to weakness", he wrote. "English gold" was not as powerful as "a sober-minded able English officer" and there was "no want of courage among Indian officers" (he quoted names). In establishing consulates not only diplomatic relations but trade would benefit as well. While there were thousands of Afghanis in India, there was scarcely one Englishman who had ventured into Afghanistan and English goods had to pass through two or three hands until they reached the Central Asian markets, "where the amount of expenses forces them to give away before inferior Russian goods".

"Should the Earl of Mayo leave the Anglo-Afghan coalition in the same state as Lord Canning had left it", he warned, the meeting at Umballah (where the Durbar was being held) will be nothing more than mere pageantry "and your political standing will not be a bit better than before".

His warning fell on deaf ears.

Did the British make a mistake in installing Yakub Khan as the ruler of Afghanistan? Vambery had met Yakub Khan grandson of

* 6 April 1869.

Dost Mohammed, when he was sixteen years old in Herat and had nearly been unmasked by him. He thought him anti-British.

The first of Vambery's letters to cause a stir and — to his own surprise — lead to an interpellation in Parliament — was on the subject of Herat. E.B. Eastwick* asked whether there was any truth in the rumours "mentioned in Mr. Vambery's letter, published in the *Times* on the 18th of this month, that Herat had been taken by Yakub Khan?

"It is evidently owing to the great political events in Europe (the Franco-Prussian war) that the English and Continental Press pay so little interest to the recent news relating to the siege or capture of Herat by Yakub Khan ..." wrote Vambery ... but if he succeeds in bringing Herat under his power the subsidies the Anglo-Indian Government so richly bestowed on him will be entirely thrown away". He blamed the policy pursued by the late Viceroy of India for this.

Vambery's claim was denied by Lord Enfield.

Three weeks later he wrote another letter to *The Times*. In it he took the British Government severely to task. "Above all I really regret that the Under-Secretary of State for Foreign Affairs is not better informed what is going on in the north of your Indian Empire than myself in my humble position as a professor of Oriental languages", he wrote, "because if such had been the case his answer to the learned member of Penryn (Eastwick) would, and ought also, to have thrown more light on the political events in that part of the world, where English interests are certainly more at stake than it is imagined in your country ... The capture of Herat is the beginning of the end of Shere Ali Khan's rule".

"Judging from my personal acquaintance with Yakub Khan", he went on, "I am fully convinced of his aversion to the English, to their alliance and to their influence in the affairs of Afghanistan ... England is the chief impediment in his ambitious way ..." and Vambery informed the public that Yakub Khan had rejected gifts presented by the Earl of Mayo on behalf of the Queen ...

If Yakub Khan was anti-British who was he in favour then? For elsewhere Vambery had written: "I do not believe that this prince who extended royal hospitality to me during my stay in his state is still saved by my former blessings; for while I stayed in his capital I had to say a prayer daily to his presence to save him from the power of the Russian arms ..."

Vambery faithfully records in his autobiography the stir his letters caused. "When recently, based on private information, I tried to alert British readers ... to Yakub Khan's machinations and the possible fall of Herat and Mr. Eastwick in an interpellation ... asked the Foreign Office whether it had similar news to mine, Lord Enfield, then Under-Secretary gave a negative answer; but already three days after this ... the offical news was received from Calcutta that Herat had fallen into the hands of the rebellious Yakub Khan. Now the British statesmen were seized by panic. One of my friends who is close to the India Office wrote to me that I would be amazed if I had been witness to the consternation which my second letter to *The Times* concerning the Afghan unrest had caused".[*]

And indeed not even three, a mere two days later than the publication of the second letter *The Times* had reported the fall of Hera as a *fait accompli*.[†]

He had been right again.

In the same letter Vambery thought it not improbably that Yakub Khan would seek an alliance with the Shah of Persia — (Herat lies very close to the border of what is now Afghanistan and Persia) — and would fight his father until he succeeded in overthrowing the throne of Afghanistan, "the chief pillars of which are the rolls of English rupees and the stands of English arms". Will the English allow him to occupy the throne or will they give Shere Ali such a support, asked Vambery, as to enable him to stand up to his own son whose cause will become in short very popular all over Afghanistan?

And in 1872 a bombshell burst: the Earl of Mayo, Viceroy of India, was murdered.

Already three years earlier — Vambery had warned of "dire consequences if Lord Mayo should be as lenient as Lord Canning ..." and in fact, a leader in *The Times* commenting on the murder put it down to the "tolerance and impartiality of the Government over which he presided". It first glance this seems a strange thing

---

[*]   9 June 1871.

[†]   No record can be found for the dates mentioned by Vambery: there is no letter in *The Times* on 18 May 1870 — 22 May turns out to have been a Sunday — but then neither was Lord Enfield Under-Secretary of State in 1870. Vambery slipped up: the year in question was 1871.

to say: tolerance and impartiality seem commendable virtues in themselves. No doubt Vambery would have applauded them as typically British in another setting. But was he right? Were they in fact interpreted as weakness in neighbouring Afghanistan?

Vambery wrote to *The Times* commenting on the murder and forecast that the disorders in Afghanistan would grow worse "if viligance and proper measures are not adopted . . ." He could not resist adding the personal touch: "I too had an opportunity of living among Mahometans", he wrote "and not sheltered by European power and influence, but mine the mendicant dress and many years of preparation . . ."

Seven years later Yakub Khan achieved a short-lived victory: he was recognised by the British as the Emir of Afghanistan, and in his turn agreed to a permanent British Embassy in Kabul. But in the very same year the British resident and his escort were murdered and the second Afghan War had broke out, he was deposed and a pro-British Khan appointed and recognised by Lord Ripon, the new Viceroy of India. The Afghan War ended in 1880 with a defeat of the British.

A battle had been fought at Maiwand and a year later an alarming story was circulated by the British press: four Britons, captured at Maiwand, had been sold into slavery . . . Colonel Stewart was on his way to investigate . . .

Vambery went into action immediately. He sent off a letter to *The Times* at once and stated categorically that the report of "four Englishmen having fallen into slavery" was impossible and "merely a story furnished by the Sepoy not worthy of implicit faith . . ."

He assured his readers that even British privates or soldiers were "such Sahibs" in the eyes of the Afghans (for each European was looked upon as a Sahib by a Central Asian). Therefore, if they were held captive at all, they could only be the prisoners of Ayub Khan himself (brother of Yakub Khan) or of near relatives, but he discounted this possibility as strongly as the idea that any "Turkoman dealer in human flesh" would have sold them to an Afghan: the value of a slave on the market was not more than £20–£25.

A slave sold for menial work would fetch an even lower price if unacquainted with Pushtu, Persian or Uzbeg which might be the case of the four Englishmen in question.

It would therefore seem a far sounder commercial proposition to the Afghans sounder commercial proposition to keep them for ransom. Besides, there had never been any report of an Englishman having been sold into slavery ... and the letter wnet on at great length in a similar strain, mentioning in conclusion that the Russians were very far from controlling the slave trade in their newly won territories. (an argument in their favour advanced by some) "The Russians do not have the power to stop it nor to know the names of the captives". He advised against official action.

Although the British had won a victory at Kandahar they later evacuated it and this was to be a source of considerable anxiety to Vambery who identified himself so totally with the British cause.

Vambery wrote immediately to Lord Lytoon, the Viceroy of India, who thought it of sufficient interest to forward to the editor of *The Times*. It ran:

"I am authorised by the distinguished Asiatic traveller and Orientalist, Professor Vambery, to forward for publication the accompanying letter which I have just received from him, upon the contemplated surrender of Kandahar".

Vambery had written:

"My Lord,

Knowing from the papers that your Lordship is to bring forward before the House of Lords that most interesting question of Kandahar, I beg leave to submit to your Lordship's particular consideration the following minutes of the undersigned, who, as a former traveller, stood in personal intercourse with the Afghans, and who as a political writer nearly twenty years ago cannot remain indifferent on seeing the unwise, nay, suicidal policy which actuated the present English statesmen with regard to the future standing of Great Britain in Asia".

Completely identifying with the British cause he went on to speak of the "moral consequences the voluntary abandoning of Kandahar must obviously have in the eyes of the Afghans, and Moslem Asiatics in general ... which will be most detrimental to your position in India". The Afghans, he argued, would interpret any giving away of territory as weakness, as fear of the Afghans, as fear of Russia ...

"England may commit all kinds of blunders in Asia", he went on, "but for Heaven's sake, do not let her show weakness, which may inevitably ruin her *prestige* with the Asiatics".

He raised a further point. "It is so often said in Liberal quarters that Kandahar will never pay the expenses of permanent occupation and that it will become a burden to the Exchequer of India". (The annual income did not amount to more than £90,000 and the cost of reputed to be tenfold higher). "Are they aware", he thundered, "that Kabul is only looked upon as the residence of the Ameer and Kandahar as the capital? Do they know that the Kandaharis are the most enterprising merchants in the whole of the Afghan nation, and that most of the Afghan traders in the distant bazaars of Central Asia, even in Kashgar and Aksu, are Kandaharis by origin?"

He went on to praise their "eminently commercial spirit" which "must be profitable to their ruler. . ." and after "order and tranquillity had been introduced to that part of Afghanistan it will not only become a flourishing place", but would prove "one of the best investments England could make in the interior of Asia".

After giving ethnographical details of the various tribes who "under certain circumstances" would become England's friends, he warned Lord Lytton "of the imminent danger which threatens your noble and great country by retracing your steps just now, when Russia is about to pave her way to the Paropamisus, it is superfluous to speak to your Lordship whose wise and energetic policy is always bent upon the dangers, and whose practical statesmanlike eye was never deceived by England's enemy".

"The people of England always speak of Merv", he continued, "and feel much gratified that Russia will not extend her conquests to that place. I certainly believe that Russia will at present not go to Merv, as its heap of ruins is out of her way there from the road leading from the Caspian to Herat has always avoided Merv".

And indeed, it was not "at present" but three years later that Russia annexed Merv.

Vambery was worried about the projected Central Asian railway extension which would Russia's line of communication "from the centre of her power to India" (which would run not through the northern steppes but from the Caucasus and through Tekke Turkoman country to Herat).

"Are people naive enough to believe", he wrote, "that ten years' long struggle and the cost of nearly 30 million of roubles — besides the sacrifice of many thousands of lives — should have no other purpose than the civilisation of the Turkomans?"

He alluded to the troubles Russia had experienced in her attempts to subdue and pacify the unruly Yomut Turkomans in the western desert, but did not see why they should not succeed with the Tekke Turkomans as well.

"If this should be done Russia will find all legitimate cause for intervention with the disorderly Afghans, and there is no exaggeration in saying that ten years will suffice to bring Russian outposts in close proximity to Kandahar and to India".

"My heart bleeds", he added, "in seeing the sinful indifference and credulity of many of your countrymen".

"When seventeen years ago", he continued, "I called your attention to the coming events in Turkestan,* I was ridiculed and called an exalted Hungarian. Alas, many of my predictions have been fulfilled since then. It pains me nitterly for having become a Cassandra . . ." and he ended his letter with an outsize melodramatic flourish, so characteristic of him: "I would prefer death", he wrote, "rather than to see how a great and free nation is brought to the brink of ruin through the carelessness of your statesmen".

He appealed to his Lordship's "high-minded and patriotic soul" and besought him most humbly to use all his available influence in favour of the retention of Kandahar (and of the continuation of the railway from Siri in India to Kandahar) and after the usual courteous formula at the end, signed himself: "Arminius Vambery, Professor of Oriental Languages at the Royal University of Buda-Pest".

A day later Vambery must have been pleased to read a report in the German press, sent by their London Correspondent, which spoke of an important meeting convened "today", in favour of the occupation of Candahar and which mentioned Vambery's letter to Lord Lytton, giving a summary of its contents.

Lord Lytton sent off a scholarly and enigmatic letter to Vambery who naturally quotes it in full in his autobiography.

---

*   Yakub Khan was exiled to India and *The Times*, reporting his death at Dehra Dun on 16 November 1923, quoted him as having come to the tent of Sir Frederick (later Lord) Roberts after his defeat in 1879 by the British, complaining about his wretched life as an Ameer and saying that he "would rather be a grass-cutter in the British camp than a ruler of Afghanistan . . ." (see p. 276).

     Vambery did not think that Yakub Khan had masterminded the murder of Sir Louis Cavagnari, the British resident. (See: *The Nineteenth Century*, July 1892).

*   11 October 1881.

Datelined Knebworth Park, Stevenage, Herts, it ran as follows:-

"Dear Professor Vambery,

I am very much obliged for you for your interesting and valuable letter about Kandahar, and you have increased my obligation by your permission to publish it, of which I have availed myself. *I little thought*, when I had the honour of making your acquaintance many years ago at Lord Houghton's *that I should live to need and receive your valued aid in endeavouring to save England's Empire in the East* from the only form of death against which not even the gods themselves can guard their favourites — death by suicide. . . ."

> Believe me, dear Professor Vambery,
> Very sincerely yours,
>
> LYTTON".

To what extent had Lytton written this letter tongue in cheek? For he certainly did not act upon it. Yet Vambery exulted in dythirambic prose. "In non-English Europe", he writes, "great statesmen seldom or never condesend t write in such terms to mere journalists", adding significantly: "And, further, what must be the feelings of the writer who knows all about England's glorious doings in Asia, and from his earliest youth had dreamed of political freedom; who, hampered hitherto by the mediaeval prejudices still prevalent in Austria, finds himself all at once able to move and act without restraint, and has not to be ashamed of his low birth? One may say what one likes against the English", he cried, "(and they have no doubt some very glaring faults), but this one thing must be allowed — before all things they are men, and only after that are they British".

Meanwhile the Russian campaign against Khiva had begun. (1873). Vambery had the temerity to take issue with SirHenry Rawlinson, the greatest living authority on Central Asia, in the columns of *The Times*, contradicting him on military matters — ("*one* Russian could fight *fifty* Tartars") — and giving such "highly amusing" details as the length of time it took an Uzbeg to light the fuse of a gun (there were 25 all told in Khiva), and the army, he added, amounted more to a rabble . . . He predicted that the Turkomans around Khiva would not remain neutral and that they would harass the Russian columns "in the most sensible way". But, he warned, they would only temporarily delay the

Russians, they would be no lasting hindrance. "As soon as Russia shall have occupied Khiva", he wrote "I doubted from the beginning her withdrawing from it — she will not fail to open up a safe route to Khorassan. This was the ulterior motive which had prompted the Russians to build a chain of fortifications "to fill the gap in Central Asia conquests . . . for the real line of Russian policy was to extend communications from the Caspian to Khorassan . . ."

Thus he saw no reason for the Russians to evacuate Khiva again "for the loss of prestige is so fatal with Orientals".

His opinions were again quoted in the House of Commons. Inexplicably Vambery does not mention this. On 22 April 1873 Eastwick made a very long speech about Central Asia and said: "No instance, said Vambery, has yet been known of the Russians ever retracing their steps in any part of Asia", and he quoted Count Perovski's proclamation on entering Central Asia: 'The Russians have come here not for a day, not yet for a year, *but for ever!*"

A measure of the growing respect in which his opinions were held was also the increasing space allotted to his letters in *The Times*. (Sometimes they take up 1½ to 2 columns or more).

Ocasionally they are self-congratulatory: "I cannot neglect the opportunity to say that your Government has at last opened its eyes to proceedings in Central Asia," he wrote on one occasion.

"By this one movement I can see myself richly rewarded for my ten years continual preaching and writing".

In the same year — 1872 — his *History of Bokhara* was published (in German, Hungarian, English and Russian). He had offered it to John Murray who rejected it.* This 410 pp long work did — in Vambery's own estimation — more harm than good to his literary reputation. It was based on Oriental manuscripts he had bought in Bokhara which he had believed to be unknown in Europe. He was wrong: he had failed to research the subject thoroughly and all but the history of modern times was already known.

The Times gave it a less than rapturous review.* "Though less interesting than we had expected", wrote the reviewer, "it hardly touches the grave questions which the name of Central Asia may suggest, it is nevertheless an instructive work and con-

*   4 June 1873.

tributes something in respect to a land which is again acquiring historical importance and may become the scene of memorable events".

"Its author, Professor Vambery", he added, "is a true scholar and has spent years travelling in Turkestan and Persia, his book possesses the real merit of knowledge and experience".

Yet he found the book "antiquarian in character — it deals too much with the extinct past. It tells too little about distant countries which now alone separate the outposts of Russia and the Indian Empire".

And finally he found it "wanting in fancy and taste, its style dry . . . inanimate, tame . . . its pages crowded with uncouth names . . ."

The *Athenaeum* published a more favourable review of the book. "Nobody knows more about this wild region than Professor Vambery", wrote the reviewer", . . . He adds new materoal in quoting the *Sheibaniade*, a Chagataic heroic poem of which there is a unique copy in the Imperial Library in Vienna . . . No one can read these last chapters without feeling that, whatever may be the effect of Russian neighbourliness on our Indian Empire, it is for the best interests of mankind thatRussia should continue her onward advance . . ." (This reflected the current view of one sector of the public who maintained that it was better "to have a well-dressed and civilised man as your neighbour as a banquet than a barbarian").

Vambery thought on the whole that the professional critics were merciless. They "seemed to take a malicious pleasure in running me down; especially . . . in Russia where I was already hated for my political opinions and activity . . ."

The book proved disastrous to him. Attack came from an unexpected quarter. Eugene Schuyler, an American diplomat at the Court of St. Petersburg, and himself the author of books on Turkestan, wrote off to the high-brow *Athenaeum* which printed his letter in full.*

"No one would cite as an authority the amusing account given by Dr. Wolff of his self-imposed mission in search of Stoddart and Conolly . . . As to the books of Vambery the most noted of modern travellers, they are nearly worthless. I have not yet been able to make up my mind whether Vambery was actually there or not.

* 4th October 1879

which is not told us by other writers and the errors are so frequent and so great, that it would seem impossible for a man to make them who had seen with his own eyes the things of which he speaks".

Schuyler gave details: the *Koktash* (the stone on which Timur's throne had stood in Samarkand) was neither blue, nor green (as Vambery had said) but whitish-grey.

Other details followed, but most damning of all — and totally unexpected — were the *fatty-tailed sheep* which Vambery had mentioned in his account. It had caused amazement and laughter among his Bokharan acquaintances, wrote Schuyler, for it was a well-known fact that in Central Asia sheep had no tail at all . . . Clearly, if further proof were needed, Vambery had never been there at all and had copied everything out from Herodotus.

Most of the Russians, the letter went on to say, did not believe either that Vambery had been there . . . and to travel as a "beggar dervish" was the worst, not the best means of seeing the country. "Perhaps we must ascribe to this the fact", Schuyler continued relentlessly, "of Mr. Vambery's failure to give a faithful picture of Bokhara life, and the mistakes and faults and want of vividness of his books are apparently owing to the want of notes, memoranda, a short memory and a too close study of the accounts left by previous travellers".

One of the greatest errors in Vambery's *History of Bokhara* was his account of the Russian advance in Central Asia . . .

"Of his more ambitious scientific books the less said the better", he said in conclusion, referring in particular to a publication dealing with the Chagataic language.* "It is utterly useless to the philological student as it is one mass of errors. There is no language bearing the name of Tchagatsi . . ."

Vambery was not slow to reply and the *Athenaeum* printed his letter a fortnight later.

"I have never pretended that my books are of any value . . .", he wrote, counter-attacking vigorously, ". . . but favourable opinions of my ethnographical, historical and philological books have been expressed by such ignoramuses as the late Lord Strangford, Sir Henry Rawlinson, Colonel Yule* and Mr. Redhouse‡. The latter makes use of my *Studies in Chagataic* in his great Turkish Dic-

---

*   25 January 1873. (No. 2361).
†   Sir Henry Yule, historian and geographer (1820-89).
‡   (Sir) James William Redhouse, Oriental scholar (1811-92)

tionary. As to Mr. Schuyler's doubts of my having been in Bokhara . . . and in Central Asia in general . . . he contradicts himself in the next line by saying that my failure may be ascribed to the disguise I assumed in my wanderings in Turkestan.

"He quotes 'serious Russian writers' by name, who nearly all corroborate my date . . . but Schuyler is wiser than all Orientalists in Europe".

He claimed Schuyler "took it into his head to represent my journey as fiction . . . (and) . . . even asserted that I, a connoisseur (sic) of Oriental languages, had never been in Bokhara, nor Samarkand, and had written my book with no other foundation than the facts I had collected in the Bosphorus, and as a proof of this assertion it was said that I described the famous nephrit stone on the tomb of Timur as green, whereas in reality it was blue . . .", and Vambery apologised (sarcastically) for not having been able to measure the *Koktash* — "my ruin would have been unavoidable" — and pointed out that the main error in Schuyler's criticism was that he had forgotten entirely the difference the last 10 years had made in the political conditions of Central Asia", adding bitingly: "I am sure had he undertaken his journey in 1863 the *Athenaeum* would never have been favoured by a letter from him; for no European was safe when I was there — and now, look, only a few weeks ago, a Miss Mittelstedt had given a concert to Russians and Tadjiks . . . !"

He admitted however that one of his greatest mistakes had been "in meddling in philological matters without first consulting the appropriate works".

A couple of months later Ashton Dilke* — "a furious Liberal and a pro-Russian" — joined in the fray. His letter was published in full by the *Athenaeum*;* he referred to Schuyler's diatribe against Vambery but was kinder in tone; while pointing out the various inaccuracies in Vambery's writings, he recognised the difficulties he was working under, yet supported Schuyler over the wretched controversy regarding the colour of the *Koktash* and added that Vambery's descriptions of life in Bokhara and Samarkand might have been drawn from Khivan life . . . in the same way his description of entering Samarkand by a certain gate was "comparable to a traveller coming from Edinburgh and entering London by the Brighton road . . ." Schuyler's allegations might be true, or might not . . . time alone would tell.

Nearly a decade later a talented journalist named O'Donovan, the 'Special' of an English paper, visited Turkestan at the height of its troubles and wrote a graphic description of his experiences as a War Correspondent. (It makes excellent reading even today).

Vambery had every reason to be grateful to him.

On his journey through Turkestan chance had led him to stay for months in the *Kibitka* (dwelling place) of an old man, named Dourdi.* "This was the same *Kibitka* in which Vambery had lived", he writes, "for notwithstanding that he succeeded in passing through unrecognised as a European, the inhabitants afterwards learned his true character, doubtless from the Russians at the naval station of Ashurada nearby.

"I heard of the famous Hungarian", he continues, "from the son of his former host.* He described the traveller as being like Timour Lenk, the great Central Asian conqueror, i.e. somewhat lame. Of course this knowledge of Vambery was not arrived at until some time after his departure . . . as otherwise it might have fared badly with him, and he certainly would not have been allowed to pass on".

Here was proof of the authenticity of his journey! But what was to confound his enemies even more — and prove Vambery's veractiy — was that O'Donovan mentioned the *fatty-tailed sheep* of Central Asia! "The animals are of the big-tailed variety", he wrote, "and all the fat of their bodies seems to concentrate itself in the tail, which cannot, on the average weigh less than 12 lbs and is the dearest portion of the carcass. When a sheep is killed, the tail is first made use of . . . the fat is melted down to the consistency of oil . . . each person dips his bread into the melted grease, now and again fishing out of a morsel of meat. Owing to the high temperature of the fat, these morsels are quite calcined and taste precisely like greasy cinders . . ."

O'Donovan's book contained many more references to the fatty-tailed sheep of Turkestan: "The sheep is everywhere of the race with fat tails; the finest are met with in Bokhara. Its flesh is the best I have tasted in the East".

Modern travel writers mention them as well.

And years later, in 1886, Vambery received a letter from

---

* Brother of Sir Charles W. Dilke.
† No. 2407, 13 December 1873.

Eugene Schuyler in Budapest.

"Dear Mr. Vambery", the letter ran, "If you are willing to overlook some hasty criticisms of mine when I was in Central Asia, and will receive me, I shall be most happy to call upon you".

Vambery reproduced this short letter in full in his autobiography and one can positively feel the satisfaction oozing from every line as he writes: "Of course I overlooked the 'hasty criticisms', gave Mr. Schuyler a warm reception, and have corresponded with him ever since".

The Russians did their best to win Vambery over to their side. One day, so Vambery tells us, he received a Russian diplomat, a "well-known statesman", in Budapest who introduced himself with the flattering remark: "When the great Greek General fled to Persia he presented himself before Cyrus the greatest enemy of the Greeks. I have come to Hungary to pay my respects to you".

"Of course", writes Vambery, "I received the wily diplomatist as pleasantly as possible", and when his visitor had looked round Vambery's modest flat, he turned to him and remarked: "You work a great deal, and yet you do not appear to be very well off," adding cryptically: "*You would probably be in better circumstances if you did not work so much*". (The italics are Vambery's).

Vambery replied with a smile that he had got used to Dervish life in Asia, that it suited him admirably both morally and physically, and that he felt no desire to change.

"Quite so", replied the Russian, and changed the subject.

Various other attempts were made wrote Vambery to turn him aside from the path he pursued and to discredit him in the eyes of England and the Continent. "But their trouble was all in vain".

14

THE RUSSIAN MENACE

On 3rd of June 1875, R.W. Hanbury*, Conservative M.P. for Tamworth, had asked the Under-Secretary for Foreign Affairs in the House of Commons whether his attention had been called to a letter in *The Times* of 2 June, in which Professor Vambery had mentioned a Russian expedition to hitherto unknown districts of the River Oxus; whether the purpose of the expedition had been communicated to the English Government; and whether . . . as stated by M. Vambery, the diplomatist M. Weinberg is a member of the expedition, and if it is of a scientific character.*

Robert Bourke, younger brother of the Earl of Mayo, Under-Secretary of State for Foreign Affairs said in reply that he had read the letter in question but that no information had been received at the Foreign Office on this subject.

This letter, published by *The Times* gave great detail of the expedition. Its composition was curious: the editor of the *Turkestan Gazette,* an astronomer and the 'diplomatist', Mr. Weinberg. "There is no doubt science will rejoice at its result", Vambery ended his long letter ironically", but the addition of a diplomatist proves that there are also other objects in view, and that the attention drawn to this new movement is not at all superfluous".

Vambery was right.

Three years later, *The Times* re-published an article written by the "well-known Oriental publicist, Arminius Vambery" which had appeared in a German paper, the *Allgemeine Zeitung* of Augsburg. In it Vambery had quoted the *Turkestan Gazette* and referred to persistent reports of Russian troop movements in Central Asia,

---

*   Robert William Hanbury (1845-1903), a politician and friend of Vambery's who had visited him in Budapest, "in a thin frock-coat without an overcoat in a rigorous winter", as Vambery mentions in his obituary. (*The Times*, 9 May 1903).

*   Verbatim, Hansard, 3 June 1875.

and in particular to the "Tartar diplomatist", Mr. Weinberg, who had lately been on a mission to see whether the Emir of Bokhara would supply provisions to the Russian army. He assured him Russia professed to have no hostile intentions against Afghanistan. The Emir agreed to allow as much flour, fruit and other victuals to be purchased by the Russian army as required; and Vambery concluded that it was evident, beyond a doubt, that the Russians were beginning to move into the interior of Asia.

The unsettled conditions of Afghanistan did not contribute either to a feeling of ease on the part of Britain; for even though the towering ranges of the Hindu Kush formed a nearly impenetrable barrier between Afghanistan and India there were quite accessible mountain passes and possibly even more accessible guides . . .

Successor of Dost Mohammed was Sher Ali Khan whom Vambery described as "of a very fickle character . . . sometimes cruel and unmerciful, as, for example towards his talented son, Yakub Khan, whose life he spares only out of consideration for England . . ." He had seen English soldiers, in their red coats, in their youth, "men whose moustaches have been shaved off", he wondered at the strange nation of the *Frengis*, laughed at them, mocked them, but also feared them. But after the unhappy ending of the British campaign in Afghanistan "he even began to doubt the devilish might of the *Frengis*". But when he ascended the throne, he seemed to change his mind, "for as is known in the whole of Asia and also in Europe, most money can be obtained from the British. This was the begin and the aim of his efforts at civilisation". At the same time, as Vambery wrote, this ruler was casting covetous looks towards St. Petersburg . . . hoping for subsidies . . ."

The animosity between the small state of Khokand and Bokhara, wrote Vambery, was of ancient date. In itself this would have been of little interest to British statesmen but the capital of Khokand was Tashkent and one of the most important cities in Central Asia. Vambery had correctly forecast its capture by the Russians. He added that Russian would find little difficulty in capturing Bokhara and the whole of Khokand as well, "for what might prove difficult for the Russian bayonet would be facilitated by intestine discord".

In Vambery's opinion the Russians had in view, in the immediate future, neither Afghanistan nor India but something else — "a stepping-stone to the latter, viz. Merv", hoping thus to anticipate the arrival of the English in Western Afghanistan.

And he proceeded to give detailed reasons why the Russians could seize Merv and the English would be unable to come up from Quetta to strike at the Russian flank. "It is possible while this is written that Merv is already in the hands of the Russians — more probably they will have commenced their march thither", he concluded his article.

On the march they were indeed, but they were not to seize Merv until six years later.

Meanwhile Vambery's *Central Asia — the Anglo-Russian Frontier Question*, originally written in German and translted by F.E. Bunnett (a lady who came in for some unkind asides), had been published. It came out at the time of the Russian campaign for Khiva and was a collection of Vambery's political writings, originally published in Leipzig. In it he discussed "the question at issue between England and Russia", not, he protests, based on his "magyar and therefore anti-Russian feelings but on facts and lengthy study".

"It found a good sale", he writes, "and although not much of a material advantage to me gave me a good deal of moral encouragement".

The *Athenaeum** was more critical than most and said: "We add a word of regret that Mr. Vambery has not found a better translator, adding with relish: ". . . there surely is no such person as Colonel Ktchirikoff". (But as any student of Russian knows the most improbably combination of sounds do exist in that language.)

Were the Russians after the Central Asiatic markets? Vambery certainly thought so.

About ten years earlier, despite the anarchy reigning in Afghanistan (and on both banks of the Oxus) there was still a relatively lively caravan traffic between the commercial cities of northwest India and the chief markets in Central Asia. A large amount of coloured cotton, muslin and silks, as well as cloth and iron wares left India for Bokhara, Karshi, Samarkand, even Khokand, via Kabul and Kandahar. From Bokhara and Karshi goods went to other parts of Turkestan, and to Herat and Maimene in Afghanistan. Although Kandahar and Kabul were nearer to Peshawar and Karachi they preferred the Russian merchandise although inferior to that of India; and although the road from India via Herat was far more convenient than from Russia, through the desert of Central Asia, British trade had been supplanted by Russia.

And although some Central Asiatics sold goods under false pretences, calling them *Ingilis Mali* (English goods), the Russians were more experienced as far as taste went than the "English manufacturers of Glasgow".

He pointed to the dangers from bandits on the Herat route, unable to resist reiterating his own experiences. ("I have seen for myself how terrible the steppes are which separate the khanates of Bokhara and Khokand in the north ... (wandering) ... through a southern stretch of it-the so-called desert of Kalata ..."

Today these dangers had decreased very much but the advantages of security and protection which Russia had stipulated in her treaties, had benefited Russian businessmen above all. "And Russia will see to it that they keep this monopoly (in Central Asia)", wrote Vambery, adding that Russian had not been able to excluse the British businessman from Turkestan, and would probably never do so ..."

Freedom-loving as Vambery was, he abhorred slavery. "I hear that this abominable trade in human beings has in recent times already become far less lucrative", he was forced to add, giving credit, albeit unwillingly, to the Russians. Yet one could not trust the Russians. Recent events had convinced *that it is Russia's intention to seize India.*

And he compared, to Russia's detriment, the benefits of British rule in India.

He referred to his own political prophecies which had now indeed come true, but in August 1863, on his way from Bokhara to Samarkand, "sitting in a Tartar cart which shook me to the core ..."he would not have believed possible. "That this most eastern point of my wanderings ... will now be visited by Russian soldiers and soon no doubt also Russian Popes who will move about with a forceful tread where I — the mightiest turban covering my forehead and neck — dared only to peer about in humility ... seems really like a fairy-tale to me ..." The news of Samarkand's fall had upset him most deeply, he added — he had never thought it would happen so quickly.

Would the Afghans under Russian domination (which he held to be a possibility) hold back from invading India? he asked, adding "While in the year 1867 the majority of the British Press and the official papers in India attacked my political views in rather strong terms and the *Pall Mall Gazette* even honoured me with the title of chief alarmist; now — a year later — since my essay on Anglo-Russian rivalry was published in *Unsere Zeit* (Our Time) their views have taken a strange turn . . .

He gave *The Times* a lashing for applauding the policy of "masterly inactivity" followed by the Viceroy of India as far back as 1867 and triumphantly quoted a leader of *The Times* a year later which vindicated his assertions . . . It seemed to Vambery as if he were hearing an echo of the words he uttered in 1864 and "which were then mocked by *The Times* who called him a Hungarian and therefore an enemy of the Russians, a traveller and therefore a person with eccentric ideas.

The Court of St. Petersburg wanted to revive the old trade routes to China, he added, wishing to beat the British, "and despite the sleepiness of the present Government in India (it) has sent out an exploratory corps to build a road from Assam to Burma and into the province of Yunnan . . . But of course the British were again beaten by the Russians . . ." despite the fact that the region are easier accessible to India than to Russia . . .?

He quoted his own experience and what his friend, *Hadji* Bilal, had told him about East Turkestan* and that was that its inhabitants considered the British Government a model of justice and order, far superior to the Chinese, so that pilgrims to Mecca preferred the difficulties of the Karakorum pass to the road via Bokhara and willingly made a big detour . . .

Discussing Persia and Turkey from his usual superior-European point of view he sneered at the Persian Government for "sending students to Paris to learn the manufacture of buttons". But he also gave news which must have interested many in Britain, namely that numerous deserters from the Sepoy army were now engaged in building fortifications in Afghanistan, and some, who had fled over the Khyber, had entered the Afghan army.

The question of over-riding importance, on everyone's mind, was: how would Afghanistan behave if overrun by the Russians? Vambery advised England to hold on to Herat: its strategic value was considerably greater "than the gentlemen of Calcutta

---

* That the region was famed for its devotion, its excellent fat and the exceptionally low price for its women (who outnumbered the men by two to one).

believed . . .", for Herat, was the key — even the gate-way — to India . . .

He noted with pleasure that British statesmen "though a little too late", began to extend their influence beyond the Khyber pass ". . . in Afghanistan the regular troops are drilled to British command, who wishes to be fashionable wears English clothes and lets his whiskers grow. Peshawar and Delhi represent Paris and London . . . the Oxus will be the first point where British and Russian culture will clash . . ."

But Vambery was wrong. The collision which he thought could "hardly be avoided" never came. The "dangerous proximity of the Russians to Northern India" was mostly in his mind for between British India and Turkestan lay the entire width of mountainous Afghanistan.

Vambery advocated friendly relations with Afghanistan; Britain should pay her a large subvention (she already paid £120,000 annually) to make the country safe and not march over the Khyber to invade it. He advised that the frontier should run over the Bolan pass and the British take possession of the 70-mile long Dadar-Quetta road in order to make the Herat-Kandahar road safer . . . adding caustically, ". . . The gentlemen in Peshawar will have hardly enough time to watch Russian movements with their telescopes from the summits of the Hindukush while the latter will already have taken possession of Herat . . ."

He discussed at length the danger of letting the Russian southward drive go unchecked, since this threatened the promised neutrality of Afghanistan; and, from his remote fastness in Budapest, he fulminated against the Gladstone administration "which is determined to preserve peace at all costs". Russia would never be content with a policy of 'so far and no further'. "The British need to wake up!" he wrote. "The men from the icy zones are firmer than the British grown soft under the Indian sun."

He was quite confident that he was right. "Just as nearly everything I prophecied so far concerning Russia's march to the south took place, in the same way my last statement will also come true . . . it (Russia) will only stop in its advance when it clashes with another civilished state head on".

The hint was clear. Despite certain Russian assurances which had recently reached Britain, he asked: "How can anyone believe that there will be a lasting relation of friendship?" He accused the

British Government of trying to escape "from the oppressive demand of manly decisive action, perhaps even of conflict. This policy of self-deception of today's Cabinet on the Thames is an unwise as it is unpractical . . . Mr. Gladstone & Co. should remember the worth of Russian promises . . ." Russia only felt bound by treaties as long as it suited her.

The *Athenaeum* gave the book a tremendous write-up. "It has been, in some degree, the fashion to decay M. Vambery and his utterances on the Central Asian question, or rather, it has been for some peculiar reason, an understood thing, that no heed should be taken of the advice which he has voluntarily given England on the subject of Russian advances in Central Asia", wrote the reviewer. "This may be attributable to the opinions of public men and authorities in England, to whom he first introduced himself on his return from his remarkable travels in Central Asia; it may also be ascribed in a measure to the inaccuracy of some of the statements which he has given to the world in his books, and to his acknowledged enmity to Russia . . ."

"We cannot allow ourselves either the time or the space to attempt any further explanation of the reason why M. Vambery has not established himself as an authority among us", he went on (and Vambery was to live to see this reversed), "nor need we be apologists so long as the book which we are now noticing in read with the attention it deserves . . . We nevertheless remark that M. Vambery's views and opinions need have no less weight in our estimation for the circumstance of his being a foreigner and a Hungarian . . ."

The review then alluded again to Vambery's inaccuracies. "Notwithstanding . . . the several errors in the account of his travels" which M. Vambery had been accused of", the reviewer added "we feel bound to own that he is a correct exponent of the Russian policy in Central Asia. "On the soundness of M. Vambery's judgments we can now barely have a doubt seeing that his forecasts in respect to the probable issues of the various Russian operations in Central Asia have all proved correct to the letter".

The writer also agreed with Vambery's suggestions (to appoint a permanent British representative in Afghanistan) and was convinced that England's civilizing influence was superior to that of Russia. "The Russians do not educate their subjects", he wrote with some perspicacity, "they train them politically . . . (and) the conquered become slaves". He regretted that Vambery had not found a better translator, and recommended the book "to the serious consideration of statesmen and politicians."

Vambery hammered four themes home with unrelenting vigour: England must stand up to Russia — Russia threatened British trade — Russia had designs on India — and, above all, war was inevitable.

On 17 April 1880 he gave a lecture to a select gathering at the Royal Society of Arts in London. The title of the lecture was "Russian Influence in Central Asia" and his distinguished audience included a number of baronets and military men. He dwelt largely on trade. Central Asia had been inundated by comparatively cheaper articles (since she had abolished duty) and exports to Russia were increasing daily. The danger of Russian monopoly was even greater for articles which had previously been imported from India and Afghanistan — the duty was prohibitive, damaging trade and the trade with Persia had been damaged as well.

Russian tea was being promoted to the exclusion of tea from India, and the heavy taxation introduced by Russia in Central Asia was worse than before.

The sale of slaves went on in three the Khanates just as before* — its abolition, "this act of humanity, of which the Russian papers boast, is of much the same nature as all others . . ."

On April 22, he read a paper at the Royal United Service Institute in London, entitled "The Past and the Future of the e Turkomans". He was introduced by Sir Henry Rawlinson as the "chief, if not the only, living authority on the question".

The paper dealt with the question not from the ethnographic point of view (as he had done 16 years earlier), but discussed the military aspect of the situation. What chances did a conqueror have? How could a future collision between the two European rival powers be avoided?

Vambery spoke of the military valour of the Turkomans (from his personal experience), their soldierly qualities, and their superior tactics which were the same as those of the ancient Huns and Magyars.

Russian use of cannons against Turkoman men, women and children at the siege of Denghil Tepe had aroused a shocked outcry in Victorian England.

Vambery rounded off his talk with a few political remarks. Law and order must be established in Persia which could thus be one a useful ally.

"Russia will not stop moving southwards until she had reached the Khyber or the Bolan pass ..." warned Vambery.

With a finger of the map, Vambery was anxiously following the latest developments, for suddenly the political spotlight had switched to Merv,* a forgotten little khanate in Central Asia, important only from a strategic point of view (in a south-easterly direction, as the crow flies, lay Kabul and from there a caravan route led over the Khyber to Peshawar in British India) and now in the news since the Russians seemed bent on annexing it.

Inveighing against the political optimists in England who were "lulled into the sleep of false security" he added: "I am at a loss to understand the joy manifested and the calmness shown by the British public on receiving the news of Russia's advance towards Merv. ... This ... would only be justifiable if England could be sure that Merv is the last step of Russia's progress towares India ... or if English statesmen agreed to let Russia come down the Suleiman range and to greet her as the long-desired neighbour on the frontiers of India.

But Britain was not as calm as all that.

Sir Charles Dilke, a prominent Liberal MP, made a speech in the Commons about Merv and the British were indeed alarmed. "The Russian annexation of Merv also caused considerable interest in Calcutta", wrote *The Times*. "The universal opinion is that it means considerable danger to India ... a danger which could have been obviated by the retention of Kandahar ..." (which Vambery had advocated) ... "... the general view is that it is hopeless to try and persuade the Government of India or of England to make any protests".

Vambery too complained of "the want of clearness and of a well-defined policy in Central Asia ..."

And rivers of ink flowed on the subject of Merv.

In 1881 Charles Marvin, who was to become a close friend of Vambery, wrote a best-seller called *Merv, the Queen of the World*, in which he enlarged on its importance and included a chapter on "The Siourge of the Man-Stealing Turkomans".

Marvin was none too scrupulous a journalist, catering to the

---

* Slavery was still a burning issue, although it had been abolished in America 17 years earlier in 1863.
* Today the ancient town of Merv lies neglected and forgotten alongside the modern town of Mary, capital of the Turkmene Soviet Socialist Republic.

sensation-loving section of the public, and his 'scoop' of 1878 was the disclosure of a secret treaty between Lord Salisbury and Count Schuvaloff which had never been meant for publication. But Marvin could not be prosecuted since he had broken no law.*

In due course Marvin made a name for himself as "*the* authority on all matters bearing on the advance of Russia in Central Asia", and was greatly commended by Vambery for his work: despite the twenty odd years difference in age the two me seemed to have formed a mutual admiration society.

Marvin's book on Merv† was fulsomely dedicated to the friend he admired so much.

"To England's Warmest and Most Disinterested Supporter in her Rivalry with Russia,
ARMINIUS VAMBERY
this work is respectfully dedicated by THE AUTHOR"

Great chunks of it were devoted to "Vambery's perilous journey through Turkmenia in the disguise of a Dervish", his sufferings, his narrow escapes and his adventures in general. "Nearly twenty years elapsed before a fresh attempt was made to acquire a knowledge of the Turkomans and the triangular region between Herat, Khiva and Bokhara", wrote Marvin, "and it does not say much for the credit of England that the explorer should have been a Hungarian, and he a cripple".

He called Vambery's *Travels in Central Asia* "undoubtedly one of the finest books of the kind we have in the English language, as well for graphic and forcible diction as for the adventures described".

It also contained a chapter entitled: "England's ingratitude to Vambery — A model English patriot" and said: "As a Russophile . . . I protest against the unmanly way that Arminius Vambery has been attacked by Russophiles for supporting England against Russia in their rivalry in the East, and, as an Englishman of the middle-class . . . I only give expression to opinion of the weightiest section of the nation in affirming that that section is deeply sensible of the Hungarian's services, and holds him and them in affectionate esteem".

Vambery, said Marvin finally, had two courses open on his return from Asia: either to join the side of Russia or of England, in

---

* The Official Secrets Act was introduced as a consequence.
* *Merv, the Queen of the World, and The Scourge of the Man-Stealing Turcomans,* W.H. Allen, London, 1883.

their quarrel about Central Asia. Had he chosen Russia he would have been "deluged with those favours which the Czar's statesmen know so well how to confer upon powerful writers who assist them" — in short, money and decorations would have been showered upon him. "Vambery's convictions, however, led him to side with England, and he refused all offers to make himself a Russian tool . . . it had cost him all his friends in Russia . . . it has even made him unpopular in his own country . . ."

Marvin wrote many similar books and collaborated with Vambery on a best-seller called *The Russian Railway to Herat and India* a project which filled the Victorians with dread — as well as *The Russians at the Gates of Herat* (1885).

He went to Russia and on his return wrote a pot-boiler, a collection of interviews with Russian military men, called *reconnoitring Central Asia*.

Marvin devoted the lion's share of this book — a summary of exploits by British officers who in the 1880s and earlier had ridden off in all directions of the compass, on official and not-so-official missions, variously disguised as Chinamen or Armenian horse-dealers, leaving London 'at the gayest time of the season . . .! to explore the distant steppes of Turkestan — to his friend Arminius.

"It was into this Central Asia — not the quiet and pacified province of Central Asia we know it today — that Vambery tramped his way in rags", he continued, "And if his sufferings, his dangers, and the distance he travelled on foot be taken into account, it will be admitted . . . that his journey not only surpasses all the succeeding pioneering exploits we have recorded, but nearly the whole of them put together".

But a chapter in his book, alarmingly entitled *Lessar's Easy Road to India*, was calculated to jolt his readers out of their complacency. It dealt with the Transcaspian railway which had been completed by the Russians in 1881, following the designs of Prince Annenkoff, who on occasion of his list visit to England had remarked to Marvin ". . . he found everybody there having most violent opinions on the Central Asiatic Question without knowing scarcely anything at all on the subject". The same complaint was made to me personally by Vambery, Marvin adds in a foot-note, on the occasion of his last visit to England.

Now the Prince had decided to extend it to India and chosen an "engineering geographer" named Lessar to conduct the survey

— of a military, as well as of an engineering character; his arrival in Meshed (in Persia) "had provoked great talk in England", for the historical highway of invasion of India ran precisely via Meshed, Herat and Kandahar.

Once the Russians were established at Herat, Marvin warned, they would be able to dominate Central Asia, Afghanistan and Persia; ". . . and if Russia extends runs her railway to India we shall need a railway of our own to fall back on in times of war". (And, indeed, a Major Chesney had elaborated a project of a railway between England and India which would shorten the journey to 7 days 13 hours and 22 minutes. He was called a dreamer).

"Rarely has an acquaintance with the Russian language been so amply utilized for English political literature as in the present case", wrote Vambery to him in a letter (1880), "for all what you write is totally unknown to the public at large, and political writers, unable to read Russian, must be grateful to you . . ."

Despite all assurances to the contrary — the "advancing locomotive" alarmed many (including Lord Salisbury) "and some alarmists saw the railway rushing at a rapid rate to the 'key of India' (Herat)".

Annenkoff hoped to see his scheme completed in his lifetime, but his dream was never realised. And today, nearly a hundred years later, there still exists no direct overland rail link between Calais and Calcutta. (And is not likely to exist until the 1980s). Afghanistan has no railway at all — let alone a terminus at Herat!

Marvin scoffed at Captain Fred Burnaby who rode off from Charing to Khiva in 1873; he called it "an everday exploit . . . of itself not a whit more remarkable than the visit of an English tourist to the capital of any Indian feudatory prince".

Captain Burnaby had not failed to consult Vambery's books before setting out on his journey and he had met the fearsome-khan, "the khan . . .", wrote Marvin, "was the ruler Vambery had to confront and bless in his dervish rags twelve years earlier . . ."

Captain Burnaby — like all his brother officers — sat down and wrote a book on his return. His *Ride to Khiva* contains passages of purple prose mentioning Vambery* — in Latin, therefore accessible only to educated — and then hardly to the ladies! It is headed *Russian Immorality in Central Asia*.

---

* A railway line from Dehli to Peshawar and in the Indus Valley was under construction.

"Year after year" Vambery had received invitations to lecture about the present and future conditions of England in Asia", for "without desiring or seeking it", a gratified Vambery noted in his autobiography, he was acknowledged in England "as the Asiatic politican and staunch friend of the realm".

His year of triumph doubtless was 1885 — a year of crisis for Britain and the year in which the Russian annexation of Pendjdeh in Afghanistan produced a war-scare.

By now Vambery had become so well known a figure that his movements made news in themselves.

On 14 April 1885 *The Times* announced that Professor Vambery was to lecture on the Central Asian question at the Royal Society of Arts, but had to add a fortnight later: "Owing to the exceptional demand for tickets the lecture on Herat is to be given at the Exeter Hall instead of the Royal Society of Arts".

Three days later — a day which *The Times* leader dealt with the Afghan frontier question — the paper published a letter by Vambery in which he announced his forthcoming visit to England, and said: "You may imagine how excited I am at seeing that my twenty years labour have not been thrown away entirely, that the great nation which I have loved since my youth has shown herself worthy of my attention". His list of lectures had not yet been quite settled, he added: he would probably lecture in London first, and then go on to Sheffield, Edinburgh, Halifax and other places. Two gentlemen, complete strangers, had already offered him hospitality in their home "and a number of congratulatory letters reach me daily from all parts of the United Kingdom".

The lecture tour came as a welcome diversion from the "not very beguiling work of proof-reading"; it did not "present any particular difficulty to the former mendicant dervish, considering the essential difference existing between a ride on camel back . . . and between a seat in the sleeping-car running directly from Vienna to Calais", and there were many places he visited "once, twice and even oftener" and where he lectured "for a modest honorarium".

He travelled through England in state.

Everywhere he was the guest "of the most distinguished and richest inhabitants of the place and thus I got an insight into the prevailing ideas and notions of the British people which increased my admiration and enthusiasm for this remarkable nation". But he accepted invitations only to the principal provincial towns, for "the labour of travelling every day to be honoured every evening with a public reception in a different place, give a lecture and attend a banquet, was too tiring and proved too much for my physical strength".

"At several railway stations the door of his compartment was flung open" and dainty luncheon baskets plentifully filled were pushed in with inscriptions such as: 'From an admirer'', or "From a grateful Englishman''.

The most remarkable of these "tokens of admiration" was shown him by Russell Shaw of London. The invitation had been sent to Budapest. On Vambery's arrival in London he was met at the station by a footman, who handed him a letter, informing him that Mr. Shaw's carriage was at his disposal. The footman looked after his luggage and drove him to no. 26, Sackville Street, where he found a richly furnished apartment "made ready for my reception". A beautiful writing desk, pen, paper, stamps, the finest cigars and liqueurs were placed at his disposal. Scarcely had he finished his toilet when the cook respectfully came to ask what his favourite dishes were and when he wished to lunch and dine. "Not until afternoon did my host appear", he adds, ':after he had begged permission to introduce himself''. He told Vambery that he could invite as many friends as he liked — and turned up again on the day of Vambery's departure, three weeks later. After that Vambery never set eyes on him again. "His was unquestionable a true type of English amiability.

In gratitude Vambery dedicated *The Coming Struggle for India*, the book that was to be his greatest triumph to him.

However he felt the strain. As an unprofessional lecturer, he "felt much exhausted" after his *debut*", and as usual, became aware of a particular pain in my jaw, owing to the strains the organs of speech were subjected to, in trying to pronounce the English sounds as faithful as possible".

Vambery received "something like twenty invitations for various meals and parties", for one day. At the one he selected, a luncheon party at Portland Place, he met Hassan Fehmi, the Turkish ambassador and confounded that diplomat, according to his story, by first addressing him in French and then "in the genuine Stambouli accent". The result was an immediate invitation to Claridges.

He met there Howard Vincent (M.P. for Sheffield from 1885).

Vambery left for Sheffield in his company the following day and upon arrival was greeted by a large crowd and a rousing ovation. "We left the compartment amidst an outburst of hurrahing, in which I joined, imagining it was intended for my travelling companion. He, however, modestly declined, and trying to make me its object, complacently drew back ... Finally, after shaking hands all round, each succeeded in getting into his own carriage and driving off ..." Had Vambery hurrah-ed himself?

The large hall was crowded, and so was the platform behind him. The enthusiastic reception and the unrelaxed attention "proved a real encouragement for the lectures I was yet to deliver".

Vambery was introduced to his audience by the Mayor of Sheffield as "a steadfast friend of England as well as a distinguished and courageous traveller". And amid cheers the Mayor quoted Lord Palmerston's remark to Vambery: "Sir, you had a nice walk across Central Asia". (Laughter). "You had a most interesting adventure".

He gave a second lecture in Sheffield and then continued to Shipley and Saltair* where he had "a like good reception, and a similar good audience in the elegant hall of the Saltaire School".

During his stay in London, at the *salon* of a lady in Wimpole Street, he met Lord Randolph Churchill, the father of Sir Winston Churchill.

There is only one reference to his contacts with the lower strata of Victorian society who he described as belonging "to a different kind of breed ... In my contact and conversation with the working-classes", he writes, "I found that they are sadly wanting in informating about the Colonies and India in general ...", "(but) the working-man (is) truly enthusiastic for the Imperial standing of his country ... really proud of his nationality ..."

The middle-classes ... the wealthier citizens (are) ... body and soul against any concessions being made to Russia ..."

Unable to resist a swipe at the Hungarian aristocracy he added: "There may be, and there are, noble idlers, fox-hunters, etc (among the aristocracy) but the by far preponderating majority are laborious, active, patriotic, highly instructed and trained, and capable to take the lead of the nation; a service for which, I am sorry to say, the Continental aristocracies are rarely fitted".

Vambery travelled to Brighton to give his lecture in the afternoon, returning on the same day and attending a large dinner-party, in spite of a cab incident in which he brusied his arm, and "partook of two dishes only"; he had to catch the night train to Newcastle-on-Tyne where he was due to deliver his lecture the following evening at 7 p.m. He was astonished that the venue for this was a theatre, since "an unusually large attendance was expected". "A continental public would be utterly shocked", he writes, "on seeing a representative of serious science, and an internal member of Academies, there where ballet-dancers usually perform . . .".

At Newcastle-on-Tyne he spoke in a large theatre "The house was filled to the top", he wrote, "one could have walked over the heads, and the galleries were full to overflowing. Tailor's apprentice, servant, tutor, Effendi, Dervish, I have been pretty well everything in my life, but a stage hero I was now to be for the first time, and although not seized with the fever of the footlights, the masses before me and their enthusiastic reception had an unusual effect upon me. I spoke for an hour and a half, often interrupted for several minutes at a time by loud applause . . ." When he referred to the danger threatening the Indian Empire, he cried out — melodramatically: "The spirits of the heroes fallen in the struggle for India, who have enabled this small island to found one of the greatest Asiatic Empires, who have made you mighty and rich, their spirits ask you now: 'Will you allow the fruits of our labour to perish, and the most precios pearl of the British crown to fall into the enemy's hands?' and the frantic 'No! No!' from all parts of the house almost moved me to tears . . ."

At the end of his lecture "many, as usual, pressed forward on the platform to shake hands", among them an elderly, well-dressed lady who took both of Vambery's hands in hers and said, her voice shaking with emotion: "Oh, my dear precious England, you have indeed done it good service. Sir, it is a glorious, golden land; continue to promote its welfare; God in heaven will reward you".

Vambery accepted further invitations to lecture at Glasgow and Edinburgh and deplored that he had no manager to advise him and arrange his tour in a more convenient ay, without first having to return to London to give his talk at Willis' Rooms.

In Scotland he lectured under the auspices of the Scottish Geographical Society at Edinburgh and Glasgow. He had met the Secretary of this Society in Budapest, as well as Mrs. Bruce who was active there and who was the daughter of David Livingstone who he had met at John Murray's house in London in 1874.

In Edinburgh he got a very warm reception and his speech "was frequently interrupted by loud cheering".

His host in Edinburgh was George Smith, former editor of the "*Friend of India*", who had reviewed Vambery's first book while still living in Calcutta.

In Glasgow, however, his host was "a wealthy flour merchant" who remains anonymous, perhaps because there was no title or mark of distinction Vambery could mention. This man had called on him a few years earlier in Budapest and, instead of presenting a letter of introduction, "the portly-looking Scotchman" had said: "Sir, I have come from Vienna to this place merely for the purpose of calling upon you, whose book I have read, and whom I have now to thank for the pleasure and instruction afforded me . . ."

On his return from Scotland Vambery lectured at Derby, Cardiff and again in London, and had many more invitations to lecture in other towns but had begun to fell exhausted "from what may be called a most trying tour". (After all, he was now 53). "Out of the eighteen days I had spent in England, nearly half of them were passed in railway travelling, and if I add to the twelve lectures delivered in various places the far more fatiguing dinners and evening parties, as well as the immense correspondence I had to carry on, with any assistance whatever . . . I made up my mind to return to Hungary as soon as possible".

One of Vambery's greatest triumphs was doubtless his lecture at Exeter Hall on the importance of Herat. "On my arrival I found the house full to overflowing with a very select audience", he writes. "Lord Houghton, who presided at this meeting, thanked me in the name of the nation, and the next day almost all the newspapers had leading articles about the services I had rendered . . ."

The Times, reporting the talk the next day, spoke of "Professor Vambery, the well-known Asiatic traveller . . ."

Vambery rose from his seat again, amid the clapping and the cheering, and expressed his thanks, stressing the hearty welcome he had had in Yorkshire. He "rejoiced to find that the indifference to Russia's southward drive had disappeared . . ."

And with an announcement of the forthcoming lecture at Willis Rooms on the subject of "England and Russia in Afghanistan — Who shall be mistress?" the meeting ended.

Four days later, on 6 May 1885, Vambery scored and even greater triumph; he considered it "the crowning point of my political labours".

It was held under the auspices of the Constitutional Union and the audience who thronged to listen to Vambery included a Field-Marshal, several peers and the late governor of Bombay.

"The heads of English aristocracy were present", writes Vambery in his autobiography "and when on the platform behind me I recognised a duke, many lords, marshals, general ex-ministers, and several famous politicians and writers of Great Britain I was really overcome.

"My thoughts wandered back into the past . . . I thought of the scorn, the contempt, and the misery to which I had been exposed as the little Jew boy and the hungry student . . . and (compared) the miserable past with the brilliant present . . .

"Modesty forbids me to speak of the manner in which Lord Hamilton, Lord Napier of Magdala, and Lord Cranbrook, and others, expressed themselves both before and after my lecture about my person and my work . . ."

Introduced by the Chairman, Sir Edward Stanhope, MP as "a gentleman who needed no introduction" . . . he was quite sure that the life and works of Arminius Vambery were familiar as household words to everyone present.

His reference to possible future trouble on the North-Western frontier drew many 'Hear! Hear!s and as Vambery rose to speak the distinguished audience cheered. The Times noted that he spoke with only an occasional glance at his notes.

There were more long, loud and prolonged cheers as Vambery bellowed: The time had come to tell Russia: "Hands Off!"

There were further 'Hear! Hear!s' and cheers as the chairman, roused to a fever pitch of patriotism, seconded Vambery: "If you want India you must first vanquish England and we will spend our last shilling and drop of blood before we let you have it!"

Lord Houghton thanked Vambery and referred to his friendship of twenty years standing; echoing Vambery' sentiments and ironically referring to Russia's efforts at civilisation he drew loud laughter.

The gist of his speech was that treachery had enabled Russia to overrun the khanates — not "courage or manliness". No reliance could be placed on Russia's assurances — and pointed to the case of Pendjdeh. Russia was now constrained to move to Herat. "If

we gave in at Pendjdeh it would be Herat next, it would be Kandahar and then the Bolan pass . . .! (Hear! Hear!) It would be most
detrimental to this country to allow Russia to get to the frontiers
of India (Cheers') With Russia at the Bolan or Khyber pass what
would be the consequences "if we waged a war and lost a battle?"
(Renewed cheers).

Talking himself into a fever of imperialist patriotism and rattling sabres from a safe distance he cried: "War with Russia is
unavoidable — the sooner it comes the better for this country!"
(Loud cheers).

He had identified himself totally with the British cause.

These stirring words came after stern phrases in which he
roundly condemned the indulgence which had allowed Russia to
go so far "for in the present emergency", he thundered "forbear-
ance shown towards Russia is the greatest sin".

Any reference to the basic friendly dispositions of the natives
brought on the cheers — "if the Amir put himself at the head of
the Afghans he would withstand Russia and have the whole
nation at his back". (Renewed cheers).

In conclusion Vambery gave the reasons which had led him "to
look to this country for the spread of Western civilisation".

And he sat down to thunderous applause.

In 1885 Vambery published a slim little book called *The Coming
Struggle for India*, written in twenty days and published simultaneously in English, German, French and Gujerati. It had the impact
of a bombshell.

Coming at a time when the question of rivalry between the
colossi in Asia had reached a seething point and the affair at Pendjdeh nearly involved England and Russia in a war, the book, written with such an unerring instinct for timing, was a runaway
success.

In substance Vambery had written: "To imagine that ambitious Russia will pursue a policy, for centuries, through the
dreary steppes of Central Asia, without any palpable results other
than the possession of the three khanates and of the Turkoman
country . . . is really more than political shortsightedness. Do people really fancy that after Russia has spent over one hundred million pounds . . . she will stop at the very gates of India . . .?"

"It caused a great sensation, far beyond its intrinsic worth," wrote Vambery modestly ". . . and it also proved a lucrative speculation".

And what is more, it was to earn him an invitation to Windsor Castle.

The *Athenaeum* gave it short shrift however.

"Herr Vambery's ópinions are well-known", wrote the reviewer. "As explained in the present publication which distrusts the loyalty of the Mohammedans in India and looks upon Afghan friendship of neutrality as a delusion; advises the construction of the railway at Kandahar and the occupation of the British troops and advocated the most friendly relations with Turkey and Persia. None of these suggestions would strike an ordinary person as very original; yet Herr Vambery is looked upon by a good many as a partisan solely inspired by hatred of Russia and not by the 'strictly humanitarian views' and love of England which he puts forward. Nor need this cause any surprise. A writer who applies such terms as 'imbecility' and 'criminal indifference' to the leading statesmen of one of the great parties of the country is sure to be opposed now and again, the more especially if he is a foreigner occupying a chair at a distant university and therefore not under provocation . . ."

Vambery had had previous criticism to face, chiefly from Liberals. In the book he quotes two specimen letters:

London, 9th February 1880

To PROFESSOR VAMBERY
The University, Buda-Pesth.
SIR, — Being I presume, a blasted Austrian or Hungarian, I can understand your sympathy with the *manly, energetic* and *wise* policy of this Government. At the same time I should advise you to keep your advice to yourself with regard to the British policy in Asia, as although you are very clever, thank God we have in this country men who are, perhaps, as far-seeing as you make yourself out to be.

Yours obediently,
A.H."

Another letter ran:

3 April 1885

". . . Did it ever occur to you that the English people (all classes) can best form an opinion on the so-called dispute between England and Russia *without the aid of a foreigner to assist them* as it is a

306

quarter of a century since you travelled in some of those parts.

What would the Hungarian people think of an Englishmen giving them advice — even by a lecture — if Hungary had a dispute with another country? Even we can see through it — the old hatred of the Hungarians towards Russia because of her aid to Austria to keep your country united to her ...

Even your Mr. Marvin is a well-known alarmist, and is of no age to have any practical experience, although he sets himself up to be even as great an authority Lord Granville, our great Foreign Minister ...''

Signed V.R.'

So much anti-Russian activity could not go unnoticed in the enemy camp in London, nor remain without a fierce Russian counter-blast. Among Vambery's fiercest opponents was Madame Olga de Novikoff who wrote under her initials* and who was one of the greatest Russian propagandists of the time. Nicknamed the "M.P. for Russia" by Disraeli, she was a close friend of Gladstone with whom she was rumoured to have had a liaison ...

She made common cause with Eugene Schuyler and wrote in one of her numerou books: "Arminius Vambery is one of the greatest Russian-haters in the world, but he admits that our soldiers have made it possible for Europeans to live at Bokhara. Formerly, Vambery himself could only visit the city disguised as a Mohammedan ...''

Calling Sir Henry Rawlinson an old Russo-phobist, she declared: "... when Russia had once cross the Steppe, there could be no permanent check in her expansion until she was arrested by the barrier of British Indian influence ...''

This could be interpreted in several ways. How far did this 'influence'' extend? Over (neutral) Afghanistan? The insertion of the word 'Indian' makes one think that Vambery had been right in writing: "... Russia will only stop in its advance when it clashes with another civilised state head on ...'' and that British vigilance had forestalled Russian intentions to extend her sphere of influence to cover Afghanistan.

Vambery in his turn retaliated vigorously: "She did her utmost to discredit me in England'', he wrote "... and suddenly discovered that I was no Hungarian, but a fraudulent Jew who had never been in Asia at all ... This skilled instrument of Russian politics on the Thames rejoiced in the friendship of Mr. Gladstone, but her childish attacks on me have had little effect in shaking my position and reputation among the British public".

It is questionable whether Vambery ever met the dangerous lady face to face, but he found an unexpected ally in Sir Charles Dilke, the Liberal MP*, who shared his dislike of her. He wrote in his diary: ". . . I breakfasted with Mr. Gladstone to meet the Duc de Broglie . . . That horrid beast, Mme. de Novikoff was there and of course the Duc took me into the corner to ask if all the scandal about her and Mr. Gladstone was true".

There was no love lost either between Vambery and Gladstone, whom he thought naive and among his bitterest political adversaries. "Amongst the few who particularly disliked my political energy was Mr. Gladstone", he wrote, "the zealous advocate of an Anglo-Russian alliance in Church and politics".

At first Gladstone is said to have remarked to a friend: "Professor Vambery's agitation seemed at first suspicious to me, but since I have heard that he is a poor man I believe in his fanaticism".

Vambery never gave up. In 1887 the Afghan border negotiations which Vambery had suggested fourteen years earlier took place and a mixed British, Russian and Afghan commission was appointed. But the situation had changed and Vambery called it "an unhappy and barren idea", feeling that even greater vigilance was called for.

In letters to the *Times* and in a fourteen-page long article, based on the close scrutiny of the Russian- and Persian-press he warned that Russia was doing her utmost to make Pendjdeh the main starting point in her southward drive.

Meanwhile the *Pamir* question had cropped up and renewed suspicion surrounded Russian movements. What were the Russians up to, dispatching "Scientific and military expeditions" to the dreary roof of the word, asked Vambery in anguished letters to the *Times*? India was their target. But he was pleased to learn that vigilant British officers had been scouting around on similar missions, that the North-West frontier had been fortified and even praised Sir Charles Dilke for favouring the extension of the Indian railway to Herat.

Today all this is forgotten. India was never invaded by the Russians and the world is busy with quite different problems.

14

AT WINDSOR CASTLE

During his visits to Britain, Vambery met many times the three generations of British royalty: Queen Victoria, King Edward VII, and King George V. He first met the young Prince of Wales at the Cosmopolitan Club in London (see Chapter 10). Vambery found him to be "a most unaffected, amiable and intelligent young man"; and it is certain that the Prince had never met anyone remotely like this small, curious, eccentric figure — alternately servile and egotistic — with a fund of strange stories to tell. This was the start of a friendship which lasted over a period of forty-five years. They were to meet several times at London, Sandringham, Windsor, and Budapest.

Not long after their first meeting at the Cosmopolitan Club, the Prince of Wales invited Vambery to lunch at Marlborough House. Vambery noted that the Prince "liked to hear the details of my adventurous career, and the more I alluded to my humble origin the more he liked the account of my past. What struck him most was my fluency in various European and Asiatic languages, for he himself was an accomplished linguist, and spoke French and German without the slightest foreign accent . . ."

Vambery never ceased to be astonished by the Prince's "great affability and kindness of heart", so different from the intolerant aristocracy on the Continent. He could not believe his eyes on one occasion when he met the Prince at dinner at the house of the Editor of the *Daily Telegraph** — "seeing him there on most intimate terms with the members of the family whose Jewish origin would have been depreciated by an everyday nobleman in Prussia and in

---

* Joseph Moses Levy (1812-1888) took over control of the *Daily Telegraph and Courier* in 1855, turning it into London's first daily penny newspaper. His son Edward (later 1st. Baron Burnham) was appointed editor at the age of 22, and he held this post for half a century. Under their management, the paper had achieved — by 1861 — a circulation of 130,000 (more than double that of *The Times*), owing to its special appeal to the middle classes.

other Continental countries, not to speak of Continental Royalty", as Vambery put it.

On another occasion, after the two had lunched together, the Prince invited Vambery to accompany him to a newly-opened park, where he had to perform the inaugural ceremony. At the park, the Prince mixed freely with the people, shaking hands and speaking with everybody, very like the Royal "walk-abouts" of today. When they returned home, the Prince asked Vambery what he thought of the ceremony. "I was admiring your Royal Highness's familiarity with everybody", replied Vambery. "In my country such things would not take place". The Prince smiled and said: "Well, Englishmen must be treated differently. If I do not bow down to them, they will crawl up and scratch me in the face!" Vambery liked to quote this anecdote, adding: "One might say it was a compulsory show of democratic tendencies, but I have witnessed scenes where he acted from his own good will, sometimes even to the dislike of the noblemen in his company. This quality of his was the main origin of his great popularity after having ascended the throne, and it touched me when my London tailor spoke, with tears in his eyes, of the good King and how he talked and shook hands with even the poorest man". Vambery noticed the same thing in Budapest, where every walk in the town cost the Prince a large amount of money, which he generously distributed to beggars.

In October 1885 the Prince spent a few days at Budapest as the guest of Count Karolyi (then Austro-Hungarian Ambassador in London). The Prince was naturally a great favourite of the Hungarian aristocracy, and he attended dinner parties and took part in hunting excursions in the country, sometimes with his Austro-Hungarian counterpart, Prince Rudolf, heir to Franz-Josef's throne. The Prince of Wales, who also met Vambery frequently, expressed his surprise at never seeing him in Hungarian "high society". Guessing the cause to be the origins of the ex-Dervish — Jewish and humble — the Prince gave a lavish dinner party for the leading members of Hungarian society, to which Vambery was invited. When Vambery arrived for the party at Karolyi's mansion, he was directed to go to the Prince's private rooms. Then, with a few reassuring words, the Prince took his arm and the two of them walked down together to the reception-room "where the flower of the Hungarian nobility had gathered", as Vambery described it. When they entered, everyone bowed deeply, as the Prince said: "Ladies and gentlemen, of course you know my friend, Professor Vambery". Everybody was forced to show Vambery the greatest consideration — albeit temporarily.

The Prince of Wales was to enforce the ex-Dervish on the "narrow-minded aristocrats" again, on his next visit to Budapest in September 1888.

There are many versions extant of this celebrated anecdote. It was long remembered; many haughty aristocrats, who had totally ignored Vambery for twenty-five years, were now obliged to acknowledge him for the first time. This version is recalled by one of Vambery's students:

A sumptuous reception was prepared for the Prince of Wales at the National Casino (the exclusive club of the Hungarian aristocracy). When the Prince arrived, his first words were: "Where is my friend Vambery?"

The barons and counts were struck dumb and looked irresolutely at one another in embarrassed silence: who was this unknown 'friend'? Eventually one of them vaguely remembered that he might be some professor living in a flat on the embankment, and a servant was instructed to bring Vambery to the reception.

But Vambery had already retired for the night and could only send word to the Prince that he would be most welcome to visit him in his flat whenever he pleased. And the very next day the Prince of Wales visited 'his friend Vambery' in his home. Immediately afterwards the National Casino elected Vambery a member, and later he became its librarian as well.

When the Prince of Wales was next honoured with a reception and a banquet at the National Casino, Vambery was at his side — fortuituously, as he was the first to point out, when the Prince was unexpectedly asked to make an impromptu speech. Vambery wrote that "the chairman took great pains to fete the princely guest by 'gushing' expressions. As far as I know the Prince was utterly unprepared, and he asked me whether he should return thanks in French or in English". Vambery advised that French would go down better with the Hungarian aristocrats. "Fancy my astonishment when I saw him rise and deliver in most elegant and idiomatic French a speech which was a masterpiece of oratorical power, and in which he recognised not only the great national qualities of the Hungarian nation, but also made happy allusions to the future in store for the chivalrous Magyars. The speech met with a most enthusiastic reception, and was much commented on by the Press".

Vambery did not meet Queen Victoria until 1889, when he was staying as a house guest with the Prince and Princess of Wales at Sandringham.

The red-letter day was 25 April, and the Queen noted the occasion in her journal: "Bertie presented Professor Vambery, a Hungarian, a wonderfully clever man, who has travelled all over the East and gone through hair-breadth escapes in Bokhara, Afghanistan, and elsewhere, having disguised himself as a Dervish. He is a man of about 60 and speaks English perfectly well, also Persian and Turkish. He is an agreeable little man, profuse in expressions of admiration for England. He knows the Sultan well, and said he was most kindly disposed to me personally. He also spoke a good deal of the poor brokenhearted Emperor and Empress of Austria and poor Rudolf".[*] This was only a few weeks after the suicide at Mayerling of the Archduke Rudolf, only son of Franz-Josef and heir to the Austrian throne.

The Prince of Wales mentioned the meeting the following week in a letter to his sister, the recently widowed Dowager German Empress: "I asked Professor Vambery (whom I know very well) to Sandringham last week, and Mama was much interested in making his acquaintance".[*]

This week was a momentous occasion, as it marked Queen Victoria's first visit to Sandringham in over seventeen years. *The Times* gave ample coverage to the event. Apart from Vambery, several important names of the local gentry were invited: Lord Henry Bentinck (the youthful M.P. for West Norfolk); Sir William Ffolkes (chairman of Norfolk County Council); and the Earl and Countess of Leicester, from Holkham Hall. The Earl, Keeper of the Privy Seal and a leading agriculturalist, held the post of Lord-Lieutenant of Norfolk for no less than sixty years. Several members of the Royal family and the Royal Household completed the list of the party: four of the Prince of Wales's five children, Prince George and the Princesses Louise, Victoria, and Maud; the Marchioness of Lorne (daughter of Queen Victoria); the Duchess of Roxburghe (lady-in-waiting); General Sir Henry Ponsonby (Queen's private secretary); Maj.-Gen. Sir Henry Ewart

[*] Queen Victoria's Journal, in the Royal Archives, Windsor Castle.
[*] Letter dated 30 April 1889, in the Royal Archives, Windsor Castle (RA Add.A4/7).

From Windsor Castle Archives. Part of letter (dated 30 April 1889) from Bertie (Prince of Wales) to his elder sister (Vicky, Dowager Empress of Germany).

(Queen's Equerry); Hon. Harry Tyrwhitt-Wilson (Prince's Equerry); Lieut.-Gen. Sir Dighton Probyn, V.C. (Comptroller and Treasurer of the Household of the Prince of Wales); Lord Suffield (Prince's Lord of the Bedchamber); Miss Elizabeth Knollys and the Dowager Countess of Morton (Princess Alexandra's ladies of the bedchamber).

Vambery really had arrived. He was the only foreign guest at the two lavish dinner parties held on 25 and 26 April. But strangely, Vambery — showing an uncharacteristic streak of modesty — hardly made any reference to these proceedings in his autobiography.

Prior to Vambery's stay at Sandringham, Harry Loveday (stage-manager of the Lyceum Theatre), and a group of carpenters and decorators, had been hard at work transforming the great drawing-room into a little theatre. The Prince of Wales had asked the greatest British actor and actress of the time, Henry Irving and Ellen Terry, to stage a private show at Sandringham specially for the Queen who had never seen them perform.

April 26 saw the arrival of Irving and Miss Terry, together with Irving's business-manager Bram Stoker and several other important members of the Lyceum company. The programme was to be *The Bells* (one of Irving's favourite set-pieces) in full, and the trial scene from *The Merchant of Venice*; the Prince of Wales thought the combination of these pieces would show both playes at their best. The scenery for the trial scene was a faithful reproduction of that which had been seen so frequently at the Lyceum, and well known to be a facsimile of the Hall at Venice.

It was an impressive scene that evening as the Queen took her place in the front row with members of the Royal family, followed by Vambery and the other guests. The big music gallery at the back was full of tenants and servants. The drawing-room looked very beautiful, as Bram Stoker noted, the white walls showing up the many stands of magnificent weapons and armour; greenery and flowers were everywhere. Many fine trophies which the Prince had brought back from India were exhibited around the room. The stage lighting was by gas. At the far end of the room was the little theatre with a proscenium opening of almost twenty feet wide, the arch painted in a pleasant colour between pink and maroon. Stoker wrote[*] later: "The Queen had

---

[*]   Bram Stoker: *Personal Reminiscences of Henry Irving* 2 vols. (Heinemann, 1906).

COURT CIRCULAR.

SANDRINGHAM, APRIL 26.

The Queen went out this morning with the Prince and Princess of Wales and the Royal Family, and visited the kitchen gardens, the thoroughbred stud, the kennels, and the Mews Industrial School.

In the afternoon Her Majesty drove with their Royal Highnesses and inspected the hackney stud at Wolferton, also visiting the church, which has been recently restored, over which the Queen was conducted by the Rev. J. Mitchell.

After taking tea at the Rectory, Her Majesty drove home through Wolferton Village.

The following have had the honour of dining with the Prince and Princess of Wales during the Queen's stay at Sandringham :—General Sir Dighton and Lady Probyn, the Earl and Countess of Romney, Lord Henry Bentinck, M.P. for the Western Division of Norfolk, Lieut.-Colonel Lord Suffield, Major Dawson, and Lieut. Evans Lombe, of the 2d Brigade Eastern Division Royal Artillery, the Rev. F. Hervey, Rector of Sandringham, Chaplain to the Queen, Lady Alfred Hervey, the Rev. J. Mitchell, Rector of Wolferton, Professor Vambéry, Sir William and Lady ffolkes, the Earl and Countess of Leicester, and Mr. Weston Jarvis, M.P. for Lynn.

kindly expressed her wish that the audience should do just as they wished as to applauding, and I must say that I have never seen or heard a more enthusiastic audience within the bounds of decorum".

The Queen had seen no dramatic entertainment of any kind since the death of the Prince Consort in 1861, except a performance by a company of London actors of a comedy by Burnand in 1881, which the Prince of Wales had induced her to attend at Abergeldie Castle. Vambery probably did not appreciate this important night in theatrical history — he made hardly any mention of it in any of his writings. In no way was he a theatre devotee, even though he was himself described by some of his acquaintances as "the greatest actor this generation ever knew", after having played the role of the dervish so successfully.

After the show, Queen Victoria presented Henry Irving and Ellen Terry with souvenirs inlaid with diamond monograms. When she had retired for the night, the Prince and Princess of Wales wined and dined the special guests at a late supper, with Vambery sitting next to Irving and Miss Terry. The great actor must have been intrigued by "the dervish", and this was to prove the beginning of a warm friendship with invitations to see him perform at the Lyceum and to dine at his favourite Beefsteak Room.

At 2.30 a.m. the whole company of actors and workmen was driven to the station where the special train was waiting. Irving declined payment of any kind, bearing the whole cost of the entertainment himself. This precedent was to establish the Royal Command Performance as we know it today.

While at Sandringham, the Duke of Clarence (eldest son of the Prince of Wales) was away,* and Vambery was allowed to take up residence in his apartments, which were situated next to those of Prince George (later King George V). Vambery was later to relate the following incident, which amused him greatly and boosted his ego still further: "One afternoon, while I was occupied with my correspondence, I received an invitation from the Queen to join her in the garden; as I wished to wash my hands before going down I rang several times for warm water, but no one came. At length the young Prince (George) came to my door, and asked me what I wanted. I told him, and he disappeared,

---

* The Duke of Clarence would die here in the same bed Vambery occupied, less than three years later (January, 1892).

316

returning in a few minutes with a large jug in his hand, which he placed, smiling, on my washstand".

He added: "Not at all bad, I thought, for the poor Jewish beggar-student of former years to be waited upon by a Prince! I have often laughed at the recollection of this incident, and have since dubbed the future sovereign of Great Britain 'The Royal Jug-bearer'!"

Another incident which Vambery recalled in later years occurred at the gala-dinner given in honour of Queen Victoria, where he was to take Princess Louise* in to dinner. The Prince of Wales, her father, took a glance at the assembled guests, then came up to them saying: "Vambery, why did you not put on orders?" Vambery, who was not fond of wearing his orders and decorations, was on the point of making some excuse when Princess Louise remarked: "Why, Papa, Professor Vambery ought to have pinned some of his books on to his coat; they would be the most suitable decorations".

Vambery certainly seemed to have made a favourable impression on Queen Victoria. Returning to London, only a few days had passed when he received the following invitation:

THE LORD STEWARD

has received her Majesty's command to invite

PROFESSOR VAMBERY

to dinner at Windsor Castle on Monday, the 6th May,

and to remain until the following day.

WINDSOR CASTLE, 5th May 1889.

A telegram also arrived bearing the same command, with the added message: "To see the library and the sights of the Castle", as Vambery noted wryly — it was not thought wise to invite the "anti-Russian author" (as he described himself) through friendship alone. There had to be a further eeason, so as to appease Russian friends and relatives of the Royal family. The reaction of the Czar Alexander III and the Czarina — who was the sister of the Princess of Wales (later Queen Alexandra) — to the British Royal Family's friendship to Vambery is not recorded.

On 6 May Vambery took the train to Windsor. He found a royal carriage awaiting him at the station, and was driven to the Castle, where Sir Henry Ponsonby, the Queen's private secretary, greeted him warmly. Vambery took a liking to Sir Henry,

* The Princess Royal, eldest sister of George V; she was then (1889) engaged to the Duke of Fife.

317

describing him as "an amiable and noble-minded man", and wrongly assumed he was the Lord Steward (an error that went uncorrected in his autobiography). Sir Henry conducted Vambery to the apartment prepared for him, and then fetched the royal birthday book. According to the custom at Court, all visitors were requested to enter their name, with day and year of birth. Vambery looked at the book in awe. "It was a noble company in whose ranks my name was to figure, for the book was full of signatures of crowned heads, princes, great artists, learned men, and noted soldiers of the day". He wondered what he should write, as the uncertainty of his date of birth made him hesitate. Sir Henry asked him with a pleasant smile the reason for his embarrassment. Vambery answered: "Sir, I do not know the exact date of my birth, and I should not like to enter a lie in the royal book", and went on to explain the circumstances.

"You need not be ashamed of that", remarked Sir Henry. "Her Majesty lays less weight upon the birth of her guests than upon their actions and merits". So Vambery entered the "conventional" date of 19 March 1832, the same date he gave to *Encyclopaedia Britannica* and various biographical dictionaries, though he could never be sure of its veracity. He commented later: "I am quite sure that among the many guests at Windsor there was never another to whom the day and year of his entry into this world were unknown".

Vambery's apartment was in one of the round towers of the Castle. "As I gazed at the lovely landscape, with the Thames winding in and out among the trees, and remembered the ideas I had formed of this royal castle when I read Shakespeare, I was deeply moved at the wonderful change in my position", wrote Vambery. "If someone had told me in the days gone by that I, who was then living in the poorest circumstances, and even suffering hunger, should one day be the honoured guest of the Queen of England and Empress of India at Windsor, that men in high position would lead me through the ancient halls, show me the royal treasures, and that I should sit next but two to the Queen at table, I should in spite of my lively imagination, have thought him a fool and have laughed in his face".

Full of admiration for his own achievements, he declared to his proud reflection in the mirror: "*Haschele Wamberger, das hast Du gut gemacht!*" ("Haschele Wamberger, you have done well!" — a story vouchsafed for its authenticity since he told it to his son.)

318

Vambery enjoyed his dinner at Windsor Castle that evening. He was the chief guest, and probably dominated the conversation. Queen Victoria commented in her journal: "Professor Vambery was very interesting, and enthusiastic about England". The other guests were Sir Archibald* and Lady Campbell, and a Mr Muther (possibly the art historian). Members of the Royal Household completed the guest-list: Lieut.-Col. William Carington (Equerry to the Queen), Lady Waterpark (newly appointed Lady-in-Waiting), and Frances Drummond (Maid of Honour).

Vambery liked and admired the Queen very much, and found her much friendlier, less cold in manner than he had been led to believe. "She certainly was a little reserved at first, but as soon as he clever brain had formed an opinion as to the character and disposition of the stranger, her seeming coldness was cast aside, and was replaced by a charming graciousness of manner, and she warmed to her subject as her interest in it grew." He declared that "the words in which she acknowledged my literary efforts on England's behalf will always be more precious to me than all the orders and treasures with which sovereigns think to have repaid me".

In Vambery's opinion, both Queen Victoria and the Prince of Wales had remarkable memories; both knew the "ins and outs" of every question and took a lively interest in most things. Vambery wrote after meeting the Queen: "In spite of her earnest mien and conversation, sparks of wit often lighted up the seemingly cold surface."

On one occasion at Sandringham, Vambery was walking in the park next to her little carriage drawn by two donkeys. She did not appear to be listening to his conversation with the gentleman-in-waiting accompanying them, but when Vambery began to speak about his adventures and experiences in Central Asia, her interest visibly increased, and she made inquiries into the smallest details. "What most surprised me", recalled Vambery, "was that she not only retained all the strange Oriental names, but pronounced them quite correctly, a rare thing in a European, especially in a lady; she even remembered the features and peculiarities of the various Asiatics who had visited her Court, and the opinions she formed were always correct".

One evening Queen Victoria chose to speak to Vambery about Turkey, and the time he had lived there. He was amazed at her memory and ability to recall the names of all the Turkish ambassadors of half a century, and spoke at length about Fuad Pasha, one of the ablest of Turkish statesmen, who had visited the Queen thirty years before. Fuad Pasha was the Grand Vizier in Constantinople during Vambery's stay there, in 1861 and 1862.

Vambery found that the Queen had more sense of the importance of strengthening British power in Asia, than many of her ministers. Even the Shah of Persia, when he visited Budapest (the same year), told him astonishing stories of the Queen's familiarity with Oriental affairs. She discussed with Vambery her studies in Hindustani, and showed him her written exercises in that language. Vambery observed with interest the two Indian servants, clothed in wide garments and enormous turbans, who waited on the Queen at table and sometimes accompanied her on excursions. "They were a living proof of the interest the Empress of India took in the establishment of British power in Asia", opined Vambery.

He was fascinated and overwhelmed by all the treasures he saw at Windsor Castle: "When I saw in the Royal Library at Windsor the numerous addresses and Presentations, and assurances of devotion from the Emir of Afghanistan and other Asiatic potentates, written on scrolls of parchment in large golden letters, or when I admired the crowns, sceptres, and Oriental arms, preserved in the Royal Treasury at Windsor, I could never tire in my admiration of the power and greatness of Britain". He would be gratified to know that several of his own books now have a permanent place in the Royal Library.

When the Queen died in 1901 and the Prince of Wales ascended the throne as Edward VII, he told Vambery to continue visiting him as often as before. The change from Prince to King would make no difference to any of his friendships, as far as he was concerned. Not long before the King's coronation, Vambery received a telegram from the King's private secretary, Sir Francis Knollys which read: "The King commands me to send you his warmest congratulations on the seventieth anniversay of your birthday".

This was followed by the following letter:

"MARLBOROUGH HOUSE,
PALL MALL, S.W.,
March 18 1902.

"DEAR PROFESSOR VAMBERY,

I am commanded by the King to inform you, that he has much pleasure in conferring upon you the third class (Commander) of the Victorian Order on your 70th birthday, as a mark of his appreciation of your having always proved so good and constant a friend to England, and as a token of His Majesty's personal regard towards you.

I beg to remain, dear Professor Vambery,
Yours very faithfully,
FRANCIS KNOLLYS."

Vambery was immensely proud of this award. He received a special telegram of congratulation from Prince George, the new Prince of Wales.

Later he used to brag to his son Rustem that, had he behaved differently, he would have been knighted or even become a Lord. "It proves", said Vambery, "that the royal birthday book at Windsor is of great value". He added boastingly: "It is only at my wish that I am not Sir Arminius, and had I wished it the second baronet would have been *Sir* Rustem, member of the English aristocracy".

Rustem replied: "I should prefer to be a University teacher — that is the title I should like to inherit from you". (Instead, Rustem was destined to become a famous lawyer and criminologist.)

Vambery was able to thank King Edward personally when he next visited London, in May 1904. His name could be found in most of the Court Circulars as he was invited by the King first to dinner at Buckingham Palace, and then to spend a few days at Windsor Castle. Vambery, who claimed that the King was anxious to see him as soon as he arrived in England, found his old friend in excellent health, and "as amiable as always".

To his consternation Vambery read, on his gilt-edged invitation, the official details of etiquette concerning court-dress; knee-breeches were now obligatory, but — owing to his malformed leg — he had never been able to wear them in his life! Always a little sensitive about his height and lameness, he feared he would resemble a jerky marionette if he 'dressed-up' at official functions. Fortunately for him, he was allowed to wear his ordinary suit — the only guest allowed to do so. He would have stood out like a sore thumb, but in his own specially-tailored trousers, he was comfortable and happy.

It seems that Vambery's anti-establishment contempt for the fancy-dress etiquette at court was something of an innovation, and future guests would follow his example. Not long afterwards, the radical M.P. John Burns was invited to Windsor Castle and insisted on wearing ordinary dress for dinner. Burns was immensely proud of his label: "Came into the world with a struggle, struggling now, and prospects of continuing it", an epithet Vambery would have appreciated.

Although Vambery's handicap could lead sometimes to a persecution complex, it did not interfere with his physical activities at all. Now in his seventies he could still go on long walks without feeling tired. On the Sunday the King took Vambery on a long guided tour of the Castle, upstairs and downstairs for two long hours, without a moment's rest. Field-Marshal Earl Roberts of Kandahar (former commander-in-chief of the British army), who accompanied them, almost collapsed with fatigue. Vambery was especially interested to see the servants' quarters, all of which had their own bathroom — and every room was, he noted, much more elegant and comfortable than his own in Budapest! He commented that many doctors and professors on the Continent might envy these servants, upon which the King said: "I am delighted to give my men all possible comfort, for good work requires good rest".

Above all else Vambery was impressed by the grandeur of the superb dining room, and declared that the royal display put all the Oriental fairy-tale splendour he had witnessed in Turkey and Persia firmly in the shade. The carafes, cutlery and plates, "all of pure shining gold", took his mind back to the time, almost forty-five years earlier, when he had dined off similar golden plates at the Merasim Kiosk in the company of Sultan Abdul Medjid. At dinner King Edward arranged for Hungarian tunes to be played in honour of his favoured guest.

Dinner usually took place at 9 p.m., the time when — at home in Budapest — "I usually creep under the blankets", to quote Vambery's own words. Vambery's customary early-to-bed routine was always changed drastically when he visited Windsor Castle, but he was robust enough not to fall by the wayside, even when the King continued to chat animatedly with him till well past midnight.

After dinner the King usually retired alone to an adjoining room where he could smoke a cigar and drink his coffee in peace. Then he would send one of his entourage to fetch the guest he specially wanted to see. On the first night this command was conveyed to Vambery by George, the Prince of Wales, and on the second by Earl Roberts. Vambery noted that the King never touched any alcoholic beverage at the table, not even the vintage wines (which Vambery himself no doubt found delicious!).

During this sojourn at Windsor Castle, in the early summer of 1904, Vambery's acquaintance with the Princess of Wales (later Queen Mary) bloomed. They shared the common link of Hungarian blood, and the conversation soon turned to Princess Mary's grandmother, whose premature brutal death caused a wave of national mourning from Austria to Transylvania in Vambery's youth.

The story is brief and poignant. In 1835 Duke Alexander of Wurttemberg met and instantly fell in love with a beautiful Hungarian girl — Claudine Rhedey — the daughter of a Transylvanain Count, and a direct descendant of the old kings of Hungary, including Arpad (founder of the Magyar dynasty in 896). In spite of her ancient pedigree, their marraige had to be a morganatic one; and Duke Alexander had to forfeit his rights to the succession of the Wurttemberg monarchy. She was created Countess Hohenstein, and was usually addressed as such rather than as the 'Duchess of Wurttemberg'. There were three children from the marriage: Claudine, Franz, and Amelie. (It was Franz who eventually became the first Duke of Teck, and father of Mary, future Queen of England.)

One fateful day, three years after the birth of her last child, Countess Hohenstein travelled to Pettau (near Vienna) to accompany her husband in order to see a review of his troops practice manoeuvres. Deciding to give her husband a pleasant surprise, she rode out to greet him and promptly met a regiment of Hussars in full attack — ironically commanded by her husband — who were advancing from the opposite direction. Her horse shied in panic, and ran directly into the midst of the Hussars. The distracted Duke saw the beautiful body of his wife crushed under the hooves of the galloping horses, over a hundred of them! Griefstricken he took the mangled and unrecognisable corpse back to his home in Stuttgart, but her father Count Rhedey insisted that the body of his daughter should be carried up to the mountain fastnesses of Transylvania, where her family had ruled for so many generations. This was done, and her body was eventually laid to rest in the little rustic church of Erdo Szent-Gyorgy.

Only a few months before his visit to Windsor, Vambery had been told by the last surviving male descendant of the Rhedey line that Claudine's grave had fallen into disrepair, was totally neglected, and lacked a memorial tablet of any kind. Vambery reported all this to Princess Mary, who appeared deeply touched on hearing these details. As it was impossible for her to visit Szent-Gyorgy personally, she entrusted Vambery with the task of refurbishing the grave and ordering the memorial tablet. King Edward commented to Vambery that this mission "should strengthen the ties which link the English Royal House and the Hungarian nation even more tightly". When Vambery took his leave from Windsor for the last time, the King gave him a beautifully bound quarto volume, *The Armoury of Windsor Castle*, personally inscribed "To Professor Vambery a souvenir from Windsor Castle by Edward VII. R et I". It became one of Vambery's most cherished possessions.

When Vambery arrived back in Budapest, his experiences at the English Court were widely reported and an 'exclusive' interview with him was published in the *Pester Lloyd* on 5 June. Vambery was still in the seventh heaven, and extolled the limitless virtues of his royal host. "It is a pleasure to hear him talk about Asia, Turkey and Persia, with the same ease and versatility as if he were discussing everyday events . . ." said Vambery, stressing that the King's chief mission was to achieve world peace. He told the interviewer: "The English constitution, as you know, limits the influence on the monarch's part, nevertheless he succeeds tactfully in imposing his political point of view . . . The whole world knows that it was he who soon after his accession to the throne ended the Boer War and established *Entente Cordiale* with France". When Vambery had congratulated the King on his successes in Paris, he replied: "Just wait and see, Vambery, the Russians will soon be finished as well".

In a long eulogy of King Edward's character, Vambery emphasized that his royal friend never discriminated in matters of class, religion, or nationality: "Scholars, artists, writers, business-men, commoners or noblemen — all are of equal worth to him. In this respect he has remained the old Prince of Wales who is never arrogant or prejudiced. He is a wonderful person who has been frequently misunderstood and misjudged in Europe ..." The King's philo-semitism was well-known. It always horrified and astonished his prejudiced relatives on the continent, especially his sister-in-law the Dowager Empress of Russia, and his nephew the Kaiser. Leading Jews who would be unacceptable in most Euro-pean Courts were numbered among his closest confidants, nota-bly his financial adviser Sir Ernest Cassel, and Sir Edward Albert Sassoon (of the well-known Baghdad family). Vambery recalled: "The proof that even the slightest trace of anti-semitism was for-eign to him is perhaps the fact that the King was guest of Mr. Sas-soon's house, on occasion of a hunt, and even ate kosher food". Possibly Vambery hoped that the Hungarian aristocrats would read this and take notice! A vain point, but he never lost an oppor-tunity to put it forward.

Vambery brought home with him a large stack of postcards and photographs, showing all the state rooms of Windsor Castle, together with the menus for breakfast, lunch, and dinner, and the accompanying music programmes. He took pains to show the interviewer the programmes of the Brahms Hungarian dances (no. 5 and 6) performed in his honour. He went on to contrast the "dazzling, princely splendour" of the Castle under King Edward, compared to the "dark and sombre atmosphere" when he had first been there. And the interview ended with details of the royal mission entrusted to him by the future Queen of England — a mission which "flatters me particularly", he said.

He lost no time in obtaining photographs of the church of Szent Gyorgy, together with a history of the place, and sent them to Princess Mary. She replied:

"MARLBOROUGH HOUSE, S.W.
July 20th 1904

"Dear Professor Vambery,

I am most grateful to you for kindly sending me the photo-graphs of the church as Szent Gyorgy; they are very interesting to me and I am so pleased to have them. Thank you too for telling me the history of the church. My eldest brother has a picture of Fran-cis Rhedey Prince of Transylvania, which formerly belonged to my father, so that it interests me doubly to hear that he is buried

325

near my grandmother. It is most kind of you suggesting that no steps should be taken with regard to the crypt until you visit Szent Gyorgy in the autumn when you will be better able to judge for yourself how much ought to be done — Though I should be quite willing to spend from £20 to £30 to renovate the crypt I must confess that I fear I cannot do anything with regard to the church and I hope you will be able to explain this to the good vicar. Thank you very much for taking so much trouble on my behalf. I am indeed grateful to you, and willingly accept your excellent advice.

> Believe me
> Yours very sincerely
> Victoria Mary"

More correspondence followed. Later in the year (5 December) she wrote: "... I quite agree with you that what I *wish* to do is merely to put up a memorial slab to my grandmother's memory, somewhere in the church, & if not giving you too much trouble I should like you to order this in Budapest & then have it sent to the church. It would be far better than sending a stone from here — The cost may be between £30 & £40 ..."

As she did not have details of either the Rhedey or Wurttemberg Arms, and did not know the dates of her grandmother's birth and death, she asked Vambery to provide these for the memorial slab. (Research provided Claudine Rhedey's dates: 1814-1841.)

The work was completed by the next spring. On 20 March 1905 Princess Mary wrote to Vambery: "... I am very glad to hear from your kind letter that the Memorial Slab is nearly finished & that you hope, before long, to be able to superintend the fixing of it near the crypt at St. Gyorgy. I assure you I am most grateful to you for all the trouble you have taken in the matter & beg you will accept my sincerest thanks ..."*

Two years later, when Vambery informed Princess Mary of the death of her cousin, Ida Rhedey, she replied to him: "... Many thanks for your kind enquiries after us, & I am glad to be able to give a good report. I am very sorry to hear that owing to age, we cannot look forward to the pleasure of seeing you again in England; we were so pleased to see you at Windsor in 1904." Having reached the age of 75, Vambery now considered

---

* An illustration of the Memorial Tablet appears in *The House of Teck* by Louis Felberman (John Long, 1911). Plate 42. H.M. Queen Elizabeth II is the great-great-ganddaughter of Claudine Rhedey, Countess Hohenstein.

himself too old to travel further than Vienna. He did not leave the confines of the Austro-Hungarian Empire again.

The friendship between Vambery and the British Royal Family did not prevent him disagreeing with them on several matters from time to time. The biggest disagreement with King Edward came in 1907 over his pact with Russia. The Anglo-Russian Entente was signed on 31 August that year in St. Petersburg by Sir Arthur Nicolson (representing Britain) and the Russian Foreign Minister Alexander Isvolsky. Discussing his views later Vambery said: "What I criticised in that agreement was the great price England paid for a rather dubious security; the fault did not lie with King Edward, but rather his advisers, who were taken in by Russia . . ."

King Edward continued to seek his advice. In September 1908, Vambery wrote a long detailed memorandum at the King's request, entitled *On the Constitutional Movement in Turkey*. It was despatched via Sir Charles Hardinge, head of the Foreign Office, who told the King: ". . . Considering his thorough knowledge of the East, I think Your Majesty will find it interesting and valuable". The King was indeed very interested in Vambery's memorandum, and kept it filed safely. It is now preserved in the Public Records Office, with a typed (partly incomplete) copy in the Royal Archives at Windsor Castle.

None of the letters Vambery sent to King Edward are known to survive, and after the King's death he was strongly advised either to destroy or return the letters he had received from his royal friend. Many touched on personal and family subjects — how personal is not known.

Just how great was Vambery's grief at the King's demise? No doubt he felt he had lost a true friend and benefactor, but even in his grief he could not help a note of egotism from creeping in. On 7 May 1910 he wrote to Sir Charles Hardinge:

"Dear Sir, I beg leave to present a copy of the paper I published under the impression of the most afflicting news of the death of His Majesty King Edward VII. I am desolate for I have lost my most generous and kindhearted Patron in the World . . ."

It was clear that Vambery admired the King more than anyone else he had ever known.

The 'paper' he mentioned, as told to the German-language *Pester Lloyd*, was entitled *My Relationship with King Edward* and was prefaced with the words: "It is well known that Professor Vambery was on intimate terms of friendship with King Edward for over four decades: he is shattered by the news of his death". In the paper Vambery stressed how close he was to the King, not failing to point out that he had been an important member of his retinue on the frequent Royal visits to Budapest. He claimed that the King shared his own contempt for some of the facile, pompous, half-witted aristocrats who fawned around him at all times. "I suppose I can now let you into a secret", wrote Vambery; "in the close circle of his friends, he smiled at these qualities of his aristocratic compatriots".

King Edward and Queen Alexandra were kindness and graciousness personified, he enthused, adding: "Up to the end of his life, the King gave me proof of his sympathy, friendship, and personal esteem for me . . . I, who was near to the King, found in him a man, who was head and shoulders above his contemporaries . . ."

After King Edward's death in 1910, innumerable obituaries and 'tributes' naturally appeared, and several of these emphasized the jovial side of the late King's character, pretending that he never took anything seriously. But it was the following paragraph from the *Dictionary of National Biography*[*] which infuriated Vambery: ". . . A man of the world, (King Edward) lacked the intellectual equipment of a thinker, and showed on occasion an unwillingness to exert his mental powers. He was no reader of books. He could not concentrate his mind on them . . . He did not sustain a conversation with much power or brilliance; but his grace and charm of manner atoned for any deficiency of matter . . ."

Vambery, who had just celebrated his 80th birthday, was asked by author Edward Legge to contribute a short essay to his book *King Edward in His True Colours*[*], which set out to discredit the malicious rumours circulating about the late King. Vambery wrote, referring to the quote (above) in the *D.N.B.*: "This is decidedly the greatest possible calumny, for I had ample opportunity of convincing myself of the contrary. Not only did I find him often reading serious works, but I know he mastered their contents, and frequently applied historical citations in support of his political views. He was thoroughly informed about England's position in Asia; he knew the intricacies of Indian policy; and, if

[*] (Smith Elder, 1912).
[*] (Eveleigh Nash, 1912).

discretion did not bridle my pen, I could quote from his conversation passages destined to be given as advice to Sultan Abdul Hamid which would justly astonish the most shrewd diplomatist . . .''

In the same book Vambery related one of his own favourite anecdotes, dating back to 1890 when he accompanied the Prince of Wales (as he then was) and his brother the Duke of Edinburgh to the Albert Hall, where the explorer Henry M. Stanley was to deliver his first lecture since returning from Africa. At a moment's notice, the Prince of Wales had to take over the job of delivering the opening speech, in place of the Duke of Edinburgh who was suddenly taken ill. "On arriving on the platform the Prince only asked me to supply him with two or three geographical proper names", claimed Vambery; "then, beginning to speak, he treated his subject with as much cleverness and perfect knowledge as if he had been a specialist on African geography and had spent years in the Ruwenzori among the pygmies . . . And yet there are writers who have said that the late King never read a book, and shunned literary people!" Vambery was now championing King Edward, just as "his dear and revered friend" had championed him in times past.

Edward Legge commented: "If there is any gratitude in the British people, now is the time for them to express it to Arminius Vambery!"

16

ESCORT TO THE SHAHS

"Where is Vambery?"

The thunderous voice contrasted strongly with the pale, sickly look of the overdressed Oriental potentate as he struggled out of his carriage at the *Nyugati p.u.* (Western) Station in Budapest. This bizarre and picturesque figure looked around eagerly at the sea of faces greeting him. His chest was a blaze of diamonds, his right hand rested on a handsome sword encrusted with jewels, a huge aigrette surmounted his headgear. Nervously stroking his long, unkempt, greying moustache, he roared again:

"*Vambery kudjast?* Where is Vambery?"

The group of Hungarian State Ministers, led by the Archduke Joseph, broke up in confusion, and a messenger was despatched hotfoot to the Academy where Vambery was summoned to the Station. Here the two men — the Oriental potentate and the venerable professor — embraced like two long-lost friends renewing an old acquaintance.

No-one was more surprised and gratified than Vambery. In fact thirty-eight years had elapsed since their last meeting. The potentate was none other than the all-powerful Muzaffer-ed-Din, "Victorious of the Faith", Shah of Persia, and this was the first time in his life that he had left the claustrophobic confines of his own country. He had ascended the throne four years previously, in 1896, totally unfitted to the task of absolute monarch. For well over thirty years before that, he had vegetated in the honorary post Governor of Azerbaijan at Tebriz, with no major responsibilities and a relatively small income.

Vambery had first seen the young nine-year-old Prince, "looking feeble and pale", at his royal investiture in 1862 (see Chapter 3). In his long, boring years at Tebriz, the young heir apparent was subjected to a very strict education which robbed him of much of his energy. Among the books he was obliged to read were the interminable journals and diaries of his autocratic father, Nasr-ed-Din Shah.

Muzaffer-ed-Din yearned to know more about the distant lands he was not allowed to see, and carefully read those journals of his father which described the pleasures of Europe. He was especially interested to read of his father's encounters with Vambery, of whom he had a distant memory . . .

Nasr-ed-Din Shah, contemporary of Queen Victoria, and autocratic ruler of Persia for nearly fifty years, remained an enigmatic personality to the rest of the world. To some he was an evil, brutal despot. Others praised him as a just ruler with cultured tastes. Vambery appears to have like him, closing his eyes to the Shah's savage cruelties: "I have not heard any other man in the whole of Iran express himself with such precision regarding Central Asia".

Early in 1864 Vambery had prepared his first written account of his travels in Central Asia for the Shah. "At that time", Vambery recalled later, "the Shah remarked in the course of conversation that I looked well, in spite of the terrible hardships and privations which I had suffered. I answered that my appearance only reflected the splendour of his Majesty, and in this way the ice was broken: the Shah responded with a gracious smile, his courtiers nodded, and I was thence forward counted among the Royal favourites". Both Vambery and the Shah were in their early thirties at this time.

Vambery would later extol the Shah's virtues: his artistry, his fine calligraphy, and especially his knowledge of literature and geography. "He is the most cultured man in Iran" he enthused, ignoring the Shah's more barbaric excesses.

Nasr-ed-Din (the name signified 'Defender of the Faith') did not like the atmosphere at his court, and found much of the etiquette boring. He much preferred to go on long excursions and hunting expeditions, especially to the area on the south-western shore of the Caspian. Vambery reported: "He does not like to stay in the palace; he dislikes the intrigues of the great dignitaries and of his women, and the servility of his officers, whom he does not trust much. For this reason he often takes his private fortune with him on his travelling and hunting expeditions". The Shah loved hunting, and often left Teheran with a large retinue in pursuit of the large and small game which were carefully preserved for his benefit. These absences — sometimes as long as nine months — meant that the 'government' became a rundown, incompetent affair, for nothing could be done without his personal authority, and he presided over every department of state.

On the subject of the Shah's harem, Vambery was given most of the details by his friends and acquaintances in Teheran: "Nasred-Din is not particularly fond of women and neglects his harem. He is very fickle in love and occasionally does everything in his power to get into his possession a beautiful Iranian girl whose glance has set his heart on fire. He divorces one wife to marry another without the least scruple, but his favourites do not usually last very long ... He soon tires of the harem and its charming inmates and is pleased to be away from them". This may explain why he fathered only the relatively small number of forty-five children over the period of five decades.

In 1856, the Shah followed the belligerent policy of his father and took Herat after a six-month siege. The British Government was forced to declare war on Persia. By the Treaty of Paris, the Shah was obliged to evacuate Afghanistan and to recognise the independence of the country. From that time onwards, he resorted to a more friendly policy towards England, and in 1866 he signed a convention which authorized the passage of the telegraph to India through is dominions. To the end of his reign he never deviated from the course he had marked out for himself after the withdrawal from Herat of showing the same friendly demeanour to both England and Russia.

Vambery, forever wary of the Russian movements on the northern frontiers of Turkey and Persia, never lost an opportunity to take up his pen and warn the British public on the subject. In 1879, following the Near-Eastern Crisis, he wrote to *The Times*:

"As may be supposed, neither the Shah nor Mirza Husein Khan, his Prime Minister, will be much afraid of the empty threat of the Russian Press. The policy of the Teheran Government in face of the Russian struggle with the hardy nomads was the most correct and the only means to get out unscathed from the trouble. Had the Persian statesmen always followed this line of policy, their country would have been saved from more than one misfortune, and the rule of the Kajars would have become much stronger than it is. An essential part in the result must be attributed to the activity and cleverness of the British Envoy at

Teheran. It is highly satisfactory to see that the period of beneficial influence which closed with the retirement of Sir Henry Rawlinson is again re-awakening, for it is only in this way that Persia
can be brought to a proper understanding of the vital interests'..*

Vambery's interest in Persia never wavered. He maintained a
large correspondence with the friends he had made, and wrote
and read widely on the language and literature of the country.
Later he encouraged the budding young explorer Sven Hedin,
and contributed a foreword to that celebrated traveller's first
book *Genom Persien,Mesopotamien och Kaukasien* (1887). Vambery
stayed with Hedin when he attended the 8th International Congress of Orientalists in Stockholm, and Hedin often used to visit
his mentor in Budapest.

Nasr-ed-Din was the first Persian monarch who ventured to
leave his dominions and to travel in foreign and 'infidel' lands, not
as a conqueror at the head of an army, but as a friendly visitor. In
the previous centuries such a step would have been unthinkable.
On his three marathon European tours in 1873, 1878 and 1889, he
became a well-known, idiosyncratic figure, with his long "flash-
ing aigrette and huge bediamonded sword" (as Lord Curzon described), examining in detail all places of interest throughout the
continent. He remained an active, robust figure, full of youthful
vigour, and always sure of keeping his greying hair and moustache dyed a raven hue.

Innumerable entertaining stories circulated about his eccentric
habits, some fabricated, but many undoubtedly true. During his
first visit to Britain, he became infatuated with Lady Margaret
Beaumont, offering to buy her for his harem at a price of
£500,000.

Of the many anecdotes concerning Nasr-ed-Din and his
breaches of etiquette, Vambery related one in which the Shah
was invited to dine with the Prince of Wales at Marlborough
House. He was said to have thrown the asparagus stumps over his
back on to the floor, and "in order not to shame his guest, the
Prince ... and all the other guests immediately did the same,
greatly to the disgust of the attendants". The Princess of Wales
was known to be similarly disgusted with the Shah — especially
after the first dinner at Marlborough House when he spat his
peach stones on to her train. Vambery thought these stories
greatly exaggerated, for the Shah never neglected to make strict

enquiries into the customs of the lands he visited.

The Shah was a veritable Pepys, dictating thousands of words to his overworked chamberlain at the end of every busy day. When each tour was completed, the mountainous reams of notes were transcribed and published for the edification of his subjects. The first two diaries were published in London in 1874 and 1879 and stand today as fascinating curiosity pieces.

The Times, in a very long review of the first Diary (11 Dec. 1874), strongly recommended the book but doubted the "Western Culture" of the Shah in regard to his knowledge and familiarity with such objects as the carpenter's tools of Peter the Great, and the *History of Ulysses*, and *Adventures of Telemaque* by Fenelon. Vambery flew to the Shah's defence in a letter to *The Times* (19 Dec. 1874) claiming the "Telemaque" has been for a long time the first reading book of French-learning Turks and Persians. It was the very book Vambery had used himself in his lessons at Constantinople and Teheran. Had he introduced it into Persia?

The Shah's 1889 reminiscences did not appear in English, though Vambery translated a few choice paragraphs for an article on the book he wrote for *The Nineteenth Century* (March 1894). "The Diary deserves to be translated", declared Vambery, "(as it) gives a rather detailed and lengthy account of various towns of England and Scotland and of many mansions and country houses of English and Scotch noblemen; nay, it affords a clear insight into the public and private life of the United Kingdom such as no other Oriental publication can boast of".

The 1889 tour was a particularly energetic one, lasting four months, and taking in Russia, Germany, England, Scotland, France, Austria, and culminating at Budapest at the end of August. Shortly before the arrival of the Shah in Hungary, Vambery, in an article in the *Pester Lloyd*, commented:

"The Shah's policy has been more prudent and successful than that of his predecessor, and to this policy is due to the fact that under his rule not an inch of Persian territory has been lost". (Here he ignored Ashurada, on the Caspian shore, which he had visited in 1863.) "He is fully aware of the hostile intentions of his northern neighbour, and he must regret the platonic manifestations of good will on the part of his English friends. As, however, Johan Bull can only be roused in moments of extreme danger, the Shah has been obliged to play a waiting game, and in that art he has displayed extraordinary skill".

The Times of 27 August 1889 printed a picturesque description of the Shah's visit to Vienna, less guarded and politic than other reports of the time:

". . . The Viennese, who take no political interest in Persia, feel beholden to his Majesty because he has made such a recreative exhibition of himself. His diamonds have been less dear to them than his delicious coolness . . . Vienna has seen its old original Shah in his old form, and his return has provoked the same outburst of merriment as always greets the appearance of certain popular characters in a harlequinade. Everything that his Majesty has done has been so done as to get talked about. Of another such man one might say that he had an astounishing faculty for doing the wrong thing, but we know that a King can do no wrong. At a Court dinner the Shah omits to give his arm to an Archduchess who is acting as his hostess, and she has to run after him. At another Court function, where the Emperor was waiting for him, he arrives, without concern, more than a quarter of an hour late. At the Zoological Gardens he borrows a stick to goad the animals and make them savage. At some public baths he and his valet play pranks with the water-cocks and flood the bath-room. In another place, having wetted his hands, his Majesty wipes them on the coat-tails of the nearest gentleman present. The Shah goes to buy a pair of spectacles, but cannot trouble himself to enter the shop, and orders that the goods shall be brought out to his carriage . . . How simple and truly royal this was, and how grateful some of us ought to be to the Shah for giving us a glimpse of royalty as it possiblly disported itself in Europe in the good old times!"

On the day that the above report was written the Shah and his large retinue sailed down the river from Vienna on the Danubian Steam Navigation Company's most luxurious vessel, the *Iris*. It was nearing dusk when they reached Budapest. Here a very large enthusiastic crowd had assembled to see the Shah land. The Archduke Joseph greeted him cordially. "The Hungarians, who are more demonstrative than the Viennese, are making much ado about the Shah's visit", reported *The Times*. "Last night up to a late hour crowds stood outside the Shah's hotel to see him appear on the balcony, and every time his Majesty showed himself he was uproariously cheered. He seemed rather to like this, for he came out often and saluted by placing his hand on his heart and then on his lips".

The Shah's first port of call was the Academy. Here Vambery greeted him with a welcoming speech delivered in true Oriental style in the Shirazi dialect. Vambery described the meeting in an article for an English magazine* soon afterwards: "I was standing in the magnificent hall of the Hungarian Academy of Sciences, surrounded by my academical colleagues, in order to receive the Shah's official visit to our Institute on his journey through Buda-Pesth. Nasr-ed-Din Shah was little altered in appearance; twenty-six years had traced few furrows on his face; his eye was as bright, his bearing as erect and dignified as before; he had somewhat increased in bulk, and his expression was less gloomy. When I greeted him in the Persian language, making use of the titles and metaphors which are in use in Persia, the Shah seemed surprised; he pushed up his spectacles, turned to the right and left to ask who I was, remained thoughtful for a moment after he had heard my name, then his colour rose, and he cordially extended his hand to renew our old acquaintance ..."

The Shah was delighted to see the 'Dervish' again and warmly shook his hands, saying to the Hungarian Minister standing at his side, "*Il parle bien, tres bien, notre langue!*" *The Times* correspondent reported, "The Shah gleefully complimented the learned professor on his knowledge of a language so little spoken in Europe". During all the Shah's European tours, as he told Vambery, he had never met with any other scholar who could speak Persian idiomatically and without foreign accent. And later in his journal the Shah declared that there were — even in Persia — few orators who for elegance and force of speech could compete with Vambery, a remark that surprised and greatly pleased the latter. "Why do not more of you learn Persian?"* asked the Shah in a loud voice, to the probable discomforture of the superior Hungarian aristocrats present. The visit of the Prince of Wales was still fresh in their mnds, and now here was another royal celebrity applauding Vambery's merits.

"Professor Arminius Vambery had been appointed interpreter to the Shah during his stay in Hungary", proclaimed *The Times*. "The learned Orientalist thus renews an acquaintanceship of long standing with His Majesty".

The first full day of the State Visit (28 August) was an extremely busy one, as Vambery escorted the Shah to all the main

---

* "The Shah's Impressions of Europe" in *The New Review* (Vol. 1) October 1889.
* *The Times*, 29 August 1889.

sights of the city, from the Academy and the Museum, to the scenic Margaret Island, a favourite resort of holiday-makers. The Shah was delighted by everything he saw, commenting that Budapest was a much more lively and busy city than Vienna.

The Shah was accompanied everywhere by his little 'pet', Aziz-i-Sultan ("the King's Affection"), an ugly and consumptive boy, who was always strutting about with an unlimited supply of pocket-money, and getting on the nerves of everyone near him. He was described as the Shah's "living talisman" or mascot. "The boy is merely a plaything which happens to please the Persian King. We fondle dogs and cats of every shape and size, while Orientals prefer children, for which no one need blame them", wrote Vambery piously, with that distaste for bringing sexual matters into the open which characterised the Victorians.

In the evening, when Vambery and the Archduke Joseph took the royal party to the Budapest Opera House for a large serving of ballet, the Shah became very bad tempered. He was sick of ballet and opera, he protested — in Vienna he had seen "nothing but ballets". He was greatly mollified by the promise that he would be taken the next day to the splendid Wulff's Circus, for a special performance to be given in his honour.

The Shah never seemed to get tired, though everyone else was exhausted and worn out at the end of the day by the continual visits and calls. Vambery was not allowed to have any rest. After ten o'clock in the evening (when he had usually gone to bed), he was summoned to the Shah's private room at the Hotel de la Reine d'Angleterre. There the Shah would fire many questions at Vambery, concerning the events, people and places he had seen during the day. All this information was transcribed into Persian writing, but the proper names he kept in their European characters, in order to avoid misspelling.

In spite of his efforts to diplay "all his European manners", Nasr-ed-Din continued to play the part of Asiatic despot and autocrat at all times. "His Grand-Vizier had sometimes to stand for hours before him", recalled Vambery later; "and when he wanted some information or other from me, I was often kept standing for a considerable time, regardless of my great fatigue; and he used closely to scrutinise my face if I dared to express an opinion different from his. In his character he certainly was more Oriental than the Sultan (Abdul Hamid), and considered this severity as indispensable to his sovereign dignity".

Next morning Vambery had to be up at the crack of dawn as all the corridors in the Hotel de la Reine d'Angleterre were thick with local tradesmen. It was a well known fact that the Shah was an 'easy sell' and that he had made a huge amount of purchases in every European city he had visited. (The acquisitions bought by the Shah in Paris alone had filled six hundred massive packing cases.) The Shah's unparalleled extravagances were a major cause of the ruinous state of the Persian economy; yet his position on the throne was strong enough to prevent any revolt at home during his long absences abroad.

Now Vambery acted as interpreter between the Shah and everyone in Budapest who had something decorative or useless to sell. The bartering went on for some time, at the end of which the Shah had paid out a total of 66,000 florins for a mountainous assortment of goods.

Later the Shah called on Sir Arthur Nicolson, formerly Charge d'Affaires at Teheran and an old acquaintance of the Shah who held him in high regard. During his four years stint as British Consul-General in Budapest, Sir Arthur (later Lord Carnock) spent much time discussing the Eastern Question and other political problems of the day with Vambery.

Nasr-ed-Din loved nothing better than to show off his beautiful jewellery. Vambery was much amused with the airs the Shah put on, "as he went about bedizened with diamonds, emeralds, rubies, and other jewels". The Shah's most treasured possession — made to his own special order — was a superb globe of jewels, then valued at one million pounds sterling. On one occasion in Budapest Vambery and the Shah were accosted by a labourer's wife who pressed up close to admire the great diamonds on the royal coat. In consternation, Vambery "motioned to the women to go out of the way, but the King said 'Let her come; she wants to see my jewels close to'. He even stopped a minute or two to let the woman stare at him to her heart's content". In later years, Vambery related anecdotes like this one to illustrate that the Shah could be better than his reputation, and that he was more of a human being than was generally depicted.

Later the same day, Vambery accompanied the Shah and the Archduke Joseph to the special performance at Wulff's Circus. *The Times* correspondent noted wryly: "It was easy to see that the antics of clowns and the exploits of a tame bear on horseback delighted his Majesty much more than studied feats of equestrianism".

During the time that Vambery remained in attendance on Nasr-ed-Din, he had ample opportunity to admire the very noticeable progress made by the Shah in the quarter-century which had elapsed since their meeting in Teheran, despite the recent derogatory comments in *The Times*. ". . . I was highly suprised by a great stride he had made in Western culture", wrote Vambery;* "he knows somethin of everything, he is anxious to be informed in all branches of Science and Art, but on the whole he is less sharp and cunning than his *cher frere* on the Bosporus, who again is superior to him in gentlemanly behaviour and manners. The Shah is a well disposed man with the outer appearance of an Asiatic tyrant, whilst the Sultan betraying in his exterior all the refinements of an European prince, is in his interior certainly more Asiatic and consequently less approachable".

Vambery naturally tried to probe first-hand into the Shah's political views, though his insinuations were usually met by evasive answers. "But in spite of his great reserve and cautiousness in political matters, I got a pretty clear insight into his political views", claimed Vambery. "Once, sailing on the Danube, I remarked that the Karun is wider but not so long as the Danube, the Kajar prince looked gravely at me and said 'Thank God, no!' ('If it had been, the English would before now have taken Teheran', was my mental comment.")

One of the more topical items which the Shah refused to be drawn upon was the Russian-built road from Askabad which had recently crossed the frontier on to Persian soil.

Budapest concluded the Shah's long European tour.

The following month saw the beginning of George (later Lord) Curzon's marathon investigation into all facets of the Persian Empire. Writing of the first stage of his journey at Constantinople, Curzon wrote: "At Pera a happy accident revealed to me the fact that my friend Professor Vambery was lodging at the same hotel, having come to the city at the invitation of the Sultan as the head of a Hungarian Commission to inquire into the historical and literary treasures stored in the palaces of Stambul. I enjoyed

---

* Curzon (G.N.): *Persia and the Persian Question* (2 vols., 1892) (Volume 1, page 59). Later in Persepolis, Curzon discovered (among the graffiti engraved by travellers to the Palace of Darius) Vambery's 1862 inscription *Eljen a Magyar!*: "On one of the western niches I observed, from his signature, that my friend Professor Vambery had also succumbed to the temptation of the surroundings."

with him a long and interesting conversation on the journey that I was about to make, and parts of which he had undertaken himself nearly thirty years before under conditions far less agreeable than those which await the modern traveller. Persia itself has not appreciably moved in the interval, but its neighbours have; and the presence of the Cossack sentry where the Turkoman raided and the Tartar reigned has multiplied tenfold the absorbing interest of the situation". (28 September 1889)*

Curzon's monumental study of Persia had to be watered down and modified before it could be published. The Shah was reported to be extremely displeased with all the astringent comments made by Curzon in his book. Curzon, like several other writers of the time, did not disguise the fact that Persia was still a country of mediaeval barbarity in many ways, not least in the assortment of gruesome punishments meted out through the whole land: from crucifixion and burning alive to the most commonly used, the bastinado.

During the latter part of Nasr-ed-Din's reign, the tortures and executions, formerly of almost daily occurence, gradually became much rarer. But throughout the whole period the Shah remained merciless in persecuting the followers of Mirza Ali Mohammed, the *Bab* ('Gateway') and founder of Babism, a new mystical movement in Islam. All Persians suspected of belonging to the sect were ruthlessly hounded from city to city, their women humiliated, and later massacred. In one publicised case a Babi was pierced through the nose and dragged by a cord through the streets. Vambery devoted a chapter to the Babis (followers of the *Bab*) in his book *Meine Wanderungen und Erlebnisse in Persien*. His descriptions of the ortures "excessive even by Persian standards" left nothing to the imagination.

The fiftieth anniversary of the Shah's accession (in lunar years) was due to take place on 6 May 1896. *The Times* reported: "In honour of the event the Emperor of Russia has presented to the Shah a field battery of Krupp guns, with a quantity of ammunition". (Vambery would have thought: "Typical!") However, the news reached Europe on 2 May 1896 — the same day that Emperor Franz Josef opened the Hungarian Millennial Exhibition in Budapest — that the Shah had been shot dead by an anarchist on entering a mosque. The assassination shocked the world, especially Sultan Abdul Hamid who was "put in a state of extreme terror" (as *The Times* described it), especially when it was disclosed that the instigator of the crime lived in Constantinople.

Muzaffar-ed-Din was a shadowy carbon copy of his father when he ascended the throne. He had been a virtual prisoner in all but name during his interminable years at Tebriz. Apart from Vambery, only a few Europeans had ever seen him.

The three long European pleasure trips undertaken by Nasr-ed-Din had left the Royal Treasury bare at his death. In 1898 Muzaffer-ed-Din appealed to Britain for financial assistance. Lord Salisbury (who had entertained the previous Shah at Hatfield, and seen his display of wealth) demurred, so the Shah turned to Russia instead. The government at St. Petersburg had no hesitation in making a large advance to meet his immediate needs, and from that moment Russian ascendancy grew in Teheran by leaps and bounds. 22,500,000 roubles (£2,500,000) were lent to the Shah at the beginning of 1900, and he lost no time in carrying out his great ambition — his own first grand tour of Europe, St. Petersburg naturally being his first stop.

In Paris the Shah narrowly escaped assassination at the hands of a fervid anti-Russian anarchist. A few weeks later he was greeted with great ceremony at the Court of Emperor Franz Josef in Vienna. Here numerous stories circulated about his behaviour, like his father eleven years before him, including one that he would habitually drink from the finger-bowls at banquets. Nevertheless, the Shah evidently adored the change and the novelty of the European capitals after spending nearly all his life marooned in a bleak Persian outpost. He took a great interest in the most recent discoveries and inventions in electricity, magnetism, and photography, which were shown him in Austria, as well as in all agricultural and industrial machinery.

Muzaffer-ed-Din had not forgotten the account in his father's journal which praised Vambery's linguistic prowess in Budapest. He now was determined to see Vambery — thirty-eight years after their first brief meeting — and on the train journey from Vienna to Budapest (26 September 1900) asked several times if he was still alive, and if he would be sure to meet him at the Hungarian capital.

Arriving in Budapest, the Shah's first question was: "Where is Vambery?" When Vambery was hurriedly summoned from the Academy, and greeted in the friendliest manner by the Shah, he was shocked by the potentate's haggard appearance: "Physically weak and insignificant as he was (in 1862), I found him now sickly and quite broken down".

He wrote shortly afterwards:* ". . . He is unfortunately a very weak man, bodily and mentally weak, for he suffers from three diseases, out of which, each of them would suffice to kill a man, his illnesses being bladder, kidneys and heart disease. He looks very tired and exhausted, he complained to me bitterly of his incessant pains and torments; and being a good hearted, kind and affectionate man, I really pitied the good King and I was much afflicted of seeing that poor ruler a prey to the varied tricks of his greedy courtiers and to the constant intrigues of the fighting parties . . ."

The Shah made no secret of his many ailments, and loved discussing them at length. Much of his time in Europe was spent at spas and health resorts.

After the meeting at the Station, the Shah invited Vambery to come with him straight to the hotel, and the two met every day during the Shah's sojourn in the city. Again Vambery acted as 'official' interpreter and escort. Unlike his father, Muzaffer-ed-Din talked quite freely and frankly about the political questions in Asia. When Vambery remarked jokingly that in Europe the Shah was looked upon as a partisan of Russia, the latter burst out laughing and said, "Am I the only one who in default of counter-arms has feigned friendship for this mighty, ambitious opponent?"

The Shah did not have a high opinion of England, and was very critical of Lord Salisbury's policies. "Britain's friendship s as cold as ice", he said, "and has always expressed itself in empty words". Vambery was seriously worried at this time about the high ascendancy of Russia over England in the Middle East, almost more than ever before. He asked the Shah why he had accepted such a large loan from Russia, and emphasized the risk of such a step.

"What were we to do?" remarked the Shah (quoted by Vambery four years later). "When my father died it was said that he had left private means to the amount of about four million pounds, and that these moneys were packed away in chests in the cellar. There was not a word of truth in all this. Instead of money my father left debts, and when I cam to the throne I was unable to pay not merely the State officials, but even the court expenses and the servants. I was forced to get a loan from somewhere, and England drove me into the arms of Russia".

Vambery believed that the Shah earnestly wanted to introduce to Persia many of the modernisations which had particularly struck him on his European tour. But the Shah, controlled by his unscrupulous Grand-Vizier, after all internal debts had been paid, squandered all the remaining money lent by Russia without conferring a single benefit on the Persian people. "(The Shah) had the best intentions in the world, was quite alive to the superior advantages of modern culture, and had a great desire to reform his country if only he had the necessary energy, money, and men", were Vambery's ingenuous comments.

The truth was that Muzaffer-ed-Din was just as much of a spendthrift as his father had been, and that each new giant loan from Russia marked another grand tour of Europe.

Vambery believed that the villain of the piece was the scheming Grand-Vizier (Amin-es-Sultan) who he had first seen eleven years earlier. He had been disgraced after the death of the late Shah, but eventually Muzaffe-ed-Din was forced to recall him to power, becoming more and more a puppet in his hands.

During his talks with the Shah at Budapest, Vambery noticed that the Grand-Vizier was omnipresent, a baleful influence, subtly pulling the strings of power. "This man, the son of a Georgian renegade from the Causasus, had pratically made the Shah the unwilling tool of his intriguing and rare abilities. He comported himself as a servant, but was in reality the master of his master and the ruler of Persia", claimed Vambery soon afterwards. "I was often an eye-witness when the two were together. The Shah, apathetically seated in his easy chair, would speak with as much authority as the words of his first minister were servile and submissive; but scarcely had he felt piercing glance of the latter than he would suddenly stop short and sink back in his armchair. Behind the door listened his secretary and faithful servant, who occasionally made his presence known by a low cough, upon which the Vizier would angrily turn towards the door, and strongly accentuating the submissive words continue his harangue. Master of the situation and with an insatiable desire for power and gain, the Grand-Vizier might possibly have been useful to the country if the violent opposition of his many rivals had not occupied all his energy, and the secret hostility of high dignitaries and the rivalry of European ambassadors at court had not effectually frustratd all attempts at any healthy reform".

Before Muzaffer-ed-Din departed from Constantinople, he

questioned Vambery closely on Turkey and the character of Sultan Abdul Hamid. After the leaders of the two adjacent Moslem empires had met in Constantinople, the Shah insisted on returning to Budapest where he spent a few more days with Vambery.

On 11 October Vambery was able to boast to the Foreign Office: ". . . in addition to my last report I have to add that the Shah took leave of me with great warmth; promising to write to me and asking me to give him occasionally my advice about political matters. He invited me to pay a visit to Persia; I declined on the excuse of my advanced age".

Writing four years later in his autobiography Vambery pitied the two Shahs and the other Asiatic despots he had known: "Their life is bare and lonely, heir enjoyment full of anxiety and fear, the hundreds of thousands who writhe before them in the dust and do them homage with bombastic titulations are their greatest enemies, and the worst victims of despotism are the despots themselves. Can one be surprised that I brought no rosy reminiscences from the Oriental courts?'

17

ADVISER TO THE SULTAN

When Vambery was asked to list his recreations for his *Who's Who* entry, he was hard pressed to think of an adequate line. He never indulged in pursuits like hunting, shooting or fishing, and thought concert and theatre-going too frivolous, so in the end he decided to give "trips to Constantinople and to the Tyrolese Mountains" as his recreations. Whereas he usually took his holidays at his summer-house in the Tyrol, only someone of Vambery's temperament would have described his trips to Constantinople as a 'recreation'.

In fact he was writing tongue-in-cheek. No visit to Constantinople could be described as a holiday. Instead, every time Vambery went to the City of the Golden Horn, he went immediately to the Yildiz Palace where the notorious Sultan Abdul Hamid was in residence. Elsewhere he described his relations with the Sultan as "not belonging to the comforts of life" — anything but recreational. But during the 1890s Vambery was generally regarded as being closer to the Sultan than any other European, though the full story was never disclosed to the public at the time.

The seeds of Vambery's relationship with Abdul Hamid were planted back in 1858 while he was living at the villa of Rifaat Pasha, in Kanlijia on the Asiatic side of the Bosporus (see Chapter 2). Already famous throughout the Ottoman capital as 'Reshid Effendi' as master linguist and tutor, he was commanded to give the first rudimentary lessons in French to Princess Fatma (daughter of Sultan Abdul Medjid) at her summer residence on the European side of the Bosporus. It was then that Vambery first encountered the young prince Hamid Effendi, then aged sixteen.

While visiting Fatma, his favourite sister, Hamid would sometimes gatecrash and interrupt the French lessons. Vambery described him later* as pale and frail-looking, leaning "with one hand

---

* A. Vambery: *Sultan Abdul Hamid* (*New Review*, 1890).

upon my knee, and fixing his black eyes upon me, he seemed anxious to snatch away every French word from my lips . . . When he addressed me with his timid, slow, and shy voice he rarely touched upon the subject of my instruction, but preferably began a conversation about his sister, her husband, and the father of the latter . . ." (who was the Grand Vizier). Only afterwards did Vambery find out the reason for his curiosity: ever since his early childhood Hamid had been trained as a consummate spy in the Imperial harem.

They met again by chance a few months later outside the palace of Bebek. Still working hard as a tutor, it was Vambery's habit to go to a shady place nearby called Chibuklu, "where, stretched on a lawn, I indulged in my studies". He related, half a century later,* a memorable occurence one day, resting on the grass, studying a difficult text written in Persian, and taking no notice of heavy footsteps approaching. Suddenly he felt a stick prodding his shoulder, and an irate voice shouting:

"Where did you learn this churlish manner to lie down and read in this indecent way?"

Frightened, he looked up into the angry face of Aziz Effendi, the Sultan's brother and heir-apparent, and one of the most important men in the Empire. (He would soon become Sultan Abdul Aziz.) Fortunately for Vambery, Hamid was at his uncle's side; he made excuses for the foreign manners of his sister's tutor, and an ugly situation was avoided. Hamid's "Oriental face and expressive eyes" made a strong impression on Vambery: "his countenance and his reserved and dignified manners left an indeliable trace on my memory", he wrote later.

Many years were to pass before the two met again.

While Vambery became known as a leading authority on the language and history of the Turkish race, Hamid Effendi succeeded to the Turkish throne in 1876 as Sultan Abdul Hamid the Second. Nicknamed 'Abdul the Damned', his autocracy and tyranny was infamous throughout Europe, for thirty-three years an absolute sovereign.

Hardly a month went by without Abdul Hamid's sly, moustachioed face being featured in the latest *Punch* cartoon. He had only been Sultan a few months when, following dissent in Serbia,

---

* A. Vambery: *Personal Recollections of Abdul Hamid and his Court* (*Nineteenth Century*, 1909).

Russia declared war on Turkey. At the beginning of 1878 the British cabinet decided to send the fleet to Constantinople, at the Sultan's request. The ships anchored off Seraglio Point, ostensibly to safeguard British nationalists and British interest in Turkey, but a popular music hall tune of the time gave a truer version:

"We don't want to fight, but by jingo if we do,
We've got the men, we've got the ships,
We've got the money too ...
The Russians shall not have Constantinople!"

The Treaty of San Stefano between Russia and Turkey was a crippling, humiliating affair for Abdul Hamid, and virtually abolished the dominion of the Ottoman Empire in Europe. However he survived the affair and proved himself over the succeeding years to be a consummate politican who kept his country going by setting the Great Powers one against the other.*

"He is not a tyrant", said Disraeli, after the Russo-Turkish war, "he is not dissolute, he is not corrupt". Disraeli was one of many to defend Abdul Hamid at this time. Far from being dissolute, the Sultan was considered to be the most temperate of men, and as such was welcomed by many of his subjects after the excesses of his mad uncle Abdul Aziz. He led a frugal, abstemious life. He preferred simple food, and wine rarely passed his lips. Western profanities like cameras were strictly forbidden. Like his neighbour, the Shah of Persia, he was a Jekyll and Hyde personality — described by many as a Satanic fiend (especially by the Christian factions in Europe), and by others as a benevolent and much maligned ruler.

There was some truth in both views. The real Abdul Hamid stood somewhere halfway between these two poles, as Vambery would describe at great length in his writings. Vambery's unique observations on this enigmatic figure covering a period of fifty years provided an invaluable source to future historians on the decline of the Ottoman Empire.

The personal acquaintance between Vambery and Abdul Hamid was not renewed until well over twenty years after their first meetings in 1858. From Vambery's unpublished correspon-

---

* Abdul Hamid apears to have liked White for he told Vambery: *"Bu baba adam dir —* he is a fatherly, i.e. kind, gentleman, who knows how to manage our susceptibilities, who has got a sparing eye for our shortcomings, whom I esteem, and whom I would also like if the policy of England would not contrast so much with the charms of his personality".

dence of the time, it appears that the Sultan first invited him to Constantinople in 1879 or 1880.

In a letter dated 3 January 1882, Vambery wrote to his friend William White,* who was then Consul-General in Bucharest: ". . . Madame Vambery and Master Rustem send you their kindest regards and are delighted at the prospect to call upon you in Bucarest the next autumn, should our old plan to revisit Constantinople be realized. I hope it will, for Abdul Hamid was so kind to invite me two years ago, and I cannot delay it any longer. . ."

Was this just name-dropping? Vambery saw White later the same year, but did not refer to a visit to Turkey at this time in any of his writings.

Abdul Hamid appears to have liked White for he told Vambery: "*Bu baba adam dir* — he is a fatherly, i.e. kind, gentleman, who knows how to manage our susceptibilities, who has got a sparing eye for our shortcomings, whom I esteem, and whom I would also like if the policy of England would not contrast so much with the charms of his personality".

Vambery commented in his autobiography later: "After my return from Central Asia, when I found other spheres of work, I kept aloof from Turkey, and I only remained in touch with the Ottoman people in so far as my philological and ethnographical studies had reference to the linguistic and ethnical part of this most Westerly branch of the great Turkish family. In my political writings, chiefly taken up with the affairs of inner Asia, the unfortunate fate of the Porte has always continued to touch me very deeply. The land of my youthful dreams, to which I am for ever indebted for its noble hospitality, and where I have felt as much at home as in my own country, could never be indifferent to me".

Eventually, in 1888 (12 August), the railway from Hungary to Constantinople was opened, and this date marked the start of Vambery's annual sojourns to the Turkish capital in earnest. (The train from Budapest to Constantinople took — the then very fast time — 42 hours).

Vambery's first publicised visit took place on 15 September 1888, and *The Times* gave him a lot of press coverage. He was

---

* *M. Vambery en Danger*, publ. Geneva, 6 August 1900.

From a collection of letters, 1876-1890, in Richard Dalby's possession from Vambery to William White (later knighted), eminent diplomatist who became British Ambassador at Constantinople 1885-1891.

HÔTEL D'ANGLETERRE
CONSTANTINOPLE

Saturday evening

My dear Sir William,

As previously announced in my letter, I am now here enjoying the hospitality of H. M. the Sultan, who will receive me tomorrow. I need scarcely say that I am anxious to see you, but in order to avoid the suspicion of my known friends — I shall postpone this call for a few days.

Yours sincerely

A. Vambery

accompanied by his colleague the Rev. Dr Vilmos Franknoi (general secretary of the Hungarian Academy of Sciences). "Professor Vambery has been received with much cordiality by his numerous friends in high Turkish circles, where he is well known through his works, and as a finished Oriental scholar", reported *The Times* (17 September).

Next day *The Times* added another piece, this time from their Vienna correspondent: "Professor Arminius Vambery, according to the *Correspondence de l'Est,* has been instrusted with the delicate mission of trying to persuade the Sultan to restore to th Hungarian Government the books which belonged to King Matthias Corvinus's library. These books fell into the hands of the Turks where Pesth was captured, and they are now deposited in the Old Seraglio". (The latter is now better known as *Top Kapi*.)

As it turned out, there was no time for Vambery to see any of the precious Hungarian manuscripts and books on this short visit. But on later visits, he was allowed to edit a few valuable old Slav manuscripts which he found in the "treasure-house of the Sultan", and which were lent to him for a considerable length of time. He claimed ". . . when, after the opening of railway communication with Turkey, I went to Stambul, I received from the Turks and their ruler a quiet, unostentatious, but all the warmer and heartier reception. Our mutual relationship only gradually manifested itself".

Owing to a major domestic crisis at Court, Vambery was unable to gain access to Abdul Hamid for some days. One of the Sultan's faithful black eunuchs had been shot dead by another eunuch in the Palace. This led to the discovery that some of the Sultan's intimate attendants, in disobedience to the strictest orders, had been secretly provided with guns and other weapons, and "were ready to use them against one another within the Palace apartments", as *The Times* related. Vambery only briefly recorded, "as an *unpleasant incident* prevented the Sultan from showing me his sympathies on my first visit, I was invited a few months later to pay another visit to the Turkish capital as his special guest".

The Times correspondent, writing from Constantinople on 23 September 1888, gave more details:

"The eunuch who recently murdered a comrade in the Palace was hanged yesterday at the police station, a large crowd witnessing the execution.

"Professor Vambery was yesterday received by the Sultan, who conferred on him the Grand Cordon of the Medjidieh Order, in recognition of his literary achievements. The Sultan expressed an opinion that the Professor's works had aided in diffusing a correct knowledge of the doctrines of Islam, so imperfectly known abroad". Vambery was there only in the role of Turcophile scholar; apparently (so we are told) the Sultan did not recognise 'Reshid Effendi', his sister's tutor of thirty years before. After the brief audience, Vambery returned to Budapest in time for the Prince of Wales's visit.

The following summer (1889) saw Vambery back in Constantinople, for a longer, more fruitful, visit. "My second visit", he claimed, "was more of a success, and my reappearance in public revived the old memory, for my fluency of speech had lent 'the foreigner' a new attraction in Turkish society. Wherever I appeared in public I was looked at somewhat doubtfully, for many who had not known me before imagined from my real Turkish Effendi conversation that I was a Turkish renegade. Thanks to my old connections, the problem was soon solved. The Turkish newspapers gave long columns about my humble person, and extolled the services which, in spite of many years' absence, I had rendered to the country".

He painted a graphic picture of his grand entry, contrasting the celebrated foreigner to the unknown, poverty-stricken young man of over thirty years before: "To make up for former neglect I received an almost regal reception. The slope up to Pera which in 1857 I had climbed a destitute young adventurer, I now drove up in a royal equipage accompanied by the court officials who had received me at the station; and when I had been installed in the apartments prepared for me by the Sultan's command, and was soon after welcomed by the Grandmaster of Ceremonies on behalf of the sovereign, that old fairy-tale-feeling came over me again. My first quarters at Puspoki's, swarming with rats; my *role* of house-dog in the isolated dwelling of Major A., my *debut* as singer and reciter in the coffee-houses, and many other reminiscences from the struggling beginning of my career in the East, flitted before my eyes in a cloudy vision of the past".

As Vambery passed through the great entrance hall of the Chit-Kiosk (where the Sultan often received visitors), various marshals, generals, and high court officials rose to greet him; and he later recalled smugly that "on many faces I detected an expression of astonishment, why, how, and for what their imperial master was doing so much honour to this insignificant, limping European, who was not even an Ambassador".

Appearing before Abdul Hamid, the two men shook hands, then the Sultan made Vambery sit down in an easy chair by his side. Vambery lost no time in strengthening his position by launching into his reminiscences of Constantinople in the late 1850s, speaking in his fluent Turkish — "of course I made my speech as elegant as I could". He called to the Sultan's memory the *Topal Khodja* (the lame teacher, as he was then called) of his late sister, Fatma Sultan. Abdul Hamid stretched out his hands towards Vambery, and said "Ah, my good sister! You gave her lessons in French; you have very much changed indeed". The ice was broken at once, claimed Vambery later, and the usually timid and distrustful monarch treated him as an old acquaintance. "At a sign the chamberlain on duty left the hall, and I remained quite alone with Sultan Abdul Hamid — a distinction thus far not vouchsafed to many Europeans, and not likely to be, as the Sultan is not acquainted with European languages, and therefore, according to the rules of court etiquette, cannot hold a face-to-face interview with foreigners", wrote Vambery.

Vambery later claimed to have been the *only* European who, dispensing with the aid of an interpreter, had free access to the Sultan. Thus his privileged, unique position was assured.

The conversation turned first to the events and mutual acquaintances of thirty years past, to the Sultan's father Abdul Medjid (to whom Vambery had once been presented), Reshid Pasha, and Stratford Canning (the *great Elchi*; Lord Stratford de Redcliffe) the celebrated British ambassador who for many years exercised much influence over the Turks. "As the conversation progressed the splendour and the nimbus of majesty disappeared before my eyes", wrote Vambery. "I saw merely a Turkish Pasha or Effendi such as I had known many in high Stambul society, only with this difference, that Sultan Abdul Hamid, by his many endowments, a wonderful memory, and a remarkable knowledge of European affairs, far surpasses many of his highly gifted subjects. Of course I became gradually freer in my conversation and when the Sultan offered me a cigarette and with his own hand struck a match for me to light it, I was quite overcome by the affability of the absolute Ruler, Padishah, and Representative of Mohammed on earth, or 'Shadow of God', as he is also called".

After Vambery had detailed all the phases of his life he had been through in the past thirty years, the Sultan admonished him for not coming to Stambul more often. He hoped that, from then on, their friendship would blossom, adding cannily that the knowledge and experience Vambery had acquired during his travels in Asia and in Europe "might be very useful to him"! Vambery was at first slightly wary: "Looking upon the Sultan standing before me, arrayed in a very costly sable fur and surrounded by princely luxury and wealth, I had some presentiment of the change which had taken place in him. I was very cautious and reserved in my conversation, and it was only gradually that I grew warmer, encouraged by his great affability and courtesy".

All the courtiers in the Palace were dumbfounded at this liaision between the Sultan of the Ottoman Empire, and a European 'Unbeliever'. Escorted to the door by Abdul Hamid, Vambery again passed through the entrance hall crowded with high dignitaries — "the surprise of these men was even greater than before, and for days together the topic of conversation in the circles of the Porte at Stambul, and in the diplomatic circles of Pera, was the extraordinary familiarity existing between the generally timid and reserved Sultan and my humble self", Vambery boasted.

Vambery gave three reasons for this unique relationship: as he pointed out, he was the first European known to the Sultan who was equally at home in the East as in the West, familiar with the language, customs and political affairs of both parts of the world, and who — in his presence — was not stiff like other Europeans, but "pliant like the Asiatics of the purest water". Abdul Hamid always referred to Vambery by his Turkish name, Reshid Effendi, and sometimes as 'Baba'. Thus, when learned Moslems were present, the Sulan could emphasize that 'Reshid Effendi' was really an "old, experienced true believer" — not an unbeliever at all. "I always appeared before him with my fez on", wrote Vambery; "I greeted him as an Oriental greets his sovereign; I used the usual bombastic forms of speech in addressing him; I sat, stood, went about, as it becomes an Oriental — in a word, I submitted to all the conventionalities which the Westerner never observes in the presence of the Sultan".

Secondly, Vambery put his popularity with the Sultan down to his "Hungarian nationality and the Turcophile character of my public activity". Abdul Hamid knew of Vambery's writings but not of his more scholarly studies, and when shown his monograph on Uiguric linguistic monuments — a work on which Vambery greatly prided himself — he was most impressed. He took an interest in Vambery's linguistic studies, yet — according to Vambery — he was not well versed in his mother-tongue. Vambery, expressing himself in the most elegant and flowery language, would be interrupted by the Sultan who said: "Please talk ordinary Turkish".

The third reason, and in Vambery's eyes the most important one, was his international renown as a writer "and more especially in the notice England had taken of my writings". The Sultan needed a better image in the press — 1876 had seen the uprisings in Bulgaria suppressed with brutality, to be followed by the even worse Armenian massacres. It was Vambery's thorough Turkishness which led the suspicious Sultan to confide in him and seek his advice. But what seemed to carry most weight with him was Vambery's friendship with the British royal family.

After Vambery's invitation from Queen Victoria to Windsor Castle, Abdul Hamid apparently became convinced that he was much more than an ordinary scholar and traveller; that he was, in fact, a confidant of the English Court and Government — two ideas which to the Sultan were inseparable. "Well, he accorded to me more liberties than to many other people in his entourage, but I never felt safe from the caprices of his fickle nature", Vambery asserted later. "In the beginning he really intended to put me in a high position if I would settle down permanently on the Bosporus; he made allusions to it, promising me all kind of wealth and dignity. I might have become an ambassador and even a Minister, but, having seen through his character, I never had the slightest desire to enter his service and contented myself with the title of a foreign friend".

In their long talks on religious matters, Vambery detected a good deal of scepticism on the Sultan's part when discussing Islam. One day Abdul Hamid suddenly asked him, "Tell me, Reshid Effendi, were you not afraid of God's punishment in playing a part of a dervish, whereas you did not believe in our religion?"

"No, Sire", was Vambery's prompt and shrewd reply; "emergencies of life very often necessitate a difference between our inner feelings and outer appearance; and is not your Majesty too, the ruler over many millions, so often obliged to show friendliness to certain persons whom you deservedly dislike and despise?" In time the Sultan gave up attempts to convert Vambery, but the fact that Vambery remained "for hours together in his room — and when I was there he kept even his most intimate chamberlain at a distance — necessarily gave rise to a good deal of speculation".

But whereas the Sultan was himself somewhat easy-going in religious matters, he demanded the most rigorous observance of the Koran from his Mohammedan subjects — stricter than ever before. "Not only had Turkish women to adopt a thicker veil and to avoid all kinds of luxury in their outer garments, but they were strictly forbidden from shopping in Pera magazines, from associating with Christian ladies, and from keeping Christian *gouvernantes* in their houses", Vambery observed. He also heard about the case of the son of a high Turkish dignitary, Military Attache in Rome, who "was suddenly dismissed from office because it had oozed out that he had taken part in a Court ball in Rome and danced with a lady". Vambery continued: "A similar fate befell a young friend of mine who was seen walking arm-in-arm with a Pera belle; whilst any Turkish lady who ventured to travel to Europe was banished for all time from the dominions of the Sultan. The rigour of these Draconic laws, aiming at the separation of his Mohammedan subjects from intercourse with Europeans, defies all description and calls forth a serious doubt as to the sanity of his Imperial mind". He was right: Abdul Hamid was a paranoiac.

Vambery continued to visit the Sultan regularly, observing and advising in turn. In his discussions with Abdul Hamid, Vambery would always take the side of Austro-Hungary and England, but he learned to be extremely careful in his expressions, "in a word", he writes, "I was dumb counsellor, and I much regret that the European diplomatists on the Bosporus did not look upon my position in this light, but laid all sorts of political intrigues to my charge". Observing and advising in turn, he never ceased to be surprised by the strange sides of the Sultan's complex character. On one of his early visits, Vambery was invited to dine with the chief dignitaries of the palace, and "was presented with a dish of strawberries, laid out in various lines according to the different shadings of the fruit, headed by a bit of paper bearing the inscription, 'From the plants reared by the hand of his Majesty'." Vambery rose to the occasion. He "took one strawberry, carried it to my forehead, kissed it in obedience and reverence to the royal donor, and offered to share the fruit with those present", he wrote. "On another occasion the servant brought me an apple and a peach of extraordinary beauty, and I had a gracious nod from the Sultan, whilst during my last invitation to his table I was greatly struck to hear Hungarian national music played by the Imperial band in the adjoining saloon, and on looking round a servant accosted me with a message from his Majesty that the Hungarian airs had been studied by the band by special order for that evening". Vambery often appeared before him in Hungarian national dress.

The Sultan must have valued his 'champion' who recorded anecdotes like the above in British newspapers and magazines; and when Vambery suffered a bad accident on a slippery pavement near his home (in early February 1893), breaking his lame leg in two places, the Sultan immediately sent him a very long telegram of condolence. A short extract was published in the Hungarian press, and caused something of a sensation. Vambery was not backward in letting his compatriots know of his influence and standing at the Turkish court.

But towards the end of the decade, it became known that Abdul Hamid was suffering continually from chronic insomia and advanced persecution mania. Unable to sleep at night, he would roam the corridors of the Palace, revolver at the ready, everwatchful for imaginary assassins. "Tired nature's sweet restorer, balmy sleep", never refreshed his tortured mind, as Vambery recalled. Guests staying at the Palace were given strict instructions never to leave their rooms at night. Vambery later wrote graphically of the long, still, silent nights he spent in his room at the Palace, "where not a shadow of a mortal was to be seen and where the swift flight of the owls was the only interruption in the dreary calm — this horrible stillness will be never forgotten by me, just as I shall always remember the frightful anxiety I felt when sitting alone at midnight in one of the rooms, whilst the heavy steps of the military watch, consisting of fiteen or twenty-five soldiers, who passed by my window, re-echoed far away in the distance, leaving a thrill in the heart of the most courageous man . . ."

The Sultan's restless nights were relieved to some extent by his most trusted aide, Izzet Bey, originally the keeper of the imperial wardrobe, and later raised to the rank of Pasha — "my and every European's most inveterate enemy", as Vambery was later to describe him. A strange and almost tender intimacy bloomed between master and servant: the Sultan and the wardrobe-keeper, who was so often by his side throughout the night as well as the day. By a deep-rooted psychological quirk, Abdul Hamid loved to hear tales of the disasters which had befallen other men; details of their acute sufferings had a soothing effect upon hiim — perhaps compensating for his own constant fear of calamity? Sometimes Izzet had to read all through the night to his master. Lying on his luxurious divan, Abdul Hamid found great solace in hearing all the details concerning the St. Bartholomew's Eve massacre, or Herod's slaughter of the Holy Innocents in Bethlehem. Other times he preferred volumes of memoirs (perhaps Vambery's *Life and Adventures* was on the list?), or detective and mystery stories. The latest work by Conan Doyle or Xavier de Montepin was promptly taken in hand by Abdul Hamid's large staff of translators and hurriedly rendered into Turkish with scant regard to style.

When Izzet Pasha became the Sultan's chief adviser, and the power behind the throne, he was detested (and envied) even more by Vambery. When Vambery pointed out the corrupting influence of Izzet, the Sultan smiled wearily and rolled up his sleeve: he caught a large flea and showed it to Vambery saying: "You see how fat and lazy it is? Full of my blood. A new one would be hungry and take more". He put the flea back and rolled down his sleeve.

As Abdul Hamid's persecution mania worsened, Vambery found he had to be on his guard every second. So mistrustful and afraid did Vambery become of the Sultan that when commanded to appear before him he took the unprecedented step of making Abdul Hamid promise he would be responsible to Queen Victoria herself for his (Vambery's) safety. "One evening", he wrote, "seated as usual alone with the Sultan in the Chit-Kiosk, sipping our tea, I fancied my tea was not quite sweet enough, and while talking I stretched out my hand towards the sugar basin, which stood near the Sultan. He gave a sudden start and drew back on the sofa. The movement suggested that he thought I had intended an attack upon his person". Vambery had a very lucky escape that time. Stories of Abdul Hamid's nervous trigger-happy fingers were legion. Once, a little slave girl who had strayed away from her mother and was found by the Sultan playing with one of his jewelled firearms was shot dead immediately in a blind moment of terror — no questions asked. And a young gardener had recently lost his life by inadvertently crossing Abdul Hamid's path when he thought he was alone ...

Vambery noticed that many of the Sultan's closest relatives — brothers, sons, cousins, and brothers-in-law — also lived in the same terror and anxiety as his unfortunate subjects, and additionally each of them had to be treated as *persona non grata*. "No outsider ventured to approach, to look at or talk with them", wrote Vambery; "and when one day on my way from the palace Chit-Kiosk to the library I met a royal prince, I had suddenly to turn into a byway as if I had met with somebody affected with a deadly disease. A prey to his unbridled passions, Sultan Abdul Hamid was easier addicted to enmity and hatred than to love and friendship, and woe betide the man who tried to come in as a mediator and appease the Imperial anger in hopeless cases. When at the height of his favour it happened that one chamberlain asked me to put his case before the Sultan, but hardly did I mention the name when the Sultan grew angry and said to me, 'Never try to act as a go-between; as an outsider you cannot mix in the internal affairs of the palace'. On another occasion when he intended to send me to London in the matter of his brother-in-law Mahmud Pasha he spoke to me of his sister Seniha Sultan (the wife of Mahmud Pasha) with a spite and hatred quite unfit for a sovereign and a brother. But of course I had to keep a dead silence during the outbreak of such Imperial fits, for any remark would only have raised his anger and caused a paroxysm, of which I was much afraid, remembering one evening when I was alone with him he had a serious fit of suffocation, and I said to myself, "If the Sultan dies in my presence I am hopelessly lost!"'" It could hardly be said that his trips to Constantinople were 'recreations'!

A 'Young Turk'-in-exile, Ali Fahri, was so worried about Vambery that he printed a brochure entitled *M. Vambery in Danger*.* In it he explained why "the famous Orientalist M. Vambery" ran the very real risk of being assassinated by Abdul Hamid.

As a result of an interview lasting far an entire day between Vambery and Tounali Bey Hilmi, a leader of the 'Young Turk' movement abroad, the latter was about to publish a book called *Reshid Effendi*. Abdul Hamid had heard of this and so, since Vambery would never deny its contents, he had lured him to Constan-

---

* Of all the Armenian revolutionary secret societies, the Hintchak was the largest and most important.

tinople under the pretext of opening a Turkish University.

Vambery, in full knowledge of the Sultan's character and foreseeing his fate (a cup of black coffee, into which a few drops of poison had been dropped) had told Tounali Bey: "Do you wish me to go to Constantinople to be poisoned? Can one entrust one's life to the Sultan? Can he have a friend? One of these days he will condemn me to death and I will be executed".

According to the author, only one expedient was left to Vambery: deny what he had said, a thing he would never do.

Vambery's life must be saved at all costs, the pamphlet concluded, and he hoped that the Austrian Ambassador in Constantinople would watch over his safety.

The latter half of Abdul Hamid's reign saw the revival and development of both the Young Turk Movement and the Armenian Revolutionary Movement. The crisis in Armenia stemmed from the period following the Treaty of San Stefano (1878), and the failure of the Great Powers to secure for the Asiatic provinces of Turkey the reforms envisaged by the Treaty of Berlin. When Russian aid ceased, the Armenians turned to Britain, where both Gladstone and Salisbury in turn warmed to the cause of the most persecuted Christian race in Asia. Armenia became increasingly a thorn in the Sultan's side, as reports of sedition and revolt reached the capital.

Already by 1890 Vambery found that the one question which obsessed the Sultan more than any other was that of Armenia. "In the face of the everlasting persecutions and hostilities of the Christian world", said the Sultan (quoted by Vambery in his autobiography), "I have been, so to speak, compelled to take these drastic measures". (The massacres in Armenia, beginning in the late 1870s, were beginning to grow in intensity.) "By taking away Rumenia and Greece, Europe has cut off the feet of the Turkish State body. The loss of Bulgaria, Servia, and Egypt has deprived us of our hands, and now by means of this Armenian agitation they want to get at our most vital parts, tear out our very entrails — this would be the beginning of total annihilation, and this we must fight against with all the strength we possess". Vambery considered him "not only an outspoken enemy, but a fanatical hater of Great Britain". He could not bring himself to believe in the power of Parliament but believed the monarch could do as he liked. "Owing to this misconception he had several times the idea of sending me with a private mission to Queen Victoria, and it was with great difficulty that he could be talked out of it", wrote Vambery. One day, when discussing Anglo-Turkish relations, Abdul Hamid "grew rather excited and said to me: 'And you really have doubt as to England's enmity against me? Look at their machinations with the Armenians, and is it out of friendship that they support the rebel Arab in Yemen? In taking away from me Egypt they have injured my title as Khalifa, for you know the right of the Khalifate rests upon the possession of the holy cities and Egypt. I can assure you I know who are my friends and enemies, and the pay-day of England will certainly come".

Vambery regarded his anger as not entirely unfounded: "For although in London good care was taken to keep aloof publicly from the disturbances in the Armenian mountains, the agitation of English agents in the North of Asia Minor is beyond all doubt. The Sultan was carefully informed of this both foolish and unreasonable movement. Whatever the Hintchakists* and other revolutionary committees of the Armenian malcontents brewed in London, Paris, New York, Marseilles, etc., full knowledge of it was received in Yildiz; the Armenians themselves had provided the secret service".

Discussing the situation next year (1891) with Vambery, Abdul Hamid declared with an air of cold determination: "I tell you, I will soon settle those Armenians. I will give them a box on the ear which will make them smart and relinquish their revolutionary ambitions". At this, Vambery became full of gloomy forebodings for the future, as he commented later: "With this 'box on the ear' he meant the massacres which soon after were instituted. The Sultan kept his word . . . That his drastic measures roused the public opinion of all Europe against the Sultan was no secret to him. He was aware of the beautiful titles given to him, 'Great Assassin', 'Sultan Rouge', 'Abdul the Damned' . . . "

Around the same time, Vambery's old acquaintance Arthur Nicolson (formerly Consul-General in Budapest) was transferred to the British Embassy in Constantinople. Nicolson wrote after his arrival: "Venice in its darkest days was light and freedom compared to the Stambul of today". The Western Powers were further outraged when the Sultan issued decrees prohibiting Christian worship and education. So far did the authorities go in this direction that even the classics of English literature, such as Shakespeare, Milton, and Scott, were confiscated. Christian writers in Turkey were even forbidden to use the word 'star', in the belief that the Magi were led by a star to worship the Messiah, and this might have encouraged the Armenians to look for a 'deliverer'. Ironically, the hypocritical Sultan always imported English literature for his personal edification, Sherlock Holmes being a special favourite.

However, when in favour at the Turkish Court, Vambery felt obliged — on several occasions — to spring to the Sultan's defence. In 1894, when there was much unfounded gossip concerning Abdul Hamid's projected visit ot Europe, he wrote to *The Times* from the Grand Hotel de Londres, Constantinople-Pera. Refuting the rumour that Queen Victoria had invited the Sultan to Britain. Vambery came to his defence: "He has got hardly the time to undertake a walk in the garden; how could he allow to himself the luxury of a holiday? To Sultan Abdul Hamid the throne is not at all a resting-place, and, having the honour to be his guest a few weeks ago, I can state from what I see that there has never been an Asiatic Prince who devoted all his energies to the welfare of his country like the present ruler of Turkey. The Press who drags this zealous Monarch into gossip does more injury than good to the spreading of Western Civilization in the East".* Abdul Hamid must have been pleased.

It was true that the Sultan — while always ruthlessly suppressing democracy — had done a great deal to modernize his country, providing schools, technical colleges, and hospitals. But at the same time, the name of Abdul Hamid was detested in Britain, and Vambery's critics, especially the Rev. Malcolm MacColl and Dr. Emile Dillon (both experts on Turkey and the Armenian situation) must have greeted his letters of this nature with scorn and contempt.

All the time, Abdul Hamid remained in absolute power, astutely setting Russia and England against each other. The growing dissension between the diplomatic representatives to the Porte was particularly gratifying to the Sultan who boasted to Vambery that there was certainly no lack of suitors for his country's favours: "I am courted by all, but I am still a virgin, and I shall not give my heart to any of them", said the Sultan, laughing

* *The Times*, 14 May 1894.

roguishly — but Vambery commented later, ". . . all the while he was in secret alliance with Russia".

October 1895 was a particularly black month for Armenia, with appalling massacres in Erzerum, Van, and Trebizond; and riots in Constantinople itself. On 7 October, in Constantinople-Pera, Vambery went to dine with General Walter Blunt Pasha. This "fine-looking old man" had spent almost twenty years in the Sultan's service — with no other duty than to attend the Selamlik and wear a handsome uniform. Also present was the General's cousin, Wilfrid Scawen Blunt, the eminent poet and diplomat. "We had a most interesting evening", wrote Wilfrid Blunt in his Diary.* "Vambery was very communicative. He talked strongly against the Sultan in this business (the Armenian disturbances in Constantinople), although he has been a favourite at the palace. He declares that, though superstitious, the Sultan is at heart a free thinker, his religion being with him a matter of policy, and he related several anecdotes bearing on this point. It is the Sultan's brother and heir presumptive, Reshid,* who is a true 'fanatic'. The Sultan has a deliberate political purpose, to diminish and drive out the Armenians, imitating in this the Emperor of Russia in his treatment of the Poles and the Jews. Vambery is of opinion that Abdul Hamid cannot long retain his throne, and agrees with me as to the desirability of renewing the Constitution of 1876. This was the best chance Turkey ever had of putting herself on a level with other European nations. It is the best chance still. But it can hrdly be under the present Sultan".

Tragically, the British newspapers were destined to be full of stories of Armenian massacres for years to come, but many of the atrocities were "too appallingly terrible for description". Dozens of reports and Government Blue Books (e.g. Turkey, No. 2 — 1896) were full of horrors, and Abdul Hamid's name was cursed throughout Europe.

In 1900 Abdul Hamid's reputation reached a new depth in the west, and during Vambery's lengthy visit that year, the Sultan made his position clear:

"I am unfortunately aware of the incapacity and of the impossibility to rely on my Ambassadors abroad. They do not care about my personal reputation, and finding myself vilified and calumni-

---

* Blunt (Wilfred Scawen): *My Diaries* Vol. 1 (Martin Secker, 1919) pp. 233-4.
* Mohammed Rashid, later Sultan Mohammed V.

ated in the European Press, I have asked you to come and to help me in that direction. You know the East as well as the West, you have shown attachment to my dynasty and to my country for more than forty years — for I remember: even my father having praised your knowledge of our history, language and literature — and I dare say you will not spare any effort to enlighten public opinion in Europe and to rehabilitate my much impaired name and reputation. It is exceedingly vexatious to find myself constantly misunderstood, to see my best intentions perverted and suspected, and it is certainly most galling to perceive that in spite of my efforts and labours, I am represented abroad as a despotic, egotistic and cruel ruler. I know your pen is influential all over the world, and without asking flattery or eulogistic expressions — I beg you to explain matters; as they are to put my plans to the Western world in the proper light".

Vambery recorded this declaration in a confidential* letter, quoting the Sultan's conversation in full thanks to his photographic memory. He believed he could keep his firm position at the Turkish court if he refrained from asking any favour from Abdul Hamid. But Vambery could not be prevented from criticising the Sultan aborad; his controversial pamphlet *La Turquie d'aujourd'hui et d'avant quarante ans* had recently been published in France to the displeasure of the Sultan.

Since the Czar of Russia had become increasingly friendly with the Sultan, Vambery found his position in Constantinople more difficult. The Czar had promised not to interfere in the affairs of Turkey — and to be, on the other hand, a personal friend and protector of his fellow autocrat. This gave rise to the rumour of a secret alliance between Russia and Turkey. Vambery continued to be up in arms against Russia, "and launched out against the perfidy, the barbarism, and the insatiable greed for land of the Northern power", as he put it succinctly, ". . . and the more I could blacken Russia politically the better service did I fancy I rendered to our European culture". The Sultan would have none of this, proclaiming to Vambery:

"Russia, the old enemy of Turkey, has acted hitherto by the unalterable decree of the Almighty, and being moved by the same heavenly power to become in future our friend, there is no reason to reuplse the tendered hand of amity, and if you are my friend,

---

* June 9 1900, letter to Sir T. Sanderson.

you must also become the friend of Russia".

Vambery replied that such a change of principle would be highly injurious to his character, to which the Sultan cried: "And you believe character to be a regulative with public men?"

At a later date, Vambery wrote: "Sultan Abdul Hamid never made a secret of his pro-Russian feelings, originating from his outspoken love of despotic rule, so flourishing in Russia. During the late Russo-Japanese war, whilst sitting with him and with Ibrahim Bey, I began to speak of the chances Turkey would have just now to attack her old enemy and to take revenge for so many aggressions. I dwelt at some length on the details of the plan, he listened attentively, and when I finished speaking he turned to me, saying, 'At what scientific work are you engaged now?' showing somewhat impolitely that he was averse to the discussion of politics with me".

Shortly after Abdul Hamid's silver jubilee Vambery paid another lengthy visit to Constantinople and was shocked by the Sultan's haggard appearance (May 1901): "Quite recently an extraordinary change has come over the man. Although but fifty-nine years old, his frame is much bent, his nerves are shattered, and his power of resistance is entirely broken. When appearing in public, he makes all possible effort to conceal his debility but when returning to privacy, he feels the much more exhausted, and begins to swoon from time to time ..."

Abdul Hamid was aging very quickly. He would study his face in the mirror, noting every grey hair and wrinkle; and he gave precise instructions for his cheeks to be rouged and his pale forehead lightly tinged with brown. His hair and beard were constantly dyed with a mixture compounded of coffee, gall-nuts and henna. When he received visiting diplomats, he wished to appear young and healthy, indestructible and eternal.

Vambery's 'recreational trips' to Constantinople were drawing to a close. Izzet Pasha, now the Sultan's most powerful adviser, had spoken against Vambery from the beginning and was laying plans to exclude every non-Mohammedan from informal meetings with the Sultan. Vambery became the object of further suspicions when he dared to suggest that philosophy and political economy should be included in the curriculum of the new University which was to be inaugurated in celebration of his Jubilee. The Sultan declared that such knowledge would undoubtedly be dangerous for his people and would be like putting a sharp knife into the hands of a young and inexperienced child. Eventually the whole plan was dropped but, ironically, the building intended for the University became the Parliament House of 1908.

The Sultan had always tried to make sure that Vambery's strong views on Turkish nationalism were never allowed to reach the ears of his subjects. Once, when Vambery had boldly asked permission to deliver a lecture in the Galata College on the ethnology of the Turkish race, the Sultan bluntly refused, saying: "We must not touch the question of nationality; all Mohammedans are brethren, and any national partition wall will cause serious dissensions".

The Young Turk Movement — who were eventually to pioneer the return of parliament in 1908 — gave the Sultan almost as much anxiety as the Armenians. He used to execrate the Young Turks in angry tones to Vambery: "Is it not sheer impudence on the part of these youngsters to presume that they know better the weal and woe of Turkey than myself? Constantly exposed to foreign attacks they aggravate our situation by interior troubles. What a pity for their sinful behaviour!" (The Young Turks were not only 'youngsters' — many older veterans joined the Movement as well.)

The Movement was very widespread throughout Europe, most of the exiles residing in London, Paris, Geneva, and Budapest. They believed passionately in *hurriyyet* (freedom), and their chief ideal was the British parliament at Westminster. Throughout the late nineteenth century, and into the twentieth, Vambery had a considerable influence through his writings on the cultural and, to some extent, on political developments in Turkey. The Young Turks admired Vambery greatly, even more than the two notable Turcophile scholars, Arthur Lumley Davids and Leon Cahun.

Writing at length on the Sultan in his autobiography (1904), Vambery said: "I must confess the character of Abdul Hamid has always been a riddle to me. I strained every nerve to penetrate him, but all in vain". Even at this late stage, Vambery could still be flattering in his descriptions of the Sultan. Perhaps he still entertained hopes that he would continue to be in favour at Constantinople.

However, five years later Abdul Hamid was deposed and sent into exile at Salonika, and Vambery then wrote in a more realistic, candid fashion of the Sultan's character: "Despite the fairly long run of my life, I never met with a man the salient features of whose character were so contradictory, so uneven and disproportionate, as with Sultan Abdul Hamid. Benevolence and wickedness, generosity and meanness, cowardice and valour, shrewdness and ignorance, moderation and excess, and many, many other qualities have alternately found expression in his acts and words. If there was a predominant feature in his character it was his timidity, the constant wavering and the apprehension of having committed a wrong step, which left an indelible mark upon all his doings. This unfortunate quality, the disastrous effect of harem education, frustrated his best intentions . . . he fell early into self-admiration, he despised the counsel of others, he grew angry and jealous at the slightest sign of mental superiority, and, favouring unbridled autocracy, he hurled his country with his own hands into hopeless ruin and destruction".

18

A FINGER IN THE PALESTINIAN PIE

The events of nearly a century ago which were eventually to lead to the founding of the modern state of Israel read like the scenario of a movie epic. The gigantic cast includes no less than two Emperors, two Grand Dukes, a Pope, a Sultan, princes and kings, statesmen and diplomats, with a supporting cast of famous men of letters, doctors, scientists, financiers, lords, millionaries and paupers and a host of anonymous but dedicated extras.

Vambery played a little known but major part in it.

The involved story is full of suspense and drama — a tale of lies and deceit, of intrigue and counter-intrigue, of hopes raised and dashed to the ground, moving swiftly from city to city and from land to land.

If we are to divide this giant epic into several parts, the star of the first part is undoubtedly Theodor Herzl, a Viennese playwright turned politician, who looked like Michelangelo's Moses and was a human dynamo.

He was born in Budapest on 2 May 1860, into a conventional Jewish middle-class family who very soon moved to Vienna where Herzl was educated and went on to read law at the University. He practised it however only for a short time (in Vienna and Salzburg), turning to journalism and play-writing instead.

His first experience of anti-semitism at the University, endemic in the Vienna of the times and especially in the *Burschenschaften* (the students' unions), as well as the fact that he had attended the Dreyfus trial in Paris as a newspaper correspondent, shaped his incipient interest in the Jewish question; in 1896 he published at his own expense a pamphlet entitled *"Der Judenstaat"* ("The Jewish State") which originally had borne the title "A Solution to the Jewish Question" and which had been turned down by two Viennese publishers.

This idea was to become the lode-star in Herzl's life and

despite the success his plays were having he now turned his attention to politics.

Two of the most picturesque characters in the giant cast were the Reverend William Hechler, Chaplain of the British embassy church in Vienna, and Count Philip Michael de Newlinsky, an impoverished Polish nobleman who at one time had been a high civil servant at the Austrian Foreign Ministry, and who was later attached to the Austrian Embassy in Constantinople; he had left and was now a journalist and a kind of roving goodwill ambassador. His first-rate contacts in Constantinople were of inestimable worth to Herzl.

Herzl's pamphlet had come to the notice of the Rev. Hechler who immediately linked it with a prophecy according to which the Caliph Omar had foretold in the 7th century AD that "forty-two moons hence" Palestine would be restored to the Jews. This had been calculated as spanning a period of 1,260 years which put the date for the fulfillment of the prophecy around 1897/98. The time was thus ripe and Rev. Hechler saw in Theodor Herzl the divine instrument ordained to fulfill this prophecy.

Newlinsky was interested and willing but how to obtain an audience with the Sultan? Newlinsky was a bit doubtful for Herzl's pamphlet had not been welcomed everywhere, especially not by the Sultan. Apart from the fact that Turkey at that moment was facing a political crisis in Crete the Sultan had told Newlinsky that he "could never give up Jerusalem and that the Mosque of Omar must always be in the hands of Islam".

Turkey was also heavily in debt.

The Turkish Debt which had been incurred in the second half of the nineteenth century ran to £233 million and by the end of 1881 had been reduced to £106 million. An Administrative Council of the Turkish Public Debt had been set up and gave the European Powers the opportunity to interfere in the internal affairs of Turkey.

Hard pressed, therefore, the Sultan had reluctantly agreed to make some reform. Jewish help — by providing publicity in the press — would be welcome.

Herzl's plan was ultimately to wring a far-reaching concession from the Sultan — Palestine — in exchange for buying off the Turkish Public Debt. It led to long and complicated negotiations during which, at one point, the Turkish Government contemplated offering 70,000 square kilometres in Palestine to Jewish settlers, in return for a 40 million franc loan and a railway concession from the Mediterranean to the Persian Gulf.

The first Zionist Congress met in Basle, in Switzerland, on 29 August 1897. It defined its aim: to create for the Jewish people a home in Palestine.

Here they were greatly at odds with Abdul Hamid II, for in 1897 Palestine (or "Egyptian Palestine" as it was then known) formed part of the Ottoman Empire. But they were also at variance with the British who had occupied Egypt in 1882.

Naturally there was nothing Herzl desired more, and nothing more urgent in his eyes than to be received by the Sultan. He had a brilliantly conceived plan up his sleeve.

Herzl tried to move heaven and earth to obtain this audience. He was prepared to go to great lengths trying to involve even the Emperor of Germany, William II.

Meanwhile however Herzl did not succeed in setting eyes on the Sultan. He had travelled to Constantinople and was received by the Grand Vizier, Khalil Rifat Pasha, whom he told that the amount of money provided would depend on the amount of territory ceded to the Jews in Palestine* and that he would only give details to the Sultan himself; he hinted, however, that the sum he had in view would be sufficient to pay off Turkey's Public Debt, and thus free her from the Debt Control Commission. The Grand Vizier did not appear favourably disposed.

Next Herzl called on a high official in the Turkish Foreign Office, Nouri Bey, who lent a willing ear — at a price.

But still no Sultan.

Newlinsky however had been received by him and reported that his Majesty would not hear of the plan. At that stage he opposed ceding even one square foot of Palestine. "Let the Jews save up their milliards", he said. "If my Empire is partitioned they will perhaps get Palestine for nothing".

The nearest he got to the Sultan was to see him driving past on his way to the mosque, splendidly arrayed, followed by an equally glittering party of high officials ... "He is a shrivelled sickly man", Herzl wrote in his diary afterwards, "with a big hooked nose and a middling full beard that looks dyed brown". He later amplified the description to include "long yellow teeth (one of which is missing) ... and (a) weak, trembling voice, wearing an imposing uniform, with brilliant decorations coloured cuffs, and a fez pressed down over his forehead".

Before he was willing to grant an audience he thought the Jews ought to consider settling in some other country — anywhere in the world but Palestine.

Herzl, naturally, was disappointed. And he sent Newlinsky scuttling around Europe in an effort to find another solution.

There were cordial relations between the German Emperor, William II, and Abdul Hamid who expressed his esteem by sending the Empress a valuable piece of jewelry. German engineers and technicians were working in Turkey and in 1898 the German Emperor was due to visit the Sultan. Herzl did all he could, working through diplomatic channels, and was assured the Kaiser would grant him an audience in Constantinople. William II was then due to travel on to the Holy Land (to inaugurate a Protestant Church) and Herzl was assured that he would be permitted to hand in an address.

He was indeed received by the monarch who proved most affable and well-disposed. He also promised to intercede with the Sultan, and wished to know what to tell him. Herzl suggested "A Chartered Company — under German protection " — in other words: Palestine.

But Herzl heard no more.

He arrived in Palestine to deliver his address, neatly typed out, in the Imperial Marquee near Jerusalem. But he had been asked to submit the text first to the German Foreign Minister, Count von Bulow, and a few moments before he delivered the address, the most important passages were deleted, so that nothing of importance to Herzl, or of the true Zionist aims, appeared in the press.

More than two years later the German ambassador in Vienna, Count Philip zu Eulenburg, told Herzl that the Sultan had declined the Kaiser's suggestion regarding the Zionists so brusquely that it was impossible to pursue the matter further.

A year later, in 1902, the Grand Duke of Baden who was very well disposed towards Herzl and the Zionist cause, received a delegation of Zionists nd "mentioned that the Kaiser had twice attempted to discuss the question of Palestine with the Sultan . . . but was met by an ostentatious lack of understanding".*

The Sultan opposed ceding even one square foot of Palestine

---

* This was the letter in which Herzl referred to "my excellent friend Professor Vambery, who is such a profoundly devoted servant of Your Imperial Majesty.
Desmond Stewart: *Herzl* (Hamish Hamilton, London, 1974 (p. 287)).

and Herzl was no nearer to his goal: an audience with His Majesty.

Meanwhile the second Zionist Congress had taken place at Basle (1898), and the Sultan, cleverly side-stepping Herzl's diplomatic overtures, replied politely to Herzl's friendly greetings — after the Congress was over.

The prospect of ever setting eyes on the Sultan receded into the distance . . .

Newlinsky's health was poor and Herzl took great precautions before he sent him to Constantinople: he sent his wife and family doctor with him. Tragically, three days after his arrival, Newlinsky dropped dead from a heart attack.

Herzl was shocked. He had lost a friend and a valuable collaborator, one who had, he thought, unrivalled connections in Constantinople. And he jotted tersely in his diary: "Practically irreplaceable".

But he did not give up. Turkish characters enter the scene and as the tale unfolds we hear stories of intrigue and counter-intrigue, of lies and deceit, and cupidity. Nearly everyone tried to exploit everyone else and use them for their own purposes. Herzl, in his contacts with Vambery, was no exception.

Nouri Bey, Secretary-General of the Turkish Foreign Office, and Izzet Bey, second secretary of the Sultan, and trusted adviser, promised to smooth the path that led to Abdul Hamid while prevaricating and all the while holding out their outstretched palms to be suitably greased. But Herzl was a match for them, and so was Vambery.

The third Congress took place in 1899 (again the venue was Basle) and Herzl was no nearer to his goal. Palestine had been decided on as the homeland for the Jews, and any earlier ideas (such as the Argentine) discarded.

Herzl was getting desperate and, knowing of the Sultan's good relations with Austria, approached the Austrian Prime Minister, Koerber, anxious for an introduction.

It is at this stage that Vambery enters the Zionist picture.

In every sense of the word he was Herzl's man.

Vambery had in fact already been approached two years earlier by some Zionist friends of Herzl's, but to no avail. He had heard of him through Max Nordau, the famous writer and Zionist and a great friend of Vambery, and of course had read his books.

Now Vambery was suddenly in the news again: he was going to Constantinople, summoned by the Sultan.

At nearly seventy Herzl had thought him too old to take an active interest in politics, a view possibly confirmed by the earlier failure to interest Vambery in Zionist affairs. But when he read the news item he felt it was time to approach him again.

As he sent the ever faithful Rev. Hechler to Budapest, who disappointingly reported back however that Vambery had already left.

Frantic telegrams were sent to Constantinople and Simon Rosenbaum, one of Herzl's contacts on the outer fringes, telegraphed that 'Schlesinger' (Vambery's code name) would "possibly introduce business (audience) in Charter affair today still".

As soon as he knew Vambery was back, Herzl sent the Rev. Hechler to Muhlbach in the Tyrol (Vambery's favourite summer resort, where he had a house), to track him down to earth. When Hecler returned he gave Herzl the surprising information — contradicting earlier information received — that Vambery had not yet mentioned Zionism to the Sultan. "Therefore", writes Herzl in his diary, "he was not 'curtly dismissed' either". He came to the conclusion that he had heard false alarms. "How am I to understand this?" he asks. "Did Vambery give Hechler ... inexact information?", adding, "*Bref*, I am going to see Vambery in the Tyrol on Saturday to find out the truth ... According to Hechler's report, Vambery is ready to help".

The journey took Herzl 14 hours by Express but it was well worth the trouble. The meeting of the two men was cordial in the extreme. Despite the great gap in age (Vambery could have been Herzl's father) the men took to each other on sight and were soon on terms of intimacy as if they were long-lost friends meeting again after an absence of years. Vambery spoke a mixture of German and English, with a liberal sprinkling of Hungarian and Yiddish words, and he immediately took Herzl into his confidence telling him things which he had never told anyone before — but carefully adjusting his revelations to suit the circumstances he found himself in.

In the beginning Herzl was impressed. "I got to know one of the most interesting men in this hobbling old Hungarian Jew who doesn't know whether he is more Turk than Englishman", he wrote in his Diary (3 May 1900) "who writes books in German, speaks twelve languages with equal mastery ... professed five religions, in two of which he has served as a priest . . . Through these many religious intimacies he has naturally become an atheist . . .

"He told me 1001 tales of the Orient, of his intimacy with the Sultan, etc . . . and he revealed, under the pledge of secrecy, that he was a secret agent of Turkey and England. The professorship in Hungary was merely a cover following upon the long torment he had suffred in a society hostile to Jews. He showed me a sheaf of secret documents which, being in Turkish, I could not read but only admire. Among them handwritten notes by the Sultan . . ."*

Herzl gave Vambery details of Zionist plans, available money, etc, as requested and Vambery, in turn, confided that the Sultan had called him in order to create a good image in the European press. Could Herzl help? Warily he entered in his Diary: "I answer evasively", adding: "Meanwhile he revealed to me the salient events in his life . . . He began in Turkey as a singer in coffee houses, 1½ years later he was an intimate of the Grand Vizier. He could sleep at the Yildiz (Palace) but thinks he might be murdered. He eats at the Sultan's table — on intimate terms, with his fingers from a dish — but cannot rid himself of the thought of poisoning. And a hundred more such picturesque things.

"I asked him: "May I call you Vambery *bacsi** as Nordau does . . .?" "My time was up. He was undecided what he would do. First of all, will he write off immediately to the Sultan for my audience?

"But he embraced and kissed me when I took leave".

A code was evolved. On Herzl's suggestion the Sultan had become "Cohn" and Yildiz Palace "the factory". (Later Vambery himself was to assume the unoriginal codename of "Schlesinger", the Grand Vizier became "number 73", and Tewfik Pasha, the Turkish ambassador in Berlin, "number 919").

Still in the train Herzl wrote a letter to Vambery *bacsi*. "Write to Cohn", he instructed him, "he should send for me. (1.) I can help him with his image. (2.) My arrival will increase his credit even if he does not accept my proposition at once. You help our cause enormously if you get me an audience". And, shrewdly assessing Vambery's most vulnerable spot, his vanity, he added:

---

*   *Diaries of Theodor Herzl*, Edited and translated with an introduction by Marvin Lowenthal, The Dial Press, New York, 1956.

*   "Uncle" — a courtesy title accorded to any older person in Hungary.

"I know what you want to erect for yourself with your autobiography: a royal sepulchre. Crown your pyramid with the chapter: 'How I helped prepare the homecoming of my people, the Jews'."

The moment Vambery had mentioned the Grand Vizier Herzl had seized the opportunity to plead his case and to win him over to the Zionist cause. To emphasize that he meant business he had offered him money. "No," Vambery had cried, waving aside with a lordly — and typically Hungarian — gesture any mention of a financial reward. "I want no money! I am a rich man. I can't eat golden beefsteaks. I have a quarter of a million and don't need half my interest. If I help you it is for the sake of the cause".

How had Vambery's change of heart come about?

At the time Vambery met Herzl he was working on his autobiography, *The Story of My Struggles*. In this book he described at length his own experiences of anti-semitism: ". . . one of the darkest stains on the escutcheon of the modern world . . . a vile baseness which cannot be justified by any religious, ethnical or social motives".

Vambery's insistence that he had faced great dangers to investigate the early history of Hungary had been met "everywhere and on all occasions by an ominous sneer, an icy indifference, or a silence which has a more deadly effect than any amount of talk". He was naturally bitter. ". . . Many, nay, most people questioned the genuineness of my Hungarianism. They criticised me and made fun of me because, they said, people of Jewish origin cannot be Hungarians, they can only be Jews and nothing ele".

So if he was now ready to help Herzl and his cause it was not because he was, from a religious point of view, bent on rescuing the Jews from the Diaspora and herding them into Palestine. But he had reached a point in his own development when he believed the salvation of the Jews lay in the possession of a national homeland (though he still felt himself to be a Hungarian patriot) and Vambery had great sympathy for any movement of national liberation.

He was also profoundly disillusioned. And he poured into Herzl's willing ear stories of his sufferings as a Jew. He was interested in Herzl's crusade — if not (as in later transpired) for idealistic reasons alone.

Herzl was certainly even more interested. Here, at last, was the "Open Sesame" to the Yildiz Kiosk. Vambery, with his experience of Constantinople, his contacts and, most important of all, his friendship with the Sultan, seemed truly heaven-sent. Where others — even the powerful Emperor of Germany — had failed, Vambery would succeed. Herzl felt sure of that. He would get him an audience and at last he would be able to put his case to the lord and master of the Promised Land. (Apart from the Argentine, alternatives such as Cyprus the Sinai peninsula and Uganda were to be discussed as suitable territories for the settlement of the Jews — the Sultan was even to suggest Mesopotamia. But for Herzl there was only one goal — Palestine).

Thus Herzl, pursuing his objective with single-minded tenacity, asked Vambery to give him a letter of introduction to the Sultan, although he would have preferred him to come to Constantinople with him as an interpreter, but Vambery shook his head and declined, afraid of the heat.

A few days after the meeting Vambery wrote from Muhlbach (21 June): "Nothing can be done with the *Mamzer-ben-nide*" (Yiddish for 'foully conceived bastard' i.e. the Sultan). "Telegrams and letters are futile at a place where the spoken word is quickly forgotten and where one deals with one of the world's arch-liars, the very personification of mistrust".

Herzl replied urging him to act. Flattering him he wrote: "I believe you to be a man of action, a man of my race, who I believe capable of every energetic action. Disraeli once said to a young Jew: 'You and I belong to a race which can do anything but fail'. My dear Vambery *bacsi*! We can do really everything, but we must be willing. Are you, Vambery *bacsi*?" And he continues: "I don't see, in view of how you describe the situation why you should not write to Cohn: 'Let him come. He will put an end to your troubles. Listen to him, have a good look at him, later you can throw him out. I don't need to tell you more. But this you must tell him — if you want to". And he signed "in sincere devotion".

Three days later Vambery replied. "He has written to the Sultan, he claims", Herzl entered in his diary; "whether the letter ever reached him is not certain".

Vambery replied to the impatient Herzl, accusing him jocularly of charging along heedlessly without a thought for the ditches. "Nevertheless he claims to have written to the Sultan", Herzl entered in his diary, "whether the letter ever reach him is

Herzl went again to Budapest, to urge Vambery to get the Sultan to invite him for a talk, threatening otherwise to withdraw any help in the press or with the loan, the conditions and amount of which varied considerably from time to time.

The 4th Zionist Congress took place in London, on 13 August 1900. Herzl had yet to meet the Sultan.

About a fortnight later he entered in his diary: "Received a comforting letter from Vambery. He has written to the Sultan about our affairs and received no negative reply", and he adds caustically: "Neither does he appear to have received one in the affirmative".

In September Herzl travelled to Budapest again. He confides to his diary: "Vambery again told me a lot about himself, and what he already had told me at Muhlbach. He gave me his word of honour that His Majesty would receive me in May. Although I don't understand how he can give me his word about something that does not depend on him".

But the days passed and on 1 October Herzl entered in his diary: "No news from Vambery. He seems to have forgotten the whole affair ..."

A month later he sent one of his aides to Budapest to invite Vambery to come with him to Constantinople.

More than a fortnight later Vambery wrote back. In his letter he said that he had written to the Sultan and asked for a telegraphic reply, whether there was any truth in the loan.* If so, he would travel to Constantinople at once and send for Herzl. "Everything", he wrote, "is in our favour".

Meanwhile Herzl had been seeing Nouri Bey's mercenary go-between, Crespi. This man told Herzl that the only reason the Turkish Government was against Zionism was because they were afraid of an intervention by the Powers, should the Jews be allowed to immigrate (into Palestine). The Powers would then immediately send warships to Jaffa and take Palestine. Herzl, as grandiloquently as Vambery, undertook to "change the Powers' mind". He asked Crespi if he could take Vambery with him and was told that "it would be an enormous advantage because Vambery has free access to the Sultan anytime he liked. And he entered in his diary: "Vambery's recommendation has helped me enormously".

---

* Nouri Bey had indicated to Herzl that the Turkish Government wanted a loan of 7-800,000 Turkish pounds, after which Herzl would be received by the Sultan. Herzl had replied in the affirmative, with the proviso that he nogotiate personally with the Sultan.

A month passed and nothing had happened. He wrote again to Vambery informing him that he would phone him the following day at the National Casino in order to give him 'Cohn's' news. "Are you ready to come with me?" (4 December)

Five days later there is another entry in Herzl's diary: "Yesterday I went to see Vambery in Pest to tell him the whole story about C . . . (Crespi)". Vambery gave financial advice and then suggested to Herzl that he was to write him two letters in French: one to be shown the Sultan officially and one, couched in more "intimate, genuine terms" which the Sultan would be allowed to get hold of, "out of indiscretion". Vambery had learnt from his Turkish masters!

A few days later Herzl heard from Vambery that his letter to the Sultan had been sent off.*

But Herzl, none too trusting, was anxious. Five days later he wrote to Vambery: "I hope you won't be put off by (the idea of) a journey in winter. Let me make you as comfortable as possible. Perhaps your son will give me the pleasure of his company?"

Another ten days later Vambery asssured Herzl (by letter) that he had written to the Grand Vizier, and there was much discussion of financial matters.

Herzl also informed Vambery that he had found a bank willing to advance the gigantic loan, adding ". . . but keep the name of the banker dark or else you might find you have pulled the chestnuts out of the fire for others . . . but my *bacsi* is too clever for that". (28 December.)

The end of the year (1900) found Vambery in Constantinople. Vambery wrote to Herzl who entered in his diary: "Vambery writes the Sultan expresses himself quite differently to him that the officialreports suggest". (Which were negative.) "He doesn't care a fig (about Palestine), all he wants is money and power".

On New Year's Eve, a letter was in the post for Vambery in which Herzl advised him what to write to 'Cohn'. "Your words will be cleverer", he added, flatteringly, "more Turkish".

And his letter was followed up on New Year's Day with further advice and suggestions on what to tell 'Cohn'.

On 4 January 1901 Vambery wrote saying that he had reported the contents of Herzl's letter to te Sultan in full but did not expect much from it.

Two months later he received a letter from Crespi which enclosed a letter written in Turkish "which he is supposed to have written to the Sultan in our interest. "I am sending this Turkish swindle to avambery for translation", he entered in his diary, "and I am asking him at the same time whether he is ready to come with me to Constantinople".

Two weeks later he had a letter from Vambery: "Vambery writes to me who his friends are in the *entourage* of Cohn, and summons me to Pest".

Who indeed were his friends?

They were certainly not to be found among the Jews on the Sultan's pay-roll (for Abdul Hamid liked the Jews who he could play off against his unruly Christian ssbjects) — as long as they kept clear of Palestine; they were by no means all enamoured of the Zionist idea. There were distinct material advantages "in being in His Majesty's employ, for . . . he gave away valuable properties, houses, and thousands of pounds to his favourites; and he gave with a free hand . . . many of his chamberlains and Court officials amassed big fortunes and quondam poor fellows became millionaires" wrote Vambery. (And he was well placed to know.) Not for them, therefore, the vision of the Holy Land and the discomforts of some 19th century Kibbutz in Palestine: they opposed Vambery.

But like a rabbit out of a hat, Vambery produced Dr. Wellisch, a Hungarian Jew in the Turkish civil service, a trusted confidant, who proved an invaluable aide through the maze nd thickets of Turkish intrigue.

Perhaps more important, though, Vambery could brief Herzl on who were his enemies. They were many.

Vambery was in the unique position to have first-hand knowledge of the men surrounding Abdul Hamid. He trusted no ne.

Izzet Bey·was the second secretary of the Sultan and Vambery's "declared enemy".

Then there was Lutfi Aga, Master of the Robes, "in his official capacity . . . but in reality the most intimate confidant of the Sultan". Vambery was contemptuous of him, "the lowest kind of servant in the household of Mahmud Nedim Pasha"' who had polished his boots. One day, while walking with the Sultan in the garden he saw this man approaching His Majesty. "In accosting the former servant somewhat boldly, I noticed a perplexity on his face, but still more remarkable was the blushing of the Sultan, who asked me whether I knew this favourite man before. 'Of course', said I, 'Lutfi was a servant in the house of Mahmud

Nedim Pasha, and often cleaned my boots . . .' *Tableau*! The most intimate man of His Majesty a shoeblack by origin."[*]

There was Tahsin Bey, the first Secretary of the Sultan and a son-in-law of one of Vambery's former pupils. Vambery described him as "a creature of Lufti Aga . . . a genuine representative of the old Turkish Effendi class, ignorant and servile, but grasping and corruptible in the extreme."[*]

He had a kind word to say for Ibrahim Bey who had the unenviable task of being the Court Interpreter and whom Vambery seems to have genuinely liked. He calls him a "kind-hearted gentleman of the old Turkish class".

Sureya Pasha remained one of Vambery's best friends.

His office was the real centre of administration and Vambery writes: "I used to spend hours in this office, as an idle spectator, where I met all the great men of the country . . ." The Sultan was in constant contact with this high official. and chamberlains were scuttling to and fro, from one palace or the other to the Secretariat a"as bearers of small letters, cautiously folded and sealed, which the secretary had to destroy or burn after having read their contents. Only once or twice I succeeded in evading the attention of the secretary, getting short speciments of the Imperial handwriting".

Were these the letters Herzl saw?

In April 1901 he went to see Vambery in Budapest. "Yesterday I called on Vambery in Pest", he writes in his Diary. "He himself suggested to go and see the Sultan because, according to his latest reiorts, he was greatly favoured at the moment. The Sultan will probably want Vambery to set up good relations between him and Edward VII whose friend Vambery is. On this occasion he intends to tell the Sultan: 'You can make a fool of Herzl. (But) be friendly with him, it costs you nothing".

Herzl had gone into involved financial discussions with Vambery with the ultimate aim of a Charter for Palestine in exchange for buying off the Turkish National Debt. Vambery's interest in the whole affair was not purely academic, as events were to show.

On the same day (11 April) Herzl writes: "Yesterday I visited

[*] Personal Recollections of Abdul Hamid II and his Court, *The Nineteenth Century*, June 1909 (Vol. 65).

Vambery in Pest. He himself proposed to me that he would go to see the Sultan, because according to his latest information he was now extremely popular. The Sultan might wish Vambery to establish a good relation with Edward VII whose friend Vambery is.'' He also records a letter he had received from Crespi, Nouri Bey's agent, which gives one a measure of the intrigues both Vambery an Herzl had to contend with. ''I am to ask Vambery'', the letter ran, ''what was contained in the parcel which he received recently from Yildiz Kiosk. And if it contained anything concerning our running negotiation''. Everyone distrusted everyone else, but Herzl also became suspicious of his good friend *Vambery bacsi* as well, for he confides to his diary:

''The style of C . . .'s letter is strange: as if he knew that something of interest to me was in the parcel. If this is true then Vambery's decision to go to Constantinople might have more serious reasons than I had thought and than he told me. Then his *bonhomie* is two-faced: h knows already that the Sultan wants to see me and is only playing around with me. We shall see''.

And Herzl kept a close watch on his good friend. Eleven days later he tried to phone him (from Vienna) at the National Casino in Budapest and was told he was leaving for Constantinople. This must have come as a relief to Herzl who for the past five or six months had been kept on tenterhooks by Vambery.

By early May Herzl had been summoned to Budapest again. He waited for Vambery to return and met him at the station. ''8 May . . . He arrived at a quarter to one (from Constantinople). With a torrent of abuse the grand old man of seventy got out of the railway carriage. The station echoed with his thunderous voice because there was no porter available. His son and I carried his luggage to my carriage''.

Always over-sensitive, ready to take umbrage at an imagined slight, Vambery ad become extremely irritable and irascible in his old age. Not only was the Orient Express nearly two hours late but he had also been kept waiting by the Sultan.

Herzl drove home with Vambery. Now Vambery turned his abuse against the Sultan ''for keeping him endlessly in Constantinople'' and assured Herzl that the Sultan would now receive him.

He described how he had been received with suspicion. ''Why are you here?'' the Sultan had asked. And Vambery had told him (whether true or not) that he had been invited by the King of England . . . Vambery was well aware that at that precise juncture it was important to the Sultan to establish goo relations with Edward VII; at the same time he had seized this opportunity to impress on the Sultan how much it would be to his benefit if he agreed to receive one of the most distinguished and influential journalists in Europe — Herzl. On the other hand he warned Herzl not to breathe a word in Constantinople about Zionism — which he called a "phantasmagoria".

Vambery also gave Herzl a recommendation to Tahsin Bey (who Vambery believed on their side, and about whose behaviour Herzl was to complain later), as well as to the implacably hostil Izzet Bey.

But "a perfect storm" assailed Vambery when Herzl told him about the financial arrangements he had made with the Nouri-Crespi group. Vambery "shouted and swore" that Herzl was being cheated and, forgetful of the fact that he could not eat golden beefsteaks (as he had said earlier on) he now ate his words and shouted that he had stayed in Constantinople for three weeks and now others were to reap the fruit. "Tact, patience and the intercession of his son", Herzl notes in his diary, "finally brought about an understanding that the Nouri group, Tahsin Bey and Vambery were each to receive a third of the commission".

When Herzl asked impatiently whether the Sultan had made a personal remark about him, Vambery gave the astonishing reply: "He does not even know your name". And Herzl jots down in his diary: "Perhaps he was merely annoyed with me because he had lent me a helping hand, or he was on edge from the journey. For how can this square with Vambery's former report that the Conference at Basle had harmed me in the Sultan's eyes?", adding drily, "Either it did me harm in his eyes, or he had never even heard of it".

But then how did anything square with anything where Vambery was concerned? He was a rich man, he could not eat "golden beefsteaks" — yet "only fools and knaves worked for nothing!"

As far as Herzl was concerned, however, the main point was that the Sultan would at last receive him. And Vambery warned him again not to speak about Zionism, for Jerusalem was as sacred to them, he said, as Mecca. "And yet they don't mind seeing a good side to Zionism as well — as a weapon against the Christians", and Vambery added: "I want Zionism to continue to exist — that's why I got you this audience".

On his way to Constantinople Herzl called on Vambery again

for his final briefing. He was given a letter for the Sultan but Herzl noted that Vambery was much cooler than he had been three days earlier. Herzl wondered whether he was alreade regretting the service he had rendered him. But the real reason lay perhaps elsewhere. Vambery wanted the money right away. "He flew into a rage and shouted and cursed that he had done everything and now others were reaping the fruits . . ." Herzl explained that he had promised a certain sum to Nouri Bey & Co. a year before and that now he had to keep his word, he knew he was being cheated . . . Finally "Vambery calmed down somewhat. But he wanted the 300,000 gulden for himself . . . Herzl could promise him only a share. The parting was rather strained".*

At Vambery's meeting with the Sultan, Abdul Hamid had exhibited the classical symptoms of paranoia: ". . . When I decided to introduce Dr. Herzl . . . I had to use all kinds of prtexts to disarm the Sultan's apprehension. He was fond of the Jews, he knew that Jewish colonisation in Palestine would serve as a counterpoise against the steadily intruding inimical Christians and would strengthen his rule in Syria. But it nevertheless cost me days and days of persuasion . . . and when he ultimately acceded to my wish and agreed to receive Dr. Herzl, he did so under the condition that I must leave Constantinople at once, which I also did. Now I am quite at a loss to discover the reason of his command and I shall probably never know it".*

This is the only mention of Herzl in Vambery's writings in English. From the casual mention of his name no one could guess that Vambery was interested in the Zionist cause at all. For the outside world he had, like Pontius Pilate, washed his hands of the whole affair.

On arrival in Constantinople, Herzl, like Vambery was kept waiting. Wellisch (Vambery's confidant) proved a safe guide through the palace intrigues, Tahsin Bey was amenable, Izzet Bey implacably hostile, and Nouri Bey and Crespi quite openly grasping.

Finally, on the fifth day after his arrival, Herzl was received in audience by the Sultan. The date was 17 May 1901.

Before the audience he was informed by Ibrahim Bey, the official Court Interpreter, that his Majesty had conferred on him the

* *Personal Recollections of Abdul Hamid II and his Court.* (Nineteenth Century, Vol. 65, June 1909).

Order of the Medidjeh second class; Herzl (briefed by Vambery perhaps for just such eventualities) refused it. The result was that a few minutes later he was awarded the highest distinction Abdul Hamid had to offer, the Grand Cordon of the Order of the Medidjeh (the same order Vambery himself possessed).

Now Herzl was introduced by his "excellent friend, Professor Vambery, who is such a profound and devoted servant of your Imperial Majesty . . ." Herzl was not impressed by the Sultan. He described him as a "small thin man, with hooknose, long yellow teeth (one of which was missing), dyed beard, and weak, trembling voice, wearing an imposing uniform, with brilliant decorations, coloured cuffs, and a fez pressed down over his head".

With typical Turkish courtesy the Sultan began by saying that he was a constant reader of Herzl's paper (*Die Neue Freie Presse*) — though he knew no German at all. Herzl, on the other hand, remembering Vambery's warning to steer clear of Zionism, mentioned that the Jews everywhere were grateful for the Sultan's good treatment to those of their race. Then, after various other remarks, he approached his object obliquely.

"When Professor Vambery informed me that His Majesty would receive me", he said, "I could not help thinking of the charming old fable of Androcles and the lion. His Majesty is the lion, perhaps I am Androcles, and perhaps there is a thorn which I could withdraw". He received permission to speak more openly and went on: "I consider the Public Debt a thorn. If this could be removed, then the life-strength of Turkey, in which I have great faith, would unfold anew". *Herzl gave further details always through the Court interpreter, for the conversation was conducted in French and Turkish, impressed the need for secrecy upon the Sultan, "and the ruler lifted his eyes to heaven, placed his hands upon his breast, and murmured 'Secret, secret!'

Obliquely Herzl hinted that the Sultan should make public a measure specially friendly to the Jews (no overt mention of Palestine).

The Sultan, equally obliquely, suggested that he could make a friendly statement to his Jewish Court jeweller who would give it to the press. He was also prepared to make a similar statement to the *Haham Bashi*, or Chief Rabbi, but Herzl refused for the latter

---

* Amos Elon: *Herzl* (Holt, Rhinehart & Winston, New York, 1975).

he said, simply spat at the mere mention of Abdul Hamid's name
. . .

After two hours Herzl was exhausted. Towards the end of the conversation he repeated his three requests: 1) complete silence; 2) a proclamation favourable to the Jews; 3) a copy of the funding plan (concerning the Public Debt) to be sent to him. Abdul Hamid agreed to all three.*

He had impressed the Sultan who later told Vambery: "This Herzl looks exactly like a Prophet, like a leader of his people. He has very clever eyes, and speaks prudently and clearly".

Ibrahim Bey said: "That is how Jesus Christ must have looked".

Having conducted some behind-the-scenes negotiations and distributed *baksheesh*, Herzl was back in Europe by the end of May and immediately set out to visit Vambery at his summer resort.

In the train from Innsbruck, Herzl noted in his Diary (29 May): "Vambery entered my compartment in Muhlbach, we continued on to Franzensfeste.* There at the inn I gave him my report. He found my achievement colossal. I told him that he had done much more than promised. Vambery replied: 'You are a noble man, not to disparage this now.' He thinks we will have the Charter (for Palestine) this year still. He intends to go to Constantinople again in September. Meanwhile I am to draw up a draft of the Charter which he will submit to the Sultan asking for his signature, without any secretary or minister ever hearing a word from him".

A month later Vambery was in London and drafted the letter to the Sultan in which he obsequiously mentioned "*Monsieur le Professeur, qui est un si profondement devoue serviteur de Votre Majeste Imperiale*" as promised to Herze long ago, no doubt sorry not to mention that he had been received in audience by the King and that his name had again appeared in the Court Circular of *The Times* (11 June 1901).

And during the same month the indefatigable Vambery, now in his 69th years, delivered a lecture in Sheffield entiled 'Russia's Progress in Asia'.

Herzl began to be very impatient, and a short while later Vam-

---

* The Hedjaz railway in Mesopotamia was a project dear to the Sultan's heart; Herzl had already tried to return a gift of £200 (Turkish) pounds made to him, by the Sultan, recommending its use for this purpose, but had been refused.

* Now Fortezza (Italy).

bery comforted him that everything moved slowly (in Constantinople).

But the summer months went by and there was still no news. And from Alt-Aussee, in Austria, Herzl's own summer resort he wrote to his "dear Vambery bacsi" in a semi-humorous style, impatient about the delay, complain ng about procrastination and suggesting to Vambery what he should write, requesting him to translate it into Turkish.

In autumn Herzl visited Vambery again in Budapest and persuaded him to write an urgent letter to the Sultan and then to go to Constantinople himself.

Nothing happened.

Next February (1902) Herzl consulted Vambery again for advice. He had received an invitation from "Cohn's Ibrahim" to come to Constantinople to discuss affairs. It had seemed too vague to him, but he had replied that he would be pleased to place himself at Ibrahim's disposal: however he wanted to know more before leaving. He ended his letter on affectionate terms: "As soon as I hear more from Cohn I will let you know and if I do go I will of course call to see you, my *bacsi*. I embrace you, your faithful Dori".

Vambery replied a week later and Herzl entered in his diary: "Vambery writes that he has news that my journey concerns the Hedjaz railway. Wellisch writes Ibrahim had told him the imperial summons was in our interest as well as in that of the Government . . ."

A bare twelve days later Herzl's tone was far less effusive, referring to "Schlesinger" in his diary, "He gave me some important tips. The main thing is that Cohn now needs me urgently. He also promised to come at once, should I call him, i.e. if we run into difficulties".

On 12 February 1902 Herzl left for Constantinople, stopping en route in Budapest for last minute instructions. He had been summoned by a telegram from Ibrahim Bey, asking him "to furnish certain explanations" and he was worried. Vambery reassured him.

He never saw the Sultan but two days later instead was conducted by Wellisch to see Ibrahim who wished to know what the object of the Zionist Congress had been. Herzl explained that it was against the absorption of the Jews by other nations, and denied that he had been responsible for a misleading newspaper report which had reported the Sultan in favour of Jewish immigration into Palestine.

Herzl stayed four days in Constantinople and on his return visited Vambery. The relationship had become much cooler and Herzl recorded in his diary: "... A quite pointless visit as I had as little news to tell him as he had to tell me. But I had to make an attempt; otherwise he would have thought that I had become unfaithful to him and ungrateful (as well). A quite unnecessary sacrifice ... the decision was taken that he would write to Tahsin — only if he received no new invitation from the Sultan.

"Vambery now believes that I will reach my goal.

"Last May he said the opposite.

"I believe him now. But when?"

Three weeks later Herzl was worried that Izzet now seemed to have gone over to his side while Tahsin Bey seemed to be against him. What could it mean? "I went to challenge Vambery about this", he wrote adding in his next diary entry: "I shall write to Vambery today, with a complaint about *his* Tahsin", concerning some devious financial machinations by Herzl who stuck doggedly to his one objective: Palestine. He had interviews with both the Pope and the King of Italy — but to no avail.

However events were to take a far more dramatic turn than even the most fertile brain of a playwright (which Herzl was) could think up.* In early February 1904 Herzl received the visit of a man calling himself Ali Nouri Bey born in Sweden, though resident in Turkey for over twenty years, a Moslem by religion and married to a Moslem princess. His scheme was nothing short of fantastic: two cruisers, with a force of 1000 men, could steam up the Bosporus and bombard Yildiz Kiosk — forcing the Sultan either to flee or surrender. A new Sultan would then be appointed, a provisional Government set up which would grant the Charter for Palestine. The adventure, he estimated, would cost about £500,000.

He suggested the Khedive of Egypt as a possible choice and Herzl promised to consider the plan.

Herzl turned it down.

No less astonishing, however, was a letter Vambery had written to Herzl nearly three years earlier. "Arminius writes to me

---

* Herzl saw Abdul Hamid as a character in a play which he planned but never wrote.

one of the most peculiar letters", Herzl had entered into his diary.
"He wants to dethrone Izzet to take his place — or to dethrone
Abdul Hamid himself". And, in fact, Vambery proposed to call in
the Young Turks to help.*

Nonplussed, Herzl replied warmly but cautiously: "My dear
Vambery *bacsi*. I have received your courageous letter full of
youthful fire with great delight. You are really a divinely inspired
man. May God keep you".*

But perhaps Vambery's grandoise ideas were not quite as fantastic as they seem. The movement of the Young Turks had begun
in the 19th century, and aimed at securing liberal reforms. Vambery was very much in sympathy with them and maintained contacts with the exiles of the movement aborad. Finally, if not by
Vambery, the Sultan was indeed deposed by the Young Turks.

After Herzl's death (in 1904), Vambery faded out of the fore-
front of the Zionist picture with unwonted quiet. He remained
active in the background, however, keeping in touch with David
Wolffsohn (Herzl's successor and President of the Zionist organi-
sation), advising him, even without the grant of a Charter, to be
satisfied with lesser concession — as well as to 'help things along'
by bribing the local authorities. This was rejected by Wolffsohn.

In 1907 Vambery was given to understand, from his friends in
Constantinople, that the Turks were interested in renewing contact with the Zionists, and Vambery wrote to Wolffsohn:

"After six years of slence . . . it may be that there is an opening
for a new dialogue. It is possible that the prospects are better than
in Herzl's time".

The exchange of letters between Vambery and Wolffsohn continued for some time. Wolffsohn was convinced that the invitation sent to Vambery by the Sultan was a direct result of his own
visit to Constantinople earlier in the year. It was Vambery's
belief however that Turkey's financial troubles were at the root
of the desire to renew contact.

In the course of the negotiations (which concerned a proposal
to permit 50,000 Jewish families to settle in the regions of Damascus, Beirut and Jerusalem over a 25-year period), Vambery was of
some help in putting Wolffsohn in contact with the Turkish officials concerned.

---

* Theodor Herzl: *Excerpts from his Diary*. (Jewish Pocket Library, Scopus Publishing Co.,
  New York, 1941).

Occasionally Vambery contributed an article on Zionist affairs, but only to German publications: he had to be careful of his public utterances. He rarely made a public speech on Zionism in the company of Herzl. One occasion was in London (10 June 1901) when he made a speech essentially in praise of Zionism and of England.* Nevertheless he claimed that he had intended to introduce Herzl to Edward VII: "If I did not succeed in managing to introduce Dr. Herzl ... to the King, I am fully conscious of the fact that my plan miscarried, not because of the King's personality, but because of his entourage".*

Did Vambery ever get his 300,000 Gulden commission (£25,00) in the end? No one knows for sure.

One thing is certain: although the Balfour Declaration establishing a Jewish homeland in Palestine was made in 1917, when Vambery was no longer alive to see it, his efforts had paved the way.

*   *The Jewish Chronicle* 14 June 1901.

*   *Pester Lloyd,* 7 May 1910.

19

SECRET AGENT

Presumably it was Arminius Vambery who sought audience of Lord Salisbury at the Foreign Office in April 1889, though it could have been the other way round. For although we now know that a meeting between the two did take place (we can imagine Vambery making his halting but self-important way from the Athenaeum, down the Duke of York steps, across the Mall to the Foreign Office) no word of it was made public then; and it was inferentially denied during Question Time in the House of Commons a few weeks later.

The facts were that on 20 June 1889 William Summers, the Member of Parliament for Huddersfield, asked Sir James Fergusson, the Under-Secretary of State for Foreign Affairs, in the House of Commons "whether there is any foundation for the statement that Professor Vambery had been on a special mission to the Sultan at the request of Lord Salisbury* and if so, whether he can inform the House what was the nature of the mission in question".

The Under-Secretary replied: "No Sir, the statement in question is without foundation".

Yet by this date there was already in the hands of the Foreign Office Vambery's voluminous report of his secret conversations with the Sultan.

Two months earlier that year Vambery had arrived in London, on the face of it to deliver a lecture at Exeter Hall on "The Cultural Progress of Turkey". At the apogee of his fame, his movements alone made news and the *Times* Correspondent in Vienna had duly reported his departure from Budapest, and the paper had published a few days later the date and venue of his lecture,†

---

* Foreign Secretary at the time.
* 9 May 1889.

access admittance to which would be "by card of invitation" only.

The lecture itelf was a huge success, the hall packed with baronets, earls and field-marshals, adorned with medals, and society ladies craning their necks to get a better view of this celebrity from distant Hungary. Vambery put the Sultan's case adroitly, stressed the progress made in science, maintained that "the light of Western culture" was beginning to penetrate all strata of society and held out hope that the harem, "that horid, inhuman custom" would disappear. Ending his speech on a patriotic note, a vote of thanks was moved by the Chairman, Sir Lepel Griffin and seconded by Sir Donald Stewart, Commander in Chief in India, and, once again, Vambery sat down amid thunderous cheers and applause.

In announcing the forthcoming lecture the *Times* had also written that "the learned Professor's paper (would) be based on observations during his recent visit to Constantinople where the Sultan gave him a private audience."

So far so good. Vambery was, most innocently and aboveboard, engaged in most scholarly enterprises. What the *Times* did not mention — simply because no one had got hold of the news — was the fact that Vambery paid a visit to Whitehall . . .

Who actually took the initiative is hard to tell, at the distance of nearly a century. But in the light of Vambery's known character it is more than likely that he presented himself at the Foreign Office, confident that he was doing the right thing, and "encouraged in his doings" by Disraeli already and by many other British statesmen.

Once again, he arrived at a most opportune moment.

He was well aware, of course, that the Sultan had taken the first step in initiating a dialogue with Lord Salisbury. Turkey was very much "in the news" and the Sultan most anxious to preserve a good image. He felt that his ultimate fate depended on Europe, and was firmly convinced that England (from motives of self-interest) would be compelled to uphold the Ottoman State. This was also Lord Salisbury's policy. The Foreign Office were therefore most anxious to find out what was going on in the Sultan's mind. As the lord and master of a vast empire which nominally included Egypt, so restive in the past, though *de facto* British-occupied since 1882 Britain had a vested interest to see that all remained quiet: only a year earlier the Conference of Constantinople had declared the Suez Canal open to ships of all nations and free from blockade.

What went on behind closed doors in Whitehall remained a closely guarded secret. All that the general public knew, from the *Times* was that Vambery had packed his bags a day after the lecture and had left for home.

They were reminded of him when they read, scarcely a month later, that he had dined with the Sultan in Constantinople and afterwards had had an hour's private conversation with His Majesty. The Sultan, it was reported, showed special interest in the subject of education and general progress in Turkey "and was much pleased to hear of the keen interest of the British people in the welfare of his country" and added a few polite political cliches.

Vambery's departure from Constantinople was delayed (all reported by the *Times* and he finally left "after a private audience with the Sultan ... having completed the arrangements which were the object of his visit". This might well have referred to his forthcoming researches, for the paper added that he would return in September "to pursue his researches connected with the eriod of Ottoman domination in Hungary. His Majesty had received Professor Vambery in the most gracious and cordial manner and promised that every facility would be afforded in the furtherance of his mission".

In point of fact, the Sultan had kept Vambery waiting for four long days before granting him a second interview, the subject of which had been wholly other than academic.

The request Abdul Hamid had sent Lord Salisbury a few years back, when the latter was Prime Minister, for the re-opening of the negotiations concerning Egypt, had met with a polite but firm refusal on the part of the Prime Minister, and subsequent attempts by Turkey to get Britain to withdraw her troops from Egypt had equally failed. Even though Russia still presented a threat from the direction of the Black Sea it did so to a lesser extent than it did to India, therefore giving greater prominence to the defence of the Suez Canal. But in both cases Britain could do with information: even though the Sultan was no longer in authority in Egypt, he still commanded the entry to the Bosporus and the Dardanelles.

When therefore Vambery arrived in Whitehall, his portmanteau packed with secrets, freshly arrived from Constantinople, the Foreign Office was all ears. They let this funny little man, so un-English in his boastfulness and arrogance, yet a scholar of world renown, unpack his baggage and sat back and listened . . .

And the result is that today there lie in the archives of the Foreign Office, gathering dust, two fat volumes labelled "PROFESSOR VAMBERY — SECRET"; they contain all that passed between the Foreign Office and Vambery, and are a record of their correspondence and accounts, covering a period of twenty-two years (1889-1911). They tell an amazing story, and reveal a lot of what went on behind the scenes.

Vambery's effusive letters and reports in his neat and spidery handwriting (the latter sometimes running to 30 foolscap pages and more, with a narrow margin pedantically ruled in pencil on the left) were neatly filed and docketed as soon as they arrived. It was the task of a civil servant to read and summarise their contents; this was not always done accurately, but with Vambery's rambling style and illegible handwriting one feels like forgiving him) and then to submit it to the Permanent Under-Secretary of State for Foreign Affairs who added his comments on the back and passed it on to his boss, the Foreign Secretary himself. The latter often initialled the letters sometimes adding comments of his own (always in red ink). Occasionally there are markings in red or blue pencil in the reports: passages which seemed of importance to the Foreign Office. Vambery's letters thus passed through the hands of Lord Salisbury, Rosebery, Iddlesleigh, Kimberley, Lansdowne and Sir Edward Grey.

Often, especially in the early part of his association with the Foreign Office, he submitted minute, often verbatim, reports of his confidential conversations with the Sultan, sometimes written on the spot, sometimes (and more often the latter) copied out at the University of Budapest (so that one sometimes wonders when on earth he found time to do his academic work) were of great interest to Whitehall. Even though they were inclined to treat him rather condescendingly, at times even curtly, they found him most useful.

They paid him generously for his information although they never called it a salary — they called it "travelling expenses", "gifts to the Palace", etc. And if the criterion of being sent on a mission is to be on someone's pay-roll, then the answer given in Parliament corresponds to the truth. Even in these matters he was, at first, a "self-made man", a free-lance, who saw himself in the role of a go-between, a mediator between Abdul Hamid and Britain. It cost him years of effort to be put on their permanent pay-roll and to receive a pension, and he was not above twisting the royal arm in the process.

All throughout their relationship the Foreign Office remained wary, not entirely trusting Vambery's discretion, for they had sized him up shrewdly. He, however, wore his heart on his sleeve: "It is the greatest pride of my life", he wrote, "to serve your glorious country ... I am Hungarian, but my heart and soul is English" (though whether his behaviour was always so measured by traditional public school standards is open to question).

In all fairness it must be said, however, that he never did anything to discredit his own country, quite on the contrary, he tried in every way to foster a good relationship between Hungary and Britain. Basically he remained a Hungarian patriot, if in some way carried away by a youthful idealism and inordinate admiration of Britian. For someone of Vambery's temperament the need for secrecy on the one hand and the desire to proclaim from the rooftops on the other his involvement with the glorious British Empire on which the sun never set, must have engendered a terrific conflict. And at times it proved too much for him as an article which appeared in a London magazine attests.*

It was the account of an interview with Vambery at his home in Budapest. And in it a very curious passage occurs.

At one point "the conversation reverted to Gladstone.† Every time that name was mentioned the old man's eyes twinkled.

"*He* called *me* a fanatic! But he was good; he was great. About the end of his second Government the Tories got up a meeting with Lord Hamilton in the chair and asked me to speak. That was in St. James's Hall. I saw Gladstone in front of me. I said all kinds of bad, political things about him but he only stared with his keen eyes and often smiled. He shook hands afterwards and asked me about Persian poets but nothing about Russia ... Do you remember Egypt? ... Gladstone thought I might help them and sent me on a mission. When I came back and reported I was asked for a *szamla*, a bill. This was a troublesome question. It had thought about it. England was rich, the service was delicate, and few others could have carried it out. I had fixed upon £200".

* C. Townley Fullam: *Westminster Review*, July 1911.
† Officially Vambery's inveterate enemy.

"But, Professor", said Gladstone, "I am afraid you could hardly expect me to entertain that".

"Then I repented and sat confused with no offer ready".

"For such a peculiarly delicate mission, so dexteriously and well carried out — bowing — we must beg you to accept — if you will permit me to amend your suggestion £500".*

"After *that*", went on Vambery, his eyes twinkling again, "I forgave him all but his Russian heresy."

What the mission was Gladstone sent him on has remained a mystery — and what was Gladstone doing at a Tory meeting? — as the author of the article asks perplexed.

Vambery himself, however, who could never keep his mouth quite tightly shut has provided an invaluable hint, for it is still rumoured in Budapest today that he had given Gladstone advice regarding Egypt in 1882 — the time of the British occupation.

If this was a fact then Vambery might well have been, in some way or other, associated with British cloak-and-dagger mano-euvres to get rid of Arabi Pasha, the awkward and nationalist Egyptian Minister of War. The plan involved both the Sultan and Gladstone and "the method resolved on was certainly one of the most extraordinary used by a civilised government in modern times, and the very last which would have been expected of one owning Mr. Gladstone as its chief. It was to beg assistance from the Sultan and to beg him to 'get rid of Arabi' . . . by one of those old-fashioned acts of treachery which were traditional with the Porte in its dealings with . . . subjects in too successful rebellion against it". (The plan involved luring Arabi on board ship and sending him off to Constantinople, or if that could not be done, for a newly appointed Turkish military Commissioner to Egypt to shoot him 'if necessary with his own hand').*

Did Vambery act as a go-between in this as well? And was 1885 the first time Gladstone set eyes on him again, to pay him for his services?

Did he also have a hand in financial dealings?

In Egypt sat the International Commission of the National Debt and on its Board was Alfred, Baron von Kremer, a noted Austrian Orientalist and a friend of Vambery. Whatever the mission consisted of it seems unlikely that Vambery ever went to

---

* This would equal about £10,000 today.
* Wilfred Scawen Blunt: *Secret History of the Occupation of Egypt*, London, T. Fisher Unwin, 1907.

Egypt himself.

Vambery with his self-avowed "secret desire for public activity" (although it might be more correct to say in this instance that he made public his desire for secret activity) would have sold his soul to the devil if it would have brought him recognition in hell. By selling it to the Foreign Office he was certainly no longer a free agent, for all his political writings and lectures, every word and gesture, would from now on be sharply watched and scrutinised; and, in fact, there were occasions when, in the eyes of the Foreign Office, he had overstepped the mark, when the things he said or wrote were in open conflict with the line British foreign policy took at the time: he was then sharply pulled up and taken to task. At other times he was given a condescending pat on the back. He was given strict instructions what to say, and, on the whole, kept on rather a short leash. The Foreign Office could be a hard task master. But, by and large, Whitehall regarded him as a useful additional source of information for Turkey, Persia — even India — but by no means as their sole source as Vambery, in his Walter Mitty-like moments of flights of fancy seems to have believed. In point of fact there must have been moments when Vambery's letters caused great amusement in the austere corridors of power, for Vambery saw a Russian spy lurking behind every bush; sometimes, no doubt, they were a reality but at others he must have appeared a Hungarian Don Quixote, tilting furiously at windmills . . .

None of this however became apparent to Vambery. The Foreign Office sent him elegantly worded, polite letters which he took at their face value. The off-the-cuff comments on the back of his letters show a quite different picture; terse and to the point they contrast neatly with Vambery's florid and effusive style, his rambling letters so full of emotion. If his letters now strike one as employing a tone of abject servility, one must, in all fairness, make allowances that in the days of the Austro-Hungarian monarchy this was the done thing when addressing one's superiors (for Vambery was very conscious of the fact that the Foreign Office were his masters) — anything else would have been interpreted as gross impertinence.

The Foreign Office greeted Vambery's effusive offers to serve the Imperial cause with British calm and sat back and listened to what he had to say. On the whole he was of great use to them, if at times a terrible nuisance. They paid him generously for his services and with monotonous (if no doubt welcome) regularity dispatched annual or bi-annual sums of £100 to £120,* always under the heading "travelling expenses" or "gifts to the Palace". It took him years of effort to get on to their permanent payroll and achieve a Life Annuity and he was not above twisting the Royal arm in the process) — but if being in the pay of someone is the criterion fo being sent on a mission than the negative reply given in Parliament was correct. Vambery was always a free-lance — even as a secret agent.

At the distance of nearly a century it is impossible to say what went on behind closed doors in Whitehall, but in the light of Vambery's known character it is a safe bet that he took the initiative.

". . . I feel bound to say a word about the rumours then prevalent", he writes brazenly trailing an elaborate red herring in his autobiography, "which made me out a secret political agent of England, the more so since a member of Parliament, Mr. Summers, has questioned the Conservative Government regarding this matter. I have never at any time stood in any official relation to the English Government. My intercoure with the Conservative and Liberal statesmen on the Thames and on the Hugli (Calcutta) has always been of a strictly private nature, and, just as my utterances in the daily papers were taken notice of by the public, so my occasional memoranda to the Ministry of Foreign Affairs have been accepted as the private information of an expert friendly to the cause of England — information for which nobody asked and for which labour I could claim no compensation from anybody".

And more follows along the same lines.

One does well to take note of this.

"My anomalous position", was touched on by Charles Marvin (in his *Merv, Queen of the World*) who blames the English Government for having neglected me and leaving me in poverty, in spite of all my services".

"I must say", he adds, "that I had at one time a modest yearly income while working with all my might for the defence of India . . . but I never suffered actual poverty and it never entered my mind to take steps to obtain material acknowledgment of my services. English statesmen least of all thought of making such an

---

* Multiply by 20 to achieve the present value — £2000–£2400 each time, a quite nice little sum.

acknowledgement".*

Adapting himself completely to the manners and customs of the Orient, keeping his ears wide open and listening at every key-hole, his method of gathering information was by no means confined to his audiences with the Sultan.

In those days "the office of the first Secretary" — Sureya Pasha, a good friend of Vambery — "was the real centre of administration of the whole Empire. I used to spend hours in this office, an idle spectator, where I met all the great men of the country". Business was carried on through chamberlains hurrying from one palace or the other to the Secretariat, bearing small letters cautiously folded and sealed, which had to be destroyed after reading. Once or twice Vambery succeeded in evading the attention of the secretary and getting short specimens of the Imperial handwriting.

Sureya Pasha's office was also a meeting-place between "members of the diplomatic circle and the Sultan. The first dragomans† of the different embassies had free access: they went straight to Sureya, sat down next to him, and, as the room was mostly full of visitors, they bent their heads to his ear and arranged their affairs whispering . . ."

The time when the French Military Attache mistook Vambery for a genuine old Turkish gentleman and spoke quite freely about his experiences during his trip in Asia Minor, where he had been sent by his Government, will have been put to good use by Vambery and later reported to Whitehall. 'Please to report to His Majesty', the French officer had said, 'that the English have got an eye on Alexandretta‡ and that their intrigues are extending far into the interior'. But the conversation was cut short, for Sureya kept looking at Vambery and finally told the Frenchman: "Monsieur le Capitaine, you evidently do not know my friend who sits there. It is Professor Vambery, the guest of the Sultan". And the spell was broken.

Vambery claims that he had a similar adventure with "Baron T

---

* And he had the effrontery to complain that the India Office declined to subscribe for twenty copies of his *Scheibaniade*, the Uzbeg heroic epic, the translation of which he had published at his own cost and which he considered one of his best works. It is now in the archives of the India Office.

† Interpreters.

‡ Today Iskenderun. A note from Salisbury to Russia in 1898 had suggested that all Asia should be divided by a line from Alexandretta to Peking into a northern (Russian) and a southern (British) sphere, but the Russians were not interested.

..." of the German Embassy, "but the shrewd Levantine was more cautious and dropped his loud conversation at once". Though he fails to explain how "Baron T . . ." turned into a Levantine.

Vambery served too as Interpreter for the Sultan and thereby astounded, so he claims, Prince M . . ., the Greek envoy, "who appeared much astonished at the confidence the Sultan had shown me". It must have astounded the Sultan no less, for "Prince M . . .", was Prince Maurocordato, the Persian and not the Greek envoy, as Vambery writes. In any case, this office was no *sinecure*, for the Sultan knew a little French and worried that the translation had not be made properly.

The Sultan pretended for a certain length of time that Vambery was his confidant . . . but Vambery was shrewd enough to see through this, even though Abdul Hamid addressed him familiarly as "Reshid Effendi". He countered by diplomatic phrases of such Oriental splendour and circumlocution that they cannot have failed to flatter the Sultan.

And no sooner had he heard the secrets than he reported them back word for word, to the Foreign Office. Although not above selling anyone's political secrets if it could be to his own advantage, it must be said in all fairness that he was by no means betraying a friend's confidences — he certainly never trusted the Sultan's professed friendship and was later, when political expediency seemed to demand it, to refer to him as "that horrible man". In any case, with so devious a character as Abdul Hamid (for whom Vambery was a perfect match) it seems more than likely that the Sultan had "leaked" his secrets into Vambery's ear, in the hope that Vambery would "leak" them to the right people in his turn.

And so it came about that an exultant Vambery presented himself in Whitehall.

But the promised invitation from the Sultan Vambery had so confidently boasted about to Lord Salisbury did not seem to be forthcoming and a furious Vambery wrote to Sir Philip Currie, the Under-Secretary for Foreign Affairs on 20 May 1889, on headed paper ('Budapest University') — the first in a long line of similar communications.

"Eight days having elapsed since my return from London without notice from the Sultan I fear his usual cautiousness has degenerated into cowardice . . . but . . . I have certain proofs of his being afraid for the services I render him . . . "

The services Vambery believed himself to be rendering to the Sultan was, in modern terminology, to project a more acceptable image of him to Britain and to the rest of Europe. But any *rapprochement* to Europe was precisely feared by the more Conservative of the Sultan's entourage and the official court organ *Tarik* in one breath extolled Vambery "as a friend and benefactor of Turkey" while flatly stating that he would not succeed in dragging the Sultan into the *Triple Alliance** nor had he any mission to befriend him with the English. And the leading papers in Constantinople took up the tune.

Vambery also feared that Russian intrigues might be behind the Sultan's delaying tactics, but decided to wait until *Ramazan* is over. "Happily I am not the man to be easily disconcerted . . . (but) if he still delays an interview (after *Ramazan*) then I might use coercive measures", he threatened, "for he has given me such secrets in hand by which I can easily compel him to continue the negotiations started on his own initiative a few months ago".

Finally the official invitation arrived and Vambery promptly informed Nicolson in Budapest, who in his turn informed Whitehall.

Currie immediately wrote off to Vambery:*

"My dear Professor, I was very glad to hear from Nicolson's telegram that you are going to Constantinople. I hope you will let me know what passes there and the Sultan's present views as to his Country and other Powers. Here there are very well informed people who think (and perhaps not without reason) that when the Russian fleet is quite ready, Nelidoff† may appear one morning at Yildiz Kiosk with a draft treaty in his pocket which he may call upon the Sultan to sign then and there. With the Russian fleet steaming up in the distance, an undefended Bosporus and the Dardanelles so well armed that no friendly succour can find its way through, what can he do but obey.

"The question is will he be warned in time and will he make the approaches to his capital from the Black Sea secure?

"Hoping that your advice may have some good effect, I am, etc".

On the same day Currie wrote to Sir William White, the British ambassador in Constantinople informing him of Vambery's

* 31 May 1889.
† The Russian ambassador in Constantinople.

visit to the Sultan. "He promised to send some notes of what he hears", he added. "He was very well received here the other day and had some talk with Lord Salisbury . . . He may I think be useful to us".

Vambery had hoped to be put up at the Palace and to keep this visit a secret. It proved a total impossibility. He was received with all pomp and circumstance and accorded a near regal reception. Instead of the Palace he was installed at the sumptuous *Hotel d'Angleterre* (at the Sultan's expense) and his arrival set the Turkish capital buzzing with rumours.

On June 12 Vambery sent off his detailed report on his conversations with the Sultan "together with a few general observations on individuality of the present ruler". There were 15 foolscap pages in all, divided into three separate sections. "I do not need calling your attention to the three different papers", he wrote to Currie, "knowing as I do your lively interest in Eastern affairs and your kind and friendly sympathies towards me. You can easily understand that my task at Yildiz Palace was an arduous one, for it is no trifle to transact business with an Oriental autocrat like Sultan Abdul Hamid".

Requesting more than once that his lengthy memorandum should be shown to Lord Salisbury, he gave a blow-by-blow account of his visit — often his report in lude verbatim report in direct speech.

He had seen the Sultan "after only four days delay" and despite the fact that Russia had "at once set her machinery against me". Abdul Hamid had been grateful to Vambery for "explaining the Turkish situation in England". There followed a verbatim passage: I: "Knowing Your Majesty's exalted mind and political sagacity I have always ridiculed the idea of Your Majesty's anti-English feelings".

And he proceeded to put over adroitly what Currie had told him to say. The reason was, he explained to the Sultan, that while he had left the forts on the entrance of the Bosporus from the Black Sea in a neglected state of defence, he had strongly fortified the Dardanelles, by putting Krupp guns in that place — "a military precaution which the English believe to be against them".

Sultan (protesting against this false belief): "Before all, I must however say (and here he grew rather excited) that as the undisputed master of my house, I have got the full right to order and adapt the keys and locks to the two doors of my house wherever I like and whenever I see the necessity".

And more followed in a similar vein. He had accidentally, said the Sultan, begun on the fortifications of the Dardanelles, but could not see why the English took umbrage . . . Italy, Austria and Greece would be fully entitled to raise a similar complaint against him. "What will Russia say if I fortify the entrance from the Black Sea, Russia, the only naval power in the north?" and he added: "Knowing as I do that the English listen to your words, tell them please that there is no idea of animosity . . ."

Abdul Hamid, added Vambery, was most anxious to reestablish the former relations of amity and good will with England but could not do it "as long as that deplorable accident of Egypt is not removed". It lowered the Sultan's dignity in the eyes of his own people and in those of the entire Mohammedan world.

Vambery did his best to be conciliatory and diplomatic and adroitly touched upon British Imperial interests — the road through the Suez Canal and often mentioned the possibility of a French occupation of Egypt if England had not done so. "An utter fallacy", retorted the Sultan, ". . . if the English would not have been overhasty I would have restored law and order on the Nile in the shortiest time".

Yet this was all bluff. The Sultan spent a sleepless night and dispatched his secretary at 1 a.m. to wake Vambery with the request to explain to him post haste what he had meant by allusions to a French *coup de main* . . .

Four days later Vambery had his second audience with the Sultan.

The subjects that came up for discussion were the same — Egypt and the Bosporus — with the addition of Armenia. Suddenly — and surprisingly — the Sultan said that "looking somewhat deeper into the nature of my questions put to him and considering my connections with the leading English statesmen, he is much inclined to suspect in me a secret agent of Great Britain . . ." If this were the case he asked Vambery to tell him the truth and "he would use quite a different and eventually a more serious language, he would say many things not touched on hitherto in what he believed to be our private conversation, whilst he would retract certain remarks which he would not have made otherwise."

Not to be caught off his guard, Vambery replied that he had absolutely nothing to do with the English Government, that he had not been sent by anybody, had not been entrusted with any secret or overt mission. "I have no right to claim even the slightest shadow of an official character", he said, "but I came on my own choice and good will and on my own suggestion only and solely for the purpose of making peace between the English and the Turks. For my 25 years of writing and political speeches in both countries it is evident and patent to everybody that my sympathies belonged to the said two nations".

But the Sultan was still suspicious. He said: "You are the only man in the world capable to act as a mediator, you have been brought up amongst us, you have served my father — you are a friend of Turkey and at the same time liked and esteemed in Europe . . . in fact you are a godsent (sic) — I will confide in you without reservation".

"The great question is who is to take the initiative", Vambery continued, "and will he send an extraordinary mission to reassume (sic) the discussion of the Egyptian question . . . for that is the stumbling block at present, and in this regard both parties will have to yield".

"My ardent desire is that my labours should not be thrown away, I found the present circumstances most favourable, and if necessary I would readily go to Constantinople to assist an eventual reassumption (sic) of the Egyptian Question".

He also promised the Sultan to go to Paris the following month to plead his case concerning Armenia at the *Congres de la Paix*. (There is no record that he did so).

Abdul Hamid touched other delicate points, such as the insurrection in Crete, encouraged by Greece* and remarked diplomatically that they belonged rather to the sphere of official *pourparlers* . . .

The interview was relatively short and Vambery reiterated that the Sultan was most anxious to reestablish friendly relations with England. The Sultan also added that he might try to get permission to have a garrison of 2000 men on the Nile, *pour sauver l'apparence*.

The Foreign Office underlined this passage in red.

Vambery considered his visit successful. The Sultan had shown himself anxious to approach England "and if you are seriously desirous to take the matter in hand", wrote to Currie, "I daresay we

---

* Lord Rosebery had taken a leading part in repressive measures against Greece in 1886 — a point Currie wished Vambery to mention at a later date.

can hope for a happy conclusion".

His policy had been "not to arouse his (the Sultan's) suspicion by any act of excessive zeal for English interests, but to instil in his mind, drop by drop, the spirit of my English policy ..."

Yet the suspicions of the Sultan's Ministers had been aroused, and they showed signs of ditrusting him as the "only European who has thoroughly penetrated the mysteries of their governmental, social and religious life": some were, he claimed, afraid of him, some jealous maintaining that he had conquered the Sultan by his command over their language and literature "and they think me a foreigner who may become a dangerous person". He suspected Russian influence.

Finally he sent his long report off and desperate for recognition he asked to be informed through Nicolson of the impression of his memorandum and whether his oral explanation was unavoidably necessary or not. "Sir William White", he added, "has met me with great frankness and kindness, he is fully alive to the usefulness of a private intermediator (sic), being convinced of the advantage of a practical orientalist opposite a thoroughly Eastern ruler.

"Requesting again the favour to remit my Memo to Lord Salisbury, I am, etc".

Vambery need not have worried. The Foreign Office were extremely pleased with his first report. "An interesting report" Currie noted on the back of it. "I think I might send him £80 for Constantinople". "Yes", added Lord Salisbury in red ink "Very interesting".

And Currie's official reply to Vambery* must have pleased him as well. "They (the reports)", said the letter, "give a striking picture of the mind of your friend and have been read with the greatest interest. I do not think we need trouble you to return here at present but I will write to you at once if there should be any occasion for your doing so". (25 June 1889).

And he enclosed the first of the welcome financial contributions.

A month later Vambery went to Constantinople again, as guest of the Sultan, and as he informed Currie, together with the chairman of the Committee of the Hungarian Academy and five other scholars, on a mission to investigate the libraries of the palace and

* 25 June 1889.

of various mosques.

He added that he would try to return to Constantinople again in September. "I shall be again the guest of the Sultan", he wrote, "and he stretches out a feeler whether I would not be inclined to go in October to London to try privately an arrangement about the Egyptian difficulty. My answer, that I must known beforehand all his ultimate desires and proposals and then I shall ask my English friends about the chances of a private discussion and if he encourages me then I might go to London as his private agent".

The *agent double* had been born.

The letter gave some details about new appointments in Egypt, spoke of a secret mission to Sheikh Senoussi, the spiritual chief of the dervishes of Kairouan, who had vanquished the Mahdi, and offered advice to the Foreign Office.

"I beg leave to render prominent and desirability of coming to an understanding with that man", he wrote, still in an atrocious style, "for he is still mischievous . . . not to mention his multifarious plots and tricks, I beg to allude to your difficulty with the Dervishes . . . I am afraid you underrate his importance", he continued, "and I am quite sure that an amicable arrangement with him . . . would greatly further English policy in the East and in the Moslem world in general . . .*

The letter dealt with the fortifications of the Bosporus, the Armenian Question and the entry of Turkey into the *Triple Alliance*.

In a postscript Vambery added: "It may interest you to know that the Sultan has asked me to come twice a year to Constantinople as his guest and that I am now in direct correspondence with him, without intermediary of the Court officials."

Vambery's tactics had produced results.

In the spring of the following year however Vambery conceived of a quite different plan.

"He (Vambery) wants to go later and lecture in India on the advantage of English rule and the wickedness of Russia", said a confidential memo of Currie. "He has asked Lord Cross to contribute to his expenses. Lord Cross said he would consult the Council but Vambery objects to it.

---

* As spiritual head of the Sunni Moslems the Sultan also held sway over the Moslem population in India.

If it is thought advisable that he would go, it would be better that his expenses should be paid from some other fund as it would be sure to leak out if the Council had dealt with it and he would be locked upon simply as the paid agent of the Government.

"It is clear from his letter that the Sultan believed Vambery to be an English agent despite all Vambery's protestations".

And he added an enigmatic sentence: "As H.M. evidently believes Vambery to be an English Agent, he no doubt does his best to make him think so".

Salisbury* added in red ink: "Cross has got a Secret Service fund if he chooses to use it' — the first official admission on the British side of Vambery's involvement.

The background to Vambery's projected trip lay in the fact that Vambery, remembering his own experiences in the East, had come to identify himself with the "down-trodden, helpless population of the East", so that "when an occasional cry was raised in some Turkish, Persian or Arabic publication for freedom, law and order . . . I felt compelled to render what assistance I could". This was the beginning of his pro-Islamic literary activity, and he touched on the subject in various lectures in England, such as during his lecture at Exeter Hall which had ended on a rousingly patriotic note:

Our Queen who ruled more than 50 million of Mahomedans, he had said, could not become the out-spoken enemy of one-sixth of her subjects, nor could Englishmen who were known for their love of liberty and equality, allow the persecution of their fellow-men because they differed from them in creed and culture. But as long as Englishmen adhered to the noble principles of justice and humanity they would be esteemed and liked all over the world, and, maintaining the glorious inheritance of its ancestors, England would remain great, powerful and happy.

There had been particularly loud cheers and Sir Donald Stewart, the former Commander-in-Chief in India, had come up to him, shaken his hands and remarked that hs writings had often stimulated the sinking courage of the officers in India and had stirred them up to endure to the end.

Vambery mentions this in his autobiography, adding that he frequently received letters of appreciation from different parts of India "thanking me for my watchfulness over occurrences in

* Secretary for India (1886-92).

Vambery, the secret agent

Central Asia, and the constant attacks I made on English statesmen who were so easily rocked to sleep in false security".

The fame of his lectures, so Vambery claims, resounded not only in Turkey but also among the Moslems of South Russia, Java and India and in Calcutta the "Mohammedan Literary Society", had been formed under the presidency of the Nawab Abdul Latif Bahadur; shortly after Vambery's lecture in Exeter Hall he received a letter from the Nawab, expressing his thanks for Vambery's interest in the affairs of Islam.

Vambery did not miss this opportunity to address a letter to the Mohammedans in India, "explaining the grounds for my Moslem sympathies", and above all, "encouraging the Hindustani to persevere in the adopted course of modern culture, and by all means tt hold fast to the English Government, the only free and humane power of the West".

This letter, dated 12 August 1889, is reproduced in full in his autobiography, as it was also by the *Times of India*, sandwiched between a report on India's export trade in flour and a financial statement by the Hongkong & Shanghai Banking Corporation.

As an after-thought he had also added that he had not quite given up the idea of visiting India, "and, circumstances permitting, of delivering some lectures in the Persian tongue to the Mohammedans of India. If I should see my way of doing so, I should like to come under the patronage of your Society, and thus try to contribute a few small stones to the noble building raised by your admirable efforts".

In other words: will you pay my travelling expenses?

For the reply from the Foreign Office had been polite but negative. If Vambery had been able to see what was going on behind the scenes he would have not have been very pleased to read a note marked PRIVATE sent by Arthur Godley* to Currie.

"Dear Currie", it ran, "Lord Cross has asked me to consult with you as to the answer to be returned to Professor Vambery who has asked for a grant from Secret Service Money, a free Railway pass, introductions etc. on the understanding that he is to visit India and preach loyalty to England and hatred of Russia —

---

* Arthur Godley who had been private secretary of Gladstone became permanent Under-Secretary for India from 1883-1909; he was later created 1st Baton Kilbracken.

especially among the Mohammedans. Lord Cross consulted me about this proposal on Friday last. I told him that he had better have nothing to do with it . . .

Do you approve?"

Vambery was in the end invited to visit India as the guest of the Mohammedan Society. (He mentions it twice in his Memoirs). Still carrying around with him, in his mental baggage, the insults and humiliations suffered in his youth "there was something very tempting to me in the thought of going to India, the land of the Rajahs, of wealth and opulence, as an admired an honoured guest. But . . . I was nearly sixty years old . . . The alluring vision of a reception in India, with eulogies and laurel-wreaths swiftly passed before my eyes, but was instantly dismissed . . ."

Which, as it turned out, was just as well and Vambery was spared a great fiasco.

An article he had written together with his letter had been published, at the Nawab's insistence, as a separate pamphlet and not only in the weekly *Reis and Rayyet** with the editor of which — Dr. Mookerjee — Vambery kept up a regular correspondence. The editor had informed him that he had taken the opportunity to make some slight corrections "which I hope improved the thing", if Vambery ever saw the letter the editor wrote to Edward Jenkins, English journalist and Conservative M.P., he never admitted it.

Alluding to the fact that errors were almost inevitable in foreign publications (when writing about India) Dr. Mookerjee said in a letter to Edward Jenkins, journalist and M.P.: "Even Professor Vambery, writing to the Nawab, has not been able to avoid it — he who is not only a great Orientalist but has travelled almost to the frontiers of India . . . He talks of coming out to India where he hopes to address the Mahomedans in Persian as if it were their own tongue. So far from Persian being one of the Indian vernaculars, none but the learned Mussulmans of the old clan know it, and few of those who have read Persian can speak it or understand it when spoken. The Professor might just as well address a Mahomedan audience in Hungarian!"*

Vambery had appeared in person when he put out his unsuccess-

*   *Prince and Peasant.*

*   F.H. Skrine: *An Indian Journalist.* Being the Life, Letters and Correspondence of Dr. Sambhu C. Mookerjee, 1889.

ful feelers concerning India, and also wished to discuss Turkey. He was seen by an underling at the Foreign Office who noted: "Professor Vambery called. He said he had come here at the request of the Sultan to ascertain the state of English feelings in regard to Armenia and Crete and to endeavour to influence it in a sense favourable to Turkey".

He was obliged to cool his heels at the Athenaeum Club and curb his impatience for Currie only saw him two days later.

There must have been important talks going on behind the scenes for Currie sent a memorandum to Salisbury: "If the British fleet remains within hailing distance (of Turkey)", he suggested, "the Sultan would be able to summon it for his protection, if Russia attempted to interfere".

But Salisbury thought otherwise: "We must be a little further forward with our naval arrangements, before this", he replied, "but otherwise I agree..."

Finally Vambery had his interview but was obliged to eat humble pie. "After returning from your office", he wrote to Currie, "and reflecting upon the very suggestive (sic) remarks contained in your conversation, I found that after all you might be right, and that the Sultan has decidedly duped me, when he assured me of his unalterable sympathies towards England...", and he went over to business: "As to the rather delicate question of my expenses incurred in travelling and the unavoidable *bakshish* at the Palace, I shall ask sixty pounds. But you will understand, that having shown myself disinterested hitherto I am rather reluctant to bother you in that regard. If Lord Salisbury is willing to give me a round sum" — and one is reminded of his first letter to John Murray — "which would bring me fifty or sixty pounds a year, I would be fully satisfied and I would never intrude for my whole life. It is a hard case to ask for remuneration for sympathies; I have withstood hitherto valiantly in spite of the general belief of the whole world..."

"I would give Vambery his money" wrote Lord Salisbury in red ink.

The instructions Currie had given Vambery concerning the fortifications of the Bosporus had made use of the same metaphor the Sultan had used: his house with two doors... If he could not persuade the Sultan to fortify the northern entrance of the Bosporus, Vambery boasted, he would give up his connections with him. And he complained that his poverty was the stumbling block.

He left for Constantinople.

On June 1 the Foreign Office received an exultant letter from him: "I have succeeded in my efforts to a certain extent", he wrote triumphantly, "I succeeded in getting an audience from the Sultan on the very day of my arrival". (For the Sultan had sent him a telegram to Budapest, urging him to come at once). ". . . Considering the fact of receiving me at once, whilst he keeps ambassadors waiting for days and weeks, my expectations in his readiness to come to terms was quite justified . . . I have got the fellow round": he exulted. "I succeeded to get a promise written by his own hand which I shall present in translation and in originals.* Forgive my want of modesty when I say that ten ambassadors could not accomplish that in years what I have done in days".*

He felt that the Russians were particularly hard on his heels. "I begin to be surrounded on all sides by spies. As long however as I keep clean from material interests", he added hypocritically, "and I do not arouse his suspicions . . . I am quite safe and nobody can shake my position".

And there followed his accounts: he was out of pocket, having spent £74 in presents to the Palace, he claimed, of which £36 had gone into the pocket of Sureya Pasha (to whom he had also given a handsome toilet case).

Currie noted: "I think he might have another £100 forwarded to Nicolson" (for although the amounts paid remained more or less the same, the manner of payment differed — always accompanied by a polite phrase, such as "Will you allow me to make a contribution to your journey . . ." But it failed to satisfy Vambery.

There was also an exchange of telegrams and letters between Currie and Nicolson marked PRIVATE & SECRET. Currie had requested Nicolson to communicate with "our friend" and arrange to "bring home the report you are preparing." In reply Nicolson wrote, "My dear Currie, The worthy pundit has asked to send you the enclosed. He has left for the Tyrol and his address there is Muhlbach, etc."

And even before Vambery arrived there to recuperate, "quite exhausted from my trip to Constantinople and particularly by having had to endure the freaks and whims of an Oriental autocrat during 14 days and nights. . . .", the Foreign Office had a letter

---

* The envoy in Persia.
* It concerned Tobacco monopolies in Turkey.

from him, complaining that at near sixty his physical powers were beginning to decline and were "not adequate to my energy and to my zeal to show myself worthy of the confidence you have shown me.

When the 25-page report arrived, the Foreign Office summarised its contents neatly: "Audience of Sultan. Urges advantage should be taken of present friendly disposition. H.M. now yielding resp. Egypt. His dislike of Sir Drummond-Wolff.† Answer required for Sultan. Question of remuneration."

That, certainly, was uppermost in Vambery's mind. For Vambery had felt compelled to add: "As to the recompensation, I leave it entirely to Lord Salisbury . . . I cannot believe that England is a country which avails herself of the services of a private man without duly remunerating him".

And to be quite sure that his report reached the right ears he had the effrontery to write to Currie: ". . . Following your patriotic zeal and high-minded character I do not deem it necessary to recommending my paper to Lord Salisbury's particular attention . . ."

Currie's reaction had been to address a confidential memo to Salisbury and to write with subtle irony: "Vambery considers that he has rendered a great service, and, dropping his modesty suggests that he should be made in some way or other independent. If this means a fixed salary", he continued, "I think it would be very unwise to give it to him, as experience shows that when no further effort is required to earn the pay none is made. I would propose to thank him for his interesting report and to send him £150 in addition to the £200 which he has already had for his travelling expenses and presents. I should ignore his hints for fixed pay".

And Salisbury initialled it approvingly in red ink.

Vambery had defined his relationship with the Sultan as "exceptional and highly interesting . . . his feigned friendship is dictated more by fear of my pen than by love or sympathy . . ." and had given an exhaustive report (25 pages long) of his personal relations with the Sultan, his policy and the general situation of the country, touching on India and Persia as well.

"Interesting", the Foreign Office had commented, "but does not lead to any practical result".

Vambery, in his alpine summer hide-out grew increasingly impatient with Foreign Office dilatoriness. Four weeks had elapsed since he had left Constantinople and "my friend has become rather anxious about the answer . . . but pardon my want of modesty", he added, in reply to a remark made by Currie, "if I venture to doubt my having been the dupe of that artist — as you properly call him. He is earnestly anxious to come to terms — as to the stumbling block on the bank of the Nile, I believe the removal is by far not so difficult as you imagine".

And, playing the secret service game to the hilt, he added: ". . . he knows you will never say good-by!" — a euphemistm for Britain never intending to leave Egypt, so transparent that even a child could have seen through it.

The £100 were duly acknowledged as well "being expenses incurred for the parcel I forwarded from Budapest . . ."

In the autumn of 1890 Vambery went again to Constantinople and spent several weeks as the guest of the Sultan. The result was another 19-page long report Currie suggesting sending Vambery another £100. "Speak to me" wrote Salisbury and one wished one knew what went on behind closed doors.

Before sending off his courteous and elegantly worded reply to Vambery, and the £100 "in case you should be put to any expense on our account", Currie had submitted the draft to Salisbury. "I have put the suggestion in the form of an inclosed Extract", he wrote, "as I do not altogether trust the Professor's discretion".

"Yes", Salisbury had replied, "that will do exceedingly well".

And the letter that went off to Budapest contained some polite phrases. "The proof of confidence you have received in the request to write weekly letters is a flattering one," said the letter, "and I hope you will take advantage of it to impress your correspondent of the friendly interest that is taken in him here. The enclosed extract from a well-informed person which has just been brought to my notice may be useful in suggesting some material for your next letter".

What Vambery did not see was the memo to Salisbury:

"Vambery has only had one tip this year", it read. "£100 last June. He has written several letters since, not of much value, but perhaps he might have another £100 as a refresher".

In December of that year Vambery sent off a 14-page letter from Budapest. He outlined a scheme for investing English capital in Turkey,* but this fell foul of British policy. "Shall I tell him that he had better say nothing to the Sultan about granting concessions to English capitalists?" asked Currie. "It will do us no good and make the Sultan suspect him of interested motives".

Salisbury initialled it which meant a tacit "yes".

Seven months elapsed until the Foreign Office heard again from Vambery. He then wrote on Athenaeum notepaper informing Currie that he was in town and had "translated literally that portion of Lord Salisbury's speech which refers to the Sultan and I have sent it to Yildiz. The Sultan will be delighted in reading it — he will be convinced that England is his only real friend in the world".

And there followed an eulogy of Salisbury's remarks on Islam. But he ended his letter on an offhanded note: "I do not bother you anymore with the question of the Government assisting me", he wrote, "since I see you cannot do anything effective for me. But I beg leave to say that the services I have rendered and am rendering continually really deserve some acknowledgment".

Unemotionally the summary read: "Professor Vambery about to leave. Asks for interview. Has translated and sent to Sultan reference to H.M. in Lord Salisbury's speech. Considers that his services deserve recognition".

And another £100 were given.

This stimulated Vambery to fresh activity. From Muhlbach he wrote barely six weeks later: "Dear Sir Philip, My recent informations from various parts of Persia, notably from Tebriz, Isfahan and Shiraz, exhibit a state of things in which I discover a serious danger to British interests in the East, and which I cannot pass in silence, believing that your official organs in the said country are either unaware of the importance of the case or that their judgment is totally different from my own ..." He approved of Salisbury's policy but thought that England should have no part in the tobacco monopoly — "this highly unpopular business ... in a word I beg the Foreign Office to keep an eye on Persia, in order not to be taken by surprise by the events in preparation".

The Foreign Office commented coolly: "According to our latest information the opposition to the Tobacco Regie is likely to calm down again".

Between then and spring 1892 Vambery sent more than half a dozen letters on the subjects of Persia and his correspondence with the Sultan.

In February 1892 the Foreign Office proposed to pay him a further contribution towards his expenses if he went to Constantinople and Currie asked Salisbury confidentially: "Shall I encourage him to go to Constantinople to pick up what he can?"

Meanwhile Vambery had been invited to the Tercentenary festivities at the University of Dublin and in April Vambery was in a bit of a quandary. But the Foreign Office was magnanimous and Currie noted on the back of his letter: "No need to return the £100".

When he returned to London he immediately wrote to Currie from the Athenaeum: "I have just returned from Dublin where my address created quite a sensation . . ." and was brazen enough to add: "I would beg you to send me some small contribution towards my journey which I have asked you. Of course I would prefer receiving it from your own hands if possible . . ."

In early 1892 there had been changes in the Government. Gladstone had taken over from Salisbury. Lord Rosebery had become the new Foreign Secretary.

Vambery immediately seized on this to try and ingratiate himself. "Ashamed of the many kindnesses I received from you without being able to render any practical services under the actual circumstances", he wrote to Currie," I thought an Essay on the Sultan and his Policy might be of some use to Lord Rosebery if he finds time to peruse it. Will you kindly submit it to his Lordship whose personal acquaintance I made six years ago. Having been invited by the late Lady Rosebery to their house at Berkeley Square. Lord Rosebery being himself a literary man of distinction will certainly appreciate a sketch made after nature under circumstances and opportunities not often available to foreign visitors of the Turkish Court".

He also asked for hints as to the language he should use.

Six months later Vambery informed the Foreign Office that he

---

* Vambery's address in Dublin was mainly on the familiar theme of Western cultural superiority and he stressed the spread of the English language in Asia and Turkey. At the banquet which included the cream of British intelligentsia and aristocracy, Vambery sat at the same table as H.H. Thakore Sahib, Prince of Gondal.

had received from a friend — "one of the leading men at the Asiatic Department of St. Petersburg, and who is personally acquainted with Count Kapnist, the Russian officer treating with Ching-Chang on the Pamir Question, the adjoint piece of information which I hasten to send you in the original ...", and he added that that he had succeeded "to open a communication with some non-Russian officers in Turkestan who send me regular information about such matters which do not ooze out in public ... These sources might be utilised to a certain extent for the English Intelligence Department which I find very defective ... although the enemies of England state the contrary".

And he proposed to discuss all this on his next visit to England.

The Foreign Office replied politely and non-committally evading the issue: "My dear Sir, Lord Kimberley desires me to return you his best thanks for your memorandum which he has taken with him into the country to read.

"He begs that you will in time let me know when you propose to start again for Constantinople, as he would like, if agreeable to you, to make a contribution towards your expenses".

And there followed the information that he might be able to get hold of the Turkish translation of the agreement between the Sultan and the French and Russian ambassadors but was not sure the document offered was not a hoax, but nevertheless had promised his informant a big sum of money if he could prove the originality of the document ...

The Pamir question (the delineation of the frontier between Russia and British territory and Afghanistan) was then becoming topical. Hardly anything had appeared in print, wrote Vambery, except his contribution in German "probably unknown to the Foreign Office" and he warned that Russia was planning mischief.

Vambery received a polite reply. Lord Rosebery, he learnt, had been much interested by his account of the Sultan and his entourage and had asked Currie to convey his thanks for his valuable paper. "Your notes will be useful to us and I enclose a small contribution which may be of use if you are travelling this autumn".

But the postscript pulled him up short. "We do not apprehend any serious results from the Russian expedition to the Pamirs", it said "... the proximity of a Russian force though objectionable is less dangerous than before. I hope you will not write to the Press in an alarmist sense. There is a fair prospect of an Agreement for an international Commission for surveying and ultimately fixing the boundary, and in any case the danger of an invasion of India from the Pamirs seems a very remote eventuality".

The letter arrived too late, for precisely on the same date* *The Times* had published another sabre-rattling letter by Vambery on the subject, warning of sinister Russian intent.

Two weeks later an excited Vambery, his beard and whiskers atwitch, sensing a Russian spy wrote off to the Foreign Office. "A few days ago", he said, "I had a rather curious visitor in the person of an Afghan called Gholam Shah, who is travelling as a Russian emissary ... his task is to convince the world of the superiority of the Russian rule. A fanatic to the excess he is vehement in his attacks and makes no secret of it that he is personally connected with the Sultan, with Emir Abdurrahman of Kabul, with the Sherif of Mecca and others ... the pale haggard look and the wild rolling eyes of the man made me rather nervous", he rambled on, "I apprehended a personal attack, but the interview ended quietly and left me full of astonishment of the extraordinary means Russia is using to further her aims in the Asiatic world".

In the same letter Vambery thanks Currie for the "receipt of your letter forwarded through H.M. Vienna Embassy in which you were so kind to inform me of the gracious reception accorded to my memorial (sic) by Lord Rosebery transmitted to me in the same time as his Lordship's kind regards which I value highly".

The Foreign Office took another long, cool look at his letter and noted on the back: "This is the scoundrel whose real name is Eliahie Bux and who married Mrs. Robinson" and wrote to Vambery:

"My dear Professor, I received your letter of the 21st. The man who calls himself Gholam Singh is neither Gholam Singh nor an Afghan, but a Hindoo oculist who has taken the name of his master. I enclose a short memo giving a short account of his matrimonial misdeeds. He seems to be one of the greatest blackguards alive. Please let me know when you have any news of your friend at Constantinople".

In an confidential inter-office memo, the Foreign Office remarked: "This is the curious case of an Englishwoman turned Mahomedan and married to an Indian swindler who seems to make a trade of marrying foolish Englishwomen".

* 9 November 1892.

In 1867, so the story goes, one Eliahie Bosche had come to Plymouth in the service of Gholam Shah, an Indian oculist who was on a round-the-world trip. They quarrelled and parted company. Eliahie set himself up as an independent oculist and in due course met a Miss Lillycrap; finding she was "well-connected and had property" he arranged to marry her; when she discovered, however, that he was a Moslem she broke off the engagement, but he pursued her and she, so terrified by his threats, "lost her reason and is now in a lunatic asylum at Exeter without hope of recovery".

Producing a fake diploma from Lahore, he set up a practice and changed his name to Bux; as Eliahie Bux, therefore, he met a Miss Lait who he married "according to the Christian rite", confessing to her after marriage that he already had a wife in Lahore. The more resilient Miss Lait suffered no nervous breakdown but merely left him.

He then moved to Newcastle and found a "domestic servant ready to marry him" whom he took to Quebec where he deserted her and "she is now earning her living as a typewriter".

Later he surfaced again in England and married a lady from Brighton at the mosque in Liverpool ". . . left for Constantinople . . . abandoned his wife and disappeared".

In Constantinople he met a resourceful Mrs Robinson, a divorcee and expatriate was receiving an allowance from the Sultan who was anxious to get the British Embassy to increase "the Sultan's bounty". It was clear that they should do nothing of the kind, added the Foreign Office memorandum.

How this liberated Mrs. Robinson had become entangled with Eliahie Bosche, alias Bux "not by any means of prepossessing appearance" is not clear; he spoke English fluently and had meanwhile left Constantinople "with some Pasha but is expected back shortly".

Rosebery had added a short comment in red ink to the brief Eliahie Bux memo. "Curious", he wrote, "inform him" (Vambery).

And in due course Vambery received a letter from the Foreign Office.

Unabashed, and apparently entirely unaware that he had made a fool of himself, he wrote: "The man called Gholam Shah, alias Bux, is still here in Budapest, intending, as he said to me, to put up as an oculist. The fellow, at all events, one of the most dangerous scoundrels, may be a Mohammedan Musulman of India, but he knows also the Afghan language and from his Persian I gather he has not any education in Moslem schools. I shall keep an eye on him, and as soon as he comes in collision with the police, he threatened, I shall cause his arrest" (although the police was then hardly likely to need him).

A political aside followed. "I gave full assurance that Lord Rosebery would not deviate from the policy of Lord Salisbury and that his* fear regarding the anti-Turkish spirit of Mr. Gladstone is groundless'.

This earned him a pat on the back. "Your language seems judicious" wrote Currie, "and there can be no objection to your continuing to speak in the same strain."

In his letter of 20 December 1892 Vambery made some strategic suggestions concerning Russia and British troop emplacements in the Hindu Kush. "England will be enabled to watch better the movements of her rival and all future complications arising from the right of possession will be cut short".

"Has been read with greatest interest" commented the Foreign Office. Most of Vambery's activities came to a sudden halt when in early 1893 he fell on the slippery pavement in Budapest and had the bad luck to break his lame leg in two parts; he was forced to stay in bed for ten days — "chained to my bed", as he wrote — and thought his leg would take another six weeks to heal.

Suffering great pain, as he wrote to Currie, he nevertheless submitted a lengthy report about Turkey: he had warned the Sultan not to meddle with England in Egypt.

Rosebery initialled the report adding to Currie: "Please talk to me about Vambery. I want to ask some questions".

The following month, in March, Vambery asked for more money to send presents on account of the Bairam festivities in Constantinople and the Foreign Office complied with his request and sent off £100 (keeping an exact record of the numbers on the banknotes sent).

There was a long gap until the autumn of that year. His silence, explained Vambery, had been due to failing health, but he wrote breathlessly that he had received a visit from a Senor Zimenes, a Spanish traveller in Central Asia, who knew everybody in Russia and had visited the Pamirs.

"How far this gentleman is animated by the spirit of scientific inquiries remains to be seen", he wrote suspiciously, "up to the present he has not given any sign of it. At all events please to inform the Indian Government to keep an eye of the man".

The idea of erecting a meteorological station on the Roof of the World is fit to arouse suspicion.

"He works hand in glove with Russian Generals and everybody in Turkestan I beseech you to consider carefully steps taken in this direction".

There must have been smiles all round, for the Foreign Office comment read: "Ximenes who has never been to the Pamirs has been unmasked as an impostor as you will see from St. Petersburg despatches" and was signed by Rosebery himself.

One can therefore imagine the surprise when Vambery received a letter from Currie a month later which read: "My dear Professor, Your friend the Spanish traveller is an impostor. He has never been further than Tashkent".

Meanwhile Vambery had sent off another letter to Whitehall in which he referred to recent correspondence with the Sultan and complained that Abdul Hamid did not want Constantinople because of his anti-Russian sentiments.

"The Armenian question is evidently uppermost in the Imperial mind" commented Currie, and Rosebery initialled it.

A little later Currie wrote privately to Lord Rosebery: "We have been in the habit of giving him £100–£150 a year. If you should think fit to continue this subvention which he has earned by his former advocacy of English views would you . . . send £100 in a sealed envelope in notes".

There was silence for a whole year. Meanwhile both Currie and Nicolson were transferred to the British Embassy in Constantinople and Vambery wrote a long letter commenting on this and accouncing his intention to visit Constantinople again the following April.

"He wants money" was Rosebery's only comment.

And in fact by March Vambery had received an invitation from the Sultan and would leave in April: his address this time would be the British Embassy.

By May a report on his conversations with the Sultan followed — 29 pages long. It dealt with the Armenian question and gave an exhaustive report of the Sultans entourage, giving names.

In June there followed another letter. "Means of reviving Eng-

419

lish influence at Constantinople", read the summary, and another £50 were despatched. But the Foreign Office continued to keep strict and detailed accounts. ("Appears had to give £65 in presents — Currie advanced £30 Turk. (£27) — balance £32 — £38 Sterling. Send him £50.")

Vambery proposed to stay two or three months in Constantinople this time and the Foreign Office was no doubt happy to know that he approved wholeheartedly of the appointment of Currie and Nicolson to Constantinople. A few words of advice followed, since Vambery felt again on top of the world. He enjoyed the confidence of the Sultan, he wrote, who knew his pronounced English tendencies and looked upon him as a mediator between England and Turkey "and I would be glad if I could be instrumental in removing the hindrances and establishing the ancient *Entente Cordiale*.

In the summer of 1894 Vambery was in England, and stayed for one week (8-15 August) at the home of his old friend, the scholar Professor F. Max Muller, at 7 Norham Gardens, Oxford. He had been invited to serve on the Committee in the Geography Section, at the Annual meeting of the British Association for the Advancement of Science, whose President was Lord Salisbury. Among the famous explorers Vambery met at Max Muller's house were Henry Godwin-Austen and Charles Doughty. At a large garden party on 14 August (in St. John's College), Vambery was entertained by Ashton's Blue Hungarian Band, playing the best-known marches and dance music of his homeland.

On his return to London, Vambery wrote to Sir Thomas Sanderson, the new Under-Secretary of State for Foreign Affairs (and his correspondent for the next eleven years): "I have just arrived here (the United Service Club) and am awaiting the orders of Lord Rosebery. I intend to leave on Wednesday and with your kind permission I shall call before leaving."

This was followed by another letter, a day later, in which he wrote in Sanderson: "Many many thanks for the trouble you have taken in my proposed interview with Lord Rosebery which however cannot take place owing to the very important discussion which took place in the House of Lords.

Announcing that he was leaving London he begged Lord Kimberley "through your kind intermittance to give me the promised assistance for my next journey to Constantinople" (mainly for presents, he added), "Sir Philip Currie has offered me funds but I do not like to take them from anybody but the Foreign Office".

"Shall I give him £100 and tell him that Sir Philip Currie and the Foreign Office are identical?" asked Sanderson, adding — and one can practically hear his sigh — "I suppose I must see him".

"I pity you", replied Lord Kimberley crisply in red ink, "I have seen him".

Lord Rosebery sent £100 — officially to provide funds for another trip to Constantinople but really as a present to Vambery.

And in due course a report of Vambery's visit to Constantinople followed (16 pages long).

Six weeks later Vambery wrote again anxiously to enquire whether the Foreign Office had received it safely and to request that it be submitted to "H.E. Lord Kimberley and tell him that I watch with eager interest the doings of the Government in Central Asia". (He had not approved of Lord Rosebery's policy in that regard).

The passage that the Foreign Office picked out, however, dealt with Armenia and Sanderson drew Kimberley's attention to page 7 dealing with this subject.

And Kimberley issued a directive: "Use account of Sultan's terror", he wrote, "which puts me in mind of Tiberius".

There was quite a long spell without news from Vambery, then — in the summer of 1895 — he sent a 10-page letter on Turkey from Murzzuschlag in Austria.

"The letter from Professor Vambery does not contain much of practical value", commented Sanderson, "I suppose I should thank him and he will no doubt expect £100 towards his expenses at Constantinople. I never feel quite sure that he is worth the money, but he is an additional source of information to Currie over there".

And Sanderson wrote to Lord Salisbury* a few days later: "(Vambery) said that he had been working for 30 years for England — Could he not have a regular allowance of £120 a year . . . The objection to an allowance in such cases is that it tends to become a pension. He would probably give up going to Constantinople . . . which must be irksome enough and we should get little or no assistance or information from him".

---

* In 1895 Lord Rosebery resigned and Lord Salisbury took over (Cons.).

In point of fact Vambery had called in person, on his way to a Geographical Congress, and without fail had asked for "a little assistance towards his expenses for Constantinople". He added that he was being denounced for saying that England was the only friend of Turkey, and could he not have a regular allowance of £120.

He had his way. By the end of the month Salisbury agreed to the annual payment of this sum, despite the fact that Sanderson had added a note: "Shall I say you cannot bind yourself or your successors to an allowance?"

"Yes, that will do," Salisbury had replied.

What had happened in the meantime was simply that the Prince of Wales had put in a good word for him, for on July 31, Vambery acknowledged Sanderson's letter from the Athenaeum Club and wrote: ". . . Having been invited by His Royal Highness the Prince of Wales, when the matter of my more than thirty years voluntary service was touched, the Prince said he will speak about me to Lord Salisbury and evidently he has done so in the meantime.

"Please send me the £120 in notes, if possible this afternoon as I shall stay in the Athenaeum Club until 4 p.m.

"I shall probably leave on Saturday or Monday for Constantinople and I shall give you a detailed account of my interview with the Sultan".

The same day a note from Sanderson to Salisbury said: "I have paid Professor Vambery his £120. I received enclosed from him this morning a reply to my note asking how he would like to have it. If he goes talking to the Prince of Wales about it, all London will know. Shall I give him a caution that any payments he receives must be kept absolutely private? I am afraid that as a foreigner he could not receive a pension from the Civil List for his writings and travels — otherwise that would be a better plan than these payments".

Vambery, his mind still not at rest, anxious for complete security, unattainable this side of the grave, had added in his letter, thanking Sanderson for his kind efforts, "although they did not lead to the desired results, I nevertheless feel satisfied for I have no doubt whoever will be at the head of the Foreign Office no one will have any cause to discontinue the payment of a modest honorarium I was asking from Lord Salisbury . . ."

The next month Vambery sent a letter dealing with the Armenian question, followed by an even longer one in November, dealing again with the same subject.

In it he said that he was regarded as a true friend of Turkey "and being less exposed to suspicion, my experience may be more accurate than that of any other foreign spectator ...". He accused the *Times* and other leading papers of gross mendacity, "and I daresay never has public opinion been mislaid (sic) in such a horrible manner as actually in England".

He therefore offered to lecture in England and in the provinces on Turkey.

Sanderson wrote a memo to Salisbury:

"It (the letter) is well-written", he said, "but takes of course a philo-Turkish view and thinks we have handled the Porte too roughly. He concludes by an offer to come over and deliver a series of lectures in the provinces which I presume you will scarcely wish to encourage".

"By no means", replied "S". (Salisbury).

There was silence from Vambery until he burst in on the Foreign Office with an excited letter in January 1896. He had discovered yet another dangerous spy.

"Hadji Mohammed Mirza Kashef, a Persian prince and a cousin of the present King of Persia, called on me today with the request to give him a letter of introduction to Lord Salisbury, being desirable to be serviceable to British interests in the East", he wrote in his atrocious style.

And he would have been most mortified to have seen the PRIVATE & SECRET memo in Sanderson's hand:

"Mahomet Mirza Kashef as a person of no particular importance", it read, "There is nothing against him but he can probably do little for us —" (Vambery had proposed to give him a letter of introduction to Sanderson) — "The Shah's relatives carry no weight as such", and a further note, possibly from Salisbury himself, read: "Requires greatest caution not to give Persian Government a notion we are opposed to them".

There was trouble with the Boers in the Transvaal and the British were defeated.* On 3 January 1896 the 'Kruger Telegram' — Kaiser Wilhelm's congratulatory despatch to the President of the South African Republic (Transvaal) — demonstrated the force of the increasing Anglophobia in Germany and caused a great outcry throughout Britain. There appeared in *The Times* of 18 January a strongly worded pro-British and anti-German letter, a full column in length, signed "A Foreigner". Naturally the Germans were furious, and their Press made wild guesses as to the "Foreigner's" identity. One newspaper declared it was Leopold II, King of the Belgians, who was in London at the time, and published a vitriolic article on him (*Norddeutsche Allegmeine Zeitung*, 21 January 1896). The King's authorship was officially denied, but the name of the real writer was not revealed until 1902, when the journalist Louis Katscher, in an article on Vambery, disclosed that it had been "the great Hungarian professor" all the time.

Vambery confirmed this in his autobiography but he never gave a satisfactory reason why this letter — out of all his one hundred letters to *the Times* — should be printed anonymously. In retrospect, the reason must lie with his dealings with the Ministers at the Foreign Office. They had warned him not to use too strong a language when lecturing or writing about Germany, so in this instance he was obliged not to sign his name to his opinions.

Vambery tried to show his pro-British sentiments in a practical way. The German Kaiser had sent a congratulatory telegram to Kruger, anti-English feeling was growing in Hungary and Austria. Vambery did his best to counteract this in an interview with the "Pester Lloyd", a German-language paper in Budapest which, in tones of utmost obsequiousness, sought his opinions on the question of Transvaal. He sent a cutting to the Foreign Office.

In May of that year he sent a long letter enclosing his report on his journey to Constantinople and his visit to the palace. "I trust Lord Salisbury will deign my rapport of some attention", he wrote, "as it is my sincere desire to be useful to England ... I think every honest man must be proud if an occasion is offered to him to support England's policy in the East".

The Foreign Office thought part of this report of interest and marked long passages in red.

Another £50 were sent.

Vambery predicted that "the fabric of the Ottoman Empire would break up" and advised the Foreign Office to keep an eye "on the anglophile portion of Turkish society — the Young Turks".

A few months later Vambery's dealt with another subject: the success of Russian endeavours to conciliate Hungarian opinion, as the concise Foreign Office summary put it, and Salisbury remared "Interesting".

By October the money had arrived and Vambery wrote to Sanderson: "Thanks for the grant, the much more wellcome under the circumstances when the earnings of my pen has greatly diminished owing to the political relations between England and Turkey on the one hand* and Austro-Hungary on the other".

He approved of the Foreign Office policy towards "that horrible man called Abdul Hamid" and suggested Salisbury make a public statement pressing for reforms but stating that England aimed at nothing but the welfare of his subjects . . . "I lay particular stress on this humble advice of mine for I see from the Moslem papers and from private letters I get that England's action is thoroughly misunderstood".

At the same time Vambery asked to be introduced to Sir Edmund Monson's successors; the outgoing British ambassador in Vienna had been a friend of his for 20 years.*

In February of the following year (1897) Vambery reported that the Sultan was furious against "English encouragement and support of the Young Turkish Party, as he believes".

He had also detailed the opinions of Kiazim Bey, who at one time had been the Sultan's private secretary and now was Turkish ambassador in Bucharest.

"A curious letter" commented Salisbury, adding "Please type", and for the first time typed copies and resumes of Vambery's letters made their appearance at the Foreign Office.

Kiazim Bey also called on Vambery a few days later so Vambery sent off another letter post-haste, in which he explained that Kiazim Bey had been sent by the Khedive of Egypt to carry out anti-English propaganda and enclosed another cutting of an interview with him published in the *Pester Lloyd*.

There was another article in the *Pester Lloyd* in September "Mole-work in Afghanistan" and Vambery took this opportunity to write to the Foreign Office anxiously again, enclosing a cutting, expatiating on the Sultan's position, dealing with Indian frontier troubles and, above all, with his allowance. "Dear Sir Thomas", he wrote, "I venture to hope that the activity I have dis-

---

* Britain had sided with Greece in the Cretan uprising and the Sultan had good cause to be angry.

* Vambery did not miss an opportunity to congratulate him on his later knighthood, *The Times*, 10 January, 1905.

played in the course of this year and particularly during the last months in the interest of the Government in Britain did not escape the notice of the Foreign Office. I beg to remind Lord Salisbury of his previous promise. I trust it will not be explained as if I would press upon a reward for my rendered services. Such services are not rendered with a material benefit", he continued, ". . . for it nothing would have been accorded I would still go on as heretofore in the persuance (sic) of my principle, but I have personnel expenses, outlays, and for this purpose I solicit the sum of last year trusting that the Government will dispense me of the inconvenience to beg every year".

Sanderson summarised it nicely: "This is an appeal from Professor Vambery to repeat the gratiuity of £120 which you have granted to him last year and the year before and to convert it into an annual pension. He has some claims on us for past services and is occasionally still useful. The Secret Service pension list has also recently been considerably reduced by deaths of pensioners. But it is rather a serious matter to create a new one".

Salisbury initialled it and a month later Vambery received his reply.

"My dear Sir", it ran. "I have shown your letter to Lord Salisbury. He wishes me to thank you for the information contained in it. He will be glad if you can from time to time let me know anything you may hear from your correspondents at Constantinople as to the Sultan's dispositions, particularly as to any maneouvres for the encouragement of Mussulman agitation in India or Afghanistan. He authorizes me to make you a payment of £120 as last year . . . (and) . . . he regrets that he cannot make any pledge as to the allowance becoming annual. But in order to make the matter as little disagreeable to you as possible, I will be ready to bring the question of gratuity before him each August or September on receiving a simple reminder from you asking me to do so". Vambery was touched and wrote an effusive letter of thanks five days later. "Dear Sir Thomas", he wrote, "Many many thanks for your kind note which was remitted to me today by Mr. Beauclerk.† Please give my best thanks to Lord Salisbury for his noble and generous behaviour towards me, his Lordship may be assured that I shall continue to devote all my energies to the interests of the principle to which I have devoted my life . . .", adding: "My remuneration was in the past and will be in the future the conscience that in defending British supremacy in Asia I served to the noble cause of Humanity, Freedom and Civilisation".

One does not know whether he was carried away by the driving-force of his own enthusiasm or deceiving himself.

For a time there had been no British Consul in Budapest and a worried Vambery, the perennial watch-dog, had written: "In default of a British Consul-General in this place who could inform you about the Hungarian public opinion with regard to the Turkish crisis, I deem it my duty to give you a few hints as to predominant opinions and views on the present situation".

A few months later the Sultan sent his private secretary to persuade a reluctant Vambery to come to Constantinople. The reason, explained Vambery once again, was that he was the only European who enjoyed the favour of a private interview, had been tutor to his favourite sister forty years ago, and was fully acquainted with the language history and religion of the Turks.

He believed the Sultan involved with "Indian Mussulmen" and ended his letter on a warning note: "I am sorry to say that the warnings I gave years ago concerning the molework of Yildiz have been disregarded. The Indian Government ought to keep a sharp eye on certain Hadjis and Mollahs".

Another cutting from the *Pester Lloyd* was enclosed and a new problem discussed: China.

In a rare moment of correct self-assessment, one is nearly tempted to say, Vambery wrote to the Foreign Office: "Dear Sir!", he said, "You will easily conceive that I dare not — I can not act as an adviser to the British Government, but, anxious, to keep up my position as a mediator between England and Turkey I would ask you to consider this report of mine and to favour me with an answer by which I can strengthen my position at Yildiz ... the Sultan must know that I am listened to in London and that he can in future confide in me such messages which are unfit for official communication".

Vambery was anxious to have backing from the Foreign Office.

In the spring of next year (1898) the Sultan invited Vambery by telegraph to come to Constantinople following the publication of a pamphlet* in which he criticised him sharply. Vambery was quite frankly afraid of the consequences. "Knowing his aversion

* *La Turquie d'aujourd'hui et d'avant quarante ans.*

and rancour against anybody who ventures to oppose him, as well as his recklessness in punishing such boldness, I ought to have considered the feasibility of a journey to Constantinople"; he wrote "my relatives and friends have dissuaded me from going, but on the other hand I knew he will not venture to touch me, and so I went on the 15th inst. (April) and stayed there twelve days during which time I had several private conversations with him of which I beg to give you a concise but nevertheless exhausting report . . ."

He concluded his letter: "It is no secret to you that diplomatists at the Turkish court, and everywhere in the East, are looked upon and treated as inimical foreigners, whereas private individuals, playing the part of go-betweens, meet always with more confidence and find easier a willing ear". And there followed more about England and Turkey.

He declared himself ready to come to London, if required and added the inevitable postscript: "I do not ask for a remuneration for the service I tried to render, excepting a contribution towards my travelling expenses".

Sanderson commented to Salisbury: "I presume Professor Vambery should be paid £100 towards his expenses in Constantinople. It does not seem very sensible to have him as an extra Ambassador", and he drafted an elegantly-worded reply.

Vambery's reply came from his summer home in Muhlbach.

He acknowledged receipt of the letter "in the above place where I am rusticating. I am suffering from insomnia and I hope that a sojourn in the mountains will deliver me from that tantalising disease.

"Please be so kind and express to his Lordship my best thanks for his generous assistance. As to the remarks upon my letter, it will be gratifying to the Sultan to learn that the English Government is not at all that implacable enemy he always believes" and concluded: "I have sent a Turkish translation of your remarks to the Sultan, and I shall send his answer in original accompanied by an English rendering.

"May I request you to send me a bill for the amount granted to this place in a registered letter".

Three and a half months later Vambery wrote again, as usual from the University in Budapest, complaining that he could not get a written answer from the Sultan and adding that Britain's successsul campaign in the North-West of India had greatly annoyed

Abdul Hamid.

"I dare say the Foreign Office has taken note of my writings in England and in various Continental countries about the Chinese question". He approved Lord Salisbury's policy.* "In conclusion allow me to remind you of the usual allowance for my expenses, which you were so kind to bring before the Secretary of State" who wrote one line on the back of the letter:

"Make usual payment of £120".

In late November Vambery gave a long report on the visit of the German Emperor to Turkey. German technicians were everywhere — there was a highly developed German technical aid programme, yet there was indignation in Turkish circles at the Sultan's lavish and extravagant hospitality. The visit was said to have cost one million Turkish pounds, "and this was spent in a time when civil and military officers are literally starving and when orphans and widows are clamouring at the gates of the ministry for finances for a bit of bread . . .", wrote Vambery, whose informant had been a Turkish court official, sent by the Sultan, to bring back the old guns lent to Hungary for the millennial exhibition.

In the spring of 1898 Vambery turned hi attention to anti-English propaganda by the French press and subsidized, he claimed, by the French Government. He enclosed a specimen of a Hungarian paper printed in Paris and of a French paper called "*Paris-Nouvelles*".

In autumn of that year Vambery announced his departure for Constantinople "to see whether there is any chance to assist the English society of capitalists who try to get a concession for the railway to Baghdad" and proposed to report upon it, but his visit was postponed to the following year.

He also asked for his annual allowance.

"Pay him £120", commented Sanderson, " — and request that he will not do anything as regards railway scheme, without consulting Sir N. O'Conor* (to whom I will write by next messenger)".

"Of course I shall communicate with Sir N. O'Conor", replied Vambery, when the letter reached him, "but in an affair like the present one, Ambassadors have got a very limited space to move

---

* The the British Ambassador in Constantinople.

429

on, and official representatives can hardly view with private agencies" (meaning himself).

Sanderson was getting a trifle annoyed. "I think I might write to Professor Vambery", he wrote to Salisbury, "remarking that he has not consulted us before advocating this English railway project, and that you will be glad to know some particulars of the scheme and the persons interested in it, in order to judge whether it is one which we consider it desirable to push" — such as the Kapnist-Rechnitzer plan* — which is not at all what we want".

A month later Vambery had to admit that he had indeed supported this plan because he thought "German ascendancy in Asia Minor may in the future be dangerous to British interests". But he would in future abstain.

The Foreign Office took note of Vambery's contrition and, not entirely trusting him, sent off a letter on the lines proposed by Sanderson.

No wonder Vambery had been cautious at the time of the Boer War.

---

* The Sultan had already been in financial and other trouble over his railway schemes. The Haidar Pasha Izmid Railway had been sold to German investors before British investors had been paid, and a Berlin-to-Baghdad extension was a pet scheme of the Kaisers.

20

FOREIGN OFFICE PENSIONER

In January 1900, shortly before the relief of Ladysmith, a lengthy interview with Vambery — on the Boer War and the very sensitive relations with Germany — was published in the Budapest *Pester Correspondence*, under the banner headline 'Uber Den Transvaalkrieg'. By this time, ill-will between Germany and England had reached a new low, and pro-Boer sentiments were becoming very pronounced in the German Press. The criticisms of Vambery's pro-English attitude were steadily increasing, and Germany was now proving to be a bigger thorn in his side than Russia (who continued to advance her interests in Persia and Afghanistan). As usual, he sent a copy of the newspaper containing the interview to Sir Thomas Sanderson at the Foreign Office.

Vambery wrote: "I have a most difficult standing at the present juncture. I write and speak frequently, I spend money upon dinners and presents to the editors of Newspapers — and still I hardly succeed to pull down the veil of ignorance and stupidity from the deluded eyes of my countrymen". He went on to describe the "shockingly strong and injurious" influence of the German Press upon the bulk of the Hungarian population.

On the same day that Vambery wrote these words, the British government suffered an ignominious loss of face after mistakenly stopping a German ship on the inadequate suspicion that she was carrying contraband.

The Foreign Office was grateful for any European marks of friendship at this critical time. "We have not many defenders on the Continent at present", commented Sanderson to Lord Salisbury, who duly sanctioned another £25 to cover the expenses described by Vambery in his letter.

Vambery wrote back at once to thank Lord Salisbury for the remittance "which I did not expect at all" (!) . . . continuing, in his usual fashion, to describe his tricky position at Budapest: ". . .

Of course, I have much to endure under the present circumstances having become the target of the mean and base attacks of the whole Continental Press, including the papers of my own country. I have got the only consolation that the high official world of Austria-Hungary is siding with me, nd our Emperor-King himself has expressed to a friend of mine his satisfaction of the trend and purpose of my writings. The whole Court feels warmly for England . . ."

In late May, Vambery was resting at his summer house in the Tyrol when he received "a most pressing invitation" from Abdul Hamid. He communicated this important news immediately to Sanderson, who in his turn sent an urgent telegram to Sir Nicholas O'Conor, the British Ambassador at Constantinople.

Vambery spent the first wek of June 1900 as the personal guest of the Sultan at Constantinople. Ostensibly he had been invited by Abdul Hamid to participate in the founding of a new University for his Silver Jubilee. But Vambery reported back to the Foreign Office: "I guessed it at once, that this was only a sham purpose. His real intention was to take my advice in political matters, and to hear my views, which he appreciates more than any of his ministers and councillors . . ."

The Sultan "poured the phial of his wrath upon the English in general", but warmly praised both Queen Victoria and Sir Nicholas O'Conor. Vambery reported: "In speaking of his present relations to England, (the Sultan) began by expressing his satisfaction with the present representative of Her Majesty the Queen, whom he styled as a benignant spring rain following the period of thunder and lightening of his predecessor". (Abdul Hamid had always detested Sir Philip Currie, O'Conor's predecessor at Constantinople.)

Vambery wrote a very detailed report for the Foreign Office, describing in length his interviews with Abdul Hamid and the other diplomats he met in the same week. Lord Salisbury read it and commented: "a remarkable paper". A copy was also sent to O'Conor in Constantinople. The Foreign Office was impressed and interested by the anecdotes concerning Vambery's meetings with important visitors to Turkey, especially those from Japan. Vambery had been invited by Abdul Hamid to a large gala-dinner, given in honour of the Japanese Prince Kotohito and Iwakura, and he listened with great interest to the conversation between the Ottoman ruler and the envoys from Japan — "which

Vambery at his desk. Note water-bottle and other souvenirs of his travels in the background.

turned mostly on military and naval topics", wrote Vambery reporting back to the Foreign Office; "(the Japanese) were much glad when I drew the attention of the Sultan to the race affinity existing between Turks and Japanese, as members of the Ural-Altaic family ..." At this critical time of worldwide anti-Brisih feeling, Japan was the most friendly country, and eighteen months later the Anglo-Japanese Alliance marked the end of Britain's 'splendid isolation'.

Vambery also acted as a go-between for the Sultan and Prince Ferdinand of Bulgaria, whose country was still under the suzerainty of Turkey. He visited Ferdinand at Sofia, on the route from Budapest to Constantinople, and a few days later conveyed the Prince's oath of feudal fidelity to Abdul Hamid. The Sultan told Vambery:

"I shall send him at once a telegram of thanks, and on your way homewards, you will meet him, and tell him, please, I never doubted in his sincerity and I never give credit to the rumours spread in the papers concerning his next declaration of independence. Bulgaria, a small and a weak principality, cannot stand on its own legs, my support is unavoidably necessary, and I shall certainly not neglect my paternal duty towards the Prince and the country entrusted to his care. Prince Ferdinand is a clever and shrewed (sic) man and he will evidently know the dangers of an adventurous career".

Vambery met Prince Ferdinand on his return to Budapest and passed on the Sultan's message. Foxy Ferdy (as he was later called), a devious and durable ruler, received it with a sarcastic smile and remarked flatteringly: "If the Sultan is clever, *you* are certainly more clever, and I daresay, you certainly know the meaning of his words ..." At this time, the Prince was already planning to wrest his country from Turkey's grip, and to proc-·laim his U.D.I.

While at Constantinople, Vambery also met the Baron Marschhal von Bieberstein, the German Ambassador, first at a sumptuous tea-party at the Yildiz, and later at the Court Theatre. Always suspicious of German diplomats, he was careful not to discuss politics with the Baron.

All this was reported back confidentially to the Foreign Office in London, and in September Vambery received his annual grant of £120 asusual.

Another detailed report from Vambery to the Foreign Office — in his own words "a highly important communication" — followed the visit of Muzaffar-ed-Din, Shah of Persia, to Budapest (see Chapter 16). The Shah had recently been given a large Russian loa, and was now the object of much criticism from the British. Unable to visit London on his European tour, he was anxious to clarify his position with Lord Salisbury's government without delay. After conferring with the Shah on 28 September, Vambery sent an urgent telegram to Sanderson:

"Shah said to me to-day: 'Pray inform Lord Salisbury that it is a mistake to suppose I am no longer a friend of England; I am as great a friend as ever I was'. Vambery." The Shah was at pains to point out that he preferred Britain to Russia, in spite of Salisbury's reluctance to lend him ay money.

In his report, Vambery stated, with his usual ring of confidence: "... My previous acquaintance with the present ruler, when he was Heir-apparent, have greatly contributed towards the confidence and intimacy which has sprung up, unexpectedly quickly, between his Persian Majesty and me. I need hardly add that my fluency in the Persian colloquial language has greatly enhanced this rather extraordinary confidence ... I got in the position of learning a good deal of the present political relations of the country, particularly such which may be unknown at the Foreign Office ..."

Not missing a trick, Vambery then sent Sanderson a short note: "I write separately requesting your favour to tell Lord Salisbury that the Shah's visit has put me in extraordinary expenses, which I would like to have reimbursed. My goodly Persians made purchases and the bill was sent to me, and I had to pay for it. It was nearly forty pounds, I had to spent. (sic) And besides, I may be pardoned in asking a slight remuneration for the work and time spent in the interest of my experience".

Like his late father Nasr-ed-Din, the Shah was an undisciplined spendthrift, and it was not unusual for him to got into the enticing shops at Paris, Vienna, and Budapest, and literally clean them out by purchasing the complete stock. During his Budapest visit, the story circulated that, deciding to buy a new pair of shoes, he went into a shop and — unable to make up his mind which pair to choose — bought the entire stock of six hundred. Usually his Minister of the Treasury would pay on the spot, but Vambery claimed that this did not always happen — and he received some bills himself after the Shah had departed.

As Sanderson pointed out, Vambery had been appointed by the Hungarian Government to be the official interpreter and guide to the Shah of Persia during his stay in Budapest, and it was they (not the British) who should pay the outstanding bills. It is not known how much money Vambery was able to squeeze out of his own Government for his services, but the Foreign Office in London decided to send him another £50 to cover his expenses and to keep him on their side.

Following the Shah's second visit to Budapest, Vambery suggested that Dr. Hugh Adcock, who had been chief physician to the Shah for many years, was long overdue for a knighthood: "This Englishman has great influence upon the Shah, he is continually rendering great services to his country and he really deserves that honour". Vambery's suggestion was apparently taken up, as Adcock was knighted only a few months later. From time to time he made various suggestions as to who, in his opinion, should be knighted, and which scholar should receive a Civil List Pension — even though he had not received any public honour from the British Government himself.

In the early part of the summer, 1901, Vambery spent three weeks in Constantinople, which would turn out to mark his last visit to the Sultan. "I had a very hard standing a the Turkish court this time", he told Sanderson, "the French and the Russians thinking it necessary to intrigue against me". As usual, he wrote a detailed confidential report on the state of affairs at Constantinople, and the Sultan's disposition towards Britain, to the Foreign Office; and a copy of the report — which, in Sanderson's words, was "long and interesting" — was despatched to the ambassador, Sir Nicholas O'Conor, "whose quiet placid and gentlemanly manner has won his (the Sultan's) affections, and whose representation is really a soothing plaster upon the wounds inflicted by his predecessor . . ." (Sir Philip Currie) Vambery was careful not to mention any details of his other mission in Constantinople, for Theodor Herzl.

In June, Vambery made a short visit to London to give Sanderson further details of his dealings with the Turkish court, but had to cut his time short owing to the illness of his wife.

Vambery received his annual allowance of £120 in September, and over the next few months, he sent several letters, giving both advice and complaints, to the Foreign Office, together with his own pamphlets and articles on many subjects, from the Anglo-Japanese talks, to Afghanistan, and the situation in the Persian Gulf. All his cuttings dealing with the Central Asian Question were forwarded to the India Office. Most of his letters touched on the German Anglophobia which was growing more acute, especially in the Berlin press.

In December Vambery sent his new pamphlet, on England and Russia in the Persian Gulf — printed in German — "in which I try to prove England's exclusive right and beneficial influence in those waters. The publication of this paper has cost me a good deal of trouble, as my pen is boycotted in Germany, what involves great moral and material loss to me", Vambery wrote to Sanderson. "But we nevertheless must go on fighting the folly and craze of the ignorant and malevolent masses, and I am sure we shall ultimately carry the point. Here in Hungary I was in the beginning ridiculed and had to experience a good deal of enmity, but now the tide begins to turn, as proved by the speech of the Hungarian Premier, and I am now to propose to an anglophil circle to send an address to Lord Kitchener in acknowledgement of his patriotism, endurance and military skill, which will conquer savage Africa to European civilisation. Nothing but perseverance can help us to overcome all kinds of obstacles", Lord Lansdowne, who had succeeded Salisbury as Foreign Secretary, agreed to pay Vambery £25 to cover the expenses of his pamphlet.

Throughout 1902, Vambery's pro-British campaign met with great success in several quarters, including some parts of the German Press. in August, to coincide with King Edward's coronation (at which the Kaiser was one of the most important guests), he sent one of his major articles from the *Weser-Zeitung*, "in order to give you an insight into the campaign I have inaugurated against German Anglophobia, and which, I am glad to say, meets with the approval of many leading German papers. As far as I learn from official sources, the German and Austro-Hungarian Governments are pleased with my doings . . ."

Thanking Sanderson on 22 September 1902 for the annual payment of £120, Vambery wrote — ". . . I have no other thought than to continue in the work I am engaged forty years ago, for the welfare of England and in the interest of Humanity. My position has been of late much aggravated through the bitter enmity of German public opinion, but I hope to overcome it . . ."

For his next important pamphlet, on the position of England in Asia, Vambery as usual asked for an advance payment from the Foreign Office to cover the printing expenses. "Shall I send him £50? He is I think of some use", wrote Sanderson to Lord Lansdowne, who agreed.

On publication the following March (1903), Vambery sent the pamphlet, entitled *England's Position in Asia, and Anglo-German relations there*, to the Foreign Office. Not only were his criticisms of Germany's foreign policy harsher than ever, but he also added, "I prove with glaring facts the many mistakes and shortcomings of Russian rule in Central Asia . . ."

The rivalry between Germany and Russia was becoming acute in Asia Minor over the Baghdad Railway scheme, and Vambery's paper (published in Europe and America) roused the anger of the Germans against him anew.

More articles and reports followed, chiefly on British influence in Persia, and on India and Tibet. His views on *Der Kampf Um Tibet* (The Struggle for Tibet), concerning the Younghusband expedition, were much criticised in the Russian Press.

Vambery's next visit to Britain, which he had planned for September 1903, had to be cancelled owing to a troublesome stomach disease, but he was mollified by the usual remittance of twelve £10 bank notes.

He had recovered his customary good health by the following May, when he came over to see his many old friends in London, as well as the Prime Minister and Sir Thomas Sanderson.

Vambery had obvious doubts concerning the future of his annual allowance, especially now that his friendship with Abdul Hamid was moribund. Following the success of his reception at Buckingham Palace, in the same week he made use of a golden opportunity by writing the following letter to Arthur Balfour, who had succeeded his uncle Lord Salisbury as Prime Minister:

"20 May 1904, THE ATHENAEUM
"Sir,
Being still under the spell of the very kind reception you have accorded to me, I take the liberty to lay before you the case I mentioned yesterday, in the following words.

It is just now forty years ago, when returning from Central Asia I began to lay before the British and Continental public my

438

experiences regarding the political situation in Central Asia, putting a particular stress upon the danger, which might threaten Great Britain by the continual encroachment of Russia in Turkestan. Through the late Sir Roderique Murchison I handed a report to Lord Palmerstone, who received me kindly and encouraged me to enlighten the public by my writings concerning this question. I have got similar encouragements from subsequent Minister-Presidents and Secretaries of Foreign Affeirs of this country, but even without them I would have gone on with my literary work having been fully convinced of the great service England has rendered to the cause of Civilisation in Asia, and that it is the duty of every friend of Light and Liberty to assist England in her noble work and to stand by her side in her struggle with Russia.

Now, Sir, the bulk of my writings on this subject in Hungarian, German, English, French and Turkish constitute many volumes. Not less numerous are the lectures and addresses I delivered on this topic in England and on the Continent, and I am happy to say that I have succeeded to impress more than once my audiences and the reading world with admiration for Englands noble mission in Asia and with the fact of her unquestionable superiority over her less civilised rival coming from the North. I need hardly say that in this, sometimes strenuous work, I have been activated merely by the desire to help poor oppressed Humanity in Asia, and to support Great Britiain, the harbour of Liberty and the headfountain of our Civilisation. Material gain was not the goal of my desire, for principals and sympathies are neither sold nor bought by money, and up to the present I was satisfied by the proud of the moral acknowledgement, I had got in your noble country.

But unfortunately our human frame is fragile and our mental power too is declining with age. I am now seventy three years old. My literary activity has not enrichened me, in fact serious literature never pays, and seeing that advanced age is in need of more comfort than usual, I must turn for assistance to the country to which I devoted all the labours and energies of a long life. It is not greed, but sheer necessity, which compels me to take this step, and You Sir, the highminded head of the present Government, you will not accuse me of want of modesty if I ask an annual help of £250 till the end of my life. As I say, it is reluctantly that I trouble you with these lines. The 46 letters of thanks I have got froo the Foreign Office have certainly amply rewarded my work, but I had to obey to imperative necessity, and I trust, you will pardon to

    Yours most obediently
    A. Vambery.

The Right Honourable
Arthur James Balfour, M.A.
Prime Minister, First Lord
of the Treasury, etc."

Two days later, Vambery was a guest at Windsor Castle, and again he took the advantage of his position by using the Royal notepaper, in writing to Sanderson:

               "May 22 1904, WINDSOR CASTLE
"Dear Sir,

You were so exceedingly kind to me on the occasion of my last visit that I must repeatedly thank you for the zeal with which you embraced my cause.

Mr. Balfour has accorded to me a warm reception and gave me his promise to do all in his power to further my object in view. He said, there is no doubt about my services rendered to the country, but there is a difficulty in my not being a British subject and he does not know how an exception is to be made.

He nevertheless said to expose to him in a letter my request, what I did and I dare say he will find his way. His Majesty and the Royal Family have accorded me a most gracious reception, I remained with H.M. the King for more than an hour and He much liked the remembrances of the pasty forty years.

I do not know whether I shall participate in the honour of seeing you again. Allow me to lay to your heart the question of my book — 'Our Culture bearers in Muslim Asia' — the publication of which I find urgently necessary, it is highly in the interest of Great Britian.

If Lord Lansdowne is willing to give me the usually accorded contribution towards any travelling's expenses, I shall be thankful for it.

    With reiterated thanks.
      Yours sincerely,
        A. Vambery."

There were urgent consultations in the Foreign Office that week. Balfour gave his letter from Vambery to Sanderson, asking how they should reply. Lord Lansdowne, anxious that all matters relating to Vambery and his allowances should remain under wraps, was afraid that the King might spread the word about his Hungarian friend and his invaluable undercover duties. He first decided to offer an initial grant of £200 towards Vambery's travel expenses in England and the translation of his new book on 'Our Culture Bearers'. With the Anglo-Russian Entente on the horizon, Landsdowne hoped that, "while defending British policy", the book would not be "too antagonistic to Russia within certain limits, as (for instance) in repressing the predatory Turkomans Russia must be admitted to have done a good deal for civilisation in the interior of Asia."

Sanderson was authorised to write to Vambery as follows:

"As regards your request to the Prime Minister, Lord Lansdowne is ready to devote a sum of £1000 to purchase a Life Annuity for you. If, as I think you told me, you are now 73 years of age, this sum would secure you an Annuity of about £140. For several reasons there are great difficulties in the way of making a promise of a Pension. The arrangement if made would be in acknowledgement of past services and would be independent of every grant which might be made for future work. If the proposal is acceptable to you, I will procure and forward the necessary papers". Together with the annual £120 which he already received, Vambery's income from the Foreign Office would therefore be more than £250 per annum (after minimal tax).

Vambery answered on 16 June (1904):

"You ask whether I am satisfied by the arrangements contained in Yr favour dated June 7. Certainly, I accept with many many heartfelt thanks the gracious proposal of Lord Lansdowne for it satisfies entirely my wants. It was never my object in view to make money through my writings for if this would have been my intention, I would have found more profitable and much easier ways & means to get it. After more than forty years hard work I am happy to see that England's position in Asia is firm and unassailable, and this is the main reward for my labours. I had no right to ask a material acknowledgement from England, and if the Government nevertheless lends me an assistance for my old age, I am most grateful for it". Regarding the additional £200 grant for his book, he asked for £50 to be sent at once in a registered letter, pending the other £150 till the next spring when he would be engaged in the work — "I might die in the winter and I would have appropriated unjust money".

It took most of the summer of 1904 to settle the details of Vambery's future Annuity, and there was much correspondence between Sanderson (at the Foreign Office) and George Hervey (at the National Debt Office). There was a large amount of red tape to unravel, as an Act of Parliament forbade the setting up of annuities on the lives of foreigners who still lived abroad.

The fact that Vambery did not know for sure whether he was born in 1831 or 1832 caused further complications. He was unable to comply with the Foreign Office's request for his Birth Certificate, as (most) Jewish births were unregistered in Hungary at that time. "In cases of this kind where the baptism did not take place in babyhood it is usual to have a continuatory declaration by a disinterested person who knows the annuitant from about the age of fifteen," was the official dictum.

In fact no Certificate of Baptism was ever forthcoming — conclusive proof that he had never been formally converted. He was as little a Protestant as he had been a Mohammedan in earlier years — but in both cases it suited him to let people believe so.

He was also, understandably, anxious to make financial arrangements from which his son, Rustem, might profit and wrote naively to the Foreign Office in this sense. They replied formally informing him that an Act of Parliament forbade the setting up of annuities on the lives of persons from outside the United Kingdom except when they were also the proprietors — annuity cards could thus not be set up in this case in the name of Rustem Vambery.

Everything was ironed out by September, when Hervey at the National Debt Office accepted the evidence furnished on Vambery's age* without further declarations, and he also accepted the claim (corrroborated by the Foreign Office) that Vambery had been connected more than forty years with "the British official world in the East".

On 1 October, Hervey sent a copy of the Life Annuity (Number 8172) with details of the first £140 to be purchased:
"The cost will be £1023.14.6.
        plus   1. 7.6. (commission)

---

* Backed up, no doubt, by the Windsor Castle visitors-book anecdote in his autobiography, which was published at the same time. (See Chapter 15).

Total: 1025.2.0. in all, and you may send me a cheque for this sum".

The Annuity of £140, vested in the name of the Permanent Under-Secretary of State for Foreign Affairs, was divided to be paid twice a year: £70 (less tax, usually 70 shillings) at the beginning of January, followed by the same amount in July. Vambery would have to submit a "certificate of Existence' each time, to prove he was still alive — a routine he did not appreciate. The Allowance, £120 per annum, from the Foreign Secretary's account, would be paid at the same time as the July Annuity.

Vambery was delighted with the new Annuity, and sent a copy of his book *The Story of My Struggles* to Sanderson, as a mark of goodwill. "To you, dear Sir", wrote Vambery, "I am most indebted for the manifold troubles you have taken on my behalf and you may rest assured that it will greatly enhance my feelings of duty and gratitude to your noble country".

Sir Thomas Sanderson was sixty-four at this time and approaching his retirement. He was a much-loved figure, known affectionately to all his colleagues at the Foreign Office as 'Lamps', but recently his long periods of overworking had caused protracted bouts of illness. Vambery wrote to him in March 1905:

"I trust you have regained your former health and vigour and that you will be long spared to the important office you are successfully filling. My health is a fairly good one. Continual work makes one forget the infirmities of age and if the pen drops off from my hand I shall soon cease to exist.

"This year I shall hardly be able to visit England inspite of the friendly invitations I get from all the parts of the United Kingdom, though I would much like to see my friends".

He now received from Sanderson the £150 (promised the previous year) to go towards the printing expenses of French and German editions of his forthcoming book on "the comparison between Russian and English civilising influence in Moslem Asia", which he had already been warned to tone down.

Vambery continued to send his advice and recent writings on the political events in Asia and elsewhere. The widespread hatred of Britain in Europe was a continual theme. "In Germany, of course, Anglophobia is steadily increasing and it is a most arduous task to get anything published which betrays the slightest sympathy to England . . ." he wrote in May 1905; ". . . it is rather striking to see the Egyptian papers, published in Turkish and Arabic, manifesting a deeply seated hatred against England and preaching publicly sedition. I wonder how Lord Cromer can suffer this . . ."

His two-volume autobiography *The Story of My Struggles* was a best-seller in England at this time, and quickly went into three editions. The publishers, T. Fisher Unwin, agreed to issue a simultaneous paperback edition for Continental readers (but still in English), and these were issued from their Leipzig and Paris offices; at bargain prices (at 3 marks and 4 francs per set respectively), these again had a wide sale. In 1905 Vambery saw the book published in a revised one-volume edition in his native Budapest under the title *Kuzdelmeim*. He tried hard to get the work translated and brought out in a German edition, but here he found himself up against a brick wall — as he described to Sanderson, from his retreat in Styria, (on 6 July):

". . . I am boycotted in Germany and no publisher ventures to publish even my 'Story of My Struggles' — what reads like a novel and has no political tendency. To give you an idea of the German narrowmindedness and coarseness I include a letter from a friend of mine, who was desirous to issue a German version of my memoirs, and to whom the reason of my being disliked in Germany is explained. Is it not childish to drag me, who is neither English nor German, in a quarrel, which I have never provoked nor supported? Well, I must tell you the Germans begin to become most tedious and unbearable".

His first autobiography for Unwins, published twenty years earlier, had suffered a similar fate being published only in England.

At the end of the year (1905) the Conservative Government, which had been in power for a decade, was ousted, and the Liberals took over the reins of power. Sir Henry Campbell-Bannerman replaced Balfour as Prime Minister, and Sir Edward Grey became Foreign Secretary (a post he would hold well into the First World War). But it was the retirement of Sir Thomas Sanderson that unsettled Vambery most of all. Worried about his future payments, he hoped the matter would be clearly introduced to Sir Charles Hardinge, the British Ambassador to Russia, who was to succeed Sanderson as the Permanent Under-Secretary for Foreign Affairs. Vambery wrote a rather panicky letter to Sanderson on 28 November:

". . . As there is not a categorical statement existing concerning my allowance, I would beg to settle this matter once for ever, so that I should not have to beg every year. Of course this latter is in connection with my future services, but can there be any doubt as to the continuance of my life long work? I dare say no Minister for Foreign Affairs will judge my request as extravagant and nobody will suspect me of greed . . ."

Vambery remained in a state of nervous activity most of the time. He had just retired from his post at Budapest University, and was very anxious that the allowances from London should continue to supplement his income at home. He need not have worried: Sanderson, now elevated to the Peerage, prepared the following Memo, entitled:

"*Professor Vambery:* history of F.O. allowance to him & method of payment.

"Professor Vambery has for many years past received gratuities from Secret Service for services rendered partly in the way of literary support in the foreign press of British policy, partly for information respecting the Sultan who is in the habit of asking him to Constantinople & treating him with considerable confidence.

In 1898 or 1899 he made an appeal to be allowed to have a regular allowance instead of these occasional grants & Lord Salisbury, while refusing to commit his successors, agreed that he should have a grant of £120 a year payable in August or Sept. in consideration of his literary services, so long as these continued; & in addition to any sums which might be paid to him on occasions of his visits to Constantinople.*

"In 1904 he came over to England & earnestly begged that he might have a life pension of £250. Both the King & Mr. Balfour favoured this appeal but it was impossible to grant him a pension from the Civil List as these are reserved for British subjects; he wished moreover that the pension should not be known.

"Lord Lansdowne eventually agreed to purchase for him a Gvmt. Life Annuity of £140, which was to be in addition to the Grant of £120 payable for literary services. The annuity is grantd for Professor Vambery's life time, but is payable to the

---

* Vambery had decided that this would be his last book, complaining that his "elasticity of mind" was "quickly disappearing with the advance of age". In a letter to John Murray (14 August 1905) he wrote: "Since your father published my first book, his son ought to publish the last one . . ."

Permanent Under Secretary of State for Foreign Affairs. Messrs. Drummond hold a Power of Attorney for collecting it. Professor Vambery sends his life certificate in half-yearly to me, & Messrs. Drummond at my request obtain payment of the instalments & give me a letter of credit for the amount in favour of Professor Vambery on the Banque Hongroisse. Professor Vambery now begs that the life annuity may be increased to £250 a year, & the yearly grant of £120 dropped. To do this would entail additional expenditure of about £840. It would somewhat simplify matters but it would leave Professor Vambery free to do nothing. His annuity might no doubt be withheld if he did anything objectionable but he s under no obligation to render us any services for it. S"
Foreign Office, Jan. 26 1906"

In 1906, Vambery's magnum opus 'Our Culture-Bearers in Moslem Asia' was published in London by John Murray under the title *Western Culture in Eastern Lands*. Still pleading poverty, he had received an advance of £120 from Murray — "the small amount of my honorarium".

Vambery sent a copy of his "literary swan-song" to the Foreign Office, and asked for £150 to cover the expenses of translation and publication in French and German. He wrote ". . . I have worked three years on the present book without any remuneration, but England will certainly not expect me to spend my own modest means in the defence of her cause . . ."

His memory was conveniently short here, as Sir Charles Hardinge reminded him: a grant of £150 for the book had already been sent to him the previous year, and £50 before that. Sir Edward Grey reluctantly sent the extra £150, debited to his own account, but told Vambery that this must definitely be the last payment connected with the book.

Several weeks later, a piqued and sensitive Vambery retorted in a letter to Hardinge: ". . . With regard to the remarks of the Secretary of State that he can not make a further grant towards the publication of this book, will you kindly say to His Excellency that I am always particular with grants asked from Foreign Office and that during the 46 years of my services to England I have never spent a farthing uselessly . . ."

In many ways Vambery did not see eye to eye with the Liberal government. Anglo-Russian discussions regarding an entente were under way. Grey refused to promise support to France in the event of German attack, while plans to widen the Kiel Canal were made, and the number of German battleships increased year by year.

Vambery continued to send his advice on political matters, especially on Germany, Turkey and Egypt. The Denshawi affair in Egypt caught his attention, and he sent several letters to Lord Cromer (via the Foreign Office) on the subject. Cromer was nearing the end of his long tenure — almost 25 years — as British resident and Consul-General (i.e. virtual ruler) in Egypt. The widespread hatred of colonial rule was revealed by the 'Denshawi outrage' (13 June 1906), when several British officers were attacked by natives, and one was killed. Vambery's Mohammedan friends in Cairo brought the virulent anglophobic writings in the local Press to his attention. In a letter to Hardinge, Cromer wrote (12 July):

"I return Vambery's letter. I do not think the Denshawi affair was political, and, on the whole, I am opposed to taking any measures against the press. But I entirely agree with what Vambery says as to the mischief which they do . . ."

Confidential news of the Turkish court-circle still filtered through to Vambery "from the Yildiz Palace, where I have got still a few reliable and trustworthy friends . . ." Still anxious to persuade the Foreign Office that he remained an important source of information, even in retirement, he wrote to Hardinge in December 1906:

". . . You will certainly smile in reading of my pretentions to be better informed than your Embassy in Constantinople. But please not to forget that I am more closely and more intimately connected with Turkey than many foreign representatives, to whom Turkish affairs will always remain a closed book".

The invitations sent to Budapest by Abdul Hamid throughout 1907 did not lead to anything, owing to Vambery's arch-enemy at the Turkish court, Izzet Pasha.

The practice of filling out his Certificate of Existence, and writing a 'begging' letter to the Foreign Office, twice a year, was beginning to prove very irksome indeed to Vambery's self-esteem. He felt it was just like asking for charity. His ego was bruised. He wished, more than anything else, that the money would flow in naturally, without any prompting whatsoever. Asking as usual for his half-yearly annuity, and £120 annual allowance, he wrote on 5 July 1907 to Hardinge:

"... (Sir Edward Grey) would put me under great obligation, if I would be relieved of the humiliation to be obliged to beg every year for this sum, which is included in the assistance accorded to me by the late Ministry.

"It is now forty five years ago since I was asked by the late Sir Ch. Alison to enquire in the steppe after Captain Wyburd of the Intelligence Department and since that time I am constantly active with my pen in the British interests in Asia. I doubt whether th Government is aware of my work done in India in furthering the British sympathies of the Mohammedans."

To prove his point, he added, while forwarding some letters from an influential editor in Lahore:

"My correspondence with the Indian Moslems is a large one and I flatter myself of having the power of influencing them. It is unfair to extol my own services, but it is the result of strenuous and persistent work and I can not leave it unmentioned ..."

The Foreign Office managed to persuade Vambery that regulations concerning allowances could not be altered, so the half-yearly applications continued as before.

The Anglo-Russian Entente, which was signed on 31 August 1907, nauseated Vambery after all his years of preaching against such an eventuality. He made his opinions plain to the Foreign Office: "I do not like it at all. You have paid a too high price for a temporary peace, for such as it is, and the humiliation undergone will not enhance British prestige in Asia. You have shown excessive caution in the face of a sick adversary, although England was not in need of doing so".

Persia, the root of so much antagonism between Russia and Britain, was now divided into three distinct spheres of influence: a large Russian sphere in the north (the most valuable part of the country); a neutral sphere in the centre; and a smaller British sphere in the south-east. Vambery received many plaintive letters from his old friends in the Caucasus and the north of Persia, with whom he till kept in touch, as he told Hardinge:

"You can hardly realise the sorrow and disappointment manifested by the writers on seeing their country forsaken by England and handed over to Russia. 'If we have to be eaten up by foreigners' — says one of the writers — 'it would be better to disappear in the clean mouth of the English instead of in the dirty and detestable mouth of Russia'. Well, the poor fellow is right . . ." Vambery enlarged on the subject in his articles for the *Pester Lloyd* in Budapest. When he next wrote to the Foreign Office for his annuity, he commented:

". . . I am sorry to say that I can not follow the new course of English politics with the same fervour as before, since I am not yet convinced of the sincerity of Russia, but keeping strictly to my principle of watching British interests in the Moslem East, I shall inform you of all the movements of the Mohammedans noticeable with regard to their awakening and the plans they nourish for the future. It would be a great mistake to ignore the cultural effort and the spirit of unity which begins to penetrate the whole body of Islam".

The British Labour Party were in complete agreement with Vambery over Russia, and much less complacent than the Conservatives and Liberals. When Sir Edward Grey announced to the House of Commons (on 27 May 1908) that King Edward would meet the Czar of Russia in his yacht off Reval (in the Baltic), the British Socialists were enraged. Keir Hardie, the leader of the Labour Party, accused the King of condoning atrocities, and Ramsay MacDonald described the Czar as a "common murderer". The King was furious with these criticisms; and when Arthur Ponsonby voted against the Russian talks, he was deleted from a list of invitations to Windsor Castle, in spite of the fact that he was a son of Queen Victoria's devoted secretary Sir Henry Ponsonby.

Although King Edward reacted furiously towards Lloyd George, Churchill, Hardie, and all the other M.P.s who sought to embarrass Sir Edward Grey's foreign policy, he always remained benevolent towards Vambery and continued to welcome his opinions. At the King's request, Vambery sent a long and detailed report *On the Constitutional Movement in Turkey* (11 September 1908). This followed closely after the victory of the Young Turk Revolution in Constantinople, when the Sultan was forced to restore the 1876 Constitution. To the relief of the Foreign Office, German influence in Turkey collapsed, to be replaced by a period of ardent anglophilia.

Reminding the Foreign Office of his long-held valuable links with the Young Turks Committee, Vambery wrote:

". . . This favourable position of mine I intend to use in the interest of peace and of a good understanding between Turkey and Austria and particularly to remove the danger of war ...

"I must further inform you that I am in direct communication with the Constantinople Committee of Young Turkey, who always ppreciated my efforts, to bring on a friendly feeling between England and Turkey, and who are glad to see now realised my former scheme. As far as I can judge from the distance, things do not look so dark and so hopeless as heretofore".

At the end of 1908, Vambery found himself involved in a series of major crises which brought Europe threateningly near to the brink of war. The ambitious Austrian Foreign Minister, Baron Alois von Aehrenthal, the grandson of a Jewish merchant who had married into the aristocracy, held the centre of the stage. Detested equally by the British, German, and Russian diplomats who dealt with him, he was a firm favourite of the Emperor Franz Josef. As a diamond jubilee present for his master, Aehrenthal annexed — without any warning — the provinces of Bosnia and Herzegovina. These two states (now part of Yugoslavia) had been administered by Austria for thirty years, though nominally they had remained Turkish suzerainty. The British and Russian governments pretended to be outraged, though a leading Turkish statesmen wrote to Vambery (he claimed) that Turkey would not take back the two provinces if they were offered to her.

Simultaneously the Prince of Bulgaria, "Foxy Ferdy," took advantage of the confusion created by the annexation, and proclaimed his own country independent, with himself as King or Czar. He had previously made several expeditions (for inside information) to Budapest, where he often conferred with Vambery. He despised the Austro-Hungarian Empire, and was once quoted as saying: "The House of Austria treats me like a dog and it certainly deserves the services of that filthy Jew Aehrenthal". (Whenever he travelled from his capital Sofia to Budapest, he always travelled in the toilets of the Orient Express to avoid recognition).

For British publication, Vambery wrote an article "On the Crisis in the Near East" for the *Nineteenth Century*, one of many pieces written over the years for that journal.

The sly Baron von Aehrenthal probably knew about Vambery's long friendship with King Edward and the respect his letters and articles received in the British press.* In November, he invited Vambery to have a series of interviews with him in Vienna. They discussed the new wave of British hostility directed against Austria following the annexations. Von Aehrenthal, wrote Vambery, "expresses his astonishment regarding the vehemently inimical language of the English Press against Austria-Hungary, the old friend of Great-Britain, whose political interests do not collide with those of England in the Near East and which has given no cause to the present latent enmity. He almost literally said: 'We are evidently a victim to the Germanophobia raging in England, for Austria-Hungary is looked upon as an advanced post of Germany in the Near East. This assumption is however an erroneous one' ..."

Vambery reported back to the Foreign Office most of the Baron's comments, and further claimed that Aehrenthal offered him money if he would write articles against England. But Vambery refused to be bought in this way. Naturally he realised that all income from London would stop if he fell in with Aehrenthal; and his reputation would suffer considerably. He therefore wrote "... I need hardly say that my actual position is a most unpleasant, nay critical one".

Aehrenthal related some half-truths about the Reval meeting, and Vambery was rash enough to quote some of these during a lecture he gave in Budapest (on 18 December). The most serious allegation he quoted was that England and Russia had plotted against the Balkan interests of Austria-Hungary. This was a direct criticism not only of King Edward but also of Sir Charles Hardinge who, as the minister in attendance, represented the British Government at all the King's conferences abroad that summer. *The Times* gave Vambery's lecture a big write-up and concluded by saying: "It would be interesting to know whether the Austro-Hungarian Foreign Office has furnished Professor Vambery with any proof of its insinuation, and, if so, in what that proof consists".

Hardinge was incensed to read this in *The Times* on 21 December, and wrote a severe letter to Vambery* at once. He knew Aehrenthal to be a real trouble-maker; and in his memoirs

---

* Towards the end of his life, Vambery's letters to *The Times* and elsewhere had deferential headlines like 'Professor Vambery's Opinion', instead of just the subject title.

* Unfortunately this letter is missing from the archives.

published forty years later, Hardinge† placed him on the short-list of four men (in his opinion) most responsible for the First World War.

Vambery replied to Hardinge (on 5 January 1909) in an apologetic but defensive style:

"Exceedingly sorry as I am to have caused you displeasure through my alluding to the rumour regarding the Reval meeting, I have to state that I have acted bona fide in repeating the words of Baron Aehrenthal, who said to me in the very beginning of my interview what prompted him mostly to the policy of annexation, was the uncertainty and the critical position caused by the Reval meeting. Could I doubt in the words of a state minister owning the confidence of the Sovereign of my country?

"I do not know on what ground Baron Aehrenthal made this statement nor had I any right to ask him the necessary explanation, but if this rumour is untrue, or as you say baseless and mischievous, then it ought to be rectified and in the interest of my own character I must insist upon the truth to come out . . ." and he went on at length in the same vein.

Hardinge responded with a short and icy reprimand on 11 January: "I accept your statement although it was quite easy for you to have ascertained from the Embassy in Vienna or the Consul General in Budapesth whether the statements made to you were true or not. Coming from you such misstatements have had a very mischievous effect which it is impossible to correct. I trust this will not occur again. If it should occur again I shall be reluctantly compelled to reconsider our relations to each othr".

When Vambery wrote again, he expostulated on the difficulties of his position, especially now that Britain and Austria-Hungary were at loggerheads. A blistering article published in *The Near East Magazine* on the Emperor Franz Josef had been brought to his attention. What on earth could he do, complained Vambery, when shown a British paper with such a "coarse and unqualificably rude attack on the old Emperor"? His compatriots were asking increduously: "And you can side with a country where such bad taste mixes in political controversy?" Vambery told Hardinge:

"I am sorry to say the tide of passion has risen too high in England and it is much to be regretted that the old and traditional

---

* Lord Hardinge of Penshurst: *Old Diplomacy* (John Murray, 1947).

friendship between the two countries has been so wantonly destroyed by uncalled for advocates.

"I trust you will give a proper estimate of the difficulty in which I find myself and not find too much fault with my behaviour".

From then on, Vambery tried to keep himself aloof from all controversy, though he found this difficult. The £140 annuity and £120 allowance continued as usual.

Harold Nicolson paints a vivid behind-the-scenes picture of the Foreign Office at this time in the biography* of his father Sir Arthur (Lord Carnock), who replaced Hardinge as Permanent Under Secretary in 1910. Hardinge, a great believer in democratic innovations, had used revolutionary methods in modernising the Foreign Office. Only a few years before, the records and letters received were folded in such a way to allow only limited space for the cramped and congested minutes of Sir Thomas Sanderson. Hardinge introduced the foolscap size and encouraged the juniors in the department to add their suggestions.

Sir Arthur Nicolson was full of admiration for the smooth system his predecessor had pioneered. But to be Head of the Foreign Office (Permanent Under Secretary) was a daunting job for a man in constant pain from rheumatism and arthritis. Problems from all over the world would accumulate in the red despatch boxes on his desk. "They filled him with nausea and despair. Never has any man so cordially disliked being Permanent Under Secretary of State", wrote Harold Nicolson in his biography. "He was so overwhelmed with a mass of subsidiary questions — some of them trivial, all of them exacting, and for most of which he had but little aptitude or interest. He would labour onwards unceasingly, cursing the fate which had condemned him to so cruel a peniteniary".

In July 1910 Hardinge, shortly before his elevation to the Peerage and the post of Viceroy to India, received an unexpected letter from Budapest. Esme Howard, the new Consul-General in Hungary, had struck up a friendship with the world-famous 'ex-dervish' (later described in his memoirs*). He had now heard some news which disturbed him:

* Nicolson, Harold: *Sir Arthur Nicolson, Bart. First Lord Carnock*, A Study in the Old Diplomacy (Constable, 1930).
* Lord Howard of Penrith: *Theatre of Life* (1935/6) Vol. 2, pp. 161-164. Hodder.

"... I use this opportunity to write o a rather tiresome little matter on which I should be glad to have your opinion — a great friend of Vambery's came to me a few days ago and told me privately he feared the old gentleman owing to advanced age was getting indiscreet. Vambery has, as you no doubt know, several letters (there are 78 in all) written to him at various times by Foreign Secretaries — other officials beginning from Lord Beaconsfield on.

"He has hitherto, so far as we know, never shown these letters to anyone, but some time ago he allowed this friend of his to read them all. The latter said to me he would certainly make no use of them but that it might be very awkward if they were seen by any unprincipled person ...

"My informant suggested that we should get hold of them now. He says he knows that the one distinction that the old man particularly covets, is the Freedom of the City. This I suppose it would be impossible to obtain for him, but perhaps on the occasion of his 80th birthday it might be possible to confer on him some other honour ..."

The Foreign Office were in a dilemma. It was suggested that £500 should be offered to Vambery for all the letters and documents. This would be a tempting reward, but there was always the chance of a rebuff on Vambery's part — in spite of his love for money, his pride could be wounded. "It is delicate ground", was Sir Edward Grey's comment.

William Tyrrell,* Grey's private secretary, took over the matter after Hardinge's departure, to avoid worrying Sir Arthur Nicolson in his first few weeks as Permanent Under-Secretary. Howard reintroduced the subject to him on 10 November:

"My dear Tyrrell,

Thanks for your letter re Vambery. I had to see him about another matter a day or two ago, and he himself mentioned the matter of the letters. I therefore sounded him as to whether we thought it might not be advisable to place them where they could not fall into unauthorized hands. He blazed up at the idea, said that nothing would induce him ever to show them to anyone and that if he ever felt himself ill he would call for me or my successor & hand them over in a sealed packet for transmission to the Foreign Office. In the event of his death before he could hand them over, his son — who is a Professor here and I believe a very good fellow — would have instructions to hand them over to the Consul General at Budapest. He further said he wanted to keep them in his own hands some time more. I naturally went no further with my proposal to buy them. I should not be surprised if he does not want to keep them in his hands as a sort of hostage for the regular payment of his allowance of £240 per annum from H.M.G.

"He is very anti-Russian and does not disguise his feelings about our entente with Russia ... He and I are very good friends for I made it a rule not to enter into any discussions with him. He's not a bad sort but tremendously self-centered and vain — perhaps not unnatural in a man who has really done a great deal and is now so old that he no longer takes pains to hide his vanity.

Yr ever

Esme Howard".

Tyrrell commented: "I felt sure the old fox would not part".

Howard had some further news on 8 December, writing this time to Sir Arthur Nicolson, as Vambery had brought the latter's name into the affair (falsely as it turned out):

"Dr. Leipnik of the Pester Lloyd has been to see me and says that Prof. Vambery spoke to him about the matter a day or two ago — Prof. Vambery told him that he had received a letter from you about the letters and that he feared you were growing suspicious of him and did not trust him not to show them to anyone. Dr. Leipnik then replied that he (Vambery) would after all do well to hand these letters back to the Foreign Office since it was impossible to tell into whose hands they might not accidentally fall. Dr. Leipnik told me he would impress this on Vambery if he got the chance. He (Leipnik) says that Vambery's son Rustem is absolutely trustworthy and will not make any bad use of the letters.

"The worst is that we cannot altogether guarantee their not falling into other hands".

(Dr. Leipnik was probably the 'great friend of Vambery's' referred to by Howard in his July letter.)

Sir Edward Grey declared in his customary bold red ink: "It is clear that we shall give offence if we try to buy the letters & all we can do is to urge when opportunity offers that Vambery should return them or take steps to ensure that they are returned after his death".

A displeased Sir Arthur Nicolson, in his next letter (21 December) to Esme Howard, made a categorical denial: he had *not* written to Vambery, nor had he received any letter from him. He then repeated Sir Edward Grey's opinions to Howard.

When Howard passed on Sir Arthur's denial to Dr. Leipnik, the latter (who knew Vambery well) nodded and said: "I felt sure the old gentleman was romancing and that Sir Arthur has never written to him".

By this time, it seemed that Leipnik had finally been able to persuade Vambery to hand over all the letters to the Foreign Office. Howard transmitted this news to Tyrrell on 22 December, and added a rider marked *V. Private*:

"Leipnik tells me that there are also several letters from King Edward of a very private character, mostly about family matters, which it would be very unfortunate to have published. These however V. is determined to keep and will hand over to his son Rustem who is, L. says, a most trustworthy & sterling fellow in whom complete reliance can be placed".

At the beginning of 1911, Vambery as usual had to fill out his Certificate of Existence, and this he took along to Howard (at the Consulate-General, Budapest), together with new bargaining conditions. After commenting at length on Persia and the Moslem World, and offering to send a detailed Memo on the subject, Vambery concluded his letter to Sir Arthur saying:

"Mr. Esme Howard has opened to me the question of returning my correspondence to London in order to prevent any indiscreet use after my death. Although still far distant from that term, I have no objections against this measure, for one never knows what may happen with the papers we leave behind. I am ready to comply with this proposal, and the gratification I would ask, is, to relieve me of the onerous task to beg annually twice for the sum the Foreign Office has decreed as a reward for the service I have rendered for more than 40 years . . ."

January 1911 was Howard's last month in Budapest — he was being transferred to Berne — and he wanted to tie up all the loose ends before his departure. Relaying some of Vambery's suggestions, he told Sir Arthur: "He would like the money to be paid to him half yearly through the British Embassy at Vienna. He would prefer this to having it done through the Consulate here — why I don't quite know — if his wishes can be met, I think it would be an excellent thing, as I am really rather nervous about some of the letters. I don't for a moment believe that he would show them if he was quite sound, but there is no mistaking the fact that he is getting old — I have wondered whether on his 80th birthday, he could be given an honorary degree at Oxford. It would please him enormously I believe. Perhaps Curzon would be willing to consider the matter more particularly as Vambery has written so much on subjects which have always especially interested Curzon . . ."

Sir Arthur Nicolson sent the following courteous reply to Vambery's leter:

"*Private*

Foreign Office
10th January 1911

My dear Professor,

Many thanks for your letter of the 5th. inst. I am looking into the question of the annual payments to you, and I hope to be able to arrange matters in a manner which will meet your wishes. I am glad to hear that you agree with us that it would be prudent to let us have the letters which are in your possession. I sincerely trust that the day is far distant when the question would assume a practical form, but as the lives of all of us are uncertain it would be well to make provision for eventualities which must occur some time or another.

"I shall be pleased to receive your Memo as I am sure that it will be interesting. The present moment in the Moslem world is well worth watching.

Many good wishes for the New Year,

Yours sincerely,
A. Nicolson".

Two days later, Sir Arthur's private secretary Viscount Errington (the son and heir of Lord Cromer) visited the National Debt Office on a delicate mission, as he recorded in a private and confidential Memo:

"*SECRET*

Sir Arthur Nicolson,

In compliance with your instructions, I went today to the National Debt & Life Annuity Office to endeavour to come to some arrangement by which the Foreign Office can meet the wishes expressed by Professor Vambery as regards the method of paying him his annuity of £140.

I saw Mr. W.G. Turpin the Sec. & Comptroller General

who informed me of the technical difficulties in the way of granting payment of any Gmt. Annuity without the necssary Life Certificate. He informed me that many aged persons refused to furnish Life Certificates and that in consequence no payments were made to them and the money was allowed to accumulate.

On pressing Mr. Turpin in the matter, he told me that he would require some valid justification to enable him to depart from the customary procedure and asked me for circumstances which would allow of his considering the matter. Owing to the technical difficulties with which Mr. Turpin was confronted and in view of the importance attached by the Foreign Office to the solution of this question, I was obliged to disclose certain of the circumstances which prompted our request.

Mr. Turpin thereupon expressed his willingness to take upon himself the responsibility of waiving the production of a Life Certificate from Professor Vambery, as required by the Regulations, on condition that the Permanent Under Secretary of State for Foreign Affairs should himself furnish half yearly a voucher to the effect that the Professor is alive. Mr. Turpin will accordingly make arrangements that the Professor's Annuity shall be continued on the lines above mentioned.

The above conversation will of course remain strictly private and confidential.

12th January   E."
Foreign Office

And in this way the red tape was neatly cut, and Vambery got his way in the end. No longer would he have to 'beg', as he put it — now the money would flow in without reminders. He could rest contented, as Sir Arthur advised him (16 January):

"... I am glad to say that I can make such arrangements as will relieve you of the procedure which you find so irksome.

In order therefore to oblige you, we will arrange that in the future the half yearly payments of your annuity as well as the annual payment of your special allowance shall be made to you through H.M.'s Ambassador at Vienna ..."

Esme Howard wrote three days later to the Foreign Office on another matter: he had just heard that Herr Rantzau, the German Consul in Budapest, had suggested to Dr. Singer (the Head Editor of the *Pester Lloyd* newspaper) that a Hungarian scholar with a knowledge of Eastern Affairs should be hired to write a book on Egyptian mtters from the Turkish point of view. "Such a book", wrote Howard, "would be considered as an unprejudiced statement by the outside world & would be quickly translated into Turkish and other languages. Rantzau suggested that Vambery should be entrusted with this job. Dr. Singer objected to this as Vambery writes poor Hungarian" (a surprising comment) "and suggested my friend Dr. Leipnik who, however, refused. It was he who told me about it. What Rantzau's exact object is, I don't pretend to understand, nor do I know whether he was acting under instructions or on his own ..."

Concerning the "famous letters", Howard wrote that Vambery "now talks about giving up 72 only. This would mean that he would keep back 7, as there are 79 I believe in all.

"I forgot to say that he asked me particularly a fortnight ago whether I thought there was any danger of his pension being cut off by the British Gvmt. if he returned the letters. I assured him that such a thing was out of the question.

"But this confirms me in the belief that he holds onto them mainly as a security for the continuance of his pension".

Sir Edward Grey advised: "We should of course be the more bound in honour to continue the pension if he surrendered all the letters, but it is evident that we cannot press him more about the letters with dignity & without making him very suspicious".

A clerk at the Foreign Office misread Howard's letter and wrote his minutes on the back: "Anti-British Book on Egypt: German intrigue to obtain publication of Professor Vambery's correspondence".

On 19 January, Vambery handed over the package containing his confidential Foreign Office Letters to Esme Howard, just before the latter's departure for London, and then wrote a grateful letter of thanks to Sir Arthur Nicolson:

"As to the letters in question, I have them handed over to Mr. Esme Howard in a sealed letter, and pray, be so kind, to acknowledge their receipt. There were originally 77 in number and I retained only one (no. 63), which is of a private and confidential character ..." The identity of this letter was never revealed.

Esme Howard brought all the letters (except '63') back to London at the end of the month and personally delivered them to the Foreign Office. Sir Arthur Nicolson acknowledged their safe receipt on 2 February, and advised Vambery of the new easier procedure for future payments of his Annuity and Allowance.

The detailed eight-page Secret Memorandum entitled *"Payments to Professor A. Vambery from Secret Service Funds"*, dated 4 March 1911, completed the files of the many years service that Vambery had given to Britain.

In 1911 the future was looking very grim indeed, and Britain was making elaborate preparations for eventual war with Germany. Vambery had become very disheartened, and he made his feelings clear at this time in a letter to his old friend and publisher John Murray:

". . . I certainly would have long ago come to see old England, if the loss of my dear friend, the late King, would not have deprived me of the great attraction of my visit. And besides, I can not conceal from you the uneasiness I feel in viewing the sad change which has taken place in your country. The present party in power is ruining the prestige of England all over the world and the former pride of mankind has become the laughing stock of the nations. That is not *my England*, which I could revisit . . ."

With all the dissatisfaction and 'humiliation' he felt he had suffered, Vambery could at least rest appeased on one point: the money he had secretly received for his services from 'his England' over the previous twenty-one years totalled well over £5000!

Some years later, Stephen Gaselee, Librarian and Keeper of the Papers at the Foreign Office, was to sum up Vambery's activity in the following words:*

"Professor Vambery, of the University of Budapest, was one of the greatest Turkish scholars of the nineteenth century; a strong friend of this country, and a bitter enemy of Russia.

"He was a useful source of information, and had the ear of the Sultan. It was accordingly usual to pay the expenses of his journey to Constantinople, whence he sent back many reports on the Porte on political affairs.

"The various payments which he received were latterly converted into a regular allowance, paid quarterly; and at the end of his life arrangements were made by which he returned into For-

---

* 3 February 1921, on the flyleaf of Volume 1 of the *"(SECRET) Professor Vambery's letters"* files.

eign Office keeping the various letters which he had received from successive Permanent Under-Secretaries of State".

21

THE DRACULA CONNECTION

The question of how Bram Stoker was inspired to write *Dracula*, the greatest horror novel of all time, has been a subject of much conjecture in recent years. It has often been stated that Arminius Vambery played an important part in the character's creation.

Vambery first met Bram Stoker, with Henry Irving and other leading members of the Lyceum Company, in the regal surroundings of Sandringham when they were guests of the Prince of Wales in April 1889. (See Chapter 15) Both Stoker and Irving immediately recognised in Vambery a fascinating and unique character, and it was inevitable that, on his next visit to Britain, Vambery would be invited to meet them again at their renowned Beefsteak Room in London.

The Beefsteak Room was the pivot of Henry Irving's social life. It was a revival of the 'Sublime Society of Beef Steaks', originally founded by John Rich in 1735 at the Covent Garden Theatre, and not to be confused with the Beefsteak Club of Irving Street (Leicester Square). The room itself had formerly been one of the Lyceum's big lumber rooms. Irving had it beautifully redecorated, stocked it with a selection of fine wines, brandy and champagne, brought in his own chef, and entertained royalty and the leading personalities of Europe there.

Bram Stoker devoted a chapter to Vambery in his *Personal Reminiscences of Henry Irving* (1906), and related: "On April 30, 1890, he came to see the play, *The Dead Heart*, and remained to supper. He was most interesting, and Irving was delighted with him. He had been to Central Asia, following after centuries the track of Marco Polo and was full of experiences fascinating to hear . . ."

It is easy to imagine Vambery in full flow, regaling his new friends with stories of romance and horror from his homeland, and there is good reason to assume that it was he who told Stoker, for the first time, of the name of the historical 'Dracula': Vlad V, a 15th. century Prince of Wallachia.

In Vambery's youth Wallachia still lay under the influence of the Ottoman Empire, while neighbouring Transylvania was situated in the south-eastern corner of Hungary. During the first half of the nineteenth century, there had been an extraordinary number of reported vampire cases from this area, especially the central and northern regions of Transylvania. Vambery had heard about several of these and no doubt described some of them in detail in the course of his conversations with Bram Stoker. 'Dracula' was well-known in Budapest.

A very widespread belief in vampirism existed in Hungary throughout Vambery's own lifetime, even as late as 1912 when the *Daily Telegraph* (15 February) carried a report from Budapest of a boy of fourteen, dead only a few days, being stuffed with garlic and pierced through the heart.

Harry Ludlam, in his book *A Biography of Dracula* (1962), tells us how Stoker's ideas for his world-famous novel were formed — following Vambery's colourful tales — combined with a "too generous helping of dressed crab at supper one night" and a "dream of a vampire king rising from the tomb to go about his ghostly business'. The "dressed crab" story was one that Stoker persistently told, but few believed him. By 1890, the plot for his novel had already begun to take shape, so Vambery's arrival on the scene was opportune. It seems inevitable that Stoker would have had many pertinent questions to ask Vambery about his homeland.

Vambery may have led Stoker to Sebastian Munster's *Cosmographia*, a 16th. century 'best-seller', which appeared in London in two abridged editions. In the original Basel edition of this book, Munster related that while Mathias Corvinus (one of the greatest Hungarian kings) was making his country the dominant power in central Europe, there reigned in Wallachia "der streng ja tyrannisch man Dracula".

Stoker consulted the *Account of the Principalities of Wallachia and Moldavia* (1820) by the British consul at Bucharest, William Wilkinson, who stated: "*Dracula* in the Wallachian language means Devil. The Wallachinas were, at that time, as they are at present, used to give this (sic) as a surname to any person who rendered himself conspicuous either by courage, cruel actions, or cunning". In his researches into the history of Eastern Europe, Vambery must have known that Transylvanian vampire stories often associated the word 'Dracul' with acts of vampirism.

Wilkinson's book was, in turn, based on the mammoth opus, *The Generall Historie of the Turkes* (1603), by the Oxford scholar Richard Knolles. In this book, Knolles described three Draculas: "Dracula, of Valachia, a man of great experience in martiall affaires", and his sons "Wladus Dracula" and "Dracula, the younger brother of Wladus" — known today respectively as Vlad III ('Dracul'), Vlad V (the 'Impaler'), and Radu (the 'Handsome').

"Wladus Dracula" (Vlad V), noted for his ferocity in battle against the invading Turks, was nicknamed the 'Impaler' because of his delight in impaling his enemies — alive — on wooden stakes. The volume by Knolles, described the times graphically:

"The year fre following, which was the yeare 1462, (Sultan) *Mahomet* having intelligence, that *Wladus Dracula* prince of VALACHIA, his tributarie, was resolved to cast from him his obedience, and to joyne himselfe unto the Hungarians, his mortall enemies . . . As he (Mahomet) marched along the countrey, he came to the place where the Bassa and the Secretarie were hanging up two high gibbets, and the dismembered Turks empailed upon stakes about them: with which sight he was grievously offended. And passing on farhter, came to a plaine containing in breadth almost a mile, and in length two miles, set full gallowes, gibbets, wheels, stakes, and other instruments of terrour, death, and torture; . . . so that a man would have thought, that all the torments the Poets faigne to bee in hell had been there put in execution. All these were such as the notable, but cruell prince (*Wladus Dracula*), jealous of his estate, had either for just desert, or some probable suspition, put to death; and with their goods rewarded his sbuldiours: whose cruell manner was, togither with the offender to execute the whole family, yea sometimes the whole kindred . . ."

Sultan Mahomet returned to Constantinople ". . . and with him *Dracula*, the younger brother of Wladus . . . *Wladus* seeing himselfe forsaken of all his subjects, and his younger brother possessed of his dominion, fled into TRANSYLVANIA, where he was by the appointment of the Hungarian king (Mathias Corvinus) apprehended and laid fast in strait prison . . ."

These were the historical foundations which laid the basis for *Dracula*. For his accurate descriptions of the Wallachian and Transylvanian countryside (which he had never visited himself), Stoker relied on the anecdotes and recollections of Vambery as well as popular travelogues of the day by such ladies as Emily Gerard (author of *The Land Beyond the Forest*, 1888), and the anonymous 'Fellow of the Carpathian Society' (*Magyarland*, 2 vols., 1881).

At the same time as his meetings with Bram Stoker, Vambery was immersed in cataloguing many of the invaluable manuscripts from part of the famed Mathias Corvinus Library, which had survived at Constantinople. *The Times* of 1 October 1889 reported from Vienna: "The Hungarian commission, which has been sent to Constantinople with Professor Arminius Vambery to explore the archives in the Imperial Library, has already made the important discovery of three volumes which belonged to the library of King Mathias Corvinus. One of these is a book of history of which no other copy is known to exist". And more discoveries followed. Vambery researched the chronicles of Antonio Bonfini (or Bonafini, as Vambery called him), the humanist Italian-born historian at the court of King Mathias Corvinus. Bonfini may have known Dracula personally, and could therefore have recorded the numerous anecdotes about the 'Impaler' firsthand.

Vambery devoted a chapter to Mathias Corvinus in his popular history of *Hungary* (1887; in Unwin's Story of the Nations series), but did not mention Dracula. His colleague and fellow-researcher at Budapest and Constantinople, Dr. Fraknoi (see Chapter 17), was an acknowledged expert — and biographer — of the life and times of Mathias Corvinus, and the Draculas of Wallachia.

Ludlam states in his biography of Stoker (basing this information on the recollections of Noel, Bram Stoker's only son) that Stoker wrote to Vambery, requesting more details about the notorious 'Impaler' and the land he lived in. He realised that Transylvania, The Land Beyond the Forest, would be an ideal setting for a vampire story. Vambery would certainly have been familiar with Johann Christian von Engel's *History of Moldavia and Wallachia* (*Geschichte der Moldau und Walachey*, 1804) which contained reprints of the rare early Dracula pamphlets. One of these pamphlets, a German publication of 1491, had been purchased by the British Museum, enabling Stoker to study it firsthand. In his role of librarian, Vambery would have known the similar pamphlet in the Magyar Nemzeti Casino in Budapest. This pamphlet described the historical Dracula as a cruel tyrant and *Wuterich* (which meant 'blood-thirsty monster'). This could have been Stoker's cue for transforming the historical Dracula into a vampire.

When Stoker wrote *Dracula*, he acknowledged his debt to Vambery by references to "my friend Arminius", speaking through the lips of Dr. Van Helsing (the celebrated vampire-hunter of the novel):*

"Thus when we find the habitation of this man-that-was, we can confine him to his coffin and destroy him, if we obey what we know. But he is clever. I have asked my friend Arminius, of Buda-Pesth University, to make his record; and, from all the means that are, he tells me of what he has been. He must, indeed, have been that Voivode Dracula who won his name against the Turk, over the great river on the very frontier of Turkey-land. If it be so, then was he no common man; for in that time, and for centuries after, he was spoken of as the cleverest and the most cunning, as well as the bravest of the sons of the 'land beyond the forest'. That mighty brain and that iron resolution went with him to his grave, and are even now arrayed against us. The Draculas were, says Arminius, a great and noble race, though now and again were scions who were held by their coevals to have had dealings with the Evil One. They learned his secrets in the Scholomance, amongst the mountains over Lake Hermanstadt, where the devil claims the tenth scholar as his due. In the records are such words as 'stregoica' — witch, 'Ordog' and 'pokol' — Satan and hell; and in one manuscript this very Dracula is spoken of as 'wampyr', which we all understand too well ..."

This description, in a nutshell, conveys what information and conclusions Vambery passed on to Bram Stoker. Regrettably a large amount of Stoker's papers vanished after his death in various directions, some being lost during the First World War. And Vambery's correspondence to Stoker cannot now be traced. Not until Harry Ludlam's *A Biography of Dracula* appeared was Bram Stoker's debt to Vambery acknowledged.

Among the later meetings between Vambery and Bram Stoker was one at the Tercentenary Celebrations of Dublin University in 1892. Both Vambery and Henry Irving were invited to receive the Honorary Degree of Doctor of Letters. Bram was there too, with his eminent brother, Dr. Thornley Stoker. As usual, Vambery delivered a speech to the distinguished assembly, glowing with generous admiration of the British people and their empire.

---

* *Dracula*. Constable, 1897 (1st edn., page 246.)

The official report described the scene vividly, as "the audience sprang to their feet as one man and cheered vociferously, carried away as they were by the force and vehemence of the orator". Afterwards, Vambery called himself, not untypically (in a letter to the Foreign Office) "a sensation"! In his tribute, Bram Stoker wrote ". . . he shone out as a star. He soared above all the speakers, making one of the finest speeches I have ever heard. Be sure that he spoke loudly against Russian aggression — a subject to which he had largely devoted himself".

An unusual twist to the links between Arminius Vambery and the lore of vampirism came in 1956, with the publication of a curious book entitled *Cavalcade of Ghosts*, six years before Ludlam's *A Biography of Dracula* appeared.

Cavalcade of Ghosts, edited by R. Thurston Hopkins, is a rather bizarre and fanciful collection of true and fictitious ghost stories. The last tale in the 'fictitious' section is called 'The Riddle of the Thetford Vampire', by a 'Michael Saltmarsh' (probably a pseudonym for Hopkins), and concerns the activities, in the Norfolk town of Thetford, of a young female refugee from Budapest. She appears to be about thirty years old, has 'flame-red hair', intense red-black eyes, and large pointed canine teeth. Her arrival coincides with a plague of bats in the town. It later transpires that she has an infamous past, is at least one hundred years old, and is — naturally — a rapacious vampire!

And the name of this delightful creature?

Naomi Vambery! — "The daughter of Arminius Vambery, Professor Oriental Languages at Pest University"!

22

JOURNEY'S END

What had happened to the pleasant young man who years before had charmed everyone he met and so delighted London society with all his tales from the Orient that he had been nicknamed 'the male *Scheherazade*'? Vambery had turned into a bitter and irascible old man. Instead of giving him serenity the advancing years had made him cantankerous and resentful, inclined to harbour a grudge for years and with the proverbial long memory of an elephant never to forget a slight, real or imaginary.

During his long career, not a whiff of scandal ever surrounded Vambery's name. If he had any extra-marital affairs, they certainly never became known. In so small a city as Budapest, and given his boastfulness and lack of discretion, it is hardly likely that any *liaison* would have remained unknown — had there ever been one.

Vambery seems to have regarded his wife Cornelia as a mere appendage — a typical *Hausfrau* of the time. Whereas he wrote endlessly about the Shah of Persia and the Sultan of Turkey, he scarcely ever referred to her in print. Even his autobiography *The Story of My Struggles* dismisses her curtly with one line, a point criticised in a review of the book by the *Athenaeum*. A visitor to the Vambery household remembers her as a modest and retiring figure, often seated in a large armchair in the dimly-lit hall — the naked bulb bereft of a lampshade owing to Vambery's extreme parsimoniousness.

From the 1880s onwards, Cornelia Vambery suffered from failing health, and frequent visits to spas were necessary. From Vambery's personal correspondence, it appears he was more concerned with the effects of his wife's illness on his home comforts than on the patient herself. As early as 1882 he wrote to Wil-

liam White (later Ambassador to Turkey):* " . . . A misfortune
has befallen me in my family, namely the serious illness of my
wife, whom I am doomed to see to fade away in a lingering death,
for she has got an incurable disease where medical skill is of no
avail. It is a great calamity but I must submit to the trial of fate!"
Reading this dramatic pronouncement, it comes as a surprise to
learn that Cornelia was still alive over thirty years later, and that
she even survived her husband. (She was not mentioned in any of
Vambery's obituaries). The "incurable disease" was never described.

Cornelia Vambery's uncle was Joseph Joachim, the most celebrated violinist of the nineteenth century. He tutored his two
young great-nieces, and they also became world-renowned violin-
ists in their own right: Jelly d'Aranyi and Adila Fachiri. When
Jelly came to London in 1909 at the age of thirteen, Vambery
supplied her with an introduction to Buckingham Palace, so she
could perform before King Edward and Queen Alexandra.

Vambery must have been elated when (in 1891) one of his
wife's first cousins, Gertrude Cornelia Joachim, married into the
highest ranks of British aristocracy. Gertrude wed Rollo Russell,
son of Lord John Russell — Prime Minister 1846-52 and 1865-6 —
and the same British Foreign Secretary to whom Charles Alison
wrote back in 1864 about Vambery on his arrival from Central
Asia. Little could Vambery have thought, on that distant occasion
(see Chapter 9), that one day he — "the obscure limping Jew" —
would be connected to Lord Russell by marriage . . .

By all accounts Vambery was, at home, a domineering and
autocratic husband and father, seeking to impose his will by force
and never seeing any standpoint but his own. Always the stern dis-
ciplinarian, his petty tyrannies would even extend into the nursery, where he would force his young son Rustem to eat food
which revolted him and made him vomit. As Rustem grew up, his
father tried to persuade him to follow in his own footsteps and
become an Orientalist. To this end, Rustem was compelled to suffer a series of five examinations, but failed all of them. He had
other inclinations, and there was little love lost between father
and son. Even on their summer holidays at Muhlbach, Vambery
would ask his secretary Vilmos Vazsonyi (later an important political figure) to try and make the young man change his mind. Small

---

* Letter in the possession of Richard Dalby.

Vambery in 1909. Photo E.O. Hoppe © Mansell Collection

wonder that Rustem usually locked the door of his room and refused to let his father in. Rustem set his heart on a career in law, and when he took these new examinations he sailed through them with flying colours. He had a thorough education at three universities: Budapest, Halle (Germany), and Geneva, where he became a LL.D. He eventually began his illustrious career as a barrister in 1897, at the age of twenty-five.

Vambery even tried to dictate his son's choice of bride. One day he spotted a particularly beautiful girl on the Korzo, the fashionable promenade in Budapest, and immediately decided she would be eminently suitable; he thought she looked as if she would bear him many healthy grandchildren. In fact the choice was well made, as Rustem fell in love with the girl, Olga Vamossy, and the couple became engaged. But then Vambery changed his mind, and turned against the marriage. He refused to listen to his son's pleadings. Rustem insisted his happiness depended on this marriage. "Bah! Happiness, happiness", growled Vambery *pere*; "what is happiness but a state of mind . . ." He did not come to the wedding which took place on 9 May 1899.

Vambery adamantly refused to help his son financially in any way. A bad situation got worse as for several years there were no grandchildren. Cornelia could only visit Olga and Rustem in secret, while old Vambery was out of town.

It is easy to imagine Vambery's thoughts as he stayed with King Edward at Windsor Castle in 1904. The four young sons of Prince George were playing happily with the King, their grandfather. One of the boys hung around his neck, another sat on his knee. "I suppose you don't have any grandchildren yet", the King asked. "No, Your Majesty", Vambery replied, gritting his teeth.

Was it overweening ambition to have the future King George and Queen Mary as his yet unborn grandchild's godparents or a wish to show off his potency at an advanced age that prompted an earthy remark on his return to Budapest?:

But soon a grandson was born; Vambery gave Olga a diamond ring and wrote to the Prince of Wales:

It is no exaggeration when I say that the only worthy reward I have found for all my sufferings was the Royal favour bestowed upon me by His Majesty, your Royal Father, and by Yourself, when yet in tender age. Now it is very natural that I cling with grateful attachment to your noble and glorious

Family and that in my desire to crown the efforts in my private life, I turn to my kindhearted benefactors.

Last week I was so happy to be favoured by destiny with my first grandchild, the offspring of my only son, whom I have brought up in an English way, and who is likewise professor of our University. Anxious to keep up my relation of devotion and gratitude in my family I beg leave from Your Royal Highness to give me the permission to name my grandchild *George* and to inscribe in the parish-register your Royal Highness as the God-father of the infant.

No other object in view leads me in this humble request of mine. My son and his wife are both members of the Protestant-Christian Church, and they will be exceedingly thankful for the Royal favour bestowed upon them. Thanking beforehand, I beg to remain Your Royal Highness' obedient servant

A. Vambery."*

There was a certain amount of humbug in this last paragraph. Vambery omitted to describe his own religious beliefs in the letter — in his autobiography published the previous year he had declared his position as a convinced free-thinker. Prince George speedily replied in the affirmative, and Vambery wrote again to Prince George in his customary style:

"Budapest University,
March 13th 1905

Your Royal Highness,

When the joyous news contained in your gracious letter arrived I had the intention of bringing about at once the christening of my grandchild and to send the certificate of baptism to your Royal Highness. This having been impossible I can not delay any longer expressing to your Royal Highness my most obedient and heartfelt thanks for the great and extraordinary Royal favour shown to me, by which my humble family has been raised to the highest rank of honour and distinction attainable by a man of such poor antecedents and hard struggles as my life was connected with.

I need hardly say that your Royal Highness' letter was a great festivity in my family, a gratification to all my friends and a surprise to the whole country, nay to the world beyond the limits of Austria-Hungary." Unable to resist a dig at the

* Royal Archives, W77/88.

Hungarian aristocrats he continued: "Your example teaches a sound and a wholesome lesson to a certain class, who like to surround themselves with the thick wall of medieval prejudice and superstition and who can not understand why the Royal Family of England is so much venerated and adored by the people of England. Well, Your Royal Highness and Your August Father fully understand the sign of time," (sic) "you will always reap the benefits of your magnanimity and wisdom and I am sure the sun of Your Glory and Happiness will never cease to shine.

God bless You and please to accept the reiterated thanks of Your grateful and obedient servant
A. Vambery."
(Royal Archives, W77/91)

Evidently Rustem and Olga had no choice over the name for their first baby. Vambery was omnipotent in the family circle. More disagreement followed the arrival of the second grandson on 9 December 1907. Rustem wanted his own name, whereas his father insisted the infant must be christened Armin. In the end his names were entered into the baptismal register: Armin Rusztem Robert Ervin Pal. (But in later years, both Armin and Ruszten were dropped, as the grandson himself preferred Robert!) At home the elder grandson George was called Bozsi' — because a Slovak nursery maid had called him 'Boze moj' ('my god'); Bozsi was a corruption, but it stuck. The younger grandson was nick-named 'Lolo', a name given to him by his mother when he was very young because she was hoping to have a girl.

Vambery mellowed towards Rustem and Olga after the grandsons were born. He encouraged them to come regularly to supper — provided they brought all their food and drinks with them. Later on the whole family had Sunday lunch together. Robert Vambery today clearly remembers these weekly visits: "As long as he lived, we went every Sunday to his house and had *ebed* (midday meal) there. This was interesting because there were always toys that were different from those we had at home. There was also a plate with *krajcars* (pennies). We could take one each." On Vambery's wealth: "He had many ornate gold cigarette cases decorated with precious stones, gifts from the rich and powerful. Before the first world war they were all sold by weight of gold. The proceeds were invested (like the rest of his money) in "Zalog-

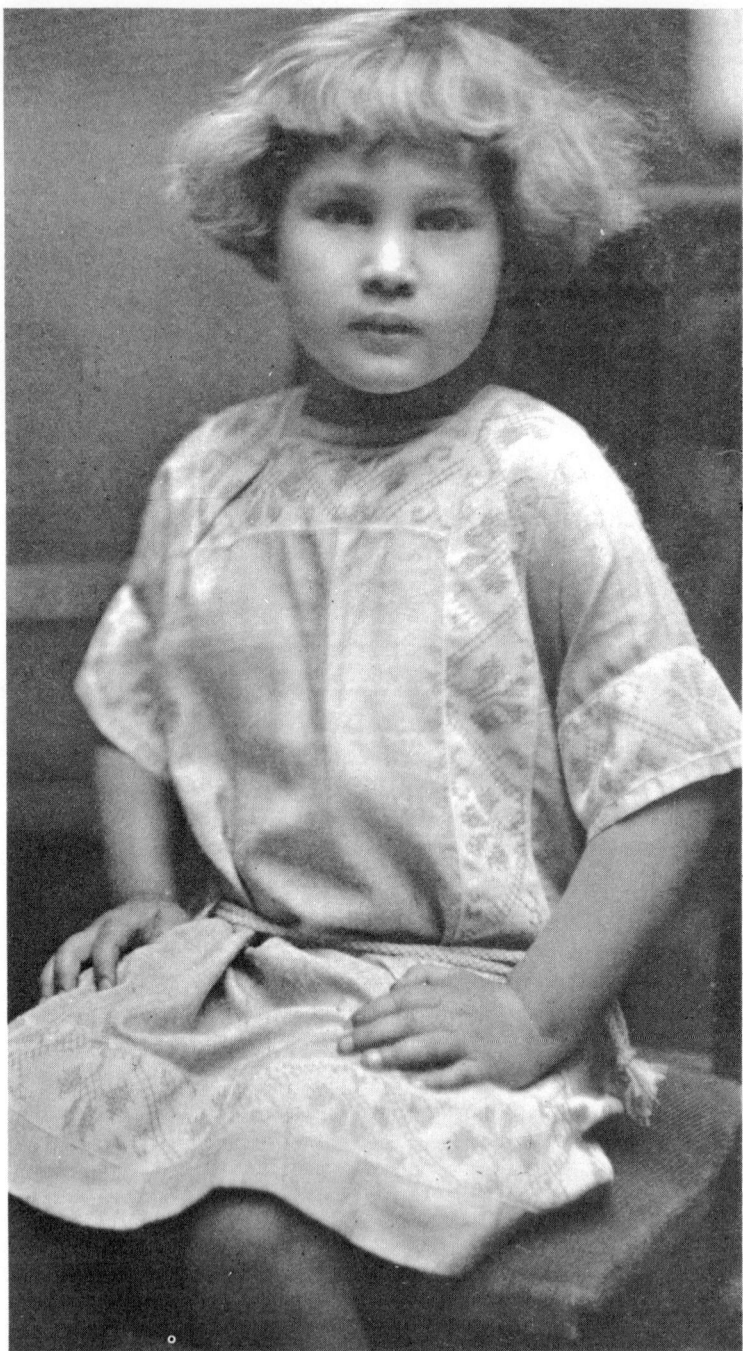

George Vambery aged 4 in 1909. Photo E.O. Hoppe. © *Mansell Collection.*

levelek" (mortgages on land — "Land is safest" he said). After the war they were paid off in practically worthless inflated money."

For many years Vambery had lived at a flat (33 Ferenc Jozsef Rakpart) on the Danube embankment on the Pest side between Erzsebet Hid (Bridge) and Ferenc Jozsef Hid (now Szabadsag Hid/Freedom Bridge). The view from his windows was superb — a view which has remained virtually unchanged to this day. He could see across the Danube to the Gellert hegy (hill) and fume at the Citadel in the east built by the Austrians to incarcerate rebellious Hungarians. (Today the Liberation Monument stands in front.) To the west he could see the Royal Palace and below it the Matthias Church. Whenever he took a few minutes relaxation, he could watch the steamers, on their way upstream to Vienna and beyond, and downstream to the Black Sea and Constantinople ... He liked to compare the view to this city, to the Pera Bridge and to the Golden Horn.

But this flat was not entirely to Vambery's liking; it lacked some modern amenities, and the toilet was on a chilly outside landing. It is said that Lord Curzon, on one of his visits to Budapest, came to call on Vambery at his flat. He found him in bed, suffering from a chill caught getting up during the night ... As a true Victorian at heart, obliged to hide even a piano leg in frills, Vambery was very embarrassed. How could he explain his predicament to his illustrious guest? Finally, however, he blurted out the truth. The story goes, that Lord Curzon, returning to England, reported this incident on a visit to Queen Victoria.

"What! A friend of mine living in such miserable conditions!" exclaimed her Majesty. "I cannot permit this — he must move at once!" And promptly some cash was despatched to Budapest. (The accounts vary from £250 to £400.) A stunned Vambery is reported to have said: "A flat at this price? Why, I could not find one in the whole of Budapest if I tried?" On the other hand, Vambery may well have invented this story, both to boost his ego in front of his friends and enemies, and to conceal the fact that he was receiving secret payments from the Foreign Office. It was bound to leak out from time to time that he was receiving generous amounts of money from England, and he had to embroider a lot of fiction in his replies to curious enquiries.

Eventually, Vambery did find a larger, more comfortable flat, only a few doors down the street: 19 Ferenc Jozsef Rakpart (now: Belgrad Rakpart 24). It was situated on the first floor, had a lift, and was in a brand new house. He was delighted with it — there were five rooms and a large bathroom (in which he is reported to have kept the overflow of Turkish papers and magazines). The move, which coincided with his retirement from the University, was complicated by the fact that he insisted on carrying many of the possessions himself. "I believe there is no man as strong as myself", he boasted. Vambery certainly remained an extremely robust figure, well into his seventies.

Several members of staff from the Academy Library were detailed to help with the move, and he was also assisted by a favourite student* who had become a friend (and whom he used to greet with a cordial *"Szervus, ocem!"* — "Hi there, younger brother!") Vambery clung ferociously to his large portfolio — containing his valuable shares, and also no doubt his secret correspondence from the Foreign Office.

Vambery spent his remaining years at this flat (with summer holidays taken as usual in Austria). In later years the house became the German legation; and today is occupied by the Hungarian Association of the United Nations. The following plaque is on the wall:

"E Hazban Elt	("In this house lived
Vambery Armin	Arminius Vambery
1832-1913	1832-1913
Vilaghiru orientalista,	World-famous Orientalist,
Kozep-azsia utazo,	Explorer of Central Asia,
A torok filologia	Outstanding scholar of
Kivalo szaktekintelye	Turkish philology,
A Magyar Tudomanyos	Member of the Hungarian
Akademia Tagja.	Academy of Science.
Budapest fovaros tanacsa	Budapest City Council
1974"	1974"

Vambery's ghost would be pleased to see it there.

Vambery's retirement coincided with the completion of his last major book, *Western Culture in Eastern Lands*. However he continued to write many articles on a wide variety of subjects, ranging from Ibn Saud's Revolt in Arabia, and Japan & the Mahometan World, to the Approach between Moslems and

E HÁZBAN ÉLT

VÁMBÉRY ÁRMIN

1832 — 1913

VILÁGHÍRÜ ORIENTALISTA,
KÖZÉP-ÁZSIAI UTAZÓ,
A TÖRÖK FILOLÓGIA
KIVÁLÓ SZAKTEKINTÉLYE,
A MAGYAR TUDOMÁNYOS
AKADÉMIA TAGJA

BUDAPEST FŐVÁROS TANÁCSA
1974.

Buddhists, and one of his favourite subjects: "When Will Turkey Cease to Exist?" Most of the learned journals and magazines in England printed his articles.

Writing predominantly in Hungarian in his early days, he now wrote mostly in German and English. It is said that even in old age he used to dictate *extempore* to a busy secretary (in the past, he had sometimes used three secretaries at one time), and often wrote and worked from memory, even in his scientific studies. But he could be a stern self-critic, by no means blind to the "blunders and defects under which so many of my literary productions laboured because of my mode of working".

His English prose usually had to be heavily edited, even though he claimed he could write it quite effortlessly. But, with some degree of insight, he felt he could not pass for a native in England — although he said he could do so in Germany, Hungary, Turkey, and Persia. Lacking the right opportunity for practice in Budapest, his recipe for keeping up a degree of fluency in various tongues was to read for half an hour or more in one particular language, ". . . and when I had thus learned to think fluently in English, German or Turkish, I also managed to obtain a certain fluency in writing." He denied that he ever had only one mother-tongue.

Vambery was a believer in the maxim: "Early to bed, early to rise, makes one healthy, wealthy and wise." He usually arose at 5.30 a.m., ate a small frugal breakfast, and concentrated on his scientific work up to 10 a.m. He would then switch to his literary and political writings which took him up to lunchtime. He would then take a break and stretch his legs, going out for a stroll — always wearing his bowler (he hated top hats) which must have given him a certain outlandish air in Budapest.

His last surviving student, Professor Gyula Germanus, remembers Vambery's daily constitutionals clearly: "Before noon he used to take a short walk on the embankment of the Danube and while trotting along, with a closed umbrella in his right hand, he usually accosted the workmen lingering on the pavement and telling them of the 'incredibly fantastic' stories of his life — dining with Queen Victoria in London, or forcing the abdication of Mr. Gladstone by his impassionate speech: 'You have squandered British money, you have squandered British blood!' The lounging tramps on the embankment stealthily but sincerely giggled over these *incredible*, but literally *true* stories, but then reverentially touched their caps as a recognition for the supposed 'fairy-tales'."

After an afternoon nap, he would appear as regular as clock-work, at 5 p.m., at the Nemzeti Casino, where he worked as a paid, part-time librarian. At home, a cook and a maid kept affairs in order.

Stories about Vambery circulated in all corners of the Moslem World. Even in a remote backwater in the Atlas Mountains of Morocco, the traveller R.B. Cunninghame Graham found himself talking one night to a Persian who was enthusing about the great 'Bamborah'. This Persian, related Graham*, had known (in Budapest) "one Bamborah, who by interior evidence and after cogitation I found to be Professor Vambery. Large hearted was this Bamborah, and speaking Persian, a Christian dervish, know-ing all the East, having read all books, explored all countries, mas-tered all sciences and learning; the friend of kings, for had not the Sultan Abdul Hamid (whom may God preserve) sent him a ring of 'diamont' worth a thousand pounds, and Bamborah had shown it whilst they sat discoursing in his hospitable house.

"In fact of all the men, Christian or Moslem, he (the Persian) had ever met, this Bamborah appeared to him the fittest to stand before a king . . ."

A revered Moslem saint and Turkish dervish, Gul Baba ('Rose Father'), had been buried in Budapest in 1541 at the time of the Turkish occupation, and pilgrims came from far and wide to visit the grave: Turks, Arabs, Persians, Afghans, Indians, Kashmirians, even Tartars from Tobolsk. Many of them came to see Vambery, of whome they had heard so much in the East. "Nothing could be more entertaining than to watch the suspicious glances cast upon me by these tattered, emaciated Moslems", wrote Vambery. "My fluency of speech in their several languages, added to the fame of my character as a Dervish, puzzled them greatly, and, encouraged by my cordiality, some made bold to ask me how much longer I intended to keep up my incognito among the unfaithful, and whether it would not be advisable for me to return to the land of the true believers." Vambery enjoyed these meet-ings much more than those with most of his own countrymen, and his customary parsimoniousness was less in evidence.

Even Hadji Bilal, his best friend on his Central Asian travels, who visited Mecca and Medina again in the 1870s, remained comp-letely firm in his belief of Vambery's Moslem identity. "He even asserted that if I had adopted an incognito at all, it was decidedly rather in Europe than in Asia, and that my *Christianity* was apocryphal", wrote Vambery triumphantly.

He had a point there for the fact that Vambery could never furnish the Foreign Office with a Certificate of Baptism is certainly proof that none had ever taken place.

A stream of acquaintances also came to visit him from Britain, to talk over old times. The journalist C. Townley Fullam came to admire Vambery as "he sat in his library, a beautiful, spacious room, overlooking the finest view upon this planet. Beneath rolled the majestic Danube . . ."

Another guest was Captain B. Granville Baker, author of *The Walls of Constantinople*. He visited Vambery several times, and in his book *The Danube with Pen and Pencil* (1911) he eulogised:

"The ancient University sheds the light of learning on a quick-witted people, and of those who keep this lamp alight and burning is one whose name should be dear to every Briton. A man who loves Old England as intensely as he loves his own fair country: Professor Vambery. Here in Pesth he lives in hale and active old age, and welcomes travelling Britons, giving them freely of the treasures of his well-stored mind. May you live long and happy years, you friend of Britons!"

Other visitors included the celebrated artist Adrian Stokes who wrote a large book on Hungary (1909), and similarly praised Vambery; and the photographer E.O. Hoppe who took a series of family portraits of the Vambery household.

The ex-dervish by this time had gained entry to every encyclopaedia of the day, even to the *King's English Dictionary* (an honour denied to the King, Edward VII, himself)! Letters poured in from all over the globe: from Turkey, India, China, Japan, America, and Australia. One day it would be a leading Japanese politician urging him to have another dig at Russia, another it would be a malcontent Hindustani blaming him for taking the 'British tyrant' under his wing, or some other Hindustani praising him for duly acknowledging the 'spirit of liberty and justice' which animated the Raj of India.

"So it goes on day after day", he wrote; "but worst of all the poor international writer fares at the hands of the Americans. The number of autograph collectors is astonishing, and many are kind enough to enclose an American stamp or a few cents for the reply postage. And then the questions I am asked! Could I inform them of the hour of my birth, in order to account for my adventurous career? And I do not even know what year I was born! An American surgeon asks me to send him a photograph of my tongue, that from its formation he may drew his conclusions as to my linguistic talent, and so on, and so on . . .''

But generally speaking, Vambery said he had survived his many vicissitudes successfully, and now had a happy outlook on life. "I never did care for a quiet, peaceful existence," he wrote, contradicting earlier statements; "and I am glad to have gained the two most precious jewels of human life — experience and independence — two treasures inseparately connected, and forming the true nucleus of human happiness . . . It has been my good fortune to contribute my mite to the enlightenment and improvement of my fellow-creatures; and when I made the joyful discovery that my books were being read all over Europe, America, and Australia, the consciousness of not having lived in vain filled me with a great happiness. I thought to myself, the father professor of the gymnasium at St. Georghen was wrong after all when he said, 'Moshele, why dost thou study? It would be better for thee to be a kosher butcher!' But more precious than all these good things is my dearly-bought experience."

Many honours and medals were given to Vambery in his later years. Besides his 1902 honour (Commander of the Victorian Order) from King Edward, Vambery was a Knight of the Imperial Leopold Order; an Officer of the Italian St. Maurice and Lazare and Crown Order; a member of the Grand Cordon of Medjidie; of Notre Dame de Guadelupe; of Sir u Khursid (Persia); and holder of the Grand Gold Medal from his own Emperor, Franz Josef. In December 1906, the Emperor of Japan conferred upon Vambery the Order of the Sacred Treasure "in recognition of the services he rendered to Japan during the late war" (Russo-Japanese War). The most striking of all the decorations was this one from Japan: it was in the shape of a beautiful enamelled sun, and was preserved in a hexagonal lacquer box. There were also decorations from Mexico and Brazil.

In 1907 Vambery was gratified to be made an Honorary Fellow of the Royal Society of Literature in London.

On 10 October 1910, the Hungarian Academy of Sciences celebrated the 50th anniversary of Vambery's membership, and presented him with a jubilee diploma in honour of the occasion. *The Times* reported: "In the course of the day Professor Vambery received congratulatory visits from a large number of Hungarian scientists and public men, as well as telegrams of congratulation from learned bodies and friends in England and America. A subscription has been opened for the purpose of founding a Vambery Scholarship in Philology."

Another anniversary followed on 19 March 1912 when Vambery celebrated his 80th 'official' birthday — and *The Times* published a special article on him on this date. Again ministers, scholars, writers, came to visit him, and the flat was filled to capacity. His favourite student remembers Vambery being extremely stingy with the Cognac and telling the servant: "Go easy there, the guests don't need so much, a little will do . . ."

Vambery was friendly with many of the younger politicians who would play a very important part in the critical years of Hungary's post-war future. Among these were Oszkar Jaszi and Vilmos Vazsonyi. When Jaszi told Vambery that he wanted to found a progressive political party in Hungary, the old man replied "You will have better prospects of success if you open a pork-butcher shop in Mecca." Later on Jaszi became president of 'Orszagos Polgari Radikalis Part', the Bourgeois-Radical party, the members of which were mainly Jewish intellectuals. (Exiled in 1919, he became Professor of Political Science at Oberlin College, Ohio.)

Vilmos Vazsonyi, secretary and friend of Vambery in the 1890s, was an ambitious lawyer who established the National Democratic Party, and asked Vambery to be the honorary president. Vazsonyi later became (in 1917) the only Jewish Minister of Justice in the Austro-Hungarian Empire, and was in fact the strongest member of the Esterhazy Government, where he represented the Socialist Party. Both Jaszi and Vazsonyi deplored the policies of the ruling Prime Minister, Count Istvan (Stephen) Tisza, who represented the aristocracy Vambery always fought against.

In his old age Vambery became interested in Bahaism. (Members of this faith look forward to the religious and political unity of all mankind.) The chief missionary at the time was Abdul-Baha, son of Baha-Ullah founder of the faith. A patriarchal, white-bearded figure, he was a well-known celebrity in Europe, and the United States, in the years before the first World War.

In April 1913, Abdul-Baha visited Budapest and the Hungarian Peace Society, of which Vambery was vice-president. After their

Family group. Vambery, his wife, his son, and Vilmos Vazsonyi.

meeting, Abdul-Baha sent him a valuable rug. In return Vambery wrote a letter of fulsome praise which outshone Oriental hyperbole: "I forward this humble petititon to the sanctified and holy presence of Abdul-Baha Abbas, who is the centre of knowledge, famous throughout the world, and loved by all mankind. O thou noble friend who art conferring guidance upon humanity — May my life be a ransom to thee!" Leaving aside the question that he may have wished to remain on the right side of this giver of rugs, the religious sentiments he expressed may have been — in part — genuine.

"This servant," Vambery continued, not quite truthfully, "in order to gain first-hand information and experience, entered into the ranks of various religions, that is, outwardly, I became a Jew, Christian, Mohammedan and Zoroastrian. I discovered that the devotees of these various religions do nothing else but hate and anathematize each other, that all their religions have become the instruments of tyranny and oppression in the hands of rulers and governors, and that they are the causes of the destruction of the world of humanity.

"Considering those evil results, every person is forced by necessity to enlist himself on the side of your Excellency, and accept with joy the prospect of a fundamental basis for a universal religion of God, being laid through your efforts.'"* He ended the letter expressing his admiration and his "utmost respect and devotion" to this new religion.

What had happened to the free-thinker?

Yet, as is often the case, when a man feels near to death, he seems to have reverted to the faith of his youth, for a friend calling unannounced on a high Jewish holiday, found Vambery wrapped in his prayer shawl, the ritual phylacteries on his forehead and an open prayer-book on his knee . . .

Vambery passed his last summer (1913) in excellent health in the neighbourhood of Vienna, but early in September symptoms of arteriosclerosis were observed. On 13 September Vambery sent a note to Rustem; perhaps he realised the end was in sight:

"My dear son! I am feeling very ill. Again I suffered the whole night and did not close an eye. Yesterday I took two powders, I was more or less alright during the day, but so much more terrible was the night. I am near to Despair. Tell the doctor this.

13/IX   Your unhappy father."

Nevertheless on the last day of his life (September 14 1913) he was well enough to dictate to his son several letters to friends in England. His death took place at home in Budapest very peacefully during the course of the night while asleep.

It was fitting that his last letter to *The Times*, on the subject of the Mohammedan Indians' attitude to British policies, appeared on the same morning he died, 15 September.

A profusion of wreaths and telegrams poured into Budapest, from the most famous monarch in the West to the most obscure maharajah in the East. A wreath from an Indian friend, Sirdar Umrad Singh, bore the inscription "Esten from India". King George V sent the following telegram to Rustem:

> "The Queen and myself deeply regret to learn the death of your distinguished father, Professor Arminius Vambery, and beg to offer you our heartfelt sympathy in your loss. George R et I."

Vambery had always believed that the idiom 'A prophet is not honoured in his own country' fitted him like a glove, so his ghost would not have been surprised to learn that the Hungarian Government, headed by Count Tisza, failed in their official duty to convey the sorrow of the nation to Vambery's widow and son. The Archduke Joseph, as personal representative of the aged Emperor Franz Josef, sent his own telegram promptly, but no message or announcement came from Count Tisza, as the Hungarian press (*Pesti Hirlap*, 19 September) noted in scathing tones.

Hungary in 1913 was still (to all intents and purposes) a feudal state; and Count Tisza represented — in Vambery's eyes — the ruling class which had cold-shouldered him for as long as he could remember. Not long before the old man's death, Tisza had conceived the idea of making Vambery a Privy Councillor. "I want no decorations", Vambery told Tisza, remembering all the humiliations he had suffered in his native land. (Foreign decorations were in quite another category.) "A sensible man whistles at rank, titles and such flourishes. In Hungary men 'break themselves' after decorations and pity enough it is that statesmen lead the way." Tisza took this as a personal affront, was deeply insulted and never forgave it to the day of Vambery's death — nor after. But Vambery did achieve an indirect revenge after his death. Several of his friends and students, including Jaszi and Vazsonyi, contributed largely to Tisza's downfall, and he was murdered soon after.

Apart from this unsavoury touch, there was a welcome surprise from an unexpected quarter at Vambery's funeral. As the coffin was lowered into the grave a lady stepped forward from among the mourners and laid a wreath of forget-me-nots and blue flowers on the coffin. This (it transpired) was the last greeting of the ancient Honved general Arthur Gorgey. Sixty-five years earlier (in 1848, while Vambery was still a youth), Gorgey had become a hero — albeit temporarily — when he commanded the forces in the War of Independence and cleared Hungary of the Austrians. His meteoric career came to a swift end when the Russian army came to the help of the Austrians, and he was compelled to surrender. When Gorgey (at his villa in Visegrad, near Budapest) heard of Vambery's death, he asked his daughter Lenke Navay to make a wreath out of the flowers in his garden and then to place it in Vambery's grave. This tribute from the old general, who was a living legend, caused something of a sensation.

Vambery was buried in the Kerepesi Cemetery at Budapest. He had rejected all idea of a public staged funeral, and the ceremony was an extremely simple one. Only the members of the family and a few close friends took part.

In England, both *The Story of My Struggles* and *The Life and Adventures* were hurriedly reprinted in new editions to meet the large demand. Innumerable tributes and obituaries appeared in many countries. Even the *Athenaeum*, often a thorn in Vambery's side, extolled his linguistic prowess and recalled the nickname he had been given decades before in Constantinople: "The Human Tower of Babel."

Vambery's obituaries, whether in the London *Times*, the *Neue Freie Presse* of Vienna or the *Pester Lloyd* of Budapest, all had one thing in common: they stressed his link with the British Royal family.

The *Times* of 17 September 1913 recalled the salient points in his career, several anecdotes concerning him, his awards and 80th birthday celebrations and mentioned Vambery's "political labours and philological researches (which) had received recognition from learned bodies in England, on the Continent and in India". With considerable insight the paper added: "Yet deeply as these tokens of esteem may have gratified him, his supreme satisfaction was always derived from the contemplation of the milestones on the road towards renown trodden by 'a little Jew boy' . . ."

In sharp contrast the *Neue Freie Presse*, the Viennese equivalent of *The Times* did not bother to report Vambery's death until 18 September, saying casually: "As is generally known, the orientalist Arminius Vambery who died the day before yesterday achieved special fame in England as a daring explorer and clever politician, and after his first lecture at the Royal Geographical Society in London . . . became the man of the day", but it did not mention his scientific work or any of his numerous publications (many of which were in German). Had Vambery not achieved fame and appreciation abroad one wonders whether his death would have been mentioned at all.

It was left to the *Royal Geographical Journal* in London to point out this value as a scientist, recalling that "for an earlier generation the name of Vambery (was) a house-hold word in connection with Asian matters" and to the "honorific donation" of £40 the Society had awarded him in 1865 "as a token of the high estimation in which we hold your adventurous journey into Asia".

Even this scientific Journal, stressed Vambery's anglophile attitude in political matters and the "warm appreciation" Vambery had met with from the English Royal family.

A day after Vambery's death the *Pester Lloyd* published two lengthy articles about him. In one the paper wrote: "Vambery was famous and honoured abroad. After his return from Central Asia he rose to fame in England but it took a long time for his fame abroad to reach his native country . . ."

In substance the article asked: "Did Vambery die too early or too late?" recalling his political prophecies and wondering whether they would prove correct. Some of them concerned Turkey and Vambery had been badly disappointed by the results of the revolution led by the Young Turks; in Asia the major showdown predicted between Britain and Russia had not yet taken place and the article ended with the words: "Perhaps Vambery died too soon after all".

An inside page article entitled "From Vambery's Life" praised him to the skies. He had preferred his homeland to Royal residences abroad; he had led a retired life, "hardly noticed by anyone; his habits had been spartan: rising at 5 am, washing himself from head to foot with the window wide open and breakfasting on tea or chocolate; his one major meal in the day was lunch, with tea as a nightcap before retiring."

No obituary of Vambery would have been complete without a reference to the fact that he had been a "welcome guest both of Queen Victoria and Abdul Hamid's".

The paper claimed that Vambery knew not only a vast number of languages but dialects as well — "at least twenty French and as many Turkish dialects" — and had on one occasion astounded his audience at a Congress in Geneva by opening it in the local patois.

It was full of praise for Vambery as a teacher, describing him as friendly, filled with benevolence towards his students, helping them where he could and doing his utmost to get them grants enabling them to go on study tours. Despite his detractors, some of his students did in fact achieve considerable fame as Orientalists in their own right.

It did not omit the several anecdotes circulating about Vambery — especially the one involving Edward VII — for Vambery had become a legend even in his life-time.

The paper informed its readers that Vambery's house had become the focal point for foreign travellers, whether from the East or West; his visitors included many famous explorers, among them Fritjof Nansen and Sven Hedin.

The paper also pointed out that King George V and the Turkish Government had been informed by telegram of Vambery's death; the Hungarian Geographical Society, of which Vambery was the founder and President of Honour had issued a special announcement and had a wreath laid on his coffin; a special meeting had been called to honour his memory. One of those, expressing their sympathy to the bereaved family, was Count Paul Teleki, its general secretary — one notable exception in Vambery's diatribes against the hereditary aristocracy. (He had tried to introduce him to the Royal Geographical Society in London).

And, finally, that the "Rector Magnificus" of the University (the Dean) had issued a special announcement on Vambery' death.

Vambery's ghost must have been gratified.

EPILOGUE

Today there is a short road in London, S.E.18, named after Vambery. It runs parallel with Plumstead Common, and lies between Vernham Road and Plum Lane, intersected by Kirk Lane. The road was built at the end of the last century and marks the spot of Marvin's home, Grosvenor House, Park Place, Plumstead, Kent, where the two men so anxiously discussed the news of the day over port and cigars.

Was it built on the instigation of Charles Marvin? Did Vambery ever know? Curiously he never mentions it once.

Not only was a London street named after Vambery, a British trawler also bore his name. The 'Vambery' hit the headlines several times in the thirties, when it was arrested (more than once) by the Icelandic authorities "for illegal fishing in territorial waters".

But no streets, squares or boats were named after Vambery in his native land, where his name fell into disgrace in the years immediately following the first world war. It was rumoured — with some justification — that he had worked for a foreign government.

Eventually the situation improved. Perhaps it was realised that he never wrote or said a thing against his country. Whatever the reasons for his reinstatement in Hungary, his portrait suddenly appeared on a stamp (value 50 fillers) in 1954 — ultimate accolade for the ex-dervish — one in a series of eight "Great Hungarians". The portrait was flattering and considerably idealised, with a camel and Central Asian minarets (of Samarkand?) shown in the background.

How pleased Vambery would be, if he could know that the Hungarian Academy of Sciences (after refusing him a loan on his return from Central Asia) now issued a special 'Vambery Armin medal', awarded for oustanding linguistic merit. The plaque on

489

Vambery's house was unveiled in 1974.

In 1970, the centenary of the founding of the Turkish Department at the Eotvos Lorand University, on the initiative of Professor Lajos Ligeti, a ceremony was held at his grave in the presence of members of the Hungarian Academy. On this occasion a simple, unimposing wooden tablet marking the grave was replaced by the present headstone. It reads:

"Vambery Armin
1832-1913
Azsiakutato egyetemi tanar
A Magyar Tudomanyos AkademiaTagya"

("Arminius Vambery
1832-1913
Explorer of Asia, University professor
Member of the Hungarian Academy of Science.")

In the same cemetery lies Pal Hunfalvy, one of Vambery's fiercest opponents in the linguistic field. His theory has won the day and it is now universally accepted that the Finno-Ugrian — and not (as Vambery maintained) the Turco-Tatar language groups — are the closest linguistic relations of Hungarian.

In Vambery's day a veritable "Ugro-Turk" war had broken out; Vambery postulated that the Turco-Tatar group was the Hungarian language's next-of-kin, and fought tooth-and-nail to defend his theory. But he received scant support from Vienna. And in any case, linguists say that he mistook the Turkish loanwords in the Hungarian language for "blood relations".

The origin of the Magyars — the mysteriousness of which drew Vambery to the East — has not been fully resolved and many theories have been put forward, ranging from Attila the Hun to even remoter ancestors, such as the Sumerians. Although Vambery contradicted himself, sometimes maintaining that he was searching for the origins of the Magyars, his greater interest lay in the language.

"What I wanted and was looking for was the ancient dialect of the Turkish languages, uninfluenced by foreign elements," he wrote; ". . . and as it happened that this dialect could not be learned from books, there was nothing left for me but to travel through those distant regions and thus acquire practically what I could not acquire theoretically".

Professor Ligeti at Vambery's grave, on the centenary of the founding of the Turkish Department of the University (1970).

VÁMBÉRY ÁRMIN
1832 — 1913

AZSIAKUTATÓ EGYETEMI TANÁR
A MAGYAR TUDOMÁNYOS AKADÉMIA
TAGJA

Finally Vambery was forced to admit defeat; he told his son that he recognised the basic Ugrian character of the Hungarian language, but that the language also bore Turco-Tatar characteristics. (No one had denied that.)

Despite the fact, however, that the Hungarian Academy of Sciences has accepted the Finno-Ugrian origin of the language as a proven fact, it by no means minimises Vambery's contribution, pointing out that its value lay chiefly in his pioneering work. Additionally, Vambery was one of the first to collect old Turkish proverbs and folk-tales.

"It is an acknowledged fact," writes the modern scholar G. Hazai, "that Vambery was the first to disclose East Turkic languages to European science, calling attention to their literature not only in field trips but also in published works. His contribution must be judged on this basis and not on his faulty views about the origin of Hungarian ... Vambery's pioneering work remains an important guide." (These works are listed in the bibliography.)

Today the only surviving friend of Arminius Vambery is Professor Abdul Karim Gyula Germanus, a sprightly nonagenarian; he is a famous linguist and Orientalist in his own right, and author of many books. He has retained the vitality and elasticity of his youth, a liveliness of spirit that many a younger man would envy. He remembers well his revered teacher:

"I myself was the last pupil of Professor Vambery at the University of Budapest, between 1903-1907, and was a constant visitor at his home, right up to his death in 1913. Our relations were more those of a benign father to his grateful son, than those of a professor to an ordinary student. I studied Turkish and Persian under his guidance, and as I knew German perfectly he gave me some texts to be translated from Turkish and Tatar, and he richly rewarded my endeavours with sums which enabled me to travel and live in Constantinople and pursue my studies there."

Professor Germanus recollects the first meeting with his "adored master":

"When I entered the University of Budapest in 1903, the professor of Turkish language and literature, the world-famous Arminius Vambery, was then over seventy. He did not like accepting those students he suspected being after no more than his autograph (which they could get if he would sign their papers), but wanted only those who wished to study in earnest. He himself rarely visited the University and those who dared approach him were obliged "the adviser in Oriental matters to the Government of Great Britain" in his flat.

"'Why do you want to learn Turkish and Persian?' he used to ask impatiently of those students who had the courage to enrol with him. 'You can remain a decent citizen without knowing a single Turkish word. I shall sign your college book as I know you only wanted my signature, but I ask you to leave me in peace!'

"I too received this reception as I stood trembling before him. The room seemed to be spinning around me. I did not even take in the magnificent collection of books which covered the entire wall. I saw only the old scholar with his high forehead, whose thirst for knowledge had led him to the tomb of Timur Lenk, among the uncouth nomads of the Central Asian deserts, and who hid a throbbing Hungarian heart under the rough mantle of a dervish. I stammered a few words, tongue-tied with awe, saying that I had already learnt Turkish by myself, but now had got stuck with Persian, although I knew some Arabic.

"He looked at me with piercing eyes and then limped to his writing-desk, lifted a thick Turkish book and placed it before me:

"'Read!' he thundered.

"With a trembling voice, but gradually feeling braver, I read and translated a section from a report of a hospital in Constantinople — one of hundreds of reports sent to him as a mark of esteem . . .

"'All right, my young friend', he said to me in a suave tone, 'I shall sign your college-book, but I do not go to the University in the afternoon, where my lectures have been announced, because at that time I am usually in the library of the National Casino. You may come to me any time in the morning . . . Read Saadi's *Gulistan*: you will get a perfect knowledge of Persian from it. And if you have any difficulty, come and see me, and I shall explain everything.'

"He then shook hands with the happiest student in the world — but first I had to learn English in order to use the Persian-English dictionary!"

Professor Germanus adds:

"The personality of Professor Vambery was fascinating. The sources of his erudition were not only books, with their often antiquated and tedious data, but he gathered his living wisdom with his fragile body out of an enthusiastic soul. Knowledge meant for him a concern of the heart, a conviction, a tool in the pursuit of truth . . ."

Compare Ignaz Goldziher, one of Vambery's earliest pupils, who later taught Arabic to Gyula Germanus. His *Diaries*, published only recently,* give quite a different picture. The reason for this famous orientalist's vitriolic attack may lie in the man's own character, and in the fact that several first-rate Hungarian philologists (led by Hunfalvy) considered Vambery a charlatan and called him a "swindler", condemning his "non-scientific methods".

Another reason for Goldziher's spitefulness may have been the fact that he felt Vambery to be a renegade and an upstart, and considered himself much better educated. Pious himself, he disapproved of Vambery's anti-family stance, so alien to Jewish custom, and condemned him for neglecting his relations, though one can hardly see what concern it was of his.

The mistrust Vambery encountered was compensated by the applause of those circles which Vambery had joined. "Above all these were the Calvinists", writes Goldziher venomously, "whom the Jewish dervish had attached himself to . . ."

Goldziher called him the "limping liar" and did not believe Vambery when the latter told him boastingly (9 April 1900):

"I earned . . . half a million Crowns, but not with science, mark you . . . Do you think I earned my wealth through my scientific studies? Ha! Ha! Ha! I have drawn a yearly salary from the English Queen and from the Sultan for political services. England has now increased my salary by £500 a year. *That* is what you call science!"

After Vambery's death Rustem moved with his wife, widowed mother, and two small sons, to a house in Buda, Orom-utca 8.

Of the two sons, only Robert survives. George died in 1928, after an attack of paratyphoid, at the age of 23.

Robert has a clear memory of Cornelia, his eccentric grandmother, who on one occasion (in August 1914) nonchalantly broke a raw egg into her soup plate in the splendid dining-room at the Sacher Hotel in Vienna, watched by goggle-eyed waiters.

Rustem was no less of an eccentric. He suffered from insomnia, and gave sleeping pills mixed into meatballs to his neighbour's noisy dog.

In his flat at Orom-utca, there were many exotic Turkish and Persian carpets of all sizes, gifts to his father, and immensely valuable. The smaller carpets were hung on the walls. A collection of nargilehs (Persian hookahs) was displayed on top of the bookcases.

Rustem Vambery became an eminent jurist and criminologist. After the first world war his attitude was so fearless and his irony so mordant that he earned himself the sobriquet of "the Hungarian Voltaire", making him attack judge and prosecutor alike, thus losing many cases. "If you want to lose your case let Rustem Vambery defend you" became a byword in Budapest. Among his many clients in the 1920s was Matyas Rakosi, later the Stalinist ruler of Hungary.

Following in his father's footsteps, Rustem became an honorary adviser to the British legation in Budapest (1921-4), and accompanied a delegation of Hungarian liberals and socialists to the first British Labour government. He addressed two committee meetings at the House of Commons; and continued his father's practice of sending regular communications to the Foreign Office, and dozens of memos on "Hungary of Today" and related subjects.

Fleeing from the Nazis in 1938, he first settled in England and later emigrated to the United States with his wife. Fortunately he was able to bring some family treasures out of the country, and the manuscript notes written by his dervish father at the peril of his life were presented to the British Museum. Here they are now preserved in a firm morocco binding, in the Department of Oriental Manuscripts.

Vambery's collection of books in Hungarian, German, English, Swedish, Polish, and many other languages, was sold to the New York Public Library. The "Vambery bequest", including 11 Persian, 2 Arabic, and 43 Turkish priceless manuscripts, had been donated to the Hungarian Academy in 1914.

Regrettably many of the larger valuables had to be left behind in Budapest, where they were stored in the cellar of the British legation. They included several carpets, and innumerable gifts such as the large silver urn inscribed to George Vambery by the Prince and Princess of Wales; and a carving set with horn handles in a wooden case, inscribed to Vambery on the occasion of his lecture tour in Sheffield in 1885. These were all lost when the legation was destroyed in the siege of Budapest (1944/5).

Rustem Vambery became the first post-war Minister at the Hungarian legation in Washington (in 1946), but later renounced his Hungarian citizenship and became a naturalised American. Like his father, he remained a very robust and active man right up to the last day of his life. On 24 October 1948, Rustem died suddenly of a heart-attack, aged 76, on the New York subway.

His widow Olga went to live in California with her son Robert, who married Hungarian-born physician Clara Erdelyi in 1947. He is now the last surviving descendant of Arminius Vambery.

Some of te gifts made to Vambery including urn from George V.

BIBLIOGRAPHY

THE WORKS OF ARMINIUS VAMBERY

As Vambery was such a prolific writer over a period lasting more than fifty-five years, a complete list of all his books, pamphlets, letters, and articles would take up more space than this biography. The following checklist has been simplified, but is the most complete to appear so far in English:

1) *Deutsch-turkisches Taschen-Woerterbuch* (Constantinople, 1858) 'Germano-Turkish pocket dictionary,' containing about 14,000 German words. It was the first German book printed in Constantinople.

2) *Abuska. Csagataj-torok szogyujtemeny.* Elobeszeddel es jegyzetek-kel kiserte Budenz Jozsef. (Pest, 1862) 'Chagataic-Turkish dictionary'. Vambery's second dictionary, also the first of its kind, and a pioneering work.

3) *Travels in Central Asia,* being the account of a journey

a) from Teheran across the Turkoman Desert on the Eastern shore of the Caspian to Khiva, Bokhara, and Samarkand, performed in the year 1863 (London, John Murray, 1864)

b) *Voyages d'un Faux Derviche dans l'Asie Centrale* Translated from the English by E.D. Forgues (Paris, 1865)

c) *Kozep-Azsiai utazas* (Pest, 1865)

d) *Reise in Mittelasien* (Leipzig, 1865)

e) *Viaggi di un falso dervish nell'Asia Centrale* (Milan, 1873)
The bestseller that carried Vambery's name around the world. Editions were published in Sweden, France, Italy, America, and many other countries, and in various European and Asiatic languages. "I can point out with pleasure that in certain parts of Central Asia I was the first European traveller", he proudly claimed, "... and have furnished many facts hitherto unknown about the ethnographical relations of the Turks in these parts."

4)
a) *Meine Wanderungen und Erlebnisse in Persien* (Pest, 1867)
b) *Vandorlasaim es elmenyeim Persziaban* (Pest, 1867)
'My Wanderings and Experiences in Persia' (not published in English) he considered of little value, except as a story of his "exciting personal adventures as a pseudo-Sunnite among the Shiites ... (and) ... in casual connection with my later wanderings in Central Asia."

5) *Cagataische Sprachstudien*, enthaltend grammatikalischen Umriss, Chrestomathie und Worterbuch der Cagataischen Sprache (Leipzig, 1867)
'Chagataic Linguistic Studies' (not published in English), on the language of the three Khanates of Turkestan. Vambery's first philological production, in which he made good use of the manuscripts he had collected in the bazaars of Khiva, Bokhara and Meshed. The East-Turkic glossary in French and in German was later used by many Turkologists. The book was severely criticised by some academics, but his researches into East-Turkic, "an entirely unknown language to Western Orientalists", was considered valuable by many.

6)
a) *Sketches of Central Asia*. Additional chapters on my Travels, Adventures, and on the Ethnology of Central Asia (London, W.H. Allen, 1868)
b) *Skizzen aus Mittelasien* (Leipzig, 1868)
c) *Vambery Armin vazlatai Kozep-Azsiabol* (Pest, 1868)
Vambery introduced the ethnographical, political, and economic data which had been omitted from *Travels in Central Asia*, and included a chapter on his Tartar Mollah Ishak. The *Athenaeum* (2097) lamented the "great number of typographical errors".

7) *Uigurische Sprachmonumente* und das Kudatku Bilik. Uigurischer Text mit Transcription und Ubersetzung nebst einem uigurisch-deutschen Worterbuche ... Facsimile aus dem Original-texte (Innsbruck/Leipzig, 1870)
'Uiguric Linguistic Monuments' (not published in English) a didactic poem in Uigur by Yusuf Khass Hajib. Vambery had very little hope that he would ever succeed in deciphering the manuscript (at Vienna); but an all-consuming curiosity plus eighteen years' study and practical knowledge of Turkic languages enabled him to do so. The Hungarian Academy of

Sciences contributed 700 Gulden towards the printing costs.

8) *Indiai tundermesek*. Erdekes olvasokonyv az erettebb ifjusag szamara. Angol utan kozli Vambery Armin. (Pest, 1870)
'Indian folklore tales', adapted by Vambery from Mary Frere's *Old Deccan Days* (London, 1868). Vambery's Hungarian edition was a bestseller, and went into several reprints.

9)
a) *Oroszorszag hatalmi allasa Azsiaban* (Pest, 1871)
b) *Russlands Machtstellung in Asien* (Leipzig, 1871)
'Power of Russia in Asia' (not translated into English) depicted the gradual progress of the Russian conquests in Asia.

10)
a) *Geschichte Bochara's oder Transoxaniens* (Stuttgart, 1872) 2 volumes
b) *Bokhara tortenete a legregibb idoktol a jelenkorig* (Pest, 1873) 2 volumes
c) *History of Bokhara*, from the earliest Period down to the Present (London, Henry King, 1873)
The book brought him "more disillusionment than joy" and he addmited that he had not studied his subject sufficiently.

11)
a) *Centralasien und die englisch-russiche Grenzfrage*. Gesammelte politische Schriften (Leipzig, 1873)
b) *Central Asia and the Anglo-Russian Frontier Question:* a series of political papers . . . translated from the German by F.E. Bunnett (London, Smith Elder, 1874)
The book was published at the time of the Khiva campaign, "when people showed a much keener interest in what took place in the inner Asiatic world."

12) *Der Islam im neunzehnten Jahrhundert* Eine culturgeschichtliche Studie. (Leipzig, 1875)
'Islam in the Nineteenth Century' dealt with "those social and political reforms which our invention and our reformatory efforts in the Middle East have called forth." The *Athenaeum* (2499) was enthusiastic: "It is a valuable contribution to the political history of the age and it appears at a most opportune moment." The book was translated into Polish (Warsaw, 1876), but not into Hungarian or English.

13)
a) *Keleti eletkepek* (Budapest, 1876)

b) *Sittenbilder aus dem Morgenlande* (Berlin, 1876)
'Moral Pictures from the Orient' (not translated into English)
dealt with the social customs and family life of Turkey, Persia, and Central Asia. Vambery claimed to have made a real
contribution to the knowledge of the Orient with both these
books.

14)
a) *Ueber die Reformfahigkeit der Turkei* ... Separate Abdruck aus
dem "Pester Lloyd" (Budapest, 1877)
b) *La Turquie est-elle susceptible de reformes?* (translated from the
German) (Budapest/Paris, 1878)

15)
a) *A torok-tatar nyelvek etymologiai szotara* (Budapest, 1877)
b) *Etymologisches Worterbuch der turko-tatarischen Sprachen.* (Leipzig,
1878)
'Etymological Dictionary of the Turkish Language' (not translated into English) the first ever published on this subject "in
which, without any precedent, I collected, criticised and compared, until I succeeded in finding out the stems and roots, and
ranged them into separate families", wrote Vambery.
"In spite of all its faults", the *Athenaeum* (2700) conceded it
"is a really valuable book which must long remain the standard work on the subject of which it treats."

16) *Die primitive Cultur des turk-tatarischen Volkes*, auf grund sprach-
licher forschungen (Leipzig, 1879)
'Primitive Culture of the Turko-Tartar People' (not
translated into English). Vambery considered this book "one
of the best productions of my pen", and was pleased with the
recognition of its value from his colleagues and fellow-philol-
ogists.

17) *Die Sprache der Turkomanen und der Diwan Machdumkuli's.* (Leipzig, 1879)
'The language of the Turkomans and the Divan
Makhdumkuli' (not translated into English). Published a hundred years after the death of Makhdumkuli, national poet of
the Turkomans.

18)
a) *A magyarok erdete* Ethnologiai tanulmany (Budapest, 1882)
b) *Der Ursprung der Magyaren* Eine ethnologische Studie. (Leipzig,
1882)
'The Origin of the Magyars' (not translated into English) was

written to refute the accusation that he was neglecting "Magyar studies". Vambery admitted that at this time "the theory of the Finnish-Ugrian descent of the Magyars held the upper hand" and his opinions in the book were naturally opposed by many philologists. (Lengthy critiques were published by Pal Hunfalvy in 1884, and Joseph Budenz in 1885.) Seven hundred copies of Vambery's book were sold in three days.

19) *Arminius Vambery: his life and adventures by himself* (London, T. Fisher Unwin, 1883)

Vambery's most successful book, enormously popular in England, America, and Australia. The first three large editions sold out in three months (at 16/- a copy, a fortune in those days). In 1886 (at Unwin's request) Vambery revised the book for a younger audience, eliminating all political and other matter that would "possess little interest for boys", and adding an "introductory chapter dedicated to the boys of England". This abridged version was a great favourite at school prize-givings. A eulogy by Max Nordau was added to the posthumous ninth edition (1914).

The book was never translated on the Continent, not even into Hungarian.

20)
a) *The Coming Struggle for India*, being an account the encroachments of Russia in Central Asia, and of the difficulties sure to arise therefrom to England. (London, Cassell, 1885)
b) *Den annalkande striden om Indien* (Stockholm, 1885)
c) *Der Zukunfts-Kampf um Indien* (Wien, 1886)
d) *La Lutte Future Pour la Possession de l'Inde* (Paris, 1886)
A 214 page volume, written in twenty days to coincide with the Russian war-scare and a follow-up to Vambery's successful lecture-tour of Britain.

21)
a) *A torok faj ethnologiai es ethnographiai tekintetben* (Budapest, 1885)
b) *Das Turkenvolk in seinen ethnologischen und ethnographischen Beziehungen geschildert* (Leipzig, 1885)
'The Turkish People in their Ethnological and Ethnographical Relationship' (not translated into English) was an endeavour to incorporate his personal experiences of the Turks. It was "favourably criticised, and I was therefore the more surprised that the book had such a very limited sale." (After ten years only 300 copies had been sold.)

22) *Die Scheibaniade.* Ein ozbegisches Heldengedicht in 76 Gesangen von Prinz Mohammed Salih aus Charezm. Text, Ubersetzung und Noten von Hermann Vambery. (Wien, 1885)

'The Sheibaniade' was a 16th. century Uzbek heroic poem — translated into German blank verse — Vambery's most cherished work, the book was printed at his own expense: nearly 1400 florins. In spite of one (flattering) review in the *Journal Asiatique*, scarcely 60 copies were sold — thus he "did not get back a fourth of the sum laid out on it."

(Shaibani, descendant of Genghis Khan, captured Samarkand Herat and Kandahar in 1500. He was the most formidable opponent of the Mogul Emperor Babur before his death in 1510.)

23)
a) *Hungary*, in Ancient, Mediaeval, and Modern Times. (London, T.Fisher Unwin, 1887)
b) *The Story of Hungary* (New York, Putnams, 1889)
c) *Historia de Hungria* (Madrid, 1891)

Commissioned by Unwins, the book appeared as Number 8 in their Story of the Nations series. Written in collaboration with Louis Heilprin, it was later translated into other languages, and had a very wide sale which "it could never have had in Hungary itself." . . . the "service hereby rendered to my compatriots", wrote Vambery, "(was) never appreciated at home" (where the book was totally ignored).

24) *Professor Vambery to Islam in Hind Greeting* (Calcutta, 1889) (A letter from A. Vambery to Nawab Abdul-Latif Bahadur, commending the work of the Mahomedan Literary Society)

25) *Die Sarten und ihre Sprache* (Wien, 1890)

26) *Aus dem Geistesleben persischer Frauen* (Wien, 1891)

Booklet dedicated to the Persian ambassador in Vienna. In the preface Vambery explained why this 18th. century manuscript (*Mazmai Mahmudi*) he had recently discovered is of interest to Orientalists: "I have been inspired to the above work since for the first time I have discovered an exhaustive discussion of the literary productions of Persian women . . ."

27) *Freiheitliche Bestrebungen im moslimischen Asien* (Berlin, 1893) 'Endeavours for Freedom in Moslem Asia' (not translated into English)

28) *A magyarsag keletkezese es gyarapodasa* (Budapest, 1895)

'The Growth and Spread of the Magyars' (not translated into English), a sequel to (18) *A magyarok erdete* based on his further researches, in which he tried to prove that "the present Magyar nation has proceeded from a gradual, scarcely definable settlement of Ural-Altaic elements in the lowlands of Hungary."

29) *La Turquie d'aujourd'hui et d'avant quarante ans* Trad. par Georges Tirard (Paris, 1898)

A short work (72 pages) written in answer to the Duke of Argyll's 'Our responsibilities for Turkey'.

30) *Noten zu den altturkischen Inschriften der Mongolei und Sibiriens* (Helsingfors, 1898)

'Notes to the Old Turkish Inscriptions of Mongolia and Siberia' (not translated into English)

31) *The Travels and Adventures of the Turkish Admiral Sidi Ali Reis, in India, Afghanistan, Central Asia, and Persia, during the years 1553-1556* (London, Luzac, 1899)

The *Mirat ul Memalik* ("Mirror of Kingdoms") translated from the Turkish by Vambery, with notes and introduction.

32) *Alt-osmanische Sprachstudien* Mit einem azerbaizanischen Text als Appendix. (Leiden, 1901)

'Old Osmanli Linguistic Studies' (not translated into English).

33)

a) *Die gelbe Gefahr* (Budapest, 1904)

b) *Le peril jaune*; etude sociale (Budapest, 1904)

'The Yellow Peril' (not translated into English), a pro-Japanese, anti-Russian publication, suggesting an Anglo-German alliance in Asia. Dedicated to Lord Lansdowne, then British Foreign Secretary.

34)

a) *The Story of My Struggles* 2 volumes (London/Leipzig, T. Fisher Unwin, 1904)

b) *Kuzdelmeim* (Budapest, 1905)

Vambery's memoirs proved to be a large bestseller like the first. Quickly reissued in one-volume, it soon went into a third edition by 1905, and after his death it appeared in the Nelson Library of Notable Books (pocket format; 1915).

"What is conspicuous from the first to the last page is a degree of egotism", declared the *Athenaeum* (4021) justifiably.

The Hungarian edition had an altered text and different illustrations. Some of his comments about the Hungarian aristocracy had to be deleted.

35)
a) *Western Cultures in Eastern Lands* (London, John Murray, 1906)
b) *Westlicher Kultureinfluss im Osten* (Berlin, 1906)
c) *Nyugat Kulturaja Keleten* (Budapest, 1906)
A comparison of the methods adopted by England and Russia in the Middle East. The *Athenaeum* (4091) reviewer now found Vambery "less belligerent and less prejudiced against everything Russian than he showed himself in some much earlier books."

36) *Jusuf und Ahmed* Ein ozbegisches Volksepos im Chiwaer Dialekte. Text, Ubersetzung und Noten von H. Vambery (Budapest, 1911)
An Uzbek national epic in Khivan dialect by Yusuf Beg. Text, translation and notes by Vambery.

37) *Reformkepes-e a Kelet?* (Budapest, 1911)

38) *A Magyarsag Bolcsojenel* A Magyar-torok rokonsag kezdete es fejlodese. (Budapest, 1914)
Posthumous volume tracing the start and progress of Hungarian-Turkish relations. The text was revised by Gy. Nemeth and M. Balla, and Vambery's son Rustem supplied the preface.

PART 2

A selection of books to which Arminius Vambery supplied chapters or introductions:

a) *Original Letters and Papers of the late Viscount Strangford* (London, 1878)

b) James Baker: *Die Turken in Europa* (Stuttgart, 1878)

c) Charles Marvin: *The Russian Railway to Herat and India* (London, 1883)

d) Sven Hedin: *Genom Persien, Mesopotamien och Kaukasien* (Stockholm, 1887)

e) Ignac Kunos: *Torok Nepmesek* (Budapest, 1889)

f) M. von Proskowetz: *Von Newastrand Nach Samarkand* (Leipzig, 1889)

g) *Voyages and Adventures of Ferdinand Mendez Pinto* (London, 1891)

h) Istvan Szamota: *Regi Magyar Utazok Europaban 1532-1770* (Budapest, 1892)

i) Marki Sandor: *Matyas Kiraly Emlekkonyv* (Budapest, 1902)

j) Hadji Khan & Wilfrid Sparroy: *With the Pilgrims to Mecca*; The Great Pilgrimage of AH 1319 (AD 1902) (London, 1905)

k) Ferenc Gaspar: *A Fold Korul* (Budapest, 1906)

l) Gyula Meszaros: *Torok Koltok* (Budapest, 1910)

m) Gyula Meszaros: *A Boszporusz Partjain* (Budapest, 1911)

n) Frigyes Vincze: *Az Oszman Irodalom Foiranyai* (Budapest, 1912)

o) Edward Legge: *King Edward in his True Colours.* (With one chapter of appreciation by A.V.) (London, 1912)

PART 3

Background Sources Consulted

Hansard, 1870; 1875; 1889

The Times, 1864-1913

The Athenaeum, 1864-1913

Pester Lloyd, 1889-1911

The Nineteenth Century, 1880-1912

Adams (W.H. Davenport): *In Perils Oft* (1885)

Alder (G.J.): *British India's Northern Frontier, 1865-1895* (1963)

Apor (Eva): *The Persian Manuscripts of the Vambery-bequest* (in the Library of the Hungarian Academy of Sciences) (1971)

Bancroft (Anne): *Religions of the East* (1974)

Bein (Alex): *Theodor Herzl* (1957)

Blunt (W.S.): *Secret History of the Occupation of Egypt* (1907)

Blunt (W.S.): *My Diaries*. 2 volumes (1919-1920)

Boulger (D.C.): *Central Asian Portraits* (1880)

Branch (Lesley): *The Wilder Shores of Love* (1954)

Burnaby (Fred): *A Ride to Khiva* (1876)

Byron (Robert): *The Road to Oxiana* (1937)

Cohen (Israel): *Theodor Herzl* (1959)

Curzon (G.N.): *Russia in Central Asia* (1889)

Curzon (G.N.): *Persia and the Persian Question*. 2 volumes (1892)

Dewdney (J.C.): *Turkey* (1961)

Eliav (Mordechai): *David Wolffsohn* (1977)

Elon (Amos): *Herzl* (1975)

Fahri (Ali): *M. Vambery en Danger* (1900)

Goldziher (I.): *Tagebuch* (1978)

Hambly (Gavin): *Central Asia* (1969)

Hazai (G.): *Bio-Bibliography of Armin Vambery* (1963)

Hedin (Sven): *My Life as an Explorer* (1926)

Heroic Adventures, Chapters in recent Exploration and Discovery (1882)

Herzl (Theodor): *Tagebucher*. 3 volumes (1922-3)

Howard of Penrith (Lord): *Theatre of Life*. 2 volumes (1935-6)

Johnston (Sir Harry) ed.: *A Book of Great Travellers* (1933)

Kinross (Lord): *The Ottoman Centuries* (1977)

Krist (Gustav): *Alone Through the Forbidden Land* (1938)

Lee (Sir Sidney): *King Edward VII* (1925)

Lewis (Bernard): *The Emergence of Modern Turkey* (rev. edn., 1968)

Lowenthal (Martin) ed.: *The Diaries of Theodor Herzl* (1956)

Ludlam (Harry): *A Biography of Dracula* (1962)

McCabe (Joseph): *A Biographical Dictionary of Modern Rationalists* (1920)

Maclean (Fitzroy): *A Person from England* (1958)

Maclean (Fitzroy): *Back to Bokhara* (1959)

Maclean (Fitzroy): *To the Back of Beyond* (1974)

Macleod (Joseph); *The Sisters d'Aranyi* (1969)

Malleson (G.B.): *Herat* (1880)

Malleson (G.B.): *Memoir of Sir Henry C. Rawlinson* (1898)

Marvin (Charles): *Merv, the Queen of the World* (1881)

Marvin (Charles): *The Russian Advance Towards India* (1882)

Marvin (Charles): *Reconnoitring Central Asia* (1884)

Nicholson (R.A.): *The Mystics of Islam* (1914)

Nicolson (Harold): *Lord Carnock* (1930)

O'Donovan (Edmund): *The Merv Oasis. 2 vols.* (1882)

'O.K.' (Olga Novikoff, nee Kireeff): *Russia and England from 1876 to 1880* (1880)

Palmer (E.H.): *Oriental Mysticism* (1974)

Palmer (F.H.E.): *Austro-Hungarian Life in Town and Country* (1904)

Paston (George): *At John Murray's* Records of a Literary Circle (1932)

Pears (Sir Edwin): *Life of Abdul Hamid* (1917)

Pratt (Edwin A.): *Notable Masters of Men* (1901)

Records of the Tercentenary Festival of Dublin University in 1892 (1894)

Recsey (Viktor): *Der weltberuhmte Orientalist, Prof. Dr. Armin Vambery* (1888)

Ripley (W.Z.): *The Races of Europe* (1900)

Schuyler (Eugene): *Turkistan. 2 volumes,* (1876)

Skrine (F.H.): *An Indian Journalist* (1895)

Stewart (Desmond): *Herzl* (1974)

Stewart (J. Massey): *Across the Russias* (1969)

Stoker (Bram): *Personal Reminiscences of Henry Irving. 2 volumes.* (1906)

Toynbee (A.J.): *Between Oxus and Jumna* (1961)

Vamos (Magda): *Resid Efendi* (1966)

INDEX

of main Places and Principal Characters

50 55

Buinak

Derbend
Samur R.

Nisovaja
Kuba

Tagai

Shemaka
SHIRWAN

10
Baku
C. Apsheron

C A S P I A N

Kizil agatch B.

Lenkoran
Ardabil
M. Sawalam
Astara
R. Lemara
Lissar

G
H
Enzelle
Herat
Perubazar
Resht
Rudi Sir

Kizil Uzen
Menjul

Sultania
Abhar
Sugsabad
R. Berid

TEHERAN
Demavend

Eywani K.
K. Irumbar
Sirdare Pass
Gehlak
Aras Koh

P E R S I A

Alexander B. Ulu-kan
Kakushechin P. Kinderli
C. Tokmak St Kinderli
Kinderli Bay Kustaru
C. Singurli Kosh-aji C
C. Sui
Kara Ata I.
Tiul dulata

Kara Boghaz
Black Gulf
Strait of Kara Boghaz

Krasnovodsk
C. Tartuk
Fort Beleovich
Krasnovodsk
Cheleken

Ogurchinsk I.
Khiva Bay

Kh.n Bugdy
Kum

S E A

Chikishlar Post
Hasan
Hasan Kuli
Gumush Tepe
Astrabad B.
Ashurada
Farahabad
R. Talar
Astrabad
Shahrud
Rostan
Kara
Shahrud
Mazas
Ramian
Jajarm

DE
Cheshmeh
Shahru
Budasht
Khan
Abbasabad
Khanahudy

Elburz Mts.
Damghan
Semnan
Lasjird
Deh nemud
Gt. Salt Desert

35

SCALES.
0   50   100   150   200
Russian Versts

0 10 20 30 40 50   100   150   200
English Miles

0 10 20 30 40 50   100   150   200
Geographical Miles

50 55